D.J.B. 2003.

Introduction to
Java
Programming
with Microsoft Visual J++ 6

Y. Daniel Liang
Purdue University at Fort Wayne
Department of Computer Science

═══════════ *An Alan R. Apt Book* ═══════════

Prentice Hall
Upper Saddle River, New Jersey 07458
http://www.prenhall.com

Library of Congress Cataloging-in-Publication Data

Liang, Y. Daniel.
　Introduction to Java programming with Microsoft Visual J++6 / Y. Daniel Liang.
　　p.　cm.
　ISBN 0-13-086912-0
　1. Java (Computer program language)　2. Microsoft Visual J++.　I. Title
　QA76.73.J38 L532 2000
　005.2'762—dc21　　　　　　　　　　　　　　　　　　　　　　　　99-058866
　　　　　　　　　　　　　　　　　　　　　　　　　　　　　　　　　　CIP

Vice president and editorial director: *Marcia Horton*
Publisher: *Alan R. Apt*
Project manager: *Ana Arias Terry*
Editorial assistant: *Toni Holm*
Marketing manager: *Jennie Burger*
Production editor: *Pine Tree Composition*
Executive managing editor: *Vince O'Brien*
Managing editor: *David A. George*
Art director: *Heather Scott*
Cover design: *John Christiana*
Manufacturing manager: *Trudy Pisciotti*
Manufacturing buyer: *Beth Sturla*
Vice president and director of production and manufacturing: *David W. Riccardi*

 © 2000 by Prentice-Hall, Inc.
Upper Saddle River, New Jersey

All rights reserved. No part of this book may be
reproduced, in any form or by any means
without permission in writing from the publisher.

The author and publisher of this book have used their best efforts in preparing
this book. These efforts include the development, research, and testing of the
theories to determine their effectiveness.

Printed in the United States of America
10　9　8　7　6　5　4　3　2　1

ISBN 0-13-086912-0

Prentice-Hall International (UK) Limited, *London*
Prentice-Hall of Australia Pty. Limited, *Sydney*
Prentice-Hall Canada Inc., *Toronto*
Prentice-Hall Hispanoamericana, S.A., *Mexico*
Prentice-Hall of India Private Limited, *New Delhi*
Prentice-Hall of Japan, Inc., *Tokyo*
Pearson Education Asia Pte. Ltd., *Singapore*
Editora Prentice-Hall do Brasil, Ltda., *Rio de Janeiro*

ABOUT THE AUTHOR

Y. Daniel Liang has B.S. and M.S. degrees in computer science from Fudan University in Shanghai and a Ph.D. degree in computer science from the University of Oklahoma. He is the author of four Java books. He has published numerous papers in international journals, taught Java courses nationally and internationally, and consulted in the areas of algorithm design, client/server computing, and database management.

Dr. Liang is currently an associate professor in the Department of Computer Science at Purdue University at Fort Wayne, where he twice received the Excellence in Research Award from the School of Engineering, Technology, and Computer Science. He can be reached via the Internet at **liangjava@yahoo.com**.

Acknowledgments

This book has benefited from the second edition of my *Introduction to Java Programming*. I would like to acknowledge the following people who helped produce *Introduction to Java Programming*: Hao Wu, Michael Willig, Russell Minnich, Balaram Nair, Ben Stonebraker, C-Y Tang, Bertrand I-P Lin, Mike Sunderman, Fen English, James Silver, Mark Temte, Bob Sanders, Marta Partington, Tom Cirtin, Songlin Qiu, Tim Tate, Carolyn Linn, Alfonso Hermida, Nathan Clement, Eric Miller, Chris Barrick, John Etchison, Louisa Klucznik, Angela Denny, Randy Haubner, Robin Drake, Betsy Brown, and Susan Kindel.

For this edition, I would like to thank Alan Apt, Ana Terry, Toni Holm, and their colleagues at Prentice Hall for organizing and managing this project, and thank Patty Donovan, Robert Milch, and Dan Boilard, and their colleagues at Pine Tree Composition for helping to produce the book.

As always, I am indebted to my wife, Samantha, for love, support, and encouragement.

To Samantha, Michael, and Michelle

INTRODUCTION

To the Instructor

There are three popular strategies in teaching Java. The first is to mix Java applets and graphics programming with object-oriented programming concepts. The second is to introduce object-oriented programming from the start. The third strategy is a step-by-step approach, first laying a sound foundation on programming elements, control structures, and methods, and then moving on to graphical user interface, applets, internationalization, multimedia, I/O, and networking.

The first strategy, starting with GUI and applets, seems attractive, but requires substantial knowledge of OOP and a good understanding of the Java event-handling model; thus, students may never fully understand what they are doing. The second strategy is based on the notion that the objects should be introduced first because Java is an object-oriented programming language. This notion, however, does not strike a chord with students. From the more than 20 Java courses I have taught, I have concluded that introducing primary data types, control structures, and methods prepares students to learn object-oriented programming. Therefore, this text adopts the third strategy, first proceeding at a steady pace through all the necessary and important basic concepts, then quickly moving to object-oriented programming, and then to using the object-oriented approach to build interesting GUI applications and applets with multimedia and networking.

This book is primarily intended for freshman programming courses, but it can also be used in teaching Java as a second language or in a short training course for experienced programmers. The book contains more material than freshmen can master in a single semester. You can cover the first 12 chapters, and use the remaining ones as time permits.

The Instructor's Manual on CD-ROM is available for instructors of this book. It contains the following resources:

- Lecture notes with suggested teaching strategies and activities
- Microsoft PowerPoint slides for lectures
- Answers to chapter reviews
- Solutions to programming exercises
- Over 400 multiple-choice and true-or-false questions and answers covering all of the chapters of the book in sequence

To obtain the Instructor's Manual, contact your Prentice-Hall sales representative.

Pedagogical Features of the Book

Introduction to Java Programming with Microsoft Visual J++ 6 uses the following elements to get the most out of the material:

- **Objectives** lists what students should have learned from the chapter. This will help them to determine whether they have met the objectives after completing the chapter.

- **Introduction** opens the discussion with a brief overview of what to expect from the chapter.

- Programming concepts are taught by representative **Examples**, carefully chosen and presented in an easy-to-follow style. Each example is described, and includes the source code, a sample run, and an example review. The source code of the examples is contained in the companion CD-ROM.

  Each program is complete and ready to be compiled and executed. The sample run of the program is captured from the screen to give students a live presentation of the example. Reading these examples is much like entering and running them on a computer.

- **Chapter Summary** reviews the important subjects that students should understand and remember. It helps students reinforce the key concepts they have learned in the chapter.

- **Chapter Review** helps students to track their progress and evaluate their learning.

- **Programming Exercises** at the end of each chapter provide students with opportunities to apply the skills on their own. The trick of learning programming is practice, practice, and practice. To that end, the book provides a large number of exercises.

- **Notes**, **Tips**, and **Cautions** are inserted throughout the text to offer valuable advice and insight on important aspects of program development:

NOTE
Provides additional information on the subject and reinforces important concepts.

TIP
Teaches good programming style and practice.

CAUTION
Helps students steer away from the pitfalls of programming errors.

What's New in this Edition

This book expands and improves upon the second edition of my *Introduction to Java Programming*. The major changes are as follows:

- Beginning with Chapter 8, "Getting Started with Graphics Programming," all the AWT user interface components are replaced with state-of-the-art Swing components.

- Visual J++ is introduced throughout the book rather than being clustered in one or two chapters. This incremental approach makes learning J++ easy, because the new features of J++ are covered in relation to the topics in each chapter.

- Chapter 12, "Internationalization," is brand-new. It was added to introduce the development of Java programs for international audiences.

- Appendix G, "Rapid Java Application Development Using Visual J++," is also new. It was added to demonstrate the use of J++ in rapid Java application development.

- Several new case studies are provided to give more examples for learning the fundamentals of programming, such as writing loops.

- Nonessential sections are marked optional and can be skipped without affecting later chapters. These sections include such topics as recursion, event adapters, anonymous inner classes, advanced layout managers, and resource bundles.

To the Student

There is nothing more important to the future of computing than the Internet. There is nothing more exciting on the Internet than Java. A revolutionary programming language developed by Sun Microsystems, Java has become the de facto standard for cross-platform applications and programming on the World Wide Web since its inception in May 1995.

Before Java, the Web was used primarily for viewing static information on the Internet using HTML, a markup language for document layout and for linking documents over the Internet. Java programs can be embedded in an HTML page and downloaded by Web browsers to bring live animation and interactive applications to Web clients.

Java is a full-featured, general-purpose programming language that is capable of developing robust and mission-critical applications. In the last three years, Java has gained enormous popularity and has quickly become the most popular and successful programming language. Today, it is used not only for Web programming, but also for developing standalone applications. Many companies that once considered Java to be more hype than substance are now using it to create distributed applications accessed by customers and partners across the Internet. For every new project being developed today, companies are asking how they can use Java to make their work easier.

Java's Design and Advantages

Java is an object-oriented programming language. Object-oriented programming is a favored programming approach that has replaced traditional procedure-based programming techniques. An object-oriented language uses abstraction, encapsulation, inheritance, and polymorphism to provide great flexibility, modularity, and reusability for developing software.

Java is platform-independent. Its programs can run on any machine with any operating system that supports the Java Virtual Machine, a software component that interprets Java instructions and carries out associated actions.

Java is distributed. Networking is inherently built-in. Simultaneous processing can occur on multiple computers on the Internet. Writing network programs is treated as simple data input and output.

Java is multithreaded. Multithreading is the capability of a program to perform several tasks simultaneously; for example, downloading a video file while playing the video at the same time. Multithreading is particularly useful in graphical user interfaces(GUI) and network programming. Multithread programming is smoothly integrated in Java. In other languages, you can only enable multithreading by calling procedures that are specific to the operating system.

Java is secure. Computers become vulnerable when they are connected with other computers. Viruses and malicious programs can damage your computer. Java is designed with multiple layers of security that ensure proper access to private data and restrict access to disk files.

Java's Versatility

Stimulated by the promise of writing programs once and running them anywhere, the computer industry gave Java its unqualified endorsement. IBM, Sun, and Apple, and many other vendors are working to integrate the Java Virtual Machine with their operating systems so that Java programs can run directly and efficiently on the native machine. Java programs run on full-featured computers, and also on consumer electronics and appliances.

Because of its great potential to unite existing legacy applications written on different platforms to run together, Java has been perceived as a universal front end for the enterprise database. The leading database companies, IBM, Oracle, Sybase, and Informix, have extended their commitment to Java by integrating it into their products. Oracle, for example, plans to enable native Java applications to run on its server, and to deliver a complete set of Java-based development tools supporting the integration of current applications with the Web.

Learning Java

Applying the concept of abstraction in the design and implementation of software projects is the key to developing software. The overriding objective of this book, therefore, is to teach students to use many levels of abstraction in solving problems and to see problems in small and in large.

This book was inspired by my students, because they taught me how to teach programming. My students told me that they wanted a book that used easy-to-follow examples to teach programming concepts. In the summer of 1996, I was looking for a Java text. I found many reference books and several books converted from C and C++ texts on the market, but I could not find the kind of book I was looking for. As a result, the idea was born to write a book that would use good examples to teach basic Java concepts.

In the pages that follow, I cover the major topics in Java programming, including programming structures, methods, objects, classes, inheritance, graphics programming, applets, exception handling, internationalization, multithreading, multimedia, I/O, and networking. Students new to object-oriented programming may take some time to become familiar with the concept of objects and classes. Once students master the principles, programming in Java is easy and productive. Students who know object-oriented programming languages like C++ and Smalltalk will find it easier to learn Java. In fact, they will find that Java is simpler than C++ and Smalltalk in many respects.

Learning Java with Visual J++

Java programs can be developed with JDK, which consists of a set of separate programs, such as compiler and interpreter, that are invoked from a command line. Besides JDK, there are more than a dozen Java development tools on the market today, such as JBuilder, Visual J++, and Visual Café. These tools support an *integrated development environment* (IDE) for rapidly developing Java programs. Editing, compiling, building, debugging, and online help are integrated in one graphical user interface. Using these tools effectively can greatly increase programming productivity.

The overriding objective of this book is to introduce the concepts and practice of Java programming. To facilitate developing and managing Java programs, the book is aided by Visual J++. With a tool like Visual J++, students can not only develop Java programs more productively, but also learn Java programming more effectively.

Microsoft Visual J++ 6 is an integrated Windows-based development tool for Java programming. Visual J++ 6 allows you to create, modify, build, run, debug, and package an application, all within a single environment. Visual J++ 6 significantly improved the earlier versions of J++ 1.1 and J++ 1.0 with many special features, such as IntelliSense, Windows Foundation classes, and Form Designer. IntelliSense is a collection of programming technologies, such as the Statement Completion feature, which helps you to write code. The Statement Completion feature guides your coding by displaying member lists and parameter information as you type.

Visual J++ is easy to learn and easy to use. For convenience and compatibility, Microsoft now uses the same IDE, referred to as *Microsoft Developer Studio* (MDS), for the latest versions of Visual J++, Visual C++, Fortran PowerStation, and Visual Basic. This IDE is very similar to the MS Office suites and certain other Microsoft products. If you have used one MS product, it is easy to learn Visual J++.

Visual J++ is an indispensable, powerful tool that will boost your programming productivity. It may take a while to become familiar with it, but your investment in time will pay off in the long run. This text takes an incremental approach to facilitate learning Visual J++. It is introduced throughout the book to help you gradually adept to programming using Visual J++.

The book is based on Java 2, and Swing components are used to build the graphics examples. Visual J++ 6 does not support Java 2, but you can use Swing components in Visual J++ by adding the Swing JAR file in the class path. Adding the Swing JAR file into the class path is discussed in Appendix F, "Using the Companion CD-ROM and Installing the Swing Library."

If you want to learn Java with JBuilder, please refer to my *Introduction to Java Programming with JBuilder 3*, published by Prentice-Hall. The pros and cons of learning Java with Visual J++ or JBuilder 3 are as follows:

- Visual J++ 6 runs significantly faster than JBuilder 3, because Visual J++ 6 is primarily a Windows-specific application. Visual J++ is more stable than JBuilder 3. Visual J++ 6 requires only 24 MB of memory on a Pentium 90 MHz processor, but you need at least 64 MB on a Pentium 133 MHz processor to run JBuilder 3.

- JBuilder 3 is a pure Java solution. It fully supports Java 2, whereas Visual J++ only supports JDK 1.1. Visual J++ 6 contains WFC (Windows Foundation Classed for Java). These classes are windows-specific and run only on Windows. For compatibility, this book does not use any WFC classes.

Visual J++ 6 is perfectly suitable for beginners to learn Java. If you have used Visual Basic or Visual C++, you will spend less time on learning Visual J++ and be able to give more attention to learning the Java language.

Organization of the Book

This book is divided into four parts that, taken together, form a comprehensive introductory course on Java programming. Because knowledge is cumulative, the early chapters provide the conceptual basis for understanding Java and guide students through simple examples and exercises; subsequent chapters progressively present Java programming in detail, culminating with the development of comprehensive Java applications. The appendixes contain a mixed bag of topics, including an HTML tutorial.

Part I: Fundamentals of Java Programming

The first part of the book is a stepping stone that will prepare you to embark on the journey of learning Java. You will begin to know Java, and will learn how to write simple Java programs with primitive data types, control structures, and methods.

Chapter 1, "Introduction to Java and Visual J++ 6," gives an overview of the major features of Java: object-oriented programming, platform-independence, Java bytecode, security, performance, multithreading, and networking. The chapter also introduces Visual J++ 6 and uses it to create, compile, and run Java applications and applets. Simple examples of writing applications and applets are provided, along with a brief anatomy of programming structures.

Chapter 2, "Java Building Elements," introduces primitive data types, operators, and expressions. Important topics include identifiers, variables, constants, assignment statements, primitive data types, operators, and shortcut operators. Java programming style and documentation are also addressed. You will learn how to run Java programs from the command line, get online help from Visual J++ 6, and customize Visual J++ 6 IDE options.

Chapter 3, "Control Structures," introduces decision and repetition statements. Java decision statements include various forms of `if` statements, the `switch` statement, and the shortcut `if` statement. Java repetition statements include the `for` loop, the `while` loop, and the `do` loop. The keywords `break` and `continue` are discussed.

Chapter 4, "Methods," introduces method creation, calling methods, passing parameters, returning values, method overloading, and recursion. Applying the concept of abstraction is the key to developing software. The chapter also introduces the use of method abstraction in problem-solving.

Part II: Object-Oriented Programming

In the book's second part, object-oriented programming is introduced. Java is a class-centric, object-oriented programming language that uses abstraction, encapsulation, inheritance, and polymorphism to provide great flexibility, modularity, and reusability in developing software. You will learn programming with objects and classes, arrays and strings, and class inheritance.

Chapter 5, "Programming with Objects and Classes," begins with objects and classes. The important topics include defining classes, creating objects, using constructors, passing objects to methods, instance and class variables, and instance and class methods. Many examples are provided to demonstrate the power of the object-oriented programming approach. Students will learn the benefits (abstraction, encapsulation, and modularity) of object-oriented programming from these examples. There are more than 500 predefined Java classes grouped in several packages. Starting with this chapter, students will gradually learn how to use Java classes to develop their own programs. The `Math` class for performing basic math operations is introduced.

Chapter 6, "Arrays and Strings," explores two important structures: arrays for processing data in lists and tables, and strings using the `String`, `StringBuffer`, and `StringTokenizer` classes. Java treats arrays as objects. Unlike the many high-level languages that treat strings as a special kind of array, it does not relate strings to arrays. Java uses strings and arrays very differently. You will also learn how to use Visual J++ 6 to debug programs.

Chapter 7, "Class Inheritance," teaches how an existing class can be extended and modified as needed. Inheritance is an extremely powerful programming technique, further extending software reusability. Java programs are all built by extending predefined Java classes. The major topics include defining subclasses, using the keywords `super` and `this`, using the modifiers `protected`, `final` and `abstract`, and casting objects and interfaces. This chapter introduces the `Object` class, which is the root of all Java classes. You will learn primitive data type wrapper classes to encapsulate primitive data type values in objects, as well as how to manage, view, and navigate code with Class Outline in Visual J++.

Part III: Graphics Programming

The third part of the book introduces Java graphics programming. Major topics include event-driven programming, creating graphical user interfaces, and writing applets. You will learn the architecture of Java graphics programming API and use the user interface components to develop graphics applications and applets.

Chapter 8, "Getting Started with Graphics Programming," introduces the concepts of Java graphics programming using Swing components. Topics include the Swing class hierarchy, event-driven programming, frames, panels, and simple layout managers (`FlowLayout`, `GridLayout`, and `BorderLayout`). The chapter also introduces drawing geometric figures in the graphics context.

Chapter 9, "Creating User Interfaces," introduces the user interface components: buttons, labels, text fields, text areas, choices, lists, check boxes, radio buttons, menus, scrollbars, and scroll panes. Today's client/server and Web-based applications use a graphical user interface (GUI, pronounced "goo-ee"). Java has a rich set of classes to help you build GUIs.

Chapter 10, "Applets and Advanced Graphics," takes an in-depth look at applets, discussing applet behavior and the relationship between applets and other Swing classes. Applets are a special kind of Java class that can be executed from the Web browser. Students will learn how to convert applications to applets, and vice versa, and how to run programs both as applications and as applets. The chapter also introduces two advanced layout mangers (`CardLayout` and `GridBagLayout`) and the use of no layout. Advanced examples of handling mouse and keyboard events are also provided. You will learn how to package and deploy Visual J++ projects.

Part IV: Developing Comprehensive Projects

The book's final part is devoted to several advanced features of Java programming. You will learn how to use these features to develop comprehensive programs; for example, using exception handling to make your program robust, using multithreading to make your program more responsive and interactive, incorporating sound and images to make your program user-friendly, using input and output to manage and process a large quantity of data, and creating client/server applications with Java networking support.

Chapter 11, "Exception Handling," teaches students how to define exceptions, throw exceptions, and handle exceptions so that their programs can either continue to run or terminate gracefully in the event of runtime errors. The chapter discusses predefined exception classes, and gives examples of creating user-defined exception classes.

Chapter 12, "Internationalization," introduces the development of Java programs for international audiences. You will learn how to format dates, numbers, currencies, and percentages for different regions, countries, and languages. You will also learn how to use resource bundles to define which images and strings are used by a component depending on the user's locale and preferences.

Chapter 13, "Multithreading," introduces threads, which enable the running of multiple tasks simultaneously in one program. Students will learn how to use the `Thread` class and the `Runnable` interface to launch separate threads. The chapter also discusses thread states, thread priority, thread groups, and the synchronization of conflicting threads.

Chapter 14, "Multimedia," teaches how to incorporate sound and images to bring live animation to Java programs. Various techniques for smoothing animation are introduced.

Chapter 15, "Input and Output," introduces input and output streams. Students will learn the class structures of I/O streams, byte and character streams, file I/O streams, data I/O streams, print streams, delimited I/O, random file access, and interactive I/O.

Chapter 16, "Networking," introduces network programming. Students will learn the concept of network communication, stream sockets, client/server programming, and reading data files from the Web server.

Appendixes

This part covers a mixed bag of topics. Appendix A lists Java keywords. Appendix B gives tables of ASCII characters and their associated codes in decimal and in hex. Appendix C shows the operator precedence. Appendix D summarizes Java modifiers and their usage. Appendix E introduces HTML basics. Appendix F contains information for using the companion CD-ROM and installing the Swing library. Appendix H introduces rapid Java application development using Visual J++ 6. Finally, Appendix G provides a glossary of key terms found in the text.

Contents at a Glance

PART I	**FUNDAMENTALS OF JAVA PROGRAMMING**	**1**
Chapter 1.	Introduction to Java and Visual J++ 6	1
Chapter 2.	Java Building Elements	45
Chapter 3.	Control Structures	79
Chapter 4.	Methods	111
PART II	**OBJECT-ORIENTED PROGRAMMING**	**139**
Chapter 5.	Programming with Objects and Classes	141
Chapter 6.	Arrays and Strings	185
Chapter 7.	Class Inheritance	231
PART III	**GRAPHICS PROGRAMMING**	**281**
Chapter 8.	Getting Started with Graphics Programming	283
Chapter 9.	Creating User Interfaces	343
Chapter 10.	Applets and Advanced Graphics	417
PART IV	**DEVELOPING COMPREHENSIVE PROJECTS**	**475**
Chapter 11.	Exception Handling	477
Chapter 12.	Internationalization	509
Chapter 13.	Multithreading	543
Chapter 14.	Multimedia	575
Chapter 15.	Input and Output	603
Chapter 16.	Networking	649
	APPENDIXES	**677**
Appendix A.	Java Keywords	679
Appendix B.	The ASCII Character Set	681
Appendix C.	Operator Precedence Chart	685
Appendix D.	Java Modifiers	689
Appendix E.	An HTML Tutorial	691
Appendix F.	Using the Companion CD-ROM and Installing the Swing Library	709
Appendix G.	Rapid Java Application Development Using Visual J++ 6	713
Appendix H.	Glossary	731

Table of Contents

PART I FUNDAMENTALS OF JAVA PROGRAMMING — 1

CHAPTER 1 Introduction to Java and Visual J++ 6 — 3

- Objectives — 3
- Introduction — 4
- The History of Java — 4
- Characteristics of Java — 4
  - Java is Simple — 5
  - Java is Object-Oriented — 5
  - Java is Distributed — 6
  - Java is Interpreted — 6
  - Java is Robust — 7
  - Java is Secure — 7
  - Java is Architecture-Neutral — 7
  - Java is Portable — 8
  - Java's Performance — 8
  - Java is Multithreaded — 8
  - Java is Dynamic — 9
- Java and the World Wide Web — 9
- The Java Language Specification — 10
- Java Development Tools and Visual J++ 6.0 — 11
- Getting Started with Visual J++ — 12
  - Creating a Project — 13
  - Menu Bar and Toolbar — 15
  - Visual J++ IDE Windows — 17
- Java Applications — 23
  - Creating a Java Program — 24
  - Compiling and Executing a Java Program — 28
- Anatomy of the Application Program — 30
  - Comments — 30
  - Reserved Words — 30
  - Modifiers — 31
  - Statements — 31
  - Blocks — 31
  - Classes — 31
  - Methods — 32
  - The *main()* Method — 32

xvii

Java Applets		32
Creating and Compiling an Applet		33
Creating an HTML File		34
Viewing Applets		37
Anatomy of the Applet Program		39
The *import* Statement		39
Class Instance		40
The *paint()* Method and the *Graphics* Class		40
The *extends* Keyword and Class Inheritance		41
Applications versus Applets		42
Chapter Summary		42
Chapter Review		43
Programming Exercises		44

CHAPTER 2   Java Building Elements   45

Objectives	45
Introduction	46
Writing Simple Programs	46
Identifiers	49
Variables	50
Declaring Variables	50
Assignment Statements	50
Declaring and Initializing Variables in One Step	51
Constants	52
Numerical Data Types	52
Numeric Literals	53
Shortcut Operators	53
Numeric Type Conversion	54
Character Data Type	55
boolean Data Type	57
Operator Precedence	59
Programming Errors	60
Compilation Errors	60
Runtime Errors	63
Logic Errors	64
Programming Style and Documentation	64
Appropriate Comments	64
Naming Conventions	65
Proper Indentation	65
Block Styles	66

	Separate Classes	66
	Case Studies	67
	Visual J++'s Online Help	71
	Visual J++ IDE Options	74
	Chapter Summary	75
	Chapter Review	76
	Programming Exercises	78
CHAPTER 3	**Control Structures**	**79**
	Objectives	79
	Introduction	80
	Using *if* Statements	80
	The Simple *if* Statement	80
	The *if . . . else* Statement	81
	Nested if Statements	82
	Running Example 3.1 in Visual J++ 6	85
	Shortcut *if* Statements	87
	Using *switch* Statements	87
	Using Loop Structures	89
	The *for* Loop	89
	The *while* Loop	94
	The *do* Loop	96
	Using the Keywords *break* and *continue*	97
	Case Studies	101
	Chapter Summary	104
	Chapter Review	105
	Programming Exercises	107
CHAPTER 4	**Methods**	**111**
	Objectives	111
	Introduction	112
	Creating a Method	112
	Calling a Method	113
	Passing Parameters	115
	Pass by Value	116
	Overloading Methods	117
	Creating Methods in Separate Classes	119
	Method Abstraction	120
	Recursion (Optional)	126
	Recursion versus Iteration (Optional)	133

	Chapter Summary	134
	Chapter Review	135
	Programming Exercises	136

PART II OBJECT-ORIENTED PROGRAMMING 139

CHAPTER 5 Programming with Objects and Classes 141

Objectives	141
Introduction	142
Objects and Classes	142
Declaring and Creating Objects	143
Constructors	147
Modifiers	150
Passing Objects to Methods	152
Instance Variables and Class Variables	157
Instance Methods and Class Methods	161
The Scope of Variables	162
Case Studies	163
Packages	170
Package-Naming Conventions	171
The CLASSPATH Environment Variable	171
Putting Classes into Packages	172
Using Packages	174
Java Application Programmer Interface	175
The *Math* Class	177
Trigonometric Methods	177
Exponent Methods	177
The *min()*, *max()*, *abs()*, and *random()* Methods	178
Chapter Summary	178
Chapter Review	179
Programming Exercises	182

CHAPTER 6 Arrays and Strings 185

Objectives	185
Introduction	186
Declaring and Creating Arrays	186
Initializing and Processing Arrays	187
Sorting Arrays	190
Searching Arrays	193
The Linear Search Approach	193
The Binary Search Approach (Optional)	195

Array of Objects	198
Copying Arrays	199
Multidimensional Arrays	202
The *String* Class	205
String Comparisons	205
String Concatenation	206
Substrings	206
String Length and Retrieving Individual Characters in a String	207
The *StringBuffer* Class	207
Appending and Inserting New Contents into a *StringBuffer*	208
The *capacity()*, *reverse()*, *length()*, *setLength()*, *charAt()*, and *setCharAt()* Methods	208
The *StringTokenizer* Class	210
Command-Line Arguments	212
Passing Arguments to Java Programs	212
Processing Command-Line Parameters	213
Debugging in Visual J++	215
Starting the Debugger	216
Controlling Program Execution	218
Setting breakpoints	219
Inspecting and Modifying Data Values	220
Debugging TestSelectionSortWithError	223
Chapter Summary	225
Chapter Review	226
Programming Exercises	228
CHAPTER 7 Class Inheritance	**231**
Objectives	231
Introduction	232
Superclasses and Subclasses	232
Using the Keyword super	234
Calling Superclass Constructors	234
Calling Superclass Methods	234
Overriding Methods	235
The Keyword *this*	237
The *protected*, *final*, and *abstract* Modifiers	238
The *protected* Modifier	238
The *final* Modifier	239
The *abstract* Modifier	239

Polymorphism	242
Casting Objects	243
The *Object* class	247
The *equals()* Method	248
The *toString()* method	248
The *clone()* Method	249
Processing Primitive Type Values as Objects	249
The *Number* Class and Its Subclasses	250
Numeric Wrapper Class Constructors	251
Numeric Wrapper Class Constants	251
Conversion Methods	251
The *valueOf()*, *parseInt()*, and *parseDouble()* Methods	252
Class-Design Guidelines	252
Case Studies (Optional)	253
Interfaces	261
Inner Classes	266
Adding New Classes, Methods, and Data to Classes in Visual J++	267
Overriding a Method in the Superclass	272
Chapter Summary	274
Chapter Review	275
Programming Exercises	278

PART III GRAPHICS PROGRAMMING 281

CHAPTER 8 Getting Started with Graphics Programming 283

Objectives	283
Introduction	284
The Java Graphics Class Hierarchy	285
Creating a Frame	288
Event-Driven Programming	289
Event and Event Source	290
Event Registration, Listening, and Handling	291
Handling Events	293
Adapters and Anonymous Inner Classes (Optional)	302
Layout Managers	305
FlowLayout	306
GridLayout	308
BorderLayout	310

	Using Panels as Containers	312
	Using Panels to Draw Graphics	314
	The *repaint()*, *update()*, *paint()*, and *paintComponent()* Methods	317
	The *Color* Class	318
	Drawing Geometric Figures	318
	The *Font* and *FontMetrics* Classes	319
	Drawing Lines	324
	Drawing Rectangles	324
	Ovals	327
	Arcs	329
	Polygons	330
	Case Studies	333
	Chapter Summary	337
	Chapter Review	337
	Programming Exercises	339
CHAPTER 9	**Creating User Interfaces**	**343**
	Objectives	343
	Introduction	344
	JavaBeans	344
	Buttons	347
	Labels	352
	Text Fields	354
	Text Areas	357
	Combo Boxes	360
	Lists	364
	Check Boxes	367
	Radio Buttons	370
	Borders	375
	Message Dialog Boxes	382
	Menus	386
	Image Icons, Keyboard Mnemonics, and Keyboard Accelerators	389
	Creating Multiple Windows	394
	Scrollbars	396
	Scroll Panes	400
	Tabbed Panes	405
	Chapter Summary	409

	Chapter Review	410
	Programming Exercises	411
CHAPTER 10	**Applets and Advanced Graphics**	**417**
	Objectives	417
	Introduction	418
	The *Applet* Classes	418
	The *init()* method	419
	The *start()* method	419
	The *stop()* method	420
	The *destroy()* method	420
	The *JApplet* Class	420
	The *<applet>* HTML Tag	424
	Running Applets in the Java Plug-In (Optional)	425
	Passing Parameters to Applets	428
	Conversions between Applications and Applets	431
	Running a Program as an Applet and an Application	437
	Mouse Events	441
	Keyboard Events	445
	Case Studies	448
	The *CardLayout* Manager (Optional)	455
	The *GridBagLayout* Manager (Optional)	458
	Using No Layout Manager (Optional)	462
	Packaging and Deploying Visual J++ Projects (Optional)	465
	Packaging and Deploying as .exe files	465
	Packaging and Deploying as .zip files	467
	Chapter Summary	467
	Chapter Review	468
	Programming Exercises	469
PART IV	**DEVELOPING COMPREHENSIVE PROJECTS**	**475**
CHAPTER 11	**Exception Handling**	**477**
	Objectives	477
	Introduction	478
	Exceptions and Exception Types	478
	Understanding Exception Handling	480
	Claiming Exceptions	480

	Throwing Exceptions	481
	Catching Exceptions	482
	Creating Custom Exception Classes	487
	Rethrowing Exceptions	494
	The *finally* Clause	495
	Cautions When Using Exceptions	495
	Chapter Summary	498
	Chapter Review	499
	Programming Exercises	506
CHAPTER 12	**Internationalization**	**509**
	Objectives	509
	Introduction	510
	Locale	510
	Processing Date and Time	513
	Formatting Numbers	527
	Resource Bundles (Optional)	532
	Chapter Summary	540
	Review Questions	540
	Exercises	540
CHAPTER 13	**Multithreading**	**543**
	Objectives	543
	Introduction	544
	The *Thread* Class	545
	Debugging Multithreaded Applications in Visual J++	549
	The *Runnable* Interface	551
	Case Studies	557
	Thread States	562
	Thread Priority	563
	Thread Groups	565
	Synchronization	565
	Chapter Summary	570
	Chapter Review	570
	Programming Exercises	571
CHAPTER 14	**Multimedia**	**575**
	Objectives	575
	Introduction	576
	Playing Audio	576
	Running Audio on a Separate Thread	581

	Displaying Images	583
	Loading Image and Audio Files in Java Applications	586
	Displaying a Sequence of Images	591
	Using MediaTracker	595
	Chapter Summary	598
	Chapter Review	598
	Programming Exercises	599
CHAPTER 15	**Input and Output**	**603**
	Objectives	603
	Introduction	604
	Stream Classes	605
	InputStream and *Reader*	606
	OutputStream and *Writer*	607
	Processing External Files	608
	Array Streams	611
	Filter Streams	611
	Data Streams	612
	Print Streams	616
	Buffered Streams	618
	Parsing Text Files	622
	Random Access Files	625
	File Dialogs	636
	Interactive Input and Output	641
	Piped Streams, String Streams, Pushback Streams, Line Number Streams, and Object Streams	643
	Chapter Summary	644
	Chapter Review	645
	Programming Exercises	646
CHAPTER 16	**Networking**	**649**
	Objectives	649
	Introduction	650
	Client/Server Computing	650
	Serving Multiple Clients	656
	Applet Clients	660
	Viewing Web Pages	665
	Retrieving Files from Web Servers	668
	Chapter Summary	673
	Chapter Review	673
	Programming Exercises	674

APPENDIXES — 677

APPENDIX A	Java Keywords	679
APPENDIX B	The ASCII Character Set	681
APPENDIX C	Operator Precedence Chart	685
APPENDIX D	Java Modifiers	689
APPENDIX E	An HTML Tutorial	691

    Getting Started — 692
    Structure Tags — 694
    Text Appearance Tags — 694
        Content-Based Tags — 694
        Physical Tags — 695
    Paragraph Style Tags — 696
    Font, Size, and Color Tags — 697
    List Tags — 698
        Ordered Lists — 699
        Unordered Lists — 699
        Definition Lists — 699
    Table Tags — 700
    Hyperlink Tags — 702
        Linking Documents on Different Computers — 702
        Linking Documents on the Same Computer — 703
        Jumping Within the Same Document — 703
    Embedding Graphics — 705
        Horizontal Bar Tags — 705
    More on HTML — 706
        Image Tags — 706

APPENDIX F	**Using the Companion CD-ROM and Installing the Swing Library**	**709**

    Installing Visual J++ 6 — 709
    Installing Swing Library in Visual J++ 6 — 709
    Using the Examples in the Book — 710

APPENDIX G	**Rapid Java Application Development Using Visual J++ 6.0**	**713**

    Form Designer Basics — 714
        Switching between Form Designer and Code Editor — 715
        The Toolbox Window — 715
        The Properties Window — 717
        Implementing Handlers — 718
    Using the Form Designer to Develop Applications — 720

	Phase 1: Creating User Interface	721
	Phase 2: Implementing Handlers	722
	Phase 3: Creating Menus	723
APPENDIX H	**Glossary**	**731**
INDEX		**739**

PART I

FUNDAMENTALS OF JAVA PROGRAMMING

By now you have heard a lot about Java and are anxious to start writing Java programs. The first part of the book is a stepping stone that will prepare you to embark on the journey of learning Java with Microsoft Visual J++. You will begin to know Java and will learn how to write simple Java programs with primitive data types, control structures, and methods.

CHAPTER 1   INTRODUCTION TO JAVA AND VISUAL J++ 6

CHAPTER 2   JAVA BUILDING ELEMENTS

CHAPTER 3   CONTROL STRUCTURES

CHAPTER 4   METHODS

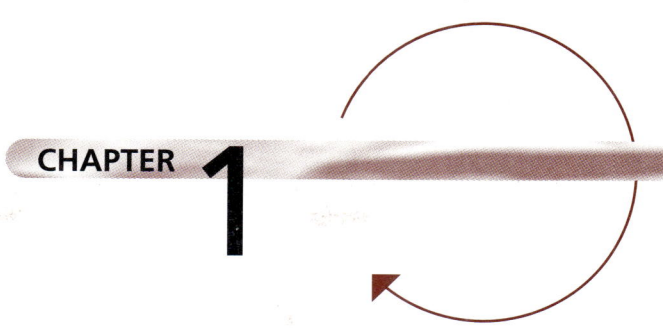

CHAPTER 1

INTRODUCTION TO JAVA AND VISUAL J++ 6

Objectives

- Learn about Java and its history.
- Understand the relationship between Java and the World Wide Web.
- Become familiar with Visual J++.
- Know how to create Java projects, and how to compile and run Java programs with Visual J++.
- Understand the Java environment.
- Write a simple Java application.
- Write a simple Java applet.

Introduction

By now you have heard quite a lot about the exciting Java programming language. It must seem as if Java is everywhere! Your local bookstores are filled with Java books. There are articles about Java in all the major newspapers and magazines. It is impossible to read a computer magazine without coming across the magic word *Java*. You must be wondering why Java is so hot. The answer is that it enables users to deploy applications on the Internet. In fact, this is its main distinguishing characteristic. The future of computing will be profoundly influenced by the Internet, and Java promises to remain a big part of that future. Java is *the* Internet programming language.

You are about to begin an exciting journey, learning a powerful programming language. Java is cross-platform, object-oriented, network-based, and multimedia-ready. After its inception in May 1995, Java quickly became a mature language for deploying mission-critical applications. This chapter begins with a brief history of Java and its programming features, followed by simple examples of Java applications and applets.

The History of Java

Java was developed by a team led by James Gosling at Sun Microsystems, a company best known for its Sun workstations. Originally called Oak, it was designed in 1991 for use in embedded consumer electronic applications. In 1995, renamed Java, it was redesigned for developing Internet applications. Java programs can be embedded in HTML pages and downloaded by Web browsers to bring live animation and interaction to Web clients.

The power of Java is not limited to Web applications, for it is a general-purpose programming language. It has full programming features and can be used to develop standalone applications. Java is inherently object-oriented. Although many object-oriented languages began strictly as procedural languages, Java was designed from the start to be object-oriented. Object-oriented programming (OOP) is a popular programming approach that is replacing traditional procedural programming techniques.

> **NOTE**
> One of the central issues in software development is how to reuse code. Object-oriented programming provides great flexibility, modularity, clarity, and reusability through method abstraction, class abstraction, and class inheritance—all of which you'll learn about in this book.

Characteristics of Java

Java has gained enormous popularity. It is the language for networking and controlling smart appliances and futuristic devices, and is perceived as a universal front end for enterprise databases. Java's rapid rise and wide acceptance can be traced to its design and programming features, particularly its promise that you can write a program once and run the program anywhere. As stated in the Java language white paper by Sun, Java is *simple, object-oriented, distributed, interpreted, robust, secure, architecture-neutral, portable, high-performance, multithreaded,* and *dynamic*. Let's analyze these often-used buzzwords.

Java is Simple

No language is simple, but Java is a bit easier than the popular object-oriented programming language C++, which was the dominant software-development language before Java. Java is partially modeled on C++, but greatly simplified and improved. For instance, pointers and multiple inheritance often make programming complicated. Java replaces the multiple inheritance in C++ with a language construct called an *interface,* and eliminates pointers.

Java uses automatic memory allocation and garbage collection, whereas C++ requires the programmer to allocate memory and collect garbage. Also, the number of language constructs is small for such a powerful language. The clean syntax makes Java programs easy to write and read. Some people refer to Java as "C++--" because it is like C++, but with more functionality and fewer negative aspects.

Java is Object-Oriented

Object-oriented programming models the real world. Everything in the world can be modeled as an object. A circle is an object, a person is an object, and a window's icon is an object. Even a mortgage can be perceived as an object. A Java program is called object-oriented because programming in Java is centered on creating objects, manipulating objects, and making objects work together.

An object has *properties* and *behaviors*. Properties are described by using *data,* and behaviors are defined by using *methods*. Objects are defined by using classes in Java. A class is like a template for the objects. An object is a concrete realization of a class description. The process of creating an object of the class is called *instantiation*. For example, you can define the class `Circle` by which to model all `Circle` objects (see Figure 1.1), with `radius` as the property and `findArea` as the method to find the area of the circle. You can create a `Circle` object by instantiating the class with a particular radius. You can create a circle with radius 2, and another circle with radius 5. You can then find the area of the respective circles by using the `findArea()` method.

A Java program consists of one or more classes. Classes are arranged in a treelike hierarchy, so that a child class can inherit properties and behaviors from its parent class. Java comes with an extensive set of predefined classes, grouped in packages. You can use them in your programs.

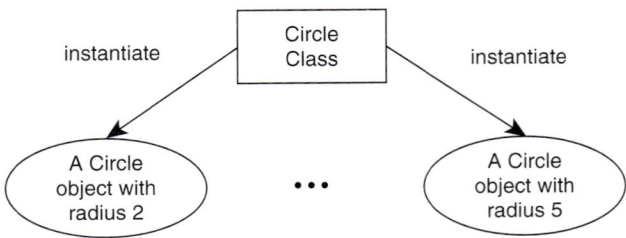

Figure 1.1 *Two* `Circle` *objects with radii 2 and 5 are created from the* `Circle` *class.*

Object-oriented programming provides great flexibility, modularity, and reusability. For years, object-oriented technology was perceived as elitist, requiring a substantial investment in training and infrastructure. Java has helped object-oriented technology enter the mainstream of computing. Its simple, clean structure makes programs easy to write and read. Java programs are quite *expressive* in terms of applications and designs.

Java is Distributed

Distributed computing involves several computers working together on a network. Java is designed to make distributed computing easy. Since networking capability is inherently integrated into Java, writing network programs is like sending and receiving data to and from a file. For example, Figure 1.2 shows three programs running on three different systems; the three programs communicate with each other to perform a joint task.

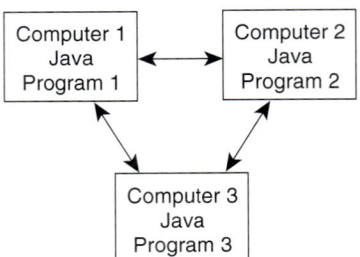

Figure 1.2 *Java programs can run on different systems that work together.*

Java is Interpreted

You need an interpreter to run Java programs. The programs are compiled into Java Virtual Machine code called *bytecode*. The bytecode is machine-independent and can run on any machine that has a Java interpreter.

Usually, a compiler translates a program in a high-level language to machine code. The code can only run on the native machine. If you run the program on other machines, it has to be recompiled on the native machine. For instance, if you compile a C program in Windows, the executable code generated by the compiler can only run on the Windows platform. With Java, you compile the source code once, and the bytecode generated by a Java compiler can run on any platform with a Java interpreter.

Java is Robust

Robust means *reliable*. No programming language can assure complete reliability. Java puts a lot of emphasis on early checking for possible errors, as Java compilers can detect many problems that would first show up at execution time in other languages. Java has eliminated certain types of error-prone programming constructs found in other languages. It does not support pointers, for example, thereby eliminating the possibility of overwriting memory and corrupting data.

Java has a runtime exception-handling feature to provide programming support for robustness. Java can catch and respond to an exceptional situation so that the program can continue its normal execution and terminate gracefully when a runtime error occurs.

Java is Secure

As an Internet programming language, Java is used in a networked and distributed environment. If you download a Java applet (a special kind of program) and run it on your computer, it will not damage your system because Java implements several security mechanisms to protect your system from being harmed by stray programs. The security is based on the premise that *nothing should be trusted*.

There is no absolute security, however. Security bugs were recently discovered in Java, but they were subtle and few, and have been addressed.

> **NOTE**
> A computer security team at Princeton University maintains a Web site devoted to Java security issues. You can find new security bugs and fixes at **www.cs.princeton.edu/sip/**.

Java is Architecture-Neutral

The most remarkable feature of Java is that it is *architecture neutral,* also known as platform-independent. With a Java Virtual Machine, you can write one program that will run on any platform. Since the major OS vendors have adopted the Java Virtual Machine, Java will soon be able to run on all machines.

Java's initial success derived from its Web programming capability. You can run Java applets from a Web browser, but Java is for more than just writing Web applets. You can also run standalone Java applications directly from operating systems using a Java interpreter. Today, software vendors usually develop multiple versions of the same product to run on different platforms (Windows, OS/2, Macintosh, and various UNIX, IBM AS/400, and IBM mainframes). Using Java, developers need to write only one version to run on all of the platforms.

Java is Portable

Java programs can be run on any platform without being recompiled, making them very portable. Moreover, there are no platform-specific features in the Java language specification. In some languages, such as Ada, the largest integer varies on different platforms. But in Java, the size of the integer is the same on every platform, as is the behavior of arithmetic. The fixed size of numbers makes the program portable.

The Java environment is portable to new hardware and operating systems. In fact, the Java compiler itself is written in Java.

Java's Performance

Java's performance is sometimes criticized. The execution of the bytecode is never as fast as a compiled language, such as C++. Because Java is interpreted, the bytecode is not directly executed by the system, but is run through the interpreter. However, the speed is more than adequate for most interactive applications, where the CPU is often idle, waiting for input or for data from other sources.

CPU speed has increased dramatically in the past few years, and this trend is likely to continue. There are many ways to improve performance. If you used the earlier Sun Java Virtual Machine (JVM), you will certainly notice that Java is slow. However, new JVMs from Borland, Microsoft, and Symantec are 10 or even 20 times faster than the first Sun JVM. These new JVMs use the technology known as just-in-time compilation. They compile bytecode into native machine code, store the native code, and reinvoke the native code when its bytecode is repeatedly executed. Sun recently unveiled the Java HotSpot Performance Engine, which includes a compiler for optimizing the frequently used code. The HotSpot Performance Engine can be plugged into a JVM to dramatically boost its performance. Thus speed will continue to improve over time.

> **NOTE**
> IBM has formed a joint lab with Sun and Netscape to improve Java performance. IBM is one of the strongest and most influential supporters of Java. It views Java as a glue that will unify different platforms and applications.

Java is Multithreaded

Multithreading is a program's capability to perform several tasks simultaneously. For example, downloading a video file while playing the video would be considered multithreading. Multithread programming is smoothly integrated in Java. In other languages, you have to call operating system-specific procedures to enable multithreading.

Multithreading is particularly useful in graphical user interface (GUI) and network programming. In GUI programming, there are many things going on at the same time. A user can listen to an audio recording while surfing a Web page. In network programming, a server can serve multiple clients at the same time. Multithreading is a necessity in visual and network programming.

Java is Dynamic

Java was designed to adapt to an evolving environment. You can freely add new methods and properties to a class without affecting its clients. For example, in the `Circle` class, you can add a new data property to indicate the color of the circle, and a new method to obtain the circumference of the circle. The original client program that uses the `Circle` class remains the same. Also, at runtime Java loads classes as they are needed.

Java and the World Wide Web

The World Wide Web is an electronic information repository that can be accessed on the Internet from anywhere in the world. You can use the Web to book a hotel room, buy an airline ticket, register for a college course, download the *New York Times,* chat with friends, and listen to live radio. There are countless activities you can do on the Internet. Today, many people spend a good part of their computer time surfing the Web for fun and profit.

The Internet is the infrastructure of the WWW. The Internet has been around for more than thirty years, but has only recently become popular. The colorful World Wide Web is the major reason for its popularity.

The primary authoring language for the Web is Hypertext Markup Language (HTML). HTML is a markup language: a simple language for laying out documents, linking documents on the Internet, and bringing images, sound, and video alive on the Web. However, it cannot interact with the user except through simple forms. Web pages in HTML essentially are static and flat.

Java programs can run from a Web browser. Because Java is a full-blown programming language, you can make programs responsive and interactive with users. Java programs that run from a Web page are called *applets*. Applets use a modern graphical user interface, including buttons, text fields, text areas, option buttons, and so on. Applets can respond to user events, such as mouse movements and keystrokes.

Figure 1.3 shows an applet in an HTML page, and Figure 1.4 shows the HTML source. The source contains an applet tag, and the applet tag specifies the Java applet. The HTML source can be seen by choosing View, HTML Source from the HotJava Web Browser.

> **NOTE**
> For a demonstration of Java applets, visit www.javasoft.com/applets/. This site contains a rich Java resource.

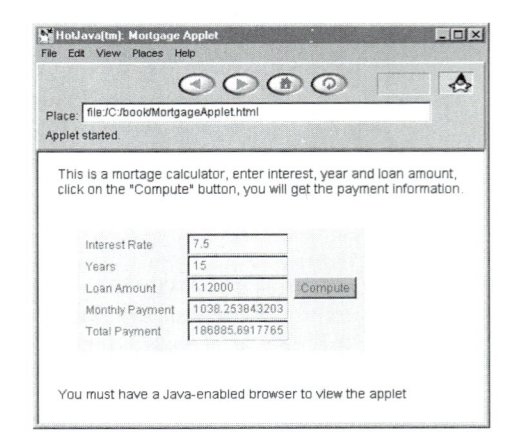

Figure 1.3 *A Java applet for computing a mortgage is embedded in an HTML page. The user can find the mortgage payment by using this applet.*

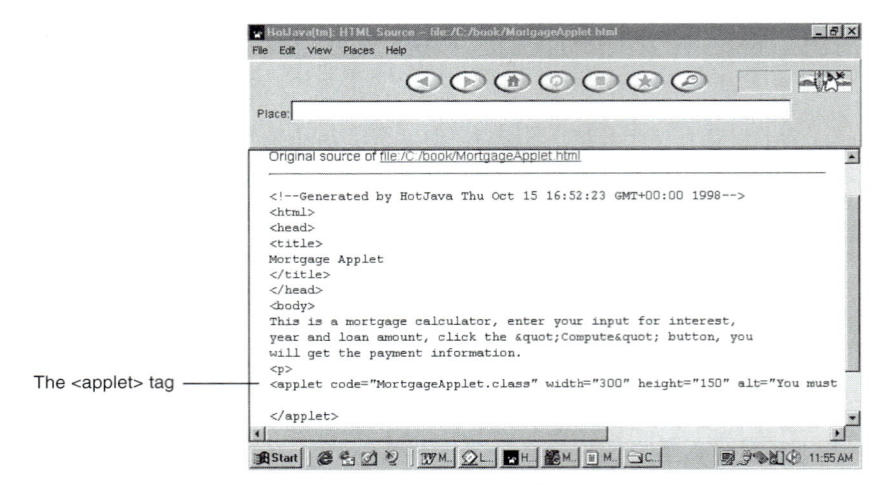

Figure 1.4 *The HTML source that contains the applet shows the tag specifying the Java applet.*

The Java Language Specification

Computer languages have strict rules of usage. You must follow the rules when writing programs or else the computer will be unable to understand them. Sun Microsystems, the originator of Java, intends to retain control of this important new computer language—and for a very good reason: to prevent it from losing its unified standards. The complete reference of Java standards can be found in *Java Language Specification* by James Gosling, Bill Joy, and Guy Steele (Addison-Wesley, 1996).

The Java language specification is a technical definition of the language that includes syntax, structures, and the *application programmer interface* (API), which contains predefined classes. The Java language is still rapidly evolving. At the JavaSoft Web site (**www.javasoft.com**), you can view the latest version and updates. Sun maintains online documentation for the API and the language specification.

Sun releases each version of Java with a Java Development Toolkit, known as JDK. This is a primitive command-line tool set that includes a compiler, an interpreter, and the Applet Viewer, as well as other useful utilities.

> **NOTE**
> Sun announced the Java 2 name in December 1998, just as it released JDK 1.2. Java 2 is the overarching brand that applies to the latest Java technology. JDK 1.2 is the first version of the Java development toolkit that supports the Java 2 technology. Not long ago, Sun's JDK 1.2 was renamed Java 2 SDK. The current version of Java 2 SDK is v 1.2.2. Since most Java programmers are familiar with the name JDK, this book uses the terms Java SDK and JDK interchangeably.

> **NOTE**
> The current version of Visual J++ does not support Java 2, but you can use the Swing components of Java 2 in Visual J++. Chapter 8, "Getting Started with Graphics Programming," discusses installing the Swing JAR files in the classpath for using Swing components in Visual J++.

Java Development Tools and Visual J++ 6.0

JDK consists of a set of separate programs, each of which is invoked from a command line. Besides JDK, there are more than a dozen Java development packages on the market today. The major development tools are

- Visual J++ by Microsoft (**www.microsoft.com**)
- JBuilder by Borland (**www.inprise.com**)
- Visual Café by Symantec (**www.symantec.com**)
- JFactory by Rouge Wave (**www.rougewave.com**)
- Sun Java Workshop (**www.javasoft.com**)
- Visual Age for Java by IBM (**www.ibm.com**)

These tools provide an *integrated development environment* (IDE) for rapidly developing Java programs. The basic functions of these tools are very similar. Editing, compiling, building, debugging, and online help are integrated in one graphical user interface. Just enter the source code in one window or open an existing file in a window, then click a button, menu item, or function key to compile the source code. The use of development tools makes it easy and productive to develop Java programs. This book introduces Java programming with Visual J++ 6.0.

Microsoft Visual J++ 6.0 is an integrated Windows-based development tool for Java programming. It allows you to create, modify, build, run, debug, and package an application, all in a single environment. Visual J++ 6.0 significantly improved the earlier versions of J++ 1.1 and J++ 1.0 with many special features, such as IntelliSense, Windows Foundation classes, and Form Designer. IntelliSense is a collection of programming technologies, such as the Statement Completion feature for assisting you to write code. The Statement Completion feature displays member lists and parameter information that guide your coding as you type.

Visual J++ 6.0 introduces Windows Foundation Classes for Java (WFC). This new application framework accesses the Microsoft Windows API, enabling you to write full-featured Windows applications with the Java programming language. The Form Designer supports Rapid Application Development (RAD) to create form-based applications with Windows Foundation classes. Using the Toolbox, you can quickly drop WFC controls onto your form and configure their properties in the Properties window.

For convenience and compatibility, Microsoft now uses the same IDE, referred to as *Microsoft Visual Studio,* for the latest versions of Visual J++, Visual C++, Fortran PowerStation, and Visual Basic. This IDE is very similar to the Microsoft Office suites and other Microsoft products. If you have used one MS product, it is easy to learn other MS products. In the next few sections, you will become acquainted with VJ++ 6 by learning how to start Visual J++, create a project, create a Java program, and compile and run a program.

Getting Started with Visual J++

Assume you have successfully installed Visual J++ 6.0 on your machine. For information on installation, please refer to Appendix F, "Installing Visual J++ 6.0."

To start Visual J++, click the Windows Start button, select Programs, Microsoft Visual J++ 6.0, Microsoft Visual J++ 6.0, as shown in Figure 1.5. The Visual J++ IDE appears, as shown in Figure 1.6.

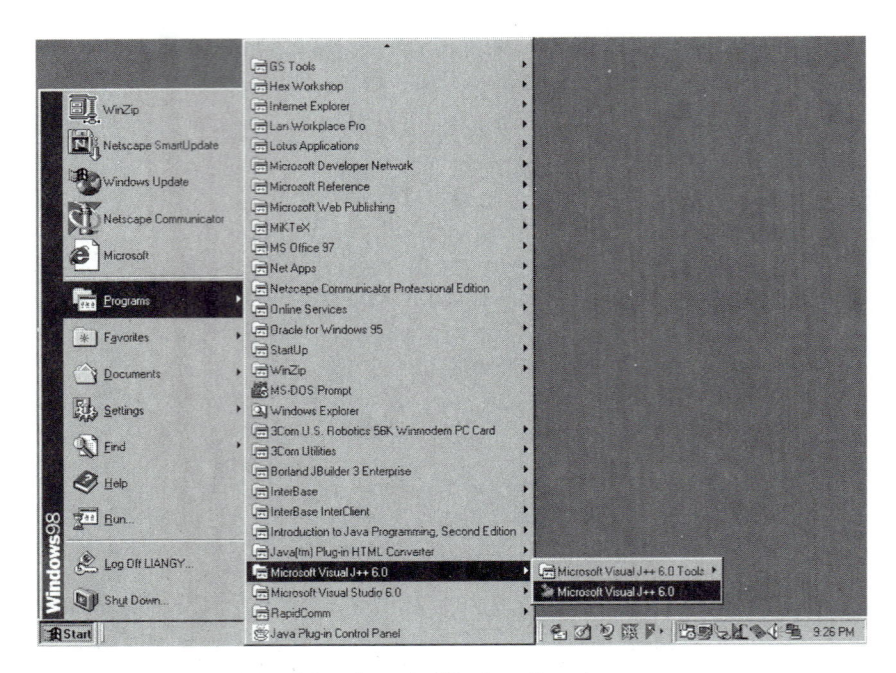

Figure 1.5 *You can start Visual J++ from the Windows Start button.*

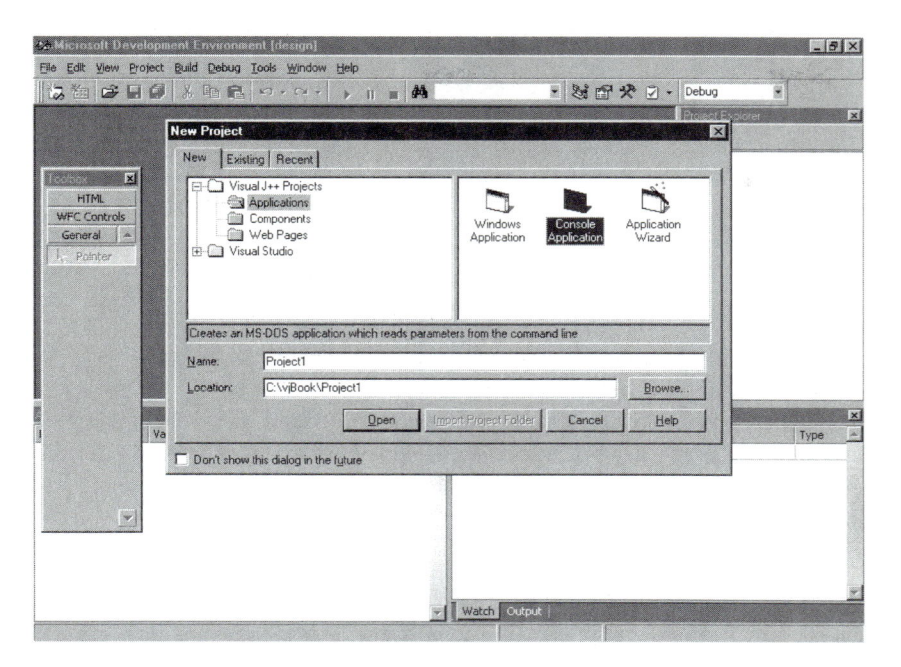

Figure 1.6 *The New Project dialog box is displayed when Visual J++ starts.*

You will see the New Project dialog box displayed in the center of the screen. In Visual J++, programs are placed in projects. Projects are directory-based. Each file and folder in the project corresponds to a file and folder on the hard disk. Creating a file to the project stores the file in the project directory on the hard disk, and vice versa. For convenience, a project will be created to hold all the programs in a chapter. For instance, all the programs in Chapter 1 will be included in a project named Project1.

Creating a Project

The following are the steps to create Project1 in the New Project dialog box:

1. If the New Project dialog is not displayed, choose File, New Project to display it.

2. In the New Project dialog, choose the New tab if it is not selected.

3. Type Project1 in the Name field and c:\vjBook\Project1 in the Location field.

4. Choose the option "Close current solution" if it is not selected. This option is *only* visible in the New Project dialog box if a current project is in use in Visual J++. This option is not shown in Figure 1.6.

5. Choose Applications under Visual J++ projects in the left pane and double-click the Console Application icon in the right pane.

You will see Project1 displayed in the Project Explorer window, as shown in Figure 1.7. A program named Class1.java was automatically created in Project1. Several supporting files for the project were also created and are stored in the directory c:\vjBook\Project1. You can display all the files in c:\vjBook\Project1 by clicking the Show All files button in the Project Explorer, as shown in Figure 1.7. The files displayed in the project with dimmed icons on the left are noneditable. These files are automatically updated by J++. You can edit the files with visible icons. For example, double-clicking the node for Class1.java, you will see the code for Class1.java displayed in the Text Editor, as shown in Figure 1.8.

The top-level node "Solution 'Project1' (1 project)" in the Project Explorer window represents a solution. A *solution* is a group of one or more projects and associated items. Every time you work in the Integrated Development Environment you are working with a solution; each instance of the IDE can contain only one solution. Information about the projects and items that make up a solution is contained in a solution .sln file with the image icon as .

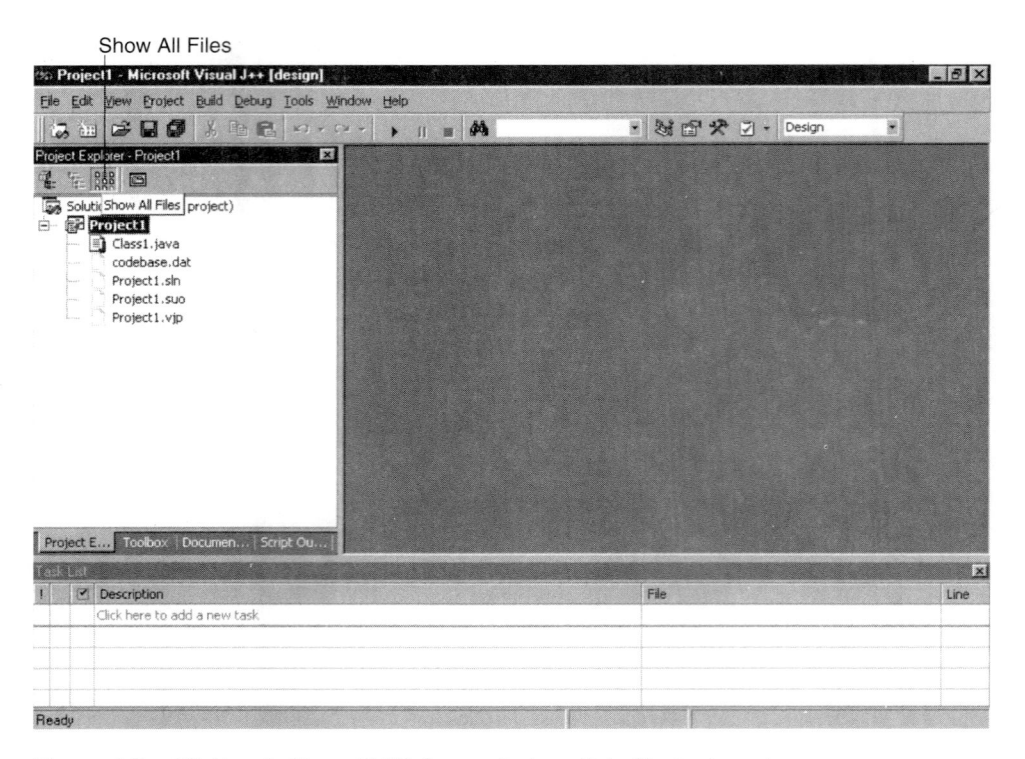

Figure 1.7 *Clicking the Show All File button displays all the files in the project.*

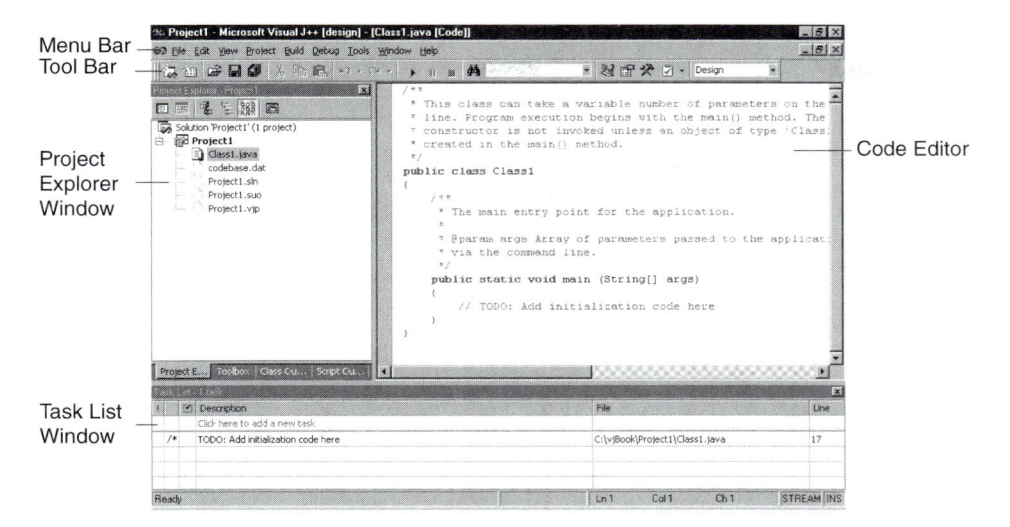

Figure 1.8 *Clicking Class1.java in the Project Explorer brings up the Text Editor.*

Menu Bar and Toolbar

As shown in Figure 1.8, the user interface primarily consists of the main menu, toolbar, and various kinds of windows. The menu bar, which is similar to that of other Windows applications, provides most of the commands you need to use Visual J++, including those for creating programs, editing programs, managing views, compiling, running, and debugging programs. The menu items are enabled and disabled in response to the current context.

The toolbar provides buttons for several frequently used commands on the menu bar. Clicking a toolbar is faster than using the menu bar. For some commands, you also can use function keys or keyboard shortcuts. For example, you can save a file in three ways:

- Select File, Save from the menu bar.
- Click the "Save" toolbar button .
- Use the keyboard shortcut Ctrl+S.

> **TIP**
> You can display a label for a toolbar button by pointing the mouse to the button without clicking. This label is known as *tooltip*.

Visual J++ has many tool bar windows. To display a toolbar window, choose View, Toolbars, or right-click on any toolbar window to display a popup menu, as shown in Figure 1.9. By default, the standard toolbar window is displayed. The toolbar window can be docked with the menu bar, as shown in Figure 1.9, or floated on top of the IDE, as shown in Figure 1.10. To make it appear floating, simply drag the toolbar window away from the menu bar area. To make it attached to menu bar, drag the toolbar window to the menu bar area.

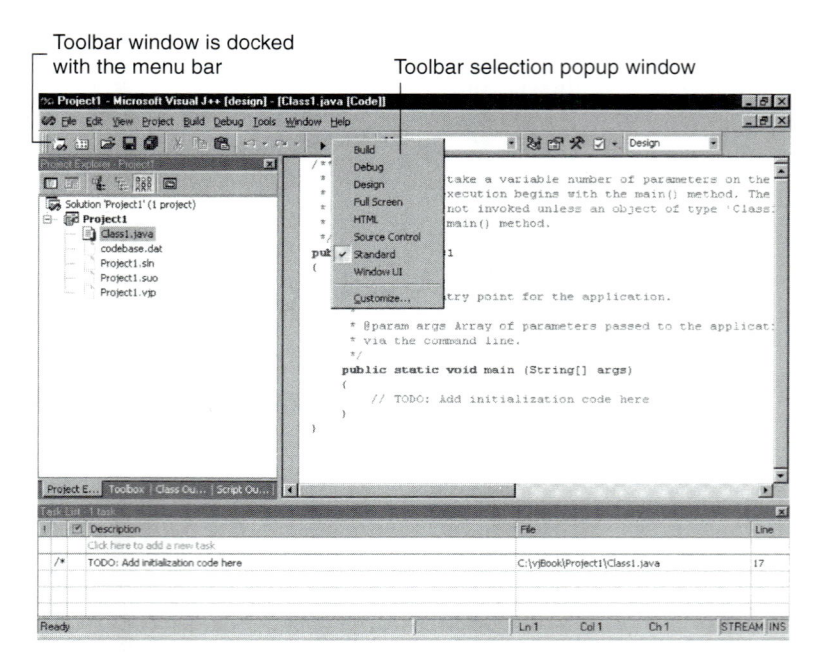

Figure 1.9 *You can display a toolbar window by clicking the toolbar item on the toolbar selection popup menu.*

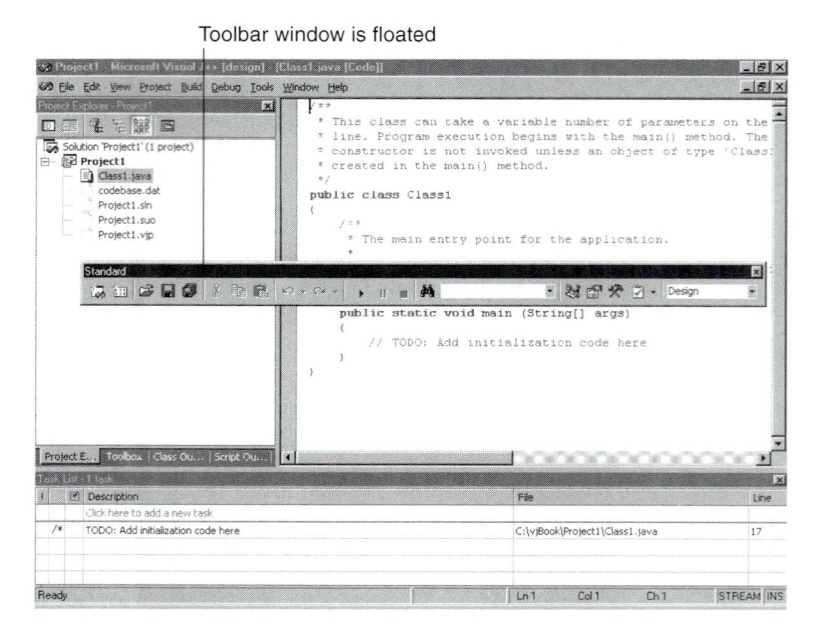

Figure 1.10 *The toolbar window can float on top of the IDE.*

Visual J++ IDE Windows

There are many kinds of windows in Visual J++ for showing project, editing files, running files, displaying compilation errors, running programs, and debugging programs. In Figure 1.11, you saw five windows inside the main window: the Project Explorer window, the Property window, the Toolbox window, the Task List window and the Text Editor window. There are over 30 different types of windows in J++ IDE. They will be introduced incrementally as the text proceeds.

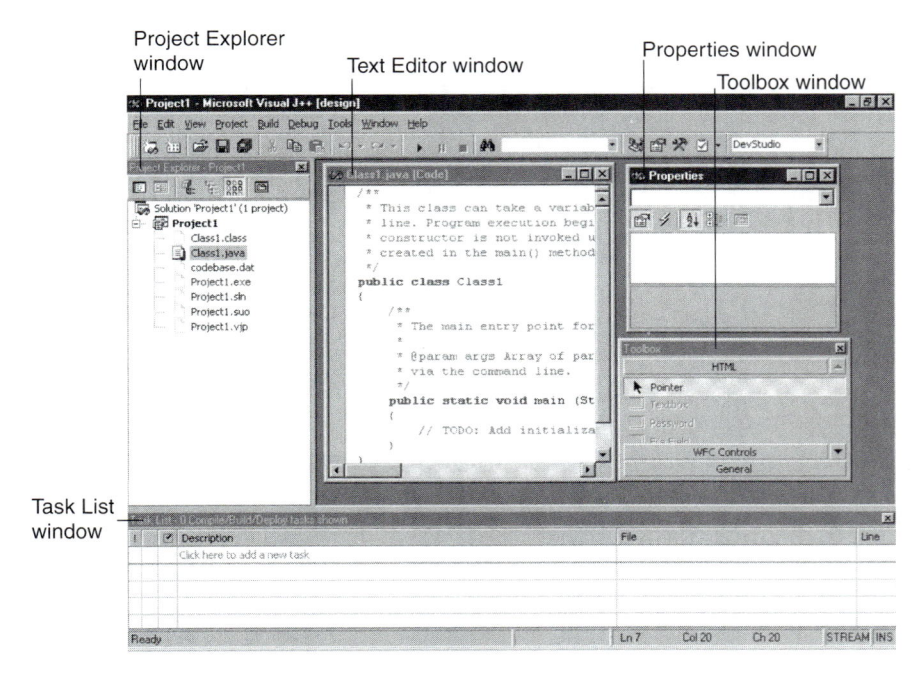

Figure 1.11 *Visual J++ IDE contains many windows for performing specific tasks.*

The windows can be classified into tool windows and document windows. *Tool windows* are windows added by the development environment. The Project Explorer window, the Property window, the Toolbox window, and the Task List window are examples of tool windows. *Document windows* are windows that contain items you create. For example, the Text Editor window is a document. You can *dock* or *link* the tool windows to minimize window clutter, and you can view only the windows you need. You can also customize your window preferences so that each time you open the development environment, you view the windows you want by defining a window layout.

Tool Windows

Although you cannot maximize or minimize a tool window, you can resize it. The new size becomes part of your current view. When a tool window is active, you can make changes to it. For example, you can add items and projects to the Project Explorer when it is active.

Tool windows can be hidden, shown, docked, linked, or moved outside the application area. To hide a tool window, simply click its close button. To show a tool window, choose an appropriate command in the View menu. For example, if the Project Explorer window is hidden, choose View, Project Explorer to show it.

You can make a tool window dockable or undockable by selecting or clearing the Dockable command on the Window menu when the window is focused or right-clicking the mouse button on the window's title bar, as shown in Figure 1.12. When a tool window is dockable, it floats on top of the other windows or snaps to a side of the application window. To move a dockable window without snapping it into place, press the CTRL key while dragging it to the location you desire. Figure 1.13 shows that the Toolbox window floats on the top of the Project Explorer window, and Figure 1.14 shows that the Toolbox window snaps to the right side of the Project Explorer window. When tool windows are no longer dockable, they behave like document windows, appearing on the Windows list of the Windows menu.

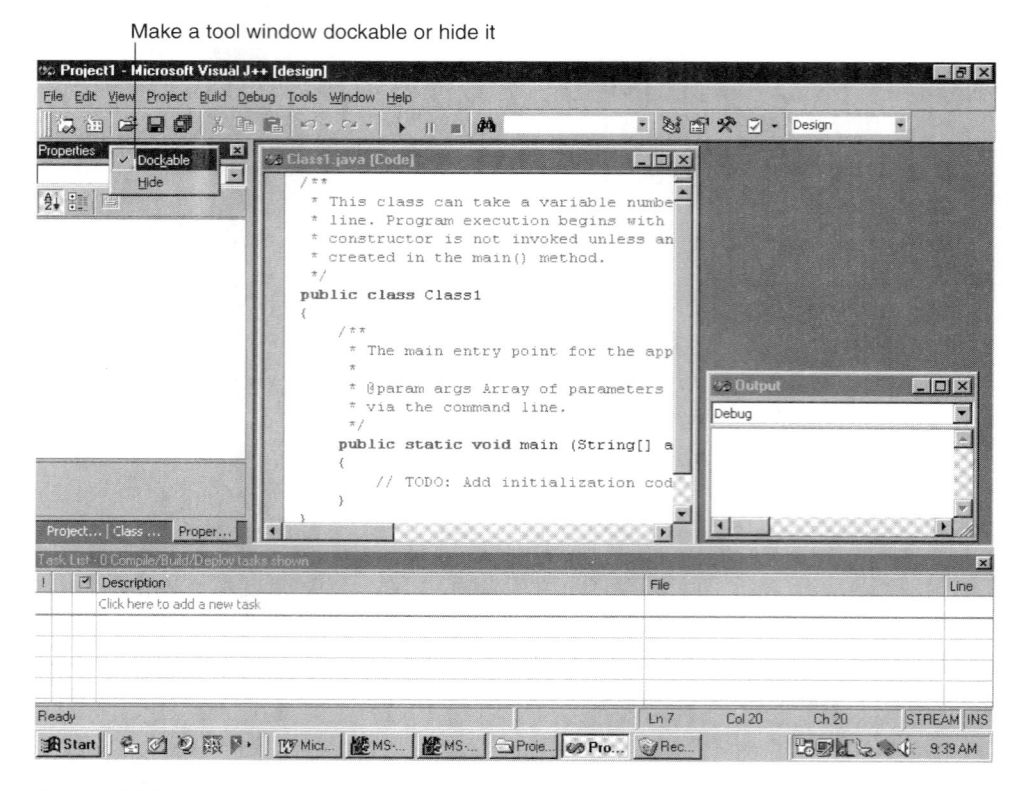

Figure 1.12 *You can set a toolbar window dockable or undockable.*

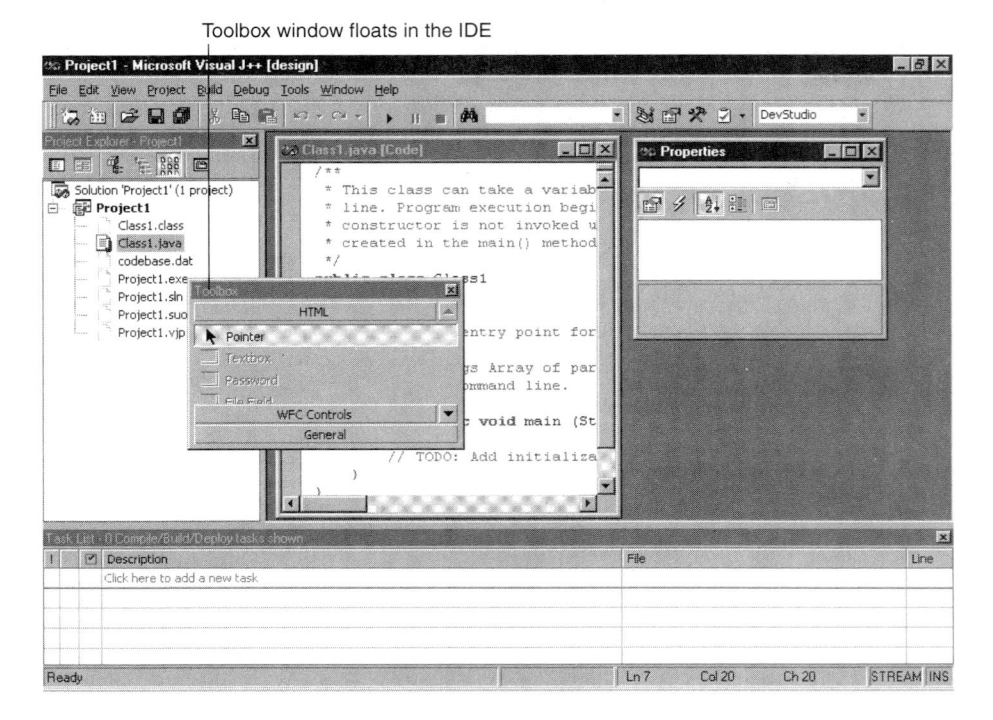

Figure 1.13 *The Toolbox window floats on the top of the Project Explorer window.*

Figure 1.14 *The Toolbox window is docked to the right side of the Project Explorer window.*

Part I Fundamentals of Java Programming

You can link tool windows together by dragging one window over another. There are two types of linking: linked windows and tab-linked windows. When you link windows horizontally, they appear as one window, with the title bar as the separator. As shown in Figure 1.15, the Project Explorer window and the Property window are linked together with separate titles. Tab-linked windows appear as one window, with tabs that allow you to navigate to the linked windows, as shown in Figure 1.16.

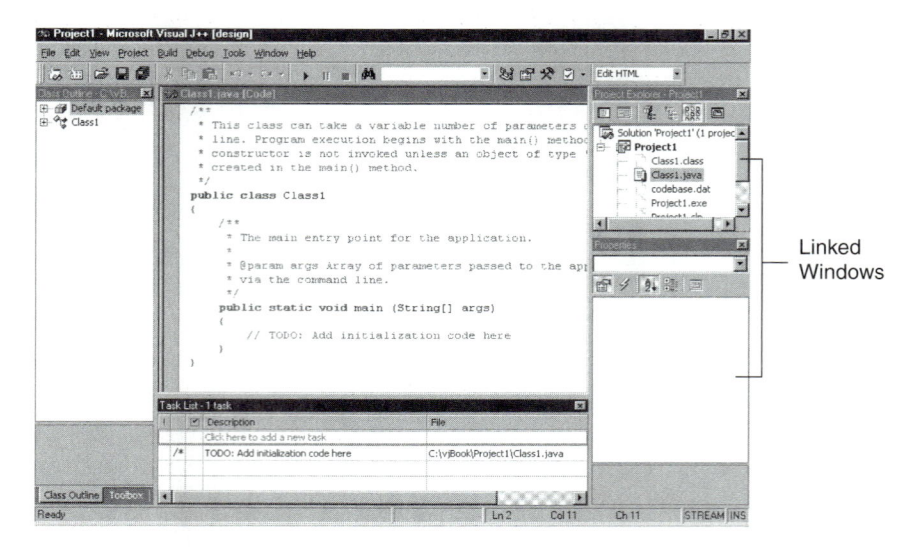

Figure 1.15 *The Project Explorer window and Properties window are linked within one window.*

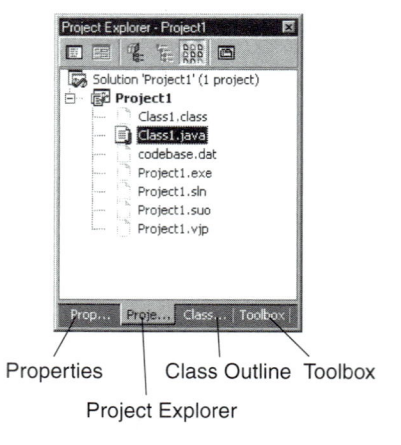

Figure 1.16 *The Properties window, Project Explorer window, Class Outline window, and Toolbar window are linked with tabs that allow you to navigate to the linked windows using tabs.*

Document Windows

Document windows are dynamically created when you open or create files or other items. For example, the Text Editor window is displayed when you click Class1.java in the Project Explorer window. A document window has the Minimize, Maximize, and Close buttons on the right of its title bar. When a document window is visible, the file is considered open and you can edit it. Closing a document window also closes the file. The current list of document windows appears in the Windows menu in the order in which they are opened, with the currently open window at the top of the list. The active document window also has a check mark to its left.

> **NOTE**
> Document windows exist only inside the application's available client area. You can close, resize, maximize, and minimize document windows, but you cannot hide, link, or dock them.

> **TIP**
> Many windows have an associated context-sensitive popup menu. You display the context menu for a window by pointing to the window and clicking the right mouse button. For example, as shown in Figure 1.17, when you click the right mouse button in the Text Editor window, a context menu pops up.

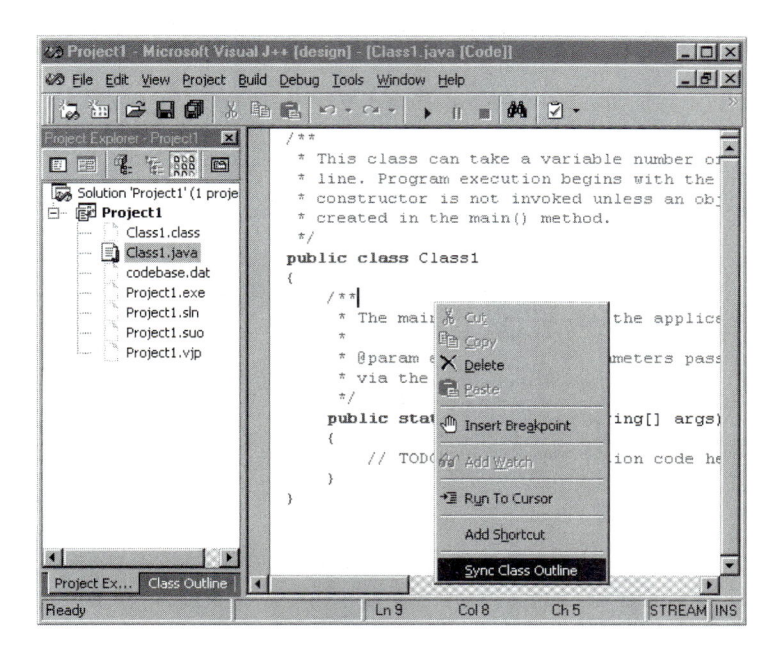

Figure 1.17 *You can reveal the window context menu by right-clicking the mouse on the window.*

Defining Window Layout

There are a variety of ways to place and organize windows in the J++ IDE. For convenience, Visual J++ provides several predefined layouts, such as Debug, Design, DevStudio, Edit HTML, and Full Screen. You can choose a layout style from the Load/Save Window's UI choice menu, as shown in Figure 1.18.

You can also create a custom layout style using the Define Window Layout, as follows:

1. Arrange the windows in your workspace.
2. Select Define Window Layout from the View menu to display the Define Window Layout dialog box, as shown in Figure 1.19.
3. In the Define Window Layout dialog box, type My Favorite Style in the View Name field. Click Add to save the current window layout style. You can now use My Favorite Style in the same way as a J++ predefined layout window.

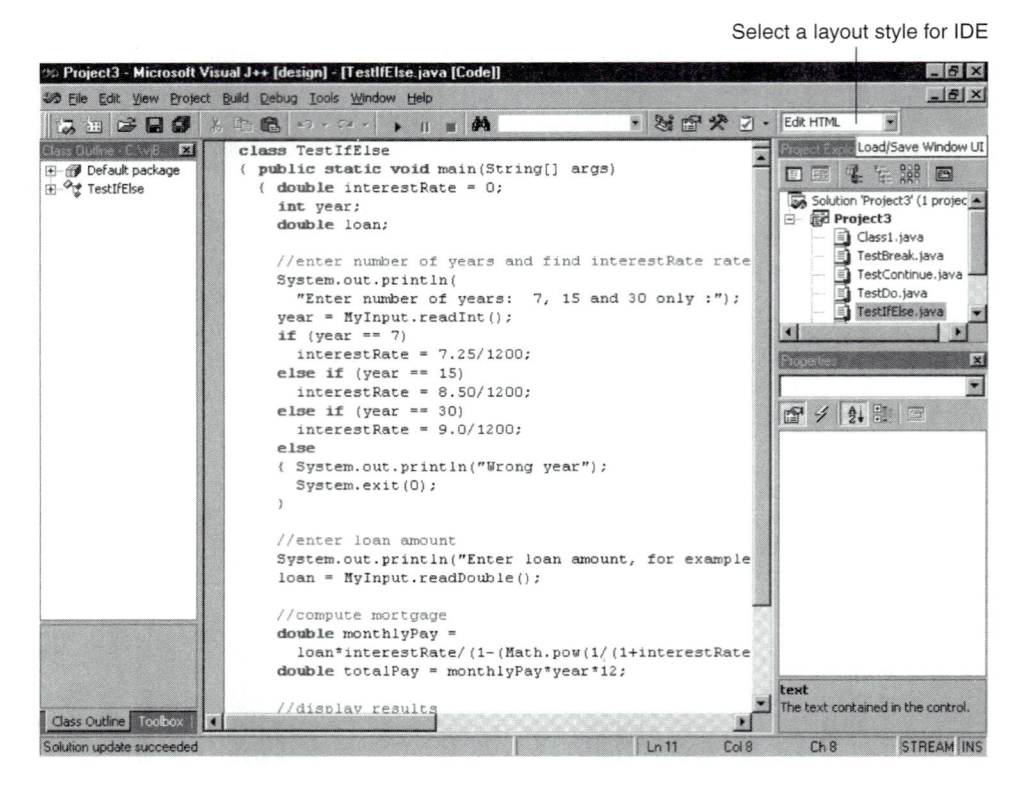

Figure 1.18 *Visual J++ makes several predefined layout styles available for you to choose.*

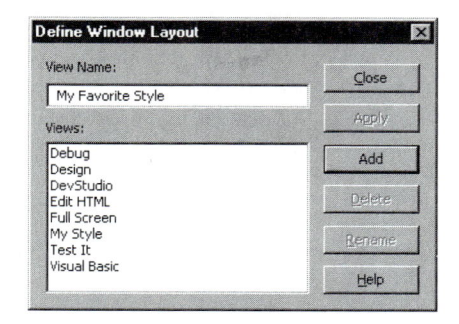

Figure 1.19 *You can use the Define Window Layout dialog box to create a new window layout style.*

Java Applications

Java programs can be of two types: applications or applets. *Applications* are standalone programs. This includes any program written with a high-level language. Applications can be executed from any computer with a Java interpreter and are ideal for developing standalone programs. Applets are special kinds of Java programs that can run directly from a Java-compatible Web browser. Applets are suitable for deploying Web projects.

Let's begin with a simple Java application program that displays the message "Welcome to Java!" on the console.

Example 1.1 A Simple Application

This program shows how to write a simple Java application and demonstrates the compilation and execution of an application.

```java
// This application program prints Welcome to Java!
public class Welcome
{
  public static void main(String[] args)
  {
    System.out.println("Welcome to Java!");
  }
}
```

Example Review

In this program, `println("Welcome to Java!")` is actually the statement that prints the message. So why do you use the other statements in the program? Because computer languages have rigid styles and strict syntax, and you need to write a code that the Java compiler understands.

Every Java program must have at least one class. Each class begins with a class declaration that defines data and methods for the class. In this example, the class name is `Welcome`.

The class contains a method called `main()`. The `main()` method in this program contains the `println()` statement. The `main()` method is invoked by the interpreter.

Creating a Java Program

There are many ways to create a Java program in Visual J++. Later in the book you will learn how to use various wizards to create certain types of Java programs. In this section, you will learn how to create Java programs without using wizards.

The following are the steps in creating a Java program for Example 1.1:

1. Choose DevStudio as the window's layout as shown in Figure 1.20. From now on, the DevStudio layout will be used to develop Visual J++ programs throughout the text.

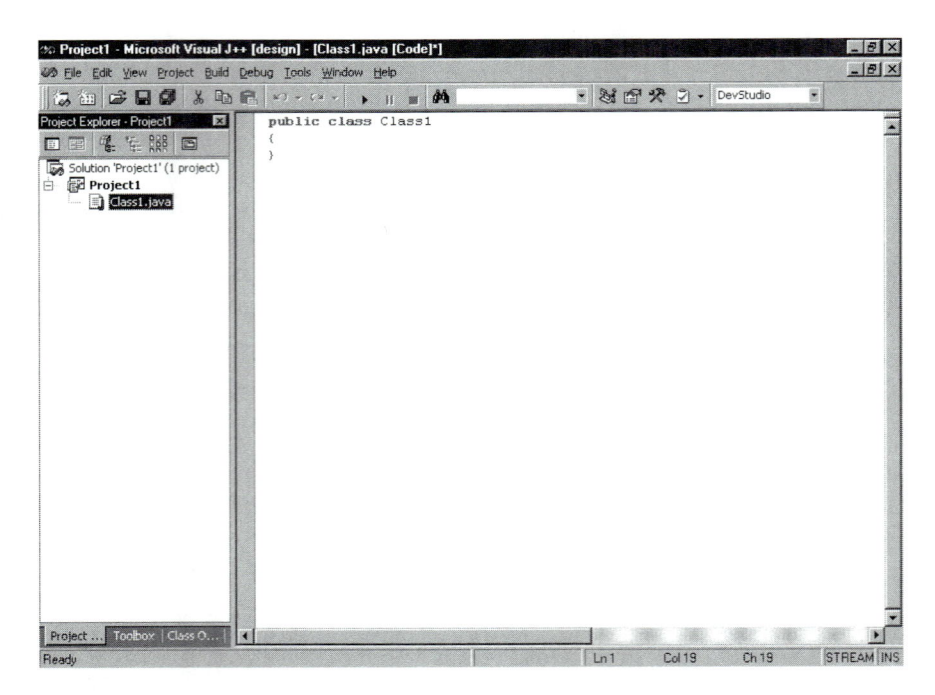

Figure 1.20   *The DevStudio layout style places all the tool windows within a single tabbed window on the left and the document windows on the right.*

2. Point to Project1 and right-click the mouse to reveal the context menu, as shown in Figure 1.21. Choose Add, Add Classes to display the Add Item dialog box, as shown in Figure 1.22.

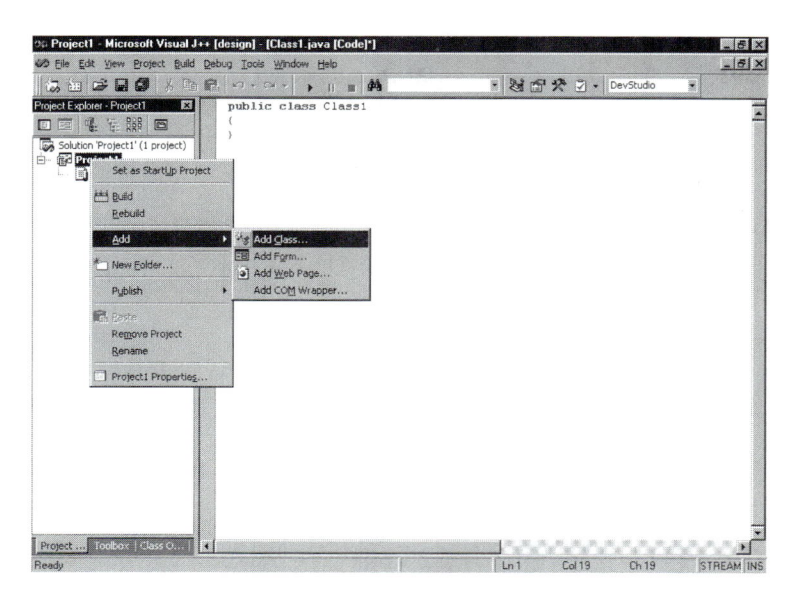

Figure 1.21 *You can create a new program and add it to the project.*

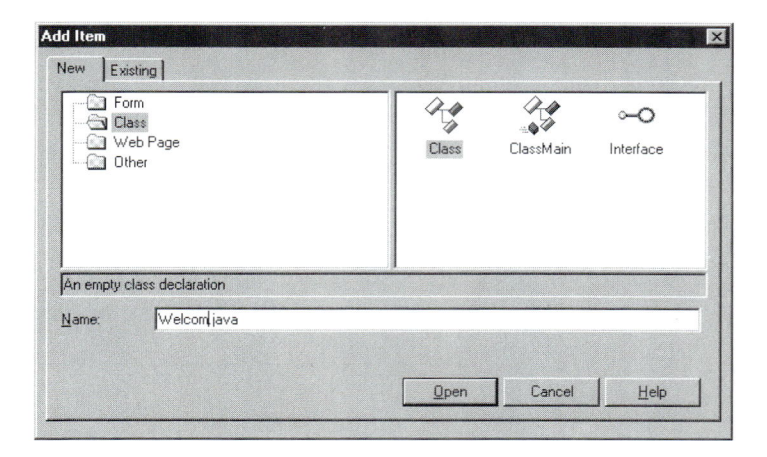

Figure 1.22 *You can use the Add Item dialog box to create a new program and add it to the project.*

3. In the Add Item dialog box, select the Class icon and type Welcome.java in the Name field. Click Open to close the Add Item dialog box. You will see Welcome.java created and added in the Project Explorer, and the Text Editor will contain the code for Welcome.java, as shown in Figure 1.23.

PART I FUNDAMENTALS OF JAVA PROGRAMMING

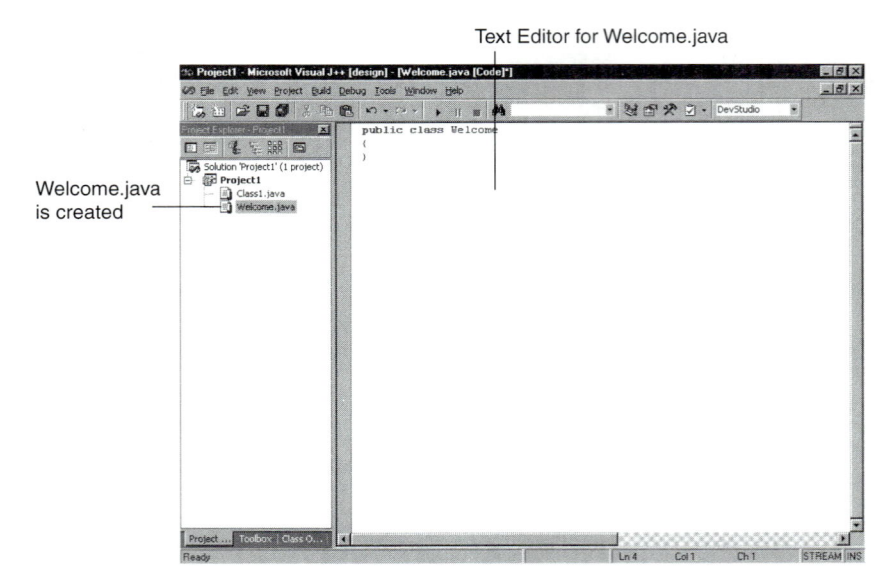

Figure 1.23 *Welcome.java was created and added to Project1, and its source code is shown in the Text Editor.*

4. Type the code for Welcome.java exactly as shown in Example 1.1. As you type, the code completion assistance automatically comes up to give you suggestions for completing the code. For instance, when you type a dot (.) after `System` and pause for a second, Visual J++ displays a popup menu with suggestions on completing the code, as shown in Figure 1.24. You can then select out from the menu to complete the code.

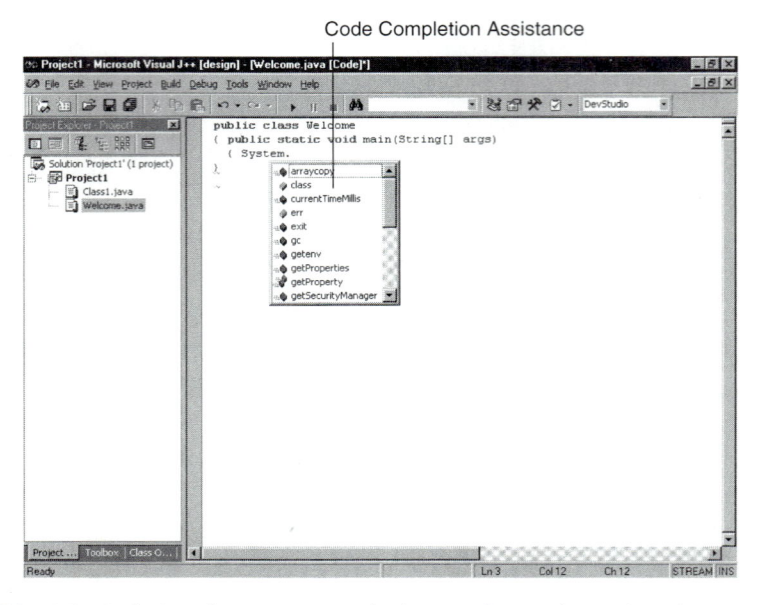

Figure 1.24 *The Code Completion Assistance displays tips for completing the code.*

5. Select File, Save All to save all your work.

> **CAUTION**
> Java source programs are case-sensitive. It would be wrong, for example, to replace `main()` in the program with `Main()`.

> **TIP**
> The file name Welcome.java should exactly match the class name Welcome. Note that both Ws are capitalized. If you mistyped the file name as welcome.java, you can change the file name as follows:
>
> 1. Right-click the file in the Project Explorer window to display a context menu, as shown in Figure 1.25.
> 2. Choose Rename in the context menu. You can now edit the file name, changing *w* to *W,* as shown in Figure 1.26.

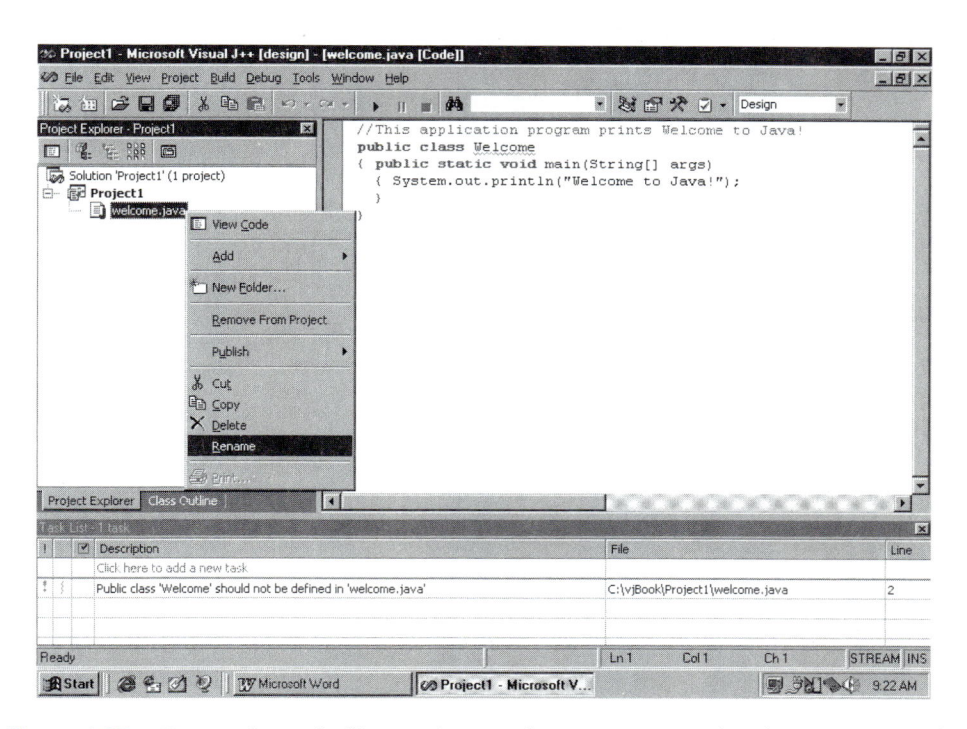

Figure 1.25 *You can change the file name by using the Rename command in the context menu of the Java source code file name in the Project Explorer window.*

Part I   Fundamentals of Java Programming

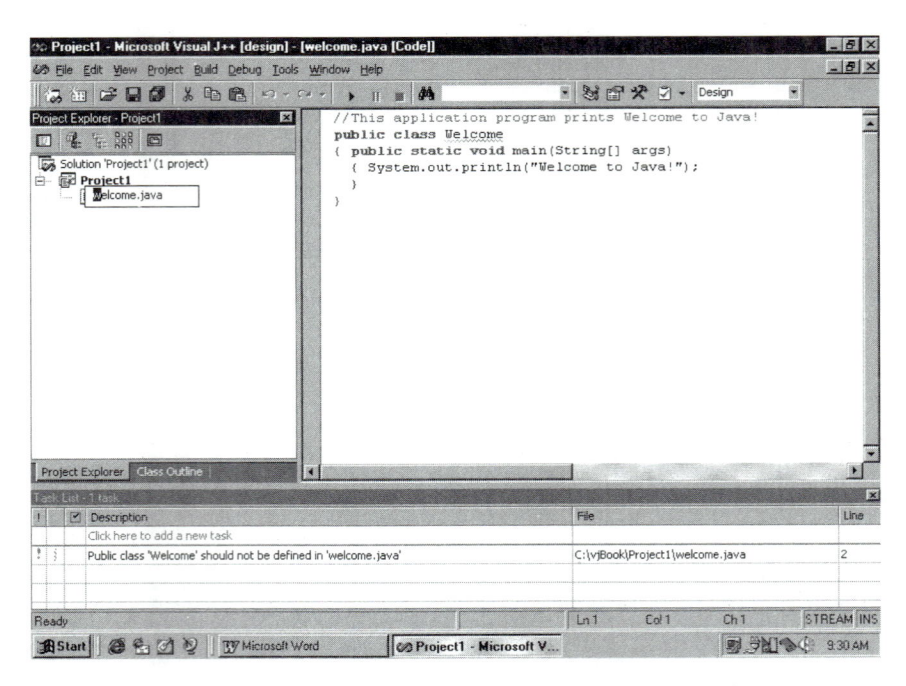

Figure 1.26   *Visual J++ allows you to change the file name in the Project Explorer.*

Compiling and Executing a Java Program

To compile the program in Visual J++, choose Build, Build from the main menu bar, or right-click the mouse at Project1 in the Project Explorer, then choose Build from the context menu, as shown in Figure 1.27.

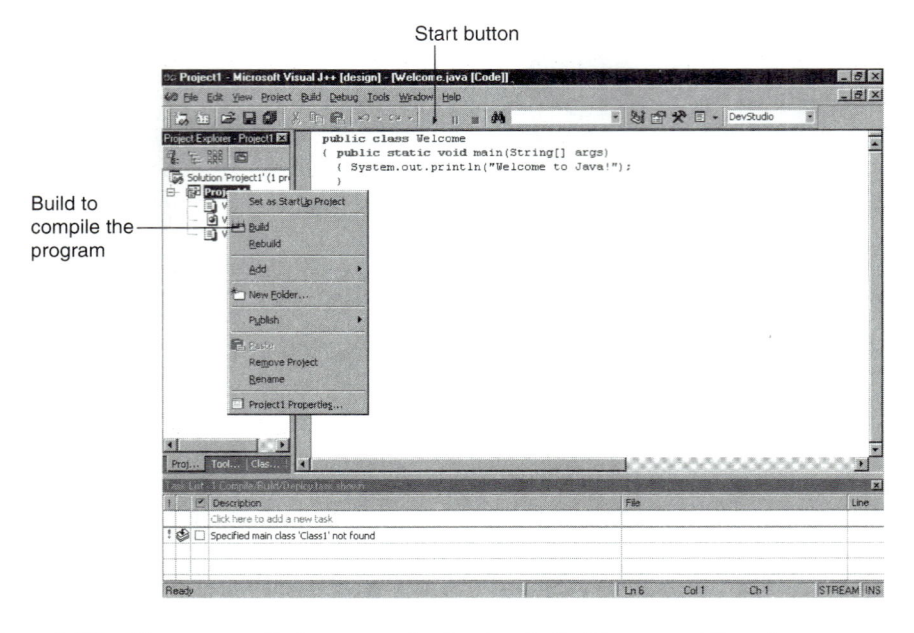

Figure 1.27   *You can compile the program by choosing the Build command from the context menu.*

If there are no syntax errors, the compiler generates a file named Welcome.class. This file, called the *bytecode*, which is similar to machine instructions, but is architecture-neutral and can run on any platform that has the Java interpreter and runtime environment. This is one of Java's primary advantages: Java bytecode can run on a variety of hardware platforms and operating systems.

> **NOTE**
> You can see that Welcome.class was created and stored in Project1 by clicking the Show All Files button in the Project Explorer window.

Before executing Welcome.class, you need to set the appropriate properties for Project1.

1. Point the mouse at Project1 in the Project Explorer and right-click it to display the context menu, as shown in Figure 1.27.

2. Choose Project1 properties in the context menu to display the Project1 Properties dialog box, as shown in Figure 1.28.

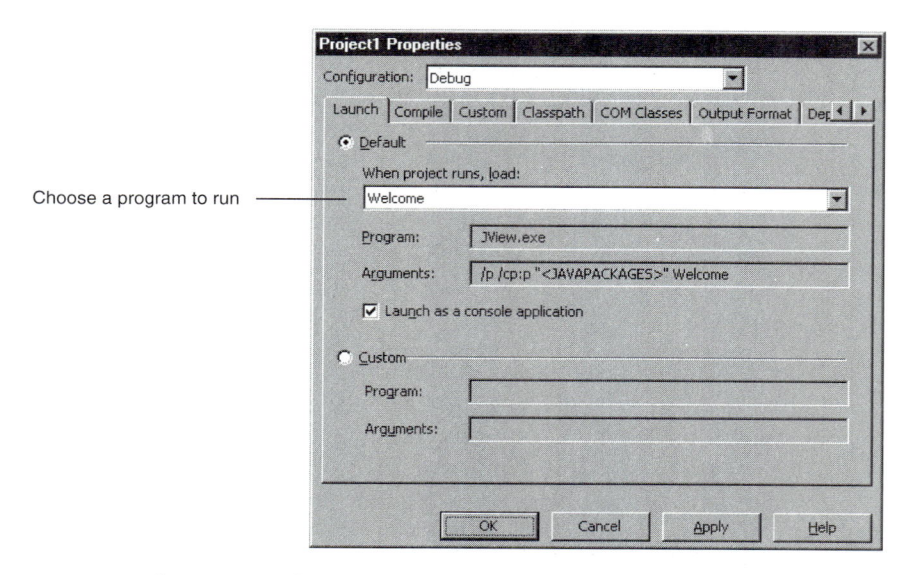

Figure 1.28 *Before executing the program, you need to specify the program in the Project Properties dialog box.*

3. On the Launch page of the Project1 Properties dialog box, choose Default in the radio button, choose Welcome to load and run, and check Launch as a console application. Click OK to close the dialog box.

To run the program, simply click the Start button ▶. as shown in Figure 1.27. Visual J++ launches a DOS window to display the output. The DOS window opens when the program starts and closes right after the program finishes. It happens too quickly to see the output. To see the console output, you can start a DOS session and use the **jview** command to run the program, as shown in Figure 1.29.

Figure 1.29 *The output of Example 1.1 displays a message: "Welcome to Java!"*

Anatomy of the Application Program

Now take a closer look at the program in Example 1.1, and examine its components:

> Comments
> Reserved words
> Modifiers
> Statements
> Blocks
> Classes
> Methods
> The `main()` method

These are the basic elements needed to construct a program. It is important to understand these terms in order to build a program.

Comments

The first line in the program is a *comment,* whose purpose is to document what the program is and how it is constructed. This helps the programmer and user communicate and understand the program. Comments are not programming statements and are ignored by the compiler. In Java, comments are preceded by two slashes (`//`) in a line, or enclosed between `/*` and `*/` in multiple lines. When the compiler sees `//`, it ignores all text after `//` in the same line. When it sees `/*`, it scans for the next `*/` and ignores any text between `/*` and `*/`.

Here are examples of the two types of comments:

```
// This application program prints Welcome to Java!
/* This application program prints Welcome to Java! */
```

Reserved Words

Reserved words, or *keywords,* are words that have a specific meaning to the compiler and cannot be used for other purposes in the program. For example, when the compiler sees the word `class`, it understands that the word after `class` is the name for the class. Other reserved words in Example 1.1 are `public`, `static`, and `void`.

> **TIP**
> Because Java is case-sensitive, `class` is a reserved word, but `Class` is not. Nonetheless, for clarity and readability, it would be best to avoid using reserved words in other forms. (See Appendix A, "Java Keywords.")

Modifiers

Java uses certain reserved words called *modifiers* that specify the properties of the data, methods, and classes, and how they can be used. Examples of modifiers are `public` and `static`. Other modifiers are `private`, `final`, `abstract`, and `protected`. A `public` data, method, or class can be accessed by other programs. A `private` data or method cannot be accessed by other programs. Modifiers are further discussed in Chapter 5, "Programming with Objects and Classes."

Statements

A *statement* represents an action or a sequence of actions. The statement `println("Welcome to Java!")` in the program is a statement to display the greeting "Welcome to Java!" Every statement in Java ends with a semicolon (;).

The following lines of code are statements:

```
x = 5;
x = x + 5;
```

The first statement assigns 5 to the variable x, and the second adds 5 to the variable x.

Blocks

The braces in the program form the *block* structure that groups statements together. The use of blocks helps the compiler to identify components of the program. In Java, each block begins with an open brace ({) and ends with a closing brace (}). Blocks can be *nested*—that is, one block can be placed within another.

The following code contains two blocks. The inner block is nested within the outer block.

```
{
  x = 5;
  x = x + 5;
  if (x > 6)
  { x = x - 1; }
}
```

Classes

The *class* is the essential Java construct. A class is a template or a blueprint for objects. Understanding classes, writing classes, and using classes are essential concepts in Java programming. The mystery of classes will continue to be unveiled throughout this book. For now, though, understand that a program is defined by using one or more classes. Every Java program has at least one class, and programs are contained inside a class definition enclosed in blocks. The class contains data declarations and method declarations.

> **NOTE**
> Each class in Java is compiled into a separate bytecode file with the extension .class.

Methods

What does `System.out.println()` mean? It is a *method*: a collection of statements that performs a sequence of operations to display a message on the console. `println()` is predefined as part of the standard Java language. It can be used even if the details of how it works are not fully understood. It is used by invoking a calling statement with arguments. The arguments are enclosed within parentheses. In this case, the argument is `"Welcome to Java!"`. You can call the same `println()` method with a different argument to print a different message.

The *main()* Method

You can create your own method. Every Java application must have a user-declared `main()` method that defines where the program begins. The `main()` method controls program flow. It will always look like this:

```java
public static void main(String[] args)
{
  // statements;
}
```

Java Applets

Applications and applets share many common programming features, although they differ slightly in some aspects. For example, every application must have a `main()` method, which contains the first sequence of instructions to be executed. The Java interpreter begins the execution of the application from the `main()` method.

Java applets, on the other hand, do not need a `main()` method: they run within the Web browser environment. Example 1.2 demonstrates the applet that displays the same message, "Welcome to Java!"

Example 1.2 A Simple Applet

This program shows how to write a simple Java applet, and demonstrates the compilation and execution of an applet.

```java
/* This is an example of Java applets */
import java.awt.Graphics;
```

```java
public class WelcomeApplet extends java.applet.Applet
{
  public void paint(Graphics g)
  {
    g.drawString("Welcome to Java!",10,10);
  }
}
```

Example Review

Applets run in a graphical environment. You need to display everything, including text, in graphical mode, and Java provides the `drawString()` method to display text in an applet.

The `drawString("Welcome to Java!", 10, 10)` method draws the string `"Welcome to Java!"` on the line. The baseline of the first character, W, in the string is displayed at the location (10, 10). The drawing area is measured in pixels, with (0,0) at the upper-left corner.

Creating and Compiling an Applet

You create and compile an applet the same way you created and compiled an application in the preceding section. Or you can use the Applet Wizard to create applets. The Applet Wizard will be introduced in Chapter 10, "Applets and Advanced Graphics."

The following are the steps in creating an applet:

1. Open Project1 if it is not opened. To open it, choose File, Open Project to display the Open Project dialog box, as shown in Figure 1.30. This dialog box resembles the New Project dialog box, as shown in Figure 1.6.

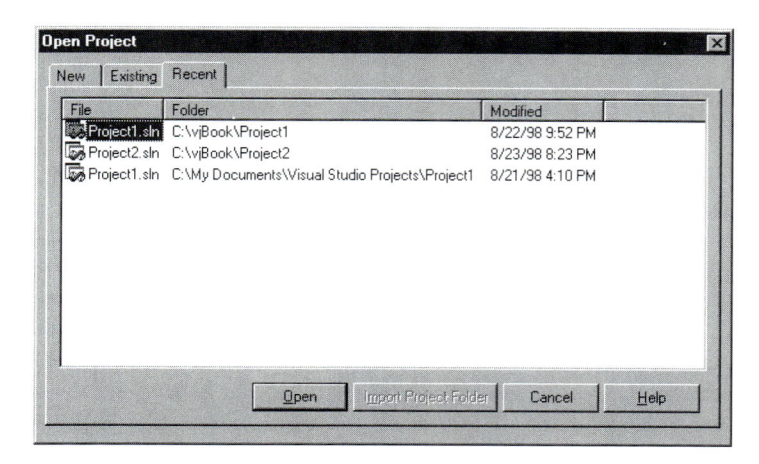

Figure 1.30 *You can use the Open Project dialog box to create a new project, or to open an existing project or a recently used project.*

2. You can open an existing project from the Existing page or from the Recent page in the Open Project dialog box. Since Project1 was recently used, it appears in the list of recent solutions. On the Recent page, double-click Project1.sln to open Project1.

3. Right-click the mouse at Project1 in the Project Explorer to reveal a context menu. Choose Add, Add Class from the menu to display the Add Item dialog box, as shown in Figure 1.22.

4. In the Add Item dialog box, choose (single-click) the Class icon and type WelcomeApplet.java in the Name field. Click Open to let J++ generate the class WelcomeApplet.java.

5. Type the code for WelcomeApplet.java exactly as shown in Example 1.2.

6. Choose File, Save All to preserve your work.

Compile the program using the Build command in the Build menu. You use the Java interpreter to run applications, but applets are executed by a Web browser from an HTML file. You need to create an HTML file to tell the browser where to get the Java applet and how to run it.

Creating an HTML File

To run an applet, embed HTML tags that refer to the applet within a Web page. HTML is a markup language that presents static documents on the Web. HTML uses tags to tell the Web browser how to render a Web page. HTML contains a tag called `<applet>` that incorporates applets into a Web page.

The following HTML file contains a tag to invoke `WelcomeApplet.class`.

```
<html>
<head>
<title>Welcome Java Applet</title>
</head>
<body>
<applet
  code = "WelcomeApplet.class"
  width = 200
  height = 50>
</applet>
</body>
</html>
```

A tag is an instruction to the Web browser. The browser interprets the tag and decides how to display or otherwise treat the subsequent contents of the HTML document. Tags are enclosed in brackets; the first word in a tag, called the *tag name*, describes tag functions. Tags can have additional attributes, sometimes with values after an equals sign, which further define the tag's action. For example, in the following tag, `<applet>` is the tag name, and `code`, `width`, and `height` are the attributes:

```
<applet code="WelcomeApplet.class" width = 100 height = 40>
```

The `width` and `height` attributes specify the rectangular viewing area of the applet.

Most tags have a *start tag* and a corresponding *end tag*. The tag has a specific effect on the region between the start tag and the end tag. For example, `<applet...>...</applet>` tells the browser to display an applet. An end tag is always the start tag's name preceded by a slash.

An HTML document begins with the `<html>` tag, which declares that the document has been written with HTML. Each document has two parts, *head* and *body*, defined by `<head>` and `<body>` tags, respectively. The head part contains the document title using the `<title>` tag and other parameters the browser can use when rendering the document, and the body part contains the actual contents of the document. The header is optional. For more information, refer to Appendix E, "An HTML Tutorial."

To create the HTML file, follow the steps below:

1. Choose Add, Add Web Page from the context menu of Project1 in the Project Explorer window to display the Add Item dialog box, as shown in Figure 1.31.

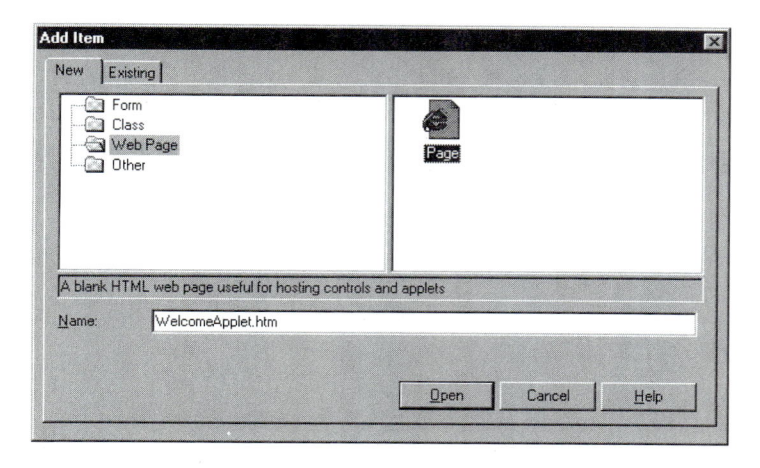

Figure 1.31 *You can use the Add Item dialog box to create an HTML file to embed the applet.*

2. On the New page of the Add Item dialog box, choose Web page on the left pane and type WelcomeApplet.htm in the Name field. Click Open to let Visual J++ generate WelcomeApplet.htm, as shown in Figure 1.32.

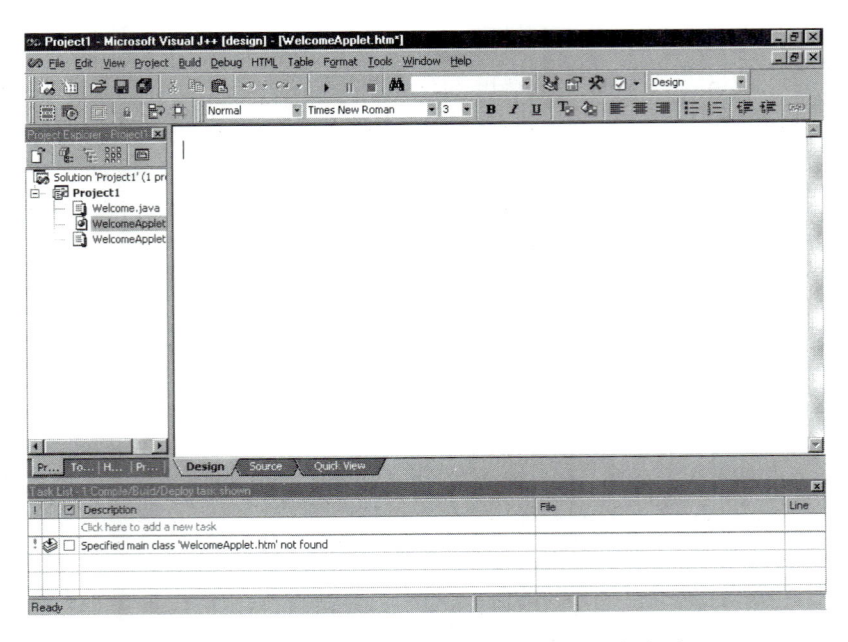

Figure 1.32 *WelcomeApplet.htm was generated using the Add Item dialog box.*

3. Choose the Source tab in the Editor window for WelcomeApplet.htm. You will see the generated HTML code, as shown in Figure 1.33.

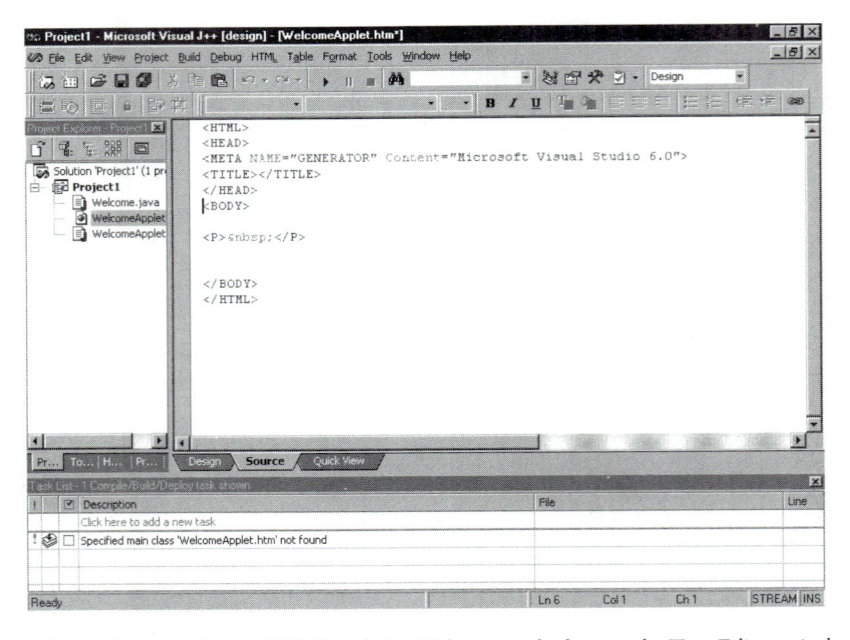

Figure 1.33 *You can edit the HTML code for WelcomeApplet.htm in the Text Editor window for WelcomeApplet.html with the Source tab selected.*

4. Insert the applet tag into the HTML code, as shown in Figure 1.34.
5. Choose File, Save All to preserve your work.

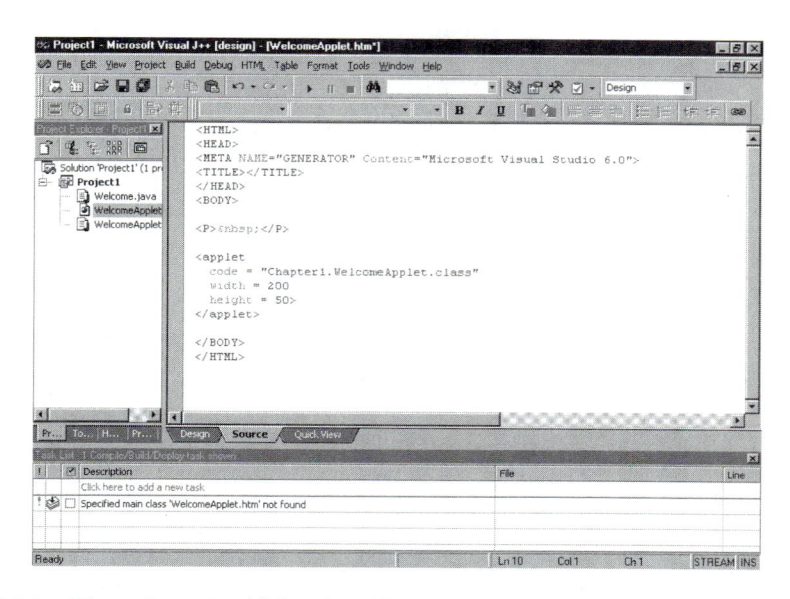

Figure 1.34 *The applet tag is added to the HTML page.*

Viewing Applets

You now can view the applet using the Internet Explorer from Visual J++. Here are the steps to view it.

1. In the Project1 Properties dialog box, choose WelcomeApplet.htm to run. You will see IExplorer.exe automatically appear in the Program field, as shown in Figure 1.35. Click OK to close the dialog box.

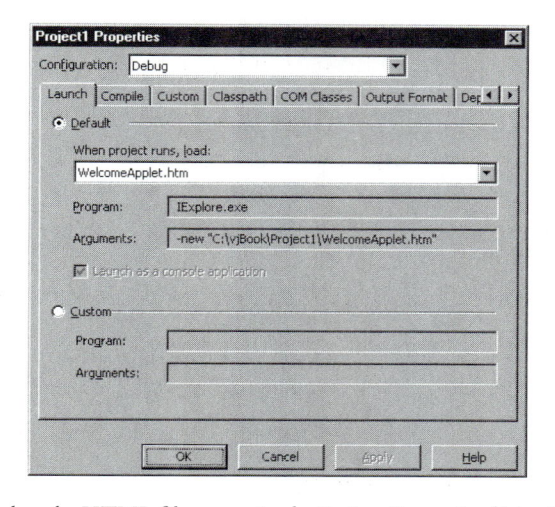

Figure 1.35 *You select the HTML file to run in the Project Properties dialog box to view the applet using the Microsoft Internet Explorer.*

2. Click the Start button to start the Microsoft Internet Explorer and view the applet, as shown in Figure 1.36.

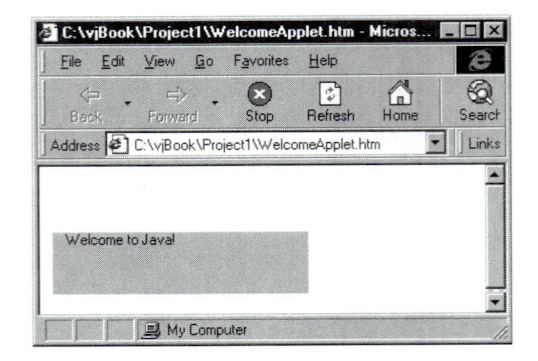

Figure 1.36 *The message "Welcome to Java!" is drawn on the browser.*

You can also use Visual J++ Quick Viewer to view a Java applet without launching the Internet Explorer. To view the applet, simply click the Quick View tab in the Editor, as shown in Figure 1.37.

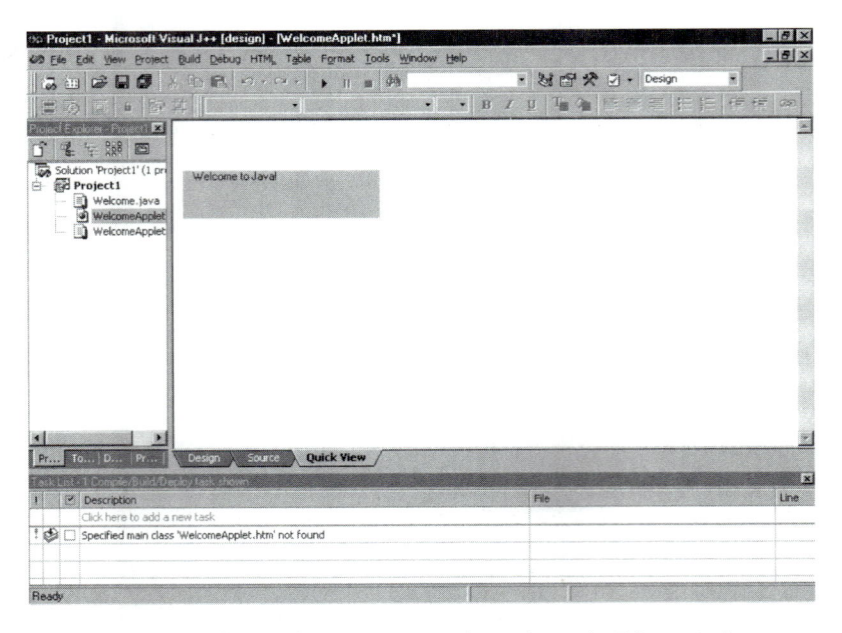

Figure 1.37 *You can use the Quick Viewer to view the applet in the Editor window.*

If you choose the Source tab again, you will not see the code for the applet tag. To see the applet as text, right-click the mouse at the applet to reveal the context menu, as shown in Figure 1.38. Choose Always View as Text.

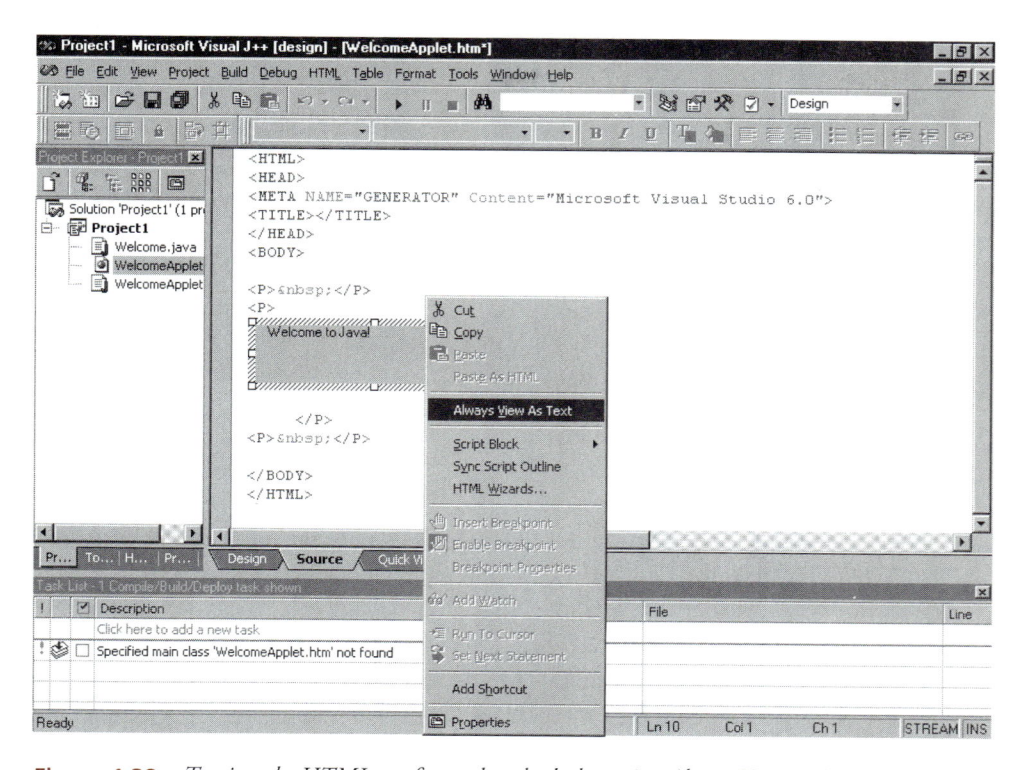

Figure 1.38 *To view the HTML tag for applet, check the option Always View As Text.*

> **NOTE**
> You can view applets from any Java-enabled Web browser on any platform. For example, the same applet can run from Netscape and HotJava on a Windows-based PC or on a UNIX workstation.

Anatomy of the Applet Program

Take a closer look at the program in Example 1.2, and examine its components: the `import` statement, the `Graphics` class, the `extends` keyword, the `paint()` method, the `drawString()` method, and the class instance. As you have seen, applications and applets have much in common. Indeed, an applet is merely a special kind of Java program with certain characteristics that make it run from a Web browser. The components mentioned here are also used in other Java programs.

The *import* Statement

The first line after the comment is an `import` statement. The `import` statement tells the compiler to include existing Java programs in the current program. In this case, the existing program is `java.awt.Graphics`. You can use the operations in `java.awt.Graphics` in your program rather than rewrite the code. This is an example of software *reusability;* that is, the same program is written once and used by many other people without having to be rewritten.

Java code is organized into packages and classes. Classes are inside packages, and packages are libraries of Java code that contain all kinds of operations ready for you to import and use. Java provides standard packages, such as `java.awt`, that come with the compiler. Users can create their own packages. `Graphics` is a class contained in the `java.awt` package. (See Chapter 5, "Programming with Objects and Classes," for more information.)

Class Instance

The g in the `paint()` method is called an *instance* for the class `Graphics`. An instance is a concrete object of the class. g can access the methods defined in `Graphics`. `drawString()` is a method in `Graphics`, which now can be used in g by a call, such as `g.drawString()`. This is exactly the way object-oriented programming works. Creating an instance from a class, the instance can use the methods defined in the class without knowing how the methods are implemented.

The *paint()* Method and the *Graphics* Class

Every applet that displays graphics must have a `paint()` method that looks like this:

```
public void paint(Graphics g) {...}
```

This method contains drawing methods to tell the Web browser what should be displayed.

Because the Web is a graphical environment, everything—including text—needs to be displayed as a graphic. The Java `Graphics` class provides operations for drawing such objects as text strings, lines, rectangles, ovals, arcs, and polygons. The drawing area is a rectangle measured in pixels with (0,0) at its upper-left corner. The following is an example:

```
public void paint(Graphics g)
{
  g.drawLine(10, 10, 50, 30);
  g.drawRect(10, 20, 20, 30);
  g.drawString("Welcome to Java", 30, 10);
}
```

The `drawLine()` method draws a line from (10, 10) to (50, 30). The `drawRect()` method draws a rectangle of width 20 and height 30; the upper-left corner of the rectangle is at (10, 20). The `drawString()` method draws the string "Welcome to Java" at (30, 10). See Figure 1.39 for the drawings.

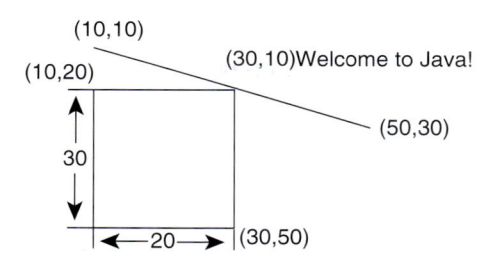

Figure 1.39 *The string* `Welcome to Java!` *is drawn at* `(30, 10)`; *a line is drawn from* `(10, 10)` *to* `(50, 30)`; *and a rectangle is drawn with its upper-left corner at* `(10, 20)` *with width of* `20` *and height of* `30`.

The *extends* Keyword and Class Inheritance

The class definition in Example 1.2 is different from the class definition in Example 1.1. Example 1.2 has an extra keyword, `extends`, which tells the compiler that the class to be defined is an extension of an existing class. In this case, the class `WelcomeApplet` extends the existing class `Applet`. The extended class `WelcomeApplet` inherits all the functionality and properties from class `Applet`. This is an example of *inheritance,* another software engineering concept. Inheritance complements and extends software reusability.

`Applet` is a class in the package `java.applet`. You could directly extend `Applet` by adding the statement `import java.applet.Applet` at the beginning of the program, as follows:

```java
import java.awt.Graphics;
import java.applet.Applet;

public class WelcomeApplet extends Applet
{
  public void paint (Graphics g)
  {
    g.drawString("Welcome to Java!", 10, 10);
  }
}
```

The `import java.applet.Applet` statement imports the `Applet` class so that it can be used in the program without explicitly referencing `Applet` as `java.applet.Applet`.

Applications versus Applets

You probably have many questions, such as whether it is necessary to write two programs—one for the application and one for the applet—and how to decide when to use applications and when to use applets. To answer these questions, it is important to understand the similarities and differences between applications and applets.

Much of the code for applications and applets is the same, but there are differences in the code dealing with their runtime environments. Applications run as stand-alone programs, as do programs written in any high-level language. Applets, however, must run from inside a Web browser. If your program is not required to run from a Web browser, choose applications. Developing Java applications is slightly faster than developing applets because you do not need to create an HTML file and load it from a Web browser to view the results.

For security reasons, the following limitations are imposed on applets to prevent destructive programs from damaging the system on which the browser is running:

- Applets are not allowed to read from, or write to, the computer's file system. Otherwise, they might damage the files and spread viruses.

- Applets are not allowed to run programs on the browser's computer. Otherwise, they might call destructive local programs and damage the local system on the user's computer.

- Applets are not allowed to establish connections between the user's computer and any other computer except for the server where the applets are stored. This restriction prevents the applet from connecting the user's computer to another computer without the user's knowledge.

However, applications can directly interact with the computer on which they are running without these limitations. Applications can be used to develop fully functional software. In fact, applications can use the same graphical features used for applets, although with applications slightly more effort would be required to create the graphical environment.

In general, you can convert a Java applet to run as an application without loss of functionality. However, because of the security limitations imposed on applets, an application cannot always be converted to run as an applet. In Chapter 10, "Applets and Advanced Graphics," you will learn how to convert applications and applets.

Chapter Summary

In this chapter, you learned about Java and the relationship between Java and the World Wide Web. Java is an Internet programming language, and since its inception in 1995, it has quickly become a premier language for building fully portable software.

Java is platform-independent, meaning that you can write the program once and run it anywhere. Java is a simple, object-oriented programming language with built-in graphics programming, input and output, exception handling, networking, and multithreading support.

The Java source file ends with the .java extension. Every class is compiled into a separate file called a bytecode that has the same name as the class and ends with the .class extension.

Every Java program is a class definition. The keyword `class` introduces a class definition. The contents of the class are included in a block. A block begins with an open brace (`{`) and ends with a close brace (`}`). The class contains at least one method. A Java application must have a `main()` method. The `main()` method is the entry point where the application program starts when it is executed.

The Java applet always extends the `Applet` class. The keyword `extends` enables new classes to inherit from an existing class. The `import` statement loads classes required for compiling and running a Java program.

Modifiers are the keywords that specify how classes and methods can be accessed. A Java applet must be a `public` class for a Web browser to access it.

Web browsers control the execution of Java applets. You must create an HTML file with an `<applet>` tag to specify the bytecode file (with the extension .class) for the applet, and the width and the height of the applet viewing area in pixels.

The Web browser calls the `paint()` method to display graphics in the applet's viewing area. The coordinates of the viewing area are measured in pixels with (`0,0`) at the upper-left corner. The `drawString()` method draws a string at a specified location in the viewing area.

You have begun to use Visual J++ to create Java applications and applets. You have learned how to create projects, create and add files into the project, and compile and run applications and applets.

Chapter Review

1.1. Briefly describe the history of Java.

1.2. Java is object-oriented. What are the advantages of object-oriented programming?

1.3. Can Java run on any machine? What is needed to run Java on a computer?

1.4. What are the input and output of a Java compiler?

1.5. List some Java development tools. Are Visual J++ and JBuilder different languages from Java, or are they dialects or extensions of Java?

1.6. What is the relationship between Java and HTML?

1.7. Explain the concept of keywords. List some Java keywords you learned in this chapter.

1.8. Is Java case-sensitive? What is the case for Java keywords?

1.9. What are the Java source file name extension and the Java bytecode file name extension?

1.10. How do you create a Java project in Visual J++?

1.11. How do you compile a Java program in Visual J++?

1.12. How do you run a Java application in Visual J++?

1.13. How do you create a Java applet in Visual J++?

1.14. Where is the .class file stored after successful compilation in Visual J++?

1.15. What is the purpose of the statement `System.out.println("Welcome to Java!")` in the Welcome.java program in Example 1.1?

1.16. What is a comment? What is the syntax for a comment in Java? Is the comment ignored by the compiler?

1.17. What is the statement to display a string on the console?

1.18. What is the `import` statement for?

1.19. What is `Graphics`, and what is the `paint()` method?

1.20. What are the differences between applications and applets? How do you run an application, and how do you run an applet? Is the compilation process different for applications and applets?

1.21. List some security restrictions of applets.

Programming Exercises

1.1. Create a project named Project1. Develop a Java application program named WelcomeHTML.java to the project. WelcomeHTML.java displays a message "Welcome to HTML" on the console. This program is similar to Example 1.1.

1.2. In Project1 created from the previous example, develop a Java applet program to display the message "Welcome to HTML" on the screen. This program is similar to Example 1.2.

CHAPTER 2

JAVA BUILDING ELEMENTS

Objectives

- Write simple Java programs.
- Understand identifiers, variables and constants.
- Use assignment statements.
- Use Java primitive data types: `byte`, `short`, `int`, `long`, `float`, `double`, `char`, and `boolean`.
- Use Java operators and write Java expressions.
- Understand the classification of programming errors.
- Become familiar with Java documentation, programming style, and naming conventions.
- Run Java programs from the command line.
- Get online help from Visual J++ 6.
- Customize Visual J++ 6 IDE options.

Introduction

In this chapter, you will be introduced to basic programming elements, such as variables, constants, data types, operators, and expressions in Java. You will learn to get online help from Visual J++ and customize the IDE options in Visual J++.

Writing Simple Programs

To begin, let's look at a simple program that computes the area of a circle. The program reads in the radius of a circle and displays its area. The program will use variables to represent the circle and the area, use a constant π, and use an expression to compute the area.

Writing this program involves designing algorithms and data structures, as well as translating algorithms into programming codes. An algorithm describes how a problem is solved in terms of the actions to be executed, and it specifies the order in which these actions should be executed. Algorithms can help the programmer plan a program before writing it in a programming language. An algorithm is often described by means of a pseudocode.

The algorithm for this program can be described as follows:

1. Read in the radius.
2. Compute the area using the following formula:

    ```
    area = radius × radius × π
    ```

3. Display the area.

Many of the problems you will meet when taking an introduction to programming course using this text can be described with simple, straightforward algorithms. As your education progresses, and you take courses on data structures, algorithm design, and analysis, you will encounter complex problems that have sophisticated solutions. You will need to design accurate, efficient algorithms with appropriate data structures in order to solve such problems.

Data structures involve data representation and manipulation. Java provides basic data types for representing integers, floats, characters, and Boolean types. Java also supports array and string types as objects. Some of the advanced data structures, such as stacks and hashing, are already supported by Java.

To novice programmers, coding is a daunting task. When you *code,* you translate the algorithm into a programming language understood by the computer. You already know that every Java program begins with a class declaration, in which the keyword `class` is followed by the class name. Assume that you have chosen `ComputeArea` as the class name. The outline of the program would look like this:

```
class ComputeArea
{
  // Data and methods to be given later
}
```

The program needs to read the radius entered by the user from the keyboard. You should consider two important issues next:

- Reading the radius.
- Storing the radius in the program.

Let's address the second issue first. How does a computer identify radius and area in the program? In order to store the radius, the program declares a symbol called *variable,* which represents the radius in the program. Variables are used to store data and computational results in the program.

Choose the descriptive names `radius` for radius and `area` for area. To let the compiler know what `radius` and `area` are, specify their data types, indicating whether they are integer, float, or others. Declare `radius` and `area` as double-precision, floating-point numbers. The program can be expanded as follows:

```
class ComputeArea
{
  static double radius, area;  // Declare radius and area
  // Method to be given later
}
```

The program declares `radius` and `area` as static variables. The reserved word `static` indicates that `radius` and `area` can be accessed by the `main()` method. Every application must have a main method that controls the execution of the program. The first step is to read in `radius`. Use the method `readDouble()`, which will be defined in the class, to read a `double` value from the keyboard. When this method is executed, the computer waits for the input from the keyboard. You will learn the details of implementing this method in Chapter 15, "Input and Output."

The second step is to compute `area`; assign the expression `radius*radius*PI` to area, where `PI` is a constant representing the number π.

In the final step, print `area` on the console by using method `System.out.println()`.

The program is completed in Example 2.1. The result is shown in Figure 2.1.

Example 2.1 Computing the Area of a Circle

This program lets the user enter the radius for a circle and then computes the area. Finally, it displays the area.

```
// ComputeArea.java: Compute the area of a circle
import java.io.*;
import java.util.*;

public class ComputeArea
{
  static double radius;
  static double area;
  static final double PI = 3.14159;
```

continues

```java
    static private StringTokenizer stok;
    static private BufferedReader br
      = new BufferedReader(new InputStreamReader(System.in), 1);

    // Main method
    public static void main(String[] args)
    {
      System.out.println("Enter radius");
      radius = readDouble();
      area = radius*radius*PI;
      System.out.println("The area for the circle of radius " +
        radius + " is " + area);
    }

    // Read a double value from the keyboard
    public static double readDouble()
    {
      double d = 0;
      try
      {
        String str = br.readLine();
        stok = new StringTokenizer(str);
        d = new Double(stok.nextToken()).doubleValue();
      }
      catch (IOException ex)
      {
        System.out.println(ex);
      }
      return d;
    }
  }
```

Example Review

To test this program, create a project named Project2 under c:\vjBook\Project2 and create a source file named ComputeArea.java. Compile the program and fix any errors. A sample run of the program is shown in Figure 2.1.

If you run the program from Visual J++, you need to set ComputeArea as the class, and check Launch as a console application on the Launch page of the Project2 Properties dialog box.

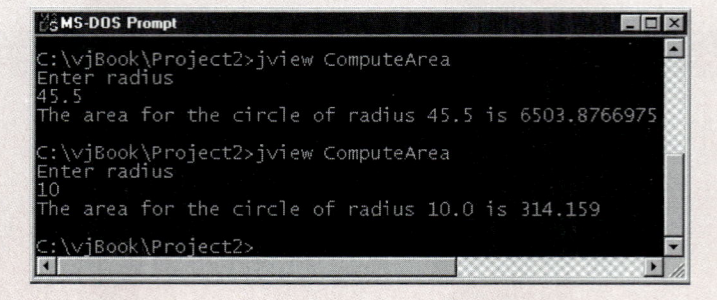

Figure 2.1   *The program receives the radius from the keyboard and displays the area of the circle.*

`System.out.println` is a system-predefined method. It can print strings and numbers. The plus sign (+) in the `System.out.println("The area for the circle of radius " + radius + " is " + area)` statement means to concatenate strings if one of the operands is a string. If both operands are numbers, the + operator will add these two numbers.

Suppose `i = 1` and `j = 2`, what is the output of the following statement?

```
System.out.println("i+j is " + i + j);
```

The output is "i+j is 12" because `"i+j is "` is concatenated with `i` first. To force `i + j` to be executed first, enclose `i + j` in the parentheses.

If you replaced

```
static double radius;
```

with

```
double radius;
```

you would get an error, because `main` is always a static method. The static method cannot reference nonstatic variables or methods. You would find the same type of error if you eliminated the word `static` from in front of the method `readDouble()`. You will learn more about method and class modifiers in Chapter 5, "Programming with Objects and Classes."

Identifiers

Just as every entity in the real world has a name, you need to choose names for the things you will refer to in your programs. Programming languages use special symbols called *identifiers* to name such programming entities as variables, constants, methods, classes, and packages. Here are the rules for naming identifiers:

- An identifier must start with a letter, an underscore (_), or a dollar sign ($).
- An identifier cannot contain operators, such as +, –, and so on.
- An identifier cannot be a reserved word. (See Appendix A, "Java Keywords," for a list of reserved words.)
- An identifier cannot be `true`, `false`, or `null`.
- An identifier can be of any length.

For example, `$2`, `Area`, `Char`, `a`, and α (the Greek alpha) are legal identifiers, while `2A` and `d+4` are illegal identifiers. Illegal identifiers do not follow the rules. The Java compiler detects illegal identifiers and reports syntax errors.

> **NOTE**
> Java uses the Unicode specification for characters. A letter does not just mean an English letter. It can be any of the tens of thousands of Unicode letters representing international languages. Therefore, α is a legal identifier.

> **TIP**
> Identifiers are used for naming variables, constants, methods, classes, and packages. Descriptive identifiers make programs easy to read. Since Java is case-sensitive, X and x are two different identifiers.

Variables

Variables are used to store data—input, output, or intermediate data. In the program in Example 2.1, radius and area were variables of double-precision, floating-point type. You can assign any float value to radius and area, and the value of radius and area can be reassigned. For example, you can write the following code to compute the area for different radii:

```
// Compute the first area
radius = 1.0;
area = radius*radius*3.14159;
System.out.println("The area is " + area + " for radius " + radius);

// Compute the second area
radius = 2.0;
area = radius*radius*3.14159;
System.out.println("The area is " + area + " for radius " + radius);
```

Declaring Variables

Variables are used to represent many different types of data. To use a variable, you declare it and tell the compiler the name of the variable as well as what type of data it represents. This is called a *variable declaration*. The syntax for declaring a variable is as follows:

```
datatype variableName;
```

Here are some examples of variable declarations:

```
int x;           // Declare x to be an integer variable;
double radius;   // Declare radius to be a double variable;
char a;          // Declare a to be a character variable;
```

The examples use data types `int`, `float`, and `char`. You will be introduced to additional data types, such as `byte`, `short`, `long`, `float`, `char`, and `boolean`, in this chapter.

Assignment Statements

After a variable is declared, you can assign a value to it by using an *assignment statement*. The syntax for the assignment is one of the following formulations:

```
variable = value;
variable = expression;
```

For example, consider the following code:

```
x = 1;              // Assign 1 to x;
radius = 1.0;       // Assign 1.0 to radius;
a = 'A';            // Assign 'A' to a;
```

> **CAUTION**
> In an assignment statement, the data type of the variable on the left must be compatible with the data type of the value on the right. For example, x = 1.0 would be illegal because the data type of x is int. You cannot assign a double value (1.0) to an int variable.

The variable name must be on the left. Thus, 1 = x would be wrong.

An expression represents a computation involving values, variables, and operators. As an example, consider this code:

```
area = radius*radius*3.14159;
```

The variable on the left can also be used in the expression on the right:

```
x = x + 1;
```

In this assignment statement, x + 1 is assigned to x. If x is 1 before the statement is executed, then x becomes 2 after the statement is executed.

> **CAUTION**
> The Java assignment statement uses the equals sign (=), not :=, which is often used in other languages.

Declaring and Initializing Variables in One Step

Variables often have initial values. You can declare a variable and initialize it in one step. For example, consider the following code:

```
int x = 1;
```

This is equivalent to the next two statements:

```
int x;
x = 1;
```

> **CAUTION**
> A variable must be declared before it can be assigned a value. A variable must be assigned a value before it can be used.

> **TIP**
> Whenever possible, declare a variable and assign its initial value in one step. This makes the program easy to read.

Constants

The value of a variable may change during the execution of the program. A constant represents permanent data that never changes. In our ComputeArea program, PI is a constant. If you use it frequently, you don't want to keep typing 3.14159; instead, you can define a constant for π. Here is the syntax for declaring a constant:

    static final datatype CONSTANTNAME = VALUE;

The word final is a Java keyword, which means the constant cannot be changed. For example, in the ComputeArea program, you defined

    static final double PI = 3.14159;

and then used it in a computation:

    area = radius*radius*PI;

CAUTION
A constant must be declared and initialized before it can be used. You cannot change the constant's value once it is declared.

Numerical Data Types

Every data type has a domain (range) of values. The compiler allocates memory space to store each variable or constant according to its data type. Java provides several primitive data types for numerical values, characters, and Boolean values. In this section, numeric data types are introduced.

Java has six numeric types: four for integers and two for floating-point numbers. Table 2.1 lists the six numeric data types, their domains, and their storage sizes.

TABLE 2.1 Numeric Data Types

Name	*Domain*	*Storage Size*
byte	-2^7 to 2^7-1	8-bit signed
short	-2^{15} to $2^{15}-1$	16-bit signed
int	-2^{31} to $2^{31}-1$	32-bit signed
long	-2^{63} to $2^{63}-1$	64-bit signed
float	$-3.4E38$ to $3.4E38$ (6 to 7 significant digits of accuracy)	32-bit IEEE 754
double	$-1.7E308$ to $1.7E308$ (14 to 15 significant digits of accuracy)	64-bit IEEE 754

Standard arithmetic operators for numerical data types include addition (+), subtraction (-), multiplication (*), division (/), and modulus (%). For examples, see the following code:

Chapter 2 Java Building Elements

```
int i1 = 34 + 1;         // i1 becomes 35
double d1 = 34.0 - 0.1;  // d1 becomes 33.9
long  i2 = 300*30;       // i2 becomes 90000
double d2 = 1.0/2.0;     // d2 becomes 0.5
int i3 = 1/2;            // i3 becomes 0; Note the result is
                         // the integer part of the division
byte i4 = 20%3;          // i4 becomes 2; Note the result is
                         // the remainder after the division
```

The result of integer division is an integer. For example, 5/2 = 2, not 2.5. The fraction part is truncated.

Numeric Literals

A *literal* is a primitive type value that appears directly in the program. For example, 34, 1,000,000, and 5.0 are literals in the following statements:

```
int i = 34;
long l = 1000000;
double d = 5.0;
```

Floating-point literals are written with a decimal point. By default, a floating-point literal is treated as a `double` type value. For example, 5.0 is considered a `double` value, not a `float` value. You can make a number a `float` or a `double` by appending the letter f, F, d, or D. For example, you can use 100.2f or 100.2F for a floating-point number, and 100.2d or 100.2D for a `double` number. A floating-point literal can also be written in scientific notation; for example, 1.23456e+2, which is equivalent to 123.456.

Shortcut Operators

Very often the current value of a variable is used, modified, and then reassigned back to the same variable. For example, consider the following code:

```
i = i + 8;
```

This statement is equivalent to

```
i += 8;
```

The += is called a *shortcut operator*. The common shortcut operators are shown in Table 2.2.

TABLE 2.2 Shortcut Operators

Operator	Example	Equivalent
+=	i+=8	i = i+8
-=	f-=8.0	f = f-8.0
*=	i*=8	i = i*8
/=	i/=8	i = i/8
%=	i%=8	i = i%8

There are two more shortcut operators for incrementing and decrementing a variable by 1. This is handy because that's how much the value often needs to be changed. These two operators are ++ and --. They can be used in prefix or suffix notation. For example:

x++ is equivalent to x = x+1;
++x is equivalent to x = x+1;
x-- is equivalent to x = x-1;
--x is equivalent to x = x-1;

Any numeric value can be applied to x. These operators are often used in loop statements. A loop statement is a structure that controls how many times an operation or a sequence of operations is performed in succession. This structure, and the subject of loop statements, is introduced in Chapter 3, "Control Structures." The prefix (++x, --x) and suffix (x++, x--) are different when they occur in the expression. If the operator is prefixed to the variable, the variable is first incremented or decremented by 1, then used in the expression. If the operator is a suffix to the variable, the variable is used in the expression first, then incremented or decremented by 1. Therefore, the prefixes ++x and --x are referred to as the *preincrement operator* and the *predecrement operator*, respectively; and the suffixes x++ and x-- are referred to as the *postincrement operator* and the *postdecrement operator*, respectively. The following code illustrates this:

```
int i=10;
int newNum;
newNum = 10*i++;
```

In this case, i++ is evaluated after the entire expression (newNum = 10*i++) is evaluated. If i++ is replaced by ++i, ++i is evaluated before the entire expression is evaluated. So newNum is 100 for the first case and 110 for the second case. In both cases, i is incremented by 1.

Here is another example:

```
double x = 1.0;
double y = 5.0;
double z = x-- + ++y;
```

After all three lines are executed, y becomes 6.0, z becomes 7.0, and x becomes 0.0.

> **TIP**
> Shortcut operators originally came from C. They were inherited by C++ and adopted by Java. Using shortcut operators makes expressions short, but it also makes them complex and difficult to read. Avoid using shortcut operators in long expressions that involve many operators.

Numeric Type Conversion

Sometimes it is necessary to mix numerical values of different types in a computation. Consider the following statements:

```
byte i = 100;
long l = i*3+4;
double f = i*3.1+l/2;
```

Are these statements correct? Java allows binary operations on numerical variables and sometimes on values of different types. When performing a binary operation involving two operands of different types, Java automatically converts the less accurate operand to the type of the other, more accurate operand. For example, if one operand is `int` and the other is `float`, the `int` operand is converted to `float`, since `float` is more accurate than `int`. If one of the operands is of the type `double`, the other is converted to `double`, since `double` has the best accuracy among all numerical types. Thus the result of 1/2 is 0, and the result of 1.0/2 is 0.5.

You can always assign a less accurate value to a more accurate variable, such as assigning a `long` value to a `float` value. You cannot, however, assign a more accurate value to a less accurate variable unless you use *type casting*. Casting is an operation that converts a value of one data type into a value of another data type. The syntax for casting gives the target type in parentheses, followed by the variable's name. For example, see the following code:

```
float f = (float)10.1;
int i = (int)f;
```

In this case, `i` has a value of 10; the fractional part in `f` is truncated. Be careful when using casting. Lost information might lead to inaccurate results, as shown in this example:

```
int i = 10000;
byte s = (short)i;
```

In the example, `s` becomes 16, which is totally distorted. To ensure correctness, you can test whether the value is in the correct target type range (see Table 2.1) before performing casting.

> **CAUTION**
> Casting is necessary if you are assigning a more accurate value to a less accurate variable, such as assigning a `double` value to an `int` variable. A compilation error would occur if casting were not used in these situations.

Character Data Type

The character data type, `char`, is used to represent a single character.

A character value is enclosed within single quotation marks. For example, consider the following code:

```
char letter = 'A';
char numChar = '4';
```

The first statement assigns character `A` to the `char` variable `letter`. The second statement assigns numerical character `4` to the `char` variable `numChar`. Note the following illegal statement:

```
char numChar = 4;
```

In this statement, 4, a numerical value, cannot be assigned to a character variable.

The `char` type only represents one character. To represent a string of characters, use a data structure called `String`. For example, the following line of code declares the message to be a string that has an initial value of "Welcome to Java!"

```
String message = "Welcome to Java!";
```

`String` is discussed in more detail in Chapter 6, "Arrays and Strings."

> **CAUTION**
> A string must be enclosed in quotation marks. A literal character is a single character enclosed in single quotation marks.

Java characters use *Unicode,* a 16-bit encoding scheme established by the Unicode Consortium to support the interchange, processing, and display of written texts in the world's diverse languages. (See the Unicode Web site at **www.unicode.org** for more information.) Unicode takes two bytes, expressed in four hexadecimal numbers that run from `'\u0000'` to `'\uFFFF'`. Most computers use ASCII code. Unicode includes ASCII code with `'\u0000'` to `'\u00FF'` corresponding to the 128 ASCII characters. (See Appendix B, "The ASCII Character Set," for a list of ASCII characters and their decimal and hexadecimal codes.)

You can use ASCII characters like `'X'`, `'1'`, and `'$'` in a Java program as well as Unicodes. Java also allows you to use the escape sequence for special characters, as shown in Table 2.3.

TABLE 2.3 Examples of Special Characters

Character Escape Sequence	*ASCII*	*Unicode*
Backspace	\b	\u0008
Tab	\t	\u0009
Linefeed	\n	\u000a
Carriage return	\r	\u000d

To illustrate, the following statements are equivalent:

```
char letter = 'A';
char letter = '\u0041';
```

Both statements assign character A to char variable letter.

You can use casting to convert a character to a numerical code, and vice versa. For example, to obtain a character's decimal code, use a casting like this:

```
int decimalCode = (int)'0'
```

The variable `decimalCode` becomes 48.

boolean Data Type

The `boolean` data type comes from Boolean algebra. The domain of the `boolean` type consists of two values: `true` and `false`. For example, the following line of code assigns `true` to the `Boolean` variable `lightsOn`.

```
boolean lightsOn = true;
```

The operators associated with Boolean values are comparison operators and Boolean operators. Comparison operators can be used in expressions that result in a Boolean value. Table 2.4 contains a list of the comparison operators.

TABLE 2.4   Comparison Operators

Operator	Name	Example	Answer
<	less than	1 < 2	true
<=	less than or equal to	1 <= 2	true
>	greater than	1 > 2	false
>=	greater than or equal to	1 >= 2	false
==	equal to	1 == 2	false
!=	not equal to	1 != 2	true

CAUTION
The equality comparison operator is two equals signs (==), not a single equals sign (=). The latter symbol is for assignment.

Boolean operators operate on Boolean values to create a new Boolean value. Table 2.5 contains a list of Boolean operators.

TABLE 2.5   Boolean Operators

Operator	Name	Description
!	not	logical negation
&&	and	logical conjunction
||	or	logical disjunction
^	exclusive or	logical exclusion

These operators are demonstrated by using examples. In the examples, the variables `width` and `height` contain the values of 1 and 2, respectively.

Table 2.6 defines the not (!) operator. The not (!) operator negates `true` to `false` and `false` to `true`. For example, `!(width == 3)` is true since `(width == 3)` is `false`.

TABLE 2.6 Truth for Operator !

Operand	!Operand
true	false
false	true

Table 2.7 defines the and (&&) operator. The and (&&) of two Boolean operands is true if and only if both operands are true. For example, (width == 1) && (height > 1) is true because (width == 1) and (height > 1) are both true.

TABLE 2.7 Truth for Operator &&

Operand1	Operand2	Operand1 && Operand2
false	false	false
false	true	false
true	false	false
true	true	true

Table 2.8 defines the or (||) operator. The or (||) of two Boolean operands is true if at least one of the operands is true. For example, (width > 1) || (height > 2) is false because (width > 1) and (height > 2) are both false.

TABLE 2.8 Truth for Operator ||

Operand1	Operand2	Operand1 || Operand2
false	false	false
false	true	true
true	false	true
true	true	true

Table 2.9 defines the exclusive or (^) operator. The exclusive or (^) of two Boolean operands is true if and only if two operands have different Boolean values. For example, (width > 1) ^ (height == 2) is true because (width > 1) is false and (height == 2) is true.

TABLE 2.9 Truth for Operator ^

Operand1	Operand2	Operand1 ^ Operand2
false	false	false
false	true	true
true	false	true
true	true	false

When evaluating p1 && p2, Java first evaluates p1, then evaluates p2 if p1 is true; if p1 is false, p2 is not evaluated. When evaluating p1 || p2, Java first evaluates p1, then evaluates p2 if p1 is false; if p1 is true, p2 is not evaluated.

Java also provides the & and | operators. The & operator works identically to the && operator, and the | operator works identically to the || operator with one exception—the & and | operators always evaluate both operands. In some rare situations, you can use the & and | operators to guarantee that the right operand is evaluated regardless of whether the left operand is true or false. For example, the expression (width < 2) & (height-- < 2) guarantees that (height-- < 2) is evaluated. Thus, the variable height will be decremented regardless of whether width is less than 2 or not.

> **TIP**
> Avoid using the & and | operators. The benefits of the & and | operators are marginal. Using the & and | operators makes the program difficult to read and could cause errors. For example, the expression (x != 0) & (100/x) results in a runtime error if x is 0.

Operator Precedence

Operator precedence determines the order in which expressions are evaluated. Suppose that you have the following expression:

```
3 + 4*4 > 5*(4+3) - i++
```

What is its value? How does the compiler know the execution order of the operators? The expression in the parentheses is evaluated first. (Parentheses can be nested, in which case the expression in the inner parentheses is executed first.) When evaluating an expression without parentheses, the operators are applied in the order shown in Table 2.10, which contains the operators you have learned in this section. (See Appendix C, "Operator Precedence Chart," for a complete list of Java operators and their precedence.)

TABLE 2.10   Operator Precedence Chart

Precedence	Operator
Highest Order	casting
	++ and -- (prefix)
	*, /, %
	+, -
	<, <=, >, =>
	==, !=
	&&
	||
	=, +=, -=, *=, /=, %=
Lowest Order	++ and -- (postfix)

> **TIP**
> You can use parentheses to force an evaluation order as well as to make a program easy to read.

Programming Errors

Programming errors are unavoidable, even for experienced programmers. Errors can be categorized into three types: compilation errors, runtime errors, or logic errors.

Compilation Errors

Errors that occur during compilation are called *compilation errors* or *syntax errors*. Compilation errors result from errors in code construction, such as mistyping a keyword, omitting some necessary punctuation, or using an opening brace without a corresponding closing brace. These errors are usually easy to detect because the compiler tells you where they are and the reasons for them. For example, compiling the following program results in a compilation error, as shown in Figure 2.2.

```java
// The program contains syntax errors
public class ShowErrors
{
  public static void main(String[] args)
  {
    i = 30;
    System.out.println(i+4);
  }
}
```

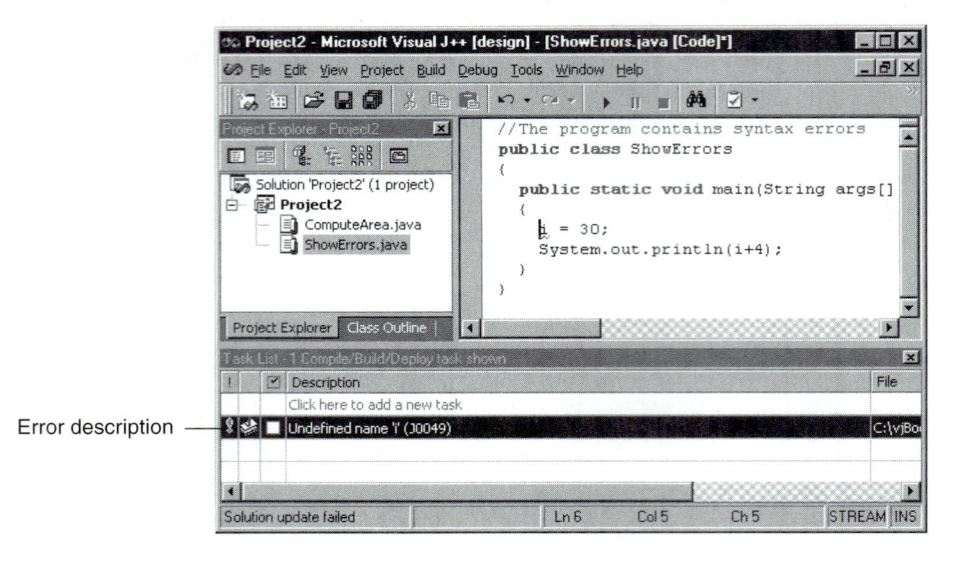

Figure 2.2 *The compiler detects a syntax error: Undefined name* i.

Chapter 2 Java Building Elements

Visual J++ makes finding and fixing syntax errors easy. As shown in Figure 2.2, compilation errors are displayed in the Task List window. Pointing the mouse and clicking on the line that shows the syntax error in the Task List window leads you to the line in the source code that caused the error.

> **TIP**
> Single errors commonly display multiple lines of compilation errors. Therefore, it is a good practice to start debugging from the top line and work downward. Fixing errors that occur earlier may fix cascading errors that occur later in the program.

Visual J++ also provides *dynamic syntax checking* to assist you when you're writing code in the Text Editor. In addition to the information the *Statement Completion Assistant* provides, you receive visual clues in the form of red squiggly lines and error tips as you build your program's statements, as shown in Figure 2.3.

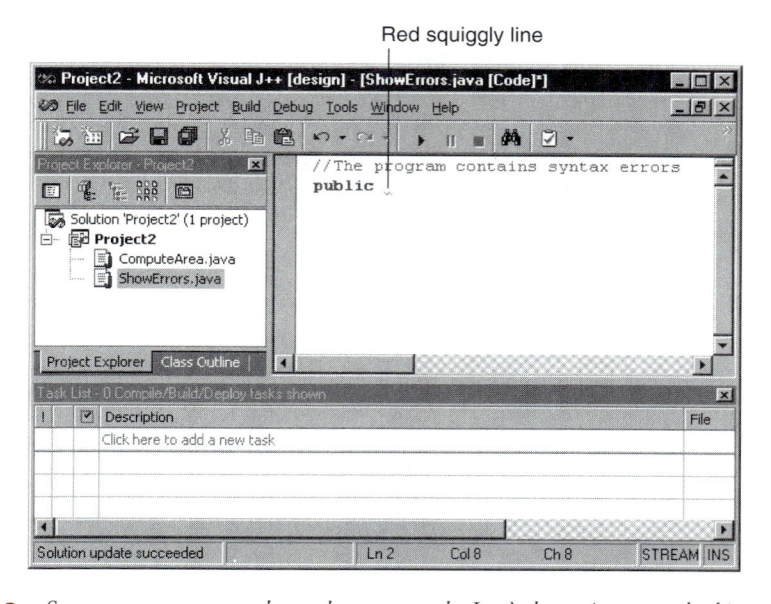

Figure 2.3 *Some syntax errors are detected as you type by J++'s dynamic syntax checking.*

When you begin typing in a .java file, red squiggly lines may appear under code elements, such as class names, member names, and symbols. Visual J++ uses red squiggly lines to tell you that your code, as currently written, has syntactic errors. The red squiggly lines may disappear when you finish typing the statement—depending upon the correctness of the completed statement.

For each syntax error marked with a red squiggly line, a task related to the syntax error will appear in the Task List window. This provides a list of the items that must be corrected before you compile your program.

> **TIP**
> You can get error tips from a red squiggly line by pointing the mouse at it. You can also view error help by choosing Error Help from the context menu at the red squiggly line, as shown in Figure 2.4. The error help document is displayed in Help Viewer, as shown in Figure 2.5.

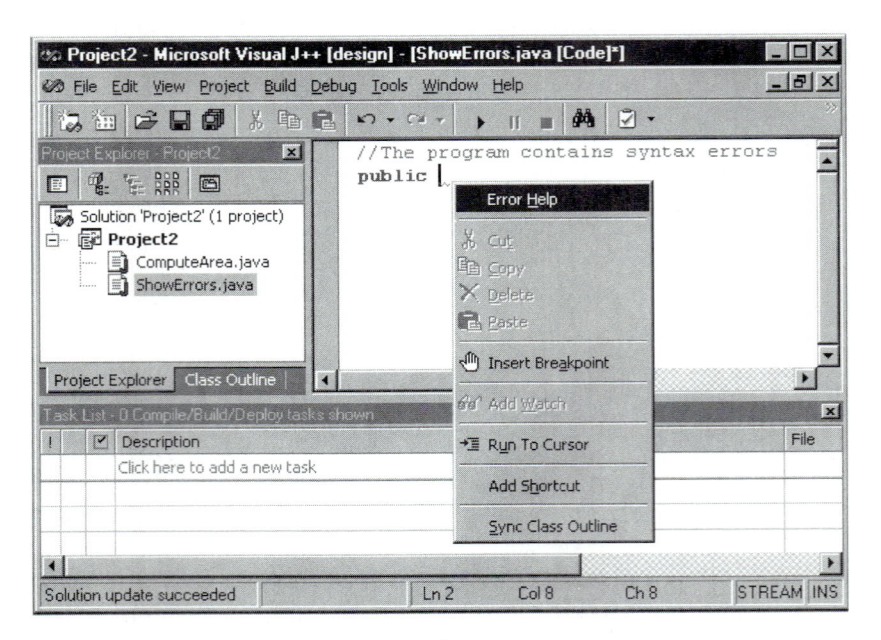

Figure 2.4 *You can get error tips from Error Help.*

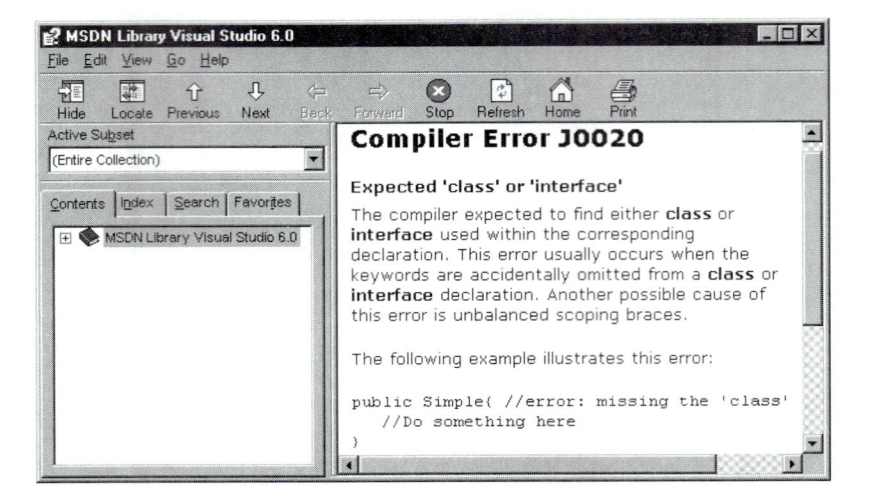

Figure 2.5 *The Error Help document is displayed in the Help Viewer.*

Runtime Errors

Runtime errors are errors that cause a program to terminate abnormally. Runtime errors occur while an application is running if the environment detects an operation that is impossible to carry out. Input error is a typical runtime error.

An *input error* occurs when the user enters an unexpected input value that the program cannot handle. For instance, if the program expects to read in a number, but instead the user enters a string, this causes data-type errors to occur in the program. To avoid the input error, the program prompts the user to enter the correct type of values. For instance, it may display a message like "Please enter an integer" before reading an integer from the keyboard.

Visual J++ IDE appears in one of three modes: design, run, and break. You can design the project, create files, edit files, build projects, and start projects in *design mode*. Once the project starts, Visual J++ enters *run mode* until it finishes or a runtime error occurs. When the program finishes normally, Visual J++ returns to design mode. If a runtime error occurs, Visual J++ enters *break mode*. For instance, if you entered a nonnumeric value like e3 when running Example 2.1, you would get an error message box, as shown in Figure 2.6. Click OK to enter the break mode, as shown in Figure 2.7. A green triangle arrow points to where the runtime error occurred in the source code. You can fix the error and continue to execute the program. Since this error was caused by incorrect input, you have to restart the program with a new, correct input.

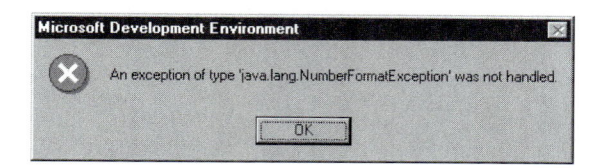

Figure 2.6 *When a runtime error occurs, an error message dialog box is displayed.*

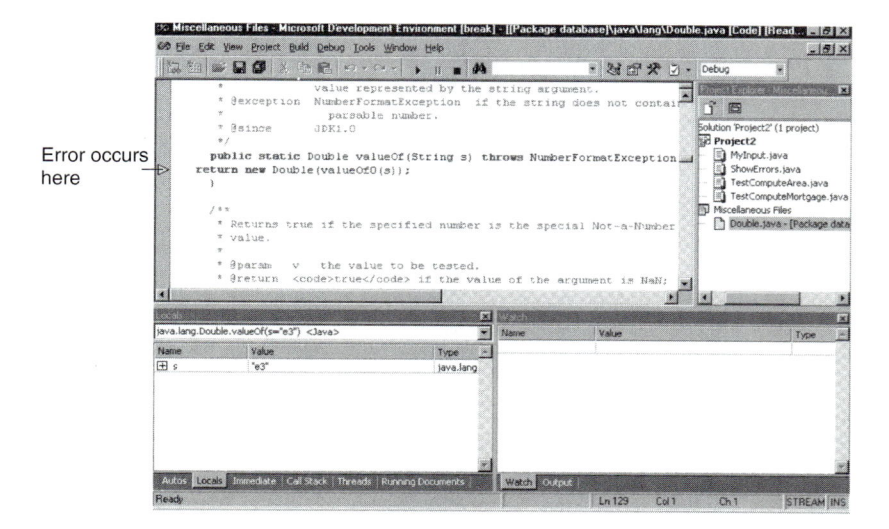

Figure 2.7 *Visual J++ enters the break mode for debugging.*

Logic Errors

Logic errors occur when a program doesn't perform the way it was intended to. Errors of this kind occur for many different reasons. Since errors are called *bugs*, the process of finding errors is called *debugging*. A common approach to debugging is to use a combination of methods to narrow down to the part of the program where the bug is located. Debugging a large program can be a daunting task. Debugging techniques are introduced in the section "Debugging in Visual J++" in Chapter 6.

Programming Style and Documentation

Programming style deals with the appearance of your program. If you were to write an entire program on one line, it would compile and run fine, but doing this would be bad programming style because the program would be hard to read. Documentation consists of explanatory remarks and comments for the program. Programming style and documentation are as important as coding. Good programming style and appropriate documentation reduce the chance for errors and make programs easy to read. Some guidelines for Java programming style and documentation are given below.

Appropriate Comments

You should include a summary at the beginning of the program to explain what the program does, its key features, its supporting data structures, and any unique techniques it uses. In a long program, you should also include comments to introduce each major step and to explain anything that is difficult to read. It is important to make your comments concise so that you do not crowd the program or make it difficult to read.

> **NOTE**
> In addition to the two comment styles, // and /*, Java supports comments of a special type, referred to as *javadoc comments*. javadoc comments begin with /** and end with */. They are generally used for documenting classes and data and methods. They can be extracted into an HTML file using JDK's `javadoc` command. You can use the `javadoc` command to obtain an HTML file for describing the package and classes. In Visual J++ 6.0, the javadoc comments are displayed in the Class Outline window, as shown in Figure 2.8.

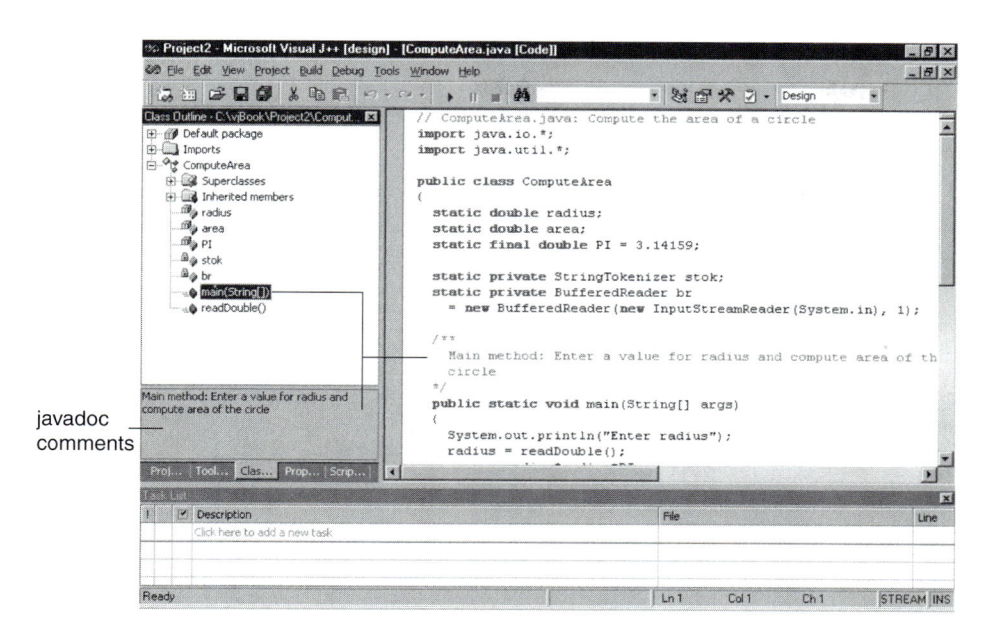

Figure 2.8 *The javadoc comments are displayed in the Class Outline window.*

Naming Conventions

Make sure that the meanings of the descriptive names you choose for variables, constants, classes, and methods are straightforward. Names are case-sensitive. The following are the conventions for naming variables, methods, and classes:

- For variables and methods, always use lowercase. If the name consists of several words, concatenate them into one, making the first word lowercase and capitalizing the first letter of each subsequent word in the name; for example, the variables `radius` and `area` and the method `readDouble()`.

- For class names, capitalize the first letter of each word in the name; for example, the class name `ComputeArea`.

- All letters in constants should be capitalized, and underscores should be used between words; for example, the constant `PI` and constant MAX_VALUE.

> **Tip**
> It is important to become familiar with naming conventions. Understanding naming conventions will help you to understand Java programs. If you stick with the naming conventions, other programmers will be more willing to accept your program.

Proper Indentation

A consistent indentation style makes your programs clear and easy to read. Indentation is used to illustrate structural relationships among the program's components or statements. Java can read the program even if all of the statements are in a straight line, but it is easier to read and maintain code that is aligned properly. You should indent each subcomponent or statement several spaces more than the structure within which it is nested.

Block Styles

A block is a group of statements surrounded by braces. A block can be written in many ways. For example, the following are equivalent:

```java
public class Test
{
  public static void main(String[] args)
  {
    System.out.println("Block Styles");
  }
}
public class Test {
  public static void main(String[] args) {
    System.out.println("Block Styles");
  }
}
```

The former is referred to as the *next-line* style, and the latter, as the *end-of-line* style. In the next-line style, the opening brace and the closing brace are on the same column; thus it is easy to see the beginning and end of the block. That is why the next-line block style is used in this book.

Separate Classes

You will frequently use readDouble to get a double floating-point number from the keyboard. Do you have to code the method readDouble() in every program that invokes readDouble? In Java, you can define a separate class for readDouble so that every program using readDouble can use it without rewriting the code.

Now let's look at a new class called MyInput. This class contains the readDouble() and the readInt() methods for reading a double and an int literal, respectively, from the keyboard.

```java
// MyInput.java: Contain the methods for reading int and double
// values from the keyboard
import java.io.*;
import java.util.*;

public class MyInput
{
  static private StringTokenizer stok;
  static private BufferedReader br
    = new BufferedReader(new InputStreamReader(System.in), 1);

  // Read an int value from the keyboard
  public static int readInt()
  {
    int i = 0;
    try
    {
      String str = br.readLine();
      StringTokenizer stok = new StringTokenizer(str);
      i = new Integer(stok.nextToken()).intValue();
    }
    catch (IOException ex)
```

```java
    {
      System.out.println(ex);
    }
    return i;
  }

  // Read a double value from the keyboard
  public static double readDouble()
  {
    double d = 0;
    try
    {
      String str = br.readLine();
      stok = new StringTokenizer(str);
      d = new Double(stok.nextToken()).doubleValue();
    }
    catch (IOException ex)
    {
      System.out.println(ex);
    }
    return d;
  }
}
```

The following case studies show how to use the `MyInput` class.

Case Studies

In the preceding sections, you learned variables, constants, primitive data types, operators, and expressions. You are now ready to use them to write interesting programs. This section presents two examples: computing mortgage payments, and breaking a sum of money down into its component units.

Example 2.2 Computing a Mortgage

This example shows you how to write a program that computes mortgage payments. The program will let the user enter the interest rate, year, and loan amount, and then will compute the monthly payment and the total payment. Finally, it will display the monthly and total final payments.

The formula to compute the monthly payment is as follows:

$$\frac{\text{principal} \times \text{monthly Interest}}{(1-(1/(1+\text{monthly Interest})))^{\text{years} \times 12}}$$

The mortgage calculation program follows, and the output is shown in Figure 2.9.

```java
// ComputeMortgage.java: Compute mortgage payments
public class ComputeMortgage
{
  // Main method
  public static void main(String[] args)
  {
    double interestRate;
    int year;
    double loan;
```

continues

```
            // Enter monthly interest rate
            System.out.println(
              "Enter yearly interest rate, for example 8.25: ");
            interestRate = MyInput.readDouble()/1200;

            // Enter number of years
            System.out.println(
              "Enter number of years as an integer, for example 5: ");
            year = MyInput.readInt();

            // Enter loan amount
            System.out.println("Enter loan amount, for example 120000.95: ");
            loan = MyInput.readDouble();

            // Calculate payment
            double monthlyPay =
              loan*interestRate/(1 - (Math.pow(1/(1 + interestRate),
                year*12)));
            double totalPay = monthlyPay*year*12;

            // Display results
            System.out.println("The monthly pay is " + monthlyPay);
            System.out.println("The total pay is " + totalPay);
          }
        }
```

Figure 2.9 *The program receives interest rate, years, and loan amount, then displays the monthly payment and total payment.*

Example Review

The methods defined in the MyInput class are readInt and readDouble. They are available for use in this program because MyInput is compiled, and its bytecode is stored in the same directory as this test program. If you get a compilation error indicating that MyInput is not defined, make sure that MyInput.class is in the directory with ComputeMortgage.java.

The method for computing b^p in the Math class is pow(b, p). The Math class, which comes with the Java runtime system, is available to all Java programs. The Math class is introduced in Chapter 5.

> **TIP**
>
> When you run the program with Visual J++ IDE as a console application, the console is closed after the program displays the result. To see the result on the console, add the following lines at the end of the `main()` method:
>
> ```
> System.out.println("**** End of the main method ****");
> System.out.println("Press Ctrl+C to close the console");
> MyInput.readDouble();
> ```
>
> When the `readDouble()` method is executed, it awaits an input from the keyboard. The use of this method here keeps the console alive. You can press Ctrl+C to close the console and terminate the program.

Example 2.3 Breaking Down a Sum of Money

This example shows you how to write a program that classifies a given amount of money into its component smaller monetary units. The program will let the user enter a decimal amount representing a total in dollars and cents, and will output a report listing the monetary equivalent in dollars, quarters, dimes, nickels, and pennies.

The program follows, and the output is shown in Figure 2.10.

```java
// BreakChanges.java: Find changes for a given amount
public class BreakChanges
{
  // Main method
  public static void main(String[] args)
  {
    double amount; // Amount entered from the keyboard

    // Receive the amount entered from the keyboard
    System.out.println(
      "Enter an amount in integer, for example 11.56");
    amount = MyInput.readDouble();

    int remainingAmount = (int)(amount*100);

    // Find the number of one dollars
    int numOfOneDollars = remainingAmount/100;
    remainingAmount = remainingAmount%100;

    // Find the number of quaters in the remaining amount
    int numOfQuarters = remainingAmount/25;
    remainingAmount = remainingAmount%25;

    // Find the number of dimes in the remaining amount
    int numOfDimes = remainingAmount/10;
    remainingAmount = remainingAmount%10;
```

continues

```java
            // Find the number of nickels in the remaining amount
            int numOfNickels = remainingAmount/5;
            remainingAmount = remainingAmount%5;

            // Find the number of pennies in the remaining amount
            int numOfPennies = remainingAmount;

            // Display results
            System.out.println("The amount " + amount + " is " +
              numOfOneDollars +
              " dollars, " + numOfQuarters + " quarters, " + numOfDimes +
              " dimes, "
              + numOfNickels + " nickels, and " + numOfPennies + " pennies");
    }
}
```

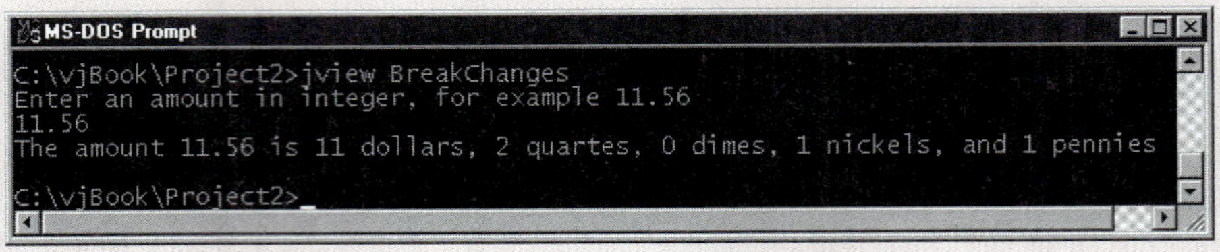

```
C:\vjBook\Project2>jview BreakChanges
Enter an amount in integer, for example 11.56
11.56
The amount 11.56 is 11 dollars, 2 quartes, 0 dimes, 1 nickels, and 1 pennies

C:\vjBook\Project2>_
```

Figure 2.10 *The program receives an amount in decimals and breaks it into singles, quarters, dimes, nickels and pennies.*

Example Review

The program extracts the maximum number of singles from the total amount and obtains the remaining amount in the variable `remainingAmount`. It then extracts the maximum number of quarters from `remainingAmount` and obtains a new `remainingAmount`. Continuing the same process, the program finds the dimes, nickels, and pennies in the remaining amount.

The variable `amount` stores the amount entered from the keyboard. This variable is not changed because the amount has to be displayed in the end. The program introduces the variable `remainingAmount` to store the changing `remainingAmount`.

The variable `amount` is a `double` decimal representing dollars and cents, it is converted to an `int` variable `remainingAmount`, which represents all cents. For instance, if `amount` is 11.54, then the initial `remainingAmount` is 1154. The division operator yields the integer part of the division. So, 1154/100 is 11. The remainder operator obtains the remainder of the division. So, 1154%100 is 54.

One serious problem with this example is the possible loss of precision when casting a `double` amount to an `int` `remainingAmount`. There are two ways to fix the problem. One is to enter the amount as an `int` value representing cents; the other is to read the decimal number as a string and extract the dollars part and cents part separately as `int` values. Processing strings will be introduced in Chapter 6, "Array and Strings."

Visual J++'s Online Help

J++ provides a large number of documents online, giving you a great deal of information on a variety of topics related to the use of Visual J++.

To access online help, choose Contents, Index, or Search from the Help menu to display the Help Viewer, as shown in Figure 2.11. You can also get the Help Viewer by pressing F1.

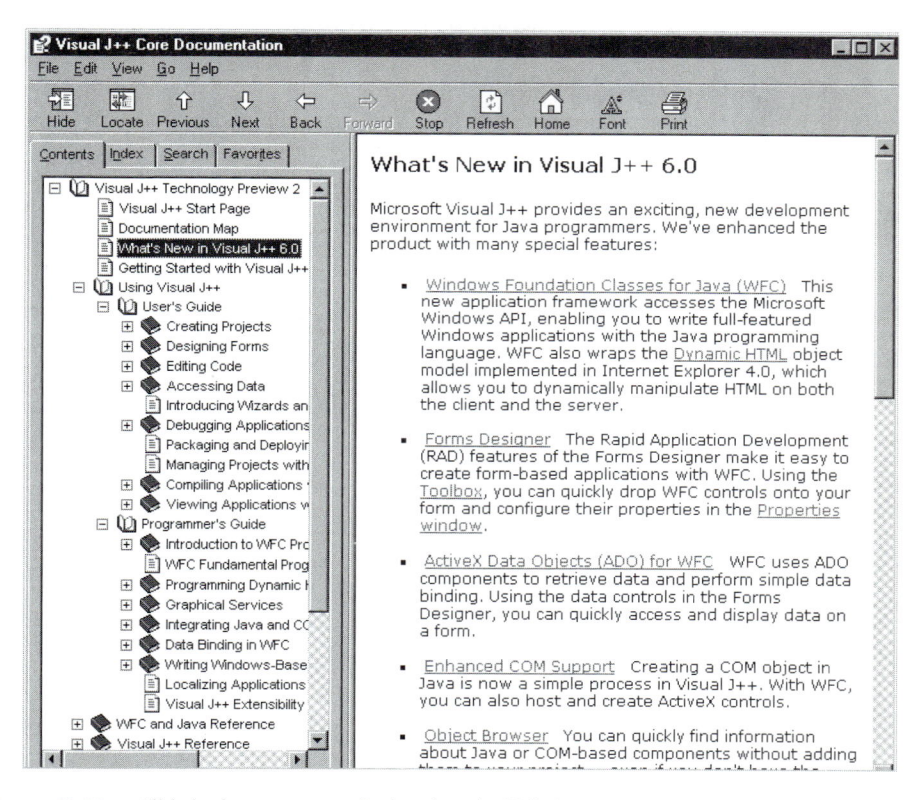

Figure 2.11 *All help documents are displayed in the Help Viewer in J++.*

The Help Viewer resembles the Internet Explorer. In fact, all the help documents are HTML files. The Help Viewer contains four tabs: Contents, Index, Search, and Favorites. The Contents page displays an expandable table of contents for the document.

The table of contents is displayed in a treelike list. To view a given topic, select the node in the tree associated with the topic. The Help Viewer then displays the document for the topic in the Content pane.

The Index page shows the index entries for the document. To display the index, simply type the first few letters in the entry. As you start typing, the index scrolls, doing an incremental search on the index entries to find the closest match, as shown in Figure 2.12. Select and double-click the index in the entry to display the document for the entry in the Content pane.

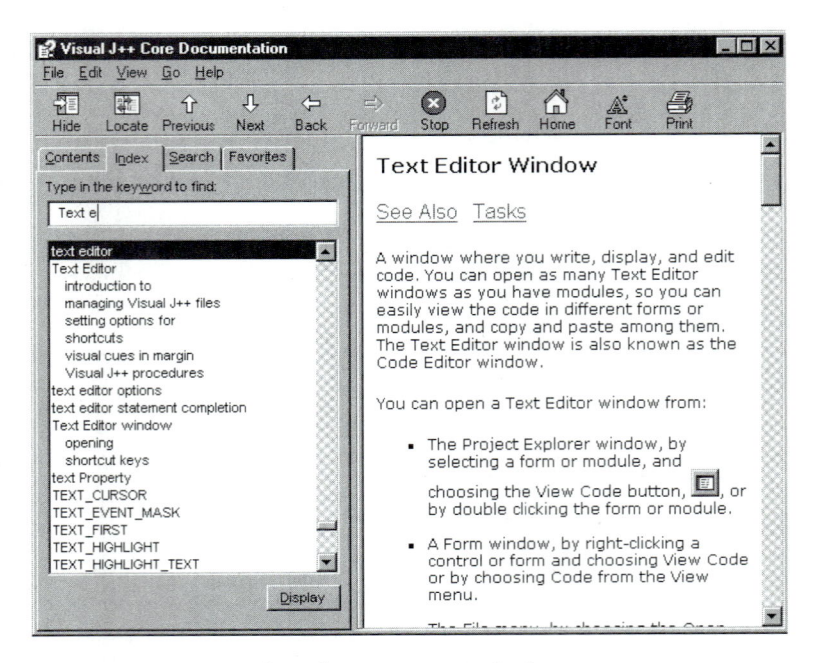

Figure 2.12 *You can type an index to locate contents in the document.*

The Search page (see Figure 2.13) enables you to search for topics that contain words similar to the one you want to search for. To search for the topic, simply type the word or words you want to search and click the List Topics button, as shown in Figure 2.13. J++ lists all the topics that match the word or words. To view a topic, select the topic and click the Display button to display it in the Content pane.

The Favorites page (see Figure 2.14) enables you to store topics in the Favorite list so they can be located without searching. To add the current topic, click the Add button. To remove a topic, select it and click the Remove button. To view a topic, select it in the Favorite list and display the topic in the Content pane.

The Help Viewer contains a Hide button that can used to hide or unhide the Search pane, and a Locate button that can be used to locate a topic for the current topic displayed in the Content pane. The Help Viewer also contains navigator buttons: **Home, Previous, Next, Back,** and **Forward.** The Home, Previous, and Next buttons are for navigating the topic in the help document in the order specified in the contents. The Back and Forward buttons are for navigating topics according to the order in which they are displayed in the Content pane.

CHAPTER 2   JAVA BUILDING ELEMENTS

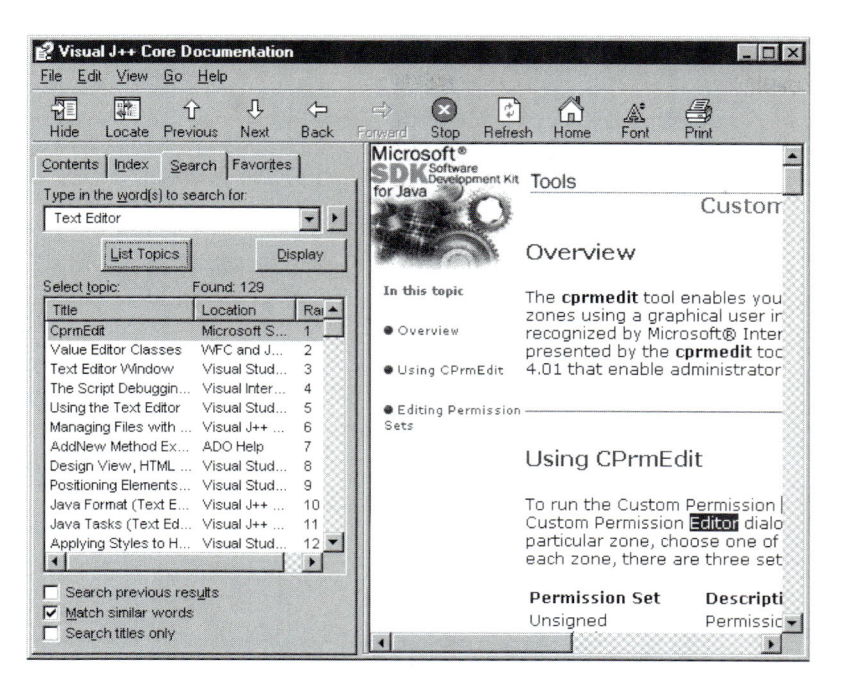

Figure 2.13   *You can view the topics that contain a word or words related to the word or words you want to search.*

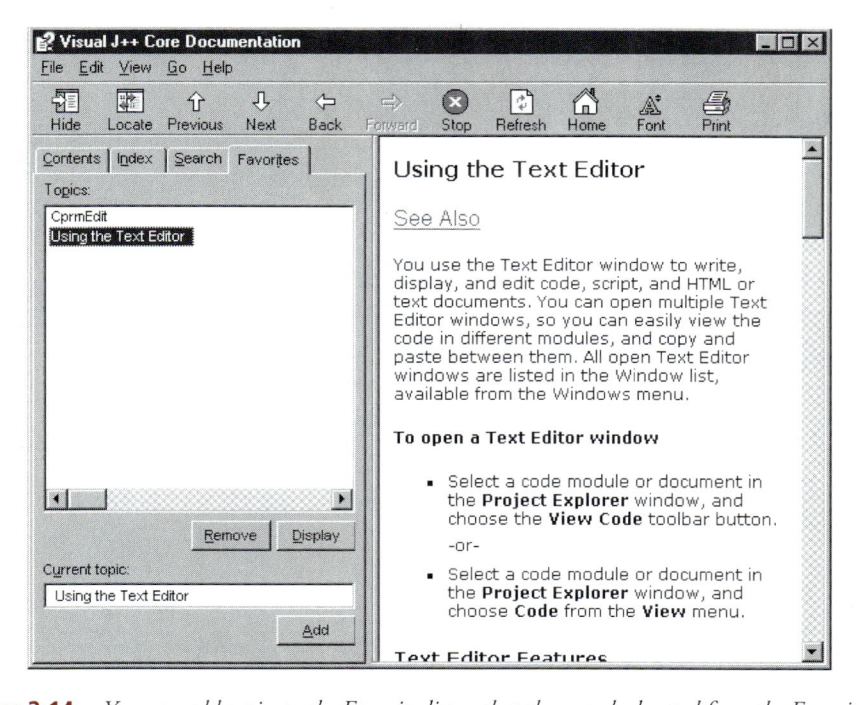

Figure 2.14   *You can add topics to the Favorite list so that they can be located from the Favorite list.*

73

> **NOTE**
> The Help menu is not the only way to get help. There are many ways to get help on a topic when you are using Visual J++. All the dialog boxes in Visual J++ have a Help button. For example, on the Launch page of the Project Properties dialog box, you can click the Help button to start Help Viewer and view the documentation on Launch.

Visual J++ IDE Options

Visual J++ allows you to customize your development environment by changing various IDE options. Options like syntax highlighting can make your programs easy to read and help you to spot errors. Other options specify whether your programs are saved before execution.

To set IDE options, choose Tools, Options to display the Options dialog box, as shown in Figure 2.15. The dialog box enables you to set the IDE options for Environment, Text Editor, Debugger, Data Tools, Form Designer, HTML, and Security.

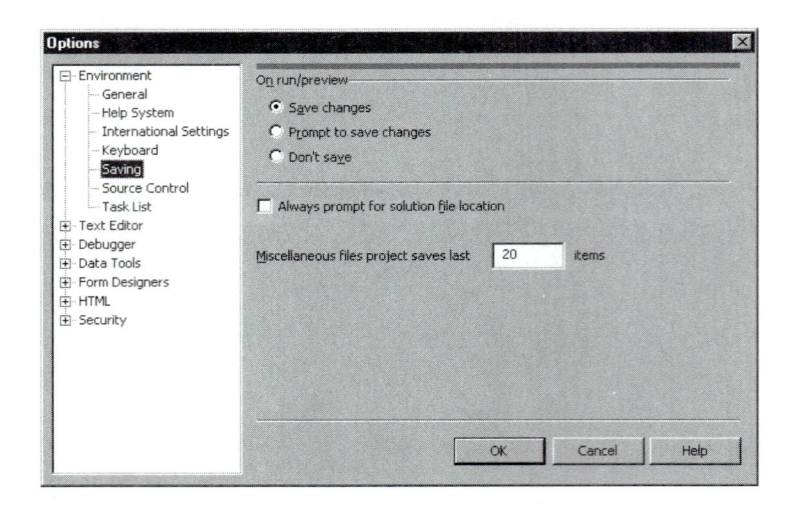

Figure 2.15 *The Options dialog box enables you to set the IDE options.*

To specify whether your program is to be saved before execution, choose Saving under the node Environment in the Navigation pane and check the Option "Save changes" in the Option pane, as shown in Figure 2.15.

You can use tabs, colors, fonts, and other editor options to set the editor's handling of text. For example, to set the tab, choose Text Editor, Tabs, and Java to display the option pane for setting tabs. Set the Tab size and Indent Size to 2, as shown in Figure 2.16. As you can see, there are options available for customization. I will alert you to them throughout the text.

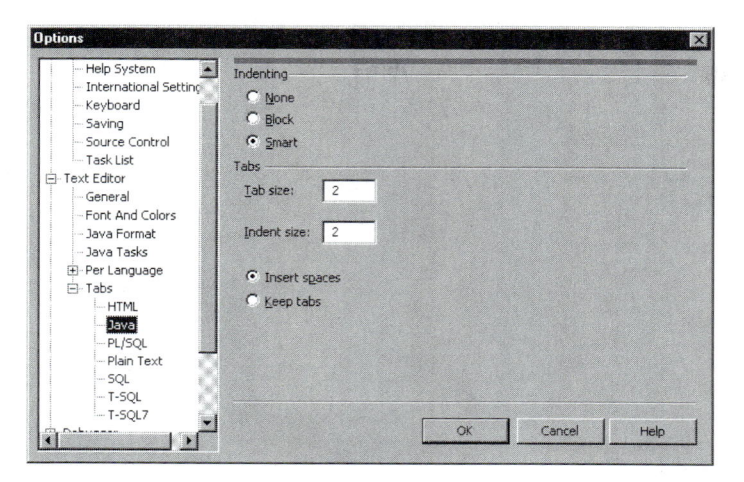

Figure 2.16 *You can set tab options for Java source code.*

Chapter Summary

In this chapter, you learned about data representation, operators, and expressions. These are the fundamental elements needed to construct Java programs. You also learned about programming errors, debugging, and programming styles. These are all important concepts and should be fully understood before you apply them.

Identifiers are used for naming programming entities, such as variables, constants, methods, classes, and packages. Variables are symbols that represent data. The value of a variable can be changed with an assignment statement. All variables must be declared with an identifier and a type before they can be used. An initial value must be assigned to a variable before it is used.

The equals sign (=) is used to assign a value to a variable. The statement with the equals sign is called an assignment statement. When a value is assigned to a variable, it replaces the previous value of the variable, which is destroyed.

A constant is a symbol representing a value in the program that is never changed. Sometimes it is called a constant variable. You cannot assign a new value to a constant.

Java provides four integer types (`byte`, `short`, `int`, `long`) that represent integers of four different sizes, and two floating-point types (`float`, `double`) that represent float numbers of two different sizes. Character type (`char`) represents a single character, and `boolean` type represents a `true` or `false` value. These are called primitive data types. Java's primitive types are portable across all computer platforms. When they are declared, the variables of these types are created and assigned with memory space.

Java provides operators that perform numerical operations: + (addition), - (subtraction), * (multiplication), / (division), and % (modulus). Integer division (/) yields an integer result. The modulus operator (%) yields the remainder after integer division.

The increment operator (++) and the decrement operator (--) increment or decrement a variable by 1. If the operator is prefixed to the variable, the variable is first incremented or decremented by 1, then used in the expression. If the operator is a suffix to the variable, the variable is used in the expression first, then incremented or decremented by 1.

In a computation involving different types of numerical values, numbers are converted to a unifying type. The unifying type is chosen according to the data type of the operands in the following order: `double`, `float`, `long`, `int`, `short`, `byte`. You can assign a value of a lower order to a variable of a higher order. However, an explicit casting operator must be used if you assign a value of a higher order (for instance, `double`) to a variable of a lower order (for instance, `int`).

The operators in arithmetic expressions are evaluated in the order determined by the rules of operator precedence. Parentheses can be used to force the order of evaluation to occur in any sequence.

You learned how to view help online, and how to customize Visual J++ 6.0 IDE options.

Chapter Review

2.1. Are the following identifiers valid?

```
applet, Applet, a++, --a, 4#R, $4, #44, apps
```

2.2. Declare the following:

- An `int` variable with an initial value of `0`.
- A `long` variable with an initial value of `10000`.
- A `float` variable with an initial value of `3.4`.
- A `double` variable with an initial value of `34.45`.
- A `char` variable with an initial value of `4`.
- A `boolean` variable with an initial value of `true`.

2.3. Assume that a = 1 and d = 1.0, and that each expression is independent. What are the results of the following expressions?

```
a = 46/9;
a = 46%9+4*4-2;
a = 45+43%5*(23*3%2);
a = 45+45*50%a--;
a = 45+1+45*50%(--a)
d += 34.23*3+d++
d -= 3.4*(a+5)*d++
a %= 3/a+3;
```

2.4. Find the largest and smallest `byte`, `short`, `int`, `long`, `float`, and `double`. Which of these data types requires the least amount of memory?

2.5. Can different types of numeric values be used together in a computation?

2.6. Describe Unicode and ASCII code.

2.7. Can the following conversions involving casting be allowed? If so, find the converted result. (Write a program to test your results.)

```
char c = 'A';
i = (int)c;

boolean b = true;
i = (int)b;

float f = 1000.34f;
int i = (int)f;

double d = 1000.34;
int i = (int)d;

int i = 1000;
char c = (char)i;

int i = 1000;
boolean b = (boolean)b;
```

2.8. What is the result of 25/4? How would you rewrite the expression if you wanted the quotient to be a floating-point number?

2.9. Are the following statements correct? If so, show the printout.

```
System.out.println("the output for 25/4 is "+ 25/4);
System.out.println("the output for 25/4.0 is "+ 25/4.0);
```

2.10. What does an explicit conversion from a `double` to an `int` do with the fractional part of the double value?

2.11. How would you write the following formula so that it produces a double value?

```
4/3(r + 34)
```

2.12. List six comparison operators.

2.13. Show the result of the following Boolean expressions if the result can be determined.

```
(true) && (3 > 4)
!(x > 0) && (x > 0)
(x > 0) || (x < 0)
(x != 0) || (x == 0)
(x >= 0) || (x < 0)
(x != 1) == !(x = 1)
```

2.14. Write a Boolean expression that evaluates to `true` if the number is between 1 and 100.

2.15. Write a Boolean expression that evaluates `true` if the number is between 1 and 100 or the number is negative.

2.16. Are the following expressions correct?

```
x > y > 0
x = y && y
x /= y
x or y
x and y
(x != 0) ¦¦ (x = 0)
```

2.17. How do you denote a comment line? a comment paragraph?

2.18. Describe compilation errors, runtime errors, and logical errors.

2.19. What are the naming conventions for class names, method names, constants, and variables? Which of the following items can be a constant, a method, a variable, or a class according to Java naming conventions?

```
MAX_VALUE, Test, read, readInt
```

2.20. What is the quick way to get the help document on a menu command in Visual J++ 6.0?

2.21. How do you set the tab positions in Visual J++ 6.0?

2.22. How do you change the colors for keywords in the source code editor in Visual J++ 6.0?

Programming Exercises

2.1. Write a program that converts Fahrenheit to Celsius. The formula for the conversion is as follows:

```
celsius = (5/9)*(fahrenheit-32)
```

Your program reads a Fahrenheit degree in double from the keyboard, then converts it to Celsius and displays the result on the console.

2.2. Write a program to compute the volume of a cylinder. Your program reads in radius and length, and computes volume using the following formulas:

```
area = radius*radius*π
volume = area*length
```

2.3. Write a program to display "Welcome to Java!" in large block letters, each letter made up of the same character it represents. The letter should be seven printed lines. For example, *W* is displayed as follows:

```
W             W
W             W
W      W      W
W    W W W    W
 W  W   W  W
  W         W
```

CHAPTER 3

CONTROL STRUCTURES

Objectives

- Understand the concept of program control.
- Use decision statements to control the execution of a program.
- Use loop structures to control the repetition of statements.
- Understand and use the keywords `break` and `continue`.
- Set classpath environment variable for accessing classes in Visual J++.

Introduction

Program control can be defined as specifying the order in which statements are executed in a computer program. The programs that you have written so far execute statements in sequence. Often, however, you are faced with situations in which you must provide alternative steps.

In Chapter 2, "Java Building Elements," if you entered a negative input for `radius` in Example 2.1, "Computing the Area of a Circle," for instance, the program would print an invalid result. If the radius is negative, you don't want the program to compute the area. Like all high-level programming languages, Java provides decision statements that let you choose actions with two or more alternative courses. You can use the decision statements in the following pseudocode to rewrite Example 2.1:

```
if the radius is negative
   the program displays a message indicating a wrong input;
else
   the program computes the area and displays the result;
```

Java supports several variations of decision statements. The three main forms are `if` statements, shortcut `if` statements, and `switch` statements.

Like other high-level programming languages, Java provides loop structures in order to control the repeated execution of statements. Suppose that you need to print the same message a hundred times. It would be tedious to have to write the message over and over again. Java provides a powerful control structure called a *loop,* which controls how many times an operation or a sequence of operations is performed in succession. Using a loop construct, you can simply tell the computer to print the message a hundred times without actually coding the print statement a hundred times. Java has three basic loop constructs: `for` loops, `while` loops, and `do` loops.

In this chapter, you will learn various decision and loop control structures.

Using *if* Statements

Java has two types of `if` statements: the simple `if` statement and the `if...else` statement. A simple `if` statement executes an action only if the condition is `true`. The actions that an `if...else` statement specifies differ based on whether the condition is `true` or `false`.

The Simple *if* Statement

The syntax for a simple `if` statement is as follows:

```
if (booleanExpression)
{
  statement(s);
}
```

The execution flow chart is shown in Figure 3.1.

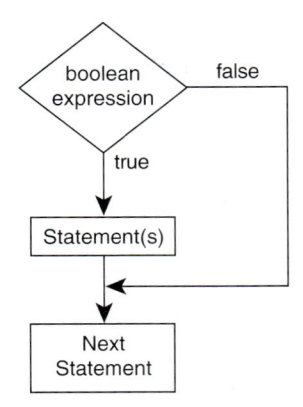

Figure 3.1 *An* if *statement executes statements if the* boolean *expression evaluates as* true.

If the booleanExpression evaluates as true, the statements in the block are executed. For example, see the following code:

```
if (radius >= 0)
{
  area = radius*radius*PI;
  System.out.println("The area for the circle of radius " +
    radius + " is " + area);
}
```

If the value of radius is greater than or equal to 0, then the area is computed and the result is displayed; otherwise, the two statements in the block will not be executed.

> **CAUTION**
> The booleanExpression is always enclosed in parentheses for all forms of the if statement.

The curly braces can be omitted if they enclose a single statement. For example:

```
if ((i >= 0) && (i <= 10))
   system.out.println("i is an integer between 0 and 10");
```

The *if . . . else* Statement

A simple if statement takes an action if the specified condition is true. If the condition is false, nothing is done. But what if you want to take alternative actions when the condition is false? You can use an if . . . else statement. The syntax for this statement is as follows:

```
if (booleanExpression)
{
  statement(s)-for-the-true-case;
}
else
{
  statement(s)-for-the-false-case;
}
```

The flow chart of the if . . . else statement is shown in Figure 3.2.

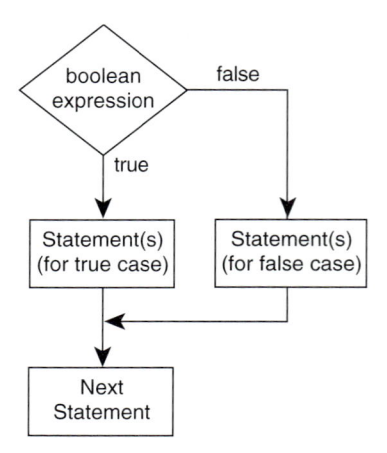

Figure 3.2 *An* if . . . else *statement executes the statements for the* true *case if the* boolean *expression evaluates as* true; *otherwise, the statements for the* false *case are executed.*

If the booleanExpression evaluates as true, the statement(s) for the true case is executed; otherwise, the statement(s) for the false case is executed. For example, consider the following code:

```
if (radius >= 0)
{
  area = radius*radius*PI;
  System.out.println("The area for the circle of radius " +
    radius + " is " + area);
}
else
{
  System.out.println("Negative input");
}
```

If radius >= 0 is true, area is computed and displayed; if it is false, the message "Negative input" is printed.

As usual, the curly braces can be omitted if there is only one statement inside them. The curly braces enclosing the System.out.println("Negative input") statement can therefore be omitted in the previous example.

Nested if Statements

The statements in an if or if...else statement can be any legal Java statement—including another if or if...else statement. The inner if statement is said to be *nested* inside the outer if statement. The inner if statement can contain another if statement; in fact, there is no limit to the depth of the nesting. For example, the following is a nested if statement:

```
if (i > k)
{
  if (j > k)
    System.out.print("i and j are greater than k");
}
else
  System.out.println("i is less than or equal to k");
```

The `if (j > k)` statement is nested inside the `if (i > k)` statement.

The nested `if` statement can be used to implement multiple alternatives. For example, the following statement assigns a letter grade to the variable grade according to the score, with multiple alternatives:

```
if (score >= 90.0)
  grade = 'A';
else
  if (score >= 80.0)
    grade = 'B';
  else
    if (score >= 70.0)
      grade = 'C';
    else
      if (score >= 60.0)
        grade = 'D';
      else
        grade = 'F';
```

The execution of this `if` statement proceeds as follows. The first condition (score >= 90.0) is tested. If it is true, the grade becomes 'A'. If it is false, the second condition (score >= 80.0) is tested. If the second condition is true, the grade becomes 'B'. If that condition is false, the third condition and the rest of the conditions (if necessary) continue to be tested until a condition is met or all of the conditions have proven to be false. If all of the conditions are false, the grade becomes 'F'. Note that a condition is tested only when all of the conditions that come before it are false.

The preceding `if` statement is equivalent to the following:

```
if (score >= 90.0)
  grade = 'A';
else if (score >= 80.0)
  grade = 'B';
else if (score >= 70.0)
  grade = 'C';
else if (score >= 60.0)
  grade = 'D';
else
  grade = 'F';
```

In fact, this is the preferred writing style for multiple alternative `if` statements. This style avoids deep indentation and makes the program easy to read.

Example 3.1 Using Nested `if` Statements

In Example 2.2, "Computing a Mortgage," you built a program that reads interest rate, year, and loan amount and computes mortgage payments. In this example, assume that the interest rate depends on the year.

Suppose that you have three different interest rates: 7.25 percent for 7 years, 8.5 percent for 15 years, and 9 percent for 30 years. The program prompts the user to enter a loan amount and the number of years of the loan, then finds the interest rate according to the number of years. The program finally displays the monthly payment amount and the total amount paid. Figure 3.3 shows a sample run of the program.

```java
// TestIfElse.java: Test if-else statements
public class TestIfElse
{
  // Main method
  public static void main(String[] args)
  {
    double interestRate = 0;
    int year;
    double loan;

    // Enter number of years
    System.out.println("Enter number of years:" +
      "7, 15 and 30 only :");
    year = MyInput.readInt();

    // Find interest rate based on year
    if (year == 7)
      interestRate = 7.25/1200;
    else if (year == 15)
      interestRate = 8.50/1200;
    else if (year == 30)
      interestRate = 9.0/1200;
    else
    {
      System.out.println("Wrong year");
      System.exit(0);
    }

    // Enter loan amount
    System.out.println("Enter loan amount, for example 120000.95: ");
    loan = MyInput.readDouble();

    // Compute mortgage
    double monthlyPay =
      loan*interestRate/(1-(Math.pow(1/(1+interestRate),year*12)));
    double totalPay = monthlyPay*year*12;

    // Display results
    System.out.println("The monthly pay is " + monthlyPay);
    System.out.println("The total pay is " + totalPay);
  }
}
```

Example Review

The program receives the year and assigns the interest rate: 7.25 percent for 7 years, 8.5 percent for 15 years, and 9 percent for 30 years. If the year value is not 7, 15, or 30, the program displays Wrong Year.

Note that an initial value of 0 is assigned to interestRate. A syntax error would occur if it had no initial value because all of the other statements that assign values to interestRate are within the if statement. The compiler thinks that these statements may not be executed and therefore reports a syntax error.

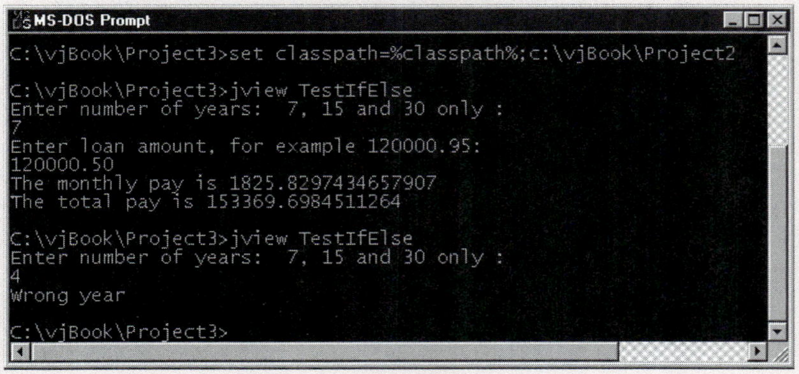

```
C:\vjBook\Project3>set classpath=%classpath%;c:\vjBook\Project2

C:\vjBook\Project3>jview TestIfElse
Enter number of years:  7, 15 and 30 only :
7
Enter loan amount, for example 120000.95:
120000.50
The monthly pay is 1825.8297434657907
The total pay is 153369.6984511264

C:\vjBook\Project3>jview TestIfElse
Enter number of years:  7, 15 and 30 only :
4
Wrong year

C:\vjBook\Project3>
```

Figure 3.3 *The program in Example 3.1 validates the input year, obtains the interest rate according to the year, receives the loan amount, and displays the monthly payment and the total payment.*

Running Example 3.1 in Visual J++ 6

As usual, create Project3 to hold all the programs introduced in Chapter 3. When you are compiling TestIfElse.java, a compilation error indicates that MyInput is not defined. MyInput was created in Project2. To make it accessible in Project3, you need to add c:\vjBook\Project2 in the ClassPath of Project3. To do so, follow the steps below.

1. Choose Project, Project3 Properties from the menu bar or from the context menu of Project3 in the Project Explorer.
2. Select the Classpath tab in the Project3 Properties dialog box, as shown in Figure 3.4.

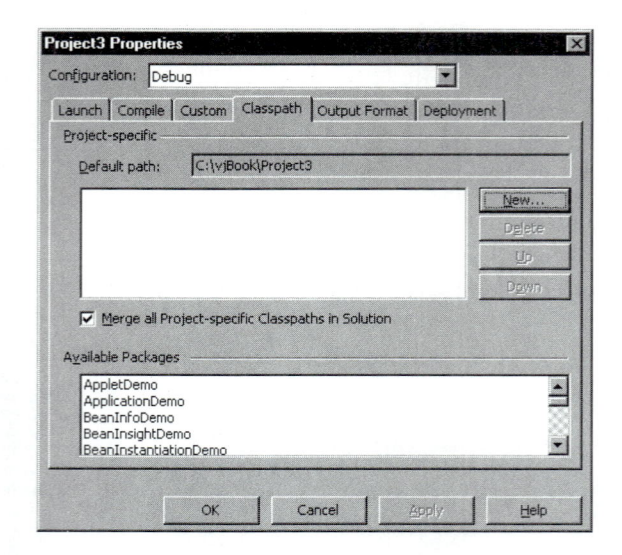

Figure 3.4 *You can set the Classpath of Project3 on the Classpath page of the Project3 Properties dialog box.*

3. Click New to display the Extend Project-specific Classpath dialog box, as shown in Figure 3.5. Enter c:\vjBook\Project2 and click OK to close this dialog box. You will see c:\vjBook\Project2 added to the list of extended classpath on the Classpath page.

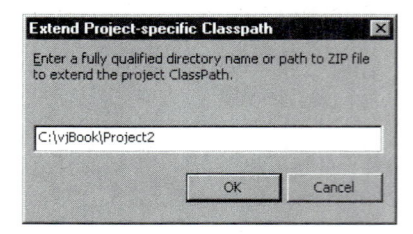

Figure 3.5 *Adding Project2 into the classpath for Project3 makes the class files in Project2 accessible to Project3.*

After Project2 is added to the classpath for Project3, Project3 can use all the class files stored in Project2. Now you can compile and run TestIfElse.java. However, the problem remains when you compile or run the program from the command line. The Project properties are only valid to Project3 within Visual J++ IDE.

To enable TestIfElse to compile and run at the command line, enter the following DOS command to set the classpath:

```
set classpath=%classpath%;c:\vjBook\Project2
```

You can incorporate this command in the autoexec.bat file on Windows 95 or Windows 98 so as to avoid typing it every time you start a new DOS window. On

Windows NT, go to the Start button and choose Control Panel, select the System icon, then modify `classpath variable` in the environment.

> **NOTE**
> If the classpath is set permanently on Windows 95, Windows 98, or Windows NT, the setting is effective in Visual J++. Thus, you do not need to set the same classpath in the IDE if it is already set permanently in autoexec.bat or in Windows NT's System properties dialog box.

Shortcut *if* Statements

You might want to assign a value to a variable that is restricted by certain conditions. For example, the following statement assigns 1 to y if x is greater than 0, and −1 to y if x is less than or equal to 0.

```
if (x > 0)
  y = 1
else
  y = -1;
```

Alternatively, you can use a shortcut `if` statement to achieve the same result:

```
y = (x > 0) ? 1 : -1;
```

The shortcut form of the `if` statement is in a completely different style. There is no explicit `if` in the statement. The syntax is as follows:

```
variable = booleanExpression ? true-result-expression :
   false-result-expression;
```

This is equivalent to the following:

```
if (booleanExpression)
  variable = true-result-expression;
else
  variable = false-result-expression;
```

> **NOTE**
> The shortcut `if` statement is also known as a *conditional expression* because it returns a value based on the condition.

> **TIP**
> The shortcut `if` statement originated in C. It is unfamiliar to many programmers who do not have a C background. Because the statement is not descriptive, you should avoid using it.

Using *switch* Statements

The `if` statement in Example 3.1 makes decisions based on a single `true` or `false` condition. There are three cases for assigning interest rates, which depend on the year value. To fully account for all the cases, nested `if` statements were used.

Clearly, overuse of the nested `if` statement makes the program difficult to read. Java provides a `switch` statement to handle multiple conditions efficiently. You could write the following `switch` statement to replace the nested `if` statement in Example 3.1:

```
switch (year)
{
  case 7:  interestRate = 7.25;
           break;
  case 15: interestRate = 8.50;
           break;
  case 30: interestRate = 9.0;
           break;
  default: System.out.println("Wrong number of Years");
}
```

The flow chart of the preceding `switch` statement is shown in Figure 3.6.

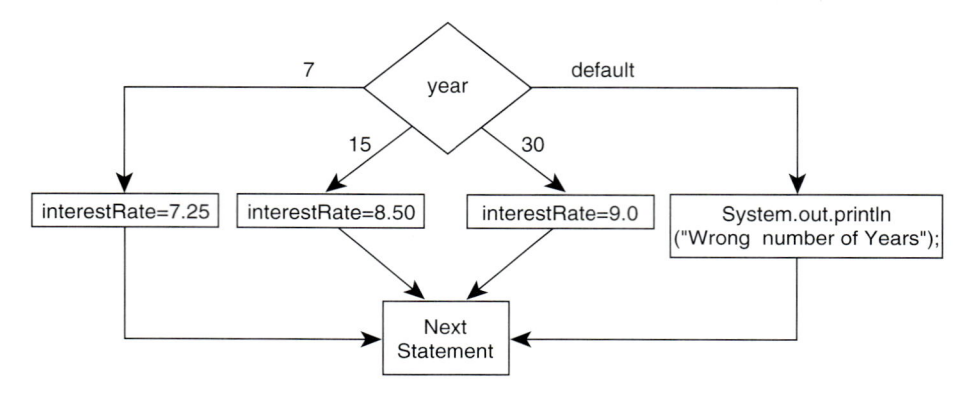

Figure 3.6 *The* `switch` *statement obtains the interest rate according to the year.*

This statement checks to see whether the year matches the value 7, 15, or 30, in that order. If matched, the corresponding statement is executed; if not matched, a message is displayed. The full syntax for the `switch` statement is as follows:

```
switch (switch-expression)
{
  case value1: statement(s)1;
               break;
  case value2: statement(s)2;
               break;
  ...
  case valueN: statement(s)N;
               break;
  default:     statement(s)-for-default;
}
```

The `switch` statement observes the following rules:

- The `switch-expression` must yield a value of `char`, `byte`, `short`, or `int` type and must always be enclosed in parentheses.

- The `value1...valueN` must have the same data type as the value of the `switch-expression`. The resulting statements in the `case` statement are executed when the value in the `case` statement matches the value of the `switch-expression`. (Each `case` statement is executed in sequential order.)

- The keyword `break` is optional. The `break` statement terminates the entire `switch` statement. If the `break` statement is not present, the next `case` statement will be executed.

- The default case, which is optional, can be used to perform actions when none of the specified cases is `true`. The default case always appears last in the `switch` block.

> **CAUTION**
> Do not forget to use the `break` statement when one is needed. For example, the following code always displays `Wrong number of Years` regardless of what year is. Suppose the year is 15. The statement `interestRate = 8.50` is executed, then the statement `interestRate = 9.0`, and finally the statement `System.out.println("Wrong number of Years")`.
>
> ```
> switch (year)
> {
>   case 7:  interestRate = 7.25;
>   case 15: interestRate = 8.50;
>   case 30: interestRate = 9.0;
>   default: System.out.println("Wrong number of Years");
> }
> ```

Using Loop Structures

Loops are structures that control repeated executions of a block of statements. The part of the loop that contains the statements to be repeated is called the *loop body*. A one-time execution of the loop body is referred to as an *iteration of the loop*. Each loop contains a loop `continue-condition`, a Boolean expression, which controls the execution of the body. After each iteration, the `continue-condition` is reevaluated. If the condition is `true`, the body is repeated. If the condition is `false`, the loop terminates.

The concept of looping is fundamental to programming. Java provides three types of loop structures: the `for` loop, the `while` loop, and the `do` loop.

The *for* Loop

The `for` loop is a common type of program loop. It is a construct that causes the loop body to be repeated for a fixed number of times. The syntax of the `for` loop is as follows:

```
for (control-variable-initializer; continue-condition;
    adjustment-statement)
{
  // Loop-body;
}
```

The flow chart of the loop is shown in Figure 3.7.

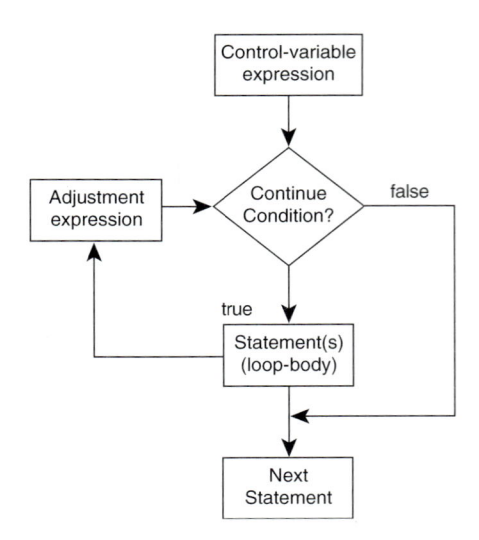

Figure 3.7 *The* `for` *loop initializes the control variable, executes the statements in the loop body, and then repeatedly evaluates the adjustment expression when the* `continue-condition` *evaluates as* `true`.

The loop construct starts with the keyword `for`, followed by the three control elements, which are enclosed by the parentheses, and the loop body, which is inside the curly braces. The control elements, which are separated by semicolons, control how many times the loop body is executed and when the loop terminates. For example, the following `for` loop prints `Welcome to Java!` 100 times:

```
int i;
for (i = 0; i<100; i++)
{
  System.out.println("Welcome to Java!");
}
```

The flow chart of the statement is shown in Figure 3.8.

The first element, `i = 0`, initializes the control variable, `i`. The control variable tracks how many times the loop body has been executed. The adjustment statement changes the value of the variable.

The next element, `i < 100`, which is the `continue-condition`, is a Boolean expression. The expression is evaluated at the beginning of each iteration. If the `continue-condition` is `true`, execute the loop body. If it is `false`, the loop terminates and the program control turns to the line following the loop.

The adjustment statement, `i++`, is a statement that adjusts the control variable. This statement is executed after each iteration. Usually, an adjustment statement either increments or decrements the control variable. Eventually, the value of the control variable forces the `continue-condition` to become `false`.

The loop control variable can be declared and initialized in the `for` loop. An equivalent statement for the previous example is as follows:

```
for (int i = 0; i<100; i++)
{
  System.out.println("Welcome to Java!");
}
```

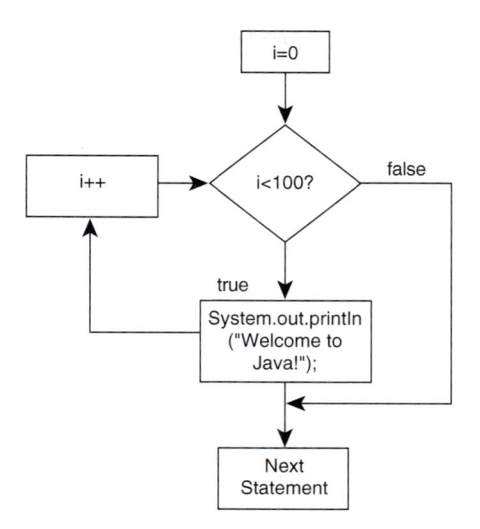

Figure 3.8 *The* `for` *loop initializes* `i` *to* `0`, *executes the* `println` *statement, and then repeatedly evaluates* `i++` *when* `i` *is less than* `100`.

If there is only one statement in the loop body, as in this example, the curly braces can be omitted.

> **NOTE**
> The three elements in a `for` loop—control-variable initializer, continue-condition, and adjustment statement—can be any statement or expression, or can be omitted. Thus the following statement, which is an infinite loop, is correct.
>
> ```
> for ( ; ; )
> {
> }
> ```

Example 3.2 Using `for` Loops

This example computes the summation of a series that starts with 0.01 and ends with 1.0. The numbers in the series will increment by 0.01, as follows: 0.01+0.02+0.03 and so on. The output of this program appears in Figure 3.9.

```java
// TestSum.java: Compute sum = 0.01 + 0.02 + … + 1;
public class TestSum
{
  // Main method
  public static void main(String[] args)
  {
    // Initialize sum
    float sum = 0;

    // Keep adding 0.01 to sum
    for (float i=0.01f; i <= 1.0f ; i = i+0.01f)
      sum += i;
```

continues

```
        // Display result
        System.out.println("The summation is " + sum);
    }
}
```

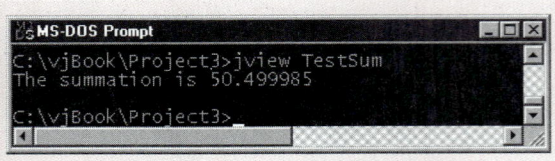

```
MS-DOS Prompt
C:\vjBook\Project3>jview TestSum
The summation is 50.499985

C:\vjBook\Project3>
```

Figure 3.9 *Example 3.2 uses a* `for` *loop to sum a series from 0.01 to 1 in increments of 0.01.*

Example Review

The `for` loop repeatedly adds the control variable `i` to the sum. This variable, which begins with 0.01, is incremented by 0.01 after each iteration. The loop terminates when `i` exceeds 1.0.

From this example, you can see that a control variable can be a `float` type. In fact, it can be any numeric data type.

You may have already noticed that the answer is not precise. This is because computers use a fixed number of bits to represent floating-point numbers, and thus cannot represent some floating-point numbers exactly. If you change `float` in the program to `double`, you will see a slight improvement in precision because a double variable takes 64 bits, whereas a float variable takes 32 bits.

CAUTION
Always use semicolons rather than commas to separate the control elements in the `for` loop header. Using commas in the `for` loop header is a common mistake.

TIP
Do not change the value of the control variable inside the `for` loop, even though it is perfectly legal to do so. Changing the value makes the program difficult to understand and could lead to subtle errors.

Example 3.3 Using Nested `for` Loops

The following program uses nested `for` loops to print a multiplication table. Nested loops are composed of an outer loop and one or more inner loops. Each time the outer loop is repeated, the inner loops are reentered, their loop control parameters are reevaluated, and all required iterations are performed. The output of the program is shown in Figure 3.10.

```java
// TestMulTable.java: Display a multiplication table
public class TestMulTable
{
  // Main method
  public static void main(String[] args)
  {
    // Display the table heading
    System.out.println("         Multiplication Table");
    System.out.println("-----------------------------------");

    // Display the number title
    System.out.print("  |  ");
    for (int j=1; j<=9; j++)
      System.out.print("   " + j);
    System.out.println(" ");

    // Print table body
    for (int i=1; i<=9; i++)
    {
      System.out.print(i+" |  ");
      for (int j=1; j<=9; j++)
      {
        // Display the product and align properly
        if (i*j < 10)
          System.out.print("   " + i*j);
        else
          System.out.print(" " + i*j);
      }
      System.out.println(" ");
    }
  }
}
```

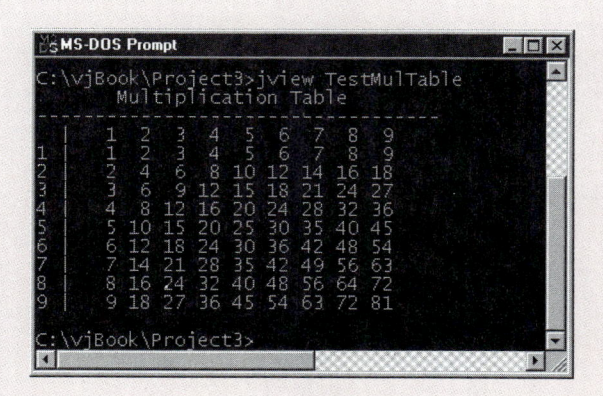

Figure 3.10 *Example 3.3 uses nested* for *loops to print a multiplication table.*

Example Review

The program displays a title on the first line, dashes (-) on the second line. The first for loop displays the numbers 1 through 9 on the third line.

The next loop is a nested for loop with the control variable i on the outer loop and j on the inner loop. For each i, the product i*j is displayed on a line in the inner loop, with j being 1, 2, 3, . . . , 9. The if statement in the inner loop is

continues

used so that the product is aligned properly. If the product is a single digit, it is displayed with a space before it.

> **CAUTION**
> The control variable must always be declared inside the control structure of the loop or before the loop. If the variable is declared inside the loop control structure, it cannot be referenced outside of the loop.

The *while* Loop

If you know the number of times you need to repeat an operation, you can use a `for` loop to control the repetitions. If the number of repeats is unknown, the `for` loop cannot help you. Suppose that you need to find the sum of all the numbers entered from the keyboard. If you know that the total number is 100, it is easy to use a `for` loop, as demonstrated in the following example:

```
int sum = 0;
for (int i = 1; i <= 100; i++)
   sum += readInt();
```

Now assume that the total number is not specified. You do know, however, that you will have all of the numbers when the input is 0—that is, the input 0 signifies the end of the input. You will need to use a `while` loop for this problem because it can handle an unspecified number of repetitions. The syntax for the `while` loop is as follows:

```
while (continue-condition)
{
   // Loop-body;
}
```

The `while` loop flow chart is shown in Figure 3.11.

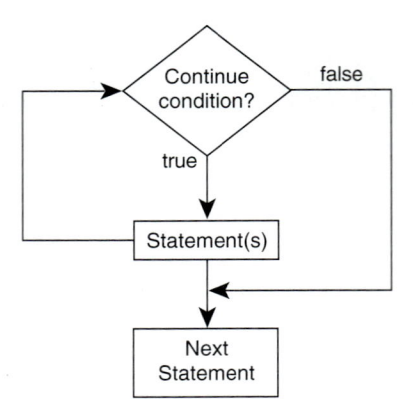

Figure 3.11 *The* `while` *loop repeatedly executes the statements in the loop body when* `continue-condition` *evaluates as* true.

The `continue-condition`, a Boolean expression, must appear inside the parentheses. It is always evaluated before the loop body is executed. If its evaluation is `true`, the loop body is executed; if its evaluation is `false`, the entire loop terminates and the program control turns to the statement that follows the `while` loop.

Example 3.4 Using a `while` Loop

This example reads and calculates an unspecified number of integers. The input 0 signifies the end of the input.

The program's sample run is shown in Figure 3.12.

```java
// TestWhile.java: Test the while loop
public class TestWhile
{
  // Main method
  public static void main(String[] args)
  {
    int data;
    int sum = 0;

    // Read an initial data
    System.out.println("Enter an int value");
    data = MyInput.readInt();

    // Keep reading data until the input is 0
    while (data != 0)
    {
      sum += data;

      System.out.println(
        "Enter an int value, the program exits if the input is 0");
      data = MyInput.readInt();
    }

    System.out.println("The sum is "+sum);
  }
}
```

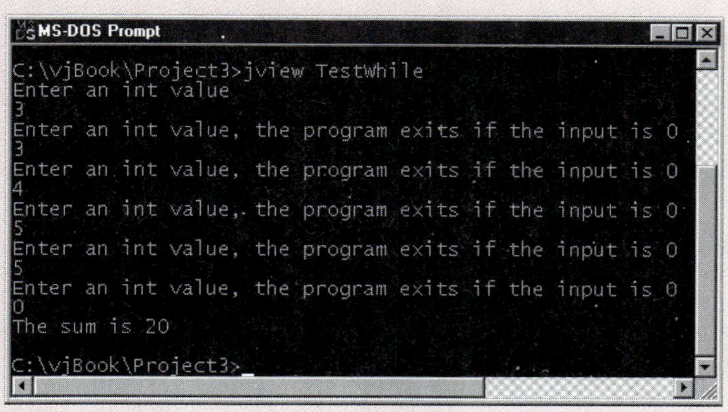

```
C:\vjBook\Project3>jview TestWhile
Enter an int value
3
Enter an int value, the program exits if the input is 0
3
Enter an int value, the program exits if the input is 0
4
Enter an int value, the program exits if the input is 0
5
Enter an int value, the program exits if the input is 0
5
Enter an int value, the program exits if the input is 0
0
The sum is 20
C:\vjBook\Project3>
```

Figure 3.12 *Example 3.4 uses a* `while` *loop to add an unspecified number of integers.*

continues

Example Review

If `data` is not 0, it is added to the sum and the next input data is read. If `data` is 0, the loop body is not executed and the `while` loop terminates.

CAUTION
Make sure that the `continue-condition` eventually becomes `false` so that the program will terminate.

TIP
Don't use floating-point values for equality checking in a loop control. Since floating-point values are approximations, using them could result in imprecise counter values and inaccurate results.

Note that if the first input read is 0, the loop body never executes, and the resulting sum is 0.

The *do* Loop

The `do` loop is a variation of the `while` loop. Its syntax is given below:

```
do
{
    // Loop body;
} while (continue-condition)
```

Its execution flow chart is shown in Figure 3.13.

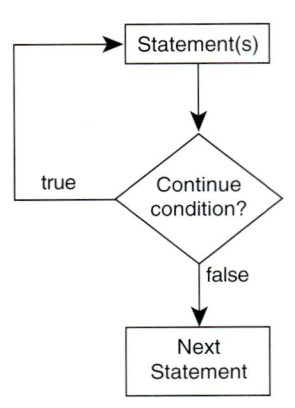

Figure 3.13 *The* do *loop body executes once when* `continue-condition` *evaluates as* `false`; *it executes repeatedly when* `continue-condition` *evaluates as* `true`.

The loop body is executed first. Then the `continue-condition` is evaluated. If the evaluation is `true`, the loop body is executed again; if it is `false`, the do loop terminates. The major difference between a `while` loop and a `do` loop is the order in which the `continue-condition` is evaluated and the loop body is executed. The `while` loop and the `do` loop have equal expressive power. Sometimes it is more convenient to choose one over the other. For example, you can rewrite Example 3.4 as follows:

```java
// TestDo.java: Test the do loop
public class TestDo
{
  // Main method
  public static void main(String[] args)
  {
    int data;
    int sum = 0;

    do
    {
      data = MyInput.readInt();
      sum += data;
    } while (data != 0);

    System.out.println("The sum is " + sum);
  }
}
```

> **TIP**
> The loop body is always executed at least once. I recommend the `do` loop if you have statements inside the loop that must be executed at least once, as in the case of the `do` loop in the preceding TestDo program. These statements must appear before the loop as well as inside the loop if you are using a `while` loop.

Using the Keywords *break* and *continue*

Two statements, `break` and `continue`, can be used in loop constructs to provide the loop with additional control:

- **break**—This keyword immediately ends the innermost loop that contains it.
- **continue**—This keyword only ends the current iteration. Program control goes to the next iteration of the loop.

You have already used the keyword `break` in a `switch` statement. You can also use `break` and `continue` in any of the three kinds of loop constructs.

The diagrams in Figure 3.14 and Figure 3.15 illustrate the functions of `break` and `continue` in a loop statement.

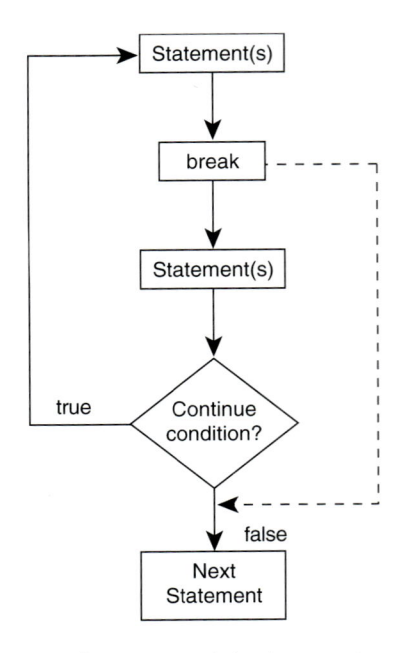

Figure 3.14 *The* break *statement forces its containing loop to exit.*

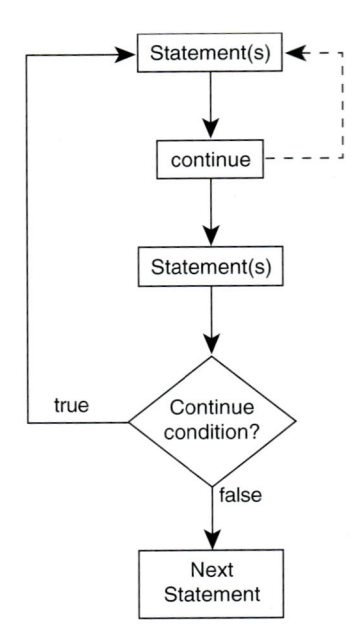

Figure 3.15 *The* continue *statement forces the current iteration of the loop to end.*

Example 3.5 Testing a *break* Statement

In this example, you will see how a `break` statement affects the results of the following program.

```
// TestBreak.java: Test the break keyword in the loop
public class TestBreak
{
  // Main method
  public static void main(String[] args)
  {
    int sum = 0;
    int item = 0;

    do
    {
      item ++;
      sum += item;
      if (sum >= 6) break;
    } while (item < 5);

    System.out.println("The sum is " + sum);
  }
}
```

Example Review

Without the `if` statement, this program calculates the sum of the numbers from 1 to 5. But with the `if` statement, the loop terminates when the sum becomes greater than or equal to 6. The output of the program is shown in Figure 3.16.

Figure 3.16 *The* break *statement in the TestBreak program forces the* do *loop to exit when* sum *is greater than 6.*

If you changed the `if` statement to the following, the output would resemble that in Figure 3.17:

```
if (sum == 5) break;
```

In this case, the `if` condition will never be `true`. Therefore, the `break` statement will never be executed.

Figure 3.17 *The* break *statement is not executed in the modified* TestBreak *program because* sum == 5 *cannot be* true.

Example 3.6 Using a *continue* Statement

In this example, you will see the effect of a continue statement on a program.

```java
// TestContinue.java: Test the continue keyword
public class TestContinue
{
  // Main method
  public static void main(String[] args)
  {
    int sum = 0;
    int item = 0;

    do
    {
      item++;
      if (item == 2) continue;
      sum += item;
    } while (item < 5);

    System.out.println("The sum is " + sum);
  }
}
```

Example Review

With the `if` statement in the program, the continue statement is executed when `item` becomes 2. The continue statement ends the current iteration so that the rest of the statement in the loop body is not executed; therefore, `item` is not added to `sum` when it is 2. The output of the program is shown in Figure 3.18.

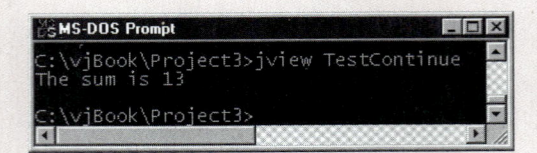

```
C:\vjBook\Project3>jview TestContinue
The sum is 13

C:\vjBook\Project3>
```

Figure 3.18 *The* continue *statement in the* `TestContinue` *program forces the current iteration to end when* `item` *equals 2.*

Without the `if` statement in the program, the output would look like Figure 3.19.

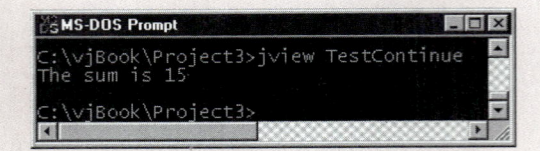

```
C:\vjBook\Project3>jview TestContinue
The sum is 15

C:\vjBook\Project3>
```

Figure 3.19 *Since the modified* `TestContinue` *program has no* continue *statement, every item is added to* `sum`.

Without the `if` statement, all of the items are added to `sum`, including when `item` is 2. Therefore, the result is 15, which is two more than it was with the `if` statement.

> **TIP**
> You can always write a program without using `break` or `continue` in a loop. See Chapter Review Question 3.20.

Case Studies

Control structures are fundamental in programming. The ability to write control statements is essential in learning Java programming. This section presents two additional examples of using decision statements and loops to solve problems.

Example 3.7 Finding the Sales Amount

You have just started a sales job in a department store. Your pay consists of a base salary and a commission. The base salary is $5,000. The following scheme is used to determine the commission rate:

Sales Amount	Commission Rate
$1–$5,000	8 percent
$5,001–$10,000	10 percent
$10,001 and above	12 percent

Your goal is to earn $30,000 in a year. Write a program that will find out the minimum amount of sales you have to generate in order to make $30,000.

Since your base salary is $5,000, you have to make $25,000 on commission to earn $30,000 in a year. What is the sales amount for a $25,000 commission? If you know the sales amount, the commission can be computed as follows:

```
if (salesAmount >= 10001)
   commission = 5000*0.08 + 5000*0.1 + (salesAmount-10000)*0.12;
else if (salesAmount >= 5001)
   commission = 5000*0.08 + (salesAmount-5000)*0.10;
else
   commission = salesAmount*0.08;
```

This suggests that you can try to find the `salesAmount` to match a given `commission` through incremental approximation. For `salesAmount` of $1, find `commission`. If commission is less than $25,000, increment `salesAmount` by 1 and find

continues

commission again. If commission is less than $25,000, repeat the process until the commission is greater than $25,000. This is a tedious job for humans, but it is exactly what a computer is good for. You can write a loop and let a computer execute it painlessly.

The complete program is given below, and a sample run of the program is shown in Figure 3.20.

```java
// FindSalesAmount.java: Find the sales amount to get the desired
// commission
public class FindSalesAmount
{
  // The commission sought
  final static double COMMISSION_SOUGHT = 25000;

  // Main method
  public static void main(String[] args)
  {
    double commission = 0;
    double salesAmount = 1;

    while (commission < COMMISSION_SOUGHT)
    {
      // Compute commission
      if (salesAmount >= 10001)
        commission = 5000*0.08 + 5000*0.1 + (salesAmount-10000)*0.12;
      else if (salesAmount >= 5001)
        commission = 5000*0.08 + (salesAmount-5000)*0.10;
      else
        commission = salesAmount*0.08;

      salesAmount++;
    }

    // Display the sales amount
    System.out.println("The sales amount " + salesAmount +
      " is needed to make a commission of $" + COMMISSION_SOUGHT);
  }
}
```

```
C:\vjBook\Project3>jview FindSalesAmount
The sales amount 210835.0 is needed to make a commission of $25000.0

C:\vjBook\Project3>
```

Figure 3.20 *The program finds the sales amount for the given commission.*

Example Review

The `while` loop is used to repeatedly compute `commission` for an incremental `salesAmount`. The loop terminates when `commission` is greater than or equal to a constant `COMMISSION_SOUGHT`.

In Exercise 3.10, you will rewrite this program to let the user enter `COMMISSION_SOUGHT` dynamically from the keyboard.

You can improve the performance of this program by using the *binary search* approach. The binary search approach is introduced in Chapter 6, "Arrays and Strings." A rewrite of this program using a binary search is proposed in Exercise 6.9.

Example 3.8 Displaying a Triangle

In this example, you will use nested loops to print the following output:

```
    1
   212
  32123
 4321234
543212345
```

Your program prints five lines. Each line consists of three parts. The first part comprises the spaces before the numbers; the second part, the leading numbers, such as 3 2 1 on line 3; and the last part, the ending numbers, such as 2 3 on line 3.

You can use an outer loop to control the lines. At the nth row, there are 5 - n leading spaces, the leading numbers are n, n-1, . . . , 1, and the ending numbers are 2, . . . , n. You can use three separate inner loops to print each part.

The complete program is given below, and a sample run of the program is shown in Figure 3.21.

```java
// PrintTriangle.java: Print a triangle pattern
public class PrintTriangle
{
  // Main method
  public static void main(String[] args)
  {
    for (int row = 1; row < 6; row++)
    {
      // Print leading spaces
      for (int column = 1; column < 6 - row; column++)
        System.out.print(" ");

      // Print leading numbers
      for (int num = row; num >= 1; num--)
        System.out.print(num);

      // Print ending numbers
      for (int num = 2; num <= row; num++)
        System.out.print(num);

      // Start a new line
      System.out.println("");
    }
  }
}
```

continues

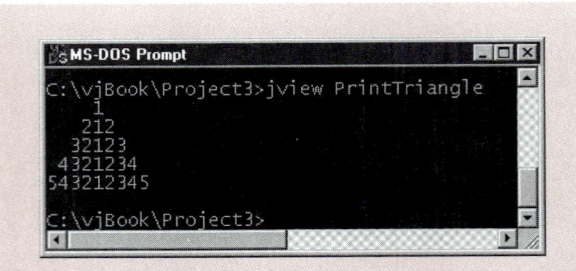

Figure 3.21 *The program uses nested loops to print numbers in a triangular pattern.*

Example Review

Printing patterns like this one and the ones in Exercises 3.4 and 3.5 is my favorite exercise for practicing loop control statements. The key is to understand the pattern and to describe it using loop control variables.

Chapter Summary

Program control specifies the order in which statements are executed in a program. In this chapter, you learned about two types of control structures: decision control and loop control.

Decision statements are for building decision steps into programs. You learned several forms of decision structures: `if` statements, `if...else` statements, nested `if` statements, `switch` statements, and shortcut `if` statements.

The various `if` statements all make control decisions based on a Boolean expression. Based on the `true` or `false` evaluation of that expression, these statements take one or two possible courses. The `switch` statement makes control decisions based on a switch variable of type `char`, `byte`, `short`, or `int`. The shortcut `if` statement is not often used.

You learned three types of repetition statements: the `for` loop, the `while` loop, and the `do` loop. In designing loops, you need to consider both the loop control structure and the loop body.

The `for` loop is generally used to execute a loop body for a predictable number of times; this number is not determined by the loop body. The loop control has three parts. The first is a control variable, which has an initial value. The second is the `continue-condition`, which determines whether the loop body is to be executed. The third part is the adjustment statement, which changes the control variable. Usually, the loop control variables are initialized and changed in the control structure.

Since the `while` loop control structure contains the `continue-condition`, which is dependent on the loop body, the number of repetitions is determined by the loop body. The `while` loop is often used for an unspecified number of repetitions.

The while loop checks the continue-condition first. If the condition is true, the loop body is executed; if it is false, the loop terminates. The do loop is similar to the while loop, except that the do loop executes the loop body first and then checks the continue-condition to decide whether to continue or to terminate.

You also learned the break and continue keywords. The break keyword immediately ends the innermost loop, which contains the break. The continue keyword only ends the current iteration.

You learned how to set classpath environment variables for accessing classes in Visual J++ IDE.

Chapter Review

3.1. Show the output of the following code, if any:

```
x = 2;
y = 3;
if (x > 2)
  if (y > 2)
  {
    int z = x + y;
    System.out.println("z is " + z);
  }
else
  System.out.println("x is " + x);
```

3.2. Show the output of the following code, if any:

```
x = 3;
y = 2;
if (x > 2)
{
  if (y > 2)
  {
    int z = x + y;
    System.out.println("z is " + z);
  }
}
else
  System.out.println("x is " + x);
```

3.3. Can you convert a switch statement to an equivalent if statement, or vice versa?

3.4. What are the advantages of using a switch statement?

3.5. What data types are required for a switch variable? If the keyword break is not used after a case is processed, what is the next statement to be executed?

3.6. What is y after the following switch statement is executed?

```
x = 3;
switch (x+3)
{
  case 6:  y = 1;
  default: y += 1;
}
```

3.7. Use a `switch` statement to rewrite the following `if` statement:

```
if (a == 1)
  x += 5;
else if (a == 2)
  x += 10;
else if (a == 3)
  x += 16;
else if (a == 4)
  x += 34;
```

3.8. What is y after the following statement is executed?

```
x = 0;
y = (x > 0) ? 1 : -1;
```

3.9. Do the following two statements result in the same value in sum?

```
for (int i=0; i<10; ++i)
{   sum += i;   }

for (int i=0; i<10; i++)
{   sum += i;   }
```

3.10. What are the three parts of a `for` loop control? Write a `for` loop that will print the numbers from 1 to 100.

3.11. What does the following statement do?

```
for (;;)
{
  do something;
}
```

3.12. If a variable is declared in the `for` loop control, can it be used after the loop exits?

3.13. Can you convert a `for` loop to a `while` loop? List the advantages of using `for` loops.

3.14. Convert the following `for` loop statement to a `while` loop and to a `do` loop:

```
long sum = 0;
for (int i=0; i<= 1000; i++)
  sum = sum + i;
```

3.15. How many times is the following loop body repeated? What is the printout of the loop?

```
int i = 1;
while (i < 10)
  if ((i++)%2==0)
    System.out.println(i);
```

3.16. What are the differences between a `while` loop and a `do` loop?

3.17. What is the keyword `break` for? Will the following program terminate? If so, give the output.

```
int balance = 1000;
while (true)
{
  if (balance < 9)
    break;
  balance = balance - 9;
}

System.out.println("balance is " + balance);
```

3.18. What is the keyword `continue` for? Will the following program terminate? If so, give the output.

```
int balance = 1000;
while (true)
{
  if (balance < 9)
    continue;
  balance = balance - 9;
}

System.out.println("balance is " + balance);
```

3.19. Can you always convert a `while` loop into a `for` loop? Convert the following `while` loop into a `for` loop.

```
int i = 1;
int sum = 0;
while (sum < 10000)
{
  sum = sum + i;
  i++;
}
```

3.20. Rewrite the programs `TestBreak` and `TestContinue` without using `break` and `continue` (see Examples 3.5 and 3.6).

3.21. What is the role of classpath, and how do you set it in Visual J++ 6.0?

Programming Exercises

3.1. Write a program that will read an integer and find out whether it is even or odd.

3.2. Write a program that will sort three integers. The integers are entered from the keyboard and stored in variables `num1`, `num2`, and `num3`, respectively. The program sorts the numbers so that `num1 <= num2 <= num3`.

3.3. Write a program that will compute sales commissions using the same scheme in Example 3.7. Your program reads the sales amount from the keyboard and displays the result on the console.

3.4. Write a nested `for` loop that will print the following output:

```
1
1 2
1 2 3
1 2 3 4
1 2 3 4 5
```

3.5. Write a nested `for` loop that will print the following output:

```
                        1
                      1 2 1
                    1 2 4 2 1
                  1 2 4 8 4 2 1
                1 2 4 8 16 8 4 2 1
              1 2 4 8 16 32 16 8 4 2 1
            1 2 4 8 16 32 64 32 16 8 4 2 1
          1 2 4 8 16 32 64 128 64 32 16 8 4 2 1
```

Hint: Here is the pseudocode solution:

```
for the row from 0 to 7
{
  Pad leading blanks in a row using a loop like this:
  for the column from 1 to 7-row
    System.out.print("   ");

  Print left half of the row for numbers 1, 2, 4, up to
  2^row using a look like this:
  for the column from 0 to row
    System.out.print((int)Math.pow(2, column)+"   ");

  Print the right half of the row for numbers
  2^row-1, 2^row-2, ..., 1 using a loop like this:
  for (int column=row-1; column>=0; col—)
    System.out.print((int)Math.pow(2, column)+"   ");

  Start a new line
  System.out.print('\n');
}
```

The `Math.pow()` method was introduced in Example 2.2. Can you write this program without using this method?

3.6. Write a program that will check whether an input integer is a prime number. (An integer is a prime number if its only divisor is 1 or itself.)

3.7. Write a program that will read an unspecified number of integers and determine how many positive and negative values have been read. Your program ends when the input is 0.

3.8. Write a program that will read integers and find the total and average of the input values. Your program ends with the input 0.

3.9. Use a `while` loop to find the smallest n such that n^2 is greater than 10,000.

3.10. Rewrite Example 3.7 as follows:

- Use a `for` loop instead of a `while` loop;
- Let the user enter COMMISSION_SOUGHT from the keyboard instead of fixing it as a constant.

3.11. You can approximate π by using the following series:

$$\pi = 4*(1-1/3+1/5-1/7+1/9-1/11+1/13+\ldots)$$

Write a program that will find out how many terms of this series you need to use before you get 3.14159.

3.12. The *cancellation error* occurs when you are manipulating a very large number with a very small number. The large number may cancel out the smaller number. For example, the result of 10000.0 + 0.000001 is equal to 10000.0 on some computers. To avoid cancellation errors and obtain more accurate results, select the order of computations carefully. For example, in computing the following series, you should compute from right to left to obtain more accurate results:

```
1 + 1/2 + 1/3 + ... + 1/n
```

Write a program to compare the results of the summation of the preceding series, computing from left to right and from right to left with n = 50000.

CHAPTER 4

METHODS

Objectives

- Understand and use methods.
- Create and invoke methods.
- Understand the role of arguments in a method.
- Use pass by value for primitive type parameters.
- Understand method overloading.
- Understand method abstraction and its use in developing software.
- Become familiar with recursion.

Introduction

In Chapter 2, "Java Building Elements," and Chapter 3, "Control Structures," you learned about methods, such as `println()`, which is used to print messages, and `readDouble()` and `readInt()`, which are used to read `double` and `int` numbers, respectively. A method is a collection of statements that are grouped together to perform an operation. When you call the method `println()`, for example, the system actually executes several statements in order to display a message on the console.

This chapter introduces several topics that involve, or are related to, methods. You will learn how to create your own methods with or without return values, invoke a method with or without parameters, overload methods using the same names, write a recursive method that invokes itself, and apply method abstraction in the program design.

Creating a Method

In general, a method has the following structure:

```
modifier returnValueType methodName(list of parameters)
{
  // Method body;
}
```

The method `readDouble()` was created in Chapter 2 to read a double value from the keyboard. Figure 4.1 illustrates the components of this method.

The method heading specifies the *modifiers, returning value type, method name,* and the *parameters* of the method. The modifier, which can be optional, specifies the

```
                       returnvaluetype
        modifier           |         methodName    parameter list
           |               |             |              |
           ↓   ↓           ↓             ↓              ↓
     public static     double     readDouble()
     {   double d = 0.0;

         try
         { String str = df.readLine();
           st = new StringTokenizer(str);
           d = new Double(st.nextToken()).doubleValue();
         } catch (IOException ex)
         { System.out.printIn(ex);}

         return d;
     }
            ↑
         return value
```

Figure 4.1 *The method* `readDouble()` *has a signature that consists of modifiers, return type, and the method name, which is followed by the method body block.*

property of the method and tells the compiler how the method can be called. Modifiers are discussed in more depth in Chapter 5, "Programming with Objects and Classes."

A method may return a value. The `returnValueType` is the data type of the value the method returns. If the method does not return a value, the `returnValueType` is the keyword `void`. For example, the `returnValueType` in the `main()` method is `void`. All methods except constructors require `returnValueType`. For a detailed discussion of constructors, see Chapter 5.

A method can have a list of parameters—*formal parameters*—in the method specification. When a method is called, its formal parameters are replaced by variables or data, which are referred to as *actual parameters*. Parameters are optional. The `readDouble()` method, for example, has no parameters.

The method body contains a collection of statements that define what the method does. Let's take a look at a method created to find which of two integers is the largest. This method, named `max()`, has two `int` parameters, `num1` and `num2`, the larger of which is returned by the method.

```
int max(int num1, int num2)
{
  if (num1 > num2)
    return num1;
  else
    return num2;
}
```

This method body simply uses an `if` statement to determine which number is larger and return the value of that number. The keyword `return` is required for nonvoid methods other than those with a `void` return value type. The return statement can also be used in a void method for terminating the method and returning to the method's caller. The method terminates when a `return` statement is executed.

> **NOTE**
> In certain other languages, methods are referred to as *procedures* and *functions*. A method with a return value type is called a *function*; a method with a `void` return value type is called a *procedure*.

> **CAUTION**
> You need to declare a data type for each parameter separately. For instance, `int i, j` should be replaced by `int i, int j`.

Calling a Method

How do you know whether a method works? You need to test it by calling it in a test program. There are two ways to call a method; the choice is based on whether the method returns a value or not.

If the method returns a value, a call to the method is usually treated as a value. For example,

```
int larger = max(3, 4);
```

calls `max(3, 4)` and assigns the result of the method to the variable `larger`. Another example of a call that is treated as a value is

```
System.out.println(max(3,4));
```

which prints the return value of the method call `max(3,4)`.

If the method returns `void`, a call to the method must be a statement. For example, the method `println()` returns `void`. The following call is a statement:

```
System.out.println("Welcome to Java!");
```

> **NOTE**
> A method with return value can also be invoked as a statement in Java. In this case, the caller simply ignores the return value. In the majority of cases, a call to a method with return value is treated as a value. In some cases, however, the caller is not interested in the return value. For example, many methods in database applications return a Boolean value to indicate whether the operation is successful. You can choose to ignore the return value if you know the operation will always succeed. I recommend, though, that you always treat a call to a method with return value as a value in order to avoid programming errors.

When a program calls a method, program control is transferred to the called method. A called method returns control to the caller when its return statement is executed or when its method-ending right brace is reached.

The example shown below gives the complete program that is used to test the `max()` method.

Example 4.1 Testing the *max()* Method

This example demonstrates how to create a test program for the `max()` method. The output of the program is shown in Figure 4.2.

```java
// TestMax.java: Demonstrate using methods
public class TestMax
{
  // Main method
  public static void main(String[] args)
  {
    int num1 = 5;
    int num2 = 2;
    int num3 = max(num1, num2);
    System.out.println("The maximum between " + num1 +
      " and " + num2 + " is " + num3);
  }
```

```
// A method for finding a max between two numbers
static int max(int num1, int num2)
{
  if (num1 > num2)
    return num1;
  else
    return num2;
}
```

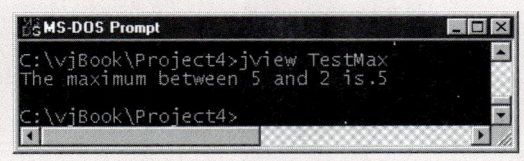

```
C:\vjBook\Project4>jview TestMax
The maximum between 5 and 2 is 5

C:\vjBook\Project4>
```

Figure 4.2 *The program invokes* `max(5, 2)` *in order to discover whether 5 or 2 is the maximum value.*

Example Review

This program contains the `main()` method and the `max()` method. The `main()` method is just like any other method, with one exception: It is invoked by the Java interpreter.

The `main()` method's heading is always the same, like the one in this example, with modifiers `public` and `static`, return type value `void`, method name `main()`, and parameters `String[] args`. `String[]` indicates that `args` is an array of `String`, which is addressed in Chapter 6, "Arrays and Strings."

The statements in `main()` may invoke other methods that are defined in the class that contains the `main()` method or in other classes. In this example, the `main()` method invokes `max(num1, num2)`, which is defined in the same class with `main()`.

Passing Parameters

The power of a method is its ability to work with parameters. You can use `println` to print any message and `max()` to find the maximum between any two numbers. When calling a method, you need to provide actual parameters, which must be given in the same order as their respective formal parameters in the method specification. This is known as *parameter order association*. For example, the following method prints a message n times:

```
void nPrintln(String message, int n)
{
  for (int i=0; i<n;  i++)
    System.out.println(message);
}
```

You can use nPrintln("Hello", 3) to print "Hello" three times. The nPrintln("Hello", 3) statement passes the actual string parameter, "Hello", to the formal parameter, message; passes 3 to n; and prints "Hello" three times. However, the statement nPrintln(3,"Hello") would be wrong. The data type of 3 does not match the data type for the first formal parameter, message, nor does the second parameter, "Hello", match the second formal parameter, n.

> **CAUTION**
> The actual parameters must match the formal parameters in type, order, and number.

Pass by Value

When invoking a method with a parameter of primitive data type, such as int, the copy of the value of the actual parameter is passed to the method. This is referred to as *pass by value*. The actual variable outside the method is not affected, regardless of the changes made to the formal parameter inside the method. Let's examine an interesting scenario in the following example, in which the formal parameter is changed in the method, but the actual parameter is not affected.

Example 4.2 Testing Pass by Value

The program given below shows the effect of passing by value. The output of the program is shown in Figure 4.3.

```java
// TestPassByValue.java: Demonstrate passing values to methods
public class TestPassByValue
{
  // Main method
  public static void main(String[] args)
  {
    // Initialize times
    int times = 3;
    System.out.println("Before the call, variable times is "+times);

    // Invoke nPrintln and display times afterwards
    nPrintln("Welcome to Java!", times);
    System.out.println("After the call, variable times is "+times);
  }

  // Method for printing the message n times
  static void nPrintln(String message, int n)
  {
    while (n > 0)
    {
      System.out.println("n = "+n);
      System.out.println(message);
      n--;
    }
  }
}
```

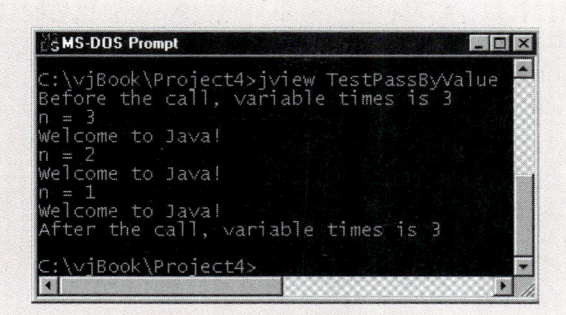

Figure 4.3 *Since the* `times` *variable is passed by value to the method* `nPrintln`, `times` *is not changed by the method.*

Example Review

A `while` loop with a changing formal parameter of `n` was used to rewrite the `nPrintln` method in the preceding section. The method `nPrintln("Welcome to Java!", times)` was then invoked. Before the call, the `times` variable was 3. Interestingly, after the call the `times` variable is still 3. This is because `n` is a parameter of primitive data type. Java passes the value of `times` to `n`. The `times` variable itself is not affected, regardless of the changes made to `n` inside the method.

Another twist is to change the formal parameter name `n` in `nPrintln()` to `times`. What effect does this have? No change occurs because it does not matter whether the formal parameter and the actual parameter have the same name. The formal parameter represents imaginary data, which do not exist until they are associated with an actual parameter.

See Chapter 5, "Programming with Objects and Classes," to learn about another mechanism for passing objects: *pass by reference*.

Overloading Methods

The `max()` method that was used earlier works only with the `int` data type. But what if you need to find which of two floating-point numbers has the maximum value? The solution is to create another method with the same name but with different parameters, as shown in the following code:

```
double max(double num1, double num2)
{
  if (num1 > num2)
    return num1;
  else
    return num2;
}
```

If you call `max()` with `int` parameters, the `max()` method that expects `int` parameters will be invoked; if you call `max()` with `double` parameters, the `max()` method that expects `double` parameters will be invoked. This is referred to as *method overloading*; that is, two methods have the same name but different parameter profiles. Java runtime system is able to determine which method to invoke based on the number and types of parameters passed to that method.

Example 4.3 Overloading the *max()* Method

In the following program, two methods are created. One finds the maximum integer; the other finds the maximum double. Both methods are named `max`. The output of the program is shown in Figure 4.4.

```
// TestMethodOverloading.java: Demonstrate method overloading
public class TestMethodOverloading
{
  // Main method
  public static void main(String[] args)
  {
    // Invoke the max method with int parameters
    System.out.println("The maximum between 3 and 4 is "
      + max(3, 4));

    // Invoke the max method with the double parameter
    System.out.println("The maximum between 3.0 and 5.4 is "
      + max(3.0, 5.4));
  }

  // Find the max between two double values
  static double max(double num1, double num2)
  {
    if (num1 > num2)
      return num1;
    else
      return num2;
  }

  // Find the max between two int values
  static int max(int num1, int num2)
  {
    if (num1 > num2)
      return num1;
    else
      return num2;
  }
}
```

```
C:\vjBook\Project4>jview TestMethodOverloading
The maximum between 3 and 4 is 4
The maximum between 3.0 and 5.4 is 5.4

C:\vjBook\Project4>
```

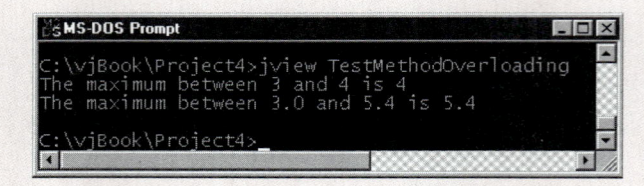

Figure 4.4. *The program invokes two different* `max` *methods*—`max(3, 4)` *and* `max(3.0, 5.4)`—*even though both have the same name.*

Example Review

Two `max()` methods were created in the same class with different parameters—one for finding maximum integers, and the other for finding maximum doubles.

When calling `max(3.0, 5.4)`, the `max()` method for finding maximum doubles is invoked. When calling `max(3, 4)`, the `max()` method for finding maximum integers is invoked.

> **TIP**
> Overloading methods can make programs clear and more readable. Methods that perform closely related tasks should be given the same name.

Creating Methods in Separate Classes

Thus far in this chapter, the methods in the examples have been placed in the same class in which they were invoked. You can create methods in separate classes so that they can be used by other classes.

Example 4.4 Computing Square Roots

In this example, you will see how a program that computes square roots is written. The square root of a number, `num`, can be approximated by repeatedly performing a calculation using the following formula:

```
nextGuess = (lastGuess + (num / lastGuess))/2
```

When `nextGuess` and `lastGuess` are almost identical, `nextGuess` is the approximated square root.

The initial guess will be the starting value of `lastGuess`. If the difference between `nextGuess` and `lastGuess` is less than a very small number, such as 0.001, you can claim that `nextGuess` is the approximated square root of `num`. The sample output of the following program is shown in Figure 4.5.

```java
// TestSquareRoot.java: Demonstrate invoking methods from other class
public class TestSquareRoot
{
  // Main method
  public static void main(String[] args)
  {
    System.out.println(
      "The square root for 9 is " + SquareRoot.sqrt(9.0));
    System.out.println(
      "The square root for 2000 is " + SquareRoot.sqrt(2000.0));
  }
}
```

continues

```java
// This class contains sqrt method
class SquareRoot
{
  // Find the square root of the value
  public static double sqrt(double num)
  {
    double nextGuess;
    double lastGuess = 1.0;
    double difference;

    do
    {
      nextGuess = (lastGuess + (num/lastGuess))*0.5;
      difference = nextGuess - lastGuess;
      lastGuess = nextGuess;
      if (difference < 0)
        difference = -difference;
    } while (difference >= 0.001);

    return nextGuess;
  }
}
```

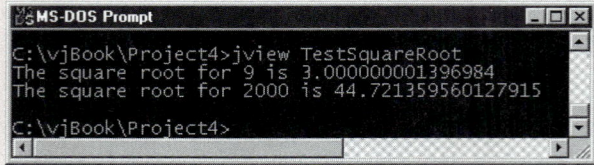

```
C:\vjBook\Project4>jview TestSquareRoot
The square root for 9 is 3.000000001396984
The square root for 2000 is 44.721359560127915

C:\vjBook\Project4>
```

Figure 4.5 *The program invokes the* `sqrt()` *method in order to compute the square root.*

Example Review

The `sqrt()` method is defined in the `SquareRoot` class. To invoke `sqrt()`, put the class name `SquareRoot` in front of the `sqrt()`.

The `sqrt()` method implements the approximation algorithm for finding the square root. In this case, the constant 0.001 is often referred to as error tolerance. The smaller the difference, the better the approximation.

Method Abstraction

The key to developing software is to apply the concept of abstraction. *Method abstraction* is defined as separating the use of a method from its implementation. This is referred to as *information hiding*. The client can use a method without knowing how the method is implemented. If you decide to change the implementation, the client program will not be affected.

When writing a large program, use the "divide and conquer" strategy in order to decompose problems into more manageable sub-problems. Apply method abstraction to make programs easy to manage. See the following example, which demonstrates the use of method abstraction in software development.

Example 4.5 Illustrating Method Abstraction in Developing a Large Project

In this example, a program is created that displays the calendar for a given month of the year. The program prompts the user to enter the year and the month, and then displays the entire calendar for the month, as shown in Figure 4.6.

Figure 4.6. *After prompting the user to enter the year and the month, the program displays the calendar for that month.*

How would you get started on such a program? Would you start coding immediately? Beginning programmers often start by trying to work out the solution to every detail. Although details are important in the final program, concern for detail in the early stages could block the problem-solving process. To make problem-solving flow as smoothly as possible, this example first uses method abstraction to isolate details from design and only later implements details.

For this example, the problem is first broken into two subproblems: get input from the user, and print the monthly calendar. At this stage, the creator of the program should be concerned with what the subproblems will achieve but not with the ways in which they will get input and print the calendar for the month. Note the structure chart, which is used to help you visualize the subproblems (see Figure 4.7).

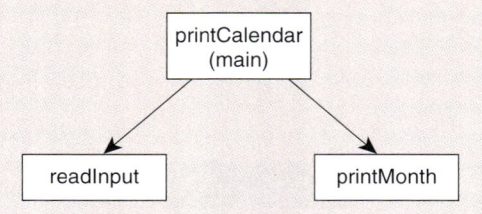

Figure 4.7 *The structure chart shows that the* `printCalendar` *problem is divided into two subproblems:* `readInput` *and* `printMonth`.

continues

Use `System.out.println()` to display a message to prompt the user for the year and the month. Then use `MyInput.readInt()` to get the input.

In order to print the calendar for a month, you need to know which day of the week is the first day of the month and how many days the month has. With this information, you can print the title and body of the calendar. Therefore, the print month problem would be further decomposed into four subproblems: get the start day, get the number of days in the month, print title, and print month body.

How would you get the start day for the first date in a month? There are several ways to find the start day. The simplest approach is to use the `Date` and `Calendar` classes in Chapter 12, "Internationalization." For now, an alternative approach is used. Assume that you know that the start day (startDay1800 = 3) for Jan 1, 1800 is Wednesday. You could compute the total number of days (totalNumOfDays) between Jan 1, 1800, and the first date of the calendar month. The start day for the calendar month is (totalNumOfDays + startDay1800) % 7.

To compute the total days (totalNumOfDays) between Jan 1, 1800 and the first date of the calendar month, you could find the total number of days between the year 1800 and the calendar year and then figure out the total number of days prior to the calendar in the calendar year. The sum of these two totals is totalNumOfDays.

You would also need to know the number of days in a month and in a year. Remember the following:

- January, March, May, July, August, October, and December have 31 days.

- April, June, September, and November have 30 days.

- February has 28 days during a regular year and 29 days during a leap year. A regular year, therefore, has 365 days, while a leap year has 366 days.

To determine whether a year is a leap year, you could use the following condition:

```
if ((year % 400 == 0) || ((year % 4 == 0) && (year % 100 != 0)))
   return true;
else
   return false;
```

To print a title, you could use `println()` to display three lines, as shown in Figure 4.8.

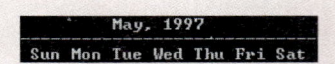

```
            May, 1997
 Sun Mon Tue Wed Thu Fri Sat
```

Figure 4.8 *The calendar title consists of three lines: month and year, a dash line, and the names of the seven days of the week.*

To print a body, you would first pad some space before the start day and then print the lines for every week, as shown for September 1999 (see Figure 4.6).

In general, a subproblem corresponds to a method in the implementation, although some are so simple that this is unnecessary. You would need to decide which modules to implement as methods and which to combine in other methods. Decisions of this kind should be based on whether the overall program would be easier to read as a result of your choice. In this example, the subproblem readInput was implemented in the main() method (see Figure 4.9).

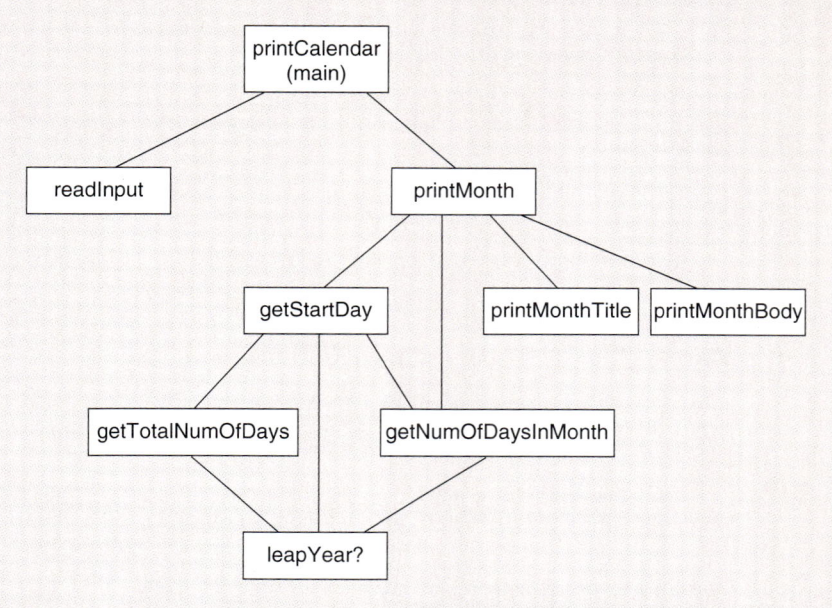

Figure 4.9 *The structure chart shows the hierarchical relationship of the subproblems in the program.*

When implementing the program, you should use the "top-down" approach. In other words, implement one method in the structure chart at a time—from the top to the bottom. You could use stubs for the methods waiting to be implemented. Implement the main() method first and then use a stub for the printMonth method. For example, let printMonth display the year and the month in the stub.

The sample run of the following program is shown in Figure 4.6.

```
// PrintCalendar.java: Print a calendar for a given month in a year
public class PrintCalendar
{
  // Main method
  public static void main(String[] args)
  {
    // The user enters year and month
    System.out.println("Enter full year");
```

continues

```java
    int year = MyInput.readInt();
    System.out.println("Enter month in number between 1 and 12");
    int month = MyInput.readInt();


    // Print calendar for the month of the year
    printMonth(year, month);
  }

  // Print the calendar for a month in a year
  static void printMonth(int year, int month)
  {
    // Get start day of the week for the first date in the month
    int startDay = getStartDay(year, month);

    // Get number of days in the month
    int numOfDaysInMonth = getNumOfDaysInMonth(year, month);

    // Print headings
    printMonthTitle(year, month);

    // Print body
    printMonthBody(startDay, numOfDaysInMonth);
  }

  // Get the start day of the first day in a month
  static int getStartDay(int year, int month)
  {
    // Get total number of days since 1/1/1800
    int startDay1800 = 3;
    long totalNumOfDays = getTotalNumOfDays(year, month);

    // Return the start day
    return (int)((totalNumOfDays + startDay1800) % 7);
  }

  // Get the total number of days since Jan 1, 1800
  static long getTotalNumOfDays(int year, int month)
  {
    long total = 0;

    // Get the total days from 1800 to year -1
    for (int i = 1800; i < year; i++)
      if (leapYear(i))
        total = total + 366;
      else
        total = total + 365;

    // Add days from Jan to the month prior to the calendar month
    for (int i = 1; i < month; i++)
      total = total + getNumOfDaysInMonth(year, i);

    return total;
  }

  // Get the number of days in a month
  static int getNumOfDaysInMonth(int year, int month)
  {
    if (month == 1 || month==3 || month == 5 || month == 7 ||
        month == 8 || month == 10 || month == 12)
      return 31;
```

```java
    if (month == 4 || month == 6 || month == 9 || month == 11)
      return 30;

    if (month == 2)
      if (leapYear(year))
        return 29;
      else
        return 28;

    return 0; // If month is incorrect.
  }

  // Determine if it is a leap year
  static boolean leapYear(int year)
  {
    if ((year % 400 == 0) || ((year % 4 == 0) && (year % 100 != 0)))
      return true;

    return false;
  }

  // Print month body
  static void printMonthBody(int startDay, int numOfDaysInMonth)
  {
    // Pad space before the first day of the month
    int i = 0;
    for (i = 0; i < startDay; i++)
      System.out.print("    ");

    for (i = 1; i <= numOfDaysInMonth; i++)
    {
      if (i < 10)
        System.out.print("   " + i);
      else
        System.out.print("  " + i);

      if ((i + startDay) % 7 == 0)
        System.out.println();
    }

    System.out.println();
  }

  // Print the month title, i.e. May, 1999
  static void printMonthTitle(int year, int month)
  {
    System.out.println("         "+getMonthName(month)+", "+year);
    System.out.println("-----------------------------");
    System.out.println(" Sun Mon Tue Wed Thu Fri Sat");
  }

  // Get the English name for the month
  static String getMonthName(int month)
  {
    String monthName = null;
    switch (month)
    {
      case 1: monthName = "January"; break;
      case 2: monthName = "February"; break;
      case 3: monthName = "March"; break;
```

continues

```
      case 4: monthName = "April"; break;
      case 5: monthName = "May"; break;
      case 6: monthName = "June"; break;
      case 7: monthName = "July"; break;
      case 8: monthName = "August"; break;
      case 9: monthName = "September"; break;
      case 10: monthName = "October"; break;
      case 11: monthName = "November"; break;
      case 12: monthName = "December";
    }

    return monthName;
  }
}
```

Example Review

The program does not validate user input. For instance, if the user enters a month not in the range between 1 and 12, or a year before 1800, the program would display an erroneous calendar. To avoid this error, you can simply add an `if` statement to check the input before printing the calendar.

This program can print calendars for a month but could easily be modified to print calendars for a whole year. Although it can only print months after January 1800, it could also be modified to trace the day of a month before 1800.

See Chapter 12, "Internationalization," to find out how to simplify the program using the `Date` and `Calendar` classes.

> **NOTE**
> Method abstraction helps modularize programs in a neat, hierarchical manner. Programs written as collections of concise methods are easier to write, debug, maintain, and modify than they would otherwise be. This writing style also promotes method reusability.

> **TIP**
> When implementing a large program, use the top-down coding approach. Start with the main method, and code and test one method at a time. Do not write the entire program at once. This approach seems to take more time for coding (because you are repeatedly compiling and running the program), but it actually saves time and makes debugging easier.

Recursion (Optional)

You have seen a method calling another method—that is, a statement contained in the method body calling another method. Can a method call itself? And what happens if it does? This section examines these questions and uses two classic examples to demonstrate recursive programming.

Recursion—a powerful mathematical concept—is the process of a method calling itself, directly or indirectly. In some cases, using recursion enables you to give a natural, straightforward, simple solution to a program that would otherwise be difficult to solve. Consider the well-known Fibonacci series problem. The Fibonacci series begins with two 1s in succession (1, 1, 2, 3, 5, 8, 13, 21, 34, and so on); each subsequent number is the sum of the previous two numbers in the series. The series can be recursively defined as follows:

```
fib(1) = 1;
fib(2) = 1;
fib(n) = fib(n-2) + fib(n-1); n > 2
```

The Fibonacci series was named for Leonardo Fibonacci, a medieval mathematician, who originated it to model the growth of the rabbit population. It can be applied in numeric optimization and in various other areas.

How do you find `fib(n)` for a given n? It is easy to find `fib(3)` because you know `fib(1)` and `fib(2)`. Assuming that you know `fib(n-2)` and `fib(n-1)`, `fib(n)` can be obtained immediately. Thus, the problem of computing `fib(n)` is reduced to computing `fib(n-2)` and `fib(n-1)`. When computing `fib(n-2)` and `fib(n-1)`, you can apply the idea recursively until n is reduced to 1 or 2.

If you call the method with n=1 or n=2, it immediately returns the result. The method knows how to solve the simplest case, which is referred to as the *base case* or the *stopping condition*. If you call the method with n>2, it divides the problem into two subproblems of the same nature. The subproblem is essentially the same as the original problem, but is slightly simpler or smaller than the original. Because the subproblem has the same property as the original, you can call the method with a different actual parameter, which is referred to as a *recursive call*.

The recursive algorithm for computing `fib(n)` can be simply described as follows:

```
if ((n==1) || (n==2))
  return 1;
else
  return fib(n-1)+fib(n-2);
```

A recursive call can result in many more recursive calls because the method is dividing a subproblem into new subproblems. For a recursive method to terminate, the problem eventually must be reduced to a stopping case. When it reaches a stopping case, the method returns a result to its caller. The caller then performs a computation and returns the result to its own caller. This process continues until the result is passed back to the original caller. The original problem can now be solved by adding the results of the two subproblems.

Example 4.6 Computing Fibonacci Numbers

In this example, a recursive method is written for computing a Fibonacci number fib(n), given index n. The test program prompts the user to enter index n, then calls the method and displays the result.

A sample run of the program is shown in Figure 4.10.

```java
// TestFibonacci.java: Find a Fibonacci number for a given index
public class TestFibonacci
{
  // Main method
  public static void main(String args[])
  {
    // Read the index
    System.out.println("Enter an index for the Fibonacci number");
    int n = MyInput.readInt();

    // Find and display the Fibonacci number
    System.out.println("Fibonacci number at index " + n +
      " is "+fib(n));
  }

  // The method for finding the Fibonacci number
  public static long fib(long n)
  {
    if ((n==1)||(n==2))   // Stopping condition
      return 1;
    else   // Reduction and recursive calls
      return fib(n-1) + fib(n-2);
  }
}
```

```
C:\vjBook\Project4>jview TestFibonacci
Enter an index for the Fibonacci number
5
Fibonacci number at index 5 is 5

C:\vjBook\Project4>jview TestFibonacci
Enter an index for the Fibonacci number
10
Fibonacci number at index 10 is 55

C:\vjBook\Project4>
```

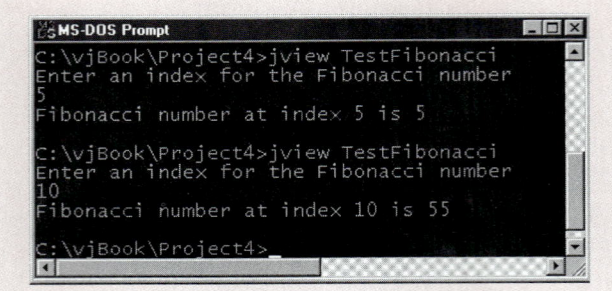

Figure 4.10 *The program prompts the user to enter an index for the Fibonacci number and then displays the number at the index.*

Example Review

The implementation of the method is, in fact, very simple and straightforward. The solution is slightly more difficult if you do not use recursion. For a hint on computing Fibonacci numbers using iterations, see Exercise 4.8.

The program does not show the considerable amount of work done behind the scenes by the computer. Figure 4.11 shows successive recursive calls for evaluating `fib(5)`. The original method, `fib(5)`, makes two recursive calls—`fib(4)` and `fib(3)`—and then returns `fib(4)+fib(3)`. But in what order are these methods called? In Java, the operands are evaluated from left to right. In Figure 4.11, the upper-left corner labels show the order in which methods are called.

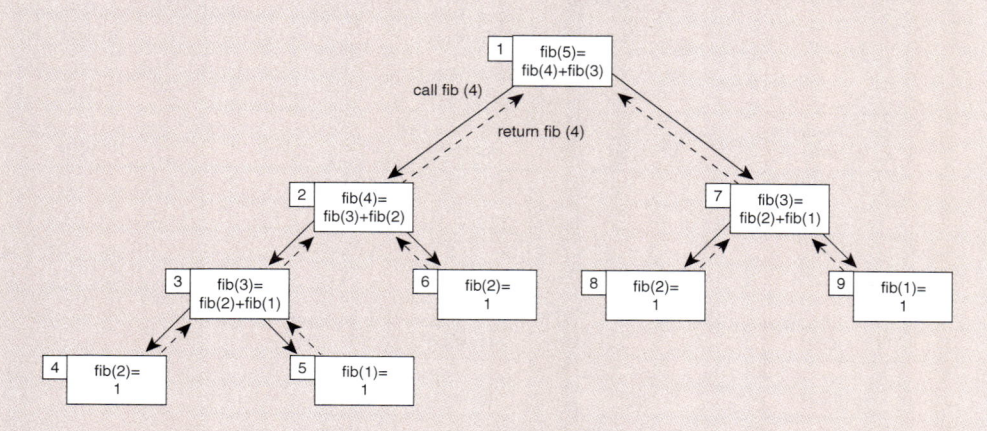

Figure 4.11 *Invoking* `fib(5)` *spawns recursive calls to* `fib()`.

As shown in Figure 4.11, there are many duplicated recursive calls. For instance, `fib(3)` is called two times, `fib(2)` is called three times, and `fib(1)` is called two times. In general, computing `fib(n)` requires twice as many recursive calls as are needed for computing `fib(n-1)`. As you try larger index values, the number of calls substantially increases.

Besides the large number of recursive calls, the computer requires more time and space to run recursive methods. See Exercise 4.8 for a more efficient method.

Each time a method is invoked, the system stores parameters, local variables, and system registers into a space known as a *stack*. When a method calls another method, the caller's stack space is kept intact, and new space is created to handle the new method call. When a method finishes its work and returns to its caller, its associated space is released. The use of stack space for recursive calls is shown in Figure 4.12.

> **NOTE**
> All recursive methods have the following common characteristics:
> - One or more base cases (the simplest case) are used to stop recursion.
> - Every recursive call reduces the original problem, bringing it increasingly close to a base case until it becomes that case.

continues

Figure 4.12 *When* `fib(5)` *is being executed, the* `fib()` *method is called recursively, causing memory space to dynamically change.*

CAUTION
Infinite recursion can occur if recursion does not reduce the problem in a manner that allows it to eventually converge into the base case.

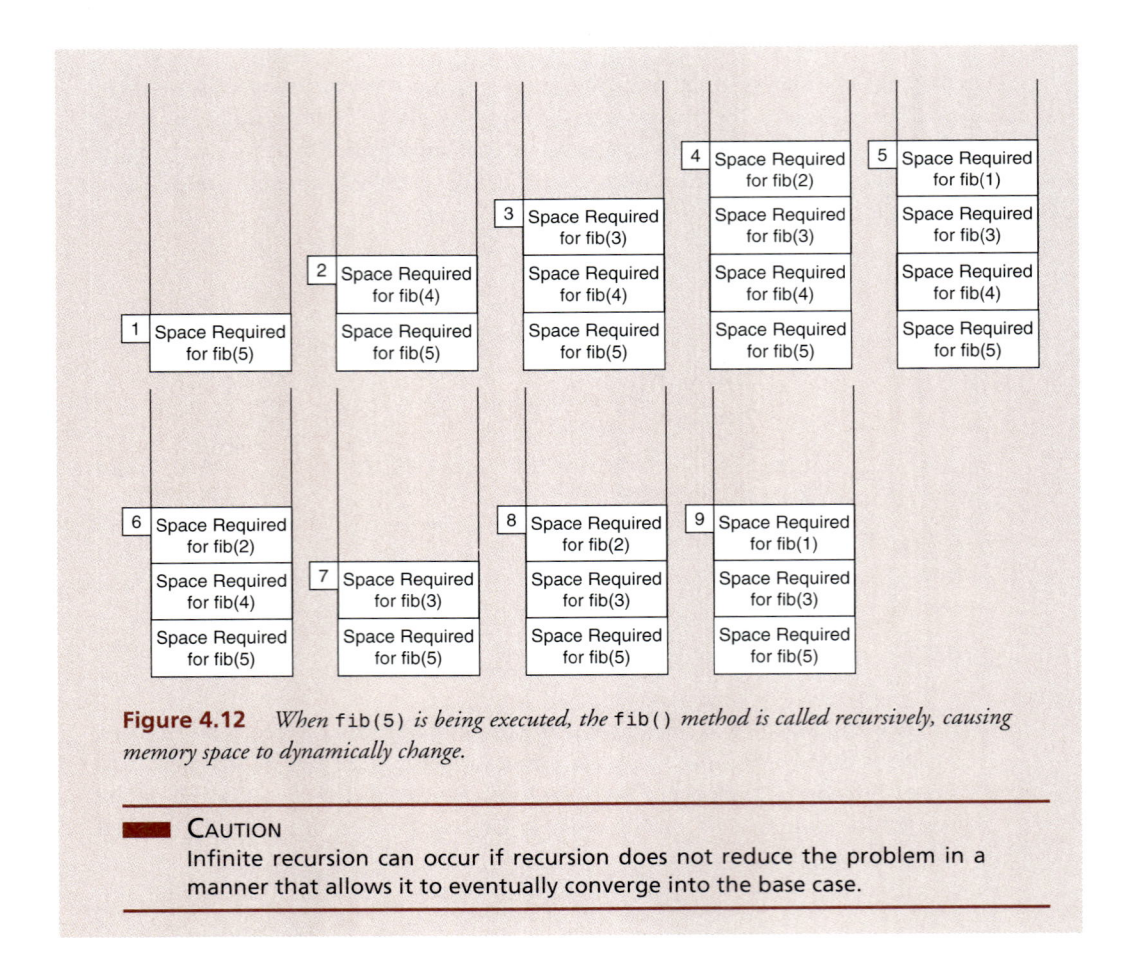

You have seen a recursive method with a return value. Here is an example of a recursive method with a return type of `void`.

Example 4.7 Solving the Towers of Hanoi Problem

This example finds a solution for the Towers of Hanoi problem. The problem involves moving a specified number of disks of a distinct size from one tower to another while observing the following rules:

- There are *n* disks labeled 1, 2, 3, . . . , *n*, and three towers labeled A, B, and C.
- No disk can be on top of a smaller disk at any time.
- Initially, all disks are placed on tower A.
- Only one disk can be moved at a time, and this disk must be the top disk of a tower.

The objective of the problem is to move all the disks from A to B with the assistance of C. For example, if you have three disks, as shown in Figure 4.13, the following steps will move all of the disks from A to B:

1. Move disk 1 from A to B.
2. Move disk 2 from A to C.
3. Move disk 1 from B to C.
4. Move disk 3 from A to B.
5. Move disk 1 from C to A.
6. Move disk 2 from C to B.
7. Move disk 1 from A to B.

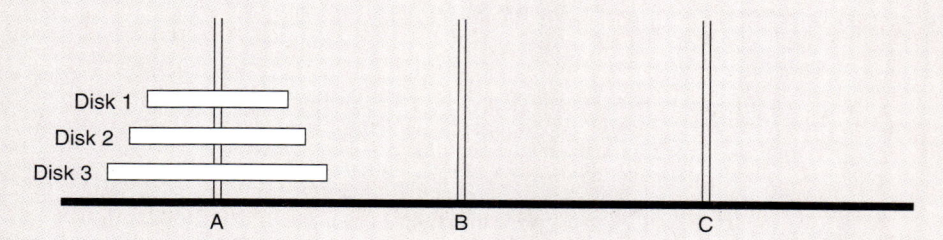

Figure 4.13 *The goal of the Towers of Hanoi problem is to move disks from tower A to tower B without breaking the rules.*

In the case of three disks, you can find the solution manually. However, the problem is quite complex for a larger number of disks—even for four. Fortunately, the problem has an inherently recursive nature, which leads to a straightforward recursive solution.

The base case for the problem is n=1. If n=1, you could simply move the disk from A to B. When n>1, you could split the original problem into the following three subproblems and solve them sequentially:

1. Move the first n-1 disks from A to C with the assistance of tower B.
2. Move disk n from A to B.
3. Move n-1 disks from C to B with the assistance of tower A.

The following method moves *n* disks from the `fromTower` to the `toTower` with the assistance of the `auxTower`:

```
void moveDisks(int n, char fromTower, char toTower, char auxTower)
```

The algorithm for the method can be described as follows:

```
if (n==1) // Stopping condition
   Move disk 1 from the fromTower to the toTower;
else
```

continues

```
    {
      moveDisks(n-1, fromTower, auxTower, toTower);
      Move disk n from the fromTower to the toTower;
      moveDisks(n-1, auxTower, toTower, fromTower);
    }
```

The sample run of the following program appears in Figure 4.14.

```java
// TowersOfHanoi.java: Find solutions for the Towers of Hanoi problem
public class TowersOfHanoi
{
  // Main method
  public static void main(String[] args)
  {
    // Read number of disks, n
    System.out.println("Enter number of disks");
    int n = MyInput.readInt();

    // Find the solution recursively
    System.out.println("The moves are:");
    moveDisks(n, 'A', 'B', 'C');
  }

  // The method for finding the solution to move n disks
  // from fromTower to toTower with auxTower
  public static void moveDisks(int n, char fromTower,
    char toTower, char auxTower)
  {
    if (n==1) // Stopping condition
      System.out.println("Move disk " + n + " from " +
        fromTower+" to " + toTower);
    else
    {
      moveDisks(n-1, fromTower, auxTower, toTower);
      System.out.println("Move disk " + n + " from " +
        fromTower + " to " + toTower);
      moveDisks(n-1, auxTower, toTower, fromTower);
    }
  }
}
```

```
C:\vjBook\Project4>jview TowersOfHanoi
Enter number of disks
4
The moves are:
Move disk 1 from A to C
Move disk 2 from A to B
Move disk 1 from C to B
Move disk 3 from A to C
Move disk 1 from B to A
Move disk 2 from B to C
Move disk 1 from A to C
Move disk 4 from A to B
Move disk 1 from C to B
Move disk 2 from C to A
Move disk 1 from B to A
Move disk 3 from C to B
Move disk 1 from A to C
Move disk 2 from A to B
Move disk 1 from C to B

C:\vjBook\Project4>
```

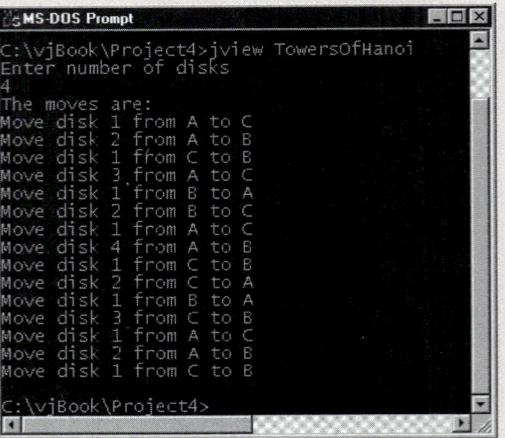

Figure 4.14 *The program prompts the user to enter the number of disks and then displays the steps that must be followed to solve the Towers of Hanoi problem.*

Example Review

This problem is inherently recursive. Using recursion enables a natural, simple solution to be found for the problem. It would be difficult to solve it without using recursion.

Consider tracing the program for n=3. The successive recursive calls are shown in Figure 4.15. As you can see, writing the program is easier than tracing the recursive calls. The system uses stacks to trace the calls behind the scenes. To some extent, recursion provides a level of abstraction that hides iterations and other details from the user.

```
                        moveDisks(3,'A','B','C')
                       moveDisks(2,'A','C','B')
                       move disk 3 from A to B
                       moveDisks(2,'C','B','A')

       moveDisks(2,'A','C','B')                    moveDisks(2,'C','B','A')
       moveDisks(1,'A','B','C')                    moveDisks(1,'C','A','B')
       move disk 2 from A to C                     move disk 2 from C to B
       moveDisks(1,'B','C','A')                    moveDisks(1,'A','B','C')

moveDisks(1,'A','B','C')  moveDisks(1,'B','C','A')  moveDisks(1,'C','A','B')  moveDisks(1,'A','B','C')
move disk 1 from A to B   move disk 1 from B to C   move disk 1 from C to A   move disk 1 from A to B
```

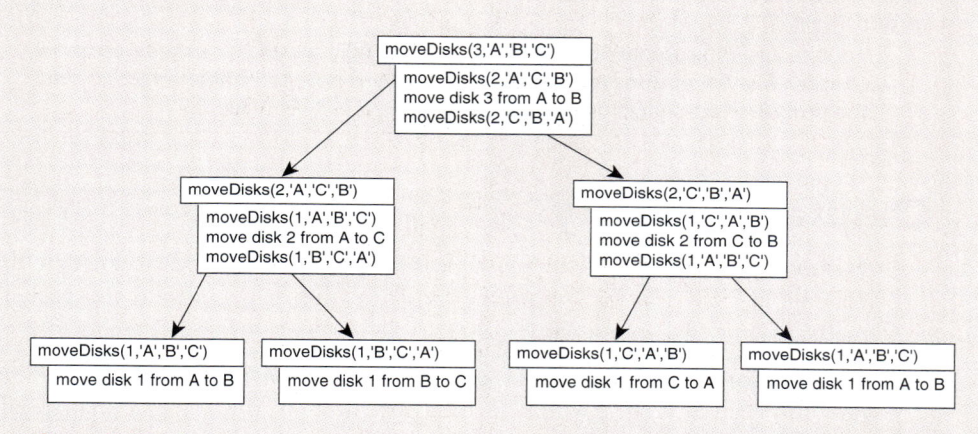

Figure 4.15 *Invoking* `moveDisks(3, 'A', 'B', 'C')` *spawns calls to* `moveDisks` *recursively.*

The `fib()` method in the previous example returns a value to its caller, but the `moveDisks()` method in this example does not return any value to its caller.

Recursion versus Iteration (Optional)

Recursion is an alternative form of program control. It is essentially repetition without a loop control. When you use loops, you specify a loop body. The repetition of the loop body is controlled by the loop control structure. In recursion, the method itself is called repeatedly. The successive recursive calls are handled behind the scenes by the system. There is always a decision structure to control the repetition.

Recursion bears substantial overhead. Each time the program calls a method, the system must assign space for all of the method's local variables and parameters. This can consume considerable memory and requires extra time to manage the additional space.

Any problem that can be solved recursively can be solved nonrecursively with iterations. Recursion has many negative aspects: it uses up too much time and too much memory. Why, then, should you use it? In some cases, using recursion enables you to specify a clear, simple solution that would otherwise be difficult to obtain.

The decision whether to use recursion or iteration should be based on the nature of the problem you are trying to solve and your understanding of the problem. The rule of thumb is to use recursion or iteration to develop an intuitive solution that naturally mirrors the problem. If an iterative solution is obvious, use it. It will generally be more efficient than the recursive option.

> **Tip**
> If you are concerned about your program's performance, avoid using recursion, because it takes more time and consumes more memory than iteration.

> **Caution**
> Your recursive program could run out of memory, causing a runtime error. In Chapter 11, "Exception Handling," you will learn how to handle errors so that the program terminates gracefully when there is a stack overflow.

Chapter Summary

Making programs modular and reusable is one of the central goals in software engineering. Java provides many powerful constructs that help to achieve this goal. The method is one such construct.

In this chapter, you have learned how to write reusable methods. You now know how to create a method with a method specification, the interface that specifies how the method can be used, and a method body that defines what the method does.

You have also learned how to call a method by passing actual parameters that replace the formal parameters in the method specification. The arguments that are passed to a method should have the same number, type, and order as the parameters in the method definition. Outside of the method, the actual values of the primitive parameters—which are passed by the value—are not affected by the method call.

In addition, you have learned that a method can be overloaded. For example, two methods can have the same name as long as their method parameter profiles differ.

You are now familiar with the "divide and conquer" strategy. The best way to develop and maintain a large program is to divide it into several subproblems that are each more manageable than the original problem. Subproblems are written in Java as classes and methods.

You learned the techniques needed to write recursive methods. Recursion is an alternative form of program control. Recursion can be used to specify simple, clear solutions for some inherently recursive problems that would otherwise be difficult to solve.

Chapter Review

4.1. What is the purpose of using a method? How do you declare a method? How do you invoke a method?

4.2. What is a return type of a main method?

4.3. What would be wrong if you did not write a return statement in a nonvoid method? Can you have a return statement in a void method, such as the following?

```java
public static void main(String[] args)
{
  int i;
  while (true)
  {
    i = MyInput.readInt();
    if (i == 0) return;
    System.out.println("i = "+i);
  }
}
```

4.4. What is method overloading? Define two methods that have the same name but different parameter types. Define two methods in a class that have identical method names and parameter profiles with different return value types or different modifiers.

4.5. How do you pass actual parameters to a method? Can the actual parameter have the same name as its formal parameter?

4.6. What is "pass by value"? Show the result of the following method call:

```java
public class Test
{
  public static void main(String[] args)
  {
    int max = 0;
    max(1, 2, max);
    System.out.println(max);
  }

  public static void max(int value1, int value2, int max)
  {
    if (value1 > value2)
      max = value1;
    else
      max = value2;
  }
}
```

4.7. A call for the method with a void return type is always a statement itself, but a call for the method with a non-void return type is always a component of an expression. Is the statement true or false?

4.8. In many other languages, you can define methods inside a method. Can you define a method inside a method in Java?

4.9. For each of the following, decide whether a void method or a non-void method is the most appropriate implementation:

- Computing a sales commission, given the sales amount and the commission rate.
- Printing a calendar for a month.
- Computing a square root.
- Testing whether a number is even and returning `true` if it is.
- Printing a message a specified number of times.

4.10. Does the `return` statement in the following method cause syntax errors?

```java
public static void main(String[] args)
{
  int max = 0;
  if (max != 0)
    System.out.println(max);
  else
    return;
}
```

4.11. What is a recursive method?

4.12. Describe the characteristics of recursive methods.

4.13. Show the printout of the following program:

```java
public class Test
{
  public static void main(String[] args)
  {
    int sum = xMethod(5);
    System.out.println("Sum is "+sum);
  }

  public static int xMethod(int n)
  {
    if (n==1)
      return 1;
    else
      return n + xMethod(n-1);
  }
}
```

Programming Exercises

4.1. Write a method to find the ceiling of a double value, and write a method to find its floor. The ceiling of a number d is the smallest integer greater than or equal to d. The floor of a number d is the largest integer less than or equal to d. For example, the ceiling of 5.4 is 6, and the floor of 5.4 is 5.

4.2. Write a method to compute the sum of the digits in an integer. Use the following method declaration:

```java
public static int sumDigits(long n)
```

For example, sumDigits(234) returns 2+3+4=9.

Hint: Use the % operator to extract digit and use the / operator to remove the extracted digit. For instance, 234%10 = 4 and 234/10 = 23. Use a loop to extract and remove the digit repeatedly until all the digits are extracted.

4.3. Write a method to compute future investment value at a given interest rate for a specified number of years. The future investment is determined using the following formula:

```
futureInvestmentValue = investmentAmount x (
   1 + interestRate)years
```

Use the flowing method declaration:

```
public static double futureInvestmentValue(
   double investmentAmount, double interestRate, int years)
```

For example, `futureInvestmentValue(10000, 0.05, 5)` returns 12762.82.

Hint: Use the `Math.pow(a, b)` method to compute a raised to the power of b.

4.4. Write a method to convert Celsius to Fahrenheit using the following declaration:

```
public static double celsToFahr(double cels)
```

Write a program that uses a `for` loop and calls the `celsToFahr` method in order to produce the following output:

```
Cels. Temp.      Fahr. Temp.
-------------------
40.00            104.00
39.00            102.20
38.00            100.40
37.00            98.60
36.00            96.80
35.00            95.00
34.00            93.20
33.00            91.40
32.00            89.60
31.00            87.80
```

4.5. Write a program to print the following table using the `sqrt` method from Example 4.4.

```
RealNumber       SquareRoot
-------------------
0                0.0000
2                1.4142
4                2.0000
6                2.4495
8                2.8284
10               3.1623
12               3.4641
14               3.7417
16               4.0000
18               4.2426
20               4.4721
```

4.6. Write a program that meets the following requirements:

- Declare a method to determine whether an integer is a prime number. Use the flowing method declaration:

  ```
  public static boolean isPrime(int num)
  ```

  An integer is a *prime number* if its only divisor is 1 or itself. For example, `isPrime(11)` returns `true` and `isPrime(9)` returns `false`.

- Use the `isPrime` method to find all the prime numbers between 1 and 100, and display every 10 prime numbers in a row as follows:

  1 2 3 5 7 11 13 17 19 23

  29 31 37 41 47 53 59 61 67

  71 73 79 83 89 97

4.7. Write a recursive method that will compute factorials. The factorial of a natural number is defined as follows:

factorial(0) = 1;

factorial(n) = factorial(n-1)*n; for n>0

4.8. Write a nonrecursive method to compute Fibonacci numbers.

Hint: To compute `fib(n)` without recursion, you need to obtain `fib(n-2)` and `fib(n-1)` first. Let `f1` and `f2` denote the two previous Fibonacci numbers. The current Fibonacci number would then be `f1+f2`. The algorithm can be described as follows:

```
f1 = 1; // For fib(1)
f2 = 1; // For fib(2)
for (int i=1; i<=n; i++)
{
  currentFib = f1+f2;
  f1 = f2;
  f2 = currentFib;
}

// After the loop, currentFib is fib(n)
```

4.9. Modify Example 4.7 so that the program finds the number of moves needed to move n disks from tower A to B.

4.10. Write a recursive method for the greatest common divisor (GCD). Given two positive integers, the GCD is the largest integer that divides them both. `GCD(m, n)` can be defined as follows:

GCD(m, n) is n if n is less than or equal to m and n divides m.

GCD(m, n) is GCD(n, m) if m is less than n.

GCD(m, n) is GCD(n, m%n), otherwise.

PART II

OBJECT-ORIENTED PROGRAMMING

In Part I, "Fundamentals of Java Programming," you learned how to write simple Java applications using primitive data types, control structures, and methods, all of which are features commonly available in conventional programming languages. Java, however, is a class-centric object-oriented programming language that uses abstraction, encapsulation, inheritance, and polymorphism to provide great flexibility, modularity, and reusability for developing software. In this part of the book you will learn how to define, extend, and work with classes and their objects.

CHAPTER 5 **PROGRAMMING WITH OBJECTS AND CLASSES**

CHAPTER 6 **ARRAYS AND STRINGS**

CHAPTER 7 **CLASS INHERITANCE**

CHAPTER 5

PROGRAMMING WITH OBJECTS AND CLASSES

Objectives

- Understand objects and classes and the relationship between them.
- Learn how to define a class and how to create an object of the class.
- Understand the roles of constructors and modifiers.
- Learn how to pass objects to methods.
- Understand instance and class variables.
- Understand instance and class methods.
- Understand the scope of variables.
- Learn how to use packages.
- Understand the organization of the Java API.
- Become familiar with the Math class.

Introduction

Programming in procedural languages like C, Pascal, BASIC, Ada, and COBOL involves choosing data structures, designing algorithms, and translating algorithms into code. An object-oriented language like Java combines the power of procedural languages with an added dimension that provides such benefits as abstraction, encapsulation, reusability, and inheritance.

In procedural programming, data and operations on the data are separate, and this methodology requires sending data to procedures and functions. Object-oriented programming places data and the operations that pertain to them within a single data structure; this approach solves many of the problems inherent in procedural programming because the data and operations are part of the same entity. The object-oriented programming approach organizes programs in a way that more closely models the real world, in which all objects are associated with both attributes and activities. Programming in Java involves thinking in terms of objects; a Java program can be viewed as a collection of cooperating objects.

This chapter introduces the fundamentals of object-oriented programming: declaring classes, creating objects, manipulating objects, and making objects work together.

Objects and Classes

Object-oriented programming (OOP) involves programming using objects. *Object* is a broad term that stands for many things. For example, a student, a desk, a circle, and even a mortgage loan can all be viewed as objects. Certain properties define an object, and certain behaviors define what it does. These properties are known as *data fields*, and the object's behaviors are defined by *methods*. Figure 5.1 shows a diagram of an object with its data fields and methods.

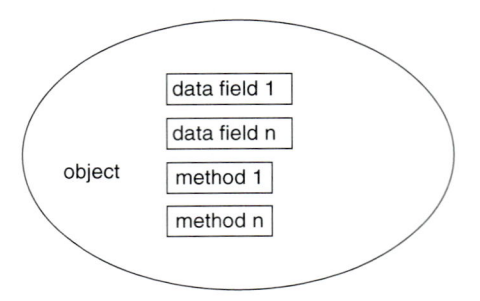

Figure 5.1 *An object contains data and methods.*

A `Circle` object, for example, has a data field `radius`, which is the property that characterizes a circle. One behavior of a circle is that its area can be computed. A `Circle` object is shown in Figure 5.2.

Chapter 5 Programming with Objects and Classes

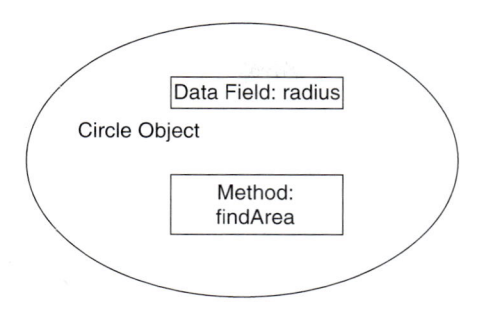

Figure 5.2 *A* `Circle` *object contains the* `radius` *data field and the* `findArea()` *method.*

Classes are constructs that define objects. In a Java class, data are used to describe properties, and methods are used to define behaviors. A class for an object contains a collection of method and data definitions. Here is an example of the class for a circle:

```
class Circle
{
  double radius = 1.0;

  double findArea()
  {
    return radius*radius*3.14159;
  }
}
```

This class is different from all of the other classes you have seen thus far. The `Circle` class does not have a main method, nor does it extend `java.applet.Applet`. Therefore, you cannot run this class; it is merely a definition used to declare and create `Circle` objects. For convenience, the class that contains the `main()` method will be referred to as the *main class* in this book.

Declaring and Creating Objects

A class is a blueprint that defines what an object's data and methods will be. An object is an instance of a class. You can create many instances of a class (see Figure 5.3). The relationship between classes and objects is analogous to the relationship between apple pie recipes and apple pies. You can make as many apple pies as you want from a single recipe.

Creating an instance is referred to as *instantiation*. In order to declare an object, you must use a variable to represent it (which is similar to declaring a variable for a primitive data type). The syntax for declaring an object is as follows:

```
ClassName objectName;
```

For example, the following statement declares the variable `myCircle` to be an instance of the `Circle` class:

```
Circle  myCircle;
```

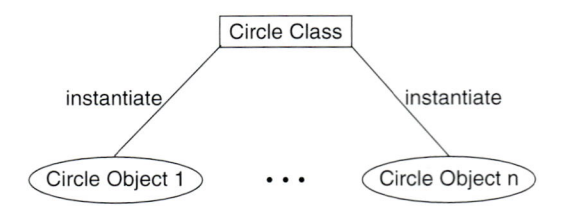

Figure 5.3 *A class can have many different objects.*

Creating an object of a class is called *creating an instance of the class*. An object is similar to a variable that has a class type. To create variables of a primitive data type, you simply declare them, as is done in the following line:

```
int i;
```

This statement creates a variable and allocates memory space for i.

However, for object variables, declaring and creating are two separate steps. The declaration of an object simply associates the object with a class, making the object an instance of that class. The declaration does not create the object. To actually create myCircle, you would need to use the operator new in order to tell the computer to create an object for myCircle and allocate memory space for it. The syntax for creating an object is as follows:

```
objectName = new ClassName();
```

For example, this statement creates an object, myCircle, and allocates memory for it:

```
myCircle = new Circle();
```

You can combine the declaration and instantiation together in one statement by using the following syntax:

```
ClassName objectName = new ClassName();
```

Below is an example of creating and instantiating myCircle in one step:

```
Circle myCircle = new Circle();
```

After an object is created, it can access its data and methods by using the following dot notation:

objectName.data — References an object's data

objectName.method — References an object's method

For example, myCircle.radius indicates what the radius of myCircle is, and myCircle.findArea() returns the area of myCircle.

> **NOTE**
> You can create an anonymous object without explicitly assigning it to a variable, as shown below:
>
> ```
> new Circle();
> ```

This statement creates an anonymous Circle object. You cannot access the contents of an anonymous object, since there is no explicit reference to it. Anonymous objects are used in Chapter 8, "Getting Started with Graphics Programming."

Example 5.1 Using Objects

The program in this example creates a `Circle` object from the `Circle` class and uses the data and method in the object. The output of the program is shown in Figure 5.4.

```java
// TestCircle.java: Demonstrate creating and using an object
public class TestCircle
{
  // Main method
  public static void main(String[] args)
  {
    Circle myCircle = new Circle();  // Create a Circle object
      System.out.println("The area of the circle of radius "
        + myCircle.radius + " is " + myCircle.findArea());
  }
}

// Define a circle
class Circle
{
  double radius = 1.0;

  // Find the area of this circle
  double findArea()
  {
    return radius*radius*3.14159;
  }
}
```

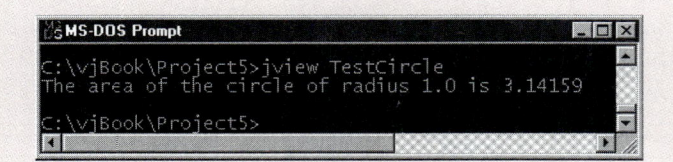

```
C:\vjBook\Project5>jview TestCircle
The area of the circle of radius 1.0 is 3.14159

C:\vjBook\Project5>
```

Figure 5.4 *This program creates a* `Circle` *object and displays its* radius *and* area.

Example Review

The program contains two classes. The first class, `TestCircle`, is the main class. Its sole purpose is to test the second class, `Circle`. Every time you run the program, the Java runtime system invokes its `main()` method in the main class.

The main class contains the `main()` method that creates an object of the `Circle` class and prints its radius and area. The `Circle` class contains the `findArea()` method and the `radius` data field.

continues

To write the `findArea()` method in a procedural programming language like Pascal, you would pass radius as argument to the method. But in the object-oriented programming, `radius` and `findArea()` are defined in the same class. The `radius` is a data member in the `Circle` class, which is accessible by the `findArea()` method. In the procedural programming languages, data and method are separated, but in the object-oriented programming language, data and methods are defined together in a class.

The `findArea()` method is an instance method, which is always invoked by an instance in which the `radius` is specified.

There are many ways to write Java programs. For instance, you can combine the two classes in the example into one, as follows:

```java
public class TestCircle
{
  double radius = 1.0;

  // Find the area of this circle
  double findArea()
  {
    return radius*radius*3.14159;
  }

  // Main method
  public static void main(String[] args)
  {
    // Create a Circle object
    TestCircle myCircle = new TestCircle();
    System.out.println("The area of the circle of radius "
        + myCircle.radius + " is " + myCircle.findArea());
  }
}
```

In this revised program, `radius` and `findArea()` are the members of the `TestCircle` class. Since `TestCircle` contains a main method, it can be executed by the Java interpreter. The main method creates `myCircle` to be an instance of `TestCircle` and displays radius and finds area in `myCircle`.

TIP
The creation of variables of primitive type is implied when the variables are declared. However, declaration and the creation of objects are separate tasks. The compiler allocates memory space for variables of primitive type when they are declared, but does not allocate space for objects when they are declared.

CAUTION
You must always create an object before manipulating it. Manipulating an object that has not been created would cause a `NullPointer` exception. Exception handling will be introduced in Chapter 11, "Exception Handling."

> **NOTE**
> The default value of a data field is `null` for object type, `0` for numerical type, `false` for boolean type, and `'\u0000'` for char type. For example, if `radius` is not initialized in the `Circle` class, Java assigns a default value of `0` to `radius`. However, Java assigns no default value to a local variable inside a method. For example, the following code is erroneous because x is not defined:
>
> ```
> class Test
> {
>   public static void main(String[] args)
>   {
>     int x;
>     System.out.println("x is " + x);
>   }
> }
> ```

Constructors

One problem with the `Circle` class that was just discussed is that all of the objects created from it have the same radius (1.0). Wouldn't it be more useful to create circles with radii of various lengths? Java enables you to define a special method in the class—known as the *constructor*—that will initialize an object's data. You can use a constructor to assign an initial radius when you are creating an object.

The constructor has exactly the same name as the class it comes from. Constructors can be overloaded, making it easier to construct objects with different initial data values. Let's see what happens when the following constructors are added to the `Circle` class:

```
Circle(double r)
{
  radius = r;
}

Circle()
{
  radius = 1.0;
}
```

When creating a new `Circle` object that has a radius of 5.0, you can use the following, which assigns 5.0 to `myCircle.radius`:

```
myCircle = new Circle(5.0);
```

If you create a circle using the following statement, the second constructor is used, which assigns the default radius 1.0 to `myCircle.radius`:

```
myCircle = new Circle();
```

> **NOTE**
> Constructors are special methods that do not require a return type—not even `void`.

Now you know why the syntax `ClassName()` is used to create the object. This syntax calls a constructor. If the class has no constructors, a default constructor (one that takes no arguments) is used, which will not initialize your object's data. If you don't use constructors, all of your objects will be the same initially.

Example 5.2 Using Constructors

In this example, a program is written that will use constructors in the `Circle` class to create two different objects. The output of the program is shown in Figure 5.5.

```java
// TestCircleWithConstructors.java: Demonstrate constructors
public class TestCircleWithConstructors
{
  // Main method
  public static void main(String[] args)
  {
    // Create a Circle with radius 5.0
    Circle myCircle = new Circle(5.0);
    System.out.println("The area of the circle of radius "
      + myCircle.radius + " is " + myCircle.findArea());

    // Create a Circle with default radius
    Circle yourCircle = new Circle();
    System.out.println("The area of the circle of radius "
      + yourCircle.radius + " is " + yourCircle.findArea());
  }
}

// Circle with two constructors
class Circle
{
  double radius;

  // Default constructor
  Circle()
  {
    radius = 1.0;
  }

  // Construct a circle with a specified radius
  Circle(double r)
  {
    radius = r;
  }

  // Find area of this circle
  double findArea()
  {
    return radius*radius*3.14159;
  }
}
```

```
MS-DOS Prompt
C:\vjBook\Project5>jview TestCircleWithConstructors
The area of the circle of radius 5.0 is 78.53975
The area of the circle of radius 1.0 is 3.14159

C:\vjBook\Project5>
```

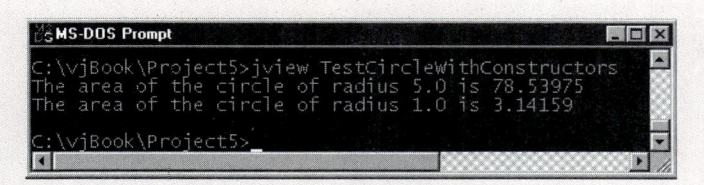

Figure 5.5 *The program constructs two circles of radii 5 and 1, and displays their radii and areas.*

Example Review

The new `Circle` class has two constructors. You can specify a radius or use the default radius to create a `Circle` object. In this example, two objects were created. The constructor `Circle(5.0)` was used to create `myCircle` with a radius of 5.0, and the constructor `Circle()` was used to create `yourCircle` with a default radius of 1.0.

These two objects (`myCircle` and `yourCircle`) have different data but share the same methods. Therefore, you can compute their respective areas by using the `findArea()` method.

You will get a compilation error message indicating duplicate definition of the `Circle` class because the `Circle` class was defined in Examples 5.1 and 5.2. To avoid getting this error, remove the TestCircle.java from the project:

1. Close TestCircle.java in the Text Editor.

2. Right-click at TestCircle.java in the Project Explorer to display its context menu, as shown in Figure 5.6.

3. Choose Remove From Project from the context menu.

TestCircle.java is now removed from Project5, but it is not deleted from the disk. You can restore it to the project program using the following steps:

1. Right-click at Project5 in the Project Explorer to reveal its context menu.

2. Choose Add from the context menu to display the Add Item dialog box, as shown in Figure 5.7.

3. On the Existing page of the Add Item dialog box, select TestCircle.java and click Open to add it into the project.

> **TIP**
> For simplicity, this book places all of each chapter's examples into one project. Normally, however, you should not use the same class names in a single project to avoid naming conflicts.

continues

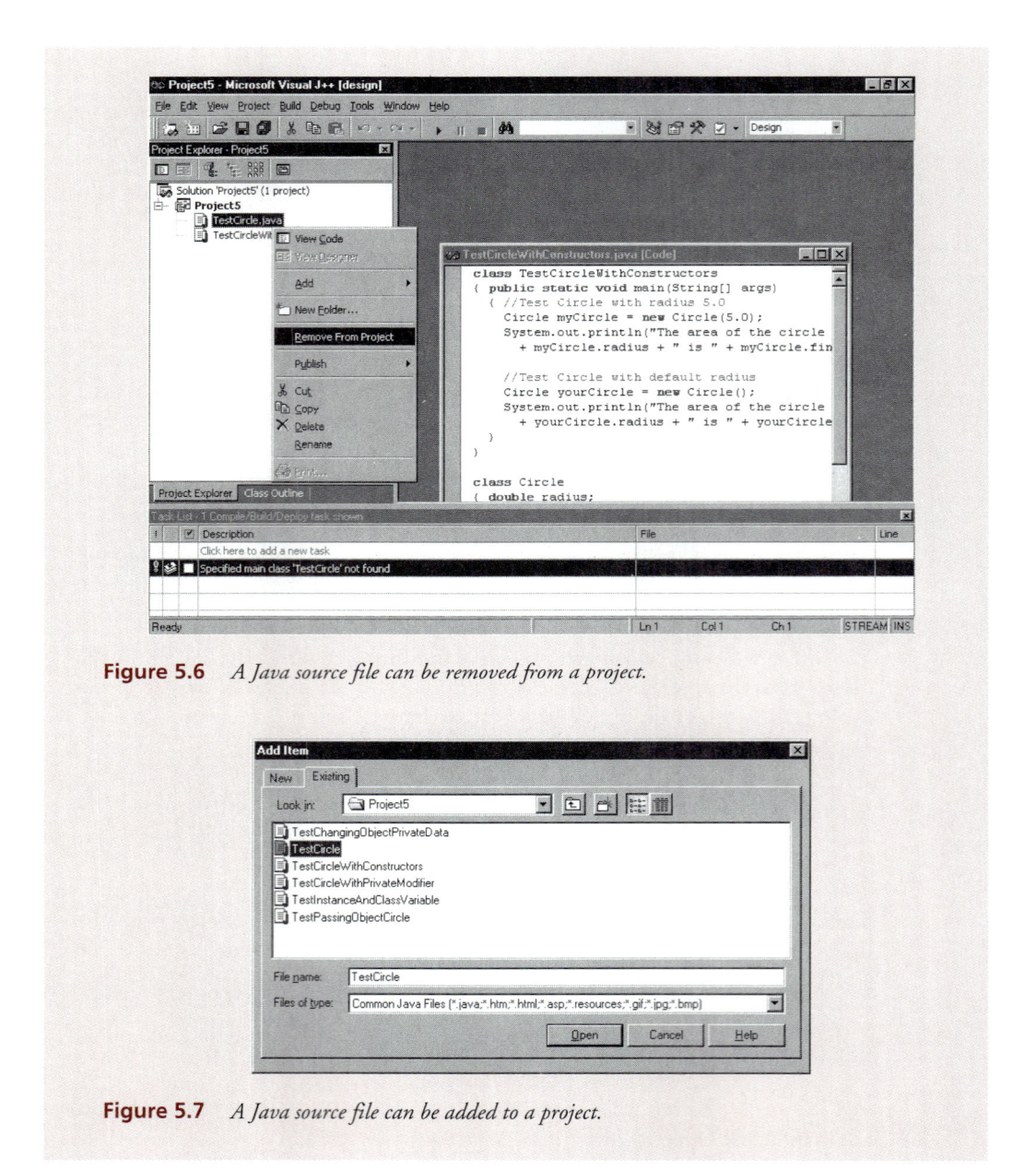

Figure 5.6 *A Java source file can be removed from a project.*

Figure 5.7 *A Java source file can be added to a project.*

Modifiers

Java provides modifiers that control access to data, methods, and classes. The following are frequently used modifiers:

- **static**—Defines data and methods. It represents class-wide information that is shared by all instances of the class. It is discussed in more detail in the sections "Instance Variables and Class Variables" and "Instance Methods and Class Methods," later in this chapter.

- **public**—Defines classes, methods, and data in such a way that all programs can access them.

- **private**—Defines methods and data in such a way that they can be accessed by the declaring class, but not by any other classes.

> **NOTE**
> The modifiers `static` and `private` apply solely to variables or methods. If `public` or `private` is not used, then by default the classes, methods, and data are accessible by any class in the same package.

> **CAUTION**
> The variables associated with modifiers are the members of the class, not local variables inside the methods. Using modifiers inside a method body would cause a compilation error.

More modifiers are described in Chapter 7, "Class Inheritance." Appendix D, "Java Modifiers," contains a table that summarizes all the Java modifiers.

Example 5.3 Using the private Modifier

In this example, private data are used for the radius to prevent clients from modifying the radius of a `Circle` object. A method, `getRadius()`, is added so that clients can retrieve the radius. This type of method is sometimes referred to as a *getter* for obtaining private data values. The output is the same as in the previous example (see Figure 5.5).

```java
// TestCircleWithPrivateModifier.java: Demonstrate private modifier
public class TestCircleWithPrivateModifier
{
  // Main method
  public static void main(String[] args)
  {
    // Create a Circle with radius 5.0
    Circle myCircle = new Circle(5.0);
    System.out.println("The area of the circle of radius "
      + myCircle.getRadius() + " is " + myCircle.findArea());

    // Create a Circle with default radius
    Circle yourCircle = new Circle();
    System.out.println("The area of the circle of radius "
      + yourCircle.getRadius() + " is " + yourCircle.findArea());
  }
}

// Declare class Circle with constructors and private data
public class Circle
{
  private double radius;
```

continues

```java
    // Default constructor
    public Circle()
    {
      radius = 1.0;
    }

    // Construct a circle with a specified radius
    public Circle(double r)
    {
      radius = r;
    }

    // Getter method for radius
    public double getRadius()
    {
      return radius;
    }

    // Find the circle area
    public double findArea()
    {
      return radius*radius*Math.PI;
    }
  }
```

Example Review

If a client program were allowed to change the radius in a circle object, programming errors might occur that would make bugs difficult to detect. In this example, the `private` modifier in the data declaration is used to prevent the client program from changing the circle's properties. As a result, the data in the object can never be changed after its creation.

If you want to access private data from the object, you can provide a getter method to retrieve the data, such as `getRadius()`.

Private data can only be accessed within its defining class. You cannot use `myCircle.radius` in the client program. A compilation error would occur if you attempted to access private data from a client.

The `Circle` class defined in this example will be used in Chapter 7, "Class Inheritance." To make it accessible by classes from a different package, you need to make the `Circle` class `public`. Since two public classes cannot be placed in the same file, the `Circle` class in this example should be placed in a separate file named Circle.java.

Passing Objects to Methods

Just as you can pass the value of variables to methods, you can also pass objects to methods as actual parameters. The following example passes the `myCircle` object as an argument to the method `printCircle()`:

```java
class TestPassingObject
{
  public static void main(String[] args)
```

```java
    {
      Circle myCircle = new Circle(5.0);
      printCircle(myCircle);
    }

    public static void printCircle(Circle c)
    {
      System.out.println("The area of the circle of radius "
        + c.getRadius() + " is " + c.findArea());
    }
  }
```

There are important differences between passing a value of variables of primitive data types and passing objects.

Passing a variable of a primitive type means that the value of the variable is passed to a formal parameter. Changing the value of the local parameter inside the method does not affect the value of the variable outside the method.

Passing an object means that the reference of the object is passed to the formal parameter. Any changes to the local object that occur inside the method body will affect the original object that was passed as the argument. In programming terminology, this is referred to as *pass by reference*.

You will see the difference in the following example.

Example 5.4 Passing Objects as Arguments

In this example, a program is written to pass a `Circle` object to the method `colorCircle()`, which changes the color of the `Circle` object. The output of the program is shown in Figure 5.8.

```java
// TestPassingObject.java: Demonstrate passing objects in methods
public class TestPassingObject
{
  // Main method
  public static void main(String[] args)
  {
    Circle myCircle = new Circle(5.0, "white");
    printCircle(myCircle);
    colorCircle(myCircle, "black");
    printCircle(myCircle);
  }

  // Change the color in the circle c
  public static void colorCircle(Circle c, String color)
  {
    c.color = color;
  }

  // Print circle information
  public static void printCircle(Circle c)
  {
    System.out.println("The area of the circle of radius "
      + c.getRadius() + " is " + c.findArea());
```

continues

```java
      System.out.println("The color of the circle is "
        + c.color);
    }
}

// Circle with a new data field: color
class Circle
{
  private double radius;
  String color;

  // Default constructor
  public Circle()
  {
    radius = 1.0;
    color = "white";
  }

  // Construct a circle with specified radius and color
  public Circle(double r, String c)
  {
    radius = r;
    color = c;
  }

  // Get radius
  public double getRadius()
  {
    return radius;
  }

  // Find circle area
  public double findArea()
  {
    return radius*radius*Math.PI;
  }
}
```

```
C:\vjBook\Project5>jview TestPassingObject
The area of the circle of radius 5.0 is 78.53981633974483
The color of the circle is white
The area of the circle of radius 5.0 is 78.53981633974483
The color of the circle is black

C:\vjBook\Project5>
```

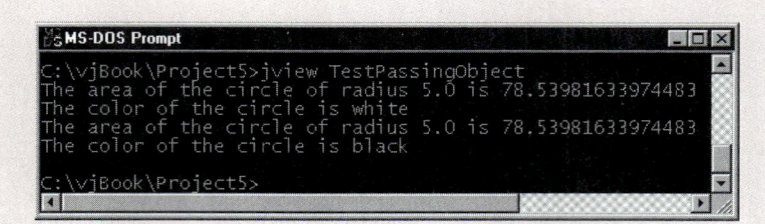

Figure 5.8 *The program passes circle objects as parameters to the method* `printCircle()`, *which displays the radius and the area.*

Example Review

The data field `radius` is private, so it cannot be changed by an assignment like the one that follows:

```
myCircle.radius = newRadius;
```

However, the data field `color` can be changed by this assignment statement:

```
myCircle.color = newColor;
```

In the `main()` method, a `"white"` object, `myCircle`, is created with a radius of 5.0. The method `colorCircle()` is then called with the argument `myCircle` and a new color, `"black"`. This call changes the color field in the `myCircle` object to `"black"` because the object's reference (and not a copy of it) was passed to the method, and that made it possible for the method to change the color value in the object `myCircle`.

Use the `private` modifier for color to prevent the user from accidentally changing the color field. If the color field is private, can it be changed safely? Yes, you can declare a method in the `Circle` class to set a new color. A method of this kind is referred to as a *setter* method. See the following example.

Example 5.5 Using a Setter Method to Change Data in a Private Field

In this example, a program is written to demonstrate a safe way to change the data in an object. The output of the program is shown in Figure 5.9.

```java
// TestChangePrivateData.java: Modify a private data using a
// setter method
public class TestChangePrivateData
{
  // Main method
  public static void main(String[] args)
  {
    Circle myCircle = new Circle(5.0, "white");
    printCircle(myCircle);
    myCircle.setColor("black");   // Modify color field in myCircle
    printCircle(myCircle);
  }

  // Print circle information
  public static void printCircle(Circle c)
  {
    System.out.println("The area of the circle of radius "
      + c.getRadius() + " is " + c.findArea());
    System.out.println("The color of the circle is "
      + c.getColor());
  }
}

// Circle class with a setter method for color
class Circle
{
  private double radius;
  private String color;
```

continues

```java
  // Default constructor
  public Circle()
  {
    radius = 1.0;
    color = "white";
  }

  // Construct a circle with a specified radius
  public Circle(double r)
  {
    radius = r;
  }

  // Construct a circle with radius and color
  public Circle(double r, String c)
  {
    radius = r;
    color = c;
  }

  // Getter method for radius
  public double getRadius()
  {
    return radius;
  }

  // Getter method for color
  public String getColor()
  {
    return color;
  }

  // Setter method for color
  public void setColor(String color)
  {
    this.color = color;
  }

  // Find circle area
  public double findArea()
  {
    return radius*radius*Math.PI;
  }
}
```

```
C:\vjBook\Project5>jview TestChangePrivateData
The area of the circle of radius 5.0 is 78.53981633974483
The color of the circle is white
The area of the circle of radius 5.0 is 78.53981633974483
The color of the circle is black

C:\vjBook\Project5>
```

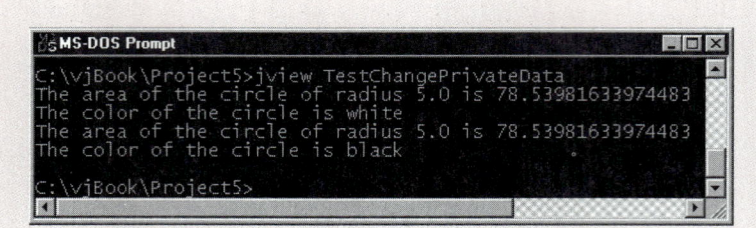

Figure 5.9 *The program views and changes the private data in the object by calling the methods in the object.*

Example Review

The `Circle` class in this example defines the setter method, `setColor()`, which allows you to change the color of the object. A setter is always a `void` type method, whereas a getter has a return type.

This example demonstrates that you can protect the data from mistakes by using a private modifier and providing a setter to change the data safely.

> **TIP**
> Provide getters and setters to the clients only if necessary. Avoid using too many getters and setters in a class.

Instance Variables and Class Variables

The variables `radius` and `color` in the `Circle` class in Example 5.5 are known as *instance variables*. Instance variables belong to each instance of the class; they are not shared among objects of the same class. For example, suppose that you create the following objects:

```
Circle myCircle = new Circle();
Circle yourCircle = new Circle();
```

The data in `myCircle` is independent of the data in `yourCircle`, and is in different memory locations (see Figure 5.10). Changes made to `myCircle`'s data do not affect `yourCircle`'s data, and vice versa.

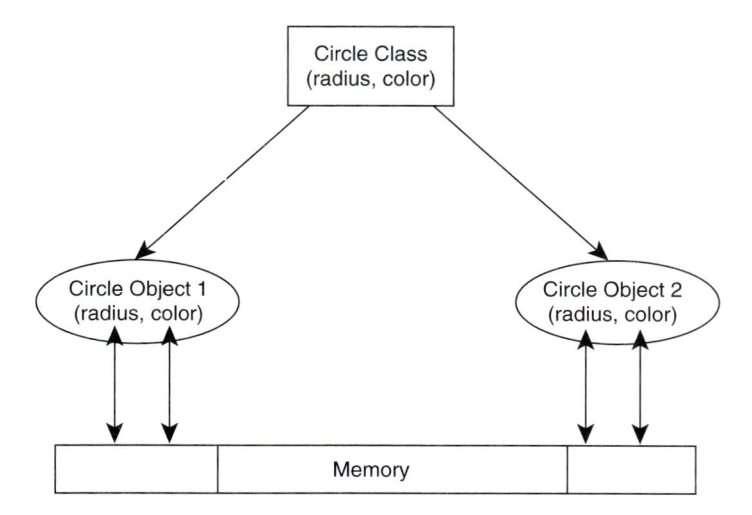

Figure 5.10 *The instance variables, which belong to the instances, have memory storage independent of each other.*

If you want the instances of a class to share data, use *class variables*. Class variables store values for the variables in a common memory location (see Figure 5.11). Because of this common location, all objects of the same class are affected if one object changes the value of a class variable.

To declare a class variable, put the modifier `static` in the variable declaration. Suppose that you want to add weight to circles. Assuming that all circles have the same weight, you can define the class variable as follows:

```
static double weight;
```

The example given below shows the effect of using instance variables and class variables.

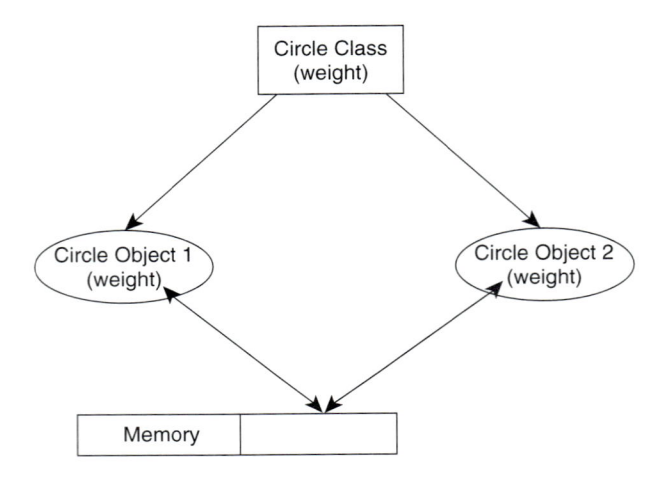

Figure 5.11 *The class variables are shared by all of the instances of the same class.*

Example 5.6 Testing Instance and Class Variables

The program in this example shows you how to use instance and class variables and illustrates the effects of using them. For this program, assume that all of the `Circle` objects are of the same weight. Thus, weight is defined as a class variable. By default, the weight is 1.0.

This program creates two circles (`myCircle` and `yourCircle`). You will see the effect of using instance and class variables after changing data in the circles. The output of the program is shown in Figure 5.12.

```java
// TestInstanceAndClassVariable.java: Demonstrate using instance and
// class variables
public class TestInstanceAndClassVariable
{
  // Main method
  public static void main(String[] args)
```

```java
    {
      // Create and display myCircle
      Circle myCircle = new Circle(4.0, "white", 5.0);
      System.out.print("myCircle:");
      printCircle(myCircle);

      // Create and display yourCircle
      Circle yourCircle = new Circle(5.0, "black", 3.0);
      System.out.print("yourCircle:");
      printCircle(yourCircle);

      // Change the weight in myCircle
      myCircle.weight = 15.5;

      // Display myCircle and yourCircle
      System.out.print("myCircle:");
      printCircle(myCircle);
      System.out.print("yourCircle:");
      printCircle(yourCircle);
    }

    // Print circle information
    public static void printCircle(Circle c)
    {
      System.out.println("radius (" + c.getRadius() +
        "), color (" + c.color +") and weight (" + c.weight + ")");
    }
}

// Circle.java: Circle class with instance and class variables
public class Circle
{
  private double radius;
  String color;
  static double weight;   // Class variable

  // Default constructor
  public Circle()
  {
    radius = 1.0;
    color = "white";
    weight = 1.0;
  }

  // Construct a circle with a specified radius
  public Circle(double r)
  {
    radius = r;
  }

  // Construct a circle with radius and color
  public Circle(double r, String c)
  {
    radius = r;
    color = c;
  }

  // Construct a circle with specified radius, color, and weight
  public Circle(double r, String c, double w)
```

continues

```java
{
  radius = r;
  color = c;
  weight = w;
}

// Getter method for radius
public double getRadius()
{
  return radius;
}

// Getter method for color
public String getColor()
{
  return color;
}

// Setter method for color
public void setColor(String color)
{
  this.color = color;
}

// Find circle area
public double findArea()
{
  return radius*radius*Math.PI;
}
}
```

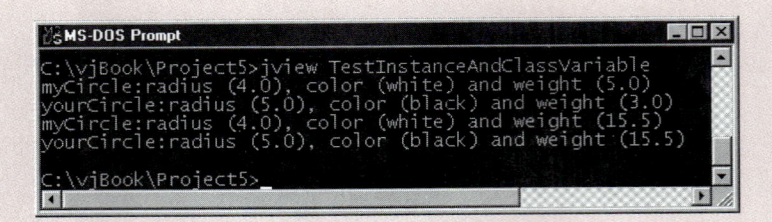

Figure 5.12 *The program uses the instance variables* radius *and* color *as well as the class variable* weight. *All of the objects have the same* weight.

Example Review

What is Math.PI used in the findArea() method? If you remembered the Java naming conventions introduced in the section "Programming Style and Documentation" of Chapter 2, "Java Building Elements," you immediately recognized that PI is a constant and Math is a class name. The Math class comes with the Java system. PI is a constant for π that is defined in the Math class. The Math class is introduced in the section "The Math Class" later in this chapter.

Note that Math.PI was used to access PI, and that c.color in the printCircle() method is used to access color. Math is the class name, and c is an object of the Circle class. To access a constant like PI, you can use either the

`ClassName.CONSTANTNAME` or the `objectName.CONSTANTNAME`. To access an instance variable like `radius`, you need to use `objectName.variableName`.

> **TIP**
> You should define a constant as `static` data that can be shared by all class objects. Do not change the value of a constant.
>
> Variables that describe common properties of objects should be declared as class variables.

Instance Methods and Class Methods

Instance methods belong to instances and can only be applied after the instances are created. They are called by the following:

```
objectName.methodName();
```

The methods defined in the `Circle` class are instance methods. Java supports class methods as well as class variables. Class methods can be called without creating an instance of the class. To define a class method, put the modifier `static` in the method declaration as follows:

```
static returnValueType staticMethod();
```

Examples of class methods are the `readDouble()` and the `readInt()` in the class `MyInput`.

Class methods are called by one of the following syntax:

```
ClassName.methodName();
objectName.methodName();
```

For example, `MyInput.readInt()` is a call that reads an integer from the keyboard. `MyInput` is a class, not an object.

> **TIP**
> A method that does not use instance variables can be defined as a class method. This method can be invoked without creating an object of the class.

> **TIP**
> I recommend that you invoke static variables and methods using ClassName.variable and ClassName.method. This improves readability because the reader can easily recognize the static and class variables and methods.

The Scope of Variables

The *scope of a variable* determines where the variable can be referenced in a program. In general, the scope of a variable is within the block where that variable is declared. You can declare a variable only once in a block. But you can declare the same variable multiple times in different blocks. For example, x is defined twice in the following program:

```
class Foo
{
  int x = 0;
  int y = 0;

  Foo()
  {
  }

  void p()
  {
    int x = 1;
    System.out.println("x = " + x);
    System.out.println("y = " + y);
  }
}
```

What is the printout for `f.p()`, in which `f` is an instance of `Foo`? To answer this question, you need to understand the scope rules that determine how a variable is accessed. The following Java scope rules are based on blocks:

- The scope of a variable is the block in which it is declared. Therefore, a variable declared in block B can be accessed in block B or in the inner block nested inside block B.

- If a variable x originally declared in block B is declared again in a block nested inside block B—block C—the scope of x that is declared in block B excludes the inner block (C).

Therefore, the printout for `f.p()` is 1 (for x) and 0 (for y), based on the following reasons:

- x is declared again in the method `p()` with an initial value of 1.

- y is declared outside the method `p()`, but is accessible inside it.

> **TIP**
> As demonstrated in the example, it is easy to make mistakes. To avoid confusion, do not declare the same variable names.

> **CAUTION**
> Do not declare a variable inside a block and then use it outside the block. Here is an example of a common mistake:
>
> ```
> for (int i=0; i<10; i++)
> {
> }
>
> int j = i;
> ```
>
> The last statement would cause an error because variable `i` is not defined outside of the `for` loop.

> **NOTE**
> A variable declared in a method is referred to as a *local variable*. You cannot declare a local variable twice in a method even though it is declared in nested blocks. For example, the following code would cause a compilation error because `x` is declared in the `for` loop body block, which is nested inside the method body block where another `x` is declared.
>
> ```
> public void xMethod()
> {
>   int x = 1;
>   int y = 1;
>
>   for (int i = 1; i<10; i++)
>   {
>     int x = 0;
>     x += i;
>   }
> }
> ```

Case Studies

By now you have formed some ideas about objects and classes and their programming features. Object-oriented programming is centered on objects; it is particularly involved with getting objects to work together. OOP provides abstraction and encapsulation. You can create the `Circle` object and find the area of the circle without knowing how the area is computed. The object may have many other data and methods.

The details of the implementation are encapsulated and hidden from the client. This is referred to as *class abstraction*. There are many real-life examples that illustrate the OOP concept.

Consider building a computer system, for instance. Your personal computer is made up of many components, such as a CPU, CD-ROM, floppy disk, motherboard, fan, and so on. Each component can be viewed as an object that has properties and methods. To get the components to work together, all you need to know is how each component is used and how it interacts with the others. You don't need to know how it works internally. The internal implementation is encapsulated and hidden from you. You can build a computer without knowing how a component is implemented.

This precisely mirrors the object-oriented approach. Each component can be viewed as an object of the class for the component. For example, you might have a class that models all kinds of fans for use on a computer with properties like fan size, speed, and so on, and methods like start, stop, and so on. A specific fan is an instance of this class with specific property values.

Consider paying a mortgage, for another example. A specific mortgage can be viewed as an object of a mortgage class. Interest rate, loan amount, and loan period are its data properties, and computing monthly payment and total payment are its methods. When you buy a house, a mortgage object is created by instantiating the class with your mortgage interest rate, loan amount, and loan period. You can then use the mortgage methods to easily find the monthly payment and total payment of your loan.

Examples 5.7 and 5.8 are case studies of designing classes.

Example 5.7 Using the Mortgage Class

In this example, a mortgage class named `Mortgage` is created with the following data fields and methods:

Data field:

> `double interest`: Represent interest rate.
>
> `int year`: Represent loan period.
>
> `double loan`: Represent loan amount.

Methods:

> `public double monthlyPay()`
>
> Return the monthly payment of the loan.
>
> `public double totalPay()`
>
> Return the total payment of the loan.

The `Mortgage` class is given below followed by a test program. Figure 5.13 shows the output of a sample run of the program.

```
// Mortgage.java: Encapsulate mortgage information
public class Mortgage
{
  private double interest;
  private int year;
  private double loan;
```

```java
  // Construct a mortgage with specified interest rate, year and
  // loan amount
  public Mortgage(double i, int y, double l)
  {
    interest = i/1200.0;
    year = y;
    loan = l;
  }

  // Getter method for interest
  public double getInterest()
  {
    return interest;
  }

  // Getter method for year
  public double getYear()
  {
    return year;
  }

  // Getter method for loan
  public double getLoan()
  {
    return loan;
  }

  // Find monthly pay
  public double monthlyPay()
  {
    return loan*interest/(1-(Math.pow(1/(1+interest),year*12)));
  }

  // Find total pay
  public double totalPay()
  {
    return monthlyPay()*year*12;
  }
}

// TestMortgageClass.java: Demonstrate using the Mortgage class
public class TestMortgageClass
{
  // Main method
  public static void main(String[] args)
  {
    // Enter interest rate
    System.out.println(
      "Enter yearly interest rate, for example 8.25: ");
    double interestRate = MyInput.readDouble();

    // Enter years
    System.out.println(
      "Enter number of years as an integer, for example 5: ");
    int year = MyInput.readInt();

    // Enter loan amount
    System.out.println(
      "Enter loan amount, for example 120000.95: ");
    double loan = MyInput.readDouble();
```

continues

```java
        // Create Mortgage object
        Mortgage m = new Mortgage(interestRate, year, loan);

        // Display results
        System.out.println("The monthly payment is " + m.monthlyPay());
        System.out.println("The total payment is " + m.totalPay());
    }
}
```

```
C:\vjBook\Project5>jview TestMortgageClass
Enter yearly interest rate, for example 8.25:
6.75
Enter number of years as an integer, for example 5:
15
Enter loan amount, for example 120000.95:
135000
The monthly payment is 1194.6277740429298
The total payment is 215032.99932772736

C:\vjBook\Project5>
```

Figure 5.13 *The program creates a* Mortgage *instance with the interest rate, year, and loan amount, and displays monthly payment and total payment by invoking the methods of the instance.*

Example Review

The Mortgage class contains a constructor, three getters, and the methods for finding monthly payment and total payment. You can construct a Mortgage object by using three parameters: interest rate, number of years, and loan amount. The three getters getInterest(), getYear(), and getLoan() return interest rate, number of years, and loan amount, respectively.

The main class reads interest rate, payment period (in years), and loan amount; creates a Mortgage object; and then obtains the monthly payment and total payment using the instance methods in the Mortgage class.

Since the Mortgage class will be used later in Chapter 10, "Applets and Advanced Graphics," this class is declared public and stored in a separate file.

Example 5.8 Using the *Rational* Class

In this example, a class for rational numbers is defined. The class provides constructors and addition, subtraction, multiplication, and division methods.

A rational number is a number with a numerator and a denominator in the form a/b, where a is a numerator and b is a denominator—for example, 1/3, 3/4, and 10/4.

A rational number cannot have a denominator of 0, but a numerator of 0 is fine. Every integer a is equivalent to a rational number a/1. Rational numbers are used in exact computations involving fractions; for example, 1/3 = 0.33333. . . . This number cannot be precisely represented in floating-point format using data type `double` or `float`. To obtain the exact result, it is necessary to use rational numbers.

There are many equivalent rational numbers; for example, 1/3 = 2/6 = 3/9 = 4/12. For convenience, 1/3 is used in this example to represent all rational numbers that are equivalent to 1/3. The numerator and the denominator of 1/3 have no common divisor except 1, so 1/3 is said to be in lowest terms.

To reduce a rational to its lowest terms, you need to find the greatest common divisor, or GCD, of the absolute values of its numerator and denominator, then divide both numerator and denominator by this value. Here is Euclid's famous algorithm for finding the GCD of two `int` values n and d:

```
t1 = Math.abs(n); t2 = Math.abs(d); // Get absolute value of n and d
r = t1 % t2; // r is the remainder of t1 divided by t2;
while (r != 0)
{
  t1 = t2;
  t2 = r;
  r = t1 % t2;
}

// When r is 0, t2 is the greatest common divisor between t1 and t2
return t2;
```

Based upon the foregoing analysis, the following data and methods are needed in the `Rational` class:

Data field:

`int numerator`: Represent the numerator of the rational number.

`int denominator`: Represent the denominator of the rational number.

Methods:

`public Rational add(Rational secondRational)`

Return the addition of this rational with another.

`public Rational subtract(Rational secondRational)`

Return the subtraction of this rational with another.

`public Rational multiply(Rational secondRational)`

Return the multiplication of this rational with another.

`public Rational divide(Rational secondRational)`

Return the division of this rational with another.

continues

The `Rational` class is presented below, followed by a test program. Figure 5.14 shows the sample run of the program.

```java
// Rational.java: Define a rational number and its associated
// operations such as add, subtract, multiply, and divide
public class Rational
{
  // Data fields for numerator and denominator
  private long numerator = 0;
  private long denominator = 1;

  // Default constructor
  public Rational()
  {
    numerator = 0;
    denominator = 1;
  }

  // Construct a rational with specified numerator and denominator
  public Rational(long n, long d)
  {
    long k = gcd(n,d);
    numerator = n/k;
    denominator = d/k;
  }

  // Find GCD of two numbers
  private long gcd(long n, long d)
  {
    long t1 = Math.abs(n);
    long t2 = Math.abs(d);
    long remainder = t1%t2;

    while (remainder != 0)
    {
      t1 = t2;
      t2 = remainder;
      remainder = t1%t2;
    }

    return t2;
  }

  // Getter method for numerator
  public long getNumerator()
  {
    return numerator;
  }

  public long getDenominator()
  {
    return denominator;
  }

  // Add a rational number to this rational
  public Rational add(Rational secondRational)
  {
    long n = numerator*secondRational.getDenominator() +
      denominator*secondRational.getNumerator();
    long d = denominator*secondRational.getDenominator();
    return new Rational(n, d);
  }
```

```java
  // Subtract a rational number from this rational
  public Rational subtract(Rational secondRational)
  {
    long n = numerator*secondRational.getDenominator()
      - denominator*secondRational.getNumerator();
    long d = denominator*secondRational.getDenominator();
    return new Rational(n, d);
  }

  // Multiply a rational number to this rational
  public Rational multiply(Rational secondRational)
  {
    long n = numerator*secondRational.getNumerator();
    long d = denominator*secondRational.getDenominator();
    return new Rational(n, d);
  }

  // Divide a rational number from this rational
  public Rational divide(Rational secondRational)
  {
    long n = numerator*secondRational.getDenominator();
    long d = denominator*secondRational.numerator;
    return new Rational(n, d);
  }

  // Override the toString() method
  public String toString()
  {
    return numerator + "/" + denominator;
  }
}

// TestRationalClass.java: Demonstrate using the Rational class
public class TestRationalClass
{
  // Main method
  public static void main(String[] args)
  {
    // Create and initialize two rational numbers r1 and r2.
    Rational r1 = new Rational(4,2);
    Rational r2 = new Rational(2,3);

    // Display results
    System.out.println(r1.toString() + " + " + r2.toString() +
      " = " + (r1.add(r2)).toString());
    System.out.println(r1.toString() + " - " + r2.toString() +
      " = " + (r1.subtract(r2)).toString());
    System.out.println(r1.toString() + " * " + r2.toString() +
      " = " + (r1.multiply(r2)).toString());
    System.out.println(r1.toString() + " / " + r2.toString() +
      " = " + (r1.divide(r2)).toString());
  }
}
```

continues

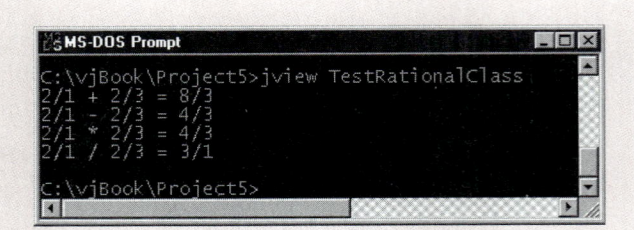

```
MS-DOS Prompt
C:\vjBook\Project5>jview TestRationalClass
2/1 + 2/3 = 8/3
2/1 - 2/3 = 4/3
2/1 * 2/3 = 4/3
2/1 / 2/3 = 3/1
C:\vjBook\Project5>
```

Figure 5.14 *The program creates two instances of the* `Rational` *class and displays their addition, subtraction, multiplication, and division by invoking the instance methods.*

Example Review

The main class creates two rational numbers, `r1` and `r2`, and displays the results of `r1+r2`, `r1-r2`, `r1xr2`, and `r1/r2`.

The rational number is encapsulated in a `Rational` object. Internally, a rational number is represented in its lowest terms; in other words, the greatest common divisor between the numerator and the denominator is 1.

The `gcd()` method is private; it is not intended for a client to use. The `gcd()` method is only for internal use by the `Rational` class.

The `abs(x)` method is defined in the `Math` class that returns the absolute value of `x`.

The equation `r1 + r2` is called in the form of `r1.add(r2)`, in which `add` (which is a method in the object `r1`) returns the following:

```
(r1.numerator*r2.denominator+r1.denominator*r1.numerator)/
   (r1.denominator*r2.denominator).
```

The `numerator` data field of the object `r1` is `r1.numerator` and the `denominator` data field of object `r1` is `r1.denominator`.

The return value of `r1 + r2` is a new Rational object.

The `r.toString()` method returns a string representation of the rational number `r` in the form numerator/denominator.

When you are dividing rational numbers, what happens if the divisor is zero? In this example, the program would terminate with a runtime exception. You need to make sure that this does not occur when you are using the division method. In Chapter 11, you will learn how to deal with the zero divisor case for a `Rational` object.

Packages

A *package* is a collection of classes. It provides a convenient way to organize classes. You can put the classes you have developed into packages and distribute them to other people. Think of packages as libraries to be shared by many users.

The Java language comes with a rich set of packages that you can use to build applications. You used the `java.awt` package in Chapter 1, "Introduction to Java and Visual J++ 6," and you will learn more about Java system predefined packages in the section "Java Application Programmer Interface," later in this chapter.

In this section, you will learn about Java package-naming conventions, and how to create and use packages.

Package-Naming Conventions

Packages are hierarchical, and you can have packages within packages. For example, `java.awt.Button` indicates that `Button` is a class in the package awt, and that awt is a package in the package `java`. You can use levels of nesting to ensure the uniqueness of package names.

Choosing unique names is important because your package may be used on the Internet by other programs. The designers of Java recommend that you use your Internet domain name in reverse order as a package prefix. Since Internet domain names are unique, this avoids naming conflicts. Suppose you want to create a package named `mypackage.io` on the host machine with the Internet domain name `liangy.ipfw.indiana.edu`. To follow the naming convention, you would name the entire package `edu.indiana.ipfw.liangy.mypackage.io`.

Java expects one-to-one mapping of the package name and the file system directory structure. For the package named `edu.indiana.ipfw.liangy.mypackage.io`, you must create a directory as shown in Figure 5.15. In other words, a package is actually a directory that contains the bytecode of the classes.

```
└── edu
    └── indiana
        └── ipfw
            └── liangy
                └── mypackage
                    └── io
```

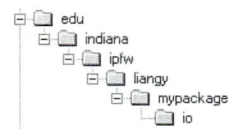

Figure 5.15 *The package* `edu.indiana.ipfw.liangy.mypackge.io` *is mapped to a directory structure in the file system.*

The CLASSPATH Environment Variable

The `edu` directory does not have to be the root directory. In order for Java to know where your package is in the file system, you must modify the environment variable `CLASSPATH` so that it points to the directory in which your package resides. For example, the following line defines three directories in `CLASSPATH`.

    CLASSPATH=.;%CLASSPATH%;C:\vjBook\Project5;

The period (.) indicating the current directory is always in `CLASSPATH`. %CLASSPATH% indicates the original class path. The directory `C:\vjBook\Project5` is in `CLASSPATH` so that you can use the package `edu.ipfw.indiana.mypackage.io` in the program.

You can add as many directories as necessary in `CLASSPATH`. The order in which the directories are specified is the order in which the classes are searched. If you have two classes of the same name in different directories, Java uses the first one it finds.

The `CLASSPATH` variable is set differently in Windows 95/98, and Windows NT, as follows:

- Windows 95/98—Edit autoexec.bat using a text editor, such as Microsoft Notepad.

- Windows NT—Go to the Start button and choose Control Panel, select the System icon, then modify `CLASSPATH` in the environment.

> **Tip**
> You must restart the system for the `CLASSPATH` variable to take effect in Windows 95 or Windows 98. On Windows NT, you have to start a new DOS window.

Putting Classes into Packages

Every class in Java belongs to a package. The class is added to the package when it is compiled. All the classes that you have used so far in this chapter were placed in the directory C:\vjBook\Project5. To put a class in a directory under C:\vjBook\Project5, you need to add the following line as the first noncomment and nonblank statement in the program:

```
package packagename;
```

Example 5.9 Putting classes into packages

This example creates the class `MyInput` and stores it in the package `edu.ipfw.liangy.mypackage.io`.

```java
package edu.indiana.ipfw.liangy.mypackage.io;

import java.io.*;
import java.util.*;

public class MyInput
{
  static private StringTokenizer stok;
  static private BufferedReader br
            = new BufferedReader(new InputStreamReader
                (System.in), 1);

  public static int readInt()
  {
    int i = 0;
    try
    {
      String str = br.readLine();
      StringTokenizer stok = new StringTokenizer(str);
```

```java
        i = new Integer(stok.nextToken()).intValue();
      }
      catch (IOException ex)
      {
        System.out.println(ex);
      }
      return i;
    }

    public static double readDouble()
    {
      double d = 0;
      try
      {
        String str = br.readLine();
        stok = new StringTokenizer(str);
        d = new Double(stok.nextToken()).doubleValue();
      }
      catch (IOException ex)
      {
        System.out.println(ex);
      }
      return d;
    }
  }
```

Example Review

The class must be defined as public for it to be accessed by other programs. The directory for the package is automatically created upon successful compilation in Visual J++. You can see the directory in the Project Explorer for Project5, as shown in Figure 5.16.

Two views are available in Project Explorer when a Java project is selected: Package View and Directory View. The views are designed to make it easier to find elements of a project. You can change the view to Directory View by clicking the Directory View button in Project Explorer or by clicking Directory View on the Project menu. You can change the view to Package View by clicking the Package View button in Project Explorer or by clicking Package View on the Project menu.

> **TIP**
> If you want to put several classes into the package, you have to create separate source files for them, because one file can have only one public class.

continues

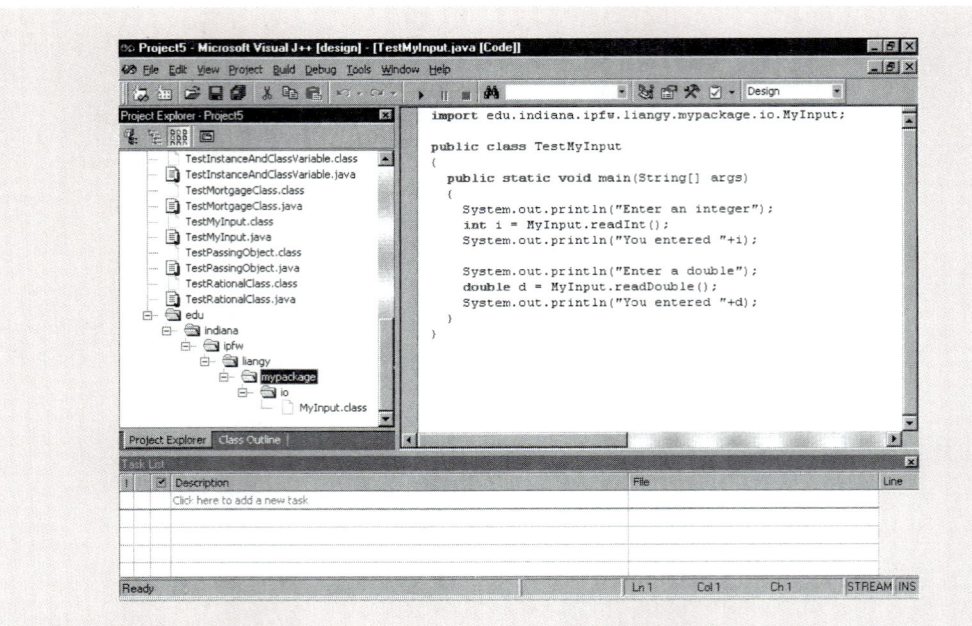

Figure 5.16 *The package* `edu.ipfw.liangy.mypackge.io` *is mapped to a directory structure in the file system.*

Using Packages

To use a class from a package in your program, add an import statement to the top of the program. For example:

```
import edu.indiana.ipfw.liangy.mypackage.io.MyInput;
```

If you wish to use all the classes in a package, indicate this with an asterisk (*). For example:

```
import mypackage.io.*;
```

This statement imports all the classes in the `mypackage.io` package.

Example 5.10 Using your own packages

This example shows a program that uses the `MyInput` class in the `edu.indiana.ipfw.liangy.mypackage.io` package. The program reads data and echo prints it. The output of the program is shown in Figure 5.17.

```java
import edu.indiana.ipfw.liangy.mypackage.io.MyInput;

public class TestMyInput
{
  public static void main(String[] args)
  {
    System.out.println("Enter an integer");
    int i = MyInput.readInt();
    System.out.println("You entered "+i);
```

```
        System.out.println("Enter a double");
        double d = MyInput.readDouble();
        System.out.println("You entered "+d);
    }
}
```

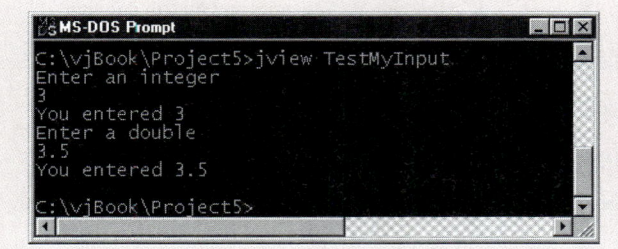

```
C:\vjBook\Project5>jview TestMyInput
Enter an integer
3
You entered 3
Enter a double
3.5
You entered 3.5

C:\vjBook\Project5>
```

Figure 5.17 *The program uses the* MyInput *class to read an* int *value and* double *value, and echo prints the values onscreen.*

Example Review

Before compiling this program, make sure that MyInput is stored in the package mypackage.io. and that the environment variable CLASSPATH is properly set. Also, please note that MyInput is defined as public, so it can be used by classes in other packages.

The program uses the import statement to get the class MyInput. You have used this class in previous examples in this book (such as Example 3.1, "Using Nested if Statements"). You did not use the import statement, however, because it was included in the same directory with these examples.

You cannot import entire packages such as mypackage.*.*. Only one asterisk (*) can be used in the import statement.

> **NOTE**
> Since this program is under Project5 there is no need to set CLASSPATH. To make edu.ipfw.liangy.myPackage.io.MyInput accessible to a project other than Project5, you need to include c:\vjBook\Project5 in the CLASSPATH for that project.

Java Application Programmer Interface

The Java Application Programmer Interface—Java 2 API—consists of numerous classes and interfaces grouped into 15 core packages, such as java.lang, java.awt, java.event, javax.swing, java.applet, java.util, java.io, and java.net. These classes provide an interface that allows Java programs to interact with the system.

- **java.lang**—Contains core Java classes (such as Object, String, System, Math, Number, Character, Boolean, Byte, Short, Integer, Long, Float, and Double). This package is implicitly imported to every Java program.

- `java.awt`—Contains classes for drawing geometrical objects, managing component layout, and creating peer-based (so called heavyweight) components, such as windows, frames, panels, menus, buttons, fonts, lists, and many others.
- `java.awt.event`—Contains classes for handling events in graphics programming.
- `javax.swing`—Contains the lightweight graphical user interface components.
- `java.applet`—Contains classes for supporting applets.
- `java.io`—Contains classes for input and output streams and files.
- `java.util`—Contains many utilities, such as date, calendar, locale system properties, vectors, hashing, and stacks.
- `java.text`—Contains classes for formatting information, such as date and time, in a number of formatting styles based on language, country, and culture.
- `java.net`—Contains classes for supporting network communications.

The `java.lang` is the most fundamental package supporting basic operations. Many of the popular classes in `java.lang` are introduced later in the book. See the following chapters for information on these classes:

- Chapter 6, "Arrays and Strings," introduces classes `java.lang.String`, `java.lang.StringBuffer`, and `java.util.StringTokenizer` for storing and processing strings.
- Chapter 7, "Class Inheritance," covers the numeric wrapper classes, such as `Integer`, and `Double`, in the `java.lang` package.
- Chapter 8, "Getting Started with Graphics Programming," and Chapter 9, "Creating User Interfaces," introduce `java.awt`, `java.awt.event`, and `javax.swing`, which are used for drawing geometrical objects, responding to mouse movements and keyboard entries, and designing graphical user interfaces.
- Chapter 10, "Applets and Advanced Graphics," introduces `java.applet`, which is used to program Java applets.
- Chapter 11, "Exception Handling," discusses using the `java.lang.Throwable` class and its subclasses for exception handling.
- Chapter 12, "Internationalization," introduces `java.util.Date`, `java.util.Calendar`, and `java.text.DateFormat` for processing and formatting date and time based on locale.
- Chapter 13, "Multithreading," focuses on the `java.lang.Thread` class and the `java.lang.Runnable` interface, which are used for multithreading.
- Chapter 14, "Multimedia," addresses the use of multimedia by several classes from `java.awt` and `java.applet`.

- Chapter 15, "Input and Output," discusses the use of `java.io` by input and output streams.
- Chapter 16, "Networking," discusses using `java.net` for network programming.

> **NOTE**
> Once you understand the concept of programming, the most important lesson in Java is learning how to use the API to develop useful programs. The core Java API will be introduced in the next few chapters.

The *Math* Class

The `Math` class contains the methods needed to perform basic mathematical functions. Two useful constants, `PI` and `E` (the base of natural logarithms), are provided in the `Math` class. You have already used `Math.PI` to obtain the π value instead of again declaring that value in the program. The constants are `double` values. Most methods operate on `double` parameters and return `double` values. The methods in the `Math` class can be categorized as trigonometric methods, exponent methods, and miscellaneous methods.

> **NOTE**
> I recommend that you browse through the class definitions for each new class you learn. You can get the class definition from Visual J++ Help or from the JDK on-line documentation at www.javasoft.com.

Trigonometric Methods

The `Math` class contains the following trigonometric methods, among many others:

```
public static double sin(double a)

public static double cos(double a)

public static double tan(double a)

public static double asin(double a)

public static double acos(double a)

public static double atan(double a)
```

Each method has a single `double` parameter, and its return type is `double`. For example, `Math.sin(Math.PI)` returns the trigonometric sine of π.

Exponent Methods

There are four methods related to exponents in the `Math` class:

```
public static double exp(double a)
// Return e raised to the power of a

public static double log(double a)
// Return the natural logarithm of a
```

```
public static double pow(double a, double b)
// Return a raised to the power of b

public static double sqrt(double a)
// Return the square root of a
```

You used the `Math.pow()` method in the mortgage calculation program. Note that the parameter in the `Math.sqrt()` method must not be negative.

The *min()*, *max()*, *abs()*, and *random()* Methods

Other useful methods in the `Math` class are the `min()` and `max()` methods, the `abs()` method, and the random generator `random()`.

The `min()` and `max()` functions return the minimum and maximum numbers between two numbers (`int`, `long`, `float`, or `double`). For example, `max(3.4, 5.0)` returns `5.0`, and `min(3, 2)` returns `2`.

The `abs()` function returns the absolute value of the number (`int`, `long`, `float`, and `double`). For example, `abs(-3.03)` returns `3.03`.

The `Math` class also has a powerful method, `random()`, which generates a random double floating-point number between 0 and 1.

> **NOTE**
> All methods and data in the `Math` class are `static`. They are class methods and class variables. Most methods operate on `double` parameters and return a `double` value.

> **TIP**
> Occasionally, you want to prohibit the user from creating an instance for a class. For example, there is no reason to create an instance from the `Math` class because all of the data and methods are of classwide information. One solution is to define a dummy private constructor in the class. The `Math` class has a private constructor, as follows:
>
> ```
> private Math() { };
> ```
>
> Therefore, the `Math` class cannot be instantiated.

Chapter Summary

In this chapter, you learned how to program using objects and classes. You learned how to define classes, create objects, and use objects. You also learned about modifiers, instance variables, class variables, instance methods, and class methods.

A class is a template for objects. It defines the generic properties of objects and provides methods to manipulate them.

An object is an instance of a class. It is declared in the same way as a primitive type variable. You use the new operator to create an object, and you use the dot (.) operator to access members of that object.

A constructor is a special method that is called when an object is created. Constructors can be overloaded. I recommend that you provide a constructor for each class so that an instance of the class is properly initialized (although it is legal to write a class without constructors).

Modifiers specify how the class, method, and data are accessed. You learned about the public, private, and static modifiers. A public class, method, or data is accessible to all clients. A private method or data is only visible inside the class. You should make instance data private. You can provide a getter method to enable clients to see the data. A class variable or a class method is defined using the keyword static.

The objects are passed to methods using pass by reference. Any changes to the object inside the method affect the object that is passed as the argument.

An instance *variable* is a variable that belongs to an instance of a class. Its use is associated with individual instances. A *class variable* is a variable shared by all instances of the same class.

An instance *method* is a method that belongs to the instance of a class. Its use is associated with individual instances. A *class method* is a method that is called without using instances.

A package is a structure for organizing classes. Java 2 API has numerous classes and interfaces that are organized into 15 core packages. Programming in Java is, in essence, using these classes to build your projects.

The Math class contains methods that perform trigonometric functions (sin, cos, tag, acos, asin, atan), exponent functions (exp, log, pow, sqrt), and some miscellaneous functions (min, max, abs, random). All of these methods operate on double values; min, max, and abs can also operate on int, long, float, and double.

Chapter Review

5.1. Describe the relationship between an object and its defining class. How do you declare a class? How do you declare an object? How do you create an object? How do you declare and create an object in one statement?

5.2. What are the differences between constructors and methods?

5.3. List the modifiers that you learned in this chapter and describe their purposes.

5.4. Describe pass by reference and pass by value. Show the output of the following program:

```java
public class Test
{
  public static void main(String[] args)
  {
    Count myCount = new Count();
    int times = 0;

    for (int i=0; i<100; i++)
      increment(myCount, times);

    System.out.println("count is " + myCount.count);
    System.out.println("times is " + times);
  }

  public static void increment(Count c, int times)
  {
    c.count++;
    times++;
  }
}

class Count
{
  public int count;

  Count(int c)
  {
    count = c;
  }

  Count()
  {
    count = 1;
  }
}
```

5.5. Suppose that the class Foo is defined as follows:

```java
public class Foo
{
  int i;
  static String s;

  void imethod()
  {
  }

  static void smethod()
  {
  }
}
```

Let f be an instance of Foo. Are the following statements correct?

```
System.out.println(f.i);
```

```
System.out.println(f.s);
```

```
f.imethod();
```

```
f.smethod();
```

```
System.out.println(Foo.i);

System.out.println(Foo.s);

Foo.imethod();

Foo.smethod();
```

5.6. What is the output of the following program?

```
public class Foo
{
  static int i = 0;
  static int j = 0;

  public static void main(String[] args)
  {
    int i = 2;
    int k = 3;

    {
      int j = 3;
      System.out.println("i + j is " + i+j);
    }

    k = i + j;
    System.out.println("k is "+k);
    System.out.println("j is "+j);
  }
}
```

5.7. What is wrong with the following program?

```
public class ShowErrors
{
  public static void main(String[] args)
  {
    int i;
    int j;

    j = MyInput.readInt();
    if (j > 3)
      System.out.println(i+4);
  }
}
```

5.8. What is wrong with the following program?

```
public class ShowErrors
{
  public static void main(String[] args)
  {
    for (int i=0; i<10; i++);
      System.out.println(i+4);
  }
}
```

5.9. Describe a package and its relationship with classes.

5.10. What is the recommended naming convention for creating your own packages?

5.11. Your packages can be stored in any directory or subdirectory. How does the compiler know where to find the packages?

Programming Exercises

5.1. Rewrite the `Rational` class with the following additional methods:

```
public boolean lessThan(Rational r)
// Return true if this Rational is < r

public boolean greaterThan(Rational r)
// Return true if this Rational is > r

public boolean equal(Rational r)
// Return true if this Rational is = r

public boolean lessThanOrEqual(Rational r)
// Return true if this Rational is <= r

public boolean greaterThanOrEqual(Rational r)
// Return true if this Rational is >= r

static Rational max(Rational r1, Rational r2)
// Return the larger one
```

Write a client program to test the new `Rational` class.

5.2. Write a program that will compute the following summation series using the `Rational` class from Example 5.8.

$$1/1 + 1/2 + 1/3 + \ldots + 1/n$$
$$1/1 + 1/2 + 1/2^2 + \ldots + 1/2^n$$

5.3. Write a class named `Rectangle` to encapsulate rectangles. The private data fields are `width`, `height`, and `color`. Use `double` for width and height, and `String` for color. The methods are `getWidth()`, `getHeight()`, `getColor()`, and `findArea()`. Suppose that all rectangles have the same color. Use a class variable for color.

```
public class Rectangle
{
  private double width, height;
  static String color;

  public Rectangle(double w, double h, String c)
  {
  }

  public double getWidth()
  {
  }

  public double getHeight()
  {
  }

  public String getColor()
  {
  }

  public double findArea()
  {
  }
}
```

Write a client program to test the class `Rectangle`. In the client program, create two `Rectangle` objects. Assign any widths and heights to the two objects. Assign the first object the color red, and the second, yellow. Display both objects' properties and find their areas.

CHAPTER 6

ARRAYS AND STRINGS

Objectives

- Understand the concept of arrays.
- Learn the steps involved in using arrays—declaring, creating, initializing, and processing arrays.
- Become familiar with sorting and search algorithms.
- Use objects as array elements.
- Become familiar with the copy array utility.
- Learn how to use multidimensional arrays.
- Recognize the difference between arrays and strings.
- Become familiar with the `String` class, the `StringBuffer` class, and the `StringTokenizer` class.
- Know how to use command-line arguments.
- Use the Visual J++ 6.0 debugger.

Introduction

In earlier chapters, you studied examples in which values were overwritten during the execution of a program. In those examples, such as Example 3.4 in Chapter 3, "Control Structures," you did not need to worry about storing former values. However, in some cases, you will have to store a large number of values in memory during the execution of a program. Suppose, for instance, that you want to sort a group of numbers. The numbers must all be stored in memory because later you have to compare each of them with all of the others.

To store the numbers requires declaring variables in the program. It is practically impossible to declare variables for each number. You need an efficient, organized approach. All of the high-level languages—including Java—provide you with a data structure, *array,* which stores a collection of the same types of data. Java treats these arrays as objects.

Strings and arrays are based on similar concepts. A string is a sequence of characters. In many languages, strings are treated as arrays of characters. But in Java, a *string* is used very differently from an array object.

Declaring and Creating Arrays

To use arrays in a program, you need to declare the arrays and the type of elements that could be stored in them. The syntax to declare an array is as follows:

```
datatype[] arrayName;
```

or

```
datatype arrayName[];
```

The following code is an example of this syntax:

```
double[] myList;
```

or

```
double myList[];
```

NOTE
The style `datatype[] arrayName` is preferred. The style `datatype arrayName[]` comes from the C language and was adopted in Java to accommodate C programmers.

Since a Java array is an object, the declaration does not allocate any space in memory for it. You cannot assign elements to an array unless it is already created.

After an array is declared, you can create it by using the `new` operator with the following syntax:

```
arrayName = new datatype[arraySize];
```

Declaration and creation can be combined in one statement, as follows:

```
datatype[] arrayName = new datatype[arraySize];
```

or

```
datatype arrayName[] = new datatype[arraySize];
```

Here is an example of such a statement:

```
double[] myList = new double[10];
```

This statement creates an array of 10 elements of `double` type, as shown in Figure 6.1. The array size must be given to specify the number of elements that could be stored in the array when allocating space for the array. After the array is created, its size cannot be changed.

double[ ] myList = new double[10]

| myList[0] |
| myList[1] |
| myList[2] |
| myList[3] |
| myList[4] |
| myList[5] |
| myList[6] |
| myList[7] |
| myList[8] |
| myList[9] |

Figure 6.1 *The array* `myList` *has 10 elements of* `double` *type and integer indices from 0 to 9.*

Initializing and Processing Arrays

When arrays are created, the elements are assigned the default value of `0` for the numeric primitive data type variables, `'\u0000'` for `char` variables, `false` for `boolean` variables, and `null` for object variables. The array elements are accessed through the index. The array indices are from `0` to `arraySize-1`. In the example in Figure 6.1, `myList` holds 10 `double` values and the indices are from `0` to `9`.

Each element in the array is represented, using the following syntax:

```
arrayName[index];
```

For example, `myList[9]` represents the last element in the array `myList`.

> **NOTE**
> In Java, an array index is always an integer that starts with 0. In many other languages, such as Ada and Pascal, the index can be an integer or another type of value.

> **CAUTION**
> Some languages use parentheses to reference an array element, as in `myList(9)`. But Java uses brackets, as in `myList[9]`.

After an array is created, you can enter values into array elements. For example, see the following loop:

```java
for (int i = 0; i < myList.length; i++)
    myList[i] = (double)i;
```

In this example, `myList.length` returns the array size (10) for `myList`.

> **NOTE**
> The size of an array is denoted by `arrayObject.length`. After an array is created, the `length` data field is assigned a value that denotes the number of elements in the array.
>
> The word `length` is a data field belonging to an array object, not to a method. Therefore, using `length()` would result in an error.

Java has a shorthand notation that creates an array object and initializes it at the same time. The following is an example of its syntax at work:

```java
double[] myList = {1.9, 2.9, 3.4, 3.5};
```

This statement creates the array `myList`, which consists of four elements. Therefore, `myList.length` is 4 and `myList[0]` is 1.9. Note that the `new` operator was not used in the syntax.

When processing array elements, you will often use a `for` loop. Here are the reasons why:

- All of the elements in the array are of the same type and have the same properties. They are even processed in the same fashion—by repeatedly using a loop.

- Since the size of the array is known, it is natural to use a `for` loop.

Example 6.1 Assigning Grades

In this example, a program is written that will read student scores (`int`) from the keyboard, get the best score, and then assign grades based on the following scheme:

Grade is A if score is >= best–10;

Grade is B if score is >= best–20;

Grade is C if score is >= best–30;

Grade is D if score is >= best–40;

Grade is F otherwise.

The program prompts the user to enter the total number of students. Then it prompts the user to enter all of the scores. Finally, it displays grades.

The output of a sample run of the program is shown in Figure 6.2.

```java
// AssigningGrade.java: Assign grade
public class AssigningGrade
{
  // Main method
  public static void main(String[] args)
  {
    int numOfStudents; // The number of students
    int[] scores; // Array scores
    int best = 0; // The best score
    char grade; // The grade

    // Get number of students
    System.out.println("Please enter number of students");
    numOfStudents = MyInput.readInt();

    // Create array scores
    scores = new int[numOfStudents];

    // Read scores and find the best score
    System.out.println("Please enter scores");
    for (int i=0; i<scores.length; i++)
    {
      scores[i] = MyInput.readInt();
      if (scores[i] > best)
        best = scores[i];
    }

    // Assign and display grades
    for (int i=0; i<scores.length; i++)
    {
      if (scores[i] >= best - 10)
        grade = 'A';
      else if (scores[i] >= best - 20)
        grade = 'B';
      else if (scores[i] >= best - 30)
        grade = 'C';
```

continues

```
        else if (scores[i] >= best - 40)
          grade = 'D';
        else
          grade = 'F';

        System.out.println("Student "+i+" score is "+scores[i]+
          " and grade is " + grade);
    }
  }
}
```

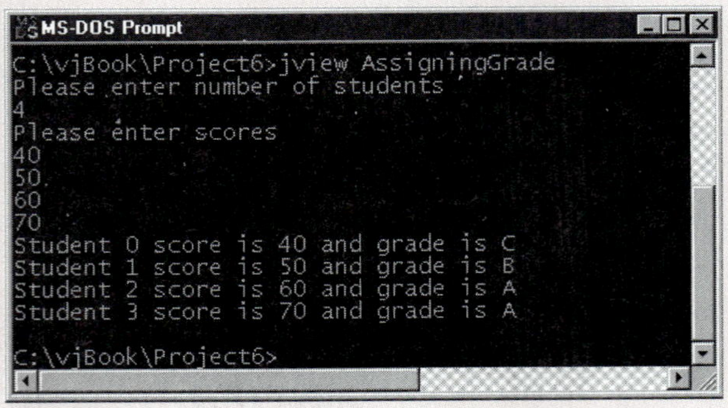

Figure 6.2 *The program receives the number of students and their scores and then assigns grades.*

Example Review

Array `scores[]` is declared in order to store scores. At the time this array is declared, its size is undetermined. After the user enters the number of students into `numOfStudents`, an array with a size of `numOfStudents` is created.

The array is not needed to find the best score, but it is needed to keep all of the scores so that grades can be assigned later on, and it is needed when scores are printed along with the students' grades.

CAUTION
Accessing an array out of bounds is a common programming error. To avoid it, make sure that you do not use an index beyond `arrayObject.length-1`.

Programmers often mistakenly reference the first element in an array with index 1, so that the index of the tenth element becomes 10. This is called the *off-by-one error*.

Sorting Arrays

Sorting is a common task in computer programming. For example, it would be used if you wanted to display the grades from the previous example in alphabetical order. There are many algorithms used for sorting. In this section, a simple, intuitive sorting algorithm, *selection sort,* is introduced.

Suppose that you want to sort a list in nondescending order. Selection sort finds the largest number in the list and places it last. It then finds the largest number remaining and places it last, and so on until the remaining list contains a single number.

Consider the following list:

    2 **9** 5 4 8 1 **6**

If you selected 9 (the largest number) and swapped it with 6 (the last in the list), the new list would be:

    2 **6** 5 4 8 1 **9**

The number 9 would now be in the correct position and thus no longer need to be considered. The list is now:

    2 6 5 4 **8** 1

If you applied selection sort to the remaining numbers, you would select 8 and swap it with 1. The new list would be:

    2 6 5 4 **1 8**

Since the number 8 has been placed in the correct position, it would no longer need to be considered. If you continued the same process, eventually the entire list would be sorted.

The algorithm can be described as follows:

```
for (int i=list.length-1; i>=1; i--)
{
  select the largest element in list[1..i];
  swap the largest with list[i], if necessary;
  //list[i] is in place. The next iteration apply on list[1..i-1]
}
```

The code is given in the following example. The `selectionSort()` method in this program works only for a list of `double` values. In Chapter 7, "Class Inheritance," you will learn the techniques for writing a generic method that will sort elements of any type in a list.

Example 6.2 Using Arrays in Sorting

In this example, the `selectionSort()` method is used to write a program that will sort a list of double floating-point numbers. The output of the program is shown in Figure 6.3.

```
// TestSelectionSort.java: Sort numbers using selection sort
public class TestSelectionSort
{
  // Main method
  public static void main(String[] args)
```

continues

```java
{
  // Initialize the list
  double[] myList = {5.0, 4.4, 1.9, 2.9, 3.4, 3.5};

  // Print the original list
  System.out.println("My list before sort is: ");
  printList(myList);

  // Sort the list
  selectionSort(myList);

  // Print the sorted list
  System.out.println(" ");
  System.out.println("My list after sort is: ");
  printList(myList);
}

// The method for printing numbers
static void printList(double[] list)
{
  for (int i=0; i<list.length; i++)
    System.out.print(list[i]);
  System.out.println(" ");
}

// The method for sorting the numbers
static void selectionSort(double[] list)
{
  double currentMax;
  int currentMaxIndex;

  for (int i=list.length-1; i>=1; i—)
  {
    // Find the maximum in the list[0..i]
    currentMax = list[i];
    currentMaxIndex = i;

    for (int j=i-1; j>=0; j—)
    {
      if (currentMax < list[j])
      {
        currentMax = list[j];
        currentMaxIndex = j;
      }
    }

    // Swap list[i] with list[currentMaxIndex] if necessary;
    if (currentMaxIndex != i)
    {
      list[currentMaxIndex] = list[i];
      list[i] = currentMax;
    }
  }
}
}
```

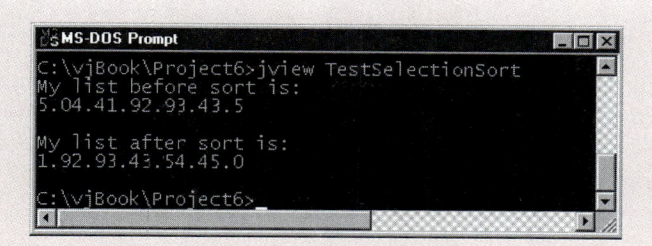

Figure 6.3 *The program invokes* `selectionSort()` *in order to sort a list of* `double` *values.*

Example Review

An array `myList` of length 6 was created. Its initial values are listed in the following single statement:

```
double[] myList = {5.0, 4.4, 1.9, 2.9, 3.4, 3.5};
```

The `selectionSort(double[] list)` method sorts any array of double elements. The method is implemented with a nested `for` loop. The outer loop (with the loop control variable `i`) is iterated in order to find the largest element in the list—which ranges from `list[0]` to `list[i]`—and exchange it with the current last element, `list[i]`.

The variable `i` is initially `list.length-1`. After each iteration of the outer loop, `list[i]` is in the right place. Eventually, all the elements are put in the right place; therefore, the whole list is sorted.

Searching Arrays

Searching is the process of looking for a specific element in the array—for example, discovering whether a certain score is included in a list of scores. Searching, like sorting, is a common task in computer programming. There are many algorithms and data structures devoted to searching. In this section, two commonly used approaches are discussed, *linear search* and *binary search*.

The Linear Search Approach

The linear search approach compares the key element, `key`, with each element in the array `list[]`. The method continues to do so until the key matches an element in the list or the list is exhausted without a match being found. If a match is made, the linear search returns the index of the element in the array that matches the key. If no match is found, the search returns -1. The algorithm can be simply described as follows:

```
for (int i=0; i<list.length; i++)
{
  if (key == list[i])
    return i;
}

return -1;
```

The example given below demonstrates a linear search.

Example 6.3 Testing Linear Search

In this example, a program is written that will implement and test the linear search method. This program creates an array of 10 random elements of int type and then displays it. The program prompts the user to enter a key for testing linear search. The output of a sample run of the program is shown in Figure 6.4.

```java
// TestLinearSearch.java: Search for a number in a list
public class TestLinearSearch
{
  // Main method
  public static void main(String[] args)
  {
    int[] list = new int[10];

    // Create the list randomly and display it
    System.out.print("The list is  ");
    for (int i=0; i<list.length; i++)
    {
      list[i] = (int)(Math.random()*10);
      System.out.print(list[i]+"  ");
    }
    System.out.println(" ");

    // Prompt the user to enter a key
    System.out.print("Enter a key  ");
    int key = MyInput.readInt();
    int index = linearSearch(key, list);
    if (index != -1)
      System.out.println("The key is found in index "+index);
    else
      System.out.println("The key is not found in the list");
  }

  // The method for finding a key in the list
  public static int linearSearch(int key, int[] list)
  {
    for (int i=0; i<list.length; i++)
      if (key == list[i])
        return i;
    return -1;
  }
}
```

```
C:\vjBook\Project6>jview TestLinearSearch
The list is  6 6 7 6 1 6 8 8 4 2
Enter a key  7
The key is found in index 2

C:\vjBook\Project6>jview TestLinearSearch
The list is  1 3 0 2 7 3 9 5 5 8
Enter a key  4
The key is not found in the list

C:\vjBook\Project6>
```

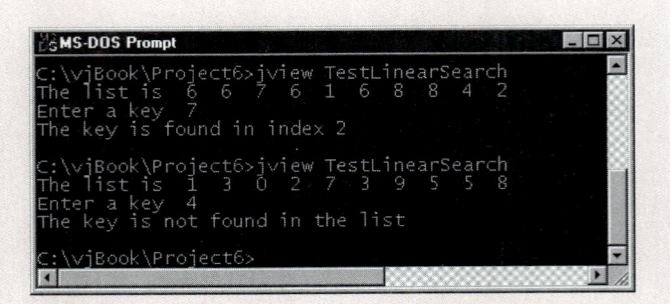

Figure 6.4 *The program uses linear search to find a key in a list of* int *elements.*

> **Example Review**
>
> `Math.random()` generates a random `double` value between 0 and 1. Therefore, `(int)(Math.random()*10)` is a random integer value between 0 and 10.
>
> In case of a match, the algorithm returns the index of the first element in the array that matches the key. In case of no match, the algorithm returns `-1`.

The linear search method compares the key with each element in the array. The elements in the array can be in any order. On average, the algorithm will have to compare half of the elements in an array. Since the execution time of a linear search increases linearly as the number of array elements increases, linear search is inefficient for a large array.

The Binary Search Approach (Optional)

Binary search is the other common search approach. For binary search to work, the array must already be in the right order. Without loss of generality, assume that the array is in nondescending order. The binary search first compares the key with the element in the middle of the array. Consider the following three cases:

- If the key is less than the middle element, you only need to search the key in the first half of the array.
- If the key is equal to the middle element, the search ends with a match.
- If the key is greater than the middle element, you only need to search the key in the second half of the array.

Clearly, the binary search method eliminates half of the array after each comparison. Suppose that the array has n elements. For convenience, let n be a power of 2. After the first comparison, there are n/2 elements left for further search; after the second comparison, there are (n/2)/2 elements left for further search. After the kth comparison, there are $n/2^k$ elements left for further search. When k = $\log_2 n$, only one element is left in the array, and you only need one more comparison. Therefore, in the worst case, you need $\log_2 n+1$ comparisons to find an element in the sorted array when using binary search. For a list of 1,024 (2^{10}) elements, binary search requires only 11 comparisons in the worst case.

The array being searched shrinks after each comparison. Let `low` and `up` denote the first index and the last index, respectively, of the array that is currently being searched. Initially, `low` is `0` and `up` is `list.length-1`. Let `binarySearch(int key, int[] list, int low, int up)` denote the method that finds the key in the list that has the specified `low` index and `up` index. The algorithm can be described recursively as follows:

```
public static int binarySearch(int key, int[] list, int low, int up)
{
  if (low > up)
    the list has been searched without a match, return -1;
```

```
    // Find mid, the index of the middle element in list[low..up]
    int mid = (low+up)/2;
    if (key < list[mid])
      // Search in list[low..mid-1] recursively.
      return binarySearch(key, list, low, mid-1);
    else if (key == list[mid])
      // A match is found
      return mid;
    else if (key > list[mid])
      // Search in list[mid+1..up] recursively.
      return binarySearch(key, list, mid+1, up);
}
```

The next example demonstrates the binary search approach.

Example 6.4 Testing Binary Search

In this example, a program is written that will implement and test the binary search method. The program first creates an array of 10 elements of `int` type. It displays this array and then prompts the user to enter a key for testing binary search. The output of sample runs of the program is shown in Figure 6.5.

```java
// TestBinarySearch.java: Search a key in a sorted list
public class TestBinarySearch
{
  // Main method
  public static void main(String[] args)
  {
    int[] list = new int[10];

    // Create a sorted list and display it
    System.out.print("The list is  ");
    for (int i=0; i<list.length; i++)
    {
      list[i] = 2*i+1;
      System.out.print(list[i]+"  ");
    }
    System.out.println(" ");

    // Prompt the user to enter a key
    System.out.print("Enter a key  ");
    int key = MyInput.readInt();
    int index = binarySearch(key, list);
    if (index != -1)
      System.out.println("The key is found in index "+index);
    else
      System.out.println("The key is not found in the list");
  }

  // Use binary search to find the key in the list
  public static int binarySearch(int key, int[] list)
  {
    int low = 0;
    int up = list.length-1;
    return binarySearch(key, list, low, up);
  }

  // Use binary search to find the key in the list between
  // list[low] list[up]
  public static int binarySearch(int key, int[] list, int low,
    int up)
```

```
    {
      if (low > up)  // The list has been exhausted without a match
        return -1;

      int mid = (low+up)/2;
      if (key < list[mid])
        return binarySearch(key, list, low, mid-1);
      else if (key == list[mid])
        return mid;
      else if (key > list[mid])
        return binarySearch(key, list, mid+1, up);

      return -1;
    }
}
```

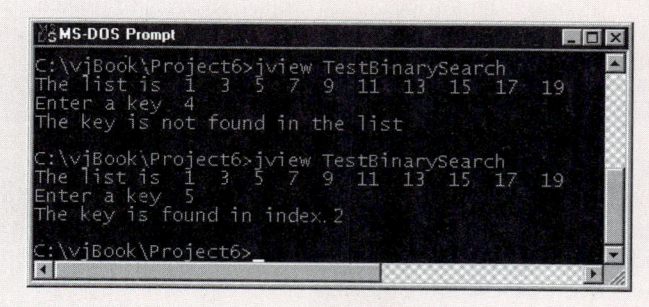

Figure 6.5 *The program uses binary search to find a key in a list of* `int` *elements.*

Example Review

There are two overloaded methods named `binarySearch` in the program: `binarySearch(int key, int[] list)` and `binarySearch(int key, int[] list, int low, int up)`. The first method finds a key in the whole list. The second method finds a key in the list with index from `low` to `up`.

The first `binarySearch()` method passes the initial array with `low = 0` and `up = list.length-1` to the second method. The second method is invoked recursively to find the key in an ever-shrinking subarray. It is a common design technique in recursive programming to choose a second method that can be called recursively.

The `return` statement in the last line of the second `binarySearch` is never executed. Its sole purpose is to fool the Java compiler. The Java compiler requires a `return` statement that is inside the method body but not embedded in an inner block. All of the other `return` statements in the second method are embedded in the `if` statements, which are inner blocks in the method.

> **NOTE**
> Linear search is useful for finding an element in a small array or an unsorted array, but it is inefficient for large arrays. If the array is sorted, binary search is more efficient.

Array of Objects

In the preceding examples, arrays of primitive type elements were created. It is also possible to create arrays of objects. For example, the following statement declares and creates an array of 10 `Circle` objects:

```
Circle[] circleArray = new Circle[10];
```

To initialize the `circleArray`, you can use a `for` loop like the one that follows:

```
for (int i=0; i<circleArray.length; i++)
{
  circleArray[i] = new Circle();
}
```

The next example demonstrates how to use an array of objects.

Example 6.5 Adding an Array of Rationals

In this example, a program is written that will summarize an array of rational numbers. The program creates `rationalArray`—an array composed of 10 `Rational` objects—and initializes it with random values, then invokes the `sum()` method to add all the rational numbers in the list. The output of a sample run of the program is shown in Figure 6.6.

```java
// TestArrayOfObjects.java: Pass an array of objects to the method
public class TestArrayOfObjects
{
  // Main method
  static public void main(String[] args)
  {
    // Create and initialize rationalArray
    Rational[] rationalArray = new Rational[10];

    // Initialize rationalArray
    System.out.println("The Rational numbers are ");
    for (int i=0; i<rationalArray.length; i++)
    {
      rationalArray[i] = new Rational(
        (int)(Math.random()*10), 1+(int)(Math.random()*10));
      System.out.print(rationalArray[i] + " ");
    }

    System.out.println(" ");

    // Compute and display the result
    System.out.println("the sum of the rational numbers is " +
      sum(rationalArray));
  }

  // Add an array of Rationals
  public static Rational sum(Rational[] rationalArray)
  {
    // Initialize sum
    Rational sum = new Rational(0, 1);
```

```
      // Add Rational elements to sum
      for (int i = 0; i < rationalArray.length; i++)
        sum = sum.add(rationalArray[i]);

      return sum;
    }
  }
```

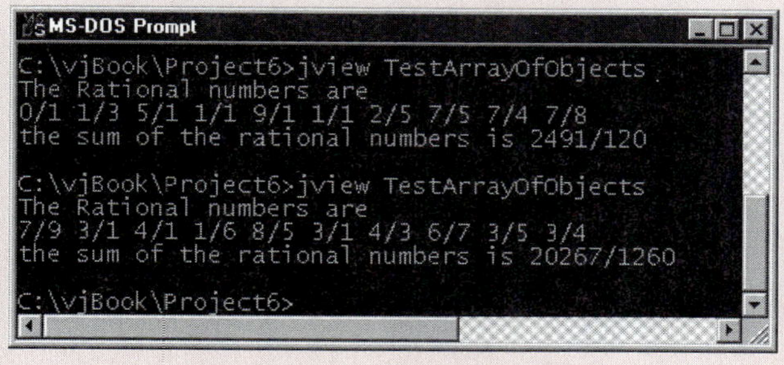

```
MS-DOS Prompt
C:\vjBook\Project6>jview TestArrayOfObjects
The Rational numbers are
0/1 1/3 5/1 1/1 9/1 1/1 2/5 7/5 7/4 7/8
the sum of the rational numbers is 2491/120

C:\vjBook\Project6>jview TestArrayOfObjects
The Rational numbers are
7/9 3/1 4/1 1/6 8/5 3/1 4/3 6/7 3/5 3/4
the sum of the rational numbers is 20267/1260

C:\vjBook\Project6>
```

Figure 6.6 *The program passes an array of* `Rational` *objects to the method* `sum()`, *which returns the sum of all the numbers in the array.*

Example Review

The program creates an array of 10 `Rational` objects and passes it to the `sum()` method that adds all the rational numbers in the array `Rational[]` and returns the sum.

The `Rational` class was introduced in the "Case Studies" section of Chapter 5, "Programming with Objects and Classes." You need to add c:\vjBook\Project5 to the classpath environment in Project6.

The rational numbers were randomly generated using the `Math.random()` method. To avoid having a denominator of 0, 1 is purposely added to the denominator.

Copying Arrays

Often, in a program, you need to duplicate an array or a part of an array. In such cases you could attempt to use the assignment statement (=), as follows:

```
newList = list;
```

It seems to work fine. But if you ran the following program, you would discover that it does not work. The example explains the reason.

Example 6.6 Copying Arrays

In this example, you will see that a simple assignment cannot copy arrays in the following program. The program simply creates two arrays and attempts to copy one to the other, using an assignment statement. The output of the program shown in Figure 6.7 demonstrates that the two arrays reference the same object after the attempted copy.

```java
// TestCopyArray.java: Demonstrate copying arrays
public class TestCopyArray
{
  // Main method
  public static void main(String[] args)
  {
    // Create an array and assign values
    int[] list = {0, 1, 2, 3, 4 ,5};

    // Create an array with default values
    int[] newList = new int[list.length];

    // Assign array list to array newList
    newList = list;

    // Display list and newList
    System.out.println("Before modifying list");
    printList("list is ", list);
    printList("newList is", newList);

    // Modify list
    for (int i=0; i<list.length; i++)
      list[i] = 0;

    // Display list and newList after modifying list
    System.out.println("After modifying list");
    printList("list is ", list);
    printList("newList is", newList);
  }

  // The method for printing a list
  public static void printList(String s, int[] list)
  {
    System.out.print(s + " ");
    for (int i=0; i<list.length; i++)
      System.out.print(list[i] + " ");

    System.out.print('\n');
  }
}
```

CHAPTER 6   ARRAYS AND STRINGS

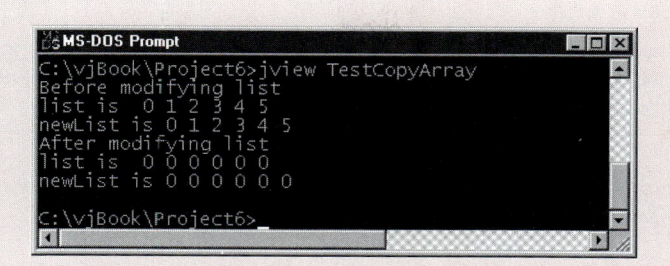

```
C:\vjBook\Project6>jview TestCopyArray
Before modifying list
list is   0 1 2 3 4 5
newList is 0 1 2 3 4 5
After modifying list
list is   0 0 0 0 0 0
newList is 0 0 0 0 0 0

C:\vjBook\Project6>
```

Figure 6.7 *When you are using an assignment statement to copy a source array to a target array, both arrays refer to the same memory location, just as objects do when they are copied using assignment statements.*

Example Review

The program creates two arrays, `list` and `newList`; assigns `list` to `newList`; and displays both `list` and `newList`. The program then changes the value in `list` and redisplays `list` and `newList`. You may have noticed that the `newList`'s value was also changed. This occurs because the assignment statement `newList = list` makes `newList` point to `list`'s memory location, as shown in Figure 6.8. Conversely, if you change the value in `newList`, `list` will see the same change.

After `list` is assigned to `newList`, the former memory space for `newList` becomes useless. The Java Virtual Machine automatically collects it so that the space can be reused.

The `print('\n')` method in the `printList()` method prints the new line character (`'\n'`), which causes the next `print` statement to print from a new line.

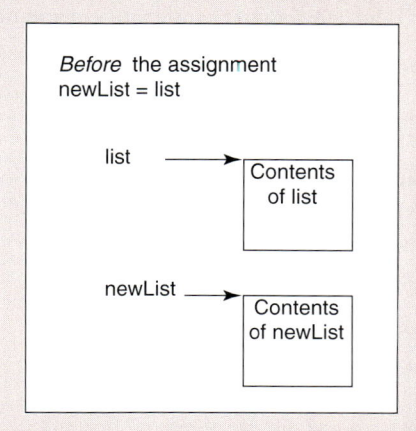

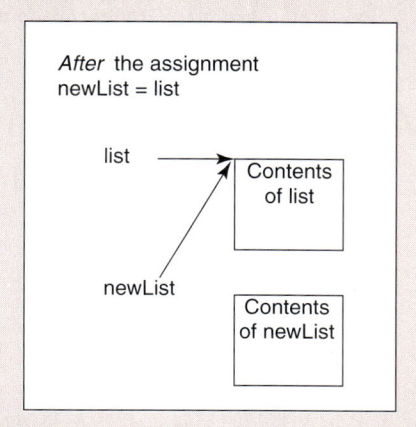

Figure 6.8 *Before the assignment statement,* `list` *and* `newList` *point to separate memory locations. After the assignment, the reference of the* `list` *array is passed to* `newList`.

201

> **NOTE**
> In Java, you can copy primitive data type variables using assignment statements, but not objects, such as arrays. Assigning one object to another object makes both objects point to the same memory location.

There are two ways to copy arrays: using a loop to copy individual elements and using the `arraycopy()` method.

One way to copy arrays is to write a loop that will copy every element, from the source array to the corresponding element in the target array. The following code, for instance, copies the `sourceArray` to the `targetArray`:

```java
for (int i = 0; i < sourceArrays.length; i++)
    targetArray[i] = sourceArray[i];
```

Another approach is to use the `arraycopy()` method in the `java.lang.System` class to copy arrays instead of using a loop. The syntax for `arraycopy` is as follows:

```java
arraycopy(sourceArray, src_pos, targetArray, tar_pos, length);
```

The parameters `src_pos` and `tar_pos` indicate the starting position in `sourceArray` and in `targetArray`, respectively. The number of elements copied from `sourceArray` to `targetArray` is indicated by `length`. For example, you can rewrite the loop using the following statement:

```java
int[] sourceArray = {2, 3, 1, 5, 10};
int[] targetArray = new int[sourceArray.length];
System.arraycopy(sourceArray, 0, targetArray, 0, sourceArray.length);
```

The `arraycopy()` method does not allocate memory space for the target array. The target array must already be created with its memory space allocated. After the copying takes place, `targetArray` and `sourceArray` have independent memory locations.

Multidimensional Arrays

Thus far, you have used one-dimensional arrays to model a linear collection of elements. To represent a matrix or a table, you can use a two-dimensional array. In Java, a two-dimensional array is declared as an array of array objects. For example, you can use the following code to declare and create a 5 by 5 matrix:

```java
int[][] matrix = new int[5][5];
```

or

```java
int matrix[][] = new int[5][5];
```

You can also use a shorthand notation to declare and initialize a two-dimensional array. For example,

```
int[][] matrix =
{
  {1, 2, 3, 4, 5},
  {2, 3, 4, 5, 6),
  {3, 4, 5, 6, 7),
  {4, 5, 6, 7, 8},
  {5, 6, 7, 8, 9}
};
```

Two subscripts are used in a two-dimensional array, one for row, and the other for the column. To assign a value 7 to a specific element at row 2 and column 0, you can use the following:

```
matrix[2][0] = 7;
```

Occasionally, you will need to represent multidimensional data structures. In Java, you can create n dimensional arrays for any integer n, as long as your computer has sufficient memory to store the array.

Example 6.7 Adding Two Matrices

In this example, a program is written that uses two-dimensional arrays to create two matrices. The program then adds the two matrices. The output of the program is shown in Figure 6.9.

```java
// TestMatrixAddition.java: Add two matrices
public class TestMatrixAddition
{
  // Main method
  public static void main(String[] args)
  {
    // Create two matrices as two dimensional arrays
    int[][] matrix1 = new int[5][5];
    int[][] matrix2 = new int[5][5];

    // Assign random values to matrix1 and matrix2
    for (int i=0; i<matrix1.length; i++)
      for (int j=0; j<matrix1[i].length; j++)
      {
        matrix1[i][j] = (int)(Math.random()*1000);
        matrix2[i][j] = (int)(Math.random()*1000);
      }

    // Print matrices
    printMatrix(matrix1);
    System.out.println();
    printMatrix(matrix2);
    System.out.println();
    System.out.println();

    // Add two matrics
    int[][] resultMatrix = new int[5][5];
    resultMatrix = addMatrix(matrix1, matrix2);

    // Print the resulting matrix
    printMatrix(resultMatrix);
  }
```

continues

```java
// The method for adding two matrices
public static int[][] addMatrix(int[][] m1, int[][] m2)
{
  int[][] result = new int[m1.length][m1[0].length];
  for (int i=0; i<m1.length; i++)
    for (int j=0; j<m1[i].length; j++)
      result[i][j] = m1[i][j] + m2[i][j];

  return result;
}

// Print a matrix
public static void printMatrix(int[][] m)
{
  for (int i=0; i<m.length; i++)
  {
    for (int j=0; j<m[0].length; j++)
      System.out.print(" "+m[i][j]);
    System.out.println();
  }
}
```

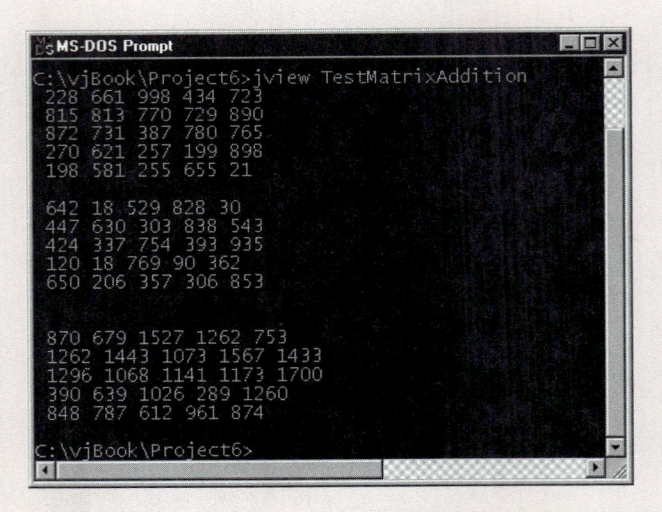

Figure 6.9 *The program adds two matrices that are represented in two-dimensional arrays.*

Example Review

The statement `int[][] matrix1 = new int[5][5]` declares and creates a 5 by 5 matrix.

Nested `for` loops are often used to process multidimensional array elements. The matrices `matrix1` and `matrix2` are initialized by using a nested `for` loop with random values.

The `addMatrix(int[][] m1, int[][] m2)` method adds `m1` and `m2` and returns the result matrix.

The *String* Class

The `java.lang.String` class represents character strings. You have already used string literals, such as the parameters in the `println()` method. The Java compiler actually converts the string literal into a string object and passes it to `println()`.

To create a string explicitly, use a syntax like this:

```
String newString = new String(s);
```

The component s is a sequence of characters enclosed inside double quotes. For example, the following statement creates a `String` object `message` for the string literal `"Welcome to Java!"`:

```
String message = new String("Welcome to Java!");
```

Since strings are frequently used, Java provides a simple notation for creating a string like this:

```
String message = "Welcome to Java!";
```

String Comparisons

Often, in a program, you need to compare the contents of two strings. You might attempt to use the == operator as follows:

```
if (string1 == string2)
  System.out.println("string1 and string2 are the same object");
else
  System.out.println("string1 and string2 are different objects");
```

However, the == operator only checks whether `string1` and `string2` refer to the same object; it does not tell you whether `string1` and `string2` contain the same contents when they are different objects. Therefore, you cannot use the == operator to find out whether two string variables have the same contents. Instead, you should use the `equals()` method for an equality comparison of the contents of objects. The code given below, for instance, can be used to compare two strings.

```
if (string1.equals(string2))
  System.out.println("string1 and string2 have the same contents");
else
  System.out.println("string1 and string2 are not equal");
```

The `compareTo()` method can also be used to compare two strings. For example, see the following code:

```
s1.compareTo(s2)
```

The method returns the value 0 if s1 is equal to s2, a value less than 0 if s1 is lexicographically less than s2, and a value greater than 0 if s1 is lexicographically greater than s2.

The actual value returned depends on the offset of the first two distinct characters in s1 and s2 from left to right. For example, suppose s1 is `"abc"` and s2 is `"abe"`, and `s1.compareTo(s2)` returns -2. The first two characters (a versus a) from s1 and s2 are compared. Because they are equal, the second two characters (b versus b) are compared. Because they are also equal, the third characters (c versus e) are compared. Since the character c is 2 less than e, the comparison returns -2.

> **CAUTION**
> Syntax errors will occur if you compare strings by using comparison operators, such as >, >=, <, <=, or !=. Instead, you have to use s1.compareTo(s2).

The `equals()` method returns `true` if two strings are equal, and `false` if they are not equal. The `compareTo()` method returns `0`, a positive integer, or a negative integer, depending on whether a string is equal to, greater than, or less than the other string.

The `String` class also provides `equalsIgnoreCase()` and `regionMatches()` methods for comparing strings. The `equalsIgnoreCase()` method ignores the case of the letters when determining whether two strings are equal. The `regionMatches()` method compares portions of two strings for equality. For more information, please refer to the JDK documentation.

> **NOTE**
> Strings are used frequently in programming. To improve efficiency and save memory, Java virtual machine makes a great effort to identify the identical strings and store them in the same memory location, but Java does not guarantee that all of the same strings are stored in the same memory location. Therefore, you must use the `equals()` method to test whether two strings have the same contents, and the `==` operator to test whether the two strings have the same references (that is, point to the same memory location).

String Concatenation

You can use the `concat()` method to concatenate two strings. For example, the following statement concatenates strings s1 and s2 into s3:

```
String s3 = s1.concat(s2);
```

Since string concatenation is heavily used in programming, Java provides a convenient way to concatenate strings. You can use the plus sign to concatenate two or more strings. For example, the following code combines the strings `message`, `" and "`, and `"HTML!"` into one string:

```
String myString = message + " and " + "HTML!";
```

Recall that you have used the + sign to concatenate a number with a string in the `println()` method. A number is converted into a string and then concatenated.

Substrings

`String` is an immutable class. After a string is created, its value cannot be changed individually. For example, you cannot change `"Java"` in `message` to `"HTML"`. So what do you do if you need to change the `message` string? You assign a new string to `message`. The following code is an example:

```
message = "Welcome to HTML!";
```

As an alternative, you can use the `substring()` method. You extract a substring from a string by using the `substring()` method in the `String` class as follows:

```
String message = message.substring(0,10) + "HTML!";
```

The string `message` now becomes `"Welcome to HTML!"`. The first character in a Java string has a position of 0.

String Length and Retrieving Individual Characters in a String

You can get the length of a string by invoking its `length()` method. For example, `message.length()` returns the length of the string `message`.

> **CAUTION**
> To get the length of an array, use the array's property `length`. To get the length of a string, use the string's `length()` method. For example, `a.length` indicates the number of elements in array `a`, while `s.length()` returns the number of characters in string `s`.

The `s.charAt(index)` method can be used to retrieve a specific character in a string `s`, where the index is between `0` and `s.length()-1`. For example, `message.charAt(0)` returns the character `W`.

> **CAUTION**
> It is incorrect to use `s[0]` to access the first character in string `s`. Instead, you must use `s.charAt(0)`.

The *StringBuffer* Class

The `StringBuffer` class is an alternative to the `String` class. In general, a string buffer can be used wherever a string is used. `StringBuffer` is more flexible than `String`. You can add, insert, or append new contents into a string buffer. However, the value of a string is fixed once the string is created.

Many of the methods in the `StringBuffer` class are synchronized to ensure that the contents of `StringBuffer` are not corrupted when running with multiple threads (this topic will be introduced in Chapter 13, "Multithreading"). The `StringBuffer` class provides three constructors:

- **`public StringBuffer()`**—Constructs a string buffer with no characters in it and an initial capacity of 16 characters.

- **`public StringBuffer(int length)`**—Constructs a string buffer with no characters in it and an initial capacity specified by the `length` argument.

- `public StringBuffer(String str)`—Constructs a string buffer so that it represents the same sequence of characters as the `string` argument. The initial capacity of the string buffer is 16 plus the length of the `string` argument.

Appending and Inserting New Contents into a *StringBuffer*

You can append new contents at the end of a string buffer or insert new contents at a specified position in a string buffer.

The `StringBuffer` class provides 10 overloaded methods to append `boolean`, `char`, `char array`, `double`, `float`, `int`, `long`, `String`, and so on, into a string buffer. For example, the following code appends strings and characters into `strBuf` to form a new string, `"Welcome to Java"`.

```
StringBuffer strBuf = new StringBuffer();
strBuf.append("Welcome");
strBuf.append(' ');
strBuf.append("to");
strBuf.append(' ');
strBuf.append("Java");
```

The `StringBuffer` class also contains nine overloaded methods to insert `boolean`, `char`, `char array`, `double`, `float`, `int`, `long`, `String`, and so on, into a string buffer. For example, consider the following code:

```
strBuf.insert(11, "HTML and ");
```

Suppose `strBuf` contains `"Welcome to Java"` before the `insert()` method is applied. This code inserts `"HTML and "` at position 11 in `strBuf` (just before `J`). The new `strBuf` is `"Welcome to HTML and Java"`.

> **NOTE**
> Every string buffer has a capacity. If its capacity is exceeded, the buffer is automatically made larger to accommodate the additional characters.

The *capacity()*, *reverse()*, *length()*, *setLength()*, *charAt()*, and *setCharAt()* Methods

The `StringBuffer` class provides many other methods for manipulating string buffers. Here are some examples:

- `public int capacity()`

    This method returns the current capacity of the string buffer. The capacity is the number of new characters that can be stored in it.

- `public synchronized StringBuffer reverse()`

    This method reverses the sequence of the string contained in the string buffer.

- `public int length()`

    This method returns the number of characters in the string buffer.

- `public synchronized setLength(int newLength)`

  This method sets the length of the string buffer. If the `newLength` argument is less than the current length of the string buffer, then the string buffer is truncated to contain exactly the number of characters given by the `newLength` argument. If the `newLength` argument is greater than, or equal to, the current length, sufficient null characters (`'\u0000'`) are appended to the string buffer so that `length` becomes the `newLength` argument. The `newLength` argument must be greater than, or equal to, 0.

- `public synchronized char charAt(int index)`

  This method returns the character at a specific index in the string buffer. The first character of a string buffer is at index 0, the next at index 1, and so on, for array indexing. The `index` argument must be greater than or equal to 0, and less than the length of this string buffer.

- `public synchronized void setCharAt(int index, char ch)`

  This method sets the character at the specified index of the string buffer to `ch`.

Example 6.8 Testing *StringBuffer*

This example gives a program that prints the multiplication table created in Example 3.3, "Using Nested `for` Loops," from Chapter 3. Rather than printing one number at a time, the program appends all the elements of the table into a string buffer. After the table is completely constructed in the string buffer, the program prints the entire string buffer on the console once. The output of the program is the same as shown in Figure 3.8.

```java
// TestMulTableUsingStringBuffer.java: Demonstrate string buffers
public class TestMulTableUsingStringBuffer
{
  // Main method
  public static void main(String[] args)
  {
    // Create a string buffer
    StringBuffer strBuf = new StringBuffer();

    // Append the title to the buffer
    strBuf.append("      Multiplication Table" + '\n');
    strBuf.append("—————————-." + '\n');

    // Append the number title to the buffer
    strBuf.append("  ¦ ");
    for (int j=1; j<=9; j++)
      strBuf.append("  " + j);
    strBuf.append('\n');

    // Append multiplication table body to the buffer
    for (int i=1; i<=9; i++)
```

continues

```java
    {
      strBuf.append(i + " | ");
      for (int j=1; j<=9; j++)
      {
        if (i*j < 10)
          strBuf.append("  "+i*j);
        else
          strBuf.append(" "+i*j);
      }
      strBuf.append(" " + '\n');
    }

    // Print the string buffer
    System.out.println(strBuf);
  }
}
```

Example Review

The program builds the multiplication table and stores it in the string buffer `strBuf` using the `append()` method. The program is the same as used in Example 3.3 except that all the `print` statements in Example 3.3 are replaced by the `strBuf.append()` statements.

The `System.out.println(strBuf)` displays the string stored in `strBuf` to the console.

This program should run faster than the one in Example 3.3 because the `print()` method is called only once to display the entire table on-screen.

TIP

You can use `StringBuffer` to construct an output string and display the whole string once to reduce I/O time and improve performance.

If the string does not require any change, you should use `String` rather than `StringBuffer`. Java can perform some optimizations for `String`, such as sharing one string among multiple references, because strings do not change after they are created.

The *StringTokenizer* Class

Another useful class for processing strings is StringTokenizer. The `java.util.StringTokenizer` class is used to break a string into pieces so that information contained in it can be retrieved and processed. For example, to get all of the words in a string like `"I am learning Java now"`, you can create an instance of the `StringTokenizer` class for the string and then retrieve individual words in the string by using the methods in the `StringTokenizer` class.

How does the `StringTokenizer` class recognize individual words? You can specify a set of characters as delimiters when constructing a `StringTokenizer` object. The delimiters break a string into pieces known as *tokens*.

Listed below are the available constructors for `StringTokenizer`.

- `public StringTokenizer(String s, String delim, boolean returnTokens)`

  This constructor constructs a `StringTokenizer` for string s with specified delimiters. If `returnTokens` is `true`, the delimiter is returned as a token.

- `public StringTokenizer(String s, String delim)`

  This constructor constructs a `StringTokenizer` for string s with specified delimiters `delim`, and the delimiter is not considered a token.

- `public StringTokenizer(String s)`

  This constructor constructs a `StringTokenizer` for string s with default delimiters `"\t\n\r"` (a space, tab, new line, and carriage return), and the delimiter is not considered a token.

You can use the following instance methods in the `StringTokenizer` class.

- `public boolean hasMoreTokens()`

  This method returns `true` if there is any token left in the string.

- `public String nextToken()`

  This method returns the next token in the string.

- `public String nextToken(String delim)`

  This method returns the next token in the string after resetting the delimiter to `delim`.

- `public public int countTokens()`

  This method returns the number of tokens remaining in the string tokenizer.

Example 6.9 Testing `StringTokenizer`

In this example, a program is written that will use a string tokenizer to retrieve words from the string `"I am learning Java. Show me how to use StringTokenizer."` and display them on the console. The output of the program is shown in Figure 6.10.

```java
// TestStringTokenizer.java: Demonstrate StringTokenizer
import java.util.StringTokenizer;

public class TestStringTokenizer
{
  // Main method
  public static void main(String[] args)
  {
    // Create a string and string tokenizer
    String s =
      "I am learning Java. Show me how to use StringTokenizer.";
    StringTokenizer st = new StringTokenizer(s);
```

continues

```
      // Retrieve and display tokens
      System.out.println("The total number of words is "+
        st.countTokens());

      while (st.hasMoreTokens())
        System.out.println(st.nextToken());
  }
}
```

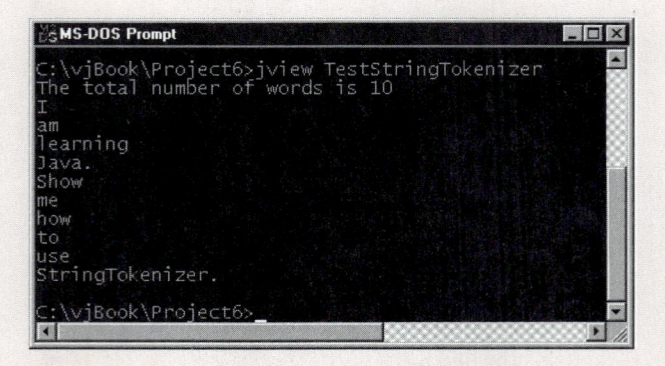

Figure 6.10 *The program uses the* `StringTokenizer` *class to extract tokens from a string.*

Example Review

The `String` class is in the `java.lang` package, so it is automatically imported. But the `StringTokenizer` class is in the `java.util` package. You need to import the `StringTokenizer` class from the `java.util` package. After all tokens are read, `st.countTokens()` is 0.

If you recreate a `StringTokenizer` instance as follows, the same words will be displayed in the program, but the dot will not be shown:

```
StringTokenizer st = new StringTokenizer(s, ". \n\t\r");
```

Command-Line Arguments

Perhaps you have already noticed the unusual declarations for the `main()` method, which has parameter args of `String[]` type. It is clear that args is an array of strings. The `main()` method is just like a regular method with parameters. You can call a regular method by passing actual parameters. Can you pass parameters to `main()`? This section will discuss how to pass and process arguments from the command line.

Passing Arguments to Java Programs

You can pass arguments to a Java program from the command line when you run the program. For example, the following command line starts the program `TestMain` with three arguments: arg0, arg1, and arg2:

```
java TestMain arg0 arg1 arg2
```

These arguments are strings, but they don't have to appear in double quotes on the command line. The arguments are separated by a space. If an argument itself contains a space, you must use double quotes to group all of the items in the argument. For example, consider the following command line:

```
java TestMain "First num" alpha 53
```

It starts the program with three arguments: `"First num"` and `alpha`, which are strings, and `53`, a numeric string. Note that `53` is actually treated as a string. You can use `"53"` instead of `53` in the command line.

Processing Command-Line Parameters

The arguments passed to the main program are stored in `args`, which is an array of strings. The first parameter is represented by `args[0]`, and `args.length` is the number of arguments passed.

Example 6.10 Using Command-Line Parameters

In this example, a program is written that will perform binary operations on integers. The program receives three parameters: an operator and two integers. To add two integers, the following command could be used:

```
java TestCommandParameters + 2 3
```

The program will display the following output:

```
2 + 3 = 5
```

The output of sample runs of the program is shown in Figure 6.11.

```java
// TestCommandParameters.java: Pass parameters from the command line
public class TestCommandParameters
{
  // Main method
  public static void main(String[] args)
  {
    // The result of the operation
    int result = 0;

    if (args.length != 3)
    {
      System.out.println(
        "Usage: java TestCommandParameters " +
          "operator operand1 operand2");
      System.exit(0);
    }

    // Determine the operator
    switch (args[0].charAt(0))
```

continues

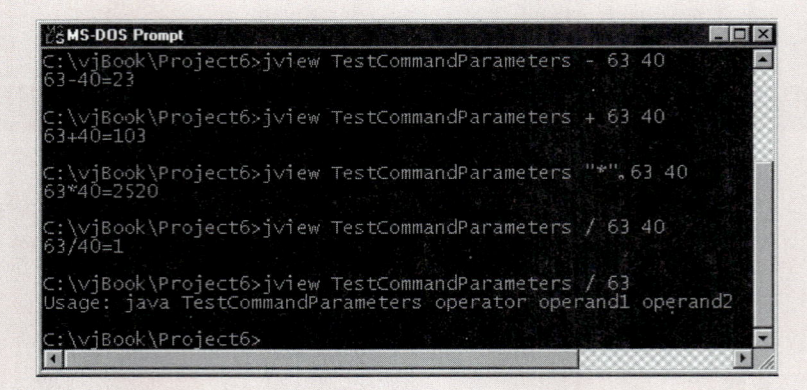

```
    {
      case '+': result = Integer.parseInt(args[1]) +
                         Integer.parseInt(args[2]);
               break;
      case '-': result = Integer.parseInt(args[1]) -
                         Integer.parseInt(args[2]);
               break;
      case '*': result = Integer.parseInt(args[1]) *
                         Integer.parseInt(args[2]);
               break;
      case '/': result = Integer.parseInt(args[1]) /
                         Integer.parseInt(args[2]);
    }

    // Display result
    System.out.println(args[1] + args[0] + args[2] + "=" + result);
  }
}
```

Figure 6.11 *The program takes three parameters (an operator and two operands) from the command line and displays the expression and the result of the arithmetic operation.*

Example Review

The program first tests whether three command-line arguments have been provided. If not, `System.exit(0)` terminates the program.

The arithmetic operations are performed according to `args[0]`, the operator.

`Integer.parseInt(args[1])` converts a digital string into an integer. The string must consist of digits. If not, the program will terminate abnormally. `Integer`, a class in `java.lang`, is introduced in Chapter 7, "Class Inheritance."

In the sample run, `"*"` is used instead of `*` for the command `java TestCommandParameters "*" 4 5`. In JDK 1.1 and above, the `*` symbol refers to all the files in the current directory when it is used on a command line. For example, the following program displays all the files in the current directory when issuing the command `java Test *`.

```
public class Test
{
  public static void main(String[] args)
  {
    for (int i=0; i<args.length; i++)
      System.out.println(args[i]);
  }
}
```

Debugging in Visual J++

Now turn your attention to *debugging*. Debugging is finding errors—*bugs*—in a program and correcting them. As you have already learned, programming errors can be separated into syntax errors, runtime errors, and logical errors. Runtime errors that cause the program to abort are reported by the Java runtime system. Syntax errors are detected and reported by the compiler. In general, they are easy to locate and to fix. Therefore, this section focuses on the more difficult problem: the logical error.

Logical errors can result in incorrect output or cause a program to terminate unexpectedly. To find logical errors, you can *hand trace* the program (that is, catch errors by reading the program) or insert print statements in order to show the values of the variables or the program's execution flow. This approach might work for a short, simple program. But for a large, complex program, such as the selection sort program in Example 6.2, the most effective approach for debugging is to use a debugger utility.

Debugger utilities let you follow the execution of a program. Although they vary from one system to another, they all support most of the following helpful features:

- Executing a single statement at a time—The debugger allows you to execute one statement at a time so that you can see the effect of each statement.

- Tracing into or stepping over a method—If a method is being executed, you can ask the debugger either to enter the method and execute one statement at a time in it or to step over the entire method. You should step over the entire method if you know that the method works. For example, you should always step over system-supplied methods like System.out.println().

- Setting breakpoints—You can also set a breakpoint at a specific statement. Your program will pause when it reaches a breakpoint and display the line with the breakpoint. You can set as many breakpoints as you want. Breakpoints are particularly useful when you know where your programming error starts. You can set a breakpoint at that line and have the program execute until it reaches the breakpoint.

- Displaying variables—The debugger lets you select several variables and display their values. As you trace through a program, the content of a variable is continuously updated.

- Using call stacks—The debugger lets you trace all of the method calls, and lists all pending methods. This feature is helpful when you need to see a large picture of the program execution flow.

- Modifying variables—Some debuggers enable you to modify the value of a variable when debugging. This is convenient when you want to test a program with different samples but do not want to leave the debugger.

The debugger utility is one of the most helpful and powerful tools in Visual J++. You can pinpoint bugs in your program with the help of the Visual J++ debugger without leaving the IDE. The Visual J++ debugger enables you to set breakpoints and execute programs line by line. As your program executes, you can watch the values stored in variables, observe which methods are being called, and know what events have occurred in the program.

This section uses the selection sort program from Example 6.2, "Using Arrays in Sorting," to demonstrate debugging in Visual J++. Suppose a mistake is made in the `selectionSort()` method, as shown in the following code listing at the highlighted line:

```java
static void selectionSort(double[] list)
{
  double currentMax;
  int currentMaxIndex;
  for (int i=list.length-1; i>=1; i—)
  {
    //find the maximum in the list[0..i]
    currentMax = list[i];
    currentMaxIndex = i;
    for (int j=i-1; j>=0; j—)
    {
      if (currentMax < list[j])
      {
        currentMax = list[i];
        currentMaxIndex = j;
      }
    }

    //swap list[i] with list[currentMaxIndex] if necessary;
    if (currentMaxIndex != i)
    {
      list[currentMaxIndex] = list[i];
      list[i] = currentMax;
    }
  }
}
```

Note that `currentMax = list[i]` should be `currentMax = list[j]`. The programmer, however, is not aware of the mistake. The debugger helps to locate the error. For convenience, let the new program be named TestSelectionSortWithError.

Starting the Debugger

The debugger automatically starts when the program encounters a runtime exception and Visual J++ enters break mode, as shown in Figure 2.6, "When a runtime error occurs, an error message dialog box is displayed." However, many programs with logic errors, such as TestSelectionSortWithError, do not raise runtime exceptions. To debug such a program, you need to use a debugging command like Step Into to start the program.

Perform the following steps to start debugging TestSelectionSortWithError:

1. Double-click TestSelectionSort.java in the Project Explorer for Project6 to display the TestSelectionSort.java in the Text Editor.

2. Choose File, Save TestSelectionSort.java As from the main menu bar to display the Save File As dialog box. Type TestSelectionSortWithError.java in the File name field. Click Save to create a new file. You will see TestSelectionSortWithError.java appearing in the Project Explorer for Project6, as shown in Figure 6.12.

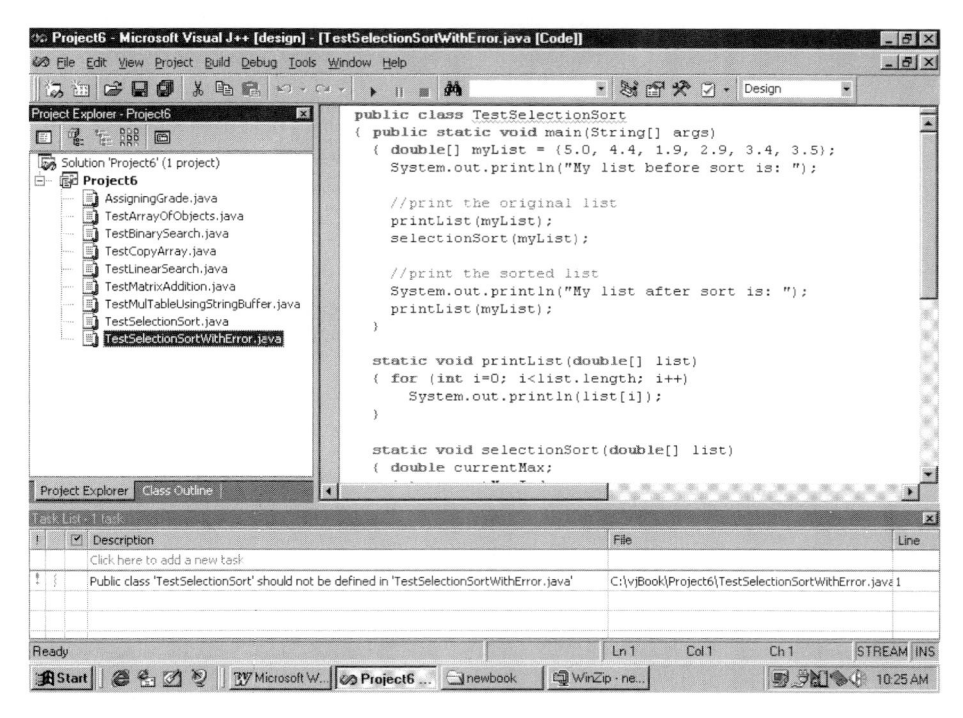

Figure 6.12 *The program TestSelectionSortWithError.java was added to the project.*

3. In the Text Editor window for TestSelectionSortWithError.java, change the class name from TestSelectionSort to TestSelectionSortWithError.

4. Build Project6 to compile TestSelectionSortWithErorr.java.

5. On the Launch page of the Project6 Properties dialog box, choose TestSelectionSortWithError to run and check Launch as a console application.

6. Choose Debug, Step Into from the main menu bar to start the debugger, as shown in Figure 6.13.

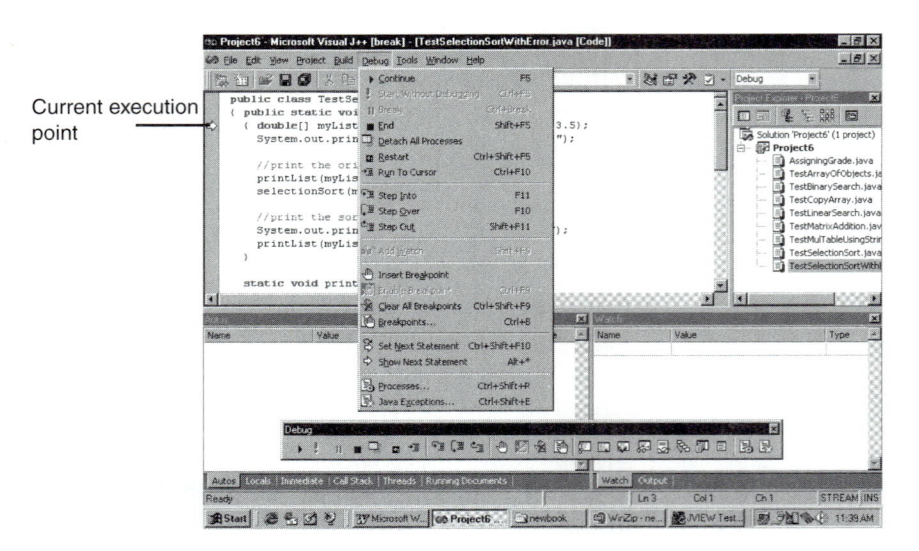

Figure 6.13 *The Debug menu contains commands for performing various debugging tasks.*

Visual J++ enters break mode when debugging starts, as shown in Figure 6.13. The window layout in the IDE is automatically set to the Debug style. The program pauses at the first line in the main() method. This line, called *the current execution point,* or *current statement,* is highlighted and has a yellow arrow to the left. The execution point marks the next statement of source code to be executed by the debugger. Whenever the program pauses, the current execution point is highlighted. You can issue debugging commands to control the execution of the program. You also can inspect or modify values of variables in the program.

Controlling Program Execution

When Visual J++ is in debugging mode, the Debug menu contains the debugging commands that can be used to control program execution (see Figure 6.13). These commands are also available from the Debug toolbar window. To show the Debug toolbar window, select View, Toolbars, Debug. The Debug toolbar window is shown in Figure 6.14.

The Visual J++ debugger enables you to control the execution of your program by using the following commands, which can be found in the Run menu or on the toolbar:

- Continue—Executes the program from the current statement until a breakpoint is encountered or the end of the program is reached.

- Run to Cursor—Runs the program starting from the current execution point, and pauses and places the execution point on the line of code containing the cursor.

- Step Into—Executes a single statement or steps into a method.

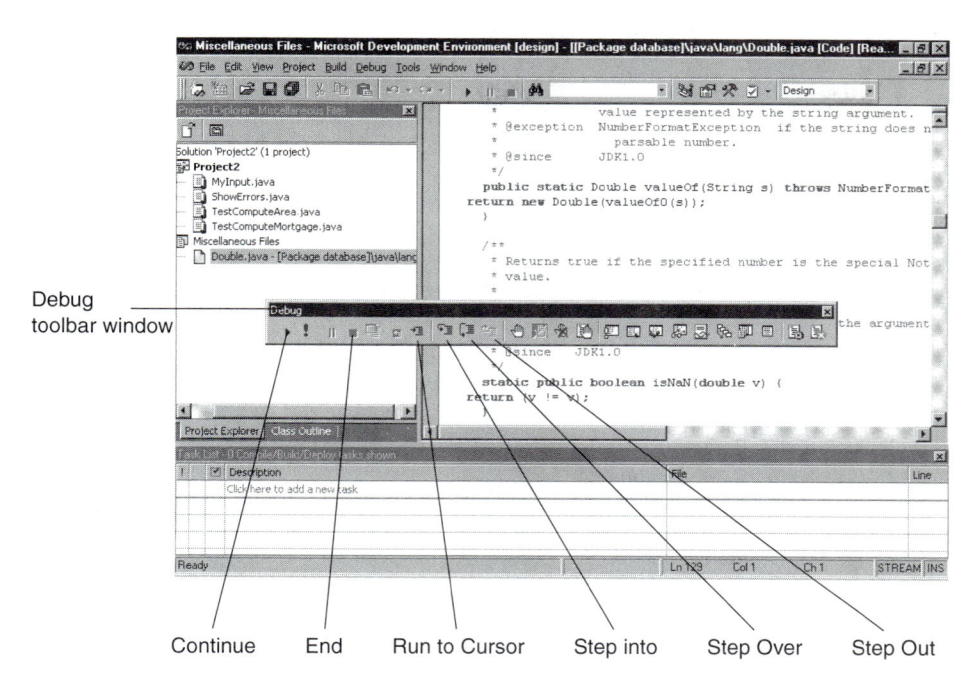

Figure 6.14 *The debugging commands appear in the Debug toolbar window.*

- Step Over—Executes a single statement. If the statement contains a call to a method, the entire method is executed without stepping through it.

- Step Out—Executes the program out of a method call, and stops at the statement immediately following the method's caller.

Setting Breakpoints

You can execute a program line by line to trace it, but this is time-consuming if you are debugging a large program. Often, you know that some parts of the program work fine. It makes no sense to execute the parts that work when you only need to trace certain lines of code that are likely to have bugs. In such cases, you can use breakpoints.

A *breakpoint* is a stop sign placed on a line of source code that tells the debugger to pause when this line is encountered. The debugger executes every line until it encounters a breakpoint, and you can then trace the part of the program at the breakpoint. Using the breakpoint, you can quickly move over sections you know work correctly and concentrate on sections causing problems.

There are several ways to set a breakpoint on a line. One quick way is to move the cursor at the cutter area of the line, then click the mouse button. You will see a solid red circle displayed in the cutter of the line, as shown in Figure 6.15. You also can set breakpoints by choosing Debug, Insert Breakpoint while the cursor rests at the line. To remove a breakpoint, simply click the red dot at the breakpoint line.

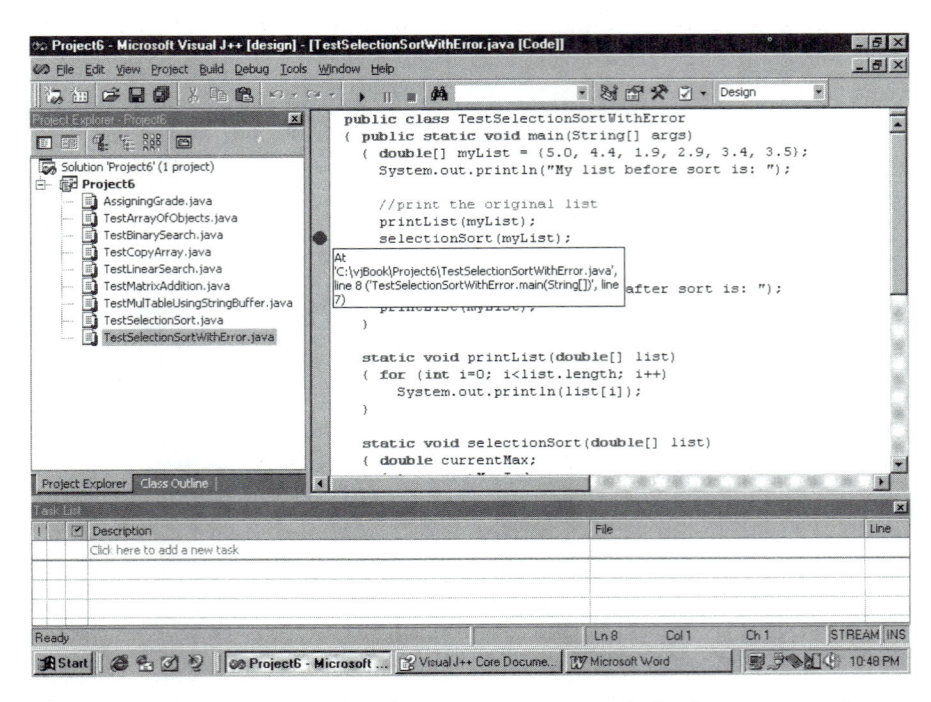

Figure 6.15 *The breakpoint tells the debugger to pause at a specific line in the source code.*

As you debug your program, you can set as many breakpoints you want, and you can remove breakpoints at any time during debugging.

> **NOTE**
> The project retains the breakpoints you have set when you exit, and the breakpoints are restored when you reopen the project.

Inspecting and Modifying Data Values

Among the most powerful features of an integrated debugger are its capability to reveal current data values and to enable programmers to modify values during debugging. You can examine the values of variables, array items, and objects, or the values of the parameters passed in a method call. You also can modify a variable value if you want to try a new value to continue debugging without restarting the program.

Visual J++ provides various type of windows that enable you to inspect and modify the values of variables. By default, these windows are grouped in two tab-linked windows, as shown in Figure 6.16.

The following are the most commonly used windows:

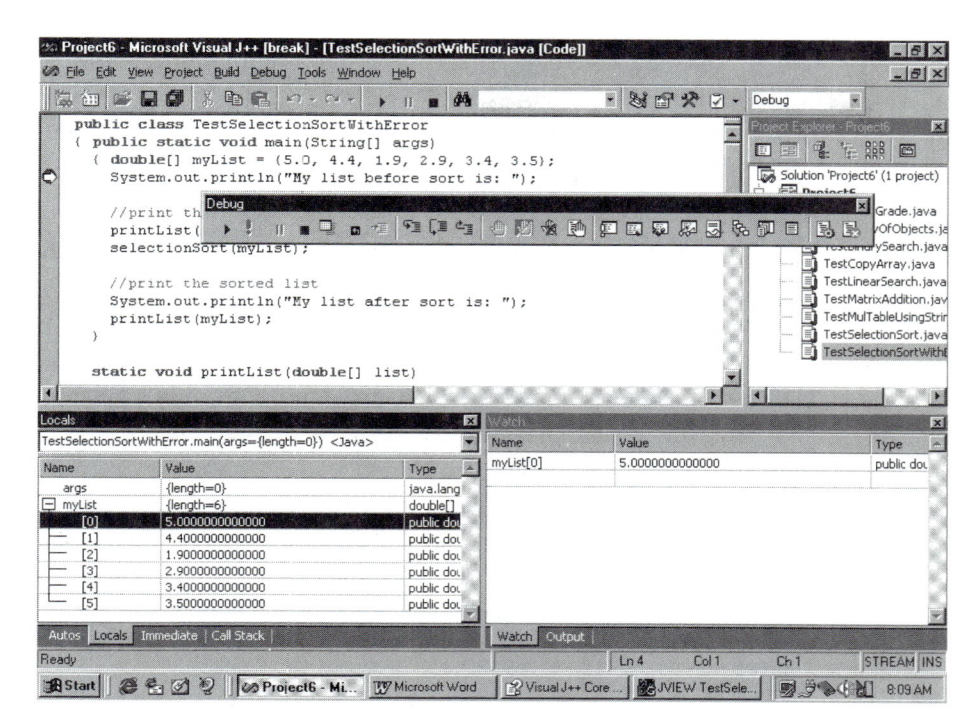

Figure 6.16 *The debug windows are displayed and grouped into two tab-linked windows when debugging starts.*

The Locals Window

The *Locals window* shows the value of any variable within the scope of the current procedure. As the execution switches from procedure to procedure, the contents of the Locals window change to reflect only the variables applicable to the current procedure. For example, since myList is a local variable, it is listed in the Locals window, as shown in Figure 6.16.

The Autos Window

The *Autos window* shows the value of any variable within the scope of the current line of execution in the current procedure. The Autos window is updated only when execution is suspended. For example, the Autos window is updated when you add a new watch, when you change the value of a variable, or when you switch between decimal and hex modes. Values that have changed since the last breakpoint are highlighted.

The Watch Window

The *Watch window* shows the values of selected variables or watch expressions. The Watch window can display a value for a selected variable or watch expression only if the current statement is in the specified context. Otherwise, the Value column shows a message indicating that the variable is not found. For example, in Figure 6.17, you selected variables `list[1]`, `list[2]`, `i`, and `j` and typed watch expression `list[1]<list[2]` in the Watch window.

The Watch window is only updated when execution is stopped at a breakpoint or exception. Values that have changed since the last break are highlighted.

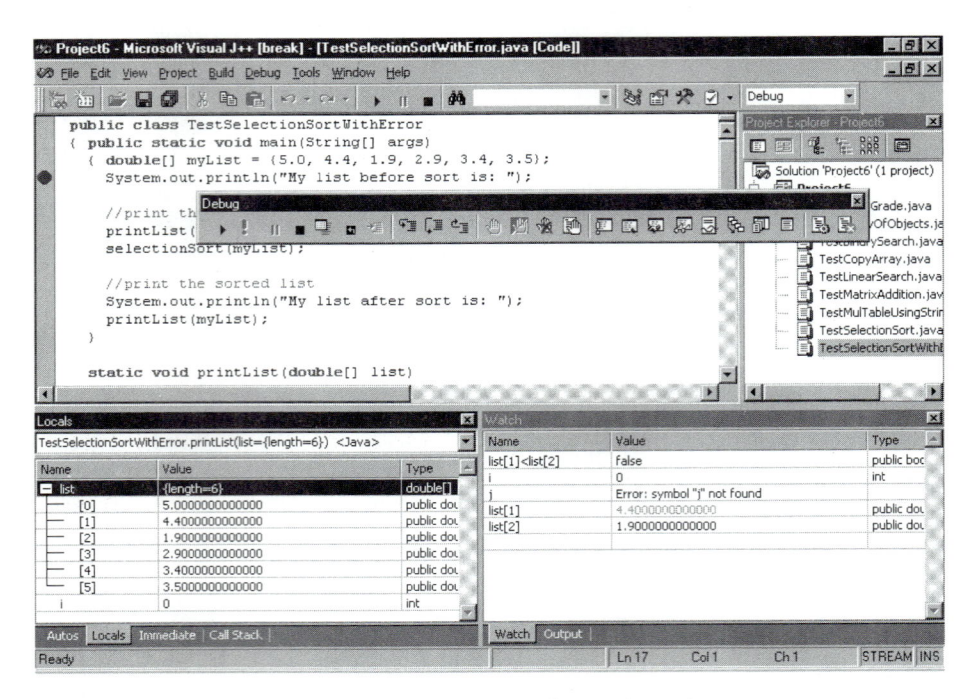

Figure 6.17 *You can add variables and expression in the Watch window.*

The Immediate Window

The *Immediate window* allows you to change the values of variables so that you can immediately see the effect of your changes. When the application is in break mode, you can evaluate expressions by typing in the Immediate window. For example, suppose you want to change the value for `list[1]` to 44 when the debugger enters the `printList` method; type `list[1] = 44`, then press RETURN, as shown in Figure 6.18. You can see the changed value in the Locals window.

There are also several other debugging windows that you will use in certain situations, depending upon the type of application you are debugging. For example, for multithreaded applications, you can use the *Threads window* to change the current thread of execution or view the threads in any attached process. Multithreaded applications will be introduced in Chapter 13, "Multithreading."

CHAPTER 6 ARRAYS AND STRINGS

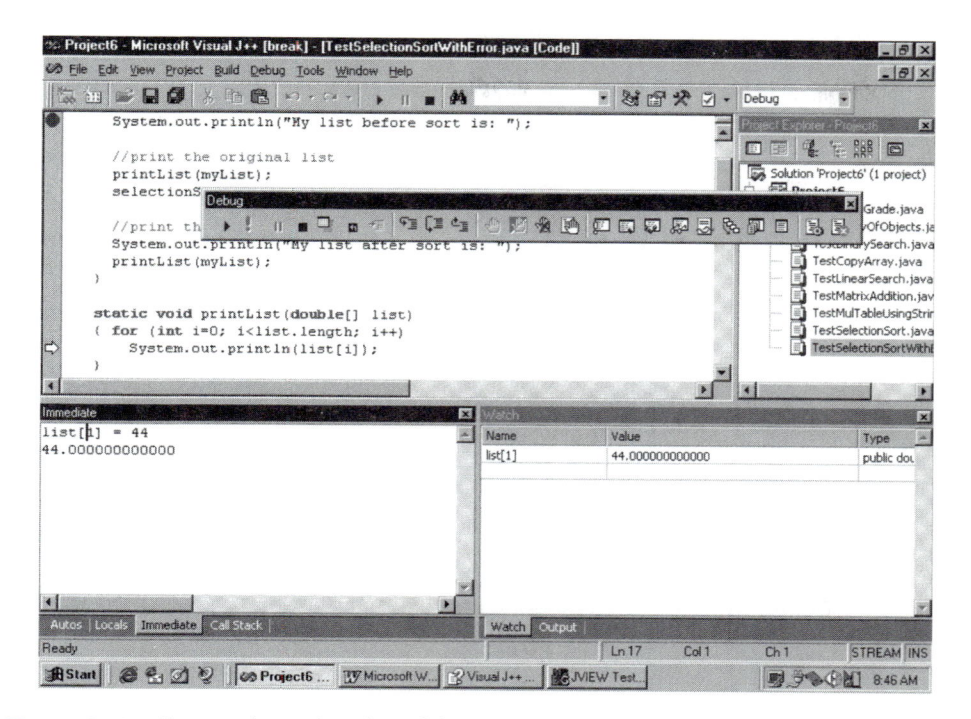

Figure 6.18 *You can change the values of the variables in the Immediate window.*

> **TIP**
> To display a debug window, click a toolbar button that represents the window. The window will be tab-linked to debug windows already in the IDE. To hide a debug window, choose the window and select Window, Hide.

> **TIP**
> Numbers can be shown in decimal or in hex in the Autos, Locals, and Watch windows. To switch between decimal and hex modes, right-click in the window to reveal the window's context menu and select Hexadecimal Display or Decimal Display to switch display modes.

Debugging *TestSelectionSortWithError*

You will use the debugger to uncover the bugs in `TestSelectionSortWithError` by performing the following steps:

1. Choose Debug, Step Into to start debugging. Visual J++ enters break mode. The IDE window layout is in the Debug style. The execution point is at the first line in the `main()` method.

2. Since you know there is nothing wrong in the code before invoking the `selectionSort` method, you can skip the lines before calling `selectionSort`

in the `main()` method by setting a breakpoint at the line for `selectionSort(myList)`, as shown in Figure 6.15.

3. Choose Debug, Continue from the main menu or click the Continue button in the Debug toolbar window to execute every line until it reaches to the breakpoint.

4. Choose Run, Step Into from the main menu or click the Step Into button from the Debug toolbar window to debug the `selectionSort()` method.

5. Add `list` to the Watch pane and select the Watch tab to monitor `list`. Check whether `list` has the correct initial values before the method starts (see Figure 6.19).

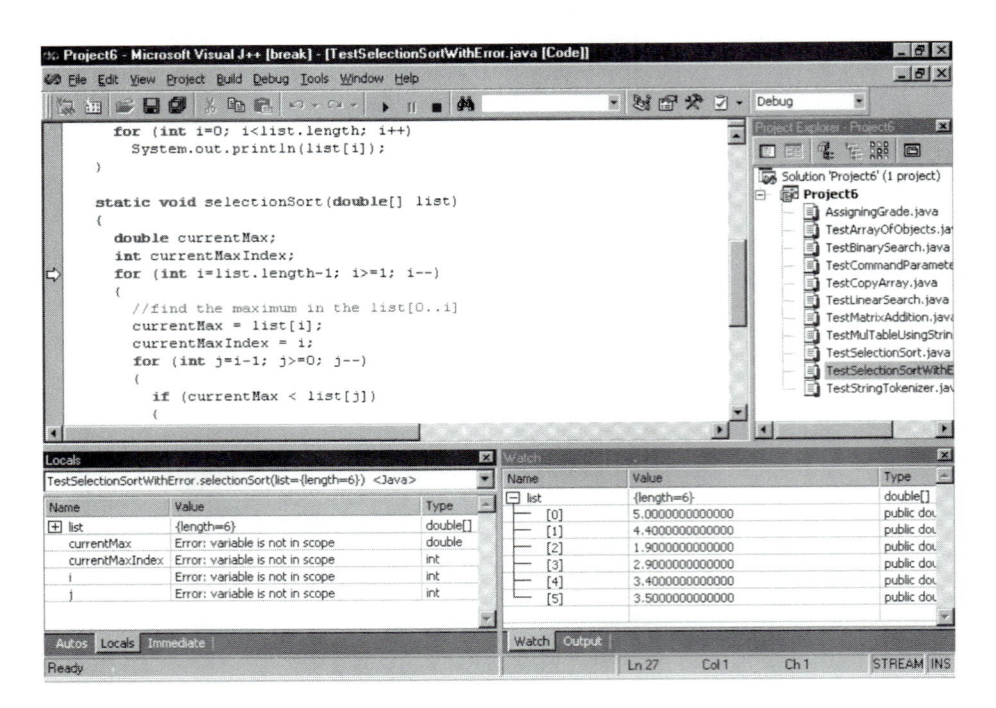

Figure 6.19 *The variable `list` was added to the Watch window.*

6. The `selectionSort()` method places the largest number at the end of the list after an iteration of the outer `for` loop. Run through the iteration at full speed by setting the cursor at the `if` statement for swapping numbers, then choose Debug, Run to Cursor.

7. You can see the value of `currentMax` in the Autos window or in the Locals window, as shown in Figure 6.20. Clearly, `currentMax` is not getting the correct value. The correct value should be 5.0. You should assign `list[j]` to `currentMax`, not `list[i]`.

8. Change `list[i]` to `list[j]` and choose Debug, Restart to restart debugger.

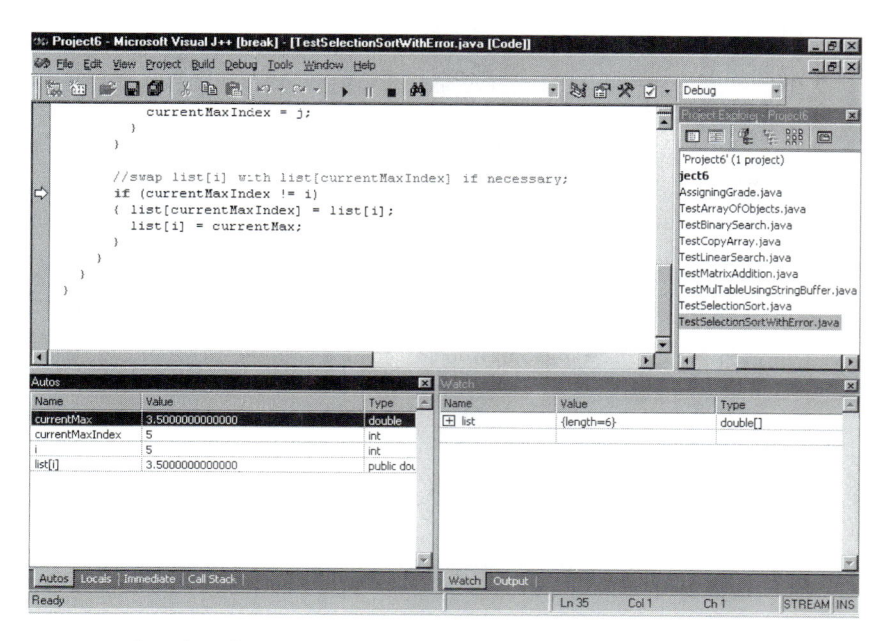

Figure 6.20 *The value of* `currentMax` *displayed in the Locals window is not the expected max value, which leads to finding the error in the program.*

TIP
The debugger is an indispensable, powerful tool that boosts your programming productivity. It may take some time to become familiar with it, but your investment will pay off in the long run.

Chapter Summary

In this chapter, you learned about using array objects to store a collection of data of the same type and using `String` objects for processing character strings. You also learned about passing and processing command-line arguments.

You learned how to declare and create arrays and how to access individual elements in an array. Java stores lists of values in arrays, which are contiguous groups of adjacent memory locations. To refer to a particular location or element of an array, you specify the name of the array and then give the index, which is placed in brackets. An index must be an integer or an integer expression.

A Java array is an object. After an array is created, its size becomes permanent and can be obtained using `arrayObject.length`. The index of an array always begins with 0. Therefore, the last index is always `arrayObject.length-1`. An out-of-bounds error would occur if you attempted to reference elements beyond the bounds of an array.

The `for` loop is often used to process all of the elements in an array. You can use `for` loops to initialize arrays, display arrays, and control and manipulate array elements.

Arrays can be passed to a method as actual parameters. An array is an object, so arrays are passed by reference; that is, the called method can modify the elements in the caller's original arrays.

You can use arrays of array objects to form multidimensional arrays. You learned a convenient syntax that can be used to declare multidimensional arrays, and you saw an example of using a multidimensional array.

Strings are objects, encapsulated in the `String` class. You learned how to create and initialize a string, compare strings, concatenate strings, use substrings, and access individual characters in strings.

The `StringBuffer` class can be used to replace the `String` class. The `String` object is immutable, but you can add, insert, or append new contents into a `StringBuffer` object. Use `String` if the string contents do not require any change, and use `StringBuffer` if the string contents change.

The `StringTokenizer` class is used to retrieve and process tokens in a string. You learned the role of delimiters, how to create a string tokenizer from a string, and how to use the `countTokens()`, `hasMoreTokens()`, and `nextToken()` methods to process a string tokenizer.

Debugging is the process of finding errors and correcting or modifying code in a program so that it can run as you expected. You learned how to use Visual J++'s debugger to find bugs.

Chapter Review

6.1. How do you declare and create an array?

6.2. Is an array an object or a primitive type value?

6.3. Is memory allocated when an array is declared? When is the memory allocated for an array?

6.4. Indicate true or false for the following statements:

- Every element in an array has the same type.
- The array size is fixed after it is declared.
- The array size is fixed after it is created.
- The element in the array must be of primitive data type.

6.5. Which of the following statements are valid array declarations?

```
int i = new int(30);
double d[] = new double[30];
Rational[] r = new Rational(1..30);
int i[] = (3, 4, 3, 2);
float f[] = {2.3, 4.5, 5.6};
char[] c = new char();
Rational[][] r = new Rational[2];
```

6.6. What is the array index type? What is the lowest index?

6.7. What is the representation of the third element in an array named a? Write a method to discover whether array a has an element that has a value of 2. If it does, find the index of that element.

6.8. What happens when your program attempts to access an array element with an invalid index?

6.9. What does the following program do?

```
public class Test
{
  public static void main(String[] args)
  {
    Rational[] r = {new Rational(2,3), new Rational(-1, 3),
                    new Rational(3,5)};
    double[] d = new double[r.length];

    for (int i=0; i<r.length; i++)
      d[i] = r[i].getNumerator() / r[i].getDenominator();
  }
}
```

6.10. Use the `arraycopy()` method to copy the following array to a target array t.

```
Circle[] source = {new Circle(3), new Circle(4),
  new Circle(5)};
```

6.11. Declare and create a 4×5 int matrix.

6.12. Suppose that s1 and s2 are two strings. Which of the following statements or expressions are incorrect?

```
String s = new String("new string");
String s3 = s1 + s2;
String s3 = s1 - s2;
s1 == s2;
s1 >= s2;
s1.compareTo(s2);
int i = s1.length();
char c = s1(0);
char c = s1.charAt(s1.length());
```

6.13. Declare a `StringTokenizer` for a string s with slash (/) and backslash (\) as delimiters.

6.14. What is the output of the following program?

```java
import java.util.StringTokenizer;

class TestStringTokenizer
{
  public static void main(String[] args)
  {
    //create a string and string tokenizer
    String s = "I/am\learning Java.";
    StringTokenizer st = new StringTokenizer(s, "/\.");

    //retrieve and display tokens
    while (st.hasMoreTokens())
      System.out.print(st.nextToken()+" ");
  }
}
```

Programming Exercises

6.1. Write a program that will read 10 integers and display the numbers in reverse order.

6.2. Use recursion to rewrite the selection sort used in Example 6.2.

6.3. Use iterations to rewrite the binary search used in Example 6.4.

6.4. Write a program that meets the following requirements:

- Create a class for students. The class must contain the student's name (`String`), ID (`int`), and status (`int`). The status indicates the student's class standing: 1 for freshman, 2 for sophomore, 3 for junior, and 4 for senior.

- Create 20 students whose names are Name1, Name2, and so on to Name20, and whose IDs and status are assigned randomly.

- Find all juniors and print their names and IDs.

6.5. Write a program that meets the following requirements:

- Write a method that will multiply two `int` square matrices. The method is declared as follows:

    ```java
    public static int[][] multiply(int[][] m1, int[][] m2)
    ```

    The algorithm for matrix multiplication can be described as follows:

    ```java
    for (int i=0; i<m.length; i++)
      for (int j=0; j<m.length; j++)
      {
        c[i][j] = 0;
        for (int k=0; k<m.length; k++)
          c[i][j] = c[i][j] + m1[i][k]*m2[k][j];
      }
    ```

- Write a main method in the same class to test the method.

6.6. Write a sort method using the bubble sort algorithm. The bubble sort algorithm makes several passes through the array. On each pass, neighboring pairs are compared successively. If a pair is in decreasing order, its values are swapped; otherwise, the values remain unchanged. The technique is called bubble sort or sinking sort because the smaller values gradually "bubble" their way to the top and the larger values sink to the bottom.

The algorithm can be described as follows:

```
boolean changed = true;
do
{
  changed = false;
  for (int j=0; j<list.length-1; j++)
    if (list[j] > list[j+1])
    {
      swap list[j] with list[j+1];
      changed = true;
    }
}
while (changed);
```

Clearly, the list is in increasing order when the loop terminates. It is easy to show that the `do` loop executes at most list.length -1 times.

6.7. Write a program that meets the following requirements:

- Write a method that will check whether a string is a palindrome: a string that reads the same forward and backward.

- Write a program that will take a string from a command-line argument to check whether it is a palindrome.

6.8. Write a program similar to the one in Example 6.10. Instead of using integers, use rationals. You will need to use the `StringTokenizer` class to retrieve numerators and denominators.

6.9. Rewrite Example 3.7, "Finding the Sales Amount," using the binary search approach. Since the sales amount is between 1 and `COMMISSION_SOUGHT/0.08`, you can use a binary search to improve Example 3.7.

CHAPTER 7

CLASS INHERITANCE

Objectives

- Understand the concept of class inheritance and the relationship between superclasses and subclasses.
- Create new classes from existing classes.
- Learn to use two keywords: `super` and `this`.
- Learn to use three modifiers: `protected`, `final`, and `abstract`.
- Understand polymorphism and objects casting.
- Become familiar with the numerical wrapper classes and its subclasses.
- Design abstract classes in generic programming.
- Become familiar with class-design guidelines.
- Understand the concept of interfaces.
- Know inner classes.
- Use Visual J++'s Class Outline.

Introduction

With object-oriented programming, you can derive new classes from existing classes. This is called *inheritance*. In Chapter 1, "Introduction to Java and Visual J++ 6," you created the `WelcomeApplet` applet by deriving it from the `Applet` class. Inheritance is an important and powerful concept in Java. In fact, every class you define in Java is inherited from an existing class, either explicitly or implicitly. The `Circle` class is actually derived implicitly from the class `Object`.

This chapter introduces the concept of inheritance. Specifically, it discusses superclasses and subclasses, the use of the keywords `super` and `this`, the `protected` modifier, the `final` modifier, the `abstract` modifier, polymorphism, casting objects, class-design guidelines, wrapper classes, the interface, and inner classes.

Superclasses and Subclasses

In Java terminology, an existing class is called a *superclass*. A class derived from a superclass is called a *subclass*. Sometimes a superclass is referred to as a *parent class* or a *base class,* and a subclass is referred to as a *child class,* an *extended class,* or a *derived class.* You can reuse or change the methods of superclasses, and you can add new data and new methods in subclasses. Subclasses usually have more functionality than their superclasses.

> **NOTE**
> Contrary to conventional interpretation, a subclass is not a subset of its superclass. In fact, a subclass usually contains more functions and more detailed information than its superclass.

Example 7.1 Demonstrating Inheritance

To demonstrate inheritance, this example creates a new class for `Cylinder` from `Circle`. The `Cylinder` class inherits all the data and methods from the `Circle` class. In addition, the `Cylinder` class has a new data field, `length`, and a new method, `findVolume()`.

The relationship of these two classes is shown in Figure 7.1.

The `Cylinder` class can be declared as follows:

```
// Cylinder.java: Class definition for describing Cylinder
public class Cylinder extends Circle
{
  private double length;

  // Default constructor
  public Cylinder()
```

```
  {
    super();
    length = 1.0;
  }

  // Construct a cylinder with specified radius and length
  public Cylinder(double r, double l)
  {
    super(r);
    length = l;
  }

  // Getter method for length
  public double getLength()
  {
    return length;
  }

  // Find cylinder volume
  public double findVolume()
  {
    return findArea()*length;
  }
}
```

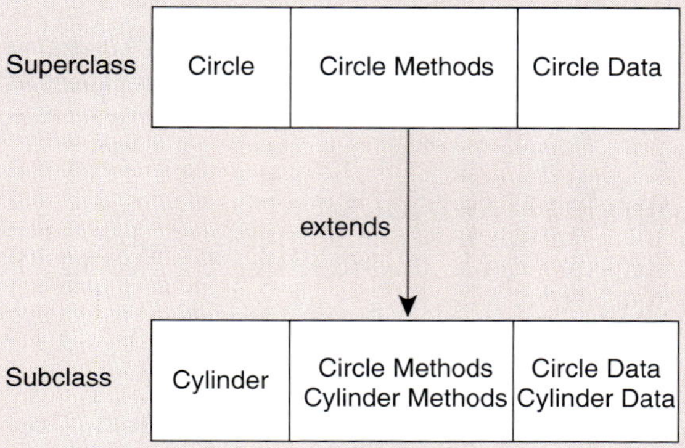

Superclass	Circle	Circle Methods	Circle Data

extends ↓

Subclass	Cylinder	Circle Methods Cylinder Methods	Circle Data Cylinder Data

Figure 7.1 *The* Cylinder *class inherits data and methods from the* Circle *class and extends the* Circle *class with its own data and methods.*

Example Review

The Cylinder class extends the circle class defined in Example 5.3, "Using the private Modifier," in Chapter 5, "Programming with Objects and Classes."

The reserved word extends tells the compiler that the Cylinder class is derived from the Circle class, thus inheriting data and methods from Circle.

The keyword super is used in the constructors. This keyword is discussed in the next section.

Using the Keyword *super*

The keyword `super` refers to the superclass of the class in which `super` appears. This keyword can be used in two ways:

- To call a superclass constructor.
- To call a superclass method.

Calling Superclass Constructors

The syntax to call a superclass constructor is:

```
super(parameters);
```

In the `Cylinder` class, for example, `super()` and `super(r)` are used to call the constructors from the `Circle` class to initialize the radius. The component `super()` must appear in the first line of the constructor and is the only way to invoke a superclass's constructor.

> **CAUTION**
> Java requires the `super()` statement to appear first in the constructor, even before data fields.
>
> It also requires using the keyword `super` to call the superclass's constructor. Invoking a superclass constructor's name in a subclass causes a syntax error.

Calling Superclass Methods

The keyword `super` can be used to reference a method other than the constructor in the superclass. The syntax can look like this:

```
super.method(parameters);
```

You could rewrite the `findVolume()` method in the `Cylinder` class as follows:

```
double findVolume()
{
  return super.findArea()*length;
}
```

It is not necessary to put `super` before `findArea()` in this case, however, because `findArea()` is a method in the `Circle` class and can be accessed in the `Cylinder` class. Nevertheless, in some cases the keyword `super` is needed.

The two examples given below demonstrate the use of inheritance and the `super` keyword.

Example 7.2 Testing Inheritance

This example shows a program that creates a `Cylinder` object and explores the relationship between the `Cylinder` and `Circle` classes by accessing the data and methods (`radius`, `findArea()`) defined in the `Circle` class and the data and methods (`length`, `findVolume()`) defined in the `Cylinder` class. The output of the program is shown in Figure 7.2.

```java
public class TestCylinder
{
  public static void main(String[] args)
  {
    // Create a Cylinder object and display its properties
    Cylinder myCylinder = new Cylinder(5.0, 2.0);
    System.out.println("The length is " + myCylinder.getLength());
    System.out.println("The radius is " + myCylinder.getRadius());
    System.out.println("The volume of the cylinder is " +
      myCylinder.findVolume());
    System.out.println("The area of the circle is " +
      myCylinder.findArea());
  }
}
```

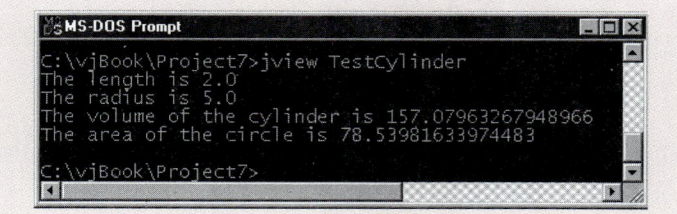

```
C:\vjBook\Project7>jview TestCylinder
The length is 2.0
The radius is 5.0
The volume of the cylinder is 157.07963267948966
The area of the circle is 78.53981633974483

C:\vjBook\Project7>
```

Figure 7.2 *The program creates a* `Cylinder` *object and accesses the data and methods defined in the* `Circle` *class and in the* `Cylinder` *class.*

Example Review

Since this program uses the `Cylinder` class, you should have created the program in Example 7.1 before compiling this program. The `Cylinder` class extends all functionality of the `Circle` class. The `myCylinder` object inherits all the data and methods in `Circle`. Therefore, it can access the `getRadius()` and `findArea()` methods defined in the `Circle` class.

A subclass cannot call a superclass's constructor without using the `super` keyword. If you replace `super()` with `Circle()` in the `Cylinder` class, you would get a compilation error.

Overriding Methods

A subclass inherits methods from a superclass. Sometimes, it is necessary for the subclass to modify the methods defined in the superclass. This is referred to as *method overriding*.

Example 7.3 Overriding the Methods in the Superclass

In this example, the `Cylinder` class defined in Example 7.1 is modified to override the `findArea()` method in the `Circle` class. The `findArea()` method in the `Circle` class computes the area of a circle, while the `findArea()` method in the `Cylinder` class computes the surface area of a cylinder. The output of the program is shown in Figure 7.3.

```java
// TestOverrideMethods.java: Test the Cylinder class that overrides
// its superclass's methods
public class TestOverrideMethods
{
  public static void main(String[] args)
  {
    Cylinder myCylinder = new Cylinder(5.0, 2.0);
    System.out.println("The length is " + myCylinder.getLength());
    System.out.println("The radius is " + myCylinder.getRadius());
    System.out.println("The surface area of the cylinder is "+
      myCylinder.findArea());
    System.out.println("The volume of the cylinder is "+
      myCylinder.findVolume());
  }
}

// New cylinder class that overrides the findArea() method defined in
// the circle class
class Cylinder extends Circle
{
  private double length;

  // Default constructor
  public Cylinder()
  {
    super();
    length = 1.0;
  }

  // Construct a cylinder with specified radius and length
  public Cylinder(double r, double l)
  {
    super(r);
    length = l;
  }

  // Getter method for length
  public double getLength()
  {
    return length;
  }

  // Find cylinder surface area
  public double findArea()
  {
    return 2*super.findArea()+(2*getRadius()*Math.PI)*length;
  }

  // Find cylinder volume
  public double findVolume()
  {
    return super.findArea()*length;
  }
}
```

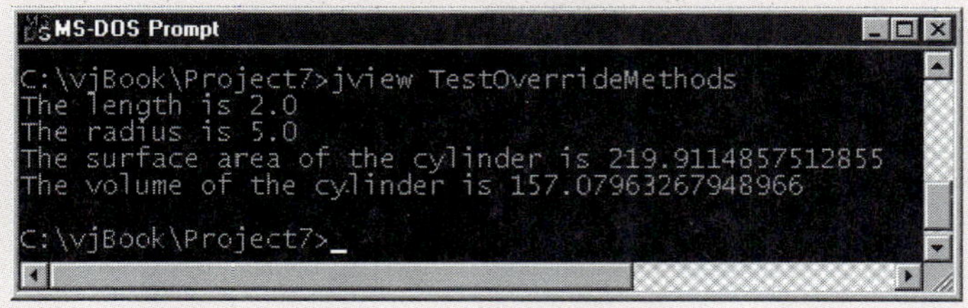

```
C:\vjBook\Project7>jview TestOverrideMethods
The length is 2.0
The radius is 5.0
The surface area of the cylinder is 219.9114857512855
The volume of the cylinder is 157.07963267948966

C:\vjBook\Project7>
```

Figure 7.3 *The* `Cylinder` *class overrides the* `findArea()` *method defined in the* `Circle` *class.*

Example Review

The example demonstrates that you can modify a method in the superclass (`Circle`) and can use `super` to invoke a method in the superclass. The `findArea()` method is defined in the `Circle` class and modified in the `Cylinder` class. Both methods can be used in the Cylinder class. To use the `findArea()` method defined in the `Circle` class, use `super.findArea()`.

A subclass of the `Cylinder` class can no longer access the `findArea()` method defined in the `Circle` class because the `findArea()` method is redefined in the `Cylinder` class.

> **NOTE**
> Since the `Cylinder` class has already been used in Example 7.1, you need to remove Cylinder.java from Project7 before compiling this example to avoid compilation errors on the duplicate class.

The Keyword *this*

The keyword `super` refers to the superclass. Occasionally, you need to reference the current class. Java provides another keyword, `this`, for referencing the current object. Use of the `this` keyword is analogous to use of `super`.

You can use `this` in the constructor. For example, you can redefine the `Circle` class as follows:

```
public class Circle
{
  private double radius;

  public Circle(double radius)
  {
    this.radius = radius;
  }

  public Circle()
  {
    this(1.0);
  }
```

```
     public double findArea()
     {
       return radius*radius*Math.PI;
     }
}
```

The line `this.radius = radius` means "assign argument `radius` to the object's data field `radius`." Here, `this` means "this object." The line `this(1.0)` invokes the constructor with a `double` value argument in the class.

> **NOTE**
> Java requires the `this()` statement to appear first in the constructor, even before data fields.

You don't need to use the `this` keyword in the `Circle` class declaration. However, the `this` keyword can be useful in certain cases discussed later in the book; for instance, you can use `new Thread(this)` to create a thread for `this` object, as described in Chapter 13, "Multithreading."

The *protected, final,* and *abstract* Modifiers

You have already used the modifiers `static`, `private`, and `public`. Three new modifiers will now be introduced: `protected`, `final`, and `abstract`. These three modifiers are used with respect to class inheritance.

The *protected* Modifier

The `protected` modifier can be applied on data and methods in a class. A protected data or a protected method in a public class can be accessed by any class in the same package or its subclasses, even if the subclasses are in a different package.

Suppose class `C1` contains a protected data named `x` in package `p1`, as shown in Figure 7.4. Consider the following scenarios:

1. If class `C2` in package `p2` is a subclass of `C1`, then `x` is accessible in `C2`, since it can be accessed by any subclass of `C1`.

2. If class `C3` in package `p1` contains an instance of `C1` named `c1`, then `x` is visible in `c1`, since `C3` and `C1` are in the same package.

3. If class `C4` in package `p2` contains an instance of `C1` named `c1`, then `x` is not visible in `c1`, because `C4` and `C1` are in different packages.

> **NOTE**
> The modifiers `private`, `public`, and `protected` are also known as *visibility modifiers,* which specify how class and class members are accessed.

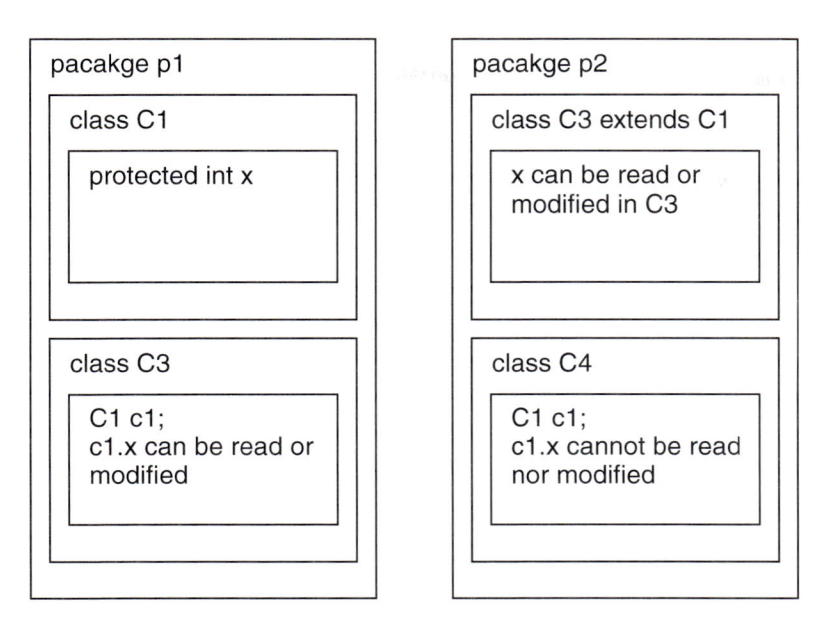

Figure 7.4 *The* `protected` *modifier can be used to prevent a non-subclass in a different package from accessing the class's data and methods.*

The *final* Modifier

You have already seen the `final` modifier used in declaring constants. Occasionally, you want to prevent classes from being extended. You can use the `final` modifier to indicate that a class is final and cannot be a parent class. The `Math` class introduced in Chapter 5, "Programming with Objects and Classes," is a `final` class.

You also can define a method to be final; a final method cannot be modified by its subclasses.

> **NOTE**
> The modifiers are used on classes and class members (data and methods), except that the `final` modifier can also be used on local variables in a method. A final local variable is a constant inside a method.

The *abstract* Modifier

In the inheritance hierarchy, classes become more specific and concrete *with each new subclass*. If you move from a subclass back up to a superclass, the classes become more general and less specific. Class design should ensure that a superclass shares features with its subclasses. Sometimes a superclass is so abstract that it cannot have any specific instances. Such classes are called *abstract classes* and are declared using the `abstract` modifier.

Abstract classes are like regular classes with data and methods, but you cannot create instances of abstract classes using the new operator. Abstract classes always contain abstract methods. An *abstract method* is a method signature without implementation. Its implementation is provided by its subclasses. The following example, for instance, shows how you can design an abstract class for all geometric objects:

```java
// GeometricObject.java: The abstract GeometricObject class
public abstract class GeometricObject
{
  protected String color;
  protected double weight;

  // Default construct
  protected GeometricObject()
  {
    color = "white";
    weight = 1.0;
  }

  // Construct a geometric object
  protected GeometricObject(String c, double w)
  {
    color = c;
    weight = w;
  }

  // Getter method for color
  public String getColor()
  {
    return color;
  }

  // Getter method for weight
  public double getWeight()
  {
    return weight;
  }

  // Abstract method
  public abstract double findArea();

  // Abstract method
  public abstract double findPerimeter();
}
```

This abstract class provides the common features (data and methods) for geometric objects. Because you don't know how to compute areas and volumes of geometric objects, `findArea()` and `findPerimeter()` are defined as abstract methods. These methods are to be implemented in the subclasses. For example, you can make `Circle` a subclass of `GeometricObject`. A possible implementation of the `Circle` class is as follows:

```java
// Circle.java: The circle class that extends GeometricObject
public class Circle extends GeometricObject
{
  protected double radius;

  // Default constructor
  public Circle()
```

```java
{
  this(1.0, 1.0, "white");
}

// Construct circle with specified radius
public Circle(double r)
{
  super("white", 1.0);
  radius = r;
}

// Construct a circle with specified radius, weight, and color
public Circle(double r, double w, String c)
{
  super(c, w);
  radius = r;
}

// Getter method for radius
public double getRadius()
{
  return radius;
}

// Find circle area
public double findArea()
{
  return radius*radius*Math.PI;
}

// Find circle perimeter
public double findPerimeter()
{
  return 2*radius*Math.PI;
}

// Override the toString() method defined in the Object class
public String toString()
{
  return "Circle radius = " + radius;
}
}
```

The data field `radius` is protected. So it can be referenced by any subclass of Circle.

For another example, you can make Rectangle a subclass of GeometricObject. A possible implementation of the Rectangle class is as follows:

```java
// Rectangle.java: The Rectangle class that extends GeometricObject
package Chapter7;

public class Rectangle extends GeometricObject
{
  protected double width;
  protected double height;

  // Default constructor
  public Rectangle()
  {
    this(1.0, 1.0, 1.0, "white");
  }
```

```java
  // Construct a rectangle with specified width and height
  public Rectangle(double width, double height)
  {
    this.width = width;
    this.height = height;
  }

  // Construct a rectangle with specified width, height, weight, and
  // color
  public Rectangle(double width, double height, double w, String c)
  {
    super(c, w);
    this.width = width;
    this.height = height;
  }

  // Getter method for radius
  public double getWidth()
  {
    return width;
  }

  // Find rectangle area
  public double findArea()
  {
    return width*height;
  }

  // Find rectangle perimeter
  public double findPerimeter()
  {
    return 2*(width + height);
  }

  // Override the toString() method defined in the Object class
  public String toString()
  {
    return "Rectangle width " + width + " and height " + height;
  }
}
```

> **TIP**
> Use abstract classes to generalize common properties and methods of subclasses. Use abstract methods to define the common methods that must be implemented in subclasses.

> **CAUTION**
> An abstract method cannot be contained in a nonabstract class. In a nonabstract subclass extended from an abstract class, all abstract methods must be implemented, even if they are not used in the subclass.

Polymorphism

Polymorphism is a Greek word meaning "many forms." In Java, polymorphism refers to the ability to determine at runtime which code to run, given multiple methods with the same name but different operations. There are many forms of polymorphism in Java. For instance, method overloading is a form of polymorphism. Java VM determines which overloaded method to invoke based on the number and types of parameters passed to that method. Another form of polymorphism involves invoking the same methods defined in different classes. Usually, a method defined in a superclass is overridden in its subclasses. Which method in a subclass is invoked depends on the type of the object and is determined at runtime.

In the preceding section, you created the `Circle` class and the `Rectangle` class. The methods `findArea()` and `findPerimeter()` defined in the `GeometricObject` class are overridden in the `Circle` class and the `Rectangle` class. Now create an array of `GeometricObject`:

```
GeometricObject geoObject[] = new GeometricObject[2];
```

Create a new circle and a rectangle, and assign them to `geoObject[0]` and `geoObject[1]`:

```
geoObject[0] = new Circle();
geoObject[1] = new Rectangle();
```

The following loop displays the area and the perimeter of the geometric objects in the array:

```
for (int i=0; i<2; i++)
{
  System.out.println("The area of object " + i + " is "
    + geoObject[i].findArea());
  System.out.println("The perimeter of object " + i + " is "
    + geoObject[i].findPerimeter());
}
```

Since `geoObject[0]` is a circle, the `findArea()` method and the `findPerimeter()` method defined in the `Circle` class are used for `geoObject[0].findArea()` and `geoObject[0].findPerimeter()`. Since `geoObject[1]` is a rectangle, the `findArea()` method and the `findPeremiter()` method defined in the `Rectangle` class are used for `geoObject[1].findArea()` and `geoObject[1].findPerimeter()`. Which of these methods are invoked is dynamically determined at runtime, depending on the type of the object.

Casting Objects

You have already used the casting operator to convert variables of one primitive type to another. Similarly, casting can also be used to convert an object of one class type to another within an inheritance hierarchy. In the preceding section, the statement

```
geoObject[0] = new Circle();
```

is known as *implicit casting*, which assigns a circle to a variable of `GeometricObject` type.

To perform an explicit casting, use a syntax similar to the one used for casting among primitive data types. Enclose the target object type in parentheses and place it before the object to be cast. For example:

```
Circle myCircle = (Circle)myCylinder;

Cylinder myCylinder = (Cylinder)myCircle;
```

The first statement converts `myCylinder` to its superclass variable `myCircle`; the second converts `myCircle` to its subclass variable `myCylinder`.

It is always possible to convert an instance of a subclass to an instance of a superclass, simply because an instance of a subclass is also an instance of its superclass. For example, an apple is an instance of the `Apple` class, which is a subclass of the `Fruit` class. An applet is always a fruit. Therefore, you can always assign an applet to a variable of the `Fruit` class. For this reason, explicit casting can be omitted in this case. For example:

```
Circle myCircle = myCylinder;
```

is equivalent to

```
Circle myCircle = (Circle)myCylinder;
```

When converting an instance of a superclass to an instance of its subclass, explicit casting must be used to confirm your intention to the compiler with the (`SubclassName`) cast notation. For the casting to be successful, you must make sure that the object to be cast is an instance of the subclass. If the superclass object is not an instance of the subclass, a runtime exception occurs. For example, an instance of the `Fruit` class cannot be cast into an instance of the `Apple` class, if the fruit is an orange. It is good practice, therefore, to ensure that the object is an instance of another object before attempting a casting. This can be accomplished by using the `instanceof` operator. For example, consider the following code:

```
Circle myCircle = new Circle();
if (myCircle instanceof Cylinder)
{
  // Perform casting if myCircle is an instance of Cylinder
  Cylinder myCylinder = (Cylinder)myCircle;
  ...
}
```

You may wonder how `myCircle` could become an instance of the `Cylinder` class and why it is necessary to perform casting. There are some cases in which a superclass becomes an instance of a subclass. To fully explore the properties and functions, you need to cast the object to its subclass. This is shown in the following example.

Example 7.4 Casting Objects

Suppose you have an array of geometric objects; some are circles and some are cylinders. This example shows a program that uses implicit casting to assign circles and cylinders to the array; it then uses explicit casting to access data and methods in the objects when processing the array. The output of a sample run of the program is shown in Figure 7.5.

```java
// TestCasting.java: Demonstrate using object casting
public class TestCasting
{
  // Main method
  public static void main(String[] args)
  {
    // Create geoObject array with two objects and initialize it
    GeometricObject[] geoObject = new GeometricObject[2];
    geoObject[0] = new Circle(5.0, 2.0, "white");
    geoObject[1] = new Cylinder(5.0, 2.0, "black", 4.0);

    // Display properties of the objects
    for (int i=0; i<2; i++)
    {
      if (geoObject[i] instanceof Cylinder)
      {
        System.out.println("Object is cylinder");
        System.out.println("Cylinder volume is " +
          ((Cylinder)geoObject[i]).findVolume());
      }
      else if (geoObject[i] instanceof Circle)
      {
        System.out.println("Object is circle");
        System.out.println("Circle area is "+
          ((Circle)geoObject[i]).findArea());
      }
    }
  }
}

// The new cylinder class that extends the circle class
class Cylinder extends Circle
{
  private double length;

  // Default constructor
  public Cylinder()
  {
    super();
    length = 1.0;
  }

  // Construct a cylinder with specified radius, and length
  public Cylinder(double r, double l)
  {
    this(r, 1.0, "white", l);
  }

  // Construct a cylinder with specified radius, weight, color, and
  // length
  public Cylinder(double r, double w, String c, double l)
  {
    super(r, w, c);
    length = l;
  }

  // Getter method for length
  public double getLength()
  {
    return length;
  }
```

continues

```java
    // Find cylinder surface area
    public double findArea()
    {
      return 2*super.findArea()+(2*getRadius()*Math.PI)*length;
    }

    // Find cylinder volume
    public double findVolume()
    {
      return super.findArea()*length;
    }
  }
```

```
C:\vjBook\Project7>jview TestCasting
Object is circle
Circle area is 78.53981633974483
Object is cylinder
Cylinder volume is 314.1592653589793

C:\vjBook\Project7>
```

Figure 7.5 *The program creates an array of objects of* `GeometricObject` *type and casts the objects to subclasses of* `GeometricObject` *in order to use the data and methods defined in the subclasses* `Circle` *and* `Cylinder`.

Example Review

The program concerns three classes: `GeometricObject`, `Circle`, and `Cylinder`. Their inheritance hierarchy is shown in Figure 7.6.

Casting can only be done when the source object is an instance of the target class. The program uses the `instanceof` operator to ensure that the source object is an instance of the target class before performing a casting.

```
GeometricObject
      ↓
    Circle
      ↓
   Cylinder
```

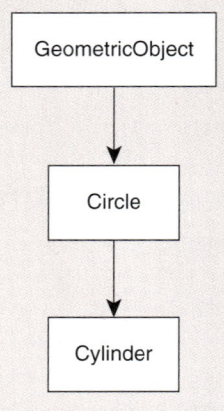

Figure 7.6 `Cylinder` *is a subclass of* `Circle`, *and* `Circle` *is a subclass of* `GeometricObject`.

The program uses implicit casting to assign a `Circle` object to `geoObject[0]` and a `Cylinder` object to `geoObject[1]`. The reason for this casting is to store the `Circle` object and the `Cylinder` object in the `geoObject` array.

In the `for` loop, the cylinder volume is displayed if the object is a cylinder; the circle area of the object is displayed if the object is a circle.

Note that the order in the `if` statement is significant. If it is reversed (for example, testing whether the object is an instance of `Circle` first), then the cylinder will never be cast into `Cylinder` because `Cylinder` is an instance of `Circle`. Try to run the program with the following `if` statement and observe the effect.

```java
if (geoObject[i] instanceof Circle)
{
  System.out.println("Object is circle");
  System.out.println("Circle area is " +
    ((Circle)geoObject[i]).findArea());
}
else if (geoObject[i] instanceof Cylinder)
{
  System.out.println("Object is cylinder");
  System.out.println("Cylinder volume is  " +
    ((Cylinder)geoObject[i]).findVolume());
}
```

NOTE
Explicit casting from `geoObject[i]` to `Cylinder` is necessary. The reason for casting to `Cylinder` is to use the `findVolume()` method, which is available only in the `Cylinder` class. However, explicit casting from `geoObject[i]` to `Circle` is not necessary, because the `findArea()` method is defined in the `GeometricObject` class and overridden in the `Circle` class. By means of polymorphism, the `findArea()` method of the `Circle` is invoked if the geometric object is a circle.

TIP
I recommend that you use the `instanceof` operator to ensure that the source object is an instance of the target class before performing a casting.

The *Object* Class

Every class in Java is descended from the `java.lang.Object` class. If no inheritance is specified when a class is defined, the superclass of the class is `Object`. Classes like `Rational`, `Mortgage`, and `GeometricObject` are implicitly the child classes of `Object` (as are all the main classes you have seen in this book so far). It is important to be familiar with the methods provided by the `Object` class so that you can use them in your classes. Three useful instance methods in the `Object` class are:

- `public boolean equals(Object object)`
- `public String toString()`
- `public Object clone()`

The *equals()* Method

The `equals()` method tests whether two objects are equal. The syntax to use `equals()` is as follows:

```
object1.equals(object2);
```

The components `object1` and `object2` are of the same class.

The default implementation of the `equals()` method in the `Object` class is as follows:

```
public boolean equals(Object obj)
{
   return (this == obj);
}
```

Thus, using the `equals()` method is equivalent to the `==` operator in the `Object` class, but it is really intended for the subclasses of the `Object` class to modify the `equals()` method to test whether two distinct objects of the same class have the same contents.

You have already used the `equals()` method to compare two strings in Chapter 6, "Arrays and Strings." The `equals()` method in the `String` class is inherited from the `Object` class and is modified in the `String` class to test whether two strings are identical in contents.

> **NOTE**
> The `==` comparison operator is used for comparing two primitive data type values, or for determining whether two objects have the same references. The `equals()` method is intended to test whether two objects have the same contents, provided that this method is modified in the defining class of the objects. The `==` operator is stronger than the `equals()` method.

The *toString()* Method

Invoking `toString()` returns a string that represents the value of this object. By default, it returns a string consisting of a class name of which the object is an instance, the at sign (@), and a number representing the object. For example, consider the following code:

```
Cylinder myCylinder = new MyCylinder(5.0, 2.0);
System.out.println(myCylinder.toString());
```

This code displays something like `Cylinder@15037e5`. This message is not very helpful or informative. Usually you should overwrite the `toString()` method so that it returns a digestible string representation of the object. For example, you can override the `toString()` method in the `Cylinder` class:

```
public String toString()
{
  return "Cylinder length = " + length;
}
```

Then `System.out.println(myCylinder.toString())` displays something like the following:

```
Cylinder length = 2
```

> **TIP**
> Alternatively, you could write `System.out.println(myCylinder)` instead of `System.out.println(myCylinder.toString())`. The Java compiler automatically translates `myCylinder` into a string by invoking its `toString()` method when it is used in the `print` method.

The *clone()* Method

Sometimes you need to make a copy of an object. Naturally, you would use the assignment statement, as follows:

```
newObject = someObject;
```

This statement does not create a duplicate object. It simply assigns the reference of `someObject` to `newObject`. To create a new object with separate memory space, you need to use the `clone()` method, as follows:

```
newObject = someObject.clone();
```

This statement copies `someObject` to a new memory location and assigns the reference of the new object to `newObject`.

> **NOTE**
> Not all objects can be cloned. For an object to be clonable, its class must implement the `java.lang.Clonable` interface. Interfaces are introduced in the section "Interfaces," in this chapter.

> **NOTE**
> The `Object` class also contains the `wait()` and `notify()` methods to control threads, which are introduced in Chapter 13, "Multithreading."

Processing Primitive Type Values as Objects

Primitive data types are not used as objects in Java. Performance is the reason for this. Because of the overhead of processing objects, the language's performance would be adversely affected if primitive data types were treated as objects. However, many Java methods require the use of objects as arguments. Java offers a convenient way to wrap a primitive data type into an object (for example, wrapping `int` into the class `Integer`). The corresponding class is called a *wrapper class* in Java terminology.

By using wrapper objects instead of a primitive data type variable, you can take advantage of generic programming. An example of generic programming is given in Example 7.5, "Designing Abstract Classes," and Example 7.6, "Extending Abstract Classes."

The wrapper classes provide constructors, constants, and conversion methods for manipulating various data types. Java provides `Boolean`, `Character`, `Double`, `Float`, `Byte`, `Short`, `Integer`, and `Long` wrappers for primitive data types. All the wrapper classes are grouped in the `java.lang` package.

> **NOTE**
> The wrapper class name for a primitive type is the same as the primitive data type name with the first letter capitalized. The exception is `Integer` and `Character`.

The next section discusses numeric wrapper classes, specifically the `Integer` and `Double` classes. For more detailed information about the wrapper classes, refer to the Java API documentation in Visual J++ Help.

The *Number* Class and Its Subclasses

Because numeric wrapper classes (`Byte`, `Double`, `Float`, `Integer`, `Long`, `Short`) are very similar, their common methods are generalized in an abstract superclass named `Number`. The `Number` class defines abstract methods to convert the represented numeric value to `byte`, `double`, `float`, `int`, `long`, and `short`. These methods are implemented in the subclasses of `Number`:

- `public byte byteValue()`

  This returns the number as a `byte`.

- `public short shortValue()`

  This returns the number as a `short`.

- `public int intValue()`

  This returns the number as an `int`.

- `public long longValue()`

  This returns the number as a `long`.

- `public float floatValue()`

  This returns the number as a `float`.

- `public double doubleValue()`

  This returns the number as a `double`.

Numeric Wrapper Class Constructors

You can construct a numeric wrapper object either from a primitive data type value or from a string representing the numeric value. The constructors are:

```
public Integer(int value)
public Integer(String s)
public Double(double value)
public Double(String s)
```

For example:

```
Double doubleObject = new Double(5.0);
```

or

```
Double doubleObject = new Double("5.0");
```

This constructs a wrapper object for `Double` value `5.0`.

```
Integer integerObject = new Integer(5);
```

or equivalently

```
Integer integerObject = new Integer("5");
```

This constructs a wrapper object for `int` value `5`.

Numeric Wrapper Class Constants

Each numerical wrapper class has constants: `MAX_VALUE` and `MIN_VALUE`. `MAX_VALUE` represents the maximum value of the corresponding primitive data type. For `Byte`, `Short`, `Integer`, and `Long`, `MIN_VALUE` represents the minimum byte, short, int, and long value. For `Float` and `Double`, `MIN_VALUE` represents the minimum *positive* float and double value. The following statements, for example, display the maximum integer (2,147,483,647), the minimum positive float (1.4E-45), and the maximum double floating-point number (1.79769313486231570e+308d).

```
System.out.println("The maximum integer is " + Integer.MAX_VALUE);
System.out.println("The minimum positive float is " +
  Float.MIN_VALUE);
System.out.println(
  "The maximum double precision floating-point number is " +
  Double.MAX_VALUE);
```

Conversion Methods

Each numeric wrapper class implements the abstract methods `doubleValue()`, `floatValue()`, `intValue()`, `longValue()`, and `shortValue()`, which are defined in the `Number` class. It also overrides the `toString()` and `equals()` methods defined in the `Object` class.

For example:

```
long l = doubleObject.longValue();
```

This converts `doubleObject`'s double value to a `long` variable l.

```
int i = integerObject.intValue();
```

This assigns the `int` value of `integerObject` to i.

```
double d = 5.9;
Double doubleObject = new Double(d);
String s = doubleObject.toString();
```

This converts `double` d to a string s.

The *valueOf(), parseInt(),* and *parseDouble()* Methods

The numeric wrapper classes have a useful class method `valueOf(String s)`. This method creates a new object, initialized to the value represented by the specified string. For example:

```
Double doubleObject = Double.valueOf("12.4");
Integer integerObject = Integer.valueOf("12");
```

The `Integer` wrapper class has some methods that are not available in `Double`. The `parseInt()` method, for example, is only available in integer wrappers `Integer` and `Long`, but not in `Double` or `Float`.

```
public static int parseInt(String s, int radix)
```

This returns the integer value represented in the string s with the specified `radix`. If `radix` is omitted, base 10 is assumed.

Since JDK 1.2, the `Double` class supports a static method `parseDouble()` with following signature for converting a numeric string into a double value.

```
public static double parseDouble(String s)
```

Class-Design Guidelines

The key to object-oriented programming is to model the application in terms of cooperative objects. Carefully designed classes are critical when a project is being developed. There are many levels of abstraction in system design. You have learned method abstraction and have applied it to the development of large programs. Methods are means to group statements. Classes extend abstraction to a higher level and provide a means of grouping methods. Classes do more than just group methods, however; they also contain data fields. Methods and data fields together describe the properties and behaviors of classes.

The power of classes is further extended by inheritance. Inheritance enables a class to extend existing classes without knowing the details of the existing classes. In the development of a Java program, class abstraction is applied to decompose the problem into a set of related classes, and method abstraction is applied to design classes.

The following are some guidelines for designing classes:

- A class should use the `private` modifier to hide its data from direct access by clients. This prevents the clients from damaging the data. A class should also hide methods not intended for client use. The `gcd()` method in the `Rational` class in Example 5.8 is private, for example, because it is only for internal use within the class. You can use getter methods and setter methods to provide users with access to the hidden data, but only to hidden data you want the user to see or to modify.

- A property that is shared by all the instances of the class should be declared as a class property. For example, the `MAX_VALUE` constant is shared by all the objects of the `Integer` class, therefore, it is declared as a class variable. A method that is not dependent on a specific instance should be declared as a class method. For instance, the `parseInt()` method in the Integer class is not tied to a specific instance of the `Integer` class, therefore, it is declared as a class method. The class properties and methods are denoted using the static modifier.

- A class should describe a single entity or a set of similar operations. You can use a class for students, for example, but do not combine students and staff in the same class. Since the `Math` class provides mathematical operations, it is natural to group the mathematical methods in one class. A single entity with too many responsibilities can be broken into several classes to separate responsibilities. The `String` class, `StringBuffer` class, and `StringTokenizer` class both deal with strings, for example, but have different responsibilities.

- Group common data fields and operations shared by other classes into a superclass, which is sometimes an abstract class. For example, the classes `Integer`, `Long`, `Float`, and `Double` share many common data fields and operations, which are grouped into an abstract class `Number`. You should use inheritance to model the is-a relationship. A student or a faculty member is a person, for example, so `Student` can be designed as a subclass of `Person`.

- Follow standard Java programming style introduced in Chapter 2. Choose informative names for classes, data fields, and methods. Always place the data declaration before constructors, and place constructors before methods. Always provide a constructor and initialize variables to avoid programming errors.

Case Studies (Optional)

This section presents a case study on designing classes for matrix operations. The operations, such as addition and multiplication, for all the matrices are similar except that their element types differ. Therefore, you can design a superclass that describes the common operations shared by matrices of all types regardless of their element types, and create subclasses tailored to specific types of matrices. Example 7.5 gives the superclass named `GenericMatrix` and Example 7.6 presents two subclasses named `IntegerMatrix` and `RationalMatrix` that extend `GenericMatrix` for handling integer matrix operations and rational matrix operations.

Example 7.5 Designing Abstract Classes

This example gives a generic class for matrix arithmetic. This class implements matrix addition and multiplication common for all types of matrices. You will use the `Integer` matrix and the `Rational` matrix to test this generic class in Example 7.6.

The generic class named `GenericMatrix` is created with the following data fields and methods:

Data field:

`Object[][] matrix`: Data representation for this matrix.

Methods:

`public Object[][] addMatrix(Object[][] secondMatrix)`

Add `secondMatrix` with this matrix.

`public Object[][] multiplyMatrix(Object[][] secondMatrix)`

Multiply `secondMatrix` with this matrix.

`public abstract Object add(Object o1, Object o2);`

Abstract method for adding two elements of the matrices.

`public abstract Object multiply(Object o1, Object o2);`

Abstract method for multiplying two elements of the matrices.

`public abstract Object zero();`

Abstract method for defining zero for the matrix element.

`public static void displayMatrix(Object[][] m)`

Display a matrix on the console.

```java
// GenericMatrix.java: Define a matrix and its associated
// operations such as add and multiply
public abstract class GenericMatrix
{
  // Representation of a matrix using a two-dimensional array
  private Object[][] matrix;

  // Construct a matrix
  public GenericMatrix(Object[][] matrix)
  {
    this.matrix = matrix;
  }

  // Add two matrices
  public Object[][] addMatrix(Object[][] secondMatrix)
  {
    // Create a result matrix
    Object[][] result =
      new Object[matrix.length][matrix[0].length];
```

```java
    // Check bounds of the two matrices
    if ((matrix.length != secondMatrix.length) ||
        (matrix[0].length != secondMatrix.length))
    {
      System.out.println(
        "The matrices do not have the same size");
      System.exit(0);
    }

    // Perform addition
    for (int i=0; i<result.length; i++)
      for (int j=0; j<result[i].length; j++)
        result[i][j] = add(matrix[i][j], secondMatrix[i][j]);

    return result;
  }

  // Multiply two matrices
  public Object[][] multiplyMatrix(Object[][] secondMatrix)
  {
    // Create result matrix
    Object[][] result =
      new Object[matrix.length][secondMatrix[0].length];

    // Check bounds
    if (matrix[0].length != secondMatrix.length)
    {
      System.out.println("Bounds error");
      System.exit(0);
    }

    // Perform multiplication of two matrices
    for (int i=0; i<result.length; i++)
      for (int j=0; j<result[0].length; j++)
    {
      result[i][j] = zero();

      for (int k=0; k<matrix[0].length; k++)
      {
        result[i][j] = add(result[i][j],
          multiply(this.matrix[i][k], secondMatrix[k][j]));
      }
    }

    return result;
  }

  // Abstract method for adding two elements of the matrices
  public abstract Object add(Object o1, Object o2);

  // Abstract method for multiplying two elements of the matrices
  public abstract Object multiply(Object o1, Object o2);

  // Abstract method for defining zero for the matrix element
  public abstract Object zero();

  // Display a matrix
  public static void displayMatrix(Object[][] m)
  {
    for (int i=0; i<m.length; i++)
```

continues

```
      {
        for (int j=0; j<m[0].length; j++)
          System.out.print(m[i][j].toString()+"  ");
        System.out.print('\n');
      }
    }
  }
}
```

Example Review

Because the element type in the matrix is not specified, the program doesn't know how to add or multiply two matrix elements and doesn't know what the zero value is for the element (for example, 0 for `int` or 0/1 for `Rational`). Therefore, `add()`, `multiply()`, and `zero()` are defined as abstract methods. These methods are implemented in the subclasses in which the matrix element type is specified.

The matrix element type is `Object`. This enables you to use an object of any class as long as you can implement the abstract `add()`, `multiply()`, and `zero()` methods.

The `addMatrix()` and `multiplyMatrix()` methods are concrete methods, defined and implemented in this generic class. They are ready to use provided that the `add()`, `multiply()`, and `zero()` methods are implemented in the subclasses.

The `displayMatrix()` method displays the matrix on the console. The `toString()` method is used to display the element.

The `addMatrix()` and `multiplyMatrix()` methods check the bounds of the matrices before performing operations. If the two matrices have incompatible bounds, the program terminates.

> **NOTE**
> Since the parameters of `add()`, `multiply()`, and `zero()` are of the `Object` type, you can pass any object type to these methods. This is another form of polymorphism in object-oriented programming, known as *generic programming*. Generic programming enables a method to operate on arguments of generic types, making it reusable with multiple types.

Example 7.6 Extending Abstract Classes

This example gives two programs that utilize the `GenericMatrix` class for integer matrix arithmetic and rational matrix arithmetic.

The program given below creates two integer matrices and performs addition and multiplication operations. The output of the program is shown in Figure 7.7.

```java
// TestIntegerMatrix.java: Test matrix operations involving
// integer values
public class TestIntegerMatrix
{
  // Main method
  public static void main(String[] args)
  {
    // Create Integer arrays m1, m2
    Integer[][] m1 = new Integer[4][4];
    Integer[][] m2 = new Integer[4][4];

    // Initialize Integer arrays m1 and m2
    for (int i=0; i<m1.length; i++)
      for (int j=0; j<m1[0].length; j++)
      {
        m1[i][j] = new Integer(i);
      }

    for (int i=0; i<m2.length; i++)
      for (int j=0; j<m2[0].length; j++)
      {
        m2[i][j] = new Integer(i+j);
      }

    // Create an instance of IntegerMatrix
    IntegerMatrix im1 = new IntegerMatrix(m1);

    // Perform integer matrix addition, and multiplication
    Object[][] m3 = im1.addMatrix((Object[][])m2);
    Object[][] m4 = im1.multiplyMatrix(m2);

    // Display m1, m2, m3, m4
    System.out.println("m1 is ...");
    IntegerMatrix.displayMatrix(m1);
    System.out.println("m2 is ...");
    IntegerMatrix.displayMatrix(m2);
    System.out.println("m1+m2 is ...");
    IntegerMatrix.displayMatrix(m3);
    System.out.println("m1*m2 is ...");
    IntegerMatrix.displayMatrix(m4);
  }
}

// Declare IntegerMatrix derived from GenericMatrix
class IntegerMatrix extends GenericMatrix
{
  // Construct an IntegerMatrix
  public IntegerMatrix(Integer[][] m)
  {
    super(m);
  }

  // Implement the add method for adding two matrix elements
  public Object add(Object o1, Object o2)
  {
    Integer i1 = (Integer)o1;
    Integer i2 = (Integer)o2;
    return new Integer(i1.intValue() + i2.intValue());
  }
```

continues

```java
    // Implement the multiply method for multiplying two matrix elements
    public Object multiply(Object o1, Object o2)
    {
      Integer i1 = (Integer)o1;
      Integer i2 = (Integer)o2;
      return new Integer(i1.intValue() * i2.intValue());
    }

    // Implement the zero method to specify zero for Integer
    public Object zero()
    {
      return new Integer(0);
    }
  }
```

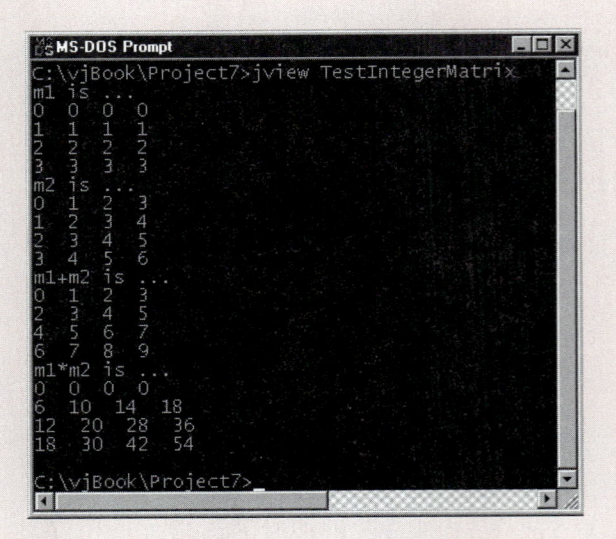

Figure 7.7 *The program creates two* int *matrices and performs addition and multiplication on them.*

The next program creates two rational matrices and performs addition and multiplication operations. The output is shown in Figure 7.8.

```java
// TestRationalMatrix.java: Test matrix operations involving
// Rational values
public class TestRationalMatrix
{
  // Main method
  public static void main(String[] args)
  {
    // Declare Rational arrays m1, m2
    Rational[][] m1 = new Rational[4][4];
    Rational[][] m2 = new Rational[4][4];

    // Initialize Rational arrays m1 and m2
    for (int i=0; i<m1.length; i++)
      for (int j=0; j<m1[0].length; j++)
```

```
      {
        m1[i][j] = new Rational(i,i+1);
        m2[i][j] = new Rational(i,i+1);
      }

    // Create RationalMatrix instance rm1
    RationalMatrix rm1 = new RationalMatrix(m1);

    // Perform Rational matrix addition, and multiplication
    Object[][] m3 = rm1.addMatrix(m2);
    Object[][] m4 = rm1.multiplyMatrix(m2);

    // Display m1, m2, m3, m4
    System.out.println("m1 is ...");
    RationalMatrix.displayMatrix(m1);
    System.out.println("m2 is ...");
    RationalMatrix.displayMatrix(m2);
    System.out.println("m1+m2 is ...");
    RationalMatrix.displayMatrix(m3);
    System.out.println("m1*m2 is ...");
    RationalMatrix.displayMatrix(m4);
  }
}

// Declare RationalMatrix derived from GenericMatrix
class RationalMatrix extends GenericMatrix
{
  // Construct a RationalMatrix for a given Rational array
  public RationalMatrix(Rational[][] m1)
  {
    super(m1);
  }

  // Implement the add method for adding two rational elements
  public Object add(Object o1, Object o2)
  {
    Rational r1 = (Rational)o1;
    Rational r2 = (Rational)o2;
    return r1.add(r2);
  }

  // Implement the multiply method for multiplying two rational
  // elements
  public Object multiply(Object o1, Object o2)
  {
    Rational r1 = (Rational)o1;
    Rational r2 = (Rational)o2;
    return r1.multiply(r2);
  }

  // Implement the zero method to specify zero for Rational
  public Object zero()
  {
    return new Rational(0,1);
  }
}
```

continues

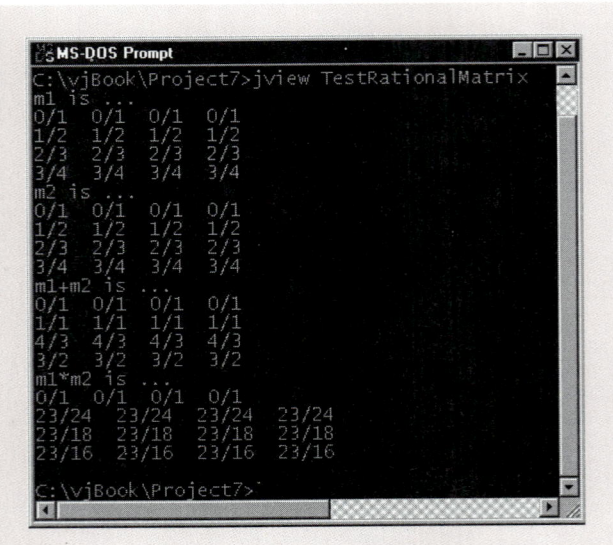

```
MS-DOS Prompt
C:\vjBook\Project7>jview TestRationalMatrix
m1 is ...
0/1   0/1   0/1   0/1
1/2   1/2   1/2   1/2
2/3   2/3   2/3   2/3
3/4   3/4   3/4   3/4
m2 is ...
0/1   0/1   0/1   0/1
1/2   1/2   1/2   1/2
2/3   2/3   2/3   2/3
3/4   3/4   3/4   3/4
m1+m2 is ...
0/1   0/1   0/1   0/1
1/1   1/1   1/1   1/1
4/3   4/3   4/3   4/3
3/2   3/2   3/2   3/2
m1*m2 is ...
0/1   0/1   0/1   0/1
23/24 23/24 23/24 23/24
23/18 23/18 23/18 23/18
23/16 23/16 23/16 23/16
C:\vjBook\Project7>
```

Figure 7.8 *The program creates two matrices of rational numbers and performs addition and multiplication on them.*

Example Review

`IntegerMatrix` and `RationalMatrix` are concrete subclasses of `GenericMatrix` for integer matrix arithmetic. These classes extend the `GenericMatrix` class and implement the `add()`, `multiply()`, and `zero()` methods.

Casting the object from type `Object` to type `Integer` in the `IntegerMatrix` class is necessary because the program has to use the `intValue()` method for integer addition and multiplication, and it is not available in `Object`. Similar casting is needed from type `Object` to type `Rational` in the `RationalMatrix` class for the same reason.

The `TestIntegerMatrix` program creates and initializes two matrices: m1 and m2. The result of adding them is stored in m3, and the result of multiplying them is stored in m4. The `TestRationalMatrix` program performs similar operations.

The statement

`IntegerMatrix im1 = new IntegerMatrix(m1);`

in `IntegerMatrix` creates im1 as an instance of `IntegerMatrix` for matrix m1, so you can use `im1.addMatrix(m2)` and `im1.multiplyMatrix(m2)` to perform matrix addition and multiplication for m1 and m2. The variable rm1 was created for the same reason in `RationalMatrix`.

Interfaces

Occasionally it is necessary to derive a subclass from several classes, thus inheriting their data and methods. If you use the `extends` keyword to define a subclass, it can have only one parent class. With interfaces, you can obtain the effect of multiple inheritance.

An interface is treated like a special class in Java. Each interface is compiled into a separate bytecode file, just like a regular class. You cannot create an instance for the interface using the `new` operator, but in most cases you can use an interface more or less the same way you use an abstract class. For example, you can use an interface as a data type for a variable, as the result of casting, and so on.

The structure of a Java interface resembles that of an abstract class in that you can have data and methods. The data, however, must be constants, and the methods can have only declarations without implementation. The syntax to declare an interface is as follows:

```
modifier interface InterfaceName
{
  // Constants declarations;
  // Methods signatures;
}
```

Suppose you want to design a generic sort method to sort elements. The elements can be an array of objects, such as students, circles, or cylinders. Because compare methods are different for different types of objects, you need to define a generic compare method to determine the order of two objects. Then you can tailor the method to comparing students, circles, or cylinders. For example, you can use student ID as the key for comparing students, radius as the key for comparing circles, and volume as the key for comparing cylinders. You can use an interface to define a generic `compareTo()` method, as follows:

```
// CompareObject.java: Interface for comparing objects
public interface CompareObject
{
  public static final int LESS = -1;
  public static final int EQUAL = 0;
  public static final int GREATER = 1;

  public int compareTo(CompareObject otherObject);
}
```

The `compareTo()` method determines the order of objects a and b of the `CompareObject` type. The method `a.compareTo(b)` returns a value of `CompareObject.LESS` (-1) if a is less than b; a value of `CompareObject.LESS` (0) if a is equal to b; or a value of `CompareObject.GREATER` (1) if a is greater than b.

A generic sort method for an array of `CompareObject` objects can be declared in a class named `Sort`, as follows:

```java
// Sort.java: Sort objects
public class Sort
{
  // Sort an array of objects using the selection sort approach
  public static void sort(CompareObject[] object)
  {
    CompareObject currentMax;
    int currentMaxIndex;

    for (int i=object.length-1; i>=1; i--)
    {
      // Find the maximum in the object[0..i]
      currentMax = object[i];
      currentMaxIndex = i;
      for (int j=i-1; j>=0; j--)
      {
        if (currentMax.compareTo(object[j]) == -1)
        {
          currentMax = object[j];
          currentMaxIndex = j;
        }
      }

      // Swap list[i] with o[currentMaxIndex] if necessary;
      if (currentMaxIndex != i)
      {
        object[currentMaxIndex] = object[i];
        object[i] = currentMax;
      }
    }
  }
}
```

The Sort class contains the static method named sort. This method is based on the same algorithm as Example 6.2, "Using Arrays in Sorting" (see Chapter 6, "Arrays and Strings"), except that here the order of two elements is determined by the compareTo() method defined in the CompareObject interface.

To use the sort() method for an array of objects of a specific type, you need to implement the CompareObject interface for that type. The following example demonstrates how the interface is used.

Example 7.7 Using Interfaces

In this example, a program is written that uses the generic sorting method to sort an array of circles in increasing order of their radii and an array of cylinders in increasing order of their volumes. The output of the program is shown in Figure 7.9.

```java
// TestSortCircleCylinder.java: Using the CompareObject interface
// and the generic sort class to sort circles and cylinders
public class TestSortCircleCylinder
{
  // Main method
  public static void main(String[] args)
  {
    // Create an array of circles
    CompareCircle[] circle = new CompareCircle[10];
    for (int i=0; i<circle.length; i++)
      circle[i] = new CompareCircle(100*Math.random(), 1.0, "white");
```

```java
    // Sort an array of circles
    Sort.sort(circle);

    // Display sorted circles
    System.out.println("Sorted circles");
    printObject(circle);

    // Create an array of cylinders
    CompareCylinder[] cylinder = new CompareCylinder[10];
    for (int i=0; i<cylinder.length; i++)
      cylinder[i] = new CompareCylinder(
        100*Math.random(), 1.0, "white", 100*Math.random());

    // Sort an array of cylinders
    Sort.sort(cylinder);

    // Display sorted cylinders
    System.out.println("Sorted cylinders");
    printObject(cylinder);
  }

  // Print cylinders
  public static void printObject(Object[] object)
  {
    for (int i=0; i<object.length; i++)
      System.out.println(object[i]);
  }
}

// CompareCircle is a subclass of Circle, which implements the
// CompareObject interface
class CompareCircle extends Circle implements CompareObject
{
  // Construct a CompareCircle with specified radius, weight, and
  // color
  public CompareCircle(double r, double w, String c)
  {
    super(r, w, c);
  }

  // Implement the compare method defined in CompareObject
  public int compareTo(CompareObject otherObject)
  {
    Circle circle = (Circle)otherObject;
    if (getRadius() < circle.getRadius())
      return LESS;
    else if (getRadius() == circle.getRadius())
      return EQUAL;
    else return GREATER;
  }
}

// CompareCylinder is a subclass of Cylinder, which implements the
// CompareObject interface
class CompareCylinder extends Cylinder implements CompareObject
{
  // Construct a CompareCylinder with radius, weight, and color
  CompareCylinder(double r, double w, String c, double l)
  {
    super(r, w, c, l);
  }
```

continues

```java
  // Implement the compare method defined in CompareObject
  public int compareTo(CompareObject otherObject)
  {
    Cylinder c = (Cylinder) otherObject;
    if (findVolume() < c.findVolume())
      return LESS;
    else if (findVolume() == c.findVolume())
      return EQUAL;
    else return GREATER;
  }

  // Override the toString method defined in the Object class
  public String toString()
  {
    return "Cylinder volume = " + findVolume();
  }
}
```

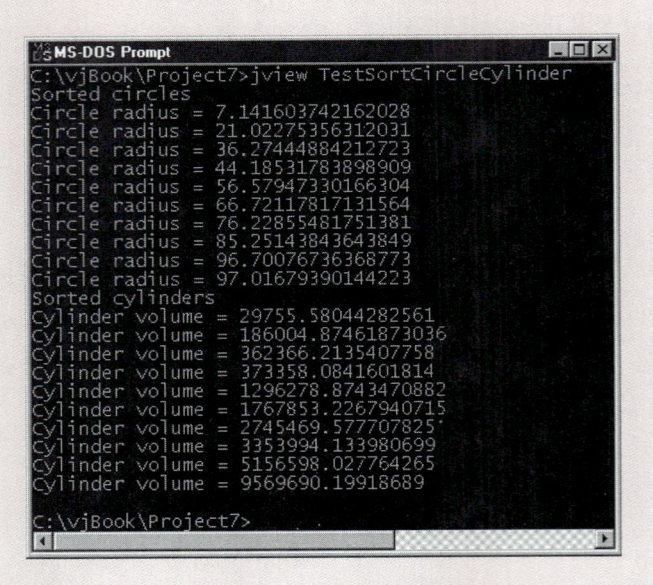

```
C:\vjBook\Project7>jview TestSortCircleCylinder
Sorted circles
Circle radius = 7.141603742162028
Circle radius = 21.02275356312031
Circle radius = 36.27444884212723
Circle radius = 44.18531783898909
Circle radius = 56.57947330166304
Circle radius = 66.72117817131564
Circle radius = 76.22855481751381
Circle radius = 85.2514384364384 9
Circle radius = 96.70076736368773
Circle radius = 97.01679390144223
Sorted cylinders
Cylinder volume = 29755.58044282561
Cylinder volume = 186004.87461873036
Cylinder volume = 362366.2135407758
Cylinder volume = 373358.0841601814
Cylinder volume = 1296278.8743470882
Cylinder volume = 1767853.2267940715
Cylinder volume = 2745469.577707825
Cylinder volume = 3353994.133980699
Cylinder volume = 5156598.027764265
Cylinder volume = 9569690.19918689

C:\vjBook\Project7>
```

Figure 7.9 *The program sorts a list of* Circle *objects by their radii and a list of* Cylinder *objects by their volumes.*

Example Review

The sort() method can be used to sort a list of any objects of the CompareObject type. Any object whose class implements the CompareObject interface is an instance of the CompareObject type. The example creates the classes CompareCircle and CompareCylinder in order to utilize the generic sorting method. The relationship of the class hierarchy is shown in Figure 7.10.

> **NOTE**
> I use a rectangular box to denote a class and a parallelogram box to denote an interface in the class hierarchy diagram, as in Figure 7.10.

```
GeometricObject ──▶ Circle ──▶ Cylinder
                      │           │
                      ▼           │
CompareObject ──▶ CompareCircle   │
      │                           ▼
      └──────────────────▶ CompareCylinder
```

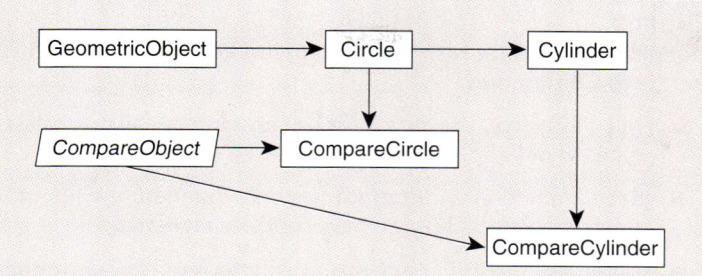

Figure 7.10 *The* `CompareCircle` *class extends* `Circle` *and implements* `CompareObject`, *and* `CompareCylinder` *extends* `Cylinder` *and implements* `CompareObject`.

The common functionality is to compare objects in this example, but the `compareTo()` methods are different for different types of objects. Therefore, the interface `CompareObject` is used to generalize common functionality and leave the detail for the subclasses to implement.

The keyword `implements` in the `CompareCircle` class indicates that `CompareCircle` inherits all data from the interface `CompareObject` and implements the methods in the interface.

The `CompareCircle` class implements the `compareTo()` method for comparing the radii of two circles, and the `CompareCylinder` class implements the `compareTo()` method for comparing the cylinders based on their volumes.

An interface provides another form of generic programming. It would be difficult to use a generic `sort()` method to sort all types of objects without using an interface in this example, because multiple inheritance is necessary to inherit the `CompareObject` class and an object's class, such as `Circle` or `Cylinder`.

Suppose you add the `compareTo()` method in the `GeometricObject` class. You can define a `sort()` method as follows:

```
public static void sort(GeometricObject[] list)
```

this new `sort()` method can be used to sort a list of circles, a list of cylinders, or a list of rectangles, provided that the classes `Circle`, `Cylinder`, and `Rectangle` implement the `compareTo()` method defined in the `GeometricObject` class. See Exercise 7.7. There is no need to use the `CompareObject` interface. This `sort()` method, however, can only be used to sort instances of the `GeometricObject` class.

The `Object` class contains the `equals()` method, which is intended for the subclasses of the `Object` class to override for comparing whether the contents of the objects are the same. Suppose the `Object` class contains the `compareTo()` method as defined in the `CompareObject` interface, the new `sort()` method can be used to compare a list of *any* objects. Whether a `compareTo()` method should be included in the `Object` class is debatable. Since the `compareTo()` method is not defined in the `Object` class, the `CompareObject` interface is created to enable a generic `sort()` method to sort a list of the `CompareObject` instances.

> **CAUTION**
> Defining an interface is similar to defining an abstract class. There are, however, a few differences:
>
> - In an interface, the data must be constants; an abstract class can have all types of data.
>
> - Each method in an interface has only a signature without implementation; an abstract class can have concrete methods.
>
> - No abstract modifier appears in an interface; you must put the abstract modifier before an abstract method in an abstract class.

> **TIP**
> Abstract classes and interfaces both can be used to achieve generic programming. You should use interfaces if multiple inheritance is needed. You should use abstract classes if single inheritance is sufficient. Generally, it is easier to use an abstract class than an interface, but interfaces are more flexible than abstract classes.

Inner Classes

An *inner class*, or *nested class*, is a class defined within the scope of another class. Here is an example of an inner class:

```java
// ShowInnerClass.java: Demonstrate using inner classes
package Chapter7;

public class ShowInnerClass
{
  private int data;

  // A method
  public void m()
  {
    // Do something
    InnerClass instance = new InnerClass();
  }

  // An inner class
  class InnerClass
  {
    // A method in the inner class
    public void mi()
    {
      // Directly reference data and method defined in its outer class
      data++;
      m();
    }
  }
}
```

The class `InnerClass` is defined inside `ShowInnerClass`. This inner class is just like any regular class, with the following features:

- An inner class can reference the data and methods defined in the outer class in which it nests, so you do not need to pass the reference of the outer class to the constructor of the inner class.

- Inner classes can make programs simple and concise. As you will see, Example 10.8, "The TicTacToe Game," the program is shorter and leaner using inner classes.

- An inner class is only for supporting the work of its containing outer class and is compiled into a class named `OutClassName$InnerClassName.class`. For example, the inner class `InnerClass` in `ShowInnerClass` is compiled into `ShowInnerClass$InnerClass.class`.

> **NOTE**
> The inner class can be further shortened with the use of an anonymous inner class. An anonymous inner class is an inner class without a name. An anonymous inner class combines declaring an inner class and creating an instance of the class in one step. Many Java development tools use inner classes to generate adapters for handling events. Event-driven programming is introduced in Chapter 8, "Getting Started with Graphics Programming."

Adding New Classes, Methods, and Data to Classes in Visual J++

You can use Class Outline to add a new class to the .java file or to add an inner class, a method, or a data member to a class.

To add a new top-level class into the .java file, right-click at a blank spot in the Class Outline window to display a context menu, as shown in Figure 7.11. Choose Add Class from the context menu to display the Add Class dialog box, as shown in Figure 7.12. Fill in the information, as shown in Figure 7.12, and click Add to generate the new class named `NewTopLevelClass`, as shown in Figure 7.13.

JDK introduces comments of a special type known as *javadoc comments*. They are often used to describe classes, methods, and data members, and are enclosed between /** and */ in the source code. If a class, method, or data member is selected that contains javadoc comments, the Javadoc pane (located below the Class Outline tree) displays the first sentence of the comment.

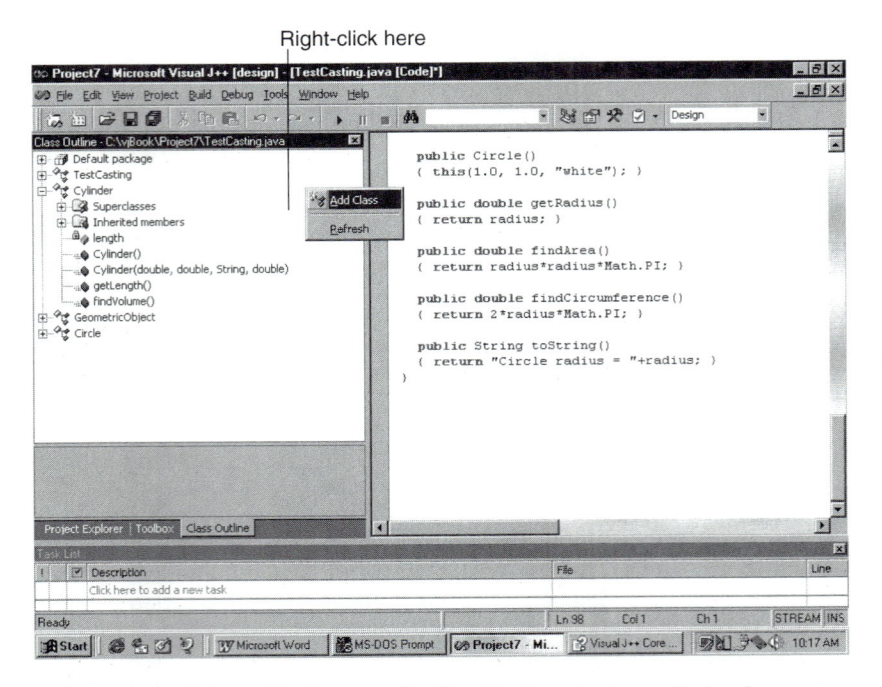

Figure 7.11 *Right-click at a blank spot in the Class Outline window to display the context menu for adding a new top-level class.*

To add a new inner class, right-click at the class in which the new inner class is nested to display a context menu, as shown in Figure 7.14. Choose Add Class to display the Add Class dialog box. This box is similar to Figure 7.12 except that you can uncheck the option "Create a nested class" to generate a top-level class in the .java file.

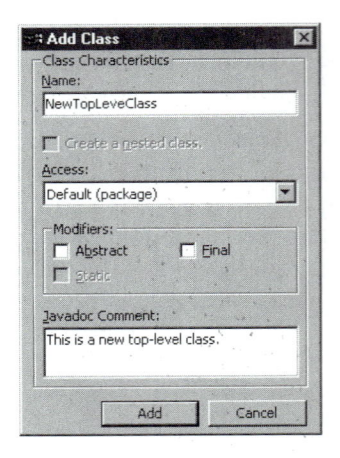

Figure 7.12 *The Add Class dialog box gathers information for a new class.*

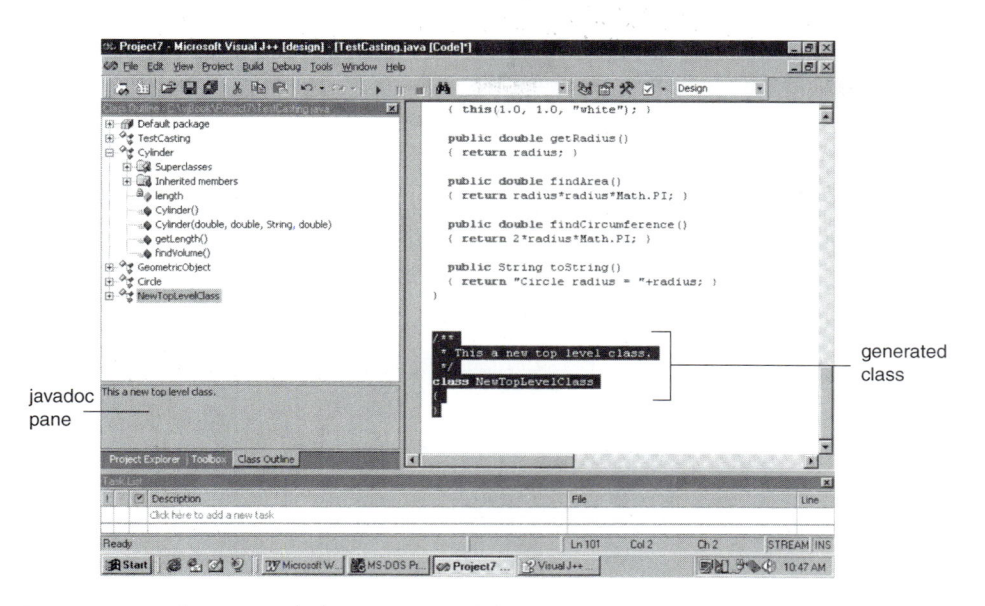

Figure 7.13 *The source code for NewTopLevelClass was generated using the Add Class dialog box.*

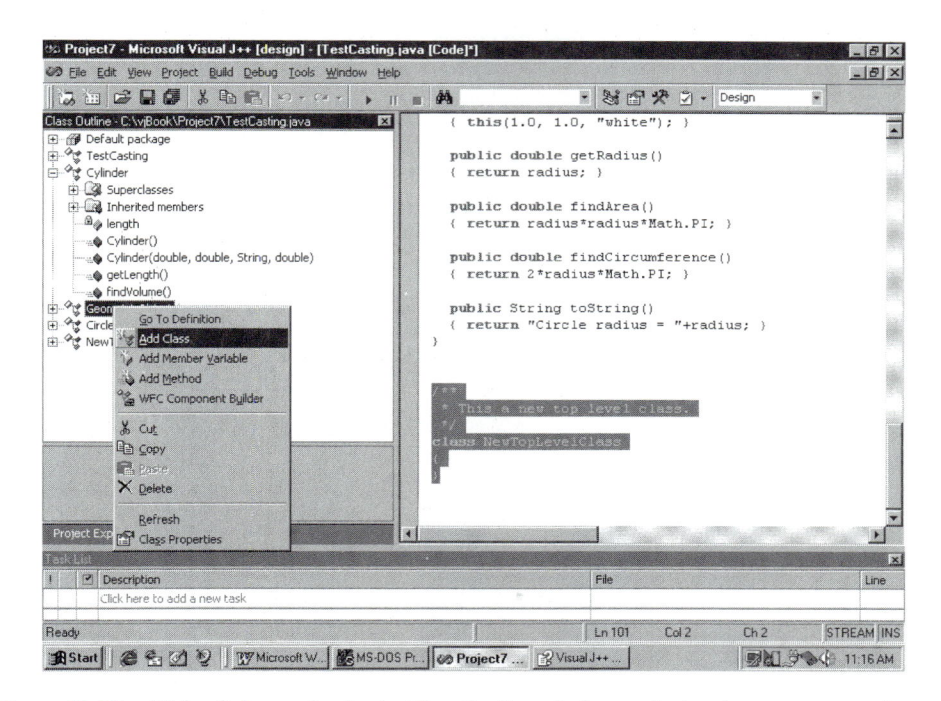

Figure 7.14 *Right-click at a class in the Class Outline window to display the context menu for adding a new inner class, methods, and data in the class.*

To create a new method, right-click at the class in which the new method is added to display the context menu. Choose Add Method from the context menu to display the Add Method dialog box, as shown in Figure 7.15. You need to specify a name for the method, and choose or type return type. To declare the parameters, click the ellipsis button to display the Edit Parameter List dialog box, as shown in Figure 7.16. Specify two parameters, `par1` and `par2` of `integer` type, and click the OK button to close the dialog box. Click the Add button to close the Add Method dialog box. The code generated by Visual J++ is shown in Figure 7.17.

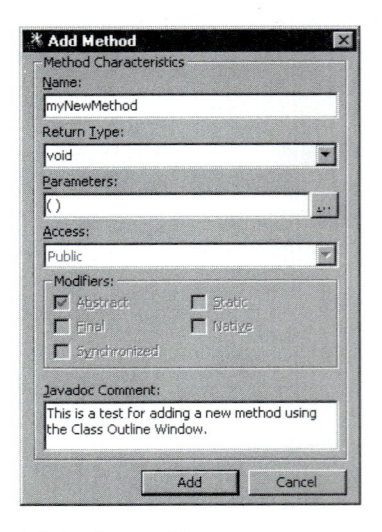

Figure 7.15 *The Add Method dialog box enables you to create a new method for the class.*

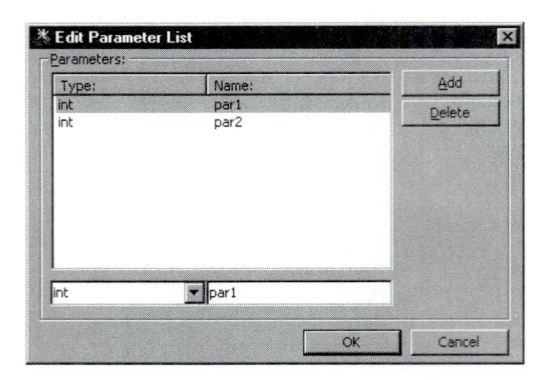

Figure 7.16 *The Edit Parameter List dialog box enables you to define parameters for the new method.*

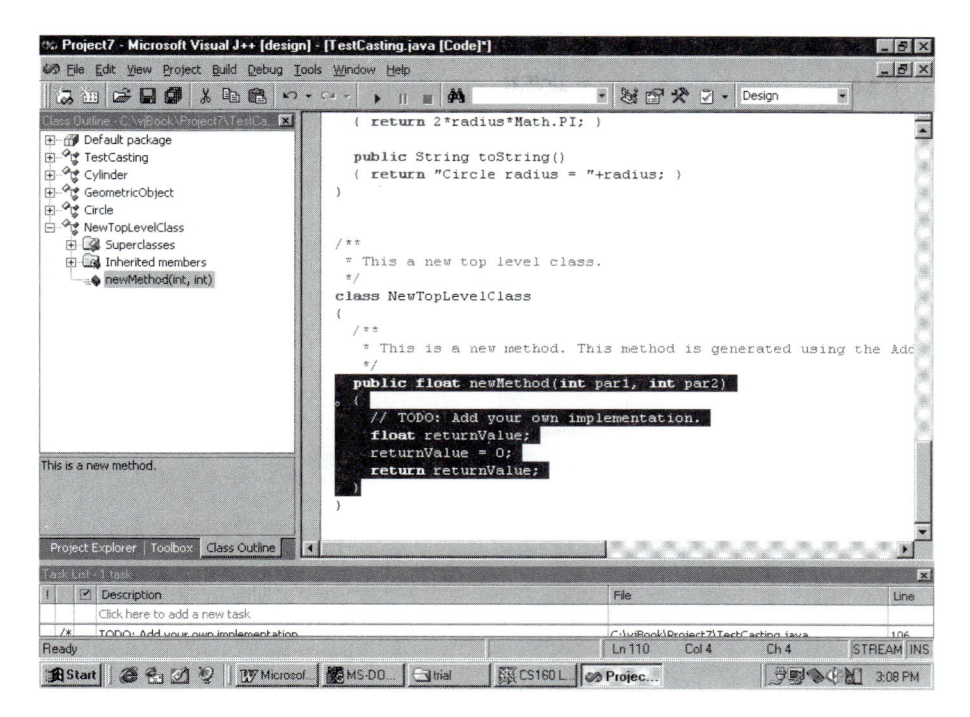

Figure 7.17 *The source code for* `newMethod()` *was generated using the Add Method dialog box.*

To create a new data member, right-click at the class in which the new data member is added to display the context menu. Choose Add Member Variable from the context menu to display the Add Member Variable dialog box, as shown in Figure 7.18. You need to specify a name for the variable, choose or type data type, choose an access modifier (default, public, private, protected) from the choice menu, and

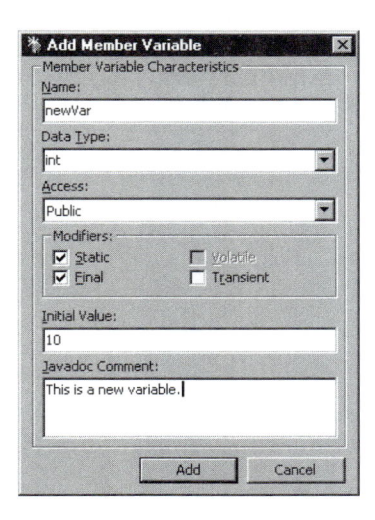

Figure 7.18 *The Add Member Variable dialog box enables you to create a new data member for the class.*

check additional modifiers (static, final, volatile, and transient). You can also specify an initial value for the variable. Click the Add button to close the dialog box. The code generated by Visual J++ is shown in Figure 7.19.

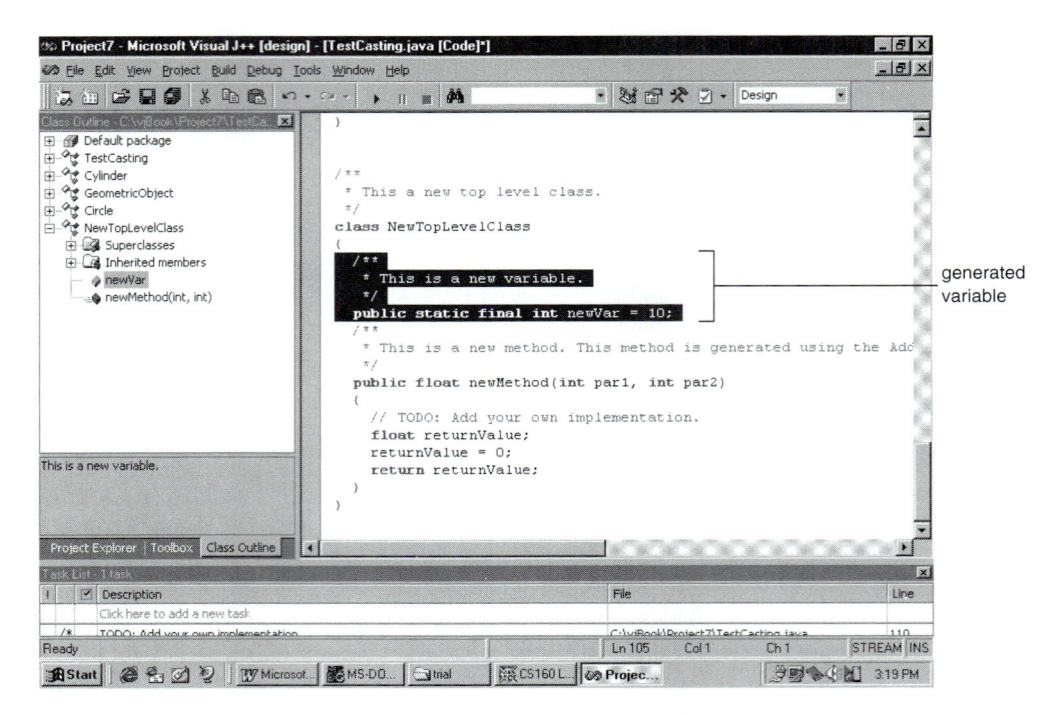

Figure 7.19 *The source code for newVar was generated using the Add Member Variable dialog box.*

■ **TIP**
Using Class Outline, you can quickly delete a definition from your .java file. To delete a definition, select the item to be deleted and press the DELETE key. The definition is removed from the source file.

■ **NOTE**
If you use the Text Editor to delete a definition, the associated item in Class Outline is automatically removed.

Overriding a Method in the Superclass

In Java programming, you often need to override a method defined in the superclass. Using Class Outline, you can quickly add a definition to override an inherited method.

> **NOTE**
> You cannot override a method that is marked as static or final.

To override an inherited method, expand the Inherited Members node of the class in the Class Outline window to display both methods and member variables; however, only methods can be overridden. Right-click the method that you want to override to display a context menu, as shown in Figure 7.20. Choose Override Method from the context menu. A declaration for the method is inserted into the .java file, where you can add your implementation. As shown in Figure 7.21, the method declaration for `toString()` was inserted in the NewTopLevelClass.

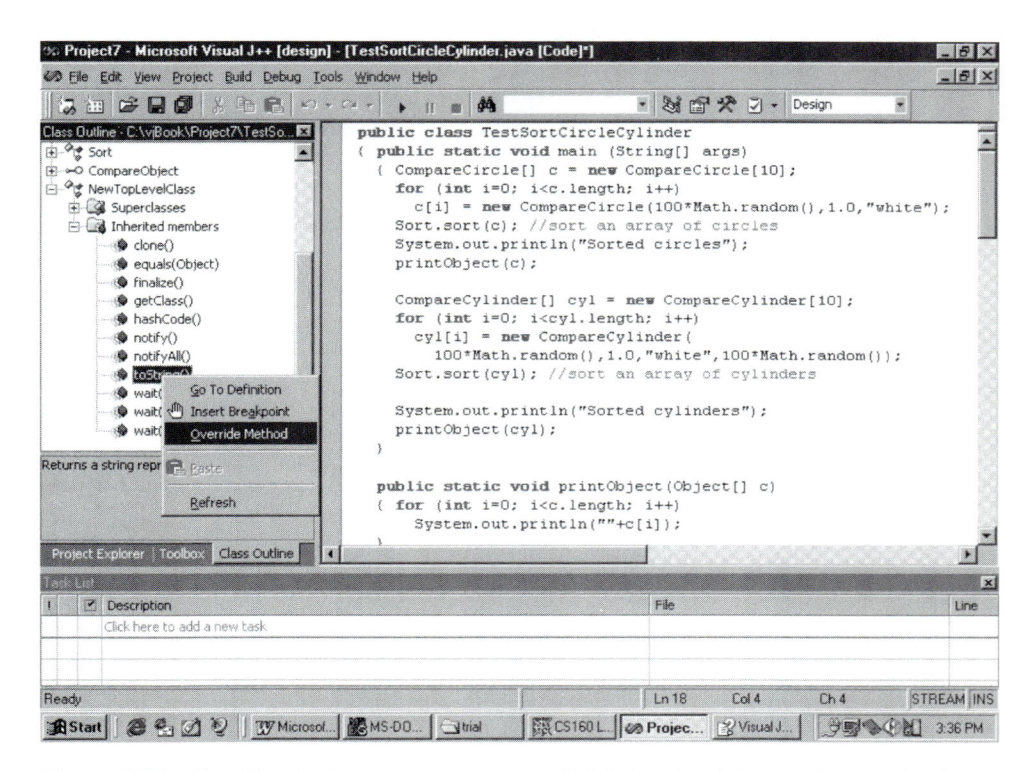

Figure 7.20 *The Class Outline can generate the method declaration defined in the superclass for implementation in subclasses.*

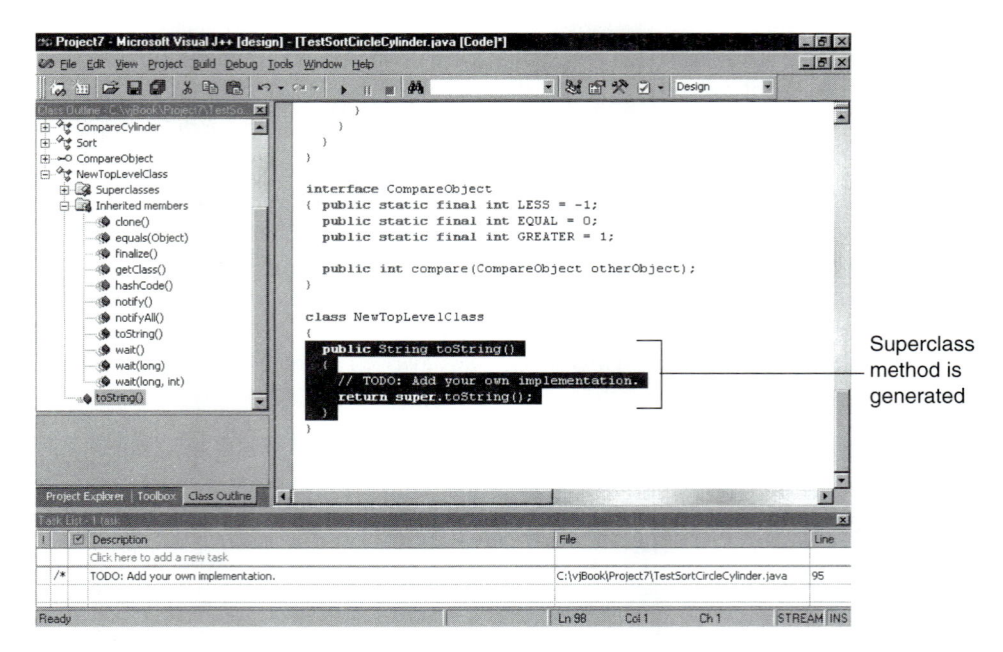

Figure 7.21 *The method declaration was automatically generated in the subclass using the Class Outline.*

Chapter Summary

In this chapter, you learned about inheritance, an important and powerful concept in object-oriented programming. You can immediately see the benefits of inheritance in Java graphics programming, exception handling, internationalization, multithreading, multimedia, I/O, network programming, and every Java program that inherits and extends existing classes.

You learned how to create a subclass from a superclass by adding new fields and methods. You can also override the methods in the superclass. The keywords `super` and `this` are used to reference the superclass and the subclass, respectively.

You learned how to use the `protected` modifier to allow data and methods to be accessed by its subclasses, even if the subclasses are in different packages.

You learned how to use the `final` modifier to prevent changes to a class, method, or variable. A final class cannot be extended. A `final` method cannot be overridden. A `final` variable is a constant.

You learned to use the `abstract` modifier to design generic superclasses. An abstract class cannot be instantiated. An abstract method contains only the method description without implementation. Its implementation is provided by subclasses.

You learned how to process numeric values as objects. Because most Java methods require the use of objects as arguments, Java provides wrapper classes for modeling primitive data types as objects. You can take advantage of generic programming by using wrapper objects instead of a primitive data type variable.

You learned how to use an interface to enable multiple inheritance. An interface cannot be instantiated. A subclass can only extend one superclass, but it can implement many interfaces to achieve multiple inheritance.

You learned how to use Visual J++'s Class Outline to add new classes, methods, and data to classes.

Chapter Review

7.1. Describe the following terms: inheritance, superclass, subclass, the keywords super and this, the modifiers protected, final, and abstract, casting objects, and interface.

7.2. Suppose you create a new Cylinder class by extending the Circle class. Identify the problems in the following classes:

```
public class Circle
{
  private double radius;

  public Circle(double radius)
  {
    radius = radius;
  }

  public double getRadius()
  {
    return radius;
  }

  public double findArea()
  {
    return radius*radius*Math.PI;
  }
}

class Cylinder
{
  private double length;

  Cylinder(double radius, double length)
  {
    Circle(radius);
    length = length;
  }

  //find the surface area for the cylinder
  public double findArea()
  {
    return findArea()*length;
  }
}
```

7.3. Indicate true or false for the following statements:

- A protected data or method can be accessed by any class in the same package.
- A protected data or method can be accessed by any class in different packages.
- A protected data or method can be accessed by its subclass in any packages.
- A final class can have instances.
- An abstract class can have instances.
- A final class can be extended.
- An abstract class can be extended.
- A final method can be overridden.
- You can always successfully cast a subclass to a superclass.
- You can always successfully cast a superclass to a subclass.
- An interface can be a separate unit and can be compiled into a bytecode file.
- The order in which modifiers appear before a class or a method is important.

7.4. Given the assumptions

```
Circle circle = new Circle(1);
Cylinder cylinder = new Cylinder(1,1);
```

are the following Boolean expressions true or false?

```
(circle instanceof Cylinder)
(cylinder instanceof Circle)
```

7.5. Are the following statements correct?

```
Cylinder cylinder = new Cylinder(1,1);
Circle circle = cylinder;
```

7.6. Are the following statements correct?

```
Cylinder cylinder = new Cylinder(1,1);
Circle circle = (Circle)cylinder;
```

7.7. Describe the difference between method overloading and method overriding.

7.8. Does every class have a `toString()` method and an `equals()` method? Where do they come from? How are they used?

7.9. Describe primitive-type wrapper classes. Why do you need these wrapper classes?

7.10. Are the following statements correct?

```
Integer i = new Integer("23");
Integer i = new Integer(23);
Integer i = Integer.valueOf("23");
Integer i = Integer.parseInt("23",8);
Double d = new Double();
Double d = Double.valueOf("23.45");
int i = (Integer.valueOf("23")).intValue();
double d = (Double.valueOf("23.4")).doubleValue();
int i = (Double.valueOf("23.4")).intValue();
String s = (Double.valueOf("23.4")).toString();
```

7.11. Can an inner class be used in a class other than the class in which the inner class nests?

7.12. What modifier should you use on a class so that a class in the same package can access it but a class in a different package cannot access it?

7.13. What modifier should you use so that a class in a different package cannot access the class, but its subclasses in any package can access it?

7.14. Which of the following class definitions defines a legal abstract class?

a.
```
class A
{
  abstract void unfinished()
  {   }
}
```

b.
```
class A
{
  abstract void unfinished();
}
```

c.
```
abstract class A
{
  abstract void unfinished();
}
```

d.
```
public class abstract A
{
  abstract void unfinished();
}
```

7.15. Which of the following is a correct interface?

a.
```
interface A
{
  void print() { };
}
```

b.
```
abstract interface A
{
  print();
}
```

c.
```
abstract interface A
{
  abstract void print() { };
}
```

d.
```
interface A
{
  void print();
}
```

Programming Exercises

7.1. Write a subclass for Triangle that extends GeometricObject. The class Triangle is defined as follows:

```
public class Triangle extends GeometricObject
{
  private double side1, side2, side3;

  // Construct a Triangle with the specified sides
  public Triangle(double side1, double side2, double side3);

  // Implement the abstract method findArea in
  // GeometricObject
  public double findArea();

  // Implement the abstract method findPerimeter in
  // GeometricObject
  public double findPerimeter();
}
```

7.2. Create a new class named NewRational that extends java.lang.Number. The new class contains all the data fields, constructors, and methods defined in the Rational class in Example 5.8, "Using the Rational Class." Additionally it must implement the abstract methods defined in the Number class. The outline of the NewRational class is as follows:

```
public class MyRational extends Number
{
  private int numerator = 0;
  private int denominator = 1;

  public byte byteValue()
  {
    //TODO: override this java.lang.Number method;
  }
```

```
    public double doubleValue()
    {
      //TODO: implement this java.lang.Number abstract method;
    }

    public float floatValue()
    {
      //TODO: implement this java.lang.Number abstract method;
    }

    public int intValue()
    {
      //TODO: implement this java.lang.Number abstract method;
    }

    public long longValue()
    {
      //TODO: implement this java.lang.Number abstract method;
    }

    // other methods and constructor from the Rational class
}
```

7.3. Modify Example 7.5 to add the following two methods for performing scalar arithmetic with matrix:

```
// Add k with each element in this.matrix
public Object[][] addScalar(Object k);

// Multiply k with each element in this.matrix
public Object[][] multiplyScalar(Object k);
```

Write a client program to test the new methods with `double` type.

7.4. Write a project to meet the following requirements:

- Write a generic class for vector arithmetic. The following is the outline of the class structure:

```
abstract class GenericVector
{
  Object[] vector;

  // Constructor
  public GenericVector(Object[] vector);

  // Vector addition, return is a new vector. For example,
  // (1, 2, 3) + (1, 2, 3) = (2, 4, 6)
  public Object[] addVector(Object[] vector);

  // Vector multiplication, return is a scalar value. For
  // example,
  // (1, 2, 3) * (1, 2, 3) = 1*1 + 2*2 + 3*3 = 11
  public Object multiplyVector(Object[] vector);

  public abstract Object add(Object o1, Object o2);

  public abstract Object multiply(Object o1, Object o2);

  public abstract Object zero();

  public static void displayVector(Object[] m);
}
```

- Write a class for `Double` vectors and `Rational` vectors, extending the abstract vector class.
- Write a client program to test the `Double` and `Rational` vector classes.

7.5. Use inner class to rewrite Example 5.5, "Changing Data in a Private Field Using a Setter." Make the `Circle` class an inner class.

7.6. Create a class named `CompareRectangle` that extends `Rectangle` and implements `CompareObject`. Implement the `compareTo()` method to compare the rectangles on their areas. Write a test class to sort a list of `CompareRectangle` objects.

7.7. Create a project that meets the following requirements:

- Add an abstract method `compareTo()` in the `GeometricObject` class as follows:

    ```
    public int compareTo(GeometricObject geoObject)
    ```

- Rewrite the `Sort` class with a new `sort()` method signature as follows:

    ```
    public static void sort(GeometricObject[] list)
    ```

- Rewrite the `Circle` class that extends the `GeometricObject` class and compare the circles on their sizes.

- Rewrite the Cylinder class that extends the GeometricObject class and compare cylinders on their volumes.

- Write a test class to sort a list of circles and a list of cylinders using the `Sort.sort()` method.

PART III

GRAPHICS PROGRAMMING

In Part II, "Object-Oriented Programming," you learned the basics of object-oriented programming. The design of the API for Java graphics programming is an excellent example of how the object-oriented principle is applied. In the chapters that follow in this part of the book, you will learn the architecture of Java graphics programming API and use the user interface components to develop graphics applications and applets.

CHAPTER 8   GETTING STARTED WITH GRAPHICS PROGRAMMING

CHAPTER 9   CREATING USER INTERFACES

CHAPTER 10   APPLETS AND ADVANCED GRAPHICS

CHAPTER 8

GETTING STARTED WITH GRAPHICS PROGRAMMING

Objectives

- Describe the Java graphics programming class hierarchy.
- Understand the concept of event-driven programming.
- Become familiar with the Java event delegation model: event registration, listening, and handling.
- Use frames, panels, and simple UI components.
- Understand the role of layout managers.
- Use the `FlowLayout`, `GridLayout`, and `BorderLayout` managers.
- Become familiar with the methods: `repaint()`, `update()`, `paint()`, and `paintComponent()`.
- Become familiar with the classes `Color`, `Font`, and `FontMetrics`.
- Be able to use the drawing methods in the `Graphics` class.

Introduction

Until now, you have only used text-based input and output. You used `MyInput.readInt()` and `MyInput.readDouble()` to read numbers from the keyboard, and `System.out.println()` to display results on the console. This is the old-fashioned way to program. Today's client/server and Web-based applications use a graphical user interface known as GUI (pronounced goo-ee).

When Java was introduced, the graphics components were bundled in a library known as *Abstract Window Toolkit* or *AWT*. For every platform on which Java runs, the AWT components are automatically mapped to the platform-specific components through their respective agents, known as *peers*. AWT is fine for developing simple GUI applications, but not for developing comprehensive GUI projects. Besides, AWT is prone to platform-specific bugs, because its peer-based approach heavily relies on the underlying platform. With the release of Java 2, the AWT user interface components were replaced by a more robust, versatile, and flexible set of a library known as the *Swing components*. Most Swing components are painted directly on canvases using Java code, except for components that are subclasses of `java.awt.Window` or `java.awt.Panel`, which must be drawn using native GUI on a specific platform. Swing components are less dependent on the target platform and use less resource of the native GUI. For this reason, Swing components that don't rely on native GUI are referred to as *lightweight components*, and AWT components are referred to as *heavyweight components*. Although AWT components are still supported in Java 2, I recommend that you learn to program using the Swing components, because the AWT user interface components will eventually fade away.

Java provides a rich set of classes to help you build graphical user interfaces. You can use various GUI-building classes—frames, panels, labels, buttons, text fields, text areas, combo boxes, check boxes, radio buttons, menus, scroll bars, scroll panes, and tabbed panes—to construct user interfaces. This chapter introduces the basics of Java graphics programming. Specifically, it discusses GUI components and their relationships, event-driven programming, and two top-level components: `JFrame` and `JPanel`. The chapter gives examples of using layout managers to place user interface components (`JButton`, `JTextField`, and so on) in `JFrame` and `JPanel`. Finally, it introduces the `Graphics` class for drawing geometric figures, such as lines, rectangles, ovals, arcs, and polygons.

> **NOTE**
> The Swing components do not replace all the classes in AWT, only the AWT user interface components—`Button`, `TextField`, `TextArea`, etc. The AWT helper classes—`Graphics`, `Color`, `Font`, `FontMetrics`, and `LayoutManager`—remain unchanged. In addition, the Swing components use the AWT event model.

> **NOTE**
> The book is completely based on Java 2, and Swing components are used to build the graphics examples. Visual J++ 6 does not support Java 2, but you can use Swing components in Visual J++ by adding the Swing JAR file in the class path. For more information, see Appendix F, "Using the Companion CD-ROM and Installing the Swing Library."

The Java Graphics Class Hierarchy

The design of Java graphics programming API is an excellent example of the use of classes, inheritances, and interfaces. The graphics API contains the essential classes listed below. Their hierarchical relationship is shown in Figure 8.1.

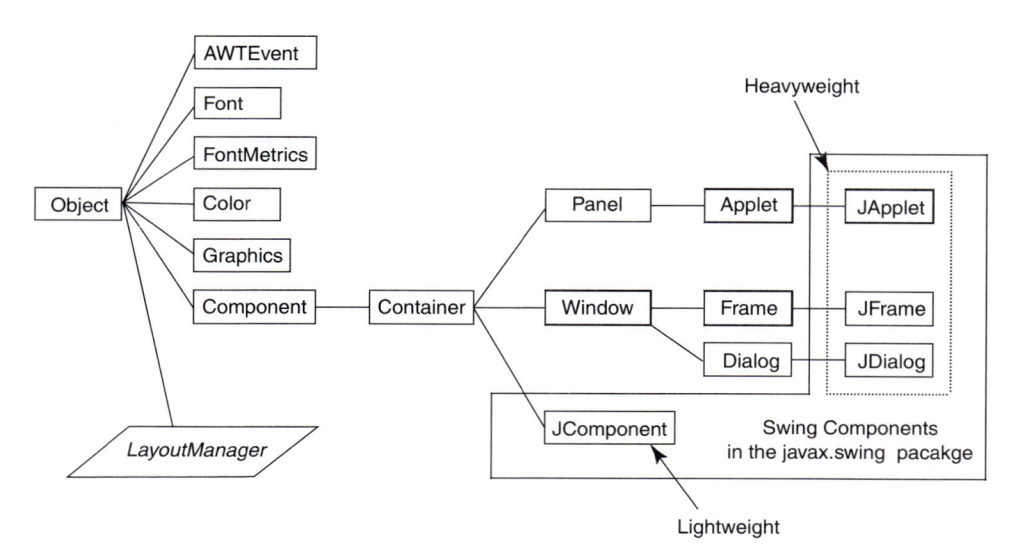

Figure 8.1 *Java graphics programming utilizes the classes shown in this hierarchical diagram.*

- **Component**—This is a superclass of all user interface classes.
- **Container**—This is used to group components. A layout manager is used to position and place components in a container in the desired location and style. Frames and panels are examples of containers.
- **JComponent**—This is a superclass of all the lightweight Swing components, which are drawn directly on canvases using Java code, rather than on specific platforms using native GUI. Its subclasses—`JButton`, `JCheckBox`, `JMenu`, `JRadioButton`, `JLabel`, `JList`, `JTextField`, `JTextArea`, `JScrollPane`—are the basic elements for constructing the GUI.
- **Window**—The `Window` class can be used to create a top-level window, but its subclasses—`JFrame` and `JDialog`—are often used instead.

- **`JFrame`**—This is a window not contained inside another window. `JFrame` is the basis that holds other Swing user interface components in Java graphical applications.

- **`JDialog`**—This is a popup window generally used as a temporary window to receive additional information from the user or to provide notification that an event has occurred.

- **`JApplet`**—This is a subclass of `Applet`. You must extend `JApplet` to create a Swing-based Java applet.

- **`JPanel`**—This is an invisible container that holds user interface components. You can place panels inside panels and in a frame in Java applications or in an applet in Java applets. `JPanel` can also be used as a canvas to draw graphics.

- **`Graphics`**—This is an abstract class that provides a graphical context for drawing strings, lines, and shapes.

- **`Color`**—This deals with the colors of graphics components. For example, you can specify background or foreground colors in a component like `JFrame` and `JPanel`, or you can specify colors of lines, shapes, and strings in drawings.

- **`Font`**—This is used to draw strings in `Graphics`. For example, you can specify the font type (SansSerif), style (bold), and size (24 points) for a string.

- **`FontMetrics`**—This is an abstract class used to get properties of the fonts used in drawings.

The `JFrame`, `JApplet`, `JDialog`, and `JComponent` classes and their subclasses are grouped in the package `javax.swing`. All the other classes in Figure 8.1 are grouped in the package `java.awt`. Most Swing components are named with a prefixed *J*. For example, the Swing version of `Button` is called `JButton` to distinguish it from its original AWT counterpart.

> **NOTE**
> Swing is a comprehensive solution to developing enterprise GUI applications. There are over 250 classes in Swing, some of which are illustrated in Figure 8.2. Since the discussion in this book is only an introduction to Java graphics programming using Swing, the components listed in the dotted rectangle are not covered. For a more detailed treatment of Swing components, including model-view architecture, look and feel, and advanced components, please refer to my *Rapid Java Application Development Using JBuilder 3*, published by Prentice Hall.

> **CAUTION**
> Do not mix Swing user interface components like `JButton` with AWT user interface components like `Button`. Do not place `JButton` in `java.awt.Panel`, and similarly do not place `Button` in `javax.swing.JPanel`. Mixing them may cause problems.

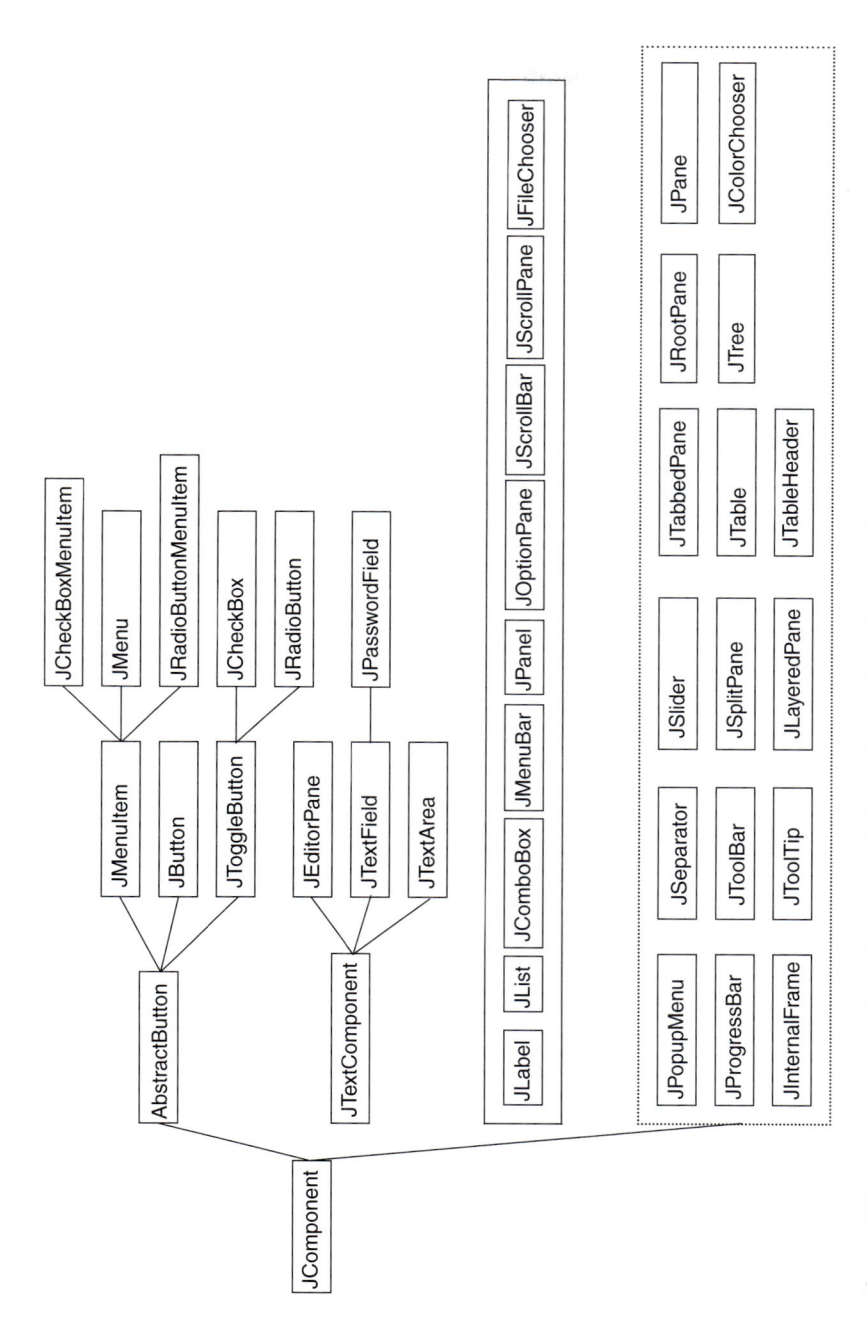

Figure 8.2 JComponent *and its subclasses are the basic elements for building graphical user interfaces.*

To create a user interface, you need to create a frame or an applet to hold other user interface components. Figure 8.3 provides examples of possible user interface layouts in a frame and an applet.

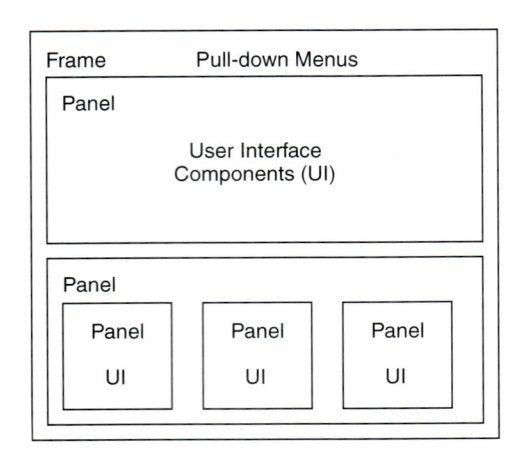

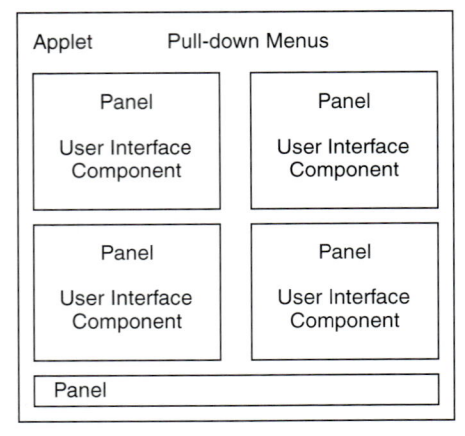

Figure 8.3 *A frame or an applet can contain menus, panels, and user interface components. Panels are used to group user interface components. Panels can contain other panels.*

Creating a Frame

The first step in graphics programming is to display a window. Java has a class named java.awt.Window that can be used to create a window, but often its subclass JFrame is used. The following program creates a frame:

```
// MyFrame.java: Display a frame
import javax.swing.*;

public class MyFrame
{
  public static void main(String[] args)
  {
    JFrame frame = new JFrame("Test Frame");
    frame.setSize(400, 300);
    frame.setVisible(true);
  }
}
```

Because JFrame is in the package javax.swing, the statement import javax.swing.* makes available all the classes from the javax.swing package, including JFrame, so that they can be used in the MyFrame class.

The following two constructors are used to create a JFrame object.

```
JFrame frame = new JFrame(String title);
```

This declares and creates a JFrame object frame with a specified title.

```
JFrame frame = new JFrame();
```

This declares and creates a JFrame object frame that is untitled.

The frame is not displayed until the frame.setVisible(true) method is applied. frame.setSize(400, 300) specifies that the frame is 400 pixels wide and 300 pixels high. If the setSize() method is not used, the frame will be sized at 0 by 0 pixels, and nothing will be seen except the title bar. Since the setSize() and setVisible() methods are both defined in the Component class, they are inherited by the JFrame class. Later you will see that these methods are also useful in many other subclasses of Component.

When you run the program MyFrame, the following window will be displayed on-screen (see Figure 8.4).

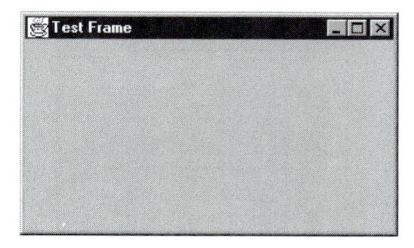

Figure 8.4 *The program creates and displays a frame with the title Test Frame.*

Suppose that you want to terminate the program. Normally, you would click the Window Close button on the upper-right corner or click the upper-left corner to reveal a menu and select Close from the menu. When you do either of these things, the window closes, but the program continues to run because you did not tell it to stop when the window is closed. The following section introduces event handling so that you can tell the program to exit when the window is closed.

> **NOTE**
> In Windows 95/98 and Windows NT, you can stop the program by pressing Ctrl+C at the DOS prompt window. With UNIX, you need to use the kill command to kill the process for the program.

Event-Driven Programming

All the programs until this chapter were object-oriented, but executed in a procedural order. You used decision and loop statements to control the flow of execution, but the program dictated the flow of execution. Java graphics programming is event driven. In event-driven programming, codes are executed when events are activated. This section introduces the Java event model.

Event and Event Source

When you run Java graphics programs, the program interacts with the user and the events drive the execution of the program. An *event* can be defined as a signal to the program that something has happened. The event is generated either by external user actions, such as mouse movements, mouse button clicks, and keystrokes, or by the operating system, such as a timer. The program can choose to respond to or ignore the event.

The GUI component on which the event is generated is called a *source object*. For example, if clicking a button triggers an event, the button is the source object. The source object can be obtained by using the getSource() method on the event. Every event is a subclass of the java.util.EventObject class. Various types of events deal with user component actions, mouse movements, and keystrokes. The hierarchical relationship of the graphics events used in this book is shown in Figure 8.5.

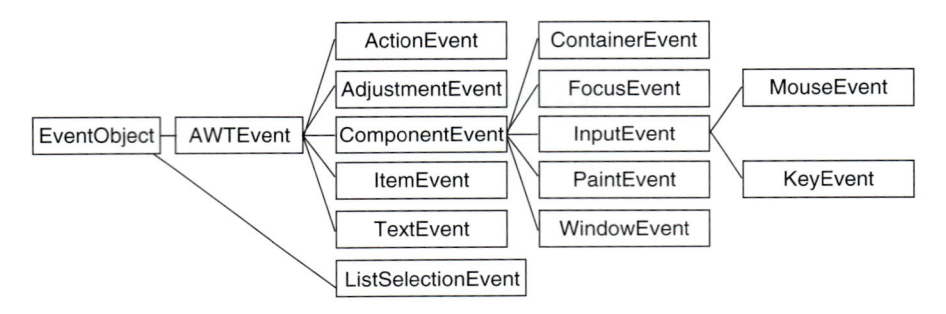

Figure 8.5 *An event is an object of one of the classes in the diagram.*

Event classes contain whatever data values are pertinent to the particular event type. For example, the KeyEvent class defines all key constants, such as VK_DOWN (for down-arrow key), and methods, such as getKeyChar() (returns character associated with the event).

NOTE
All the event classes in Figure 8.5 are included in the java.awt.event package except the ListSelectionEvent, which is in the javax.swing.event package. The AWT events were originally designed for the AWT components, but many Swing components fire them.

Table 8.1 lists external user actions, source objects, and event types generated.

NOTE
If a component can generate an event, any subclass of the component can generate the same type of event. For example, every GUI component can generate MouseEvent, KeyEvent, FocusEvent, and ComponentEvent, since Component is the superclass of all GUI components.

TABLE 8.1 User Action, Source Object, and Event Type

User Action	Source Object	Event Type Generated
Clicked on a button	`JButton`	`ActionEvent`
Changed text	`JTextComponent`	`TextEvent`
Pressed return on a text field	`JTextField`	`ActionEvent`
Selected a new item	`JComboBox`	`ItemEvent, ActionEvent`
Select item(s)	`JList`	`ListSelectionEvent`
Checked a box	`JCheckBox`	`ItemEvent, ActionEvent`
Checked a box	`JRadioButton`	`ItemEvent, ActionEvent`
Selected a menu item	`JMenuItem`	`ActionEvent`
Moved the scroll bar	`JScrollBar`	`AdjustmentEvent`
Window opened, closed, iconified, deiconified, or closing	`Window`	`WindowEvent`
Component added or removed from the container	`Container`	`ContainerEvent`
Component moved, resized, hidden, or shown	`Component`	`ComponentEvent`
Component gained or lost focus	`Component`	`FocusEvent`
Key released or pressed	`Component`	`KeyEvent`
Mouse movement	`Component`	`MouseEvent`

Event Registration, Listening, and Handling

Java uses a delegation-based model for event handling: An external user action on a source object triggers an event. An object interested in the event receives the event. Such an object is called a *listener*. Not all objects can receive events. To become a listener, an object must be registered as a listener by the source object. The source object maintains a list of listeners and notifies all the registered listeners by invoking the event-handling method, known as *handler,* on the listener object to respond to the event, as shown in Figure 8.6.

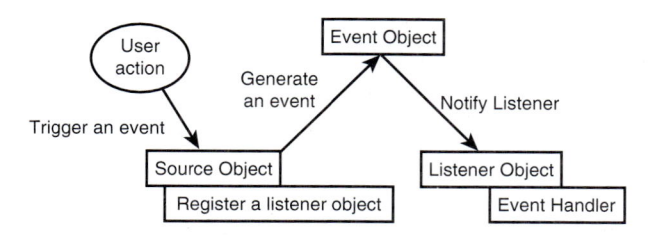

Figure 8.6 *An event is triggered by user actions on the source object; the source object generates the event object and invokes the handler of the listener object to process the event.*

For example, if a JFrame object is interested in the external events on a JButton source object, it must register with the JButton object. The registration is done by invoking a method from the JButton object to declare that the JFrame object is a listener for the JButton object. When you click the button, the JButton object generates an ActionEvent event and notifies the listener by invoking a method defined in the listener to handle the event.

> **NOTE**
> A source object and a listener object may be the same. A source object may have many listeners. It maintains a queue for all them.

Registration methods are dependent on event type. For ActionEvent, the method is addActionListener. In general, the method is named addXListener for XEvent.

For the system to invoke the handler on a listener, the listener must implement the standard handler. The handler is defined in the corresponding event listener interface. Java provides a listener interface for every type of graphics event. For example, the corresponding listener interface for ActionEvent is ActionListener; each listener for ActionEvent should implement the ActionListener interface.

Table 8.2 lists event types, the corresponding listener interfaces, and the methods defined in the listener interfaces.

TABLE 8.2 Events, Event Listeners, and Listener Methods

Event Class	Listener Interface	Listener Methods (Handlers)
ActionEvent	ActionListener	actionPerformed(ActionEvent e)
ItemEvent	ItemListener	itemStateChanged(ItemEvent e)
WindowEvent	WindowListener	windowClosing(WindowEvent e)
		windowOpened(WindowEvent e)
		windowIconified(WindowEvent e)
		windowDeiconified(WindowEvent e)
		windowClosed(WindowEvent e)
		windowActivated(WindowEvent e)
		windowDeactivated(WindowEvent e)
ContainerEvent	ContainerListener	componentAdded(ContainerEvent e)
		componentRemoved(ContainerEvent e)
ComponentEvent	ComponentListener	componentMoved(ComponentEvent e)
		componentHidden(ComponentEvent e)
		componentResized(ComponentEvent e)
		componentShown(ComponentEvent e)

Event Class	Listener Interface	Listener Methods (Handlers)
`FocusEvent`	`FocusListener`	`focusGained(FocusEvent e)`
		`focusLost(FocusEvent e)`
`TextEvent`	`TextListener`	`textValueChanged(TextEvent e)`
`KeyEvent`	`KeyListener`	`keyPressed(KeyEvent e)`
		`keyReleased(KeyEvent e)`
		`keyTyped(KeyEvent e)`
`MouseEvent`	`MouseListener`	`mousePressed(MouseEvent e)`
		`mouseReleased(MouseEvent e)`
		`mouseEntered(MouseEvent e)`
		`mouseExited(MouseEvent e)`
		`mouseClicked(MouseEvent e)`
	`MouseMotionListener`	`mouseDragged(MouseEvent e)`
		`mouseMoved(MouseEvent e)`
`AdjustmentEvent`	`AdjustmentListener`	`adjustmentValueChanged(AdjustmentEvent e)`

> **NOTE**
> In general, the listener interface is named `XListener` for `XEvent`, except for `MouseMotionListener`.

Handling Events

A listener object must implement the corresponding listener interface. For example, a listener for a `JButton` source object must implement the `ActionListener` interface. The `ActionListener` interface contains the `actionPerformed(ActionEvent e)` method. This method must be implemented in the listener class. Upon receiving notification, it is executed to handle the event.

An event object is passed to the handling method. The event object contains information pertinent to the event type. You can get useful data values from the event object for processing the event. For example, for an event object e of the `MouseEvent` type, you can use `e.getX()` and `e.getY()` to obtain the location of the mouse pointer; in the `ActionEvent`, you can use `e.getSource()` to obtain the source object in order to determine whether it is a button, a check box, a radio button or a menu item.

Three examples on the use of event handling are given below. The first is for the `WindowEvent`, the second for the `MouseEvent`, and the last for the `ActionEvent`.

Example 8.1 Creating a Centered Frame with Exit Handling

This example creates a new frame class that extends the `JFrame` class with exit handling and a new method for centering the frame. The program displays the frame in the center of the screen when it starts and exits when the window is closing.

The closing window event is the `WindowEvent` type, and its corresponding listener interface is `WindowListener`; therefore, the program must implement the `WindowListener` interface.

By default, a frame is displayed in the upper-left corner of the screen. To display a frame at a specified location, you can use the `setLocation(x, y)` method in the `JFrame` class. This method places the upper-left corner of a frame at location (x, y).

To center a frame on the screen, you need to know the width and height of the screen and the frame in order to determine the frame's upper-left coordinates. The screen's width and height can be obtained using the `java.awt.Toolkit` class:

```
Dimension screenSize = Toolkit.getDefaultToolkit().getScreenSize();
int screenWidth = screenSize.width;
int screenHeight = screenSize.height;
```

Therefore, the upper left x and y coordinates of the frame `frame` can be:

```
Dimension frameSize = frame.getSize();
int x = (screenWidth - frameSize.width)/2;
int y = (screenHeight - frameSize.height)/2;
```

The `java.awt.Dimension` class encapsulates the width and height of a component (in integer precision) in a single object.

The new frame class `MyFrameWithExitHandling` is given as follows:

```
// MyFrameWithExitHandling.java: Define a new frame with exit
// capability and the center() method
import java.awt.*;
import java.awt.event.*;
import javax.swing.JFrame;

public class MyFrameWithExitHandling extends JFrame
  implements WindowListener
{
  // Main method
  public static void main(String[] args)
  {
    MyFrameWithExitHandling frame =
      new MyFrameWithExitHandling("Test Frame");
    frame.setSize(200, 200);
    frame.center();
    frame.setVisible(true);
  }
```

```java
// Default constructor
public MyFrameWithExitHandling()
{
  super();
  addWindowListener(this);  // Register listener
}

// Constructor a frame with a title
public MyFrameWithExitHandling(String title)
{
  super(title);
  addWindowListener(this); // Register listener
}

// Center the frame
public void center()
{
  // Get the screen dimension
  Dimension screenSize =
    Toolkit.getDefaultToolkit().getScreenSize();
  int screenWidth = screenSize.width;
  int screenHeight = screenSize.height;

  // Get the frame dimension
  Dimension frameSize = this.getSize();
  int x = (screenWidth - frameSize.width)/2;
  int y = (screenHeight - frameSize.height)/2;

  // Determine the location of the left corner of the frame
  if (x < 0)
  {
    x = 0;
    frameSize.width = screenWidth;
  }

  if (y < 0)
  {
    y = 0;
    frameSize.height = screenHeight;
  }

  // Set the frame to the specified location
  this.setLocation(x, y);
}

// Handler for window closed event
public void windowClosed(WindowEvent event)
{
}

// Handler for window deiconified event
public void windowDeiconified(WindowEvent event)
{
}

// Handler for window iconified event
public void windowIconified(WindowEvent event)
{
}
```

continues

```java
      // Handler for window activated event
      public void windowActivated(WindowEvent event)
      {
      }

      // Handler for window deactivated event
      public void windowDeactivated(WindowEvent event)
      {
      }

      // Handler for window opened event
      public void windowOpened(WindowEvent event)
      {
      }

      // Handler for window closing event
      public void windowClosing(WindowEvent event)
      {
        dispose();
        System.exit(0);
      }
    }
```

Example Review

The main method creates a `JFrame` instance, sets the window size for the frame using `setSize()`, centers the frame on the screen using the `center()` method, and makes it visible using `setVisible(true)`. The frame will not be shown without `setVisible(true)`.

The `WindowEvent` can be generated by the `Window` class or any subclasses of `Window`. Since `JFrame` is a subclass of `Window`, it can generate `WindowEvent`.

`MyFrameWithExitHandling` extends `JFrame` and implements `WindowListener`. The `WindowListener` interface defines several abstract methods (`windowActivated`, `windowClosed`, `windowClosing`, `windowDeactivated`, `windowDeiconified`, `windowIconified`, `windowOpened`) for handling window events when the window is activated, closed, closing, deactivated, deiconified, iconified, or opened.

When a window event such as activation occurs, the `windowActivated()` method is triggered. You should implement the `windowActivated()` method with a concrete response if you want this event to be processed.

Because all these methods in the `WindowListener` interface are abstract, you must implement them all even if your program does not care about some of the events. In `MyFrameWithExitHandling`, all the window event handlers are implemented, although only the `windowClosing()` handler is needed. When the window is in the process of closing, the event triggers the `windowClosing()` method to execute. `System.exit(0)` terminates the program.

For an object to receive event notification, it must register as an event listener. `addWindowListener(this)` registers the object of `MyFrameWithExitHandling` as a window event listener so that it can receive notification about the window event. `MyFrameWithExitHandling` is both a listener and a source object.

The `dispose()` method disposes the frame object when the object is no longer needed.

The `center()` method is defined in `MyFrameWithExitHandling`. Invoking it causes the frame to appear in the center of the screen. This method uses the `java.awt.Toolkit` to obtain platform-dependent information, such as the screen dimension in this example. The `java.awt.Dimension` encapsulates the width and height of a component.

> **TIP**
> For all Java graphics applications, you can simply extend the `MyFrameWith-ExitHandling` class to inherit `JFrame` with exit handling and the `center()` method.

Example 8.2 Handling Simple Mouse Events

This example gives a program that creates a frame and displays a solid square at the mouse pointer when the mouse is pressed. The output of the program is shown in Figure 8.7.

```java
// TestMouseEvent.java: Display a filled square at the mouse pointer
// when the mouse is pressed
import java.awt.event.*;
import javax.swing.*;
import java.awt.*;

public class TestMouseEvent extends MyFrameWithExitHandling
  implements MouseListener
{
  private int x, y = 0; // x, y coordinates

  // Default constructor
  public TestMouseEvent()
  {
    setTitle("TestMouseEvent");
    addMouseListener(this); // Register listener
  }

  // Main method
  public static void main(String[] args)
  {
    TestMouseEvent frame = new TestMouseEvent();
    frame.setSize(200, 200);
    frame.setVisible(true);
  }

  // When the mouse is pressed, the mouse pointer location
  // will be stored in (x, y)
  public void mousePressed(MouseEvent e)
```

continues

```java
    {
      // Get (x, y) coordinates using getX() and getY() methods
      x = e.getX();
      y = e.getY();
      repaint();
    }

    public void mouseClicked(MouseEvent e)
    {
    }

    public void mouseEntered(MouseEvent e)
    {
    }

    public void mouseExited(MouseEvent e)
    {
    }

    public void mouseReleased(MouseEvent e)
    {
    }

    // Draw a small solid square around the point (x, y)
    public void paint(Graphics g)
    {
      g.fillRect(x-5, y-5, 10, 10);
    }
  }
```

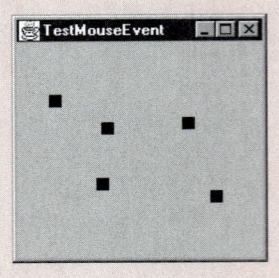

Figure 8.7 *When the mouse button is pressed, a solid square appears that surrounds the area where the mouse pointed.*

Example Review

This program extends `MyFrameWithExitHandling`. For all Java graphics applications throughout the book, you can extend the `MyFrameWithExitHandling` class to inherit `JFrame` with exiting capability without rewriting the same code.

Pressing a mouse button triggers a mouse event (`MouseEvent`) and causes the system to invoke the `mousePressed()` method. This method obtains the location of the mouse pointer by using the `e.getX()` and `e.getY()` methods.

The `repaint()` method, defined in the `Component` class, is invoked in the `mousePressed()` method. Invoking `repaint()` causes the `paint()` method to be called. The `paint()` and `repaint()` methods will be further discussed in the section "The `repaint()`, `update()`, `paint()`, and `paintComponent()` Methods."

The `paint()` method displays graphics on the frame. The `paint()` method is defined in the `Component` class. You should always override it to tell the system what you want to paint.

The `g.fillRect()` method is in the `Graphics` class to display a filled rectangle. The parameters in `fillRect()` specify where the rectangle is drawn. Drawing geometric shapes is introduced in the section "Drawing Geometric Figures," later in this chapter.

> **TIP**
> To debug event-driven programs, you can insert a breakpoint at a statement in a handling method that you want to trace. For example, if you want to trace the `mousePressed()` handler, insert a breakpoint at the first line in this method. When the mouse is pressed, the `mousePressed()` handler is invoked, and the program is paused at the breakpoint, as shown in Figure 8.8.

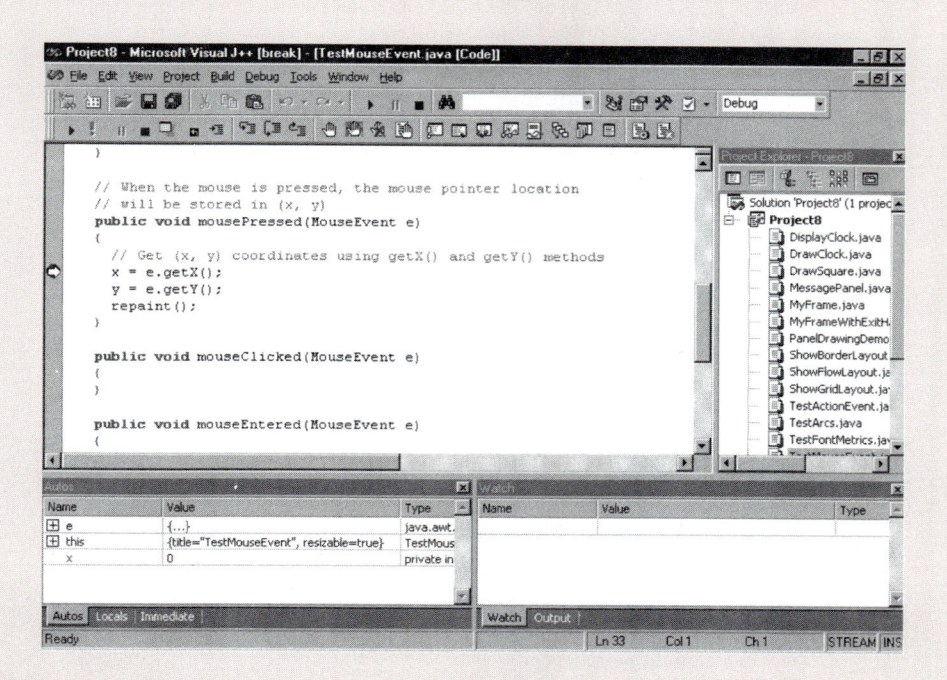

Figure 8.8 *The program pauses at the breakpoint in the* `mousePressed()` *handler.*

continues

> **NOTE**
> Although the example draws graphics directly on the frame, that is actually not a good practice. Frame is designed as a container to hold other UI components. You should draw graphics on a panel. Panels will be introduced in the section "Using Panels" later in this chapter.

Example 8.3 Handling Simple Action Events

This example presents a program that displays a Close button in the window. You can terminate the program by clicking the Close button in the window or on the title bar. Figure 8.9 shows the output of the program.

```java
// TestActionEvent.java: Create a Close button in the frame
import javax.swing.*;
import java.awt.*;
import java.awt.event.*;

public class TestActionEvent extends MyFrameWithExitHandling
  implements ActionListener
{
  // Create an object for "Close" button
  private JButton jbtClose = new JButton("Close");

  // Default constructor
  public TestActionEvent()
  {
    // Set the window title
    setTitle("TestActionEvent");

    // Set FlowLayout manager to arrange the components
    // inside the frame
    getContentPane().setLayout(new FlowLayout());

    // Add button to the frame
    getContentPane().add(jbtClose);

    // Register listener
    jbtClose.addActionListener(this);
  }

  // Main method
  public static void main(String[] args)
  {
    TestActionEvent frame = new TestActionEvent();
    frame.setSize(100, 80);
    frame.setVisible(true);
  }

  // This method will be invoked when a button is clicked.
  public void actionPerformed(ActionEvent e)
  {
    if (e.getSource() == jbtClose)
      System.exit(0);
  }
}
```

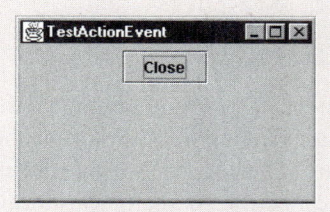

Figure 8.9 *You can close the program by clicking the Close button inside the frame or on the title bar.*

Example Review

The `JFrame` uses a content pane, which is a container that holds UI components inside the frame. The method `getContentPane()` returns the content pane. The statement `getContentPane().setLayout(new FlowLayout())` specifies that the components in the content pane are arranged using the `FlowLayout` style. By default, the content pane of `JFrame` uses `BorderLayout`.

`FlowLayout` is one of the layout management styles discussed in the next section, "Layout Managers." The layout manager tells the system how to lay out the components in the container. The `FlowLayout` manager places the components in the container from left to right and row by row.

The statement `new FlowLayout()` creates an anonymous object of the `FlowLayout` class; the object is anonymous because it is not directly referenced in the program. However, the statement `jbtClose = new JButton("Close")` creates a `JButton` object named `jbtClose`, because `jbtClose` needs to be referenced in the program.

The `getContentPane().add(jbtClose)` method adds the button `jbtClose` into the frame. `JButton` is a user interface component. Its use is further discussed in Chapter 9, "Creating User Interfaces."

The statement `jbtClose.addActionListener(this)` registers `this` (referring to `TestActionEvent`) to listen to `ActionEvent` on `jbtClose`.

Clicking the Close button causes the `actionPerformed()` method to be invoked. The `e.getSource()` method returns the source object.

> **CAUTION**
> Missing listener registration is a common mistake in event handling. Because the system doesn't notify the listener, the listener cannot act on the event.

Adapters and Anonymous Inner Classes (Optional)

The Java event model, as shown in Figure 8.6, has the flexibility to allow modifications and variations. One useful variation of the model is to create an adapter for handling the events. The adapter is registered as the listener for the source object. When an event occurs, the source object notifies the adapter. The adapter either handles the event or delegates the handling to another object, referred to as the *target object*, as shown in Figure 8.10.

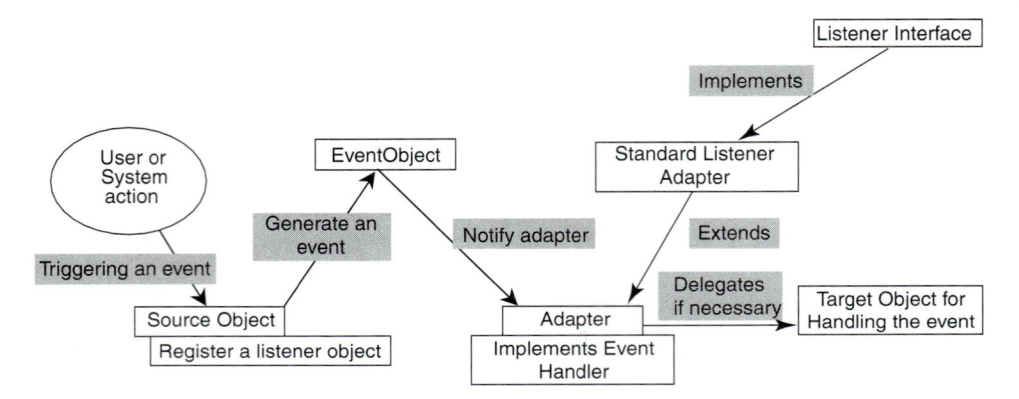

Figure 8.10 *The adapter listens for the event and either handles it or delegates handling to the target object.*

The adapter class should implement the listener interface for the listener it intends to listen, or should extend a convenience adapter class for a listener interface. Java provides a convenience adapter class for each listener interface with multiple handlers. The convenience adapter is a simple implementation of the listener interface, containing empty methods for each method defined in the interface. The convenience adapter class is named *X*Adapter for *X*Listener. For example, MouseListener's corresponding adapter is MouseAdapter. The ActionListener interface does not have a convenience adapter because it contains only one handler (actionPerformed).

You can use the adapter to rewrite Example 8.2, as follows:

```
// TestMouseEventUsingStandardAdapter.java:
// Using standard adapter
import java.awt.event.*;
import javax.swing.*;
import java.awt.*;

public class TestMouseEventUsingStandardAdapter
  extends MyFrameWithExitHandling
{
  int x, y = 0; // x, y coordinates
```

```java
    // Default constructor
    public TestMouseEventUsingStandardAdapter()
    {
      setTitle("TestMouseEventUsingStandardAdapter");

      // Register adapter as a listener
      addMouseListener(new StandardMouseAdapter(this));
    }

    // Main method
    public static void main(String[] args)
    {
      TestMouseEventUsingStandardAdapter frame =
        new TestMouseEventUsingStandardAdapter();
      frame.setSize(200, 200);
      frame.setVisible(true);
    }

    // Draw a small solid square around the point (x, y)
    public void paint(Graphics g)
    {
      g.fillRect(x-5, y-5, 10, 10);
    }

    // The real handler for the mousePressed event
    public void processMousePressed(MouseEvent e)
    {
      // Get (x, y) coordinates using getX() and getY() methods
      x = e.getX();
      y = e.getY();
      repaint();
    }
  }

  // Standard adapter
  class StandardMouseAdapter extends MouseAdapter
  {
    TestMouseEventUsingStandardAdapter adaptee;

    StandardMouseAdapter(TestMouseEventUsingStandardAdapter adaptee)
    {
      this.adaptee = adaptee;
    }

    // Delegate it to the handler to the adaptee
    public void mousePressed(MouseEvent e)
    {
      adaptee.processMousePressed(e);
    }
  }
```

The adapter `StandardMouseAdapter` serves as an intermediary class interposed between an event source and the target. The reference of the target object is passed to the adapter, since the adapter has to invoke the method in the target object for handling the event. You can shorten the program by implementing `StandardMouseAdapter` as an inner class inside the target class, as follows:

```java
// TestMouseEventUsingInnerClass.java: Display a filled square at the
// mouse pointer when the mouse is pressed (Using event adapters)
import java.awt.event.*;
import javax.swing.*;
import java.awt.*;
```

```java
public class TestMouseEventUsingInnerClass
  extends MyFrameWithExitHandling
{
  int x, y = 0; // x, y coordinates

  // Default constructor
  public TestMouseEventUsingInnerClass()
  {
    setTitle("TestMouseEventUsingInnerClass");

    // Register adapter as a listener
    addMouseListener(new InnerClassMouseAdapter());
  }

  // Main method
  public static void main(String[] args)
  {
    TestMouseEventUsingInnerClass frame =
      new TestMouseEventUsingInnerClass();
    frame.setSize(200, 200);
    frame.setVisible(true);
  }

  // Draw a small solid square around the point (x, y)
  public void paint(Graphics g)
  {
    g.fillRect(x-5, y-5, 10, 10);
  }

  // The real handler for the mousePressed event
  public void processMousePressed(MouseEvent e)
  {
    // Get (x, y) coordinates using getX() and getY() methods
    x = e.getX();
    y = e.getY();
    repaint();
  }

  class InnerClassMouseAdapter extends MouseAdapter
  {
    // Delegate it to the handler to the parent class
    public void mousePressed(MouseEvent e)
    {
      processMousePressed(e);
    }
  }
}
```

The program can be further shortened by using an anonymous inner class. An *anonymous inner class* is an inner class without a name. An anonymous inner class combines declaring an inner class and creating an instance of the class in one step, as shown in the following code.

```java
// TestMouseEventUsingAnonymousInnerClass.java:
// Using anonymous inner class for event adapter
import java.awt.event.*;
import javax.swing.*;
import java.awt.*;

public class TestMouseEventUsingAnonymousInnerClass
  extends MyFrameWithExitHandling
{
  int x, y = 0; // x, y coordinates
```

```
  // Default constructor
  public TestMouseEventUsingAnonymousInnerClass()
  {
    setTitle("TestMouseEventUsingAnonymousInnerClass");

    // Register adapter as a listener
    addMouseListener(new MouseAdapter()
    {
      // Delegate it to the handler to the parent class
      public void mousePressed(MouseEvent e)
      {
        processMousePressed(e);
      }
    });
  }

  // Main method
  public static void main(String[] args)
  {
    TestMouseEventUsingAnonymousInnerClass frame =
      new TestMouseEventUsingAnonymousInnerClass();
    frame.setSize(200, 200);
    frame.setVisible(true);
  }

  // Draw a small solid square around the point (x, y)
  public void paint(Graphics g)
  {
    g.fillRect(x-5, y-5, 10, 10);
  }

  // The real handler for the mousePressed event
  public void processMousePressed(MouseEvent e)
  {
    // Get (x, y) coordinates using getX() and getY() methods
    x = e.getX();
    y = e.getY();
    repaint();
  }
}
```

> **NOTE**
> Adapters are convenient in some situations, but are not really needed when creating code manually. For this reason, I regard this section as optional. The examples are all developed without using adapters. Nonetheless, adapters are extremely useful for automatically associating listener objects with source objects in Java builder tools like JBuilder.

Layout Managers

In many other windowing systems, the user interface components are arranged by using hard-coded pixel measurements. For example, put a button at location (10, 10) in the window. Using hard-coded pixel measurements, the user interface might look fine on one system but become unusable on another. Java's layout managers provide a level of abstraction that automatically maps your user interface on all windowing systems.

The Java GUI components are placed in containers. Each container has a layout manager that arranges the GUI components within it. Note that in Example 8.3, you did not specify where to place the Close button in the frame. Java knows where to place the button because the layout manager works behind the scenes to place components in the correct locations. The five basic layout managers are `FlowLayout`, `GridLayout`, `GridBagLayout`, `BorderLayout`, and `CardLayout`. These classes implement the `LayoutManager` interface.

Layout managers are set in containers, such as `JFrame`, `JPanel`, and `JApplet`. The syntax to set a layout manager is as follows:

```
container.setLayout(new specificLayout());
```

To add a component to the container, use the `add()` method. To remove a component from the container, use the `remove()` method. For example, the following statement add `jbtClose` to the container.

```
container.add(jbtClose);
```

The following sections introduce the `FlowLayout`, `GridLayout`, and `BorderLayout` managers. The `CardLayout` and `GridBagLayout` are introduced in Chapter 10, "Applets and Advanced Graphics."

FlowLayout

`FlowLayout` is the simplest layout manager. The components are arranged in the container from left to right in the order in which they were added. When one row becomes filled, a new row is started. You can specify the way the components are aligned by using one of three constants: `FlowLayout.RIGHT`, `FlowLayout.CENTER`, or `FlowLayout.LEFT`. You can also specify the gap between components in pixels. `FlowLayout` has three constructors:

- public FlowLayout(int align, int hGap, int vGap)

    This constructs a new `FlowLayout` with the specified alignment, horizontal gap, and vertical gap. The gaps are the distances in pixels between components.

- public FlowLayout(int alignment)

    This constructs a new `FlowLayout` with a specified alignment and a default gap of five pixels horizontally and vertically.

- public FlowLayout()

    This constructs a new `FlowLayout` with a default center alignment and a default gap of five pixels horizontally and vertically.

Example 8.4 Testing the *FlowLayout* Manager

This example enables a program to arrange components in a frame by using the `FlowLayout` manager with a specified alignment and horizontal and vertical gaps. The program uses the following simple code to arrange 10 buttons in a frame. The output is shown in Figure 8.11.

```java
// ShowFlowLayout.java: Demonstrate using FlowLayout
import javax.swing.JButton;
import java.awt.Container;
import java.awt.FlowLayout;

public class ShowFlowLayout extends MyFrameWithExitHandling
{
  // Default constructor
  public ShowFlowLayout()
  {
    // Get the content pane of the frame
    Container container = getContentPane();

    // Set FlowLayout, aligned left with horizontal gap 10
    // and vertical gap 20 between components
    container.setLayout(new FlowLayout(FlowLayout.LEFT, 10, 20));

    // Add buttons to the frame
    for (int i=1; i<=10; i++)
      container.add(new JButton("Component " + i));
  }

  // Main method
  public static void main(String[] args)
  {
    ShowFlowLayout frame = new ShowFlowLayout();
    frame.setTitle("Show FlowLayout");
    frame.setSize(200, 200);
    frame.setVisible(true);
  }
}
```

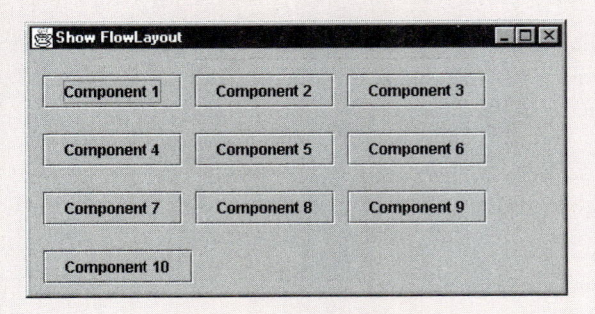

Figure 8.11 *The components are added to fill in the rows one after another in the container with the* `FlowLayout` *manager.*

continues

> **Example Review**
>
> If you resize the frame, the components are automatically rearranged to fit in the new window.
>
> If you replace the `setLayout` statement with `setLayout(new FlowLayout (FlowLayout.LEFT, 0, 0))`, you will see all the buttons left-aligned with no gaps.
>
> An anonymous object `new FlowLayout()` was created in the program. The `setLayout(new FlowLayout())` is equivalent to the following code:
>
> ```
> FlowLayout layout = new FlowLayout();
> setLayout(layout);
> ```
>
> This code creates an explicit reference to the object `layout` of the `FlowLayout` class. This explicit reference is not necessary, because the object is not directly referenced in the program.
>
> ---
>
> ■ **CAUTION**
> Do not forget to put the `new` operator before `LayoutManager` when setting a layout style; for example, `setLayout(new FlowLayout())`.

GridLayout

The `GridLayout` manager arranges components in a grid (matrix) formation with the number of rows and columns defined by the constructor. The components are placed in the grid from left to right, starting with the first row, then the second, and so on, in the order in which they are added. The `GridLayout` manager has three constructors:

- `public GridLayout(int rows, int columns, int hGap, int vGap)`

    This constructs a new `GridLayout` with the specified number of rows and columns, along with specified horizontal and vertical gaps between components in the container.

- `public GridLayout(int rows, int columns)`

    This constructs a new `GridLayout` with the specified number of rows and columns. The horizontal and vertical gaps are zero.

- `public GridLayout()`

    This constructs a new `GridLayout` with one column per component in a single row.

You can specify the number of rows and columns in the grid. The basic rule is as follows:

- The number of rows or the number of columns can be zero, but not both. If one is zero and the other is nonzero, the nonzero dimension is fixed and the zero dimension is determined dynamically by the layout manager. For example, if you specify zero rows and three columns for a grid that has 10 components, `GridLayout` creates three fixed columns of four rows, with the last row containing one component. If you specify three rows and zero columns for a grid that has 10 components, `GridLayout` creates three fixed rows of four columns, with the last row containing two components.

- If both the number of rows and the number of columns are nonzero, the number of rows is the dominating parameter; that is, the number of rows is fixed, and the layout manager dynamically calculates the number of columns. For example, if you specify three rows and three columns for a grid that has 10 components, `GridLayout` creates three fixed rows of four columns, with the last row containing two components.

Example 8.5 Testing the *GridLayout* Manager

This example presents a program that arranges components on a frame with `GridLayout`. The program gives the following code to arrange 10 buttons in a grid of four rows and three columns. Its output is shown in Figure 8.12.

```java
// ShowGridLayout.java: Demonstrate using GridLayout
import java.awt.GridLayout;
import java.awt.Container;
import javax.swing.JButton;

public class ShowGridLayout extends MyFrameWithExitHandling
{
  // Default constructor
  public ShowGridLayout()
  {
    // Get the content pane of the frame
    Container container = getContentPane();

    // Set GridLayout, 4 rows, 3 columns, and gaps 5 between
    // components horizontally and vertically
    container.setLayout(new GridLayout(4, 3, 5, 5));

    // Add buttons to the frame
    for (int i=1; i<=10; i++)
      container.add(new JButton("Component "+i));
  }

  // Main method
  public static void main(String[] args)
  {
    ShowGridLayout frame = new ShowGridLayout();
    frame.setTitle("Show GridLayout");
    frame.setSize(200, 200);
    frame.setVisible(true);
  }
}
```

continues

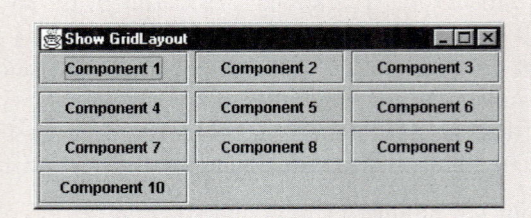

Figure 8.12 *The* `GridLayout` *manager divides the container into grids, then the components are added to fill in the cells, row by row.*

Example Review

If you resize the frame, the layout of the buttons remains unchanged (that is, the number of rows and columns does not change, and the gaps don't change either).

All components in the layout are given equal size in `GridLayout`.

Replacing the `setLayout` statement with `setLayout(new GridLayout(3, 10))` would yield three rows and *four* columns, with the last row containing two components. The columns parameter is ignored if the rows parameter is nonzero. The actual number of columns is calculated by the layout manager.

> **NOTE**
> In `FlowLayout` and `GridLayout`, the order in which the components are added to the container is important. It determines the order of the components in the container.

BorderLayout

The `BorderLayout` manager divides the window into five areas: East, South, West, North, and Center. Components are added to a `BorderLayout` by using `add(Component, index)`, where `index` is a constant `BorderLayout.EAST`, `BorderLayout.SOUTH`, `BorderLayout.WEST`, `BorderLayout.NORTH`, or `BorderLayout.CENTER`. You can use one of the following two constructors to create a new `BorderLayout`:

- `public BorderLayout(int hGap, int vGap)`

    This constructs a new `BorderLayout` with the specified horizontal and vertical gaps between the components.

- `public BorderLayout()`

    This constructs a new `BorderLayout` without horizontal or vertical gaps.

The components are laid out according to their preferred sizes and where they are placed. The north and south components can stretch horizontally; the east and west components can stretch vertically; the center component can stretch both horizontally and vertically to fill any empty space.

Example 8.6 Testing the *BorderLayout* Manager

This example enables a program to place five buttons in the window by using the `BorderLayout` manager. The program presents the following code to place East, South, West, North, and Center buttons in the frame by using `BorderLayout`. The output of the program is shown in Figure 8.13.

```java
// ShowBorderLayout.java: Demonstrate using BorderLayout
import java.awt.Container;
import java.awt.BorderLayout;
import javax.swing.JButton;

public class ShowBorderLayout extends MyFrameWithExitHandling
{
  // Default constructor
  public ShowBorderLayout()
  {
    // Get the content pane of the frame
    Container container = getContentPane();

    // Set BorderLayout with horizontal gap 5 and vertical gap 10
    container.setLayout(new BorderLayout(5, 10));

    // Add buttons to the frame
    container.add(new JButton("East"), BorderLayout.EAST);
    container.add(new JButton("South"), BorderLayout.SOUTH);
    container.add(new JButton("West"), BorderLayout.WEST);
    container.add(new JButton("North"), BorderLayout.NORTH);
    container.add(new JButton("Center"), BorderLayout.CENTER);
  }

  // Main method
  public static void main(String[] args)
  {
    ShowBorderLayout frame = new ShowBorderLayout();
    frame.setTitle("Show BorderLayout");
    frame.pack();
    frame.setVisible(true);
  }
}
```

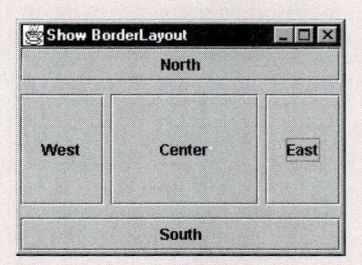

Figure 8.13 `BorderLayout` *divides the container into five areas, each of which can hold a component.*

continues

Example Review

The buttons are added to the frame. Note that the `add()` method for `BorderLayout` is different from `FlowLayout` and `GridLayout`. With `BorderLayout` you specify where to put the components.

It is unnecessary to place components to occupy all the areas. If you remove the East button from the program and rerun it, you will see that the center stretches rightward to occupy the East area.

> **NOTE**
> For convenience, `BorderLayout` interprets the absence of an index specification as `BorderLayout.CENTER`. For example, `add(component)` is the same as `add(Component, BorderLayout.CENTER)`.

> **TIP**
> Always explicitly set a layout style for a container, even though `BorderLayout` is used by default for the content pane of a `JFrame`.

Using Panels as Containers

Suppose that you want to place 10 buttons and a text field on a frame. The buttons are placed in grid formation, but the text field is placed on a separate row. It is difficult to achieve the desired look by placing all the components in a single container. With Java graphics programming, you can divide a window into panels. Panels act as smaller containers to group user interface components. You add the buttons in one panel, and then add the panel into the frame.

The Swing version of panel is `JPanel`. The constructor in the `JPanel` class is `JPanel()`. To add a button to the panel p, for instance, you can use:

```
JPanel p = new JPanel();
p.add(new JButton("ButtonName"));
```

By default, `JPanel` uses `FlowLayout`. Panels can be placed inside a frame or inside another panel. The following statement places panel p into frame f:

```
f.getContentPane().add(p);
```

> **NOTE**
> To add a component to `JFrame`, you actually add it to the content pane of `JFrame`. To add a component to a panel, you add it directly to the panel using the `add()` method.

Example 8.7 Testing Panels

This example uses panels to organize components. The program creates a panel that holds ten buttons labeled 0, 1, 2, and so on to 9, using the `GridLayout` manager. The panel is placed in the frame by using the `BorderLayout` manager. The number is displayed in the text field when a number button is clicked. The output is shown in Figure 8.14.

```java
// TestPanels.java: Use panels to group components
import java.awt.*;
import java.awt.event.*;
import javax.swing.*;

public class TestPanels extends MyFrameWithExitHandling
  implements ActionListener
{
  // Declare a text field to display a selected number
  private JTextField jtfNum;

  // Create an array of buttons
  private JButton jbtNum[] = new JButton[10];

  // Default constructor
  public TestPanels()
  {
    // Get the content pane of the frame
    Container container = getContentPane();

    // Set BorderLayout for the frame
    container.setLayout(new BorderLayout());

    // Create panel p for the buttons and set GridLayout
    JPanel p = new JPanel();
    p.setLayout(new GridLayout(3, 4));

    // Add buttons to the panel and register listener for each button
    for (int i=0; i<=9; i++)
    {
      p.add(jbtNum[i] = new JButton(" "+i));
      jbtNum[i].addActionListener(this);
    }

    // Create a new text field
    jtfNum = new JTextField();

    // Add the panel and the text field to the frame
    container.add(p, BorderLayout.CENTER);
    container.add(jtfNum, BorderLayout.SOUTH);
  }

  // Main method
  public static void main(String[] args)
  {
    TestPanels frame = new TestPanels();
    frame.setTitle("TestPanels");
    frame.setSize(200,250);
    frame.setVisible(true);
  }
```

continues

```java
      // Handler for button actions
      public void actionPerformed(ActionEvent e)
      {
        String actionCommand = e.getActionCommand();
        if (e.getSource() instanceof JButton)
          jtfNum.setText(actionCommand);
      }
    }
```

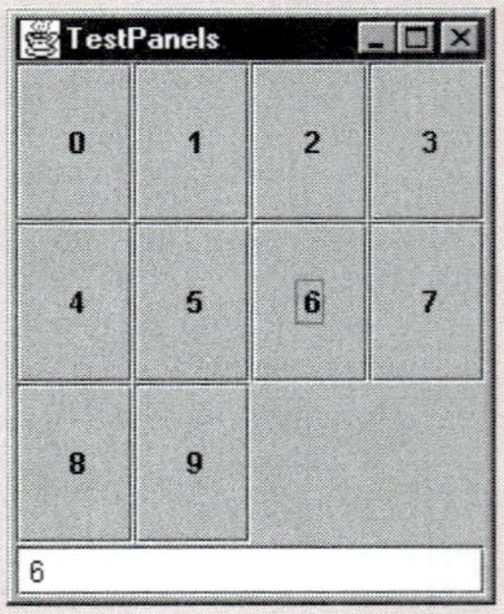

Figure 8.14 *The program uses a panel to group the buttons labeled 0 through 9 and displays the button label on a text field when the button is clicked.*

Example Review

JPanel p is used to group the number buttons by using the GridLayout manager. The program places panel p in the center of the frame and a text field below the panel.

The statement jtfNum = new JTextField() creates an instance of JTextField. Text field is a GUI component that can be used for user input as well as to display values. Text field will be introduced in Chapter 9, "Creating User Interfaces."

Clicking a button triggers the actionPerformed() method to display the label of the button in the text field. If you resize the window, you will see that the button size changes, but all the components remain in the same relative position.

Using Panels to Draw Graphics

Panels are invisible and are used as small containers that group components to achieve a desired layout look. Another important use of JPanel is for drawing graphics.

To draw on a panel, you create a new class that extends JPanel and override the paintComponent() method to tell the panel how to draw graphics. You can then display strings, draw geometric shapes, and view images on the panel. Although you can display strings in a frame or directly in an applet, I recommend that you use JPanel to draw messages and shapes and to show images; this way your drawing does not interfere with other components.

Example 8.8 Drawing on Panels

This example presents a program to create a subclass of `JPanel` that will display a message. You can use the mouse to move the message. The message moves as the mouse drags and is always displayed at the mouse point. The output of the program is shown in Figure 8.15.

```java
// PanelDrawingDemo.java: Draw on a JPanel
import java.awt.*;
import java.awt.event.*;
import javax.swing.*;

public class PanelDrawingDemo extends MyFrameWithExitHandling
{
  // Default constructor
  public PanelDrawingDemo()
  {
    // Create a PaintPanel instance for drawing a message
    PaintPanel p = new PaintPanel("Welcome to Java");

    // Place a drawing panel in the frame
    getContentPane().setLayout(new BorderLayout());
    getContentPane().add(p);
  }

  // Main method
  public static void main(String[] args)
  {
    PanelDrawingDemo frame = new PanelDrawingDemo();
    frame.setTitle("Panel Drawing Demo");
    frame.setSize(300,200);
    frame.setVisible(true);
  }

  // PaintPanel draws a message. This class is defined as inner class
  class PaintPanel extends JPanel implements MouseMotionListener
  {
    private String message;
    private int x = 10;
    private int y = 10;

    // Construct a panel to draw string s
    public PaintPanel(String s)
    {
      message = s;
      this.addMouseMotionListener(this);
      repaint();
    }

    // Tell the panel how to draw things
    public void paintComponent(Graphics g)
    {
      // It is necessary to invoke this method to clear the viewing
      // area
      super.paintComponent(g);

      // Draw the message at (x, y)
      g.drawString(message, x, y);
    }
```

continues

```
      public void mouseMoved(MouseEvent e)
      {
      }

      // Handler for mouse dragged event
      public void mouseDragged(MouseEvent e)
      {
        // Get the new location and repaint the screen
        x = e.getX();
        y = e.getY();
        repaint();
      }
    }
  }
```

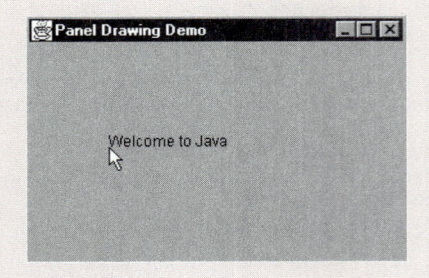

Figure 8.15 *The program displays "Welcome to Java" on a panel placed in a frame.*

Example Review

The class `PaintPanel` extends `JPanel` and implements `MouseMotionListener`. The `PaintPanel` class is used to display a message. The message is passed to `PaintPanel` through the constructor when creating an object of `PaintPanel`.

The `MouseMotionListener` interface contains two handlers, `mouseMoved()` and `mouseDragged()`, for handling mouse motion events. When you move the mouse with the button pressed, the `mouseDragged()` method is invoked to repaint the viewing area and display the message at the mouse point.

You used the `fillRect()` method in the `Graphics` class to display a solid square on a frame in Example 8.2. You also used the `drawString()` method to display a string on an applet in Example 1.2, "Writing a Simple Applet." The `drawString()` method in this example draws on the panel. The `drawString(s, x, y)` method draws a string s whose left end of the baseline starts at (x, y).

The Swing components use the `paintComponent()` method to draw things. The `paintComponent()` method is invoked to paint the graphics context. Invoking `super.paintComponent()` is necessary to clear the viewing area before a new drawing is displayed. If this method was not invoked, the previous drawings would not be cleared.

The `repaint()` method is defined in the `Component` class. Invoking `repaint()` causes `paintComponent()` method to be called.

The *repaint()*, *update()*, *paint()*, and *paintComponent()* Methods

In Java graphics programming, drawings are painted in graphics mode. The `repaint()`, `update()`, `paint()`, and `paintComponent()` methods cause strings, lines, figures, and images to be displayed on frames, applets, and panels. It is important to understand the roles of these methods.

The `update()`, `paint()`, and `paintComponent()` methods take a `Graphics` object as a parameter. The paintings are drawn on this object. The Java system automatically creates a default graphics context, an object of the `Graphics` class, and passes it to these methods. This object is local to the methods and cannot be used outside of them.

The `repaint()`, `update()`, and `paint()` methods are defined in the `Component` class and are modified in the `JComponent` class. The `repaint()` method is invoked to refresh the viewing area. Typically, you call it if you have new things to display. Never override this method. It calls the `update()` method. In the `Component` class, the `update()` method first clears the viewing area and then invokes the `paint()` method. Sometimes, clearing the entire viewing area is not needed, and repeated erasing and painting cause flickering. Therefore, the `update()` method was modified in `JComponent` to invoke the `paint()` method directly so as to avoid clearing the viewing area. However, in many cases, the background needs to be cleared before repainting, so the Swing component introduces the `paintComponent()` method that clears the background before repainting. In addition, a technique known as *double buffering* was implemented with all the Swing components to eliminate flickering. This technique is particularly useful for displaying a sequence of images. From now on, all the paintings will be displayed on Swing components such as `JPanel`.

> **NOTE**
> For Swing lightweight components, you should always use `paintComponent()` method rather than the `paint()` method. The `paintComponent()` method should never be invoked directly. It is invoked either by the `update()` method as result of calling the `repaint()` method or by the Java system when your viewing area changes.

> **NOTE**
> The `repaint()` method lodges a request to update the viewing area and returns immediately. Its effect is asynchronous, and if several requests are outstanding, it is likely that only the last `paintComponent()` will be done.

> **CAUTION**
> The `paintComponent()` method is for drawing strings, geometric figures, and images. They are not for displaying user interface components. The UI components are displayed in the container using the `setVisible()` method.

The *Color* Class

You can set colors for GUI components by using the `java.awt.Color` class. Colors are made of red, green, and blue components, each of which is represented by a byte value that describe its intensity, ranging from 0 (darkest shade) to 255 (lightest shade). This is commonly known as the RGB model.

The syntax to create a `Color` object is

```
Color color = new Color(r, g, b);
```

in which r, g, and b specify a color by its red, green, and blue components; for example:

```
Color color = new Color(128, 100, 100);
```

You can use the `setBackground(Color c)` and `setForeground(Color c)` methods to set a component's background and foreground colors.

Following is an example of setting the background by using `Color c`:

```
JPanel myPanel = new JPanel();
myPanel.setBackground(c);
```

Alternatively, you can use one of the 13 standard colors (`black`, `blue`, `cyan`, `darkGray`, `gray`, `green`, `lightGray`, `magenta`, `orange`, `pink`, `red`, `white`, `yellow`) defined as constants in `java.awt.Color`. For example, the following code sets the background color of the panel to yellow.

```
JPanel myPanel = new JPanel();
myPanel.setBackground(Color.yellow);
```

> **NOTE**
> The standard color names are constants, but they are named as variables with lowercase for the first word and uppercase for the first letters of subsequent words. Thus the color names violate the Java naming convention.

Drawing Geometric Figures

In this section you will learn how to draw figures in the `Graphics` context. Java provides a set of methods in the `Graphics` class that make it easy to draw geometric figures. These methods are contained in the `Graphics` class.

All the drawing methods have arguments that specify the locations of the subjects to be drawn. The Java coordinate system has *x* in the horizontal axis and y in the vertical axis, with the origin (`0, 0`) at the upper-left corner of the screen. The *x* coordinate increases to the right, and the *y* coordinate increases downward. All measurements in Java are made in pixels, as shown in Figure 8.16.

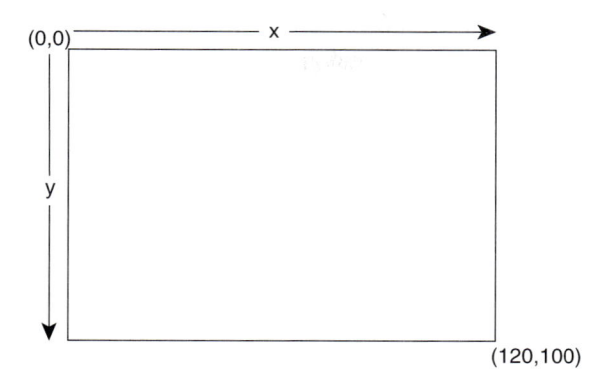

Figure 8.16 *The Java graphics coordinate system is measured in pixels, with (0, 0) at its upper-left corner.*

To draw geometric figures, you must either override the `paintComponent()` method or create a `Graphics` object and draw graphics there. In many cases, it is easier to draw graphics by overriding `paintComponent()` in a subclass of `JPanel`. In some cases, however, you must create your own `Graphics` object to draw graphics by using the `getGraphics()` method. You will learn when and how to use the `getGraphics()` method in Example 10.6, "Handling a Complex Mouse Event" in Chapter 10, "Applets and Advanced Graphics."

The `paintComponent()` method takes a `Graphics` object as an argument. The `Graphics` object contains a collection of settings, such as fonts and colors. You can set fonts and colors for drawing text, shapes, and images.

The *Font* and *FontMetrics* Classes

You can set the font for the subjects you draw and use font metrics to measure font size. Fonts and font metrics are encapsulated in two AWT classes: `Font` and `FontMetrics`.

Whatever font is current will be used in the subsequent drawing. To set a font, you need to create a `Font` object from the `Font` class. The syntax is:

```
Font myFont = new Font(name, style, size);
```

You can choose a font name from `SansSerif`, `Serif`, `Monospaced`, `Dialog`, or `DialogInput`, and choose a style from `Font.PLAIN`, `Font.BOLD`, and `Font.ITALIC`. The styles can be combined, as in the following code:

```
Font myFont = new Font("SansSerif ", Font.BOLD, 16);
Font myFont = new Font("Serif", Font.BOLD+Font.ITALIC, 12);
```

You can use `FontMetrics` to compute the exact length and width of a string, which is helpful for measuring the size of a string in order to display it in the right position. For example, you can center strings in the viewing area with the help of the `FontMetrics` class. A `FontMetrics` is measured by the following attributes (see Figure 8.17):

- **Leading**—Pronounced *ledding*, this is the amount of space between lines of text.
- **Ascent**—This is the height of a character, from the baseline to the top.
- **Descent**—This is the distance from the baseline to the bottom of a descending character, such as *j*, *y*, and *g*.
- **Height**—This is the sum of leading, ascent, and descent.

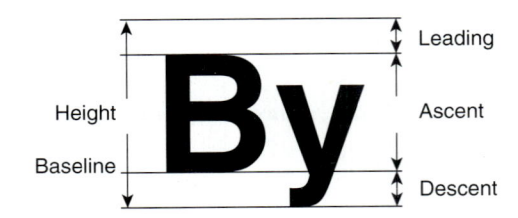

Figure 8.17 *The* `FontMetrics` *class can be used to determine the font properties of characters.*

To get a `FontMetrics` object for a specific font, use

```
g.getFontMetrics(Font f); or
g.getFontMetrics(); // Get FontMetrics for current font
```

You can use the following instance methods to obtain font information:

```
public int getAscent()
public int getDescent()
public int getLeading()
public int getHeight()
public int stringWidth(String str)
```

Example 8.9 Using *FontMetrics*

This example presents a program that displays "Welcome to Java" in SansSerif 20-point bold, centered in the frame. The output of the program is shown in Figure 8.18.

```
// TestFontMetrics.java: Draw a message at the center of a panel
import java.awt.Font;
import java.awt.FontMetrics;
import java.awt.Graphics;
import javax.swing.JPanel;

public class TestFontMetrics extends MyFrameWithExitHandling
{
  // Main method
  public static void main(String[] args)
  {
    TestFontMetrics frame = new TestFontMetrics();
    frame.setSize(300, 200);
    frame.setTitle("TestFontMetrics");
    frame.setVisible(true);
  }
}
```

```java
    // Default constructor
    public TestFontMetrics()
    {
      MessagePanel messagePanel = new MessagePanel("Welcome to Java");
      messagePanel.setCentered(true);
      getContentPane().add(messagePanel);
    }
}

// MessagePanel.java: Display a message on a JPanel
import java.awt.Font;
import java.awt.FontMetrics;
import java.awt.Dimension;
import java.awt.Graphics;
import javax.swing.JPanel;

public class MessagePanel extends JPanel
{
  private String message = "Welcome to Java"; // Message to display

  // (x, y) coordinates where the message is displayed
  private int xCoordinate = 20;
  private int yCoordinate = 20;

  // Indicating whether the message is displayed in the center
  private boolean centered;

  // font used to display message
  private Font font = new Font("SansSerif", Font.BOLD, 20);

  // Default constructor
  public MessagePanel()
  {
    repaint();
  }

  // Constructor with a message parameter
  public MessagePanel(String message)
  {
    this.message = message;
    repaint();
  }

  public String getMessage()
  {
    return message;
  }

  public void setMessage(String message)
  {
    this.message = message;
  }

  public int getXCoordinate()
  {
    return xCoordinate;
  }

  public void setXCoordinate(int x)
  {
    this.xCoordinate = x;
  }
```

continues

```java
    public int getYCoordinate()
    {
      return yCoordinate;
    }

    public void setYCoordinate(int y)
    {
      this.yCoordinate = y;
    }

    public Font getFont()
    {
      return font;
    }

    public void setFont(Font font)
    {
      this.font = font;
    }

    public boolean isCentered()
    {
      return centered;
    }

    public void setCentered(boolean centered)
    {
      this.centered = centered;
    }

    public void paintComponent(Graphics g)
    {
      super.paintComponent(g);

      if (centered)
      {
        // Get font metrics for the font
        FontMetrics fm = g.getFontMetrics(font);

        // Find the center location to display
        int w = fm.stringWidth(message);  // Get the string width
        int h = fm.getAscent(); // Get the string height
        xCoordinate = (getSize().width-w)/2;
        yCoordinate = (getSize().height+h)/2;
      }

      g.drawString(message, xCoordinate, yCoordinate);
    }

    public Dimension getPreferredSize()
    {
      return new Dimension(200, 100);
    }

    public Dimension getMinimumSize()
    {
      return new Dimension(200, 100);
    }
}
```

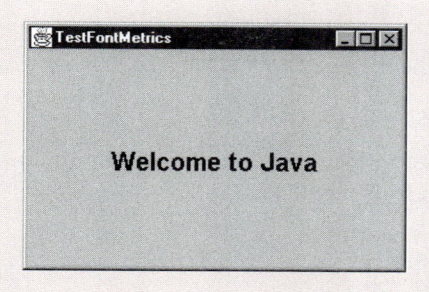

Figure 8.18 *The program uses the* `FontMetrics` *class to measure the string width and height, and displays it at the center of the frame.*

Example Review

The example contains two classes: `TestFontMetrics` and `MessagePanel`. `TestFontMetrics` creates an instance of `MessagePanel` to display a message at the center of the panel. `TestFontMetrics` and `MessagePanel` are stored in separate files, because `MessagePanel` is public and will be used by classes in other packages.

The `MessagePanel` class has the properties message, xCoordinate, yCoordinate, and centered. xCoordinate and yCoordinate specify where the message is displayed if centered is false. If centered is true, the message is displayed at the center of the panel.

The statement `Font f = new Font("SansSerif", Font.BOLD, 20)` creates a new font with the specified style and size. `g.setFont(f)` sets font for g. The statement `FontMetrics fm = g.getFontMetrics(f)` obtains a `FontMetrics` instance for font f.

The `getSize()` method defined in the `Component` class returns the size of this component in the form of a `Dimension` object. The `height` field of the `Dimension` object contains the component's height, and the `width` field of the `Dimension` object contains the component's width.

Since the centered property is set to true, the message is displayed in the center of the panel. Resizing the frame results in the message always being displayed in the center of the panel.

The `getPreferredSize()` method defined in `Component` is overridden in `MessagePanel` to specify a preferred size for the layout manager to consider when laying out a `MessagePanel` object.

Drawing Lines

You can use the method shown below to draw a straight line:

```
drawLine(x1, y1, x2, y2);
```

The components (x1, y1) and (x2, y2) are the starting and ending points of the line, as shown in Figure 8.19.

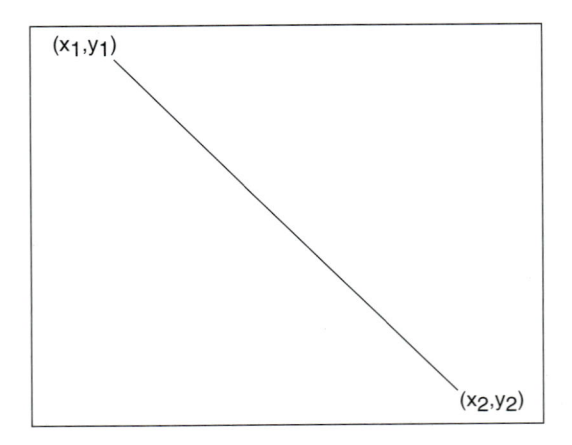

Figure 8.19   *The* `drawLine()` *method draws a line between two specified points.*

Drawing Rectangles

Java provides six methods for drawing rectangles in outline or filled with color. You can draw plain rectangles, rounded rectangles, or 3D rectangles.

To draw a plain rectangle, use:

```
drawRect(x, y, w, h);
```

To draw a rectangle filled with color, use the following code:

```
fillRect(x, y, w, h);
```

The component x, y is the upper-left corner of the rectangle, and w and h are the width and height of the rectangle (see Figure 8.20).

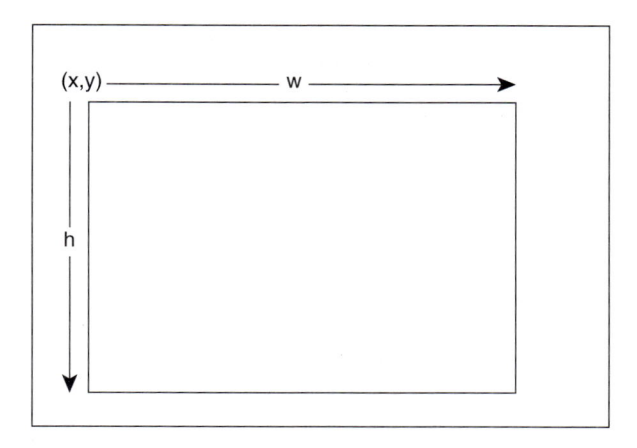

Figure 8.20 *The* `drawRect()` *method draws a rectangle with specified upper-left corner* (x, y), *width, and height.*

To draw a rounded rectangle, use the following code:

```
drawRoundRect(x, y, w, h, aw, ah);
```

To draw a rounded rectangle filled with color, use this code:

```
fillRoundRect(x, y, w, h, aw, ah);
```

The components x, y, w, and h are the same as in the `drawRect()` method, the parameter aw is the horizontal diameter of the arcs at the corner, and ah is the vertical diameter of the arcs at the corner (see Figure 8.21).

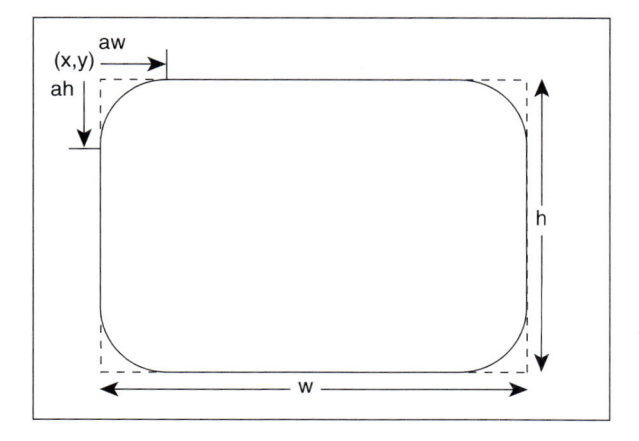

Figure 8.21 *The* `drawRoundRect()` *method draws a rounded-corner rectangle.*

325

To draw a 3D rectangle, use

```
draw3DRect(x, y, w, h, raised);
```

in which x, y, w, and h are the same as in drawRect(). The last parameter, a Boolean value, indicates whether the rectangle is raised or indented from the surface.

The next example demonstrates these methods. The output is shown in Figure 8.22.

```java
// TestRect.java: Demonstrate drawing rectangles
import java.awt.Graphics;
import java.awt.Color;
import javax.swing.JPanel;

public class TestRect extends MyFrameWithExitHandling
{
  // Default constructor
  public TestRect()
  {
    setTitle("Show Rectangles");
    getContentPane().add(new RectPanel());
  }

  // Main method
  public static void main(String[] args)
  {
    TestRect frame = new TestRect();
    frame.setSize(300,250);
    frame.setVisible(true);
  }
}

class RectPanel extends JPanel
{
  public void paintComponent(Graphics g)
  {
    super.paintComponent(g);

    g.drawRect(30,30,100,100); // Draw a rectangle

    // Draw a rounded rectangle
    g.drawRoundRect(140, 30, 100, 100, 60, 30);
    g.setColor(Color.yellow); // Set new color

    // Draw a 3D rectangle
    g.fill3DRect(30, 140, 100, 100, true);
  }
}
```

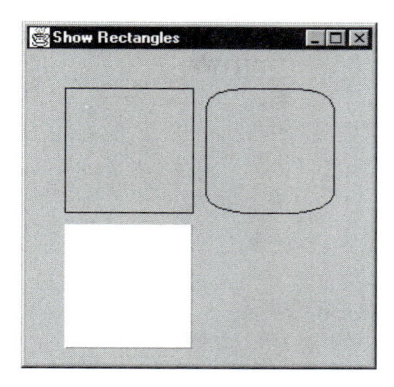

Figure 8.22 *The program draws a rectangle, a rounded rectangle, and a 3D rectangle.*

Ovals

You can use `drawOval()` or `fillOval()` to draw an oval in outline or filled solid. In Java, the oval is drawn based on its bounding rectangle; therefore, give the parameters as if you were drawing a rectangle.

Here is the syntax for drawing an oval:

```
drawOval(x, y, w, h);
```

To draw a filled oval, use the following code:

```
fillOval(x, y, w, h);
```

The parameters x and y indicate the top-left corner of the bounding rectangle, and w and h indicate the width and height, respectively, of the bounding rectangle, as shown in Figure 8.23.

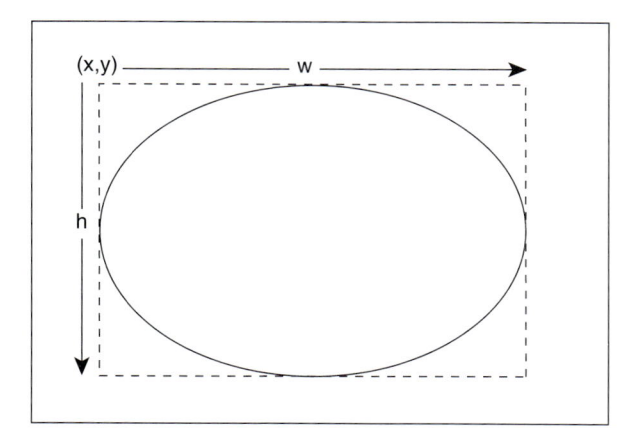

Figure 8.23 *The `drawOval()` method draws an oval based on its bounding rectangle.*

The following is an example of how to draw ovals, with the output in Figure 8.24.

```java
// TestOvals.java: Demonstrate drawing ovals
import java.awt.Color;
import java.awt.Graphics;
import javax.swing.JPanel;

public class TestOvals extends MyFrameWithExitHandling
{
  // Default constructor
  public TestOvals()
  {
    setTitle("Show Ovals");
    getContentPane().add(new OvalsPanel());
  }

  // Main method
  public static void main(String[] args)
  {
    TestOvals frame = new TestOvals();
    frame.setSize(250, 250);
    frame.setVisible(true);
  }
}

// The class for drawing the ovals on a panel
class OvalsPanel extends JPanel
{
  public void paintComponent(Graphics g)
  {
    super.paintComponents(g);

    g.drawOval(10, 30, 100, 60);
    g.drawOval(130, 30, 60, 60);
    g.setColor(Color.yellow);
    g.fillOval(10, 130, 100, 60);
  }
}
```

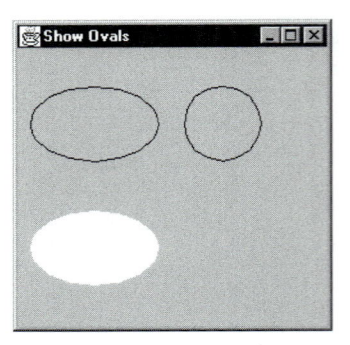

Figure 8.24 *The program draws an oval, a circle, and a filled oval.*

Arcs

Like an oval, an arc is drawn based on its bounding rectangle. An arc is conceived as part of an oval. The syntax to draw or fill an arc is as follows:

```
drawArc(x, y, w, h, angle1, angle2);

fillArc(x, y, w, h, angle1, angle2);
```

The parameters x, y, w, and h are the same as in the drawOval() method; the parameter angle1 is the starting angle; angle2 is the spanning angle (that is, the ending angle is angle1+angle2). Angles are measured in degrees and follow the usual mathematical conventions (that is, 0 degrees is at 3 o'clock, and positive angles indicate counterclockwise rotation; see Figure 8.25).

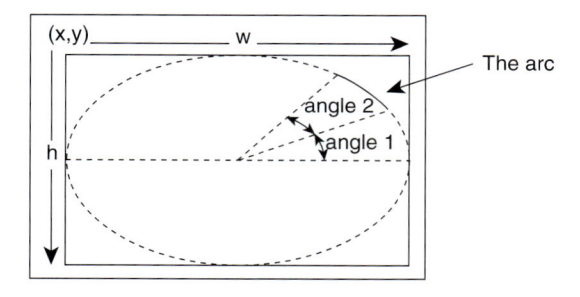

Figure 8.25 *The* drawArc() *method draws an arc based on an oval with specified angles.*

Shown below is an example of how to draw arcs; the output is shown in Figure 8.26.

```
// TestArcs.java: Demonstrate drawing arcs
import java.awt.Color;
import java.awt.Graphics;
import javax.swing.JPanel;

public class TestArcs extends MyFrameWithExitHandling
{
  // Default constructor
  public TestArcs()
  {
    setTitle("Show Arcs");
    getContentPane().add(new ArcsPanel());
  }

  // Main method
  public static void main(String[] args)
  {
    TestArcs frame = new TestArcs();
    frame.setSize(250, 300);
    frame.setVisible(true);
  }
}
```

```
// The class for drawing arcs on a panel
class ArcsPanel extends JPanel
{
  public void paintComponent(Graphics g)
  {
    super.paintComponent(g);

    g.drawArc(10, 30, 100, 60, 20, 120); // Draw an arc
    g.setColor(Color.yellow); // Set new color
    g.fillArc(10, 150, 100, 60, 120, 300); // Draw another arc
  }
}
```

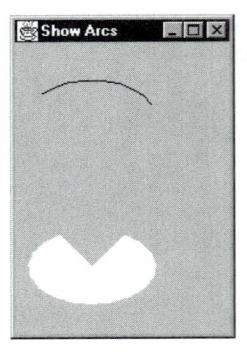

Figure 8.26 *The program draws an arc and a filled arc.*

Polygons

The `Polygon` class encapsulates a description of a closed, two-dimensional region within a coordinate space. This region is bounded by an arbitrary number of line segments, each of which is one side (or edge) of the polygon. Internally, a polygon comprises a list of (x, y) coordinate pairs in which each pair defines a vertex of the polygon, and two successive pairs are the endpoints of a line that is a side of the polygon. The first and final pairs of (x, y) points are joined by a line segment that closes the polygon.

Java enables you to draw a polygon in two ways: by using the direct method or by using the `Polygon` object.

The direct method draws a polygon by specifying all the points in the `drawPolygon()` method. The syntax is as follows:

```
drawPolygon(x, y, n);
```

```
fillPolygon(x, y, n);
```

The parameters x and y are arrays of x-coordinates and y-coordinates, and n indicates the number of points. For example:

```
int x[] = {40, 70, 60, 45, 20};
int y[] = {20, 40, 80, 45, 60};
g.drawPolygon(x, y, x.length);
g.fillPolygon(x, y, x.length);
```

The drawing method opens the polygon by drawing lines between point (x[i], y[i]) and point (x[i+1], y[i+1]) for i = 0, ... , length-1; it closes the polygon by drawing a line between the first and last points (see Figure 8.27).

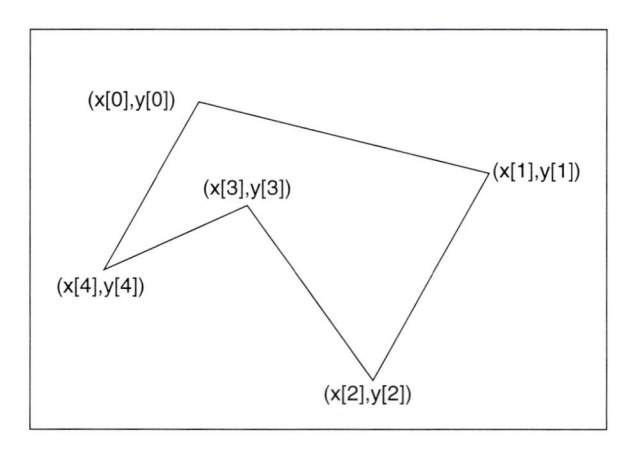

Figure 8.27 *The* drawPolygon() *method draws a polygon with specified points.*

You can also draw a polygon by first creating a Polygon object, then adding points to it, and finally displaying it. To create a Polygon object, use

```
Polygon poly = new Polygon();
```

or

```
Polygon poly = new Polygon(x, y, n);
```

The parameters x, y, and n are the same as in the previous drawPolygon() method. Here is an example of how to draw a polygon in Graphics g:

```
Polygon poly = new Polygon();
poly.addPoint(20,30);
poly.addPoint(40,40);
poly.addPoint(50,50);
g.drawPolygon(poly);
```

The addPoint() method adds a point to the polygon. The drawPolygon() method also takes a Polygon object as a parameter.

Next is an example of how to draw a polygon with the output shown in Figure 8.28.

```
// TestPolygon.java: Demonstrate drawing polygons
import java.awt.Graphics;
import java.awt.Polygon;
import javax.swing.JPanel;

public class TestPolygons extends MyFrameWithExitHandling
{
  // Default constructor
  public TestPolygons()
```

```java
    {
      setTitle("Show Polygons");
      getContentPane().add(new PolygonsPanel());
    }

    // Main method
    public static void main(String[] args)
    {
      TestPolygons frame = new TestPolygons();
      frame.setSize(200,250);
      frame.setVisible(true);
    }
  }

  // Draw a polygon on the panel
  class PolygonsPanel extends JPanel
  {
    public void paintComponent(Graphics g)
    {
      super.paintComponent(g);

      // Create a Polygon object
      Polygon poly = new Polygon();

      // Add points to the polygon
      poly.addPoint(10, 30);
      poly.addPoint(60, 45);
      poly.addPoint(35, 55);
      poly.addPoint(90, 85);
      poly.addPoint(100, 155);
      poly.addPoint(50, 155);

      // Draw the polygon
      g.drawPolygon(poly);
    }
  }
```

Figure 8.28 *The program draws a polygon by using the* `drawPolygon()` *method.*

> **NOTE**
> Prior to JDK 1.1, a polygon was a sequence of lines that were not necessarily closed. But in JDK 1.1, a polygon is always closed. Nevertheless, you can draw a nonclosed polygon by using the drawPolyline(int[] x, int[] y, int nPoints) method, which draws a sequence of connected lines defined by arrays of x and y coordinates. The figure is not closed if the first point differs from the last point.

Case Studies

This case study presents an example that combines several drawing methods and trigonometric methods to draw a clock showing the current time in a frame. To draw a clock, you need to draw a circle and three hands for second, minute, and hour. To draw a hand, you need to specify the two ends of the line. As shown in Figure 8.29, one end is the center of the clock at (xCenter, yCenter), and the other end at (xEnd, yEnd) is determined by the following formula:

```
xEnd = xCenter + handLength × sin(θ)
yEnd = yCenter - handLength × cos(θ)
```

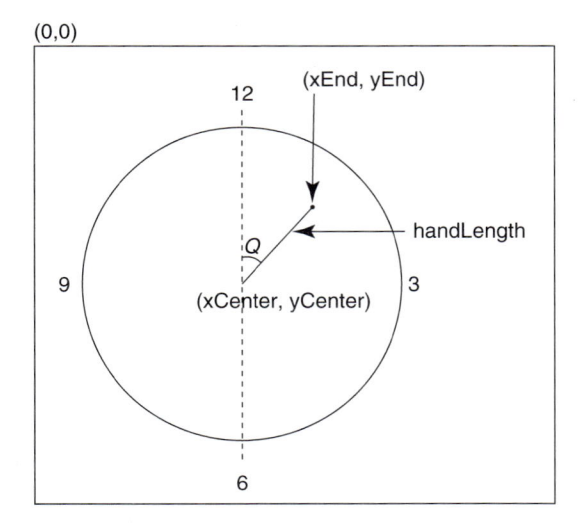

Figure 8.29 *The end point of a clock hand can be determined given the spanning angle, the hand length, and the center point.*

The angle θ is in radians. Let second, minute, and hour denote the current second, minute, and hour.

The angle for the second hand is

```
second × (2π/60)
```

The angle for the minute hand is

```
(minute + second/60)×(2π/60)
```

The angle for hour hand is

```
(hour + minute/60 + second/(60×60))) × (2π/12)
```

For simplicity, you can omit the seconds in computing the angles of the minute hand and the hour hand, since they are very small and can be neglected. Therefore the end points for the second hand, minute hand, and hour hand can be computed as:

```
xSecond = xCenter + secondHandLength × sin(second × (2π/60))
ySecond = yCenter - secondHandLength × cos(second × (2π/60))
xMinute = xCenter + minuteHandLength × sin(minute × (2π/60))
yMinute = yCenter - minuteHandLength × cos(minute × (2π/60))
xHour = xCenter + hourHandLength × sin((hour + minute/60)(2π/60)))
yHour = yCenter - hourHandLength × cos((hour + minute/60)
  × (2π/60)))
```

Example 8.10 Drawing a Clock

This example presents a program that displays a clock based on the specified hour, minute, and second. The hour, minute, and second are passed to the program as command-line arguments like this:

```
java DisplayClock hour minute second
```

The program is given next, and its output is shown in Figure 8.30.

```java
// DisplayClock.java: Display a clock in a panel
import java.awt.*;
import javax.swing.*;

public class DisplayClock extends MyFrameWithExitHandling
{
  // Main method with three auguments:
  // args[0]: hour
  // args[1]: minute
  // args[2]: second
  public static void main(String[] args)
  {
    // Declare hour, minute, and second values
    int hour = 0;
    int minute = 0;
    int second = 0;

    // Check usage and get hour, minute, second
    if (args.length > 3)
    {
      System.out.println(
        "Usage: java DisplayClock hour minute second");
      System.exit(0);
    }
    else if (args.length == 3)
```

```java
      {
        hour = new Integer(args[0]).intValue();
        minute = new Integer(args[1]).intValue();
        second = new Integer(args[2]).intValue();
      }
      else if (args.length == 2)
      {
        hour = new Integer(args[0]).intValue();
        minute = new Integer(args[1]).intValue();
      }
      else if (args.length == 1)
      {
        hour = new Integer(args[0]).intValue();
      }

      // Create a frame to hold the clock
      DisplayClock frame = new DisplayClock();
      frame.setTitle("Display Clock");
      frame.getContentPane().add(new DrawClock(hour, minute, second));
      frame.setSize(300, 350);
      frame.setVisible(true);
  }
}

// DrawClock.java: Display a clock in JPanel
import java.awt.*;
import javax.swing.*;

public class DrawClock extends JPanel
{
  private int hour;
  private int minute;
  private int second;
  protected int xCenter, yCenter;
  protected int clockRadius;

  // Construct a clock panel
  public DrawClock(int hour, int minute, int second)
  {
    this.hour = hour;
    this.minute = minute;
    this.second = second;
  }

  // Draw the clock
  public void paintComponent(Graphics g)
  {
    super.paintComponent(g);

    // Initialize clock parameters
    clockRadius =
      (int)(Math.min(getSize().width, getSize().height)*0.7*0.5);
    xCenter = (getSize().width)/2;
    yCenter = (getSize().height)/2;

    // Draw circle
    g.setColor(Color.black);
    g.drawOval(xCenter - clockRadius,yCenter - clockRadius,
      2*clockRadius, 2*clockRadius);
```

continues

```java
            g.drawString("12",xCenter-5, yCenter-clockRadius);
            g.drawString("9",xCenter-clockRadius-10,yCenter+3);
            g.drawString("3",xCenter+clockRadius,yCenter+3);
            g.drawString("6",xCenter-3,yCenter+clockRadius+10);

            // Draw second hand
            int sLength = (int)(clockRadius*0.9);
            int xSecond =
              (int)(xCenter + sLength*Math.sin(second*(2*Math.PI/60)));
            int ySecond =
              (int)(yCenter - sLength*Math.cos(second*(2*Math.PI/60)));
            g.setColor(Color.red);
            g.drawLine(xCenter, yCenter, xSecond, ySecond);

            // Draw minute hand
            int mLength = (int)(clockRadius*0.75);
            int xMinute =
              (int)(xCenter + mLength*Math.sin(minute*(2*Math.PI/60)));
            int yMinute =
              (int)(yCenter - mLength*Math.cos(minute*(2*Math.PI/60)));
            g.setColor(Color.blue);
            g.drawLine(xCenter, yCenter, xMinute, yMinute);

            // Draw hour hand
            int hLength = (int)(clockRadius*0.6);
            int xHour = (int)(xCenter +
              hLength*Math.sin((hour+minute/60.0)*(2*Math.PI/12)));
            int yHour = (int)(yCenter -
              hLength*Math.cos((hour+minute/60.0)*(2*Math.PI/12)));
            g.setColor(Color.green);
            g.drawLine(xCenter, yCenter, xHour, yHour);

            // Display current time in string
            g.setColor(Color.red);
            String time = "Hour: " + hour + " Minute: " + minute +
              " Second: " + second;
            FontMetrics fm = g.getFontMetrics();
            g.drawString(time, (getSize().width -
              fm.stringWidth(time))/2, yCenter+clockRadius+30);
        }
    }
```

Example Review

The `DisplayClock` class obtains command-line arguments for hour, minute, and second and uses this information to create an instance of `DrawClock`. `DrawClock` is responsible for drawing the clock on a panel.

The program enables the clock size to adjust as the frame resizes. Every time you resize the window, `paintComponent()` is automatically called to paint the new window. The `paintComponent()` method displays the clock in proportion to the window size.

The numeric time (consisting of hour, minute, and second) is displayed below the clock. The program uses font metrics to determine the size of the time string and display it in the center.

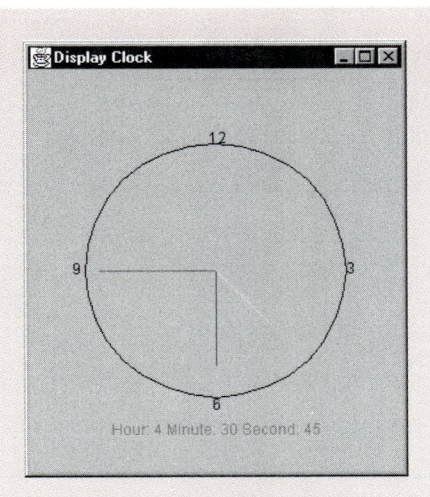

Figure 8.30 *The program displays a clock that shows the time with the specified hour, minute, and second.*

Chapter Summary

In this chapter, you learned Java graphics programming using the container classes, UI component classes, and helper classes.

The container classes, such as `JFrame`, `JPanel`, and `JApplet`, are used to contain other components. The UI component classes, such as `JButton`, `JTextField`, `JTextArea`, `JComboBox`, `JList`, `JRadioButton`, and `JMenu`, are subclasses of `JComponent`. They are used to facilitate user interaction. These classes are referred to as Swing UI components and are grouped in the `javax.swing` package.

The helper classes, such as `Graphics`, `Color`, `Font`, `FontMetrics`, `Dimension`, and `LayoutManager`, are used by components and containers to draw and place objects. These classes are grouped in the `java.awt` package.

Java graphics programming is event driven. The code is executed when events are activated. An event is generated by user actions, such as mouse movements, keystrokes, or clicking buttons. Java uses a delegation-based model to register listeners and handle events. External user actions on the source object generate events. The source object notifies listener objects of events by invoking the handlers implemented by the listener class.

Chapter Review

8.1. Describe the Java graphics class hierarchy.

8.2. Describe the methods in `Component`, `Frame`, `JFrame`, `JComponent`, and `JPanel`.

8.3. Describe the difference between the original AWT UI components, such as `java.awt.Button`, and the Swing components, such as `javax.swing.JButton`.

8.4. Can a button generate `WindowEvent`? Can a button generate a `MouseEvent`? Can a button generate an `ActionEvent`?

8.5. Determine whether the following statements are true or false:

- You can add a component to a button.
- You can add a button to a frame.
- You can add a frame to a panel.
- You can add a panel to a frame.
- You can add any number of components to a panel, a frame, or an applet.
- You can derive a class from `JPanel`, `JFrame`, or `JApplet`.

8.6. Describe how to register a listener object and how to implement a listener interface.

8.7. Describe the information contained in an `AWTEvent` object and an object of its subclasses. Find the variables, constants, and methods defined in these event classes.

8.8. How do you override a method defined in the listener interface? Do you need to override all the methods defined in the listener interface?

8.9. What is the event type for a mouse movement? What is the event type for getting key input?

8.10. Describe the `paintComponent()` method. Where is it defined? How is it invoked? Can you use the `paintComponent()` method to draw things directly on a frame?

8.11. Why do you need to use the layout managers?

8.12. Can you use the `setTitle()` method in a panel? Is a panel visible?

8.13. Describe `FlowLayout`. How do you create a `FlowLayout` manager? How do you add a component to a `FlowLayout` container? Is the number of components that can be added to a `FlowLayout` container limited?

8.14. Describe `GridLayout`. How do you create a `GridLayout` manager? How do you add a component to a `GridLayout` container? Is the number of components that can be added to a `GridLayout` container limited?

8.15. Describe `BorderLayout`. How do you create a `BorderLayout` manager? How do you add a component to a `BorderLayout` container? List the exact names of the five sections in a `BorderLayout`. Can you add multiple components in the same section?

8.16. Suppose that you want to draw a new message below an existing message. Should the x, y coordinate increase or decrease?

8.17. How do you set colors and fonts in a graphics context? How do you find the current color and font style?

8.18. Describe the drawing methods for lines, rectangles, ovals, arcs, and polygons.

8.19. What methods do you use to detect mouse movements?

8.20. What methods do you use to obtain an input character from a keyboard event?

8.21. Write a statement to draw the following shapes:

- Draw a thick line from (10, 10) to (70, 30). You must draw several lines next to each other to create the effect of one thick line.
- Draw a rectangle of width 100 and height 50 with the upper-left corner at (10, 10).
- Draw a rounded rectangle with width 100, height 200, corner horizontal diameter 40, and corner vertical diameter 20.
- Draw a circle with radius 30.
- Draw an oval with width 50 and height 100.
- Draw the upper half of a circle with radius 50.
- Draw a polygon connecting the following points: (20, 40), (30, 50), (40, 90), (90, 10), (10, 30).
- Draw a 3D cube like the one in Figure 8.31.

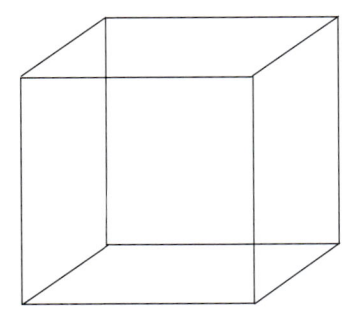

Figure 8.31 *Use the* `drawLine()` *method to draw a 3D cube.*

Programming Exercises

8.1. Write a program to meet the following requirements (see Figure 8.32):

- Create a frame and set its content pane's layout to `FlowLayout`.
- Create two panels and add the panels to the frame.

- Each panel contains three buttons. The panel uses `FlowLayout`.
- When a button is clicked, display a message indicating that button is clicked on the console.

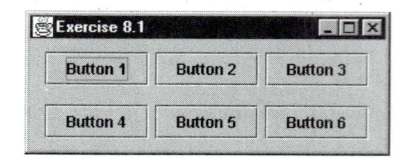

Figure 8.32 *The first three buttons are placed in one panel, and the remaining three buttons are placed in another panel.*

8.2. Rewrite the preceding program to create the same user interface. Instead of using `FlowLayout` for the frame's content pane, use `BorderLayout`. Place one panel in the south of the content pane and the other panel in the center of the content pane.

8.3. Rewrite the preceding program to create the same user interface. Instead of using `FlowLayout` for the panels, use `GridLayout` of two rows and three columns.

8.4. Rewrite the preceding program to create the same user interface. Instead of creating buttons and panels separately, you must define the panel class that extends the `JPanel` class. Place three buttons in your panel class, and create three panels from the user-defined panel class.

8.5. Write a program that displays the mouse position when the mouse is pressed (see Figure 8.33).

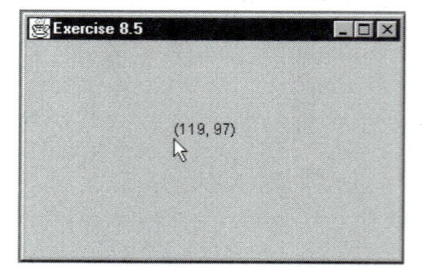

Figure 8.33 *When you click the mouse, the pixel coordinates are shown.*

8.6. Write a program that displays a multiplication table in a panel using the drawing methods, as shown in Figure 8.34.

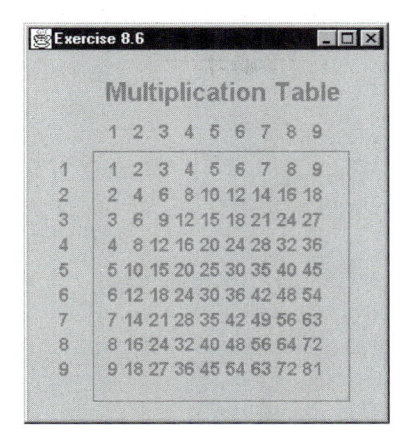

Figure 8.34 *The program displays a multiplication table.*

8.7. Write a program that draws the diagram for the function shown below (see Figure 8.35). (Hint: Create arrays `x[]` and `y[]` for coordinates and use `drawPolyline` to connect the points.)

```
f(x) = x²;
```

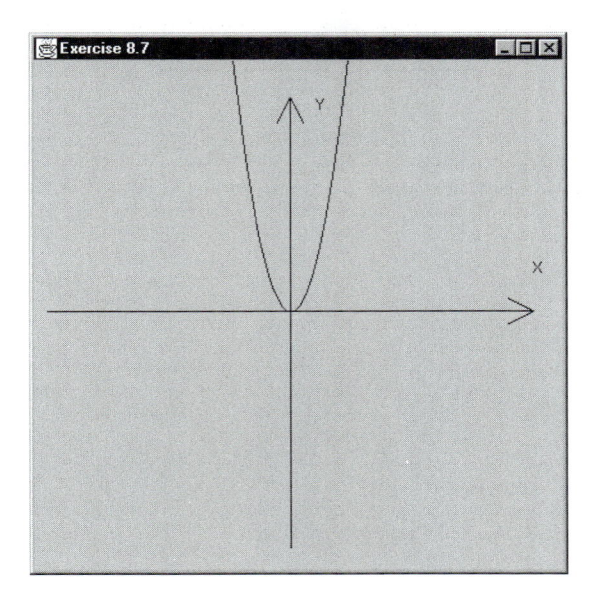

Figure 8.35 *The program draws a diagram for function $f(x) = x^2$.*

8.8. Write a generic class that draws the diagram for a function. The class is defined as follows:

```
public abstract class DrawFunction extends JPanel
{
  abstract double f(double x);
```

```
// Draw the function
public void drawFunction()
{
}
}
```

Implement the `drawFunction()` method. Test the class with the following functions:

```
f(x) = x²;
f(x) = cos(x)+5sin(x);
f(x) = log(x) + x²;
```

8.9. Write a program that draws a fan with four blades, as shown in Figure 8.36. Draw the circle in blue and the blades in red. (Hints: Use the `fillArc()` method to draw the blades.)

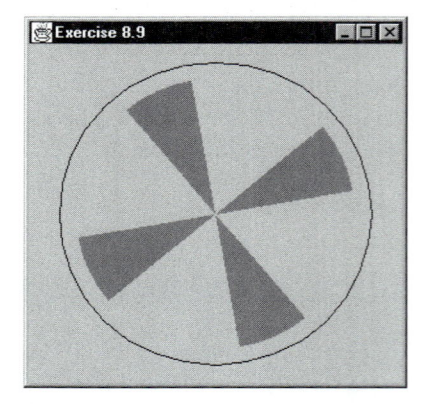

Figure 8.36 *The drawing methods are used to draw a fan with four blades.*

CHAPTER 9

CREATING USER INTERFACES

Objectives

- Become familiar with the JavaBeans concept.
- Know various user interface components: `JButton`, `JLabel`, `JTextField`, `JTextArea`, `JComboBox`, `JList`, `JCheckBox`, `JRadioButton`, `JMenuBar`, `JMenu`, `JMenuItem`, `JCheckBoxMenuItem`, `JRadioButtonMenuItem`, `JScrollBar`, `JScollPane`, and `JTabbedPane`.
- Create interactive graphical user interfaces using these components.
- Use borders to visually group user interface components.
- Know how to use the message dialog boxes.
- Create multiple windows in an application.
- Implement the listener interface for the user interface components.

Introduction

A graphical user interface (GUI) makes the system easy and fun to use. Creating a GUI requires creativity and knowledge of how the GUI components work. Since the GUI components in Java are very flexible, you can create an extensive array of different user interfaces.

Visual J++ provides tools for visually designing and programming Java classes. This enables you to rapidly assemble the elements of a user interface (UI) for a Java application or applet with minimum coding. No tools, however, can do everything, so you may have to modify the program they produce. This makes it imperative to understand the basic concepts of Java graphics programming before using the visual tools. Therefore you should finish Chapter 10, "Applets and Advanced Graphics," before starting to use Visual J++'s visual design tools. Appendix G, "Rapid Java Application Development Using Visual J++ 6," provides an introduction to Visual J++'s Form Designer.

This chapter concentrates on creating user interfaces. In particular, it discusses the various GUI components that make up a user interface and how to make those components work.

JavaBeans

All the Swing components are JavaBeans. JavaBeans is a software component architecture that extends the power of the Java language by enabling well-formed objects to be manipulated visually at design time in a pure Java builder tool, such as JBuilder, Visual Café, or IBM Visual Age for Java. Such well-formed objects are referred to as *JavaBeans* or simply *beans*. The classes that define the beans, referred to as *JavaBeans components* or *bean components*, or simply *components*, conform to the JavaBeans component model with the following requirements:

- A bean must be a public class.

- A bean must have a public default constructor (one that takes no arguments), though it can have other constructors, if needed. For example, a bean named `MyBean` must either have a constructor with the signature

    ```
    public MyBean();
    ```

    or have no constructors if its superclass has a default constructor.

- A bean must implement the `java.io.Serializable` or `java.io.Externalizable` interface to ensure persistent state. JavaBeans can be used in a wide variety of tools, such as Lotus, Delphi, MS Visual Basic, and MS Word. When JavaBeans are used in other tools, bean persistence may be required. Some tools need to save the beans and restore them later. Bean persistence ensures that the tools can reconstruct the properties and consistent behaviors of the bean to the state when it was saved. For more information on bean persistence and serialization, please refer to my *Rapid Java Application Development Using JBuilder 3*.

- A bean usually has properties with correctly constructed public accessor methods that enable the properties to be seen and updated visually by a builder tool.

- A bean may have events with correctly constructed public registration methods that enable the bean to add and remove listeners. If the bean plays a role as the source of events, it must provide registration methods for registering listeners. For example, you can register a listener for `ActionEvent` using the `addActionListener()` method of a `JButton` bean.

The first three requirements must be observed by the beans, and therefore are referred to as the *minimum JavaBeans component requirements.* The last two requirements are dependent on implementations. It is possible to write a bean without accessor methods and event registration methods.

> **NOTE**
> At present, Visual J++ 6 does not support JavaBeans. Visual J++'s Form Designer uses the Microsoft proprietary Windows Foundation Classes for Java.

A JavaBean component is a special kind of Java class. The relationship of a JavaBean component and a Java class is illustrated in Figure 9.1.

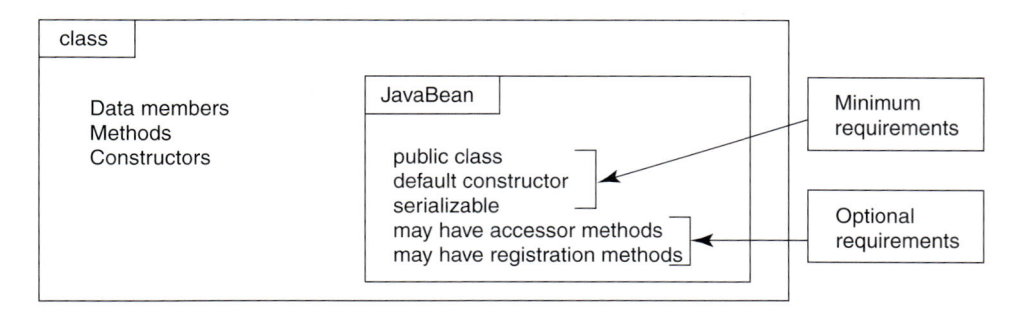

Figure 9.1 *A JavaBean component is a serializable public class with a default constructor.*

The getter method is named `get<PropertyName>()`, which takes no parameters and returns an object of the type identical to the property type. For example, `getContentPane()` is the getter method for the property `contentPane` in the `JFrame` class, which returns an object of the `Container` type. For a property of the `boolean` type, the getter method should be named `is<PropertyName>()`, which returns a `boolean` value. For example, `isVisible()` is the getter method for the `visible` property in the `JFrame` class, which returns `true` if the frame is visible.

The setter method is named `set<PropertyName>`, which takes a single parameter identical to the property type and returns `void`. For example, `setLayout` is the setter method for the `layout` property in the `Container` class for setting the `layout` property value.

Once you understand the basics of Java graphics programming, such as containers, layout managers, and event handling, you will be able to learn new components to explore their properties. All but a few Swing components, such as `JFrame`, `JApplet`, and `JDialog`, are subclasses of `JComponent`. Many of the properties of the Swing components are defined in the `JComponent` class. Here is a list of frequently used properties in `JComponent`:

- `toolTipText`—The text displayed when the mouse points on the component without clicking. This text is generally used to give the user a tip about the function of the component.

- `font`—The font used to display text on the component.

- `background`—The background color of the component.

- `foreground`—The foreground color of the component.

- `doubleBuffered`—Specifies whether the component is painted using double buffering. This is a technique for reducing flickering. In AWT programming, you have to manually implement this technique in the program. With Swing, this capability is automatically supported if the `doubleBuffered` property is set to `true`. By default, it is `true`.

- `border`—Specifies a border of the component. The border types and styles will be introduced in the section "Borders" later in this chapter.

- `preferredSize`—Indicates the ideal size at which the component looks best. This property may or may not be considered by the layout manager, depending on its rules. For example, a component uses its preferred size in a container with a `FlowLayout` manager, but its preferred size may be ignored if it is placed in a container with a `GridLayout` manager.

- `minimumSize`—Specifies the minimum size for the component to be useful. For most of the Swing components, `minimumSize` is the same as `preferredSize`. Layout managers generally respect `minimumSize` more than `preferredSize`.

- `maximumSize`—Specifies the maximum size the component needs so that the layout manager won't waste space by giving it to a component that does not need it. For instance, `BorderLayout` could limit the center component's size to its maximum size, and then either give the space to edge components or limit the size of outer window when resized.

`font`, `background`, `foreground`, `preferredSize`, `minimumSize`, and `maximumSize` are defined in `java.awt.Component` and inherited in `javax.swing.JComponent`.

The principal benefit of JavaBeans is for use in the Java builder tools for rapid Java application development. As shown in Figure 9.2, you can set the properties of a `JButton` instance in JBuilder's visual designer during design time. For complete coverage of JavaBeans, please refer to my *Rapid Java Application Development Using JBuilder 3*.

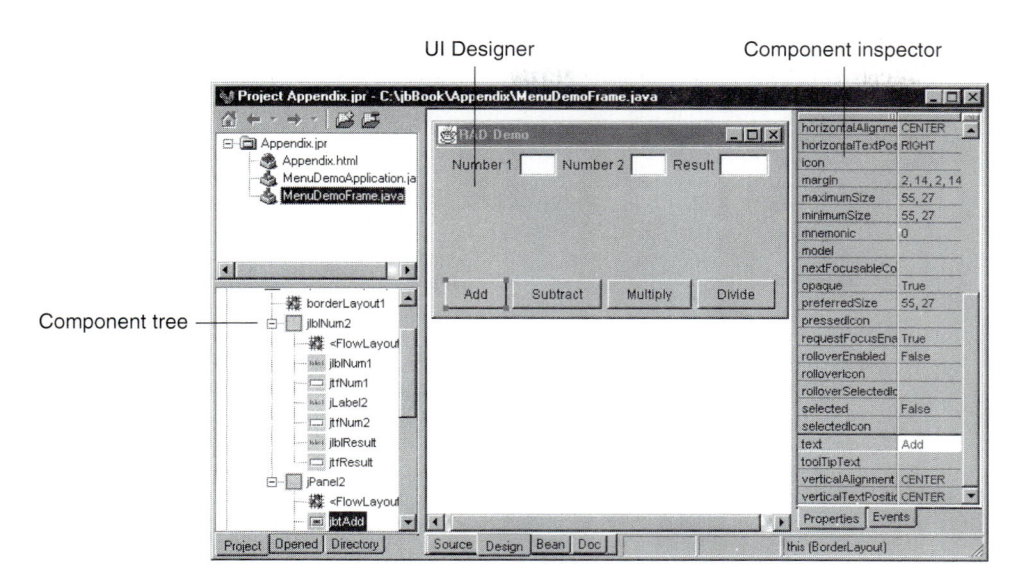

Figure 9.2 *You can set the properties of a JavaBeans instance, such as a JButton, at design time.*

Buttons

A *button* is a component that triggers an event when clicked. The Swing version of a button is named JButton. Its default constructor creates an empty button. In addition, JButton has the following constructors:

- public JButton(String text)

    This creates a button labeled with the specified text.

- public JButton(Icon icon)

    This creates a button with the specified icon.

- public JButton(String text, Icon icon)

    This creates a button with the specified text and icon.

An icon is a fixed-size picture; typically it is small and used to decorate components. An icon can be obtained from an image file by using the ImageIcon class, such as

    Icon icon = new ImageIcon("photo.gif");

javax.swing.ImageIcon is a subclass of javax.swing.Icon.

NOTE
Java currently supports two image formats: GIF (Graphics Interchange Format) and JPEG (Joint Photographic Experts Group). The image filenames for these types end with .gif and .jpg, respectively. If you have a bitmap file, or image files in other formats, you can use image-processing utilities to convert them into GIF or JPEG format for use in Java.

Since `JButton` is a subclass of `JComponent`, all the properties in `JComponent` can be used in `JButton`. Additionally, `JButton` has the following useful properties:

- `text`—The label on the button. You can set a label using the `setText()` method.

- `icon`—The image icon on the button. You can set an icon using the `setIcon()` method.

- `mnemonic`—Specifies a shortcut key. You can select the button by pressing the ALT key and the mnemonic key at the same time.

- `horizontalAlignment`—One of the three values, `SwingConstants.LEFT`, `SwingConstants.CENTER`, and `SwingConstants.RIGHT`, that specify how the label is placed horizontally on a button. The default alignment is `SwingConstants.CENTER`.

- `verticalAlignment`—One of the three values, `SwingConstants.TOP`, `SwingConstants.CENTER`, and `SwingConstants.BOTTOM`, that specify how the label is placed vertically on a button. The default alignment is `SwingConstants.CENTER`.

- `horizontalTextPosition`—One of the three values, `SwingConstants.LEFT`, `SwingConstants.CENTER`, and `SwingConstants.RIGHT`, that specify the horizontal position of the text relative to the icon. The default alignment is `SwingConstants.RIGHT`.

- `verticalTextPosition`—One of the three values, `SwingConstants.LEFT`, `SwingConstants.CENTER`, and `SwingConstants.RIGHT`, that specify the vertical position of the text relative to the icon. The default alignment is `SwingConstants.CENTER`.

Buttons can generate many types of events, but often you need to respond to an `ActionEvent`. In order to make a button responsive to an `ActionEvent`, you must implement the `actionPerformed()` method in the `ActionListener` interface. The following code is an example of how to handle a button event. The code prints out "Button clicked" on the console when the button is clicked.

```java
public void actionPerformed(ActionEvent e)
{
  // Make sure the event source is a button.
  if (e.getSource() instanceof JButton)
    System.out.println("Button clicked!");
}
```

Example 9.1 Using Buttons

This example gives a program that displays a message on a panel and uses two buttons, <= and =>, to move the message on the panel to the left or right. The output of the program is shown in Figure 9.3.

```java
// ButtonDemo.java: Use buttons to move message in a panel
import java.awt.*;
import java.awt.event.ActionListener;
import java.awt.event.ActionEvent;
import javax.swing.*;

public class ButtonDemo extends MyFrameWithExitHandling
  implements ActionListener
{
  // Declare a panel for displaying message
  private MessagePanel messagePanel;

  // Declare two buttons to move the message left and right
  private JButton jbtLeft, jbtRight;

  // Main method
  public static void main(String[] args)
  {
    ButtonDemo frame = new ButtonDemo();
    frame.pack();
    frame.center();
    frame.setVisible(true);
  }

  public ButtonDemo()
  {
    setTitle("Button Demo");

    // Create MessagePanel instance and set colors
    messagePanel = new MessagePanel("Welcome to Java");
    messagePanel.setBackground(Color.yellow);

    // Create Panel jpButtons to hold two Buttons "<=" and "right =>"
    JPanel jpButtons = new JPanel();
    jpButtons.setLayout(new FlowLayout());
    jpButtons.add(jbtLeft = new JButton());
    jpButtons.add(jbtRight = new JButton());

    // Set button text
    jbtLeft.setText("<=");
    jbtRight.setText("=>");

    // Set keyboard mnemonics
    jbtLeft.setMnemonic('L');
    jbtRight.setMnemonic('R');

    // Set icons
    //jbtLeft.setIcon(new ImageIcon("images/left.gif"));
    //jbtRight.setIcon(new ImageIcon("images/right.gif"));

    // Set toolTipText on the "<=" and "=>" buttons
    jbtLeft.setToolTipText("Move message to left");
    jbtRight.setToolTipText("Move message to right");

    // Place panels in the frame
    getContentPane().setLayout(new BorderLayout());
    getContentPane().add(messagePanel, BorderLayout.CENTER);
    getContentPane().add(jpButtons, BorderLayout.SOUTH);
```

continues

```java
    // Register listeners with the buttons
    jbtLeft.addActionListener(this);
    jbtRight.addActionListener(this);
  }

  // Handler for button events
  public void actionPerformed(ActionEvent e)
  {
    if (e.getSource() == jbtLeft)
    {
      left();
    }
    else if (e.getSource() == jbtRight)
    {
      right();
    }
  }

  // Move the message in the panel left
  private void left()
  {
    int x = messagePanel.getXCoordinate();
    if (x > 10)
    {
      // Shift the message to the left
      messagePanel.setXCoordinate(x-10);
      messagePanel.repaint();
    }
  }

  // Move the message in the panel right
  private void right()
  {
    int x = messagePanel.getXCoordinate();
    if (x < getSize().width - 20)
    {
      // Shift the message to the right
      messagePanel.setXCoordinate(x+10);
      messagePanel.repaint();
    }
  }
}
```

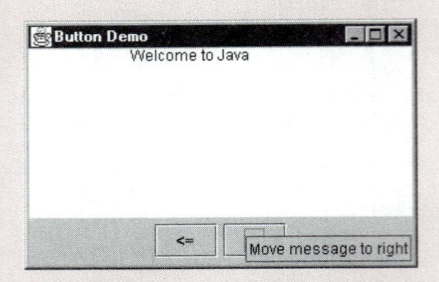

Figure 9.3 *Clicking the <= and => buttons causes the message on the panel to move to the left or right, respectively.*

Example Review

The program displays a message on a panel and places two buttons, <= and =>, on a panel below the message panel. The `MessagePanel` class, created in Example 8.9, "Using FontMetrics," displays a message on a panel. When you click a button, the handler, `actionPerformed()`, determines which button is clicked and invokes the `left()` or `right()` method to move the message.

Each button has a tool tip text, which appears when the mouse is set on the button without clicking, as shown in Figure 9.3.

You can set an icon image on the button by using the `setIcon()` method. If you replace the `setText()` method with the `setIcon()` method, as follows:

```
jbtLeft.setIcon(new ImageIcon("images/left.gif"));
jbtRight.setIcon(new ImageIcon("images/right.gif"));
```

the labels are replaced by the icons, as shown in Figure 9.4. "images/left.gif" is located in "c:\jbBook\Chapter9\images\left.gif" in Windows. Note that the back slash is the Windows file path notation. In Java, the forward slash should be used.

Figure 9.4 *You can set an icon on a* `JButton`.

You can set both icons and labels on a button at the same time, if you wish. By default, the labels and icons are centered horizontally and vertically.

The button can also be accessed by using the keyboard mnemonics. Pressing ALT+L is equivalent to clicking the <= button, since you set the mnemonic property to 'L' in the left button. If you change the left button text to "Left" and the right button to "Right," the L and R in the captions of these buttons will be underlined, as shown in Figure 9.5.

Figure 9.5 *The buttons can be accessed by using the keyboard mnemonics.*

Labels

A *label* is a display area for a short text, an image, or both. It is often used to label other components (usually text fields). As with other components, the layout managers can place labels inside a container. The default constructor of `JLabel` creates an empty label. Other constructors for `JLabel` are as follows:

- `public JLabel(String text, int horizontalAlignment)`

    This creates a label with the specified string and horizontal alignment (`SwingConstants.LEFT`, `SwingConstants.RIGHT`, or `SwingConstants.CENTER`).

- `public JLabel(String text)`

    This creates a label with a specified text.

- `public JLabel(Icon icon)`

    This creates a label with an icon.

- `public JLabel(Icon icon, int horizontalAlignment)`

    This creates a label with the specified image and horizontal alignment.

- `public JLabel(String text, Icon icon, int horizontalAlignment)`

    This creates a label with the specified text, image, and horizontal alignment.

For example, the following statement creates a label with the string `"Interest Rate"`:

```
JLabel myLabel = new JLabel("Interest Rate");
```

The following statement creates a label with the specified image in the file "images/map.gif":

```
JLabel mapLabel = new JLabel(new ImageIcon("images/map.gif"));
```

`JLabel` inherits all the properties from `JComponent` and shares many properties with `JButton`, such as `text`, `icon`, `horizontalAlignment`, and `verticalAlignment`.

Example 9.2 Using Labels

This example gives a program that uses a label as an area for displaying images. There are 52 images in image files named L1.gif, L2.gif, ..., L52.gif stored in the images directory under c:\jbBook\Chapter9. You can use two buttons, Prior and Next, to browse the images, as shown in Figure 9.6.

```
// LabelDemo.java: Use label to display images
import java.awt.*;
import java.awt.event.*;
import javax.swing.*;
```

```java
public class LabelDemo extends MyFrameWithExitHandling
  implements ActionListener
{
  // Declare an ImageIcon array. There are total 52 images
  private ImageIcon[] imageIcon = new ImageIcon[52];

  // The current image index
  private int currentIndex = 0;

  // Buttons for browsing images
  private JButton jbtPrior, jbtNext;

  // Label for displaying images
  private JLabel jlblImageViewer = new JLabel();

  final int TOTAL_NUMBER_OF_IMAGES = 52;

  // Main Method
  public static void main(String[] args)
  {
    LabelDemo frame = new LabelDemo();
    frame.setSize(500, 500);
    frame.center();
    frame.setVisible(true);
  }

  // Default Constructor
  public LabelDemo()
  {
    setTitle("Label Demo");

    // Load images into imageIcon array
    for (int i=1; i<=52; i++)
    {
      imageIcon[i-1] = new ImageIcon("images/L" + i + ".gif");
    }

    // Show the first image
    jlblImageViewer.setIcon(imageIcon[currentIndex]);

    // Set center alignment
    jlblImageViewer.setHorizontalAlignment(SwingConstants.CENTER);
    //jlblImageViewer.setVerticalAlignment(SwingConstants.CENTER);

    // Panel jpButtons to hold two buttons for browsing images
    JPanel jpButtons = new JPanel();
    jpButtons.add(jbtPrior = new JButton());
    jbtPrior.setIcon(new ImageIcon("images/left.gif"));
    jpButtons.add(jbtNext = new JButton());
    jbtNext.setIcon(new ImageIcon("images/right.gif"));

    // Add jpButton and the label to the frame
    getContentPane().add(jlblImageViewer, BorderLayout.CENTER);
    getContentPane().add(jpButtons, BorderLayout.SOUTH);

    // Register listeners
    jbtPrior.addActionListener(this);
    jbtNext.addActionListener(this);
  }
```

continues

```java
// Handle ActionEvent from buttons
public void actionPerformed(ActionEvent e)
{
  if (e.getSource() == jbtPrior)
  {
    // Make sure index is nonnegative
    if (currentIndex == 0) currentIndex = TOTAL_NUMBER_OF_IMAGES;
    currentIndex = (currentIndex - 1)%TOTAL_NUMBER_OF_IMAGES;
    jlblImageViewer.setIcon(imageIcon[currentIndex]);
  }
  else if (e.getSource() == jbtNext)
  {
    currentIndex = (currentIndex + 1)%TOTAL_NUMBER_OF_IMAGES;
    jlblImageViewer.setIcon(imageIcon[currentIndex]);
  }
 }
}
```

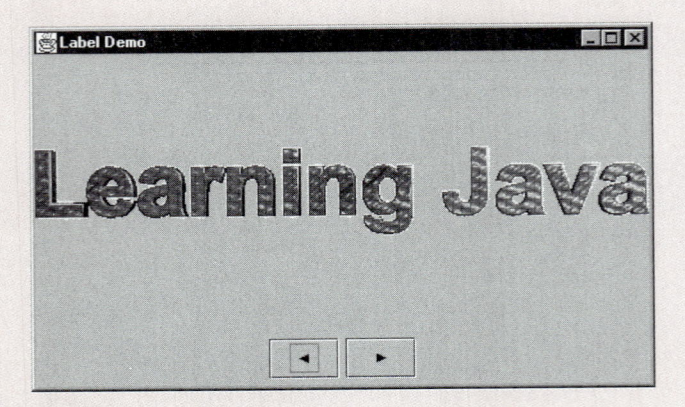

Figure 9.6 *You can use the label to display images.*

Example Review

The images are stored in files L1.gif, L2.gif, . . . , and L52.gif, and are loaded to an array of ImageIcon in a for loop.

By default, the icon is centered vertically, but left aligned horizontally. The following statement ensures that the image is displayed in the center of the viewing area.

```java
jlblImageViewer.setHorizontalAlignment(SwingConstants.CENTER);
```

Text Fields

A *text field* is an input area where the user can type in characters. Text fields enable the user to enter in variable data, such as a name or a description. The default constructor of JTextField creates an empty text field. Other constructors of JTextField are as follows:

■ `public JTextField(int columns)`

This creates an empty text field with the specified number of columns.

- `public JTextField(String text)`

This creates a text field initialized with the specified text.

- `public JTextField(String text, int columns)`

This creates a text field initialized with the specified text and the column size.

In addition to such properties as `text` and `horizontalAlignment`, `JTextField` has the following properties:

- `editable`—A `boolean` property indicating whether the text field can be edited by the user.
- `columns`—The width of the text field.

`JTextField` can generate `ActionEvent` and `TextEvent`, among many other events. Pressing Enter in a text field triggers the `ActionEvent`. Changing contents in a text field triggers the `TextEvent`.

Here is an example of how to react to an `ActionEvent` on a text field.

```
public void actionPerformed(ActionEvent e)
{
  // Make sure it is a text field
  if (e.getSource() instanceof JTextField)
    // Processing the event
    ...
}
```

Example 9.3 Using Text Fields

This example gives a program that enters two numbers in two text fields and displays their sum in the third text field when you press the Add button. The output of the program is shown in Figure 9.7.

```
// TextFieldDemo.java: Add two numbers in the text fields
import java.awt.*;
import java.awt.event.*;
import javax.swing.*;

public class TextFieldDemo extends MyFrameWithExitHandling
  implements ActionListener
{
  // Declare three text fields
  private JTextField jtfNum1, jtfNum2, jtfResult;
  private JButton jbtAdd; // Declare "Add" button

  // Main method
  public static void main(String[] args)
  {
    TextFieldDemo frame = new TextFieldDemo();
    frame.pack();
    frame.center();
    frame.setVisible(true);
  }
```

continues

```java
// Constructor
public TextFieldDemo()
{
  setTitle("TextFieldDemo");
  setBackground(Color.yellow);
  setForeground(Color.black);

  // Use panel p1 to group text fields
  JPanel p1 = new JPanel();
  p1.setLayout(new FlowLayout());
  p1.add(new Label("Number 1"));
  p1.add(jtfNum1 = new JTextField(3));
  p1.add(new Label("Number 2"));
  p1.add(jtfNum2 = new JTextField(3));
  p1.add(new Label("Result"));
  p1.add(jtfResult = new JTextField(4));
  jtfResult.setEditable(false);   // Set jtfResult noneditable

  // Use panel p2 for the button
  JPanel p2 = new JPanel();
  p2.setLayout(new FlowLayout());
  p2.add(jbtAdd = new JButton("Add"));

  // Set FlowLayout for the frame and add panels to the frame
  getContentPane().setLayout(new BorderLayout());
  getContentPane().add(p1, BorderLayout.CENTER);
  getContentPane().add(p2, BorderLayout.SOUTH);

  // Register listener
  jbtAdd.addActionListener(this);
}

// Handle the add operation
public void actionPerformed(ActionEvent e)
{
  if (e.getSource() == jbtAdd)
  {
    // Get int values from text fields and use trim() to
    // trim extraneous space in the text field
    int num1 = (Integer.parseInt(jtfNum1.getText().trim()));
    int num2 = (Integer.parseInt(jtfNum2.getText().trim()));
    int result = num1 + num2;

    // Set result in TextField jtfResult
    jtfResult.setText(String.valueOf(result));
  }
}
}
```

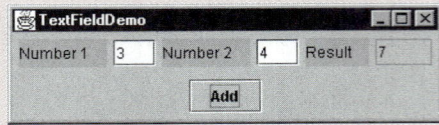

Figure 9.7 *The addition of Number 1 and Number 2 shows in the Result when you click the Add button.*

Example Review

The program uses two panels, `p1` and `p2`, to contain the components. The panel `p1` is for the labels and text fields, and `p2` is for the Add button. You can place the button directly in the frame instead of in `p2`, but in this case the button will look very long because it will stretch to fill in the entire south area of the `BorderLayout`.

Instead of using the `setSize()` method to set the size for the frame, this program uses the `pack()` method, which automatically sizes up the frame according to the size of the components placed in it.

The `jtfNum1.getText()` method returns the text in the text field `jtfNum1`, and `jtfResult.setText(s)` sets the specified string into text field `jtfResult`.

The `trim()` method is useful to remove blank space from both ends of a string. If you run the program without applying `trim()` to the string, a runtime exception may occur when the string is converted to an integer.

Using `jtfResult.setEditable(false)` prevents the user from editing the Result text field. By default, editing is enabled on all text fields.

Text Areas

If you want to let the user enter multiple lines of text, you have to create several instances of `JTextField`. The solution is to use `JTextArea`, which enables the user to enter multiple lines of text.

The default constructor of `JTextArea` creates an empty text area. Other constructors of `JTextArea` are listed below:

- `public JTextArea(int rows, int columns)`

  This creates a text area with the specified number of rows and columns.

- `public JTextArea(String text, int rows, int columns)`

  This creates a text area with the specified text and the number of rows and columns specified.

In addition to `text`, `editable`, and `columns`, `JTextArea` has the following properties:

- `lineWrap`—A `boolean` property indicating whether the line in the text area is automatically wrapped.
- `wrapStyleWord`—A `boolean` property indicating whether the line is wrapped on word or character. The default value is `false`, which indicates that the line is wrapped on character boundaries.
- `rows`—The number of lines in the text area.
- `lineCount`—The number of lines in the text.

- `tabSize`—The number of characters inserted when the Tab key is pressed.

You can use the following methods to insert, append, and replace text:

- `public void insert(String s, int pos)`

    This inserts string `s` in the specified position in the text area.

- `public void append(String s)`

    This appends string `s` to the end of the text.

- `public void replaceRange(String s, int start, int end)`

    This replaces partial texts in the range from position `start` to position `end` with string `s`.

`JTextArea` does not handle scrolling, but you can create a `JScrollPane` object to hold an instance of `JTextArea` and let the `JScrollPane` handle scrolling for `JTextArea`, as follows:

```
// Create a scroll pane to hold text area
JScrollPane scrollPane = new JScrollPane(jta = new JTextArea());
getContentPane().add(scrollPane, BorderLayout.CENTER);
```

`JScrollPane` will be further discussed in the section "Scroll Panes" later in this chapter.

Example 9.4 Using Text Areas

This example gives a program that lets the user enter text from a text field and then append it to a text area. A sample run of the program is shown in Figure 9.8.

```
// TextAreaDemo.java: Append text in a text field to the text area
import java.awt.*;
import java.awt.event.*;
import javax.swing.*;

public class TextAreaDemo extends MyFrameWithExitHandling
  implements ActionListener
{
  private JTextField jtf;
  private JButton jbt;
  private JTextArea jta;

  // Main method
  public static void main(String[] args)
  {
    TextAreaDemo frame = new TextAreaDemo();
    frame.pack();
    frame.center();
    frame.setVisible(true);
  }

  // Constructor
  public TextAreaDemo()
  {
    setTitle("Test TextArea");
```

```java
        // Create panel p to hold the text field and button
        JPanel p = new JPanel();
        p.setLayout(new FlowLayout());
        p.add(jtf = new JTextField(20));
        p.add(jbt = new JButton("Store"));

        // Create a scroll pane to hold text area
        JScrollPane scrollPane = new JScrollPane(jta = new JTextArea());

        // Set lineWrap true
        jta.setLineWrap(true);

        // Set FlowLayout for the frame and add components in it
        getContentPane().setLayout(new BorderLayout());
        getContentPane().add(scrollPane, BorderLayout.CENTER);
        getContentPane().add(p, BorderLayout.SOUTH);

        // Register listeners
        jtf.addActionListener(this);
        jbt.addActionListener(this);
    }

    // ActionEvent handler
    public void actionPerformed(ActionEvent e)
    {
        jta.append(jtf.getText().trim());
    }
}
```

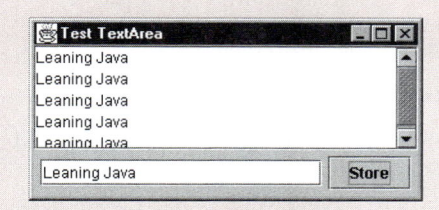

Figure 9.8 *The text in the text field is appended to the text area when you click the Store button.*

Example Review

The program groups the text field and the button in a panel and places the panel below the text area. The text area is inside a `JScrollPane`, which provides scrolling functions for the text area. Scrollbars automatically appear if there is more text than the physical size of the text area, and disappears if the text is deleted and the remaining text does not exceed the text area size.

The `lineWrap` property is set to true so that the line is automatically wrapped when the text cannot fit in one line.

When you click the Store button or press the ENTER key in the text field, the handler, `actionPerformed()`, takes the string from the text field and appends it to the text area, using the `append()` method.

The text area is editable. You can type characters or delete characters directly into the text area. You also can highlight to select characters in the text area.

Combo Boxes

A *combo box,* also known as *choice,* is a simple list of items from which the user can choose. It is useful in limiting a user's range of choices and avoids the cumbersome validation of data input. You can easily choose and extract the value in a combo box.

To create a `JComboBox`, simply use its default constructor. The following properties are often useful:

- `selectedIndex`—An `int` value indicating the index of the selected item in the combo box.
- `selectedItem`—A selected item whose type is `Object`.

The following methods are useful for operating a `JComboBox` object:

- `public void addItem(Object item)`

    This adds the item of any object into the combo box.

- `public Object getItemAt(int index)`

    This gets an item from the combo box at the specified index.

- `public void removeItem(Object anObject)`

    This removes an item from the item list.

- `public void removeAllItems()`

    This removes all items from the item list.

Here is an example of how to create a combo box and add items to the object:

```
JComboBox jcb = new JComboBox();
jcb.addItem("Item 1");
jcb.addItem("Item 2");
jcb.addItem("Item 3");
add(jcb);
```

This creates a `JComboBox` with three items in the combo box.

To get data from a `JComboBox` menu, you can use `getSelectedItem()` to return the currently selected item, or you can use the `e.getItem()` method to get the item from the `itemStateChanged(ItemEvent e)` handler.

`JComboBox` can generate `ActionEvent` and `ItemEvent` among many other events. Whenever a new item is selected, `JComboBox` generates `ItemEvent` twice, one for deselecting the previously selected item, and the other for selecting the currently selected item. `JComboBox` generates an `ActionEvent` after generating `ItemEvent`. To respond to an `ItemEvent`, you need to implement the `itemStateChanged(ItemEvent e)` handler for processing a choice. Here is an example of how to get data from the `itemStateChanged(ItemEvent e)` handler:

```java
public void itemStateChanged(ItemEvent e)
{
  // Make sure the source is a combo box
  if (e.getSource() instanceof JComboBox)
    String s = (String)e.getItem();
}
```

Example 9.5 Using Combo Boxes

This example gives a program that lets users enter their name, department, university, state, and zip code, and store the information in a text area. The state is a JComboBox item. Figure 9.9 shows a sample run for the program.

```java
// ComboBoxDemo.java: Use combo box to select values
import java.awt.*;
import java.awt.event.*;
import javax.swing.*;

public class ComboBoxDemo extends MyFrameWithExitHandling
  implements ItemListener, ActionListener
{
  private JComboBox jcboState;
  private JTextField jtfName = new JTextField(32);
  private JTextField jtfDepartment = new JTextField(32);
  private JTextField jtfUniversity = new JTextField(20);
  private JTextField jtfZip = new JTextField(5);
  private JTextArea jta = new JTextArea(5, 30);
  private JButton jbtStore = new JButton("Store");
  private String state;

  // Main method
  public static void main(String[] args)
  {
    ComboBoxDemo frame = new ComboBoxDemo();
    frame.pack();
    frame.setVisible(true);
  }

  // Constructor
  public ComboBoxDemo()
  {
    setTitle("ComboBoxDemo");

    // Panel p1 to hold name field
    JPanel p1 = new JPanel();
    p1.setLayout(new FlowLayout(FlowLayout.LEFT));
    p1.add(new JLabel("Name"));
    p1.add(jtfName);

    // Panel p2 to hold department field
    JPanel p2 = new JPanel();
    p2.setLayout(new FlowLayout(FlowLayout.LEFT));
    p2.add(new JLabel("Department"));
    p2.add(jtfDepartment);
```

continues

```java
    // Panel p3 to hold university field
    JPanel p3 = new JPanel();
    p3.setLayout(new FlowLayout(FlowLayout.LEFT));
    p3.add(new JLabel("University"));
    p3.add(jtfUniversity);

    // Panel p4 to hold state and zip field
    JPanel p4 = new JPanel();
    p4.setLayout(new FlowLayout(FlowLayout.LEFT));
    p4.add(new JLabel("State"));
    p4.add(jcboState = new JComboBox());
    p4.add(new JLabel("  Zip"));
    p4.add(jtfZip);

    // Initialize choice items
    jcboState.addItem("MA");
    jcboState.addItem("IN");
    jcboState.addItem("OK");
    jcboState.addItem("PA");
    jcboState.setSelectedIndex(1);

    // Panel jpAddress to group p1, p2, p3 and p4
    JPanel jpAddress = new JPanel();
    jpAddress.setLayout(new GridLayout(4,1));
    jpAddress.add(p1);
    jpAddress.add(p2);
    jpAddress.add(p3);
    jpAddress.add(p4);

    // Panel p5 to hold text area and button
    JPanel p5 = new JPanel();
    p5.setLayout(new FlowLayout(FlowLayout.LEFT));
    p5.add(jta);
    p5.add(jbtStore);

    // Add panels to the frame
    getContentPane().setLayout(new BorderLayout());
    getContentPane().add(jpAddress, BorderLayout.CENTER);
    getContentPane().add(p5, BorderLayout.SOUTH);

    // Register listener
    jcboState.addItemListener(this);
    jcboState.addActionListener(this);
    jbtStore.addActionListener(this);
  }

  // Obtain state code
  public void itemStateChanged(ItemEvent e)
  {
    if (e.getSource() instanceof JComboBox)
    {
      state = (String)e.getItem();
      storeToTextArea();
    }
  }

  // Respond to the button action
  public void actionPerformed(ActionEvent e)
  {
    if (e.getSource() == jbtStore)
      storeToTextArea();
  }
```

```java
        // Store information to the text area
        private void storeToTextArea()
        {
          // Clear text area
          jta.setText(null);

          // Get selected item if needed
          if (state == null)
            state = (String)jcboState.getSelectedItem();

          // Retrieve address information from text field and combo box
          // and append it in the text area
          jta.append(jtfName.getText()+'\n');
          jta.append(jtfDepartment.getText()+'\n');
          jta.append(jtfUniversity.getText()+'\n');
          jta.append(state+", "+jtfZip.getText());
        }
      }
```

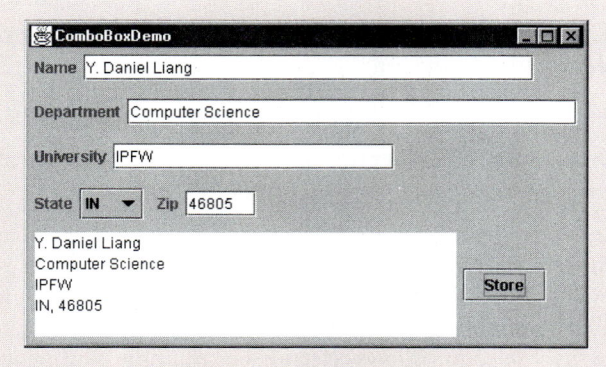

Figure 9.9 *When the Store button is clicked, the name, department, university, state, and zip code are displayed in the text area.*

Example Review

The frame listens to `ActionEvent` for the Store button and `ItemEvent` for the `JComboBox` item, so it implements `ActionListener` and `ItemListener`.

The program uses several panels to organize the user interface. The state field is a choice item with sample values `MA`, `IN`, `OK`, and `PA`. When the user selects a choice, the handler, `itemStateChanged(ItemEvent e)`, gets the selected item and stores it in the state string.

When the user clicks the Store button, the `actionPerformed()` handler is executed, which invokes the `storeToTextArea()` method to display the address collected from the user input.

When the user selects an item in the combo box, the `ItemStateChanged` handler is executed, which invokes the `storeToTextArea()` method to display the address collected from the user input. You can get the selected item by using `e.getItem()` in the `itemStateChanged(ItemEvent e)` handler, or simply by using `jcboState.getSelectedItem()`.

Instead of using the `ItemEvent`, you can rewrite the program to use `ActionEvent` for handling combo box item selection.

Lists

A *list* is a component that basically performs the same function as a combo box but enables the user to choose a single value or multiple values. The Swing `JList` is very versatile. Its advanced features are beyond the scope of this book. This section demonstrates selecting string items from a list.

To create a list with a set of strings, use the following constructor:

```
public JList(Object[] stringItems)
```

where `stringItems` is an array of `String`.

The following properties are often useful:

- `selectedIndex`—An `int` value indicating the index of the selected item in the list.
- `selectedIndices`—An array of `int` values representing the indices of the selected items in the list.
- `selectedValue`—The first selected value in the list.
- `selectedValues`—An array of objects representing selected values in the list.
- `selectionMode`—One of the three values (`SINGLE_SELECTION`, `SINGLE_INTERVAL_SELECTION`, `MULTIPLE_INTERVAL_SELECTION`) that indicate whether a single item, single-interval item, or multiple-interval item can be selected. Single selection allows only one item to be selected. Single-interval selection allows multiple selections, but the selected items must be contiguous. Multiple-interval selection allows selections of multiple contiguous items. The default value is `MULTIPLE_INTERVAL_SELECTION`.
- `visibleRowCount`—The preferred number of rows in the list that can be displayed without a scrollbar. The default value is 8.

Lists do not scroll automatically. To make a list scrollable, create a scroll pane and add the list to it. This is the same way that you make a text area scrollable.

`JList` generates `javax.swing.event.ListSelectionEvent` to notify the listeners of the selections. The listener must implement the `valueChanged()` handler to process the event. Here is an example of how to get a selected item from the `valueChanged(ListSelectionEvent e)` handler:

```
public void valueChanged(ListSelectionEvent e)
{
  String selectedItem = (String)jlst.getSelectedValue();
}
```

Example 9.6 Using Lists

This example gives a program that lets users select a country name in a list and display the country's flag in a label. Figure 9.10 shows a sample run of the program.

```java
// ListDemo.java: Use list to select a country and display the
// selected country's flag
import java.awt.*;
import java.awt.event.*;
import javax.swing.*;
import javax.swing.event.*;

public class ListDemo extends MyFrameWithExitHandling
  implements ListSelectionListener
{
  // Declare an ImageIcon array for the national flags of 9 countries
  private ImageIcon[] imageIcon = new ImageIcon[9];

  // Label for displaying images
  private JLabel jlblImageViewer = new JLabel();

  // The list for selecting countries
  JList jlst;

  // Main Method
  public static void main(String[] args)
  {
    ListDemo frame = new ListDemo();
    frame.setSize(450, 200);
    frame.setTitle("List Demo");
    frame.center();
    frame.setVisible(true);
  }

  // Default Constructor
  public ListDemo()
  {
    // Load images into imageIcon array
    imageIcon[0] = new ImageIcon("images/us.gif");
    imageIcon[1] = new ImageIcon("images/ca.gif");
    imageIcon[2] = new ImageIcon("images/uk.gif");
    imageIcon[3] = new ImageIcon("images/germany.gif");
    imageIcon[4] = new ImageIcon("images/fr.gif");
    imageIcon[5] = new ImageIcon("images/denmark.gif");
    imageIcon[6] = new ImageIcon("images/norway.gif");
    imageIcon[7] = new ImageIcon("images/china.gif");
    imageIcon[8] = new ImageIcon("images/india.gif");

    // Show the first image
    jlblImageViewer.setIcon(imageIcon[0]);

    // Set center alignment
    jlblImageViewer.setHorizontalAlignment(SwingConstants.CENTER);
    //jlblImageViewer.setVerticalAlignment(SwingConstants.CENTER);

    // Create a string of country names
    String[] countries = {"United States of America", "Canada",
      "United Kingdom", "Germany", "France", "Denmark", "Norway",
      "China", "India"};

    // Create a list with the country names
    jlst = new JList(countries);

    // Add jpButton and the label to the frame
    getContentPane().add(jlblImageViewer, BorderLayout.CENTER);
    getContentPane().add(new JScrollPane(jlst), BorderLayout.WEST);
```

continues

```
      // Register listeners
      jlst.addListSelectionListener(this);
   }

   // Handle list selection
   public void valueChanged(ListSelectionEvent e)
   {
      jlblImageViewer.setIcon(imageIcon[jlst.getSelectedIndex()]);
   }
}
```

Figure 9.10 When the country in the list is selected, a corresponding flag image is displayed in a label.

Example Review

The frame listens to `ListSelectionEvent` for handling the selection of country names in the list, so it implements `ListSelectionListener`. `ListSelectionEvent` and `ListSelectionListener` are defined in the `javax.swing.event` package, so this package is imported in the program.

The program loads the images of nine countries into an image array and creates a list of the nine countries in the same order as in the image array. Thus the index 0 of the image array corresponds to the first country on the list.

The list is placed in a scroll pane so that it can be scrolled when the number of items in the list extends beyond the viewing area.

When the user selects an item in the list, the `valueChanged()` handler is executed, which gets the index of the selected item and sets its corresponding image icon in the label to display the country's flag.

The example constructs a list with a fixed set of strings. If you want to add new items to the list or delete existing items, you have to use the the list model. The use of list models is explained in *Rapid Java Application Development Using JBuilder 3*.

Check Boxes

A *check box* is a component that enables the user to toggle a choice on or off, like a light switch.

To create a check box, use the following constructor:

- `public JCheckBox()`

  This default constructor creates an unselected empty check box.

- `public JCheckBox(String text)`

  This creates an unselected check box with the specified text.

- `public JCheckBox(String text, boolean selected)`

  This creates a check box with a text and specifies whether the check box is initially selected.

- `public JCheckBox(Icon icon)`

  This creates an unselected check box with an icon.

- `public JCheckBox(Icon icon, boolean selected)`

  This creates a check box with an icon and specifies whether the check box is initially selected.

- `public JCheckBox(String text, Icon icon)`

  This creates an unselected check box with an icon and a text.

- `public JCheckBox(String text, Icon icon, boolean selected)`

  This creates a check box with an icon and a text, and specifies whether the check box is initially selected.

In addition to `text`, `icon`, `mnemonic`, `verticalAlignment`, `horizontalAlignment`, `horizontalTextPosition`, and `verticalTextPosition`, `JCheckBox` has the following property:

- `selected`—Specifies whether the check box is selected.

`JCheckBox` can generate `ActionEvent` and `ItemEvent` among many other events. The following code shows you how to implement `itemStateChanged()` to determine whether a box is checked or unchecked in response to an `ItemEvent`:

```
public void itemStateChanged(ItemEvent e)
{
  // Make sure the source is a JCheckBox
  if (e.getSource() instanceof JCheckBox)
    if (jchk1.isSelected())
      // Process the selection for jchk1;
    if (jchk2.isSelected())
      // Process the selection for jchk2;
}
```

Example 9.7 Using Check Boxes

This example gives a program that displays a message in overlapping font styles. The message can be displayed in bold and italic at the same time, or can be displayed in the center of the panel. The output of a sample run of the program is given in Figure 9.11.

```java
// CheckBoxDemo.java: Use check boxes to select one or more choices
import java.awt.BorderLayout;
import java.awt.FlowLayout;
import java.awt.Color;
import java.awt.Font;
import java.awt.event.*;
import javax.swing.*;

public class CheckBoxDemo extends MyFrameWithExitHandling
  implements ItemListener
{
  // Declare check boxes
  private JCheckBox jchkCentered, jchkBold, jchkItalic;

  // Declare a panel for displaying message
  private MessagePanel messagePanel;

  // Main method
  public static void main(String[] args)
  {
    CheckBoxDemo frame = new CheckBoxDemo();
    frame.pack();
    frame.setVisible(true);
  }

  // Constructor
  public CheckBoxDemo()
  {
    setTitle("Checkbox Demo");

    // Create the message panel
    messagePanel = new MessagePanel();
    messagePanel.setMessage("Welcome to Java!");
    messagePanel.setBackground(Color.yellow);

    // Put three check boxes in panel p
    JPanel p = new JPanel();
    p.setLayout(new FlowLayout());
    p.add(jchkCentered = new JCheckBox("Centered"));
    p.add(jchkBold = new JCheckBox("Bold"));
    p.add(jchkItalic = new JCheckBox("Italic"));

    // Set keyboard mnemonics
    jchkCentered.setMnemonic('C');
    jchkBold.setMnemonic('B');
    jchkItalic.setMnemonic('I');

    // Place messagePanel and p in the frame
    getContentPane().setLayout(new BorderLayout());
    getContentPane().add(messagePanel, BorderLayout.CENTER);
    getContentPane().add(p, BorderLayout.SOUTH);
```

```
      // Register listeners on jchkCentered, jchkBold, and jchkItalic
      jchkCentered.addItemListener(this);
      jchkBold.addItemListener(this);
      jchkItalic.addItemListener(this);
    }

    // Handle check box selection
    public void itemStateChanged(ItemEvent e)
    {
      if (e.getSource() instanceof JCheckBox)
      {
        // Determine a font style
        int selectedStyle = 0;
        if (jchkBold.isSelected())
          selectedStyle = selectedStyle+Font.BOLD;
        if (jchkItalic.isSelected())
          selectedStyle = selectedStyle+Font.ITALIC;

        // Set font for the message
        messagePanel.setFont(new Font("Serif", selectedStyle, 20));
        if (jchkCentered.isSelected())
          messagePanel.setCentered(true);
        else
          messagePanel.setCentered(false);

        // Make sure the message is repainted
        messagePanel.repaint();
      }
    }
  }
```

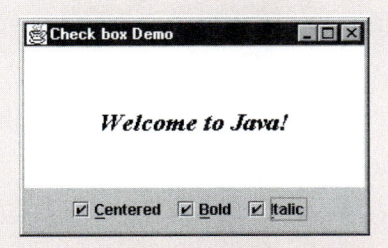

Figure 9.11 *The program uses three* `JCheckBox` *components to let the user choose the font style for the message displayed and specify whether the message is centered.*

Example Review

The program displays the message using the `MessagePanel` class. The check boxes are labeled "Centered," "Bold," and "Italic." The user can toggle a check box on and off to select or deselect it.

Upon selecting a check box, the handler, `itemStateChanged(ItemEvent e)`, is invoked to determine the state of each check box and combines all selected fonts. The font styles are `int` constants: `Font.BOLD` and `Font.ITALIC`. Font styles are combined by adding together the selected integers representing the fonts.

continues

> The `selected` property determines whether a check box is selected. The value of this property is synchronized with the display. If it is true, then the check box is selected.
>
> The keyboard mnemonics 'C', 'B', and 'I' are set on the check boxes "Centered," "Bold," and "Italic," respectively. You can use a mouse gesture or the shortcut keys to select a check box.
>
> Since invoking the methods `setFont()` and `setCentered()` in `MessagePanel` does not repaint the viewing area in the panel, you must invoke the `repaint()` method to refresh the panel.

Radio Buttons

Radio buttons, also known as *option buttons,* enable you to choose a single item from a list of choices. In appearance radio buttons resemble check boxes, but check boxes display a square that is either checked or blank, whereas radio buttons display a circle that is either filled (if selected) or blank (not selected).

The constructors of `JRadioButton`, shown directly below, are similar to the constructors of `JCheckBox`.

- `public JRadioButton()`

    This default constructor creates an unselected empty radio button.

- `public JRadioButton(String text)`

    This creates an unselected radio button with the specified text.

- `public JRadioButton(String text, boolean selected)`

    This creates a radio button with a text and specifies whether the radio button is initially selected.

- `public JRadioButton(Icon icon)`

    This creates an unselected radio button with an icon.

- `public JRadioButton(Icon icon, boolean selected)`

    This creates a radio button with an icon and specifies whether the radio button is initially selected.

- `public JRadioButton(String text, Icon icon)`

    This creates an unselected radio button with an icon and a text.

- `public JRadioButton(String text, Icon icon, boolean selected)`

    This creates a radio button with an icon and a text, and specifies whether the radio button is initially selected.

Here is how to create a radio button with a text and an icon:

```
JRadionButton jrb = new JRadioButton(
  "My Radio Button", new ImageIcon("imagefile.gif"));
```

The radio buttons are added to a container just like a button. To group the radio buttons, you need to create an instance of `java.swing.ButtonGroup` and use the `add()` method to add them to it, as follows:

```
ButtonGroup btg = new ButtonGroup();
btg.add(jrb1);
btg.add(jrb2);
```

This code creates a radio button group so that `jrb1` and `jrb2` are selected mutually exclusively.

`JRadioButton` has such properties as `text`, `icon`, `mnemonic`, `verticalAlignment`, `horizontalAlignment`, `selected`, `horizontalTextPosition`, and `verticalTextPosition`.

`JRadioButton` can generate `ActionEvent` and `ItemEvent` among many other events. The following code shows you how to implement the `itemStateChanged()` handler to determine whether a box is checked or unchecked in response to an `ItemEvent`:

```
public void itemStateChanged(ItemEvent e)
{
  // Make sure the source is a JRadioButton
  if (e.getSource() instanceof JRadioButton)
    if (jrb1.selected())
      // Process the selection for jrb1
    else if (jrb2.isSelected())
      // Process the selection for jrb2
}
```

Example 9.8 Using Radio Buttons

This example gives a program that simulates traffic lights. The program lets the user select one of three lights: red, yellow, or green. When a radio button is selected, the light is turned on, and one light can be on at a time. No light is on when the program starts. Figure 9.12 contains the output of a sample run of the program.

```
// RadioButtonDemo.java: Use radio buttons to select a choice
import java.awt.*;
import java.awt.event.*;
import javax.swing.*;

public class RadioButtonDemo extends MyFrameWithExitHandling
   implements ItemListener
{
  // Declare radio buttons
  private JRadioButton jrbRed, jrbYellow, jrbGreen;

  // Declare a radio button group
  private ButtonGroup btg = new ButtonGroup();

  // Declare a traffic light display panel
  private Light light;
```

continues

```java
    // Main method
    public static void main(String[] args)
    {
      RadioButtonDemo frame = new RadioButtonDemo();
      frame.setSize(250, 170);
      frame.setVisible(true);
    }

    // Constructor
    public RadioButtonDemo()
    {
      setTitle("RadioButton Demo");

      // Add traffic light panel to panel p1
      JPanel p1 = new JPanel();
      p1.setSize(200, 200);
      p1.setLayout(new FlowLayout(FlowLayout.CENTER));
      light = new Light();
      light.setSize(40, 90);
      p1.add(light);

      // Put the radio button in Panel p2
      JPanel p2 = new JPanel();
      p2.setLayout(new FlowLayout());
      p2.add(jrbRed = new JRadioButton("Red", false));
      p2.add(jrbYellow = new JRadioButton("Yellow", false));
      p2.add(jrbGreen = new JRadioButton("Green", false));

      // Set keyboard mnemonics
      jrbRed.setMnemonic('R');
      jrbYellow.setMnemonic('Y');
      jrbGreen.setMnemonic('G');

      // Group radio buttons
      btg.add(jrbRed);
      btg.add(jrbYellow);
      btg.add(jrbGreen);

      // Place p1 and p2 in the frame
      getContentPane().setLayout(new BorderLayout());
      getContentPane().add(p1, BorderLayout.CENTER);
      getContentPane().add(p2, BorderLayout.SOUTH);

      // Register listeners for check boxes
      jrbRed.addItemListener(this);
      jrbYellow.addItemListener(this);
      jrbGreen.addItemListener(this);
    }

    // Handling checkbox events
    public void itemStateChanged(ItemEvent e)
    {
      if (jrbRed.isSelected())
        light.red(); // Set red light
      if (jrbYellow.isSelected())
        light.yellow(); // Set yellow light
      if (jrbGreen.isSelected())
        light.green(); // Set green light
    }
}
```

```java
// Three traffic lights shown in a panel
class Light extends JPanel
{
  private boolean red;
  private boolean yellow;
  private boolean green;

  public Light()
  {
    red = false;
    yellow = false;
    green = false;
  }

  // Set red light on
  public void red()
  {
    red = true;
    yellow = false;
    green = false;
    repaint();
  }

  // Set yellow light on
  public void yellow()
  {
    red = false;
    yellow = true;
    green = false;
    repaint();
  }

  // Set green light on
  public void green()
  {
    red = false;
    yellow = false;
    green = true;
    repaint();
  }

  // Display lights
  public void paintComponent(Graphics g)
  {
    super.paintComponent(g);

    if (red)
    {
      g.setColor(Color.red);
      g.fillOval(10, 10, 20, 20);
      g.setColor(Color.black);
      g.drawOval(10, 35, 20, 20);
      g.drawOval(10, 60, 20, 20);
      g.drawRect(5, 5, 30, 80);
    }
    else if (yellow)
    {
      g.setColor(Color.yellow);
      g.fillOval(10, 35, 20, 20);
```

continues

```java
      g.setColor(Color.black);
      g.drawRect(5, 5, 30, 80);
      g.drawOval(10, 10, 20, 20);
      g.drawOval(10, 60, 20, 20);
    }
    else if (green)
    {
      g.setColor(Color.green);
      g.fillOval(10, 60, 20, 20);
      g.setColor(Color.black);
      g.drawRect(5, 5, 30, 80);
      g.drawOval(10, 10, 20, 20);
      g.drawOval(10, 35, 20, 20);
    }
    else
    {
      g.setColor(Color.black);
      g.drawRect(5, 5, 30, 80);
      g.drawOval(10, 10, 20, 20);
      g.drawOval(10, 35, 20, 20);
      g.drawOval(10, 60, 20, 20);
    }
  }

  // Set preferred size
  public Dimension getPreferredSize()
  {
    return new Dimension(40, 90);
  }
}
```

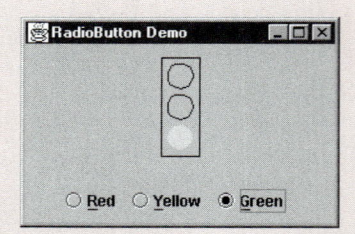

Figure 9.12 *The radio buttons are grouped to let you select one color in the group to control traffic lights.*

Example Review

The lights are displayed on a panel. The program groups the radio buttons in a panel and places it below the traffic light panel. The `BorderLayout` is used to arrange these components.

The `Light` class, a subclass of `JPanel`, contains the methods `red()`, `yellow()`, and `green()` to control the lights. For example, use `light.red()` to turn on the red light, where light is an instance of `Light`.

The program creates a `ButtonGroup` btg and puts three `JRadioButton` instances (red, yellow, and green) in the group. When the user checks a box in the group, the handler, `itemStateChanged(ItemEvent e)`, determines which radio button is selected, using the `isSelected()` method, and turns on the corresponding light.

The `getPreferredSize()` method is overridden to set the preferred size to 40 by 90. This is just the right size for displaying the traffic lights.

Borders

Borders are one of the interesting new Swing component features. You can set a border on any object of the `JComponent` class, but often it is useful to set a titled border on a `JPanel` that groups a set of related user interface components.

There are several basic types of borders to choose from. The titled border is the most useful of them. To create a titled border, use the following statement:

```
Border titledBorder = new TitledBorder("A Title");
```

`Border` is the interface for all types of borders. `TitledBorder` is an implementation of `Border` with a title. You can create a border as desired by using the following properties:

- `title`—The title of the border.
- `titleColor`—The color of the title.
- `titleFont`—The font of the title.
- `titleJustification`—Specifies `Border.LEFT`, `Border.CENTER`, or `Border.RIGHT` for left, center, or right title justification.
- `titlePosition`—One of the six values (`Border.ABOVE_TOP`, `Border.TOP`, `Border.BELOW_TOP`, `Border.ABOVE_BOTTOM`, `Border.BOTTOM`, `Border.BELOW_BOTTOM`) that specify the title position above the border line, on the border line, or below the border line.
- `border`—The `TitledBorder` itself has the `border` property for building composite borders.

The other types of borders can be created by using the following classes:

- `BevelBorder`—Creates a 3D-look border that can be lowered or raised. To construct a `BevelBorder`, use the following constructor, which creates a `BevelBorder` with the specified `bevelType` (`BevelBorder.LOWERED` or `BevelBorder.BevelBorder`)

  ```
  public BevelBorder(int bevelType)
  ```

- `EtchedBorder`—Creates an etched border that can be etched-in or etched-out. You can use its default constructor to construct an `EtchedBorder` with a lowered border. `EtchedBorder` has a property `etchType` with the value `LOWERED` or `RAISED`.

- `LineBorder`—Creates a line border of arbitrary thickness of a single color. To create a `LineBorder`, use the following constructor:

  ```
  public LineBorder(Color c, int thickness)
  ```

- `MatteBorder`—Creates a matte-like border padded with the icon images. To create a `MatteBorder`, use the following constructor:

  ```
  public MatteBorder(Icon tileIcon)
  ```

- `EmptyBorder`—Creates a border with border space but no drawings. To create an `EmptyBorder`, use the following constructor:

  ```
  public EmptyBorder(int top, int left, int bottom, int right)
  ```

> **NOTE**
> All the border classes and interfaces are grouped in the package `javax.swing.border`.

Swing also provides the `javax.swing.BorderFactory` class, which contains static methods for creating borders. Some of the static methods are:

- `public static TitledBorder createTitledBorder(String title)`
- `public static Border createLoweredBevelBorder()`
- `public static Border createRaisedBevelBorder()`
- `public static Border createLineBorder(Color color)`
- `public static Border createLineBorder(Color color, int thickness)`
- `public static Border createEtchedBorder()`
- `public static Border createEtchedBorder(Color highlight, Color shadow)`
- `public static Border createEmptyBorder()`
- `public static MatteBorder createEmptyBorder(int top, int left, int bottom, int right)`
- `public static MatteBorder createMatteBorder(int top, int left, int bottom, int right, Color color)`
- `public static MatteBorder createMatteBorder(int top, int left, int bottom, int right, Icon tileIcon)`
- `public static Border createCompoundBorder(Border outsideBorder, Border insideBorder)`

For example, to create an etched border, use the following statement:

```
Border border = BorderFactory.createEtchedBorder();
```

Example 9.9 Using Borders

This example gives a program that creates and displays various types of borders. You can select a border with a title or without a title. For a border without a title, you can choose a border style from Lowered Bevel, Raised Bevel, Etched, Line, Matte, or Empty. For a border with a title, you can specify the title position and justification. You can also embed another border into a titled border. Figure 9.13 displays a sample run of the program.

```java
// BorderDemo.java: Use borders for JComponent components
import java.awt.*;
import java.awt.event.ActionListener;
import java.awt.event.ActionEvent;
import javax.swing.*;
import javax.swing.border.*;

public class BorderDemo extends MyFrameWithExitHandling
  implements ActionListener
{
  // Declare a panel for displaying message
  private MessagePanel messagePanel;

  // A check box for selecting a border with or without a title
  private JCheckBox jchkTitled;

  // Radio buttons for border styles
  private JRadioButton jrbLoweredBevel, jrbRaisedBevel,
    jrbEtched, jrbLine, jrbMatte, jrbEmpty;

  // Radio buttons for titled border options
  private JRadioButton jrbAboveBottom, jrbBottom,
    jrbBelowBottom, jrbAboveTop, jrbTop, jrbBelowTop,
    jrbLeft, jrbCenter, jrbRight;

  // TitledBorder for the message panel
  private TitledBorder messagePanelBorder = new TitledBorder("");

  // Main method
  public static void main(String[] args)
  {
    BorderDemo frame = new BorderDemo();
    frame.pack();
    frame.setVisible(true);
  }

  // Constructor
  public BorderDemo()
  {
    setTitle("Border Demo");

    // Create a MessagePanel instance and set colors
    messagePanel = new MessagePanel
      ("Display the border type");
    messagePanel.setCentered(true);
    messagePanel.setBackground(Color.yellow);
    messagePanel.setBorder(messagePanelBorder);
```

continues

```java
    // Place title position radio buttons
    JPanel jpPosition = new JPanel();
    jpPosition.setLayout(new GridLayout(3, 2));
    jpPosition.add(
      jrbAboveBottom = new JRadioButton("ABOVE_BOTTOM"));
    jpPosition.add(jrbAboveTop = new JRadioButton("ABOVE_TOP"));
    jpPosition.add(jrbBottom = new JRadioButton("BOTTOM"));
    jpPosition.add(jrbTop = new JRadioButton("TOP"));
    jpPosition.add(
      jrbBelowBottom = new JRadioButton("BELOW_BOTTOM"));
    jpPosition.add(jrbBelowTop = new JRadioButton("BELOW_TOP"));
    jpPosition.setBorder(new TitledBorder("Position"));

    // Place title justification radio buttons
    JPanel jpJustification = new JPanel();
    jpJustification.setLayout(new GridLayout(3,1));
    jpJustification.add(jrbLeft = new JRadioButton("LEFT"));
    jpJustification.add(jrbCenter = new JRadioButton("CENTER"));
    jpJustification.add(jrbRight = new JRadioButton("RIGHT"));
    jpJustification.setBorder(new TitledBorder("Justification"));

    // Create panel jpTitleOptions to hold jpPosition and
    // jpJustification
    JPanel jpTitleOptions = new JPanel();
    jpTitleOptions.setLayout(new BorderLayout());
    jpTitleOptions.add(jpPosition, BorderLayout.CENTER);
    jpTitleOptions.add(jpJustification, BorderLayout.EAST);

    // Create Panel jpTitle to hold a check box and title position
    // radio buttons, and title justification radio buttons
    JPanel jpTitle = new JPanel();
    jpTitle.setBorder(new TitledBorder("Border Title"));
    jpTitle.setLayout(new BorderLayout());
    jpTitle.add(jchkTitled = new JCheckBox("Titled"),
      BorderLayout.NORTH);
    jpTitle.add(jpTitleOptions, BorderLayout.CENTER);

    // Group radio buttons for title position
    ButtonGroup btgTitlePosition = new ButtonGroup();
    btgTitlePosition.add(jrbAboveBottom);
    btgTitlePosition.add(jrbBottom);
    btgTitlePosition.add(jrbBelowBottom);
    btgTitlePosition.add(jrbAboveTop);
    btgTitlePosition.add(jrbTop);
    btgTitlePosition.add(jrbBelowTop);

    // Group radio buttons for title justification
    ButtonGroup btgTitleJustification = new ButtonGroup();
    btgTitleJustification.add(jrbLeft);
    btgTitleJustification.add(jrbCenter);
    btgTitleJustification.add(jrbRight);

    // Create Panel jpBorderStyle to hold border style radio buttons
    JPanel jpBorderStyle = new JPanel();
    jpBorderStyle.setBorder(new TitledBorder("Border Style"));
    jpBorderStyle.setLayout(new GridLayout(6, 1));
    jpBorderStyle.add(jrbLoweredBevel =
      new JRadioButton("Lowered Bevel"));
    jpBorderStyle.add(jrbRaisedBevel =
      new JRadioButton("Raised Bevel"));
```

```java
      jpBorderStyle.add(jrbEtched = new JRadioButton("Etched"));
      jpBorderStyle.add(jrbLine = new JRadioButton("Line"));
      jpBorderStyle.add(jrbMatte = new JRadioButton("Matte"));
      jpBorderStyle.add(jrbEmpty = new JRadioButton("Empty"));

      // Group radio buttons for border styles
      ButtonGroup btgBorderStyle = new ButtonGroup();
      btgBorderStyle.add(jrbLoweredBevel);
      btgBorderStyle.add(jrbRaisedBevel);
      btgBorderStyle.add(jrbEtched);
      btgBorderStyle.add(jrbLine);
      btgBorderStyle.add(jrbMatte);
      btgBorderStyle.add(jrbEmpty);

      // Create Panel jpAllChoices to place jpTitle and jpBorderStyle
      JPanel jpAllChoices = new JPanel();
      jpAllChoices.setLayout(new BorderLayout());
      jpAllChoices.add(jpTitle, BorderLayout.CENTER);
      jpAllChoices.add(jpBorderStyle, BorderLayout.EAST);

      // Place panels in the frame
      getContentPane().setLayout(new BorderLayout());
      getContentPane().add(messagePanel, BorderLayout.CENTER);
      getContentPane().add(jpAllChoices, BorderLayout.SOUTH);

      // Register listeners
      jchkTitled.addActionListener(this);
      jrbAboveBottom.addActionListener(this);
      jrbBottom.addActionListener(this);
      jrbBelowBottom.addActionListener(this);
      jrbAboveTop.addActionListener(this);
      jrbTop.addActionListener(this);
      jrbBelowTop.addActionListener(this);
      jrbLeft.addActionListener(this);
      jrbCenter.addActionListener(this);
      jrbRight.addActionListener(this);
      jrbLoweredBevel.addActionListener(this);
      jrbRaisedBevel.addActionListener(this);
      jrbLine.addActionListener(this);
      jrbEtched.addActionListener(this);
      jrbMatte.addActionListener(this);
      jrbEmpty.addActionListener(this);
    }

    // Handler for ActionEvents on check box and radio buttons
    public void actionPerformed(ActionEvent e)
    {
      // Get border style
      Border border = new EmptyBorder(2, 2, 2, 2);

      if (jrbLoweredBevel.isSelected())
      {
        border = new BevelBorder(BevelBorder.LOWERED);
        messagePanel.setMessage("Lowered Bevel Style");
      }
      else if (jrbRaisedBevel.isSelected())
      {
        border = new BevelBorder(BevelBorder.RAISED);
        messagePanel.setMessage("Raised Bevel Style");
      }
```

continues

```java
      else if (jrbEtched.isSelected())
      {
        border = new EtchedBorder();
        messagePanel.setMessage("Etched Style");
      }
      else if (jrbLine.isSelected())
      {
        border = new LineBorder(Color.black, 5);
        messagePanel.setMessage("Line Style");
      }
      else if (jrbMatte.isSelected())
      {
        border = new MatteBorder(20, 20, 20, 20,
          new ImageIcon("images/swirl.gif"));
        messagePanel.setMessage("Matte Style");
      }
      else if (jrbEmpty.isSelected())
      {
        border = new EmptyBorder(2, 2, 2, 2);
        messagePanel.setMessage("Empty Style");
      }

      if (jchkTitled.isSelected())
      {
        // Get the title position and justification
        int titlePosition = TitledBorder.DEFAULT_POSITION;
        int titleJustification = TitledBorder.DEFAULT_JUSTIFICATION;

        if (jrbAboveBottom.isSelected())
          titlePosition = TitledBorder.ABOVE_BOTTOM;
        else if (jrbBottom.isSelected())
          titlePosition = TitledBorder.BOTTOM;
        else if (jrbBelowBottom.isSelected())
          titlePosition = TitledBorder.BELOW_BOTTOM;
        else if (jrbAboveTop.isSelected())
          titlePosition = TitledBorder.ABOVE_TOP;
        else if (jrbTop.isSelected())
          titlePosition = TitledBorder.TOP;
        else if (jrbBelowTop.isSelected())
          titlePosition = TitledBorder.BELOW_TOP;

        if (jrbLeft.isSelected())
          titleJustification = TitledBorder.LEFT;
        else if (jrbCenter.isSelected())
          titleJustification = TitledBorder.CENTER;
        else if (jrbRight.isSelected())
          titleJustification = TitledBorder.RIGHT;

        messagePanelBorder = new TitledBorder("A Title");
        messagePanelBorder.setBorder(border);
        messagePanelBorder.setTitlePosition(titlePosition);
        messagePanelBorder.setTitleJustification(titleJustification);
        messagePanelBorder.setTitle("A Title");
        messagePanel.setBorder(messagePanelBorder);
      }
      else
      {
        messagePanel.setBorder(border);
      }
    }
  }
```

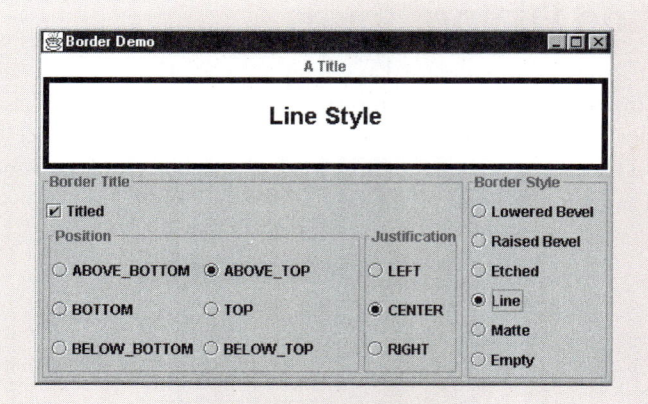

Figure 9.13 *The program demonstrates various types of borders.*

Example Review

This example uses many panels to group UI components to achieve the desired look. Figure 9.13 illustrates the relationship of these panels. The Border Title panel groups all the options for setting title properties. The position options are grouped in the Position Panel. The justification options are grouped in the Justification panel. The Border Style panel groups the radio buttons for choosing Lowered Bevel, Raised Bevel, Etched, Line, Matte, and Empty borders.

The `MessagePanel` displays the selected border with or without a title, depending on the selection of the title check box. The `MessagePanel` also displays a message indicating which type of border is being used, depending on the selection of the radio button in the Border Style panel.

The `TitledBorder` can be mixed with other borders. To do so, simply create an instance of `TitledBorder`, and use the `setBorder()` method to embed a new border into the `TitledBorder`.

The `MatteBorder` can be used to display icons on the border, as shown in Figure 9.14.

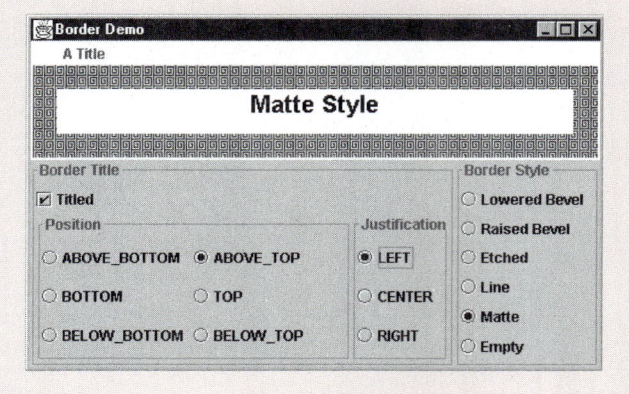

Figure 9.14 `MatteBorder` *can display icons on the border.*

Message Dialog Boxes

A *dialog box* is normally used as a temporary window to receive additional information from the user or to provide notification that some event has occurred. You can build a variety of dialog boxes in Java. This section introduces the *message dialog box*. This simple and frequently used dialog box displays a message to alert the user, as shown in Figure 9.15.

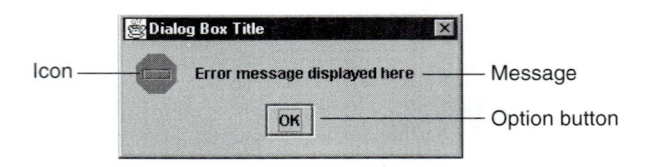

Figure 9.15 *A message dialog box displays a message.*

To display a message dialog box, as shown in Figure 9.15, use the static `showMessageDialog()` method in the `JOptionPane` class, as follows:

```
public static void showMessageDialog(Component parentComponent,
                                     Object message,
                                     String title,
                                     int messageType)
```

The `parentComponent` is the parent component of the dialog box, from which the dialog box is launched. The `message` is the object to display. Often you use a string for `message`. The `title` is the title of the dialog box. The `messageType` determines the type of message to be displayed. There are five message types:

- ERROR_MESSAGE
- INFORMATION_MESSAGE
- PLAIN_MESSAGE
- WARNING_MESSAGE
- QUESTION_MESSAGE

Each type, except for the PLAIN_MESSAGE type, has an associated icon. You can use the following method to supply your own icon:

```
public static void showMessageDialog(Component parentComponent,
                                     Object message,
                                     String title,
                                     int messageType,
                                     Icon icon)
```

Example 9.10 Using Message Dialogs

This example gives a program that displays student exam grades. The user enters the SSN and the password, then clicks the Find Score button (see Figure 9.16) to show the student name and the grade. If the SSN is incorrect, a message dialog box displays the message SSN not found, as shown in Figure 9.17. If the password is incorrect, a message dialog box displays Password does not match SSN, as shown in Figure 9.18. In either case, the user must click the OK button in the message dialog box to go back to the main frame.

```java
// DialogDemo.java: Use message dialog box to select information
import java.awt.*;
import java.awt.event.*;
import javax.swing.*;

public class DialogDemo extends MyFrameWithExitHandling
  implements ActionListener
{
  // Create sample student information in arrays
  // with name, SSN, password, and grade
  private String[][] student =
    {
      {"John Willow", "111223333", "a450", "A"},
      {"Jim Brown", "111223334", "b344", "B"},
      {"Bill Beng", "111223335", "33342csa", "C"},
      {"George Wall", "111223336", "343rea2", "D"},
      {"Jill Jones", "111223337", "34g", "E"}
    };

  // Declare text fields for last name, password, full name and score
  private JTextField jtfSSN;
  private JPasswordField jpfPassword;
  private JTextField jtfName;
  private JTextField jtfGrade;
  private JButton jbtFind;

  // Main method
  public static void main(String[] args)
  {
    DialogDemo f = new DialogDemo();
    f.pack();
    f.setVisible(true);
  }

  public DialogDemo()
  {
    setTitle("Find The Score");

    // Panel jpLables to hold labels
    JPanel jpLabels = new JPanel();
    jpLabels.setLayout(new GridLayout(4, 1));
    jpLabels.add(new JLabel("Enter SSN"));
    jpLabels.add(new JLabel("Enter Password"));
    jpLabels.add(new JLabel("Name"));
    jpLabels.add(new JLabel("Score"));
```

continues

```java
      // Panel jpTextFields to hold text fields and password
      JPanel jpTextFields = new JPanel();
      jpTextFields.setLayout(new GridLayout(4, 1));
      jpTextFields.add(jtfSSN = new JTextField(10));
      jpTextFields.add(jpfPassword = new JPasswordField(10));
      jpTextFields.add(jtfName = new JTextField(10));
      jpTextFields.add(jtfGrade = new JTextField(10));

      // Panel p1 for holding jpLables and jpTextFields
      JPanel p1 = new JPanel();
      p1.setLayout(new BorderLayout());
      p1.add(jpLabels, BorderLayout.WEST);
      p1.add(jpTextFields, BorderLayout.CENTER);

      // Panel p2 for holding the Find button
      JPanel p2 = new JPanel();
      p2.setLayout(new FlowLayout(FlowLayout.RIGHT));
      p2.add(jbtFind = new JButton("Find Score"));

      // Place panels into the frame
      getContentPane().setLayout(new BorderLayout());
      getContentPane().add(p1, BorderLayout.CENTER);
      getContentPane().add(p2, BorderLayout.SOUTH);

      // Register listener for jbtFind
      jbtFind.addActionListener(this);
    }

    public void actionPerformed(ActionEvent e)
    {
      // Find the student in the database
      int index = find(jtfSSN.getText().trim(),
        new String(jpfPassword.getPassword()));

      if (index == -1)
      {
        JOptionPane.showMessageDialog(this, "SSN not found",
          "For Your Information", JOptionPane.INFORMATION_MESSAGE);
      }
      else if (index == -2)
      {
        JOptionPane.showMessageDialog(this,
          "Password does not match SSN",
          "For Your Information", JOptionPane.INFORMATION_MESSAGE);
      }
      else
      {
        // Display name and score
        jtfName.setText(student[index][0]);
        jtfGrade.setText(student[index][3]);
      }
    }

    // Find the student who matched user name and password
    // return the index if found; return -1 if SSN is not in
    // the database, and return -2 if password does not match SSN
    public int find(String SSN, String pw)
    {
      // Find a student who matches SSN and pw
      for (int i=0; i<student.length; i++)
        if (student[i][1].equals(SSN) && student[i][2].equals(pw))
          return i;
```

```
            // Determine if the SSN is in the database
            for (int i=0; i<student.length; i++)
              if (student[i][1].equals(SSN))
                return -2;

            // Return -1 since the SSN and pw do not match
            return -1;
        }
    }
```

Figure 9.16 *The main frame lets the user enter the SSN and password, and then click the Find button to display name and score.*

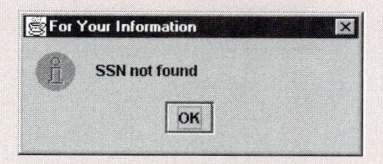

Figure 9.17 *The message box displays the error message* Last name not found*.*

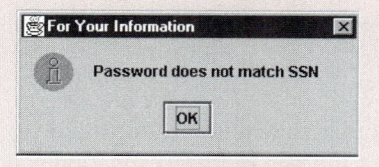

Figure 9.18 *The message box displays the error message* Password does not match SSN*.*

Example Review

The message dialog box is *modal,* which means that no other window can be accessed before the message dialog is dismissed.

The student information is stored in the two-dimensional array student[][]. Each element in the array consists of name, SSN, password, and grade. If the SSN and password match student[i][1] and student[i][2] for some i, the name (student[i][0]) and the grade (grade[i][3]) are displayed in the main frame.

When the program starts, the main frame comes up first, as shown in Figure 9.16. If the user enters a wrong SSN, the message SSN not found appears in the dialog box, as shown in Figure 9.17. If the user enters a correct SSN, but a

continues

wrong password, the message Password does not match SSN appears in the dialog box, as shown in Figure 9.18. When the correct SSN and password are received, the user's name and grade are displayed in the frame, as shown in Figure 9.16.

The statement

```
JOptionPane.showMessageDialog(this, "SSN not found",
        "For Your Information", JOptionPane.INFORMATION_MESSAGE);
```

displays a message dialog box of the INFORMATION_MESSAGE type with the message "SSN not found" and the title "For Your Information."

The find(SSN, pw) method defined in the main frame returns the index of the student array element that matches the SSN and the password, returns -1 if the SSN is not found, and returns -2 if password does not match the SSN.

The JPasswordField component, a subclass of JTextField, is specifically designed to receive the password. The characters entered in a JPasswordField are echo displayed in * to protect them from being seen by bystanders. To get the password, you need to use the getPassword() method, which returns the password in an array of char, not a string.

Menus

Menus make selection easier, and are widely used in window applications. Java provides five classes to implement menus—JMenuBar, JMenu, JMenuItem, JCheckBoxMenuItem, and JRadioButtonMenuItem.

JMenuBar is the top-level menu component used to hold the menus. Menus consist of *menu items* that the user can select (or toggle on or off). A menu item can be an instance of JMenuItem, JCheckBoxMenuItem, or JRadioButtonMenuItem.

The sequence of implementing menus in Java is as follows:

1. Create a menu bar and associate it with a frame.

    ```
    JFrame frame = new JFrame();
    frame.setSize(300, 200);
    frame.setVisible(true);
    JMenuBar jmb = new JMenuBar();
    frame.setJMenuBar(jmb);   // Attach a menu bar to a frame
    ```

    This code creates a frame and a menu bar, and sets the menu bar in the frame.

2. Create menus.

    You can use the following constructor to create a menu:

    ```
    public JMenu(String label)
    ```

The following is an example of creating menus:

```
JMenu fileMenu = new JMenu("File");
JMenu helpMenu = new JMenu("Help");
jmb.add(fileMenu);
jmb.add(helpMenu);
```

This creates two menus labeled `File` and `Help`, as shown in Figure 9.19. The menus will not be seen until they are added to `JMenuBar`.

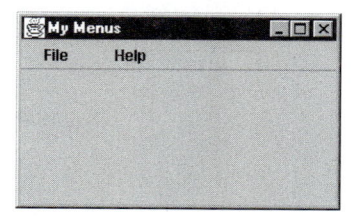

Figure 9.19 *The menu bar appears below the title bar on the frame.*

3. Create menu items and add them to menus.

```
fileMenu.add(new JMenuItem("New"));
fileMenu.add(new JMenuItem("Open"));
fileMenu.addSeparator();
fileMenu.add(new JMenuItem("Print"));
fileMenu.addSeparator();
fileMenu.add(new JMenuItem("Exit"));
```

This code adds the menu items New, Open, a separator bar, Print, another separator bar, and Exit in this order into the File menu, as shown in Figure 9.20.

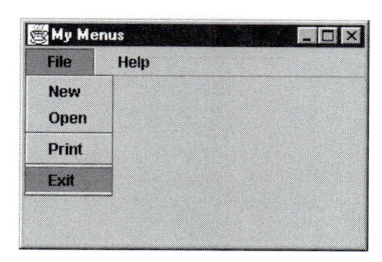

Figure 9.20 *Clicking a menu on the menu bar reveals the items under the menu.*

The `addSeparator()` method adds a separate bar in the menu.

3.1. Creating submenu items.

You can also embed menus inside menus so that the embedded menus become submenus. Here is an example:

```
JMenu softwareHelpSubMenu = new JMenu("Software");
JMenu hardwareHelpSubMenu = new JMenu("Hardware");
helpMenu.add(softwareHelpSubMenu);
```

```
helpMenu.add(hardwareHelpSubMenu);
softwareHelpSubMenu.add(new JMenuItem("Unix"));
softwareHelpSubMenu.add(new JMenuItem("NT"));
softwareHelpSubMenu.add(new JMenuItem("Win95"));
```

This code adds two submenus, `softwareHelpMenu` and `hardwareHelpMenu`, in `helpMenu`. The menu items `Unix`, `NT`, and `Win95` are added to `softwareHelpMenu` (see Figure 9.21).

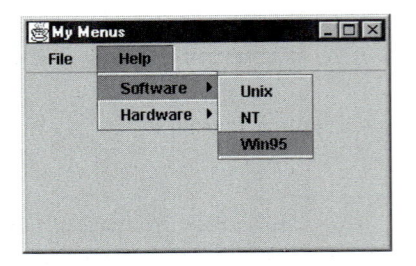

Figure 9.21 *Clicking a menu item reveals the secondary items under the menu item.*

3.2. Creating check box menu items.

You can also add a `JCheckBoxMenuItem` to a `JMenu`. `JCheckBoxMenuItem` is a subclass of `JMenuItem` that adds a Boolean state to the `JMenuItem`, and displays a check when its state is true. You can click the menu item to turn it on and off. For example, the following statement adds the check box menu item `Check it` (see Figure 9.22).

```
helpMenu.add(new JCheckBoxMenuItem("Check it"));)
```

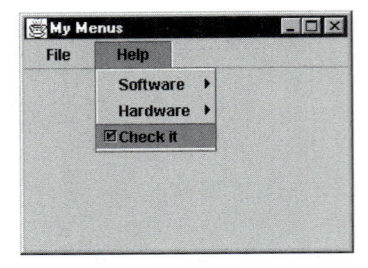

Figure 9.22 *A check box menu item lets you check or uncheck a menu item just like a check box.*

3.3. Creating radio button menu items.

You can also add radio buttons in a menu, using the `JRadioButtonMenuItem` class. This is often useful when you have a group of mutually exclusive choices in the menu. For example, the following statements add a submenu named Color and a set of radio buttons for choosing a color (see Figure 9.23):

```
JMenu colorHelpSubMenu = new JMenu("Color");
helpMenu.add(colorHelpSubMenu);

JRadioButtonMenuItem jrbmiBlue, jrbmiYellow, jrbmiRed;
colorHelpSubMenu.add(jrbmiBlue =
  new JRadioButtonMenuItem("Blue"));
colorHelpSubMenu.add(jrbmiYellow =
  new JRadioButtonMenuItem("Yellow"));
colorHelpSubMenu.add(jrbmiRed =
  new JRadioButtonMenuItem("Red"));

ButtonGroup btg = new ButtonGroup();
btg.add(jrbmiBlue);
btg.add(jrbmiYellow);
btg.add(jrbmiRed);
```

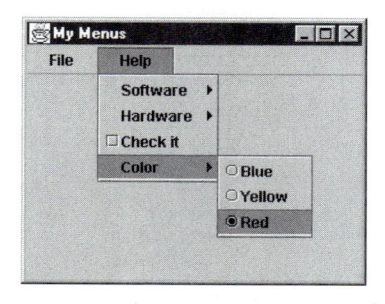

Figure 9.23   *You can use* `JRadioButtonMenuItem` *to choose a mutually exclusive menu choice.*

4. The menu items generate `ActionEvent`. Your program must implement the `actionPerformed()` handler to respond to the menu selection. The following is an example:

```
public void actionPerformed(ActionEvent e)
{
  String actionCommand = e.getActionCommand();

  // Make sure the source is JMenuItem
  if (e.getSource() instanceof JMenuItem)
    if ("New".equals(actionCommand))
      respondeToNew();
}
```

This code executes the method `respondToNew()` when the menu item labeled New is selected.

Image Icons, Keyboard Mnemonics, and Keyboard Accelerators

The menu components `JMenu`, `JMenuItem`, `JCheckBoxMenuItem`, and `JRadioButtonMenuItem` have the `icon` and `mnemonic` properties. For example, using the following code, you can set icons for the New and Open menu items, and set keyboard mnemonic for File, Help, New, and Open:

```
JMenuItem jmiNew, jmiOpen;
fileMenu.add(jmiNew = new JMenuItem("New"));
fileMenu.add(jmiOpen = new JMenuItem("Open"));
jmiNew.setIcon(new ImageIcon("images/new.gif"));
jmiOpen.setIcon(new ImageIcon("images/open.gif"));
helpMenu.setMnemonic('H');
fileMenu.setMnemonic('F');
jmiNew.setMnemonic('N');
jmiOpen.setMnemonic('O');
```

The new icons and mnemonics are shown in Figure 9.24. You can also use JMenuItem constructors like the ones that follow to construct and set an icon or mnemonic in one statement.

```
public JMenuItem(String label, Icon icon);
public JMenuItem(String label, int mnemonic);
```

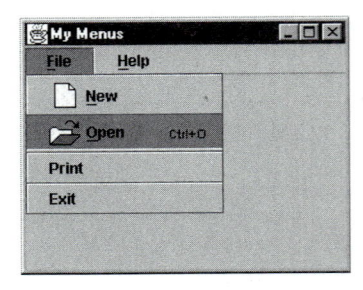

Figure 9.24 *You can set image icons, keyboard mnemonics, and keyboard accelerators in menus.*

To select a menu, you press the ALT key and the mnemonic key. For example, press ALT+F to select the File menu, and then press ALT+O to select the Open menu item. Keyboard mnemonics is useful, but it only lets you select menu items from the currently open menu. Key accelerators, however, let you select a menu item directly by pressing the CTRL and accelerator keys. For example, by using the following code, you can attach the accelerator key CTRL+O to the Open menu item:

```
jmiOpen.setAccelerator(KeyStroke.getKeyStroke
  (KeyEvent.VK_O, ActionEvent.CTRL_MASK));
```

The setAccelerator() method takes an object KeyStroke. The static method getKeyStroke() in the KeyStroke class creates an instance of the key stroke. VK_O is a constant representing the O key, and CTRL_MASK is a constant indicating that the CTRL key is associated with the keystroke.

Example 9.11 Using Menus

This example gives a program to create a user interface that does arithmetic. The interface contains labels and text fields for Number 1, Number 2, and Result. The Result text field displays the result of the arithmetic operation between Number 1 and Number 2.

The program has four buttons labeled Add, Subtract, Multiply, and Divide. The program will also create a menu to perform the same operation. The user can choose the operation either from buttons or from menu selections. Figure 9.25 contains a sample run of the program.

```java
// MenuDemo.java: Use menus to move message in a panel
import java.awt.*;
import java.awt.event.*;
import javax.swing.*;

public class MenuDemo extends MyFrameWithExitHandling
  implements ActionListener
{
  // Text fields for Number 1, Number 2, and Result
  private JTextField jtfNum1, jtfNum2, jtfResult;

  // Buttons "Add", "Subtract", "Multiply" and "Divide"
  private JButton jbtAdd, jbtSub, jbtMul, jbtDiv;

  // Menu items "Add", "Subtract", "Multiply","Divide" and "Close"
  private JMenuItem jmiAdd, jmiSub, jmiMul, jmiDiv, jmiClose;

  // Main Method
  public static void main(String[] args)
  {
    MenuDemo frame = new MenuDemo();
    frame.pack();
    frame.setVisible(true);
  }

  // Default Constructor
  public MenuDemo()
  {
    setTitle("Menu Demo");

    // Create menu bar
    JMenuBar jmb = new JMenuBar();

    // Set menu bar to the frame
    setJMenuBar(jmb);

    // Add menu "Operation" to menu bar
    JMenu operationMenu = new JMenu("Operation");
    operationMenu.setMnemonic('O');
    jmb.add(operationMenu);

    // Add menu "Exit" in menu bar
    JMenu exitMenu = new JMenu("Exit");
    exitMenu.setMnemonic('E');
    jmb.add(exitMenu);

    // Add menu items with mnemonics to menu "Operation"
    operationMenu.add(jmiAdd= new JMenuItem("Add", 'A'));
    operationMenu.add(jmiSub = new JMenuItem("Subtract", 'S'));
    operationMenu.add(jmiMul = new JMenuItem("Multiply", 'M'));
    operationMenu.add(jmiDiv = new JMenuItem("Divide", 'D'));
    exitMenu.add(jmiClose = new JMenuItem("Close", 'C'));

    // Set keyboard accelerators
    jmiAdd.setAccelerator(
      KeyStroke.getKeyStroke(KeyEvent.VK_A, ActionEvent.CTRL_MASK));
```

continues

```java
      jmiSub.setAccelerator(
        KeyStroke.getKeyStroke(KeyEvent.VK_S, ActionEvent.CTRL_MASK));
      jmiMul.setAccelerator(
        KeyStroke.getKeyStroke(KeyEvent.VK_M, ActionEvent.CTRL_MASK));
      jmiDiv.setAccelerator(
        KeyStroke.getKeyStroke(KeyEvent.VK_D, ActionEvent.CTRL_MASK));

      // Panel p1 to hold text fields and labels
      JPanel p1 = new JPanel();
      p1.setLayout(new FlowLayout());
      p1.add(new JLabel("Number 1"));
      p1.add(jtfNum1 = new JTextField(3));
      p1.add(new JLabel("Number 2"));
      p1.add(jtfNum2 = new JTextField(3));
      p1.add(new JLabel("Result"));
      p1.add(jtfResult = new JTextField(4));
      jtfResult.setEditable(false);

      // Panel p2 to hold buttons
      JPanel p2 = new JPanel();
      p2.setLayout(new FlowLayout());
      p2.add(jbtAdd = new JButton("Add"));
      p2.add(jbtSub = new JButton("Subtract"));
      p2.add(jbtMul = new JButton("Multiply"));
      p2.add(jbtDiv = new JButton("Divide"));

      // Add panels to the frame
      getContentPane().setLayout(new BorderLayout());
      getContentPane().add(p1, BorderLayout.CENTER);
      getContentPane().add(p2, BorderLayout.SOUTH);

      // Register listeners
      jbtAdd.addActionListener(this);
      jbtSub.addActionListener(this);
      jbtMul.addActionListener(this);
      jbtDiv.addActionListener(this);
      jmiAdd.addActionListener(this);
      jmiSub.addActionListener(this);
      jmiMul.addActionListener(this);
      jmiDiv.addActionListener(this);
      jmiClose.addActionListener(this);
    }

    // Handle ActionEvent from buttons and menu items
    public void actionPerformed(ActionEvent e)
    {
      String actionCommand = e.getActionCommand();

      // Handle button events
      if (e.getSource() instanceof JButton)
      {
        if ("Add".equals(actionCommand))
          calculate('+');
        else if ("Subtract".equals(actionCommand))
          calculate('-');
        else if ("Multiply".equals(actionCommand))
          calculate('*');
        else if ("Divide".equals(actionCommand))
          calculate('/');
      }
      else if (e.getSource() instanceof JMenuItem)
```

```java
      {
        // Handling menu item events
        if ("Add".equals(actionCommand))
          calculate('+');
        else if ("Subtract".equals(actionCommand))
          calculate('-');
        else if ("Multiply".equals(actionCommand))
          calculate('*');
        else if ("Divide".equals(actionCommand))
          calculate('/');
        else if ("Close".equals(actionCommand))
          System.exit(0);
      }
    }

    // Calculate and show the result in jtfResult
    private void calculate(char operator)
    {
      // Obtain Number 1 and Number 2
      int num1 = (Integer.parseInt(jtfNum1.getText().trim()));
      int num2 = (Integer.parseInt(jtfNum2.getText().trim()));
      int result = 0;

      // Perform selected operation
      switch (operator)
      {
        case '+': result = num1 + num2;
                  break;
        case '-': result = num1 - num2;
                  break;
        case '*': result = num1 * num2;
                  break;
        case '/': result = num1 / num2;
      }

      // Set result in jtfResult
      jtfResult.setText(String.valueOf(result));
    }
  }
```

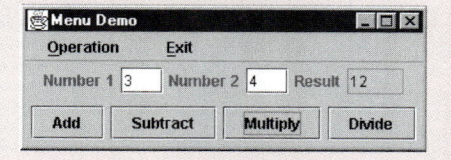

Figure 9.25 *Arithmetic operations can be performed by clicking buttons or by choosing menu items from the Operation menu.*

Example Review

The program creates a menu bar, `jmb`, which holds two menus: `operationMenu` and `exitMenu`. The `operationMenu` contains four menu items, Add, Subtract, Multiply, and Divide, for doing arithmetic. The `exitMenu` contains the menu item Close for exiting the program. The menu items in the Operation menu are created with keyboard mnemonics and accelerators.

continues

> The user enters two numbers in the number fields. When an operation is chosen from the menu, its result, involving two numbers, is displayed in the Result field. The user may also click the buttons to perform the same operation.
>
> The private method `calculate(char operator)` retrieves operands from the text fields in Number 1 and Number 2, applies the binary operator on the operands, and sets the result in the Result text field.

Creating Multiple Windows

Occasionally, you may want to create multiple windows in an application. Suppose that your application has two tasks: displaying traffic lights and doing arithmetic calculations. You can design a main frame with two buttons representing the two tasks. When the user clicks one of the buttons, the application opens a new window to perform the specified task. The new windows are called *subwindows,* and the main frame is called the *main window.*

To create a subwindow from an application, you usually need to create a subclass of `JFrame` that defines the task and tells the new window what to do. You can then create an instance of subclass in the application and launch the new window by setting the frame instance to be visible.

Example 9.12 Creating Multiple Windows

This example creates a main window with two buttons: Simple Calculator and Traffic Lights. When the user clicks Simple Calculator, a new window appears that lets the user perform add, subtract, multiply, and divide operations. When the user clicks Traffic Lights, another window appears that displays traffic lights.

The Simple Calculator frame named `MenuDemo` is given in Example 9.11, and the Traffic Lights frame named `RadioButtonDemo` is given in Example 9.8. They can be used directly in this example without modification.

Figure 9.26 contains the output of a sample run of the program.

```
// MultipleWindowsDemo.java: Use multiple windows in an application
import java.awt.*;
import java.awt.event.*;
import javax.swing.*;

public class MultipleWindowsDemo
  extends MyFrameWithExitHandling implements ActionListener
{
  // Declare and create a frame: an instance of MenuDemo
  MenuDemo calcFrame = new MenuDemo();

  // Declare and create a frame: an instance of RadioButtonDemo
  RadioButtonDemo lightsFrame = new RadioButtonDemo();

  // Declare two buttons for displaying frames
  private JButton jbtCalc;
  private JButton jbtLights;
```

```java
public static void main(String[] args)
{
  MultipleWindowsDemo frame = new MultipleWindowsDemo();
  frame.pack();
  frame.setVisible(true);
}

public MultipleWindowsDemo()
{
  setTitle("Multiple Windows Demo");

  // Add buttons to the main frame
  getContentPane().setLayout(new FlowLayout());
  getContentPane().add(jbtCalc = new JButton("Simple Calculator"));
  getContentPane().add(jbtLights = new JButton("Traffic Lights"));

  // Register the main frame as listener for the buttons
  jbtCalc.addActionListener(this);
  jbtLights.addActionListener(this);
}

public void actionPerformed(ActionEvent e)
{
  String actionCommand = e.getActionCommand();
  if (e.getSource() instanceof JButton)
    if ("Simple Calculator".equals(actionCommand))
    {
      // Show the MenuDemo frame
      calcFrame.pack();
      calcFrame.setVisible(true);
    }
    else if ("Traffic Lights".equals(actionCommand))
    {
      // Show the traffic light demo frame
      lightsFrame.pack();
      lightsFrame.setVisible(true);
    }
}
}
```

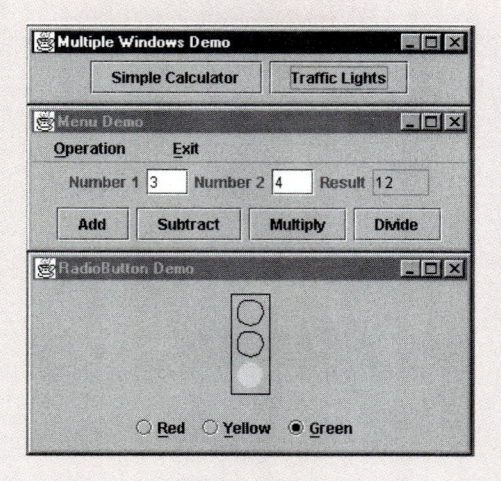

Figure 9.26 *Multiple windows can be displayed simultaneously, as shown in this program.*

continues

Example Review

The program creates `calcFrame` to be an instance of `MenuDemo`, and creates `lightsFrame` to be an instance of `RadioButtonDemo`. The classes `MenuDemo` and `RadioButtonDemo` are given in Examples 9.11 and 9.8, respectively.

The program creates two buttons—Simple Calculator and Traffic Lights—and adds them to the main frame. When a button is clicked, the `ActionEvent` handler determines which source object triggered the event. If the source object is the Simple Calculator button, the window for performing arithmetic calculations is launched with `calcFrame.pack()` and `calcFrame.setVisible(true)`. If the source object is the Traffic Lights button, the window for displaying lights is launched.

Interestingly, the `MenuDemo` class and the `RadioButtonDemo` class are used in this application without any changes. What about the `main()` method in the `MenuDemo` and in the `RadioButtonDemo`? The `main()` method is ignored because the bytecode for `MenuDemo` or `RadioButtonDemo` is not directly invoked by the Java interpreter.

The program has an annoying problem. When you close a subwindow, the whole program exits. This is because the subwindows are frames that extend `MyFrameWithExitHandling`. Can the new windows be closed without terminating the whole program? There are several ways to fix the problem.

One way is to replace `system.exit(0)` in `MyFrameWithExitHandling` with `setVisible(false)`, which in effect closes the subwindow but does not terminate the main frame. The other approach is to change the label of the buttons in the main frame. For example, when you click the Simple Calculator button, the Calculator window appears, and the name of the button changes to Hide Calculator. When you click the Hide Calculator button, the window is closed and the name of the button changes back to Simple Calculator (see Exercise 9.8).

> ■ **CAUTION**
> You cannot add an instance of `JFrame` to a container. For example, adding `calcFrame` or `lightsFrame` to the main frame would cause a runtime exception. However, you can create a frame instance and set it to be visible to launch a new window.

Scrollbars

A *scrollbar* is a control that enables the user to select from a range of values. Scrollbars appear in two styles, *horizontal* and *vertical,* as shown in Figure 9.27.

You can use the following constructors to create a scrollbar:

■ `public JScrollBar()`

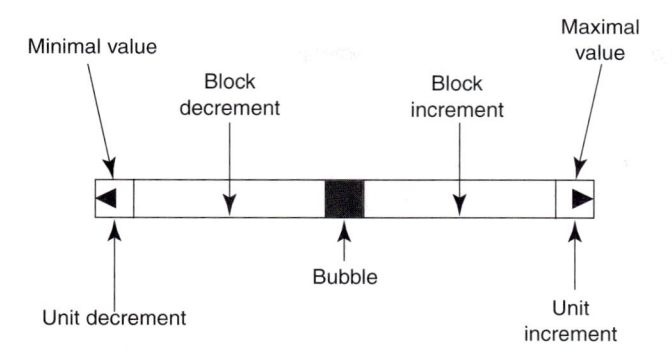

Figure 9.27 *A scrollbar represents a range of values graphically.*

This constructs a new vertical scrollbar.

- `public JScrollBar(int orientation)`

  This constructs a new scrollbar with the specified orientation (`JScrollBar.HORIZONTAL` or `JScrollBar.VERTICAL`).

- `public JScrollbar(int orientation, int value, int visible, int minimum, int maximum)`

  This constructs a new scrollbar with the specified orientation, initial value, visible bubble size, and minimum and maximum values.

`JScrollBar` has the following properties:

- `orientation`—Specifies horizontal or vertical style, with `JScrollBar.HORIZONTAL` (0) for horizontal and `JScrollBar.VERTICAL` (1) for vertical.

- `maximum`—The maximum value the scrollbar represents when the bubble reaches the right end of the scrollbar for horizontal style or the bottom of the scrollbar for vertical style.

- `minimum`—The minimum value the scrollbar represents when the bubble reaches the left end of the scrollbar for horizontal style or the top of the scrollbar for vertical style.

- `visibleAmount`—The relative width of the scrollbar's bubble. The actual width appearing on the screen is determined by the maximum value and the value of `visibleAmount`.

- `value`—Represents the current value of the scrollbar. Normally, a program should change a scrollbar's value by calling the `setValue()` method. The `setValue()` method simultaneously and synchronously sets the minimum, maximum, visible amount, and value properties of a scrollbar, so that they are mutually consistent.

- `blockIncrement`—The value added (subtracted) when the user activates the block increment (decrement) area of the scrollbar, as shown in Figure 9.27.

The `blockIncrement` property, which is new in JDK 1.1, supersedes the `pageIncrement` property used in JDK 1.02.

- **`unitIncrement`**—The value added (subtracted) when the user activates the unit increment (decrement) area of the scrollbar, as shown in Figure 9.27. The `unitIncrement` property, which is new in JDK 1.1, supersedes the `lineIncrement` property used in JDK 1.02.

> **NOTE**
> The actual width of the scrollbar's track is `maximum+visibleAmount`. When the scrollbar is set to its maximum value, the left side of the bubble is at `maximum`, and the right side is at `maximum+visibleAmount`.

Normally, the user changes the value of the scrollbar by making a gesture with the mouse. For example, the user can drag the scrollbar's bubble up and down, or click in the scrollbar's unit increment or block increment areas. Keyboard gestures can also be mapped to the scrollbar. By convention, the Page Up and Page Down keys are equivalent to clicking in the scrollbar's block increment and block decrement areas.

When the user changes the value of the scrollbar, the scrollbar generates an instance of `AdjustmentEvent`, which is passed to any registered listeners. An object that wishes to be notified of changes to the scrollbar's value should implement `adjustmentValueChanged()` method in the `AdjustmentListener` interface defined in the package `java.awt.event`.

Example 9.13 Using Scrollbars

This example uses horizontal and vertical scrollbars to control a message displayed on a panel. The horizontal scrollbar is used to move the message to the left or the right, and the vertical scrollbar to move it up and down. The sample run of the program is shown in Figure 9.28.

```java
// ScrollBarDemo.java: Use scrollbars to move the message
import java.awt.*;
import java.awt.event.*;
import javax.swing.*;

public class ScrollBarDemo extends MyFrameWithExitHandling
  implements AdjustmentListener
{
  // Declare scrollbars
  JScrollBar jscbHort, jscbVert;

  // Declare a MessagePanel
  MessagePanel messagePanel;

  // Main method
  public static void main(String[] args)
```

```java
    {
      ScrollBarDemo frame = new ScrollBarDemo();
      frame.pack();
      frame.setVisible(true);
    }

    // Constructor
    public ScrollBarDemo()
    {
      setTitle("ScrollBar Demo");

      // Create a vertical scrollbar
      jscbVert = new JScrollBar();
      jscbVert.setOrientation(Adjustable.VERTICAL);

      // Create a horizontal scrollbar
      jscbHort = new JScrollBar();
      jscbHort.setOrientation(Adjustable.HORIZONTAL);

      // Add scrollbars and message panel to the frame
      messagePanel = new MessagePanel("Welcome to Java");
      getContentPane().setLayout(new BorderLayout());
      getContentPane().add(messagePanel, BorderLayout.CENTER);
      getContentPane().add(jscbVert, BorderLayout.EAST);
      getContentPane().add(jscbHort, BorderLayout.SOUTH);

      // Register listener for the scrollbars
      jscbHort.addAdjustmentListener(this);
      jscbVert.addAdjustmentListener(this);
    }

    // Handler for scrollbar adjustment actions
    public void adjustmentValueChanged(AdjustmentEvent e)
    {
      if (e.getSource() == jscbHort)
      {
        // getValue() and getMaximumValue() return int, but for better
        // precision, use double
        double value = jscbHort.getValue();
        double maximumValue = jscbHort.getMaximum();
        double newX = (value*messagePanel.getSize().width/
          maximumValue);
        messagePanel.setXCoordinate((int)newX);
        messagePanel.repaint();
      }
      else if (e.getSource() == jscbVert)
      {
        // getValue() and getMaximumValue() return int, but for better
        // precision, use double
        double value = jscbVert.getValue();
        double maximumValue = jscbVert.getMaximum();
        double newY = (value*messagePanel.getSize().height/
          maximumValue);
        messagePanel.setYCoordinate((int)newY);
        messagePanel.repaint();
      }
    }
}
```

continues

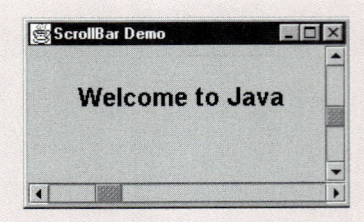

Figure 9.28 *The scrollbars move the message on a panel horizontally and vertically.*

Example Review

The program creates an instance of `MessagePanel` (`messagePanel`) and two scrollbars (`jscbVert` and `jscbHort`). `messagePanel` is placed in the center of the frame; `jscbVert` and `jscbHort` are placed in the east and south sections of the frame, respectively.

You can specify the orientation of the scrollbar in the constructor or use the `setOrientation()` method. By default, the property value for `maximum` is 100, for `minimum` is 0, for `pageIncrement` is 10, and for `visibleAmount` is 10.

When the user drags the bubble, or clicks the increment or decrement unit, the value of the scrollbar changes. An instance of `AdjustmentEvent` is generated and passed to the listener by invoking the `adjustmentValueChanged` handler. Since there are two scrollbars in the frame, the `e.getSource()` method is used to determine the source of the event. The vertical scrollbar moves the message up and down, and the horizontal bar moves the message to right and left.

The maximum value of the vertical scrollbar corresponds to the height of the panel, and the maximum value of the horizontal scrollbar corresponds to the width of the panel. The ratio between current value and the maximum of the horizontal scrollbar is the same as the ratio between the x value and the width of the panel. Similarly, the ratio between current value and the maximum of the vertical scrollbar is the same as the ratio between the y value and the height of the panel.

Scroll Panes

Often you need to use a scrollbar to scroll the contents of an object that cannot be completely fit into the viewing area. `JScrollBar` can be used for this purpose, but you have to *manually* write the code to implement scrolling with it. `JScrollPane` is a component that supports *automatic* scrolling without coding. It was used to scroll text area in Example 9.4. In fact, it can be used to scroll any subclass of `JComponent`.

A `JScrollPane` can be viewed as a specialized container with a view port for displaying the contained component. In addition to horizontal and vertical scrollbars, a `JScrollPane` can have a column header, a row header, and corners, as shown in Figure 9.29.

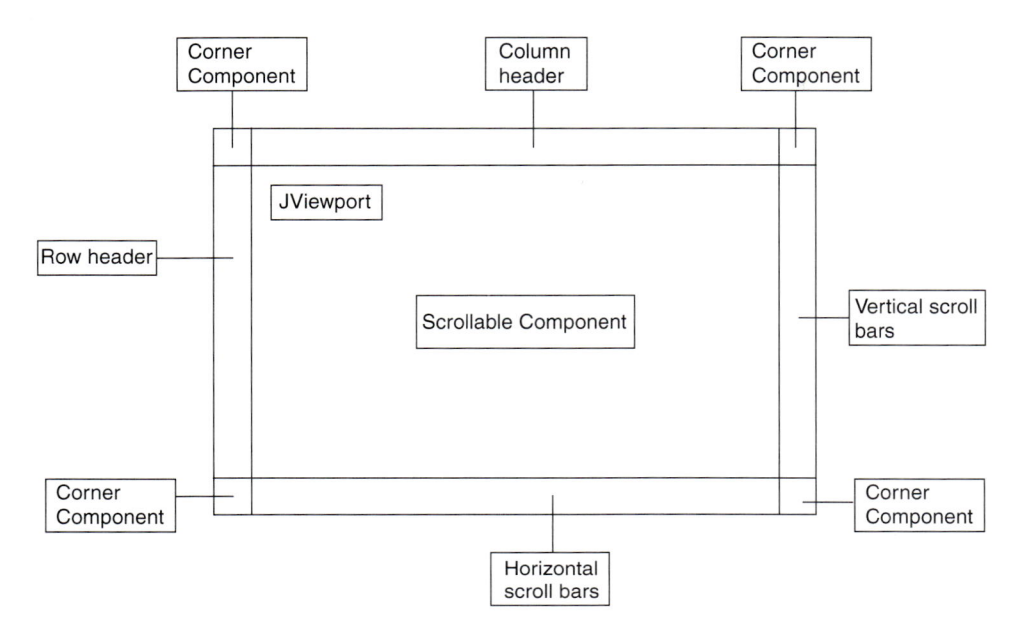

Figure 9.29 *A* `JScrollPane` *has a view port, optional horizontal and vertical bars, optional column and row headers, and optional corners.*

The view port is an instance of `JViewport` through which a scrollable component is displayed. When you add a component to the scroll pane, you are actually placing it in the scroll pane's view port.

To construct a `JScrollPane` instance, use the following constructors:

- `public JScrollPane()`

    Creates an empty scroll pane with a view port and no viewing component where both horizontal and vertical scrollbars appear when needed.

- `public JScrollPane(Component view)`

    Creates a scroll pane and view port to display the contents of the specified component, where both horizontal and vertical scrollbars appear whenever the component's contents are larger than the view.

- `JScrollPane(Component view, int vsbPolicy, int hsbPolicy)`

    Creates a scroll pane that displays the view component in a view port whose view position can be controlled with a pair of scrollbars.

- `JScrollPane(int vsbPolicy, int hsbPolicy)`

    Creates an empty scroll pane with specified scrollbar policies.

The constructor always creates a view port regardless of whether the viewing component is specified. The `vsbPolicy` parameter can be one of the following three values:

- `JScrollPane.VERTICAL_SCROLLBAR_AS_NEEDED`
- `JScrollPane.VERTICAL_SCROLLBAR_NEVER`

- `JScrollPane.VERTICAL_SCROLLBAR_ALWAYS`

The `hsbPolicy` parameter can be one of the following three values:

- `JScrollPane.HORIZONTAL_SCROLLBAR_AS_NEEDED`
- `JScrollPane.HORIZONTAL_SCROLLBAR_NEVER`
- `JScrollPane.HORIZONTAL_SCROLLBAR_ALWAYS`

The following properties of `JScrollPane` are often useful:

- `horizontalScrollBarPolicy`—Determines when the horizontal scrollbar appears in the scroll pane.
- `verticalScrollBarPolicy`—Determines when the vertical scrollbar appears in the scroll pane.
- `viewportView`—Specifies the component to be viewed in the view port.
- `viewportBorder`—Specifies a border around the view port in the scroll pane.
- `rowHeaderView`—Specifies the row header view component to be used in the scroll pane.
- `columnHeaderView`—Specifies the column header view component to be used in the scroll pane.

To set a corner component, use the following method:

```
public void setCorner(String key,
                      Component corner)
```

The legal values for the key are:

- `JScrollPane.LOWER_LEFT_CORNER`
- `JScrollPane.LOWER_RIGHT_CORNER`
- `JScrollPane.UPPER_LEFT_CORNER`
- `JScrollPane.UPPER_RIGHT_CORNER`

Example 9.14 Using Scroll Panes

This example uses a scroll pane to browse a large map. The program lets you choose a map from a combo box and display it in the scroll pane, as shown in Figure 9.30.

```java
// ScrollPaneDemo.java: Use scroll pane to view large maps
import java.awt.*;
import java.awt.event.*;
import javax.swing.*;
import javax.swing.border.*;

public class ScrollPaneDemo extends MyFrameWithExitHandling
  implements ItemListener
```

```java
{
  // Create images in labels
  private JLabel lblIndianaMap =
    new JLabel(new ImageIcon("images/indianaMap.gif"));
  private JLabel lblOhioMap =
    new JLabel(new ImageIcon("images/ohioMap.gif"));

  // Declare a scroll pane to scroll map in the labels
  private JScrollPane jspMap;

  // Main method
  public static void main(String[] args)
  {
    ScrollPaneDemo frame = new ScrollPaneDemo();
    frame.setSize(300, 300);
    frame.setVisible(true);
  }

  // Default constructor
  public ScrollPaneDemo()
  {
    setTitle("ScrollPane Demo");

    // Create a scroll pane with northern California map
    jspMap = new JScrollPane(lblIndianaMap);

    // Create a combo box for selecting maps
    JComboBox jcboMap = new JComboBox();
    jcboMap.addItem("Indiana");
    jcboMap.addItem("Ohio");

    // Panel p to hold combo box
    JPanel p = new JPanel();
    p.setLayout(new BorderLayout());
    p.add(jcboMap);
    p.setBorder(new TitledBorder("Select a map to display"));

    // Set row header, column header and corner header
    jspMap.setColumnHeaderView(
      new JLabel(new ImageIcon("images/horizontalRuler.gif")));
    jspMap.setRowHeaderView(
      new JLabel(new ImageIcon("images/verticalRuler.gif")));
    jspMap.setCorner(JScrollPane.UPPER_LEFT_CORNER,
      new CornerPanel(JScrollPane.UPPER_LEFT_CORNER));
    jspMap.setCorner(ScrollPaneConstants.UPPER_RIGHT_CORNER,
      new CornerPanel(JScrollPane.UPPER_RIGHT_CORNER));
    jspMap.setCorner(JScrollPane.LOWER_RIGHT_CORNER,
      new CornerPanel(JScrollPane.LOWER_RIGHT_CORNER));
    jspMap.setCorner(JScrollPane.LOWER_LEFT_CORNER,
      new CornerPanel(JScrollPane.LOWER_LEFT_CORNER));

    // Add the scroll pane and combo box panel to the frame
    getContentPane().add(jspMap, BorderLayout.CENTER);
    getContentPane().add(p, BorderLayout.NORTH);

    // Register listener
    jcboMap.addItemListener(this);
  }
```

continues

```java
    public void itemStateChanged(ItemEvent e)
    {
      String selectedItem = (String)e.getItem();
      if (selectedItem.equals("Indiana"))
      {
        // Set a new view in the view port
        jspMap.setViewportView(lblIndianaMap);
      }
      else if (selectedItem.equals("Ohio"))
      {
        // Set a new view in the view port
        jspMap.setViewportView(lblOhioMap);
      }

      // Revalidate the scroll pane
      jspMap.revalidate();
    }
  }

  // A panel displaying a line used for scroll pane corner
  class CornerPanel extends JPanel implements ScrollPaneConstants
  {
    // Line location
    private String location;

    // Constructor
    public CornerPanel(String location)
    {
      this.location = location;
    }

    // Draw a line depending on the location
    public void paintComponent(Graphics g)
    {
      super.paintComponents(g);

      if (location == "UPPER_LEFT_CORNER")
        g.drawLine(0, getSize().height, getSize().width, 0);
      else if (location == "UPPER_RIGHT_CORNER")
        g.drawLine(0, 0, getSize().width, getSize().height);
      else if (location == "LOWER_RIGHT_CORNER")
        g.drawLine(0, getSize().height, getSize().width, 0);
      else if (location == "LOWER_LEFT_CORNER")
        g.drawLine(0, 0, getSize().width, getSize().height);
    }
  }
}
```

Example Review

The program creates a scroll pane to view image maps. The image maps are created using the ImageIcon class and placed in labels. To view an image, the label that contains the image is placed in the scroll pane's view port.

The scroll pane has a main view, a header view, a column view, and four corner views. Each view is a subclass of Component. Since ImageIcon is not a subclass of Component, it cannot be directly used as a view in the scroll pane. Instead the program places an ImageIcon to a label and uses the label as a view.

Figure 9.30 *The scroll pane can be used to scroll contents automatically.*

The `CornerPanel` is a subclass of `JPanel`, which is used to display a line. How the line is drawn depends on the `location` of the corner. The `location` is a string, passed in as a parameter in the `CornerPanel`'s constructor. The `CornerPanel` class also implements the `ScrollPaneConstants` interface. The constants indicating the four corners are available in `CornerPanel`.

Whenever a new map is selected, the label for displaying the map image is set to the scroll pane's view port. The `validate()` method must be invoked to cause the new image to be displayed. The `validate()` method causes a container to lay out its subcomponents again after the components it contains have been added to or modified.

Tabbed Panes

`JTabbedPane` is a useful Swing component that provides a set of mutually exclusive tabs for accessing multiple components. Usually you place the panels inside a `JTabbedPane` and associate a tab with each panel. `JTabbedPane` is easy to use, since the selection of the panel is handled automatically by clicking the corresponding tab. You can switch between a group of panels by clicking on a tab with a given title and/or icon.

To construct a `JTabbedPane` instance, use the following constructors:

- `public JTabbedPane()`

    Creates an empty tabbed pane.

- `public JTabbedPane(int tabPlacement)`

    Creates an empty `JTabbedPane` with the specified tab placement of either `SwingConstants.TOP`, `SwingConstants.BOTTOM`, `SwingConstants.LEFT`, or `SwingConstants.RIGHT`.

You can also set the tab placement using the following method:

```
public void setTabPlacement(int tabPlacement)
```

By default, the tabs are placed at top.

To add a component to a JTabbedPane, use the following add() method:

```
add(Component component, Object constraints)
```

Where component is the component to be displayed when this tab is clicked and constraints can be a title for the tab.

Example 9.15 Using Tabbed Panes

This example uses a tabbed pane with four tabs to display four types of figures: Square, Rectangle, Circle, and Oval. You click the corresponding tab to select a figure to be displayed. You can also use the radio buttons to specify the tab placement. A sample run of the program is shown in Figure 9.31.

```java
// TabbedPaneDemo.java: Use tabbed pane to select figures
import java.awt.*;
import java.awt.event.*;
import javax.swing.*;
import javax.swing.border.TitledBorder;

public class TabbedPaneDemo extends MyFrameWithExitHandling
  implements ItemListener
{
  // Create a tabbed pane to hold figure panels
  private JTabbedPane jtpFigures = new JTabbedPane();

  // Radio buttons for specifying where tab is placed
  private JRadioButton jrbTop, jrbLeft, jrbRight, jrbBottom;

  // Main method
  public static void main(String[] args)
  {
    TabbedPaneDemo frame = new TabbedPaneDemo();
    frame.setSize(200, 300);
    frame.center();
    frame.setVisible(true);
  }

  // Constructor
  public TabbedPaneDemo()
  {
    setTitle("Tabbed Pane Demo");

    jtpFigures.add(new FigurePanel(FigurePanel.SQUARE), "Square");
    jtpFigures.add(
      new FigurePanel(FigurePanel.RECTANGLE), "Rectangle");
    jtpFigures.add(new FigurePanel(FigurePanel.CIRCLE), "Circle");
    jtpFigures.add(new FigurePanel(FigurePanel.OVAL), "Oval");

    // Panel p to hold radio buttons for specifying tab location
    JPanel p = new JPanel();
    p.add(jrbTop = new JRadioButton("TOP"));
```

```java
      p.add(jrbLeft = new JRadioButton("LEFT"));
      p.add(jrbRight = new JRadioButton("RIGHT"));
      p.add(jrbBottom = new JRadioButton("BOTTOM"));
      p.setBorder(new TitledBorder("Specify tab location"));

      // Group radio buttons
      ButtonGroup btg = new ButtonGroup();
      btg.add(jrbTop);
      btg.add(jrbLeft);
      btg.add(jrbRight);
      btg.add(jrbBottom);

      // Place tabbed pane and panel p into the frame
      this.getContentPane().add(jtpFigures, BorderLayout.CENTER);
      this.getContentPane().add(p, BorderLayout.SOUTH);

      // Register listeners
      jrbTop.addItemListener(this);
      jrbLeft.addItemListener(this);
      jrbRight.addItemListener(this);
      jrbBottom.addItemListener(this);
    }

    // Handling radio button selection
    public void itemStateChanged(ItemEvent e)
    {
      if (jrbTop.isSelected())
        jtpFigures.setTabPlacement(SwingConstants.TOP);
      else if (jrbLeft.isSelected())
        jtpFigures.setTabPlacement(SwingConstants.LEFT);
      else if (jrbRight.isSelected())
        jtpFigures.setTabPlacement(SwingConstants.RIGHT);
      else if (jrbBottom.isSelected())
        jtpFigures.setTabPlacement(SwingConstants.BOTTOM);
    }
}

// The panel for displaying a figure
class FigurePanel extends JPanel
{
  final static int SQUARE = 1;
  final static int RECTANGLE = 2;
  final static int CIRCLE = 3;
  final static int OVAL = 4;
  private int figureType = 1;

  // Constructing a figure panel
  public FigurePanel(int figureType)
  {
    this.figureType = figureType;
  }

  // Drawing a figure on the panel
  public void paintComponent(Graphics g)
  {
    super.paintComponent(g);

    // Get the appropriate size for the figure
    int width = getSize().width;
    int height = getSize().height;
    int side = (int)(0.80*Math.min(width, height));
```

continues

```
          switch (figureType)
          {
            case 1:
              g.drawRect((width-side)/2, (height-side)/2, side, side);
              break;
            case 2:
              g.drawRect((int)(0.1*width), (int)(0.1*height),
                (int)(0.8*width), (int)(0.8*height));
              break;
            case 3:
              g.drawOval((width-side)/2, (height-side)/2, side, side);
              break;
            case 4:
              g.drawOval((int)(0.1*width), (int)(0.1*height),
                (int)(0.8*width), (int)(0.8*height));
              break;
          }
        }
      }
```

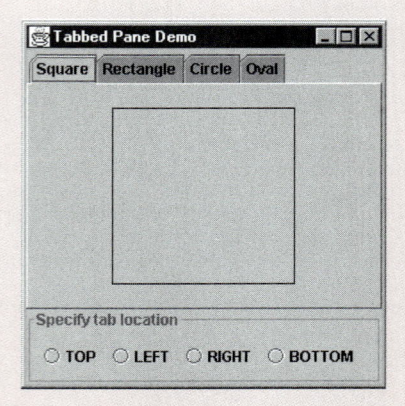

Figure 9.31 *A tabbed pane can be used to access multiple components using tabs.*

Example Review

The program creates a tabbed pane that holds four panels, each of which displays a figure. A panel is associated with a tab. Tabs are created using the `add()` method and are titled Square, Rectangle, Circle, and Oval.

By default, the tabs are placed at the top of the tabbed pane. You can use the radio button to select a different placement, as shown in Figure 9.32.

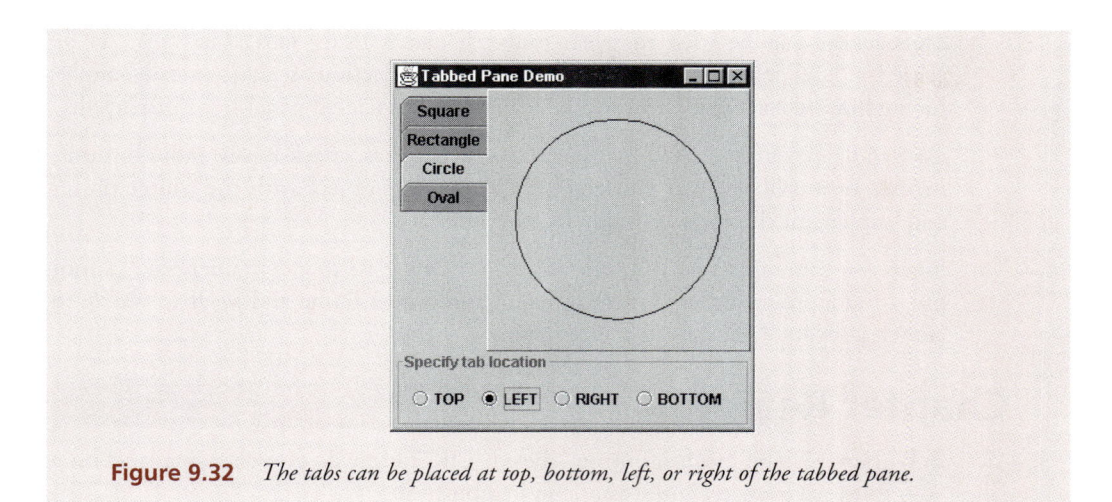

Figure 9.32 *The tabs can be placed at top, bottom, left, or right of the tabbed pane.*

Chapter Summary

In this chapter, you learned how to create graphical user interfaces using `JButton`, `JLabel`, `JTextField`, `JTextArea`, `JComboBox`, `JList`, `JCheckBox`, `JRadioButton`, Border (`TitledBorder`, `BevelBorder`, `LineBorder`, `EtchedBorder`, `MatteBorder`, and `EmptyBorder`), message dialog boxes, `JMenuBar`, `JMenu`, `JMenuItem`, `JCheckBoxMenuItem`, `JRadioButtonMenuItem`, `JScrollBar`, and `JScrollPane`.

`JButton` is used to activate actions. The user expects something to happen when a button is clicked. Clicking a button generates the `ActionEvent` and invokes the listener to invoke the `actionPerformed()` method.

`JLabel` is an area for displaying texts or images, or both. `JTextField` is used to accept user input into a string. `JTextArea` can accept multiple lines of strings.

`JComboBox` is a simple list of values to choose from. `JList` allows multiple selections. `JCheckBox` is for specifying whether the item is selected or not. `JRadioButton` is similar to `JCheckBox`, but is generally used to select a value exclusively.

A dialog box is commonly used to gather information from the user or show information to the user. This chapter introduced the `showMessageDialog()` method in the `JOptionPane` class, which can be used to display a simple message box.

Menus can be placed in a frame or an applet. A menu bar is used to hold the menus. You must add a menu bar to the frame or applet using the `setJMenuBar()` method, add menus to the menu bar, and add menu items to a menu.

Scrollbars are the controls for selecting from a range of values. You can create scrollbars using the `JScrollBar` class and specify horizontal or vertical scrollbars using the `setOrientation()` method. `JScrollPane` provides automatical scrolling, so it is convenient to use in most cases.

`JTabbedPane` can be used to select multiple panels using tabs. The tabs can be placed at top, left, right, or bottom. Since tab selection is automatically implemented in `JTabbedPane`, clicking a tab causes the associated panel to be displayed.

To handle events generated by buttons, combo boxes, check boxes, radio buttons, menus, or scrollbars, you must register the listener object with the source object and implement the corresponding listener interface.

Since you cannot add an instance of the Window class to a container, you cannot put a frame into a frame. However, you can create a frame and set it to visible to launch a separate window in the program.

Chapter Review

9.1. How do you create a button labeled "OK"? How do you change a label on a button? How do you set an icon in a button?

9.2. How do you create a label named "Address"? How do you change the name on a label? How do you set an icon in a label?

9.3. How do you create a text field with a width of 10 characters and the default text "Welcome to Java"?

9.4 How do you create a text area with 10 rows and 20 columns? How do you insert three lines into the text area? How do you create a scrollable text area?

9.5. How do you create a combo box, add three items to it, and retrieve a selected item?

9.6. How do you create a check box? How do you determine whether a box is checked?

9.7. How do you create a radio button? How do you group the radio buttons together? How do you determine whether a radio button is selected?

9.8. Can you have a border for any subclass of `JComponent`? How do you set a titled border for a panel?

9.9. How do you create the menus File, Edit, View, Insert, Format, and Help, and add menu items Toolbar, Format Bar, Ruler, Status Bar, and Options to the View menu? (See Figure 9.33.)

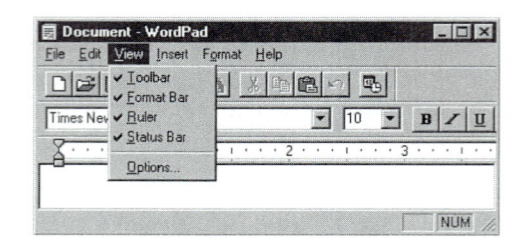

Figure 9.33 *Create a menu like this in WordPad, with menus and menu items.*

9.10. How do you create a vertical scrollbar? What event can a scrollbar generate?

9.11. How do you create a scroll pane to view an image file?

9.12. Describe how to create a simple message dialog box. Describe the message types used in the `JOptionPane` class.

9.13. Describe how to create and show multiple frames in an application.

9.14. What method causes the layout manager to lay out the components in a container again? When should a container be laid out again?

9.15. Suppose you want to display the same component named c in the four corners of a scroll pane named jsp. What would be wrong with using the following statements?

```
jsp.setCorner(JScrollPane.UPPER_LEFT_CORNER, c);
jsp.setCorner(JScrollPane.UPPER_RIGHT_CORNER, c);
jsp.setCorner(JScrollPane.LOWER_RIGHT_CORNER, c);
jsp.setCorner(JScrollPane.LOWER_LEFT_CORNER, c);
```

(Since each corner view is an individual component, you need to create four separate objects.)

Programming Exercises

9.1. Rewrite Example 9.1 to add a group of radio buttons to select background colors. The available colors are red, yellow, white, gray, and green (see Figure 9.34).

Figure 9.34 *The <= and => buttons move the message on the panel, and you can also set the color for the message.*

9.2. Rewrite Example 9.3 to handle double values and perform subtract, multiply, and divide operations in addition to the add operation (see Figure 9.35).

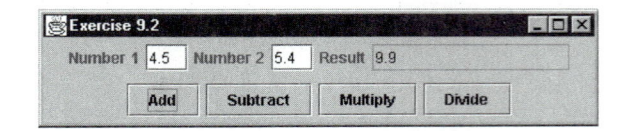

Figure 9.35 *The program does addition, subtraction, multiplication, and division on double numbers.*

9.3. Write a program that meets the following requirements:

- Create a text field, a text area, and a combo box in a panel using `FlowLayout`.
- Create a button labeled Store and place it in a panel using `FlowLayout`.
- Place the preceding two panels in a frame.
- The action of the Store button is to retrieve the item from the text field and store it in a text area or a combo box.
- When an item in the combo box is selected, it is displayed in the text field.

9.4. Write a program that converts Celsius and Fahrenheit temperatures, as shown in Figure 9.36. If you enter a value in the Celsius degree text field and press the Enter key, the Fahrenheit temperature is displayed in the Fahrenheit text field. Likewise, if you enter a value in the Fahrenheit degree text field, the corresponding Celsius degree is displayed in the Celsius text field.

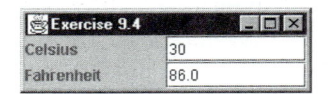

Figure 9.36 *The program converts Celsius to Fahrenheit, and vice versa.*

9.5. Write a program that draws various figures on a panel. The user selects a figure from a radio button. The selected figure is then displayed on the panel (see Figure 9.37).

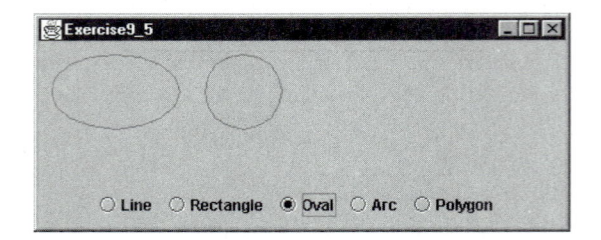

Figure 9.37 *The program displays lines, rectangles, ovals, arcs, or polygons when you select a shape type.*

9.6. Write a program that calculates the future value of an investment at a given interest rate for a specified number of years. The formula for the calculation is as follows:

$$futureValue = investmentAmount \times (1 + interestRate)^{years}$$

Use text fields for interest rate, investment amount, and years. Display the future amount in a text field when the user clicks the Calculate button or chooses Calculate from the Operation menu (see Figure 9.38). Show a message dialog box when the user clicks the About menu item from the Help menu.

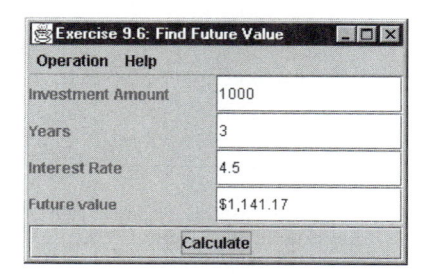

Figure 9.38 *The user enters the investment amount, years, and interest rate to compute future value.*

9.7. Use `JTabbedPane` to write a program to display flags for USA, UK, Germany, Canada, China, and India (see Figure 9.39).

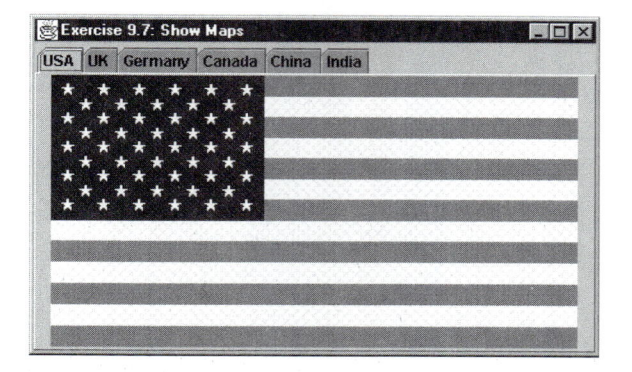

Figure 9.39 *You can show the map by selecting a tab in the tabbed pane.*

9.8. Rewrite Example 9.12, "Creating Multiple Windows," as follows:

- When the user clicks the Simple Calculator button, the Calculator window appears and the name of the button changes to Hide Calculator. When the user clicks the Hide Calculator button, the window is closed, and the name of the button changes back to Simple Calculator.

- Modify the function of the Traffic Lights button in the same way as in the preceding item.

9.9. Write a program that uses the scrollbars to select the foreground color for a label, as shown in Figure 9.40. Three horizontal scrollbars are used for selecting red, green, and blue components of the color. Use a title border on the panel that holds the scrollbars.

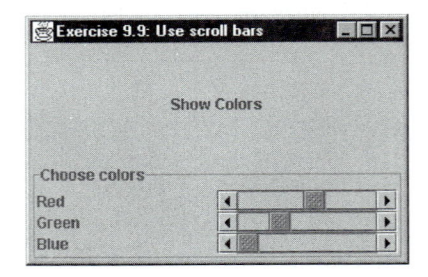

Figure 9.40 *The foreground color changes in the label as you adjust the scrollbars.*

9.10. Write a program that computes sales amount or commission, as shown in Figure 9.41. When the user types a sales amount in the Sales Amount text field and presses the Enter key, the commission is displayed in the Commission text field. Likewise, when the user types a commission, the corresponding sales amount is displayed. The commission rates are the same as in Example 3.7, "Finding Sales Amount." The commission rates are displayed using labels.

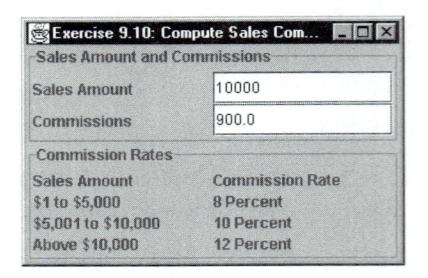

Figure 9.41 *The sales amount and the commission are synchronized. You can compute sales amount given the commission or compute commission given the sales amount.*

9.11. Write a program that sets the alignment and text position properties of a button dynamically, as shown in Figure 9.42.

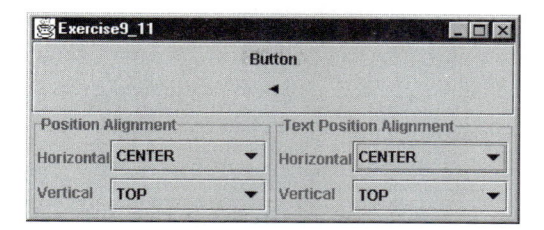

Figure 9.42 *You can set the alignment and text position properties of a button dynamically.*

9.12. Write a program that sets the horizontal alignment and column size properties of a text field dynamically, as shown in Figure 9.43.

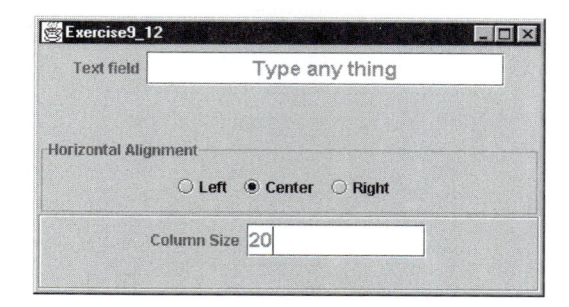

Figure 9.43 *You can set the horizontal alignment and column size properties of a text field dynamically.*

9.13. Write a program that demonstrates the wrapping styles of the text area. The program uses a check box to indicate whether the text area is wrapped. In the case where the text area is wrapped, you need to specify whether it is wrapped by characters or by words, as shown in Figure 9.44.

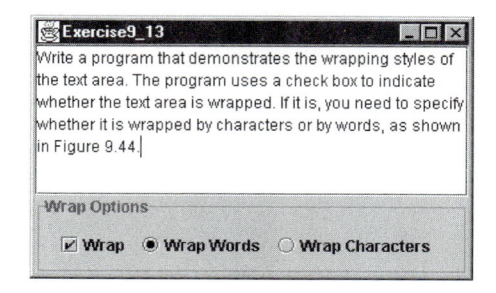

Figure 9.44 *You can set the options to wrap a text area by characters or by words dynamically.*

9.14. Write a program that demonstrates selecting items in a list. The program uses a combo box to specify a selection mode, as shown in Figure 9.45. When you select items, they are displayed in a label below the list.

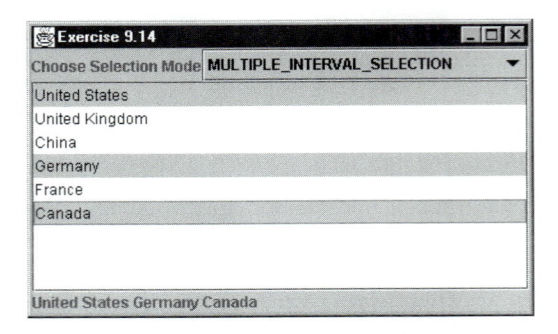

Figure 9.45 *You can choose single selection, single-interval selection, or multiple-interval selection in a list.*

CHAPTER 10

APPLETS AND ADVANCED GRAPHICS

Objectives

- Understand how the Web browser controls and executes applets.
- Become familiar with the `init()`, `start()`, `stop()`, and `destroy()` methods in the `Applet` class.
- Pass parameters to applets from HTML.
- Convert between applications and applets.
- Write a Java program that can run as an application and as an applet.
- Handle mouse events and keystrokes.
- Understand and use `CardLayout` and `GridBagLayout`, or use no layout managers.
- Package and Deploy Visual J++ Projects.

Introduction

Java's early success was attributed to applets. Running from a Java-enabled Web browser, applets can bring dynamic interaction and live animation to an otherwise static HTML page. It is safe to say that Java would be nowhere today without applets. They make Java appealing, attractive, and popular.

In this book so far, you have mostly used Java applications in examples that introduce Java programming. Everything you have learned about writing applications, however, also applies to writing applets. Because applets are invoked from a Web page, Java provides special features that enable applets to run from a Web browser.

In this chapter, you will learn how to write Java applets, discover the relationship between applets and the Web browser, and explore the similarities and differences between applications and applets. You also will see more complex examples of handling mouse events and keystrokes, and using advanced layout managers.

The *Applet* Classes

As shown in Chapter 1, "Introduction to Java and Visual J++ 6," every Java applet extends the `java.applet.Applet` class. The `Applet` class provides the essential framework that enables your applets to be run by a Web browser. Every Java application has a main method that is executed when the application starts. Unlike applications, applets do not have a main method. Applets depend on the browser to call the methods. Every applet has a structure like the following:

```
public class MyApplet extends java.applet.Applet
{
  ...
  // Called by the browser when the Web page containing
  // this applet is initially loaded
  public void init()
  {
    ...
  }

  // Called by the browser after the init() method and
  // every time the Web page is visited.
  public void start()
  {
    ...
  }

  // Called by the browser when the page containing this
  // applet becomes inactive.
  public void stop()
  {
    ...
  }

  // Called by the browser when the Web browser exits.
  public void destroy()
  {
    ...
  }

  // Other methods if necessary...
}
```

The browser controls the applets using the `init()`, `start()`, `stop()`, and `destroy()` methods. By default, these methods do nothing. To perform specific functions, they need to be modified in the user's applet so that the browser can call your code properly. Figure 10.1 shows how the browser calls these methods.

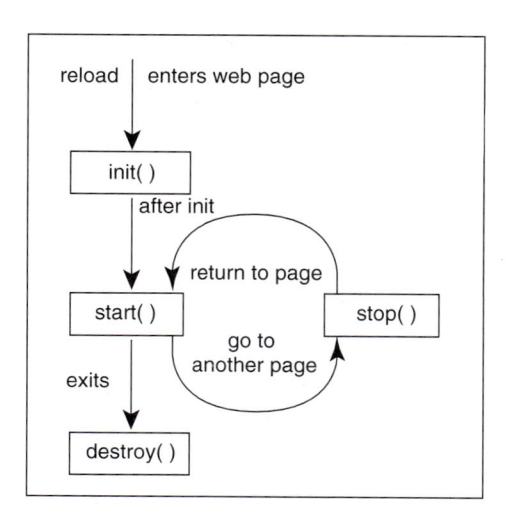

Figure 10.1 *The Web browser uses the* `init()`, `start()`, `stop()`, *and* `destroy()` *methods to control the applet.*

The *init()* method

The `init()` method is invoked when the applet is first loaded and again if it is reloaded.

A subclass of `Applet` should override this method if the subclass has an initialization to perform. The functions usually implemented with this method include creating new threads, loading images, setting up user interface components, and getting parameters from the `<applet>` tag in the HTML page. Chapter 13, "Multithreading," discusses threads in more detail; passing `Applet` parameters is discussed later in this chapter.

The *start()* method

The `start()` method is invoked after the `init()` method. It is also called whenever the applet becomes active again after a period of inactivity. The `start()` method is called, for example, when the user returns to the Web page containing the applet after surfing other pages.

A subclass of `Applet` overrides this method if the subclass has any operation that needs to be performed whenever the Web page containing the applet is visited. An applet with animation, for example, might want to use the `start()` method to resume animation.

The *stop()* method

The `stop()` method is the opposite of the `start()` method. The `start()` method is called when the user moves back to the page containing the applet. The `stop()` method is invoked when the user moves off the page.

A subclass of `Applet` overrides this method if the subclass has any operation that needs to be performed each time the Web page containing the applet is no longer visible. When the user leaves the page, any threads the applet has started—but not completed—will continue to run. You should override the `stop()` method to suspend the running threads so that the applet does not take up system resources when it is inactive.

The *destroy()* method

The `destroy()` method is invoked when the browser exits normally to inform the applet that it is no longer needed and should release any resources it has allocated. The `stop()` method is always called before the `destroy()` method.

A subclass of `Applet` overrides this method if the subclass has any operation that needs to be performed before it is destroyed. Usually, you won't need to override this method unless you need to release specific resources, such as threads that the applet created.

The *JApplet* Class

The `Applet` class is an AWT class and does not work well with Swing components. To use Swing components in Java applets, you should create a Java applet that extends `javax.swing.JApplet`, which is a subclass of `java.applet.Applet`. `JApplet` inherits all the methods from the `Applet` class. In addition, it provides support for laying out Swing components.

To add a component to a `JApplet`, you need to add it to the content pane of a `JApplet` instance, which is the same as adding a component to a `JFrame` instance. By default, the content pane of `JApplet` uses `BorderLayout`.

Example 10.1 Using Applets

This example shows an applet that computes mortgages. The applet enables the user to enter the interest rate, the number of years, and the loan amount. Clicking the Compute button displays the monthly payment and the total payment. The applet and the HTML code containing the applet are provided in the following code. Figure 10.2 contains a sample run of the applet.

```java
// MortgageApplet.java: Applet for computing mortgage payments
import java.awt.*;
import java.awt.event.*;
import javax.swing.*;
import javax.swing.border.TitledBorder;
```

```java
public class MortgageApplet extends JApplet
  implements ActionListener
{
  // Declare and create text fields for interest rate
  // year, loan amount, monthly payment, and total payment
  private JTextField jtfInterestRate = new JTextField(10);
  private JTextField jtfYear = new JTextField(10);
  private JTextField jtfLoan = new JTextField(10);
  private JTextField jtfMonthlyPay = new JTextField(10);
  private JTextField jtfTotalPay = new JTextField(10);

  // Declare and create a Compute Mortgage button
  private JButton jbtCompute = new JButton("Compute Mortgage");

  // Initialize user interface
  public void init()
  {
    // Set properties on the text fields
    jtfMonthlyPay.setEditable(false);
    jtfTotalPay.setEditable(false);

    // Panel p1 to hold labels and text fields
    JPanel p1 = new JPanel();
    p1.setLayout(new GridLayout(5,2));
    p1.add(new Label("Interest Rate"));
    p1.add(jtfInterestRate);
    p1.add(new Label("Years "));
    p1.add(jtfYear);
    p1.add(new Label("Loan Amount"));
    p1.add(jtfLoan);
    p1.add(new Label("Monthly Payment"));
    p1.add(jtfMonthlyPay);
    p1.add(new Label("Total Payment"));
    p1.add(jtfTotalPay);
    p1.setBorder(new
      TitledBorder("Enter interest rate, year and loan amount"));

    // Panel p2 to hold the button
    JPanel p2 = new JPanel();
    p2.setLayout(new FlowLayout(FlowLayout.RIGHT));
    p2.add(jbtCompute);

    // Add the components to the applet
    getContentPane().add(p1, BorderLayout.CENTER);
    getContentPane().add(p2, BorderLayout.SOUTH);

    // Register listener
    jbtCompute.addActionListener(this);
  }

  // Handler for the "Compute" button
  public void actionPerformed(ActionEvent e)
  {
    if (e.getSource() == jbtCompute)
    {
      // Get values from text fields
      double interest =
        (Double.valueOf(jtfInterestRate.getText())).doubleValue();
      int year =
        (Integer.valueOf(jtfYear.getText())).intValue();
      double loan =
        (Double.valueOf(jtfLoan.getText())).doubleValue();
```

continues

```java
      // Create a mortgage object
      Mortgage m = new Mortgage(interest, year, loan);

      // Display monthly payment and total payment
      jtfMonthlyPay.setText(String.valueOf(m.monthlyPay()));
      jtfTotalPay.setText(String.valueOf(m.totalPay()));
    }
  }
}
```

```html
<!-- HTML code, this code is separated from the preceding Java code>
<html>
<head>
<title>Mortgage Applet</title>
</head>
<body>
This is a mortgage calculator, enter your input for interest, year
and loan amount, click the "Compute" button, you will get the payment
information.<p>
<applet
  code = "MortgageApplet.class"
  width = 300
  height = 150
  alt="You must have a JDK1.2-enabled browser to view the applet">
</applet>
</body>
</html>
```

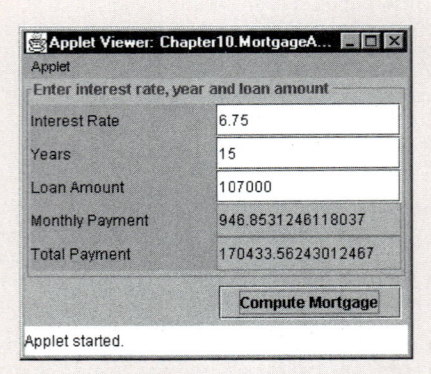

Figure 10.2 *The applet computes the monthly payment and the total payment when provided with the interest rate, number of years, and loan amount.*

Example Review

You need to use the `public` modifier for the `MortgageApplet`; otherwise, the Web browser cannot load the applet.

`MortgageApplet` implements `ActionListener` because it listens for button actions.

The `init()` method initializes the user interface. The program overrides this method to create user interface components (labels, text fields, and a button), and places them in the applet.

The only event handled is the Compute button. When this button is clicked, the `actionPerformed()` method gets the interest rate, year, and loan from the text fields. It then creates a `Mortgage` object to obtain the monthly payment and the total payment. Finally, it displays the monthly and total payments in their respective text fields.

The `Mortgage` class is responsible for computing the payments. This class was introduced in Example 5.7, "Using the `Mortgage` Class" (see Chapter 5, "Programming with Objects and Classes").

The monthly and total payments are not displayed in currency format. To display a number as currency, see Chapter 12, "Internationalization."

Applets are embedded in HTML using the `<applet>` tag, which is discussed in the next section. The `code` parameter specifies the location of the applet bytecode file. The `width` and `height`, both in pixels, specify the initial size of the applet.

As usual, all the Java source files and HTML files in this chapter are put in the directory c:\vjBook\Project10. Create MortgageApplet.java and Mortgage Applet.htm for the Java source code and the HTML code in Project10.

Since `Mortgage` was defined in C:\vjBook\Project5, you need to add C:\vjBook\Project5 in the Classpath in the Project10 Properties dialog box.

You can use Internet Explorer or JVIEW to run this applet. To run it with Internet Explorer, choose MortgageApplet.htm to load on the Launch page of the Project10 Properties dialog box. To run it with JVIEW, choose MortgageApplet.Java instead. You may get a warning message indicating that a main class is not found; ignore it and proceed to view the applet. When running the applet using JVIEW, the applet viewer utility is invoked, as shown in Figure 10.3.

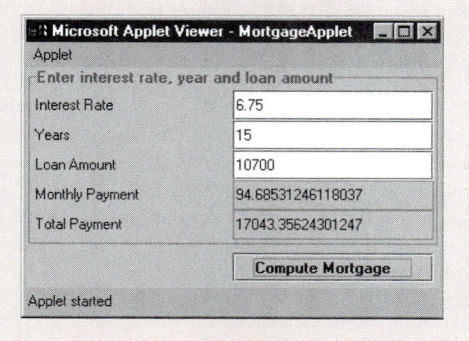

Figure 10.3 *The applet viewer utility is used to run an applet from Visual J++.*

continues

You can also view the applet by clicking the Quick View tab in the Text Editor window for MortgageApplet.htm, as shown in Figure 10.4. I recommend that you use Quick View to test applets. Quick View is convenient and takes less system resource.

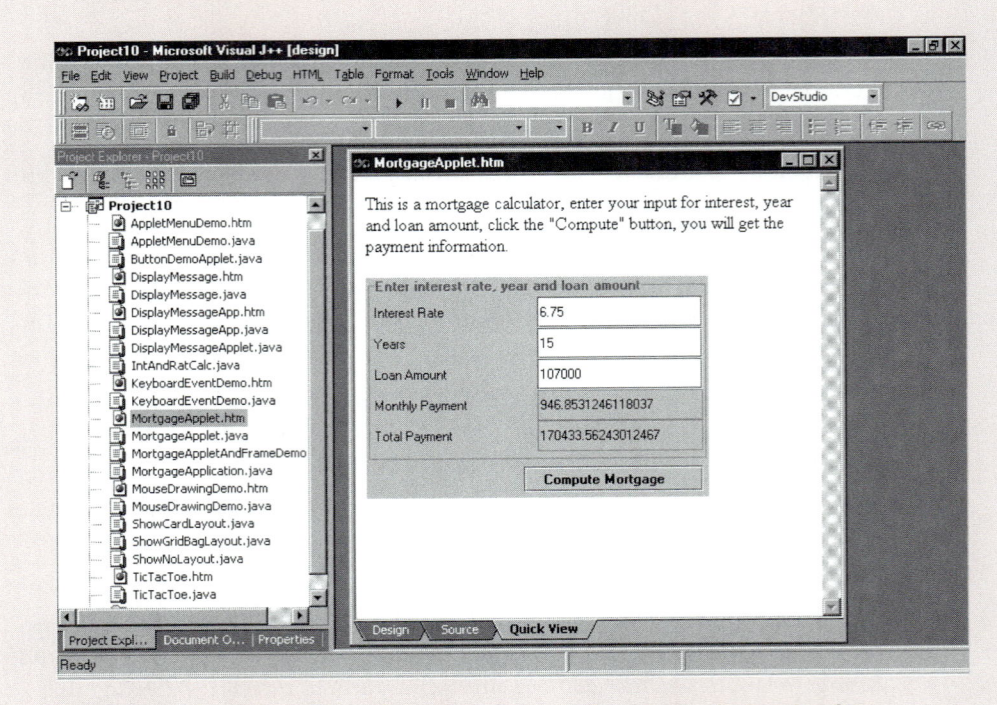

Figure 10.4 *The Quick View tab enables you to view the applet in the HTML editor.*

The <applet> HTML Tag

To run applets, you must create an HTML file with the <applet> tag to specify the applet bytecode file, the applet viewing area dimension (width and height), and other associated parameters. The syntax of the <applet> tag is as follows:

```
<applet
  code=classfilename.class
  width=applet_viewing_width_in_pixels
  height=applet_viewing_height_in_pixels
  [archive=archivefile]
  [codebase=applet_url]
  [vspace=vertical_margin]
  [hspace=horizontal_margin]
  [align=applet_alignment]
  [alt=alternative_text]
>
<param name=param_name1 value=param_value1>
<param name=param_name2 value=param_value2>
...
<param name=param_name3 value=param_value3>
</applet>
```

The `code`, `width`, and `height` attributes are required; all others are optional. The `<param>` tag is introduced in the section "Passing Parameters to Applets." The meanings of the other attributes are as follows:

- **`archive`**—You can use this attribute to instruct the browser to load an archive file that contains all the class files needed to run the applet. The archiving allows the Web browser to load all the classes from a single compressed file only once, thus reducing loading time and improving performance. To create archives, see the section "Packaging and Deploying Visual J++ Projects," later in this chapter.

- **`codebase`**—If this attribute is not used, the Web browser loads the applet from the directory in which the HTML page is located. If your applet is located in a different directory from the HTML page, you must specify the `applet_url` for the browser to load the applet. This attribute enables you to load the class from anywhere on the Internet. The classes used by the applet are dynamically loaded when needed.

- **`vspace`** and **`hspace`**—These two attributes specify the size, in pixels, of the blank margin to leave around the applet vertically and horizontally.

- **`align`**—This attribute specifies how the applet will be aligned in the browser. One of nine values is used: `left`, `right`, `top`, `texttop`, `middle`, `absmiddle`, `baseline`, `bottom`, or `absbottom`.

- **`alt`**—This attribute specifies the text to be displayed in case the browser cannot run Java.

> **NOTE**
> The W3 consortium (**www.w3.org**) has introduced the `<object>` tag as a replacement for the `<applet>` tag. The `<object>` tag has more options and is more versatile than the `<applet>` tag. Nonetheless, this book will continue to use the `<applet>` tag, since not all Web browsers support the `<object>` tag at this time.

Running Applets in the Java Plug-In (Optional)

When Java was first introduced in 1995, the only Web browser for viewing Java applets was the HotJava browser by Sun. Netscape quickly updated Navigator 2 to support JDK 1.0. Microsoft followed suit to support JDK 1.0 in Internet Explorer 3. As Java rapidly evolves, browser vendors are falling behind in their effort to keep up with Java updates. Consequently, your Java applets may not be viewable on certain Web browser. To address this problem, Sun introduced the Java Plug-In technology, which enables browsers to install the Java Plug-In so that applets can be viewed consistently on any platform.

To use the Java Plug-In, you have to convert your simple HTML file to a rather complex HTML file using the Java Plug-in HTML Converter supplied by JavaSoft. The converter can be downloaded from

www.javasoft.com/products/plugin/1.2/converter.html

To install it, unzip it and save it in a directory. To use the converter, change the directory to where the HTMLConvert.class is located and type

```
jview HTMLConverter
```

at the DOS prompt to display a window titled "Java Plug-in HTML Converter," as shown in Figure 10.5. Check the One File radio button, specify the simple HTML file with the <applet> tag in the text field followed after the label "One File," and select an appropriate conversion template in the Template File text field, as shown in Figure 10.5.

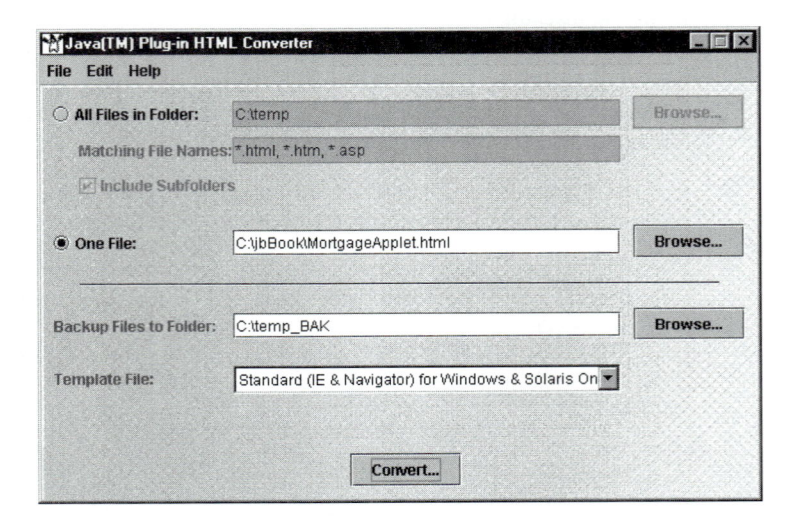

Figure 10.5 *The HTML converter translates a simple HTML file to one that uses the Java Plug-In.*

Press the Convert button to process the conversion. The generated HTML file contains the script that prompts you to download and install the Java Plug-In if it is not installed on your machine. You can run it from Netscape or Internet Explorer. Figures 10.6 and 10.7 are the sample run of the MortgageApplet running on Netscape and Internet Explorer.

CHAPTER 10 APPLETS AND ADVANCED GRAPHICS

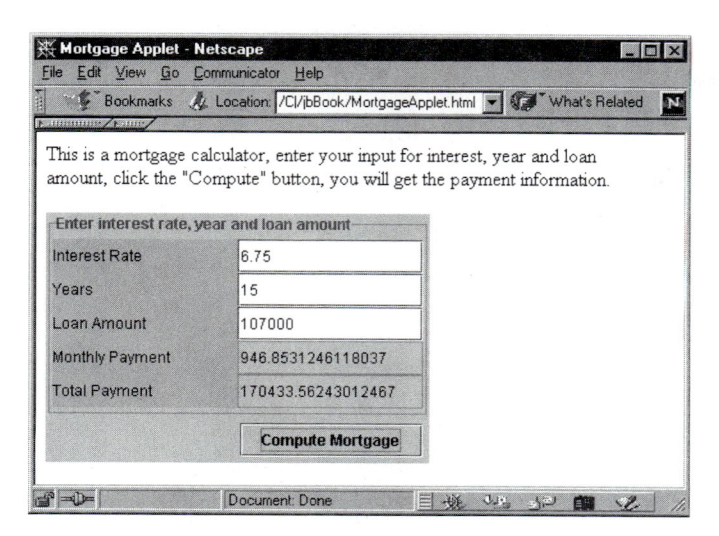

Figure 10.6 *The MortgageApplet runs on Netscape using the Java Plug-In.*

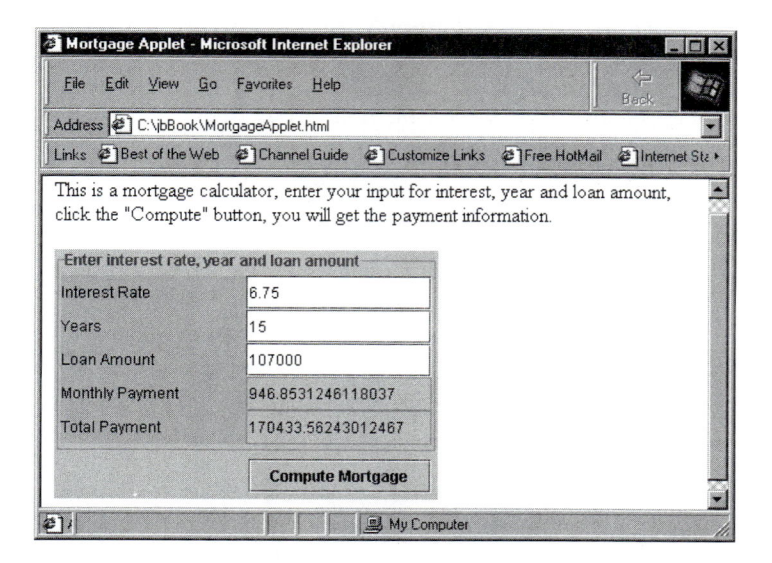

Figure 10.7 *The MortgageApplet runs on Internet Explorer using the Java Plug-In.*

> **TIP**
> Using the Java Plug-In is somewhat inconvenient, because you have to use the converter to generate an HTML file. If your applet does not use any Java 2 features except the Swing components, as in all the examples presented so far in this text, you can view your applets from Netscape or Internet Explorer. To enable Netscape or Internet Explorer to display Java applets with Swing components, install swingall.jar in Netscape or Internet Explorer as follows:
>
> For Netscape, add swingall.jar in the \Netscape\Communicator\Program\Java\Classes directory.
>
> For Internet Explorer, add swingall.jar in the classpath. On Windows 95 or Windows 98, insert the following line in the autoexec.bat file:
>
> ```
> set classpath=%classpath%;c:\swingall.jar
> ```
>
> On Windows NT, add it to classpath on the Environment variable page in the System dialog box.

Passing Parameters to Applets

In Chapter 6, "Arrays and Strings," you learned how to pass parameters to Java applications from a command line. The parameters were entered from the Java interpreter and were passed as an array of strings to the main() method. When the application starts, the main() method can use these arguments. There is no main() method in an applet, however, and applets are not run from the command line by the Java interpreter.

How, then, can applets accept arguments? In this section, you will learn how to pass parameters to Java applets.

To be passed to an applet, parameters must be declared before the applet starts, and must be read by the applet when it is initialized. The parameters are declared using the <param> tag in the HTML file. The <param> tag must be embedded in the <applet> tag and has no end tag. The syntax for the <param> tag is as follows:

```
<param name=parametername value=parametervalue>
```

This tag specifies a parameter and its corresponding value.

> **NOTE**
> There is no comma separating the parameter name from the parameter value in the HTML code.

Suppose you want to write an applet to display a message. The message is passed as a parameter. In addition, you want the message to be displayed at a specific location. The start location of the message is also passed as a parameter in two values, x coordinate and y coordinate. Assume the applet is named DisplayMessage. The parameters and their values are listed in Table 10.1.

TABLE 10.1 Parameter Names and Values for the `DisplayMessage` Applet

Parameter Name	Parameter Value
MESSAGE	"Welcome to Java"
X	20
Y	30

The HTML source file might look like this:

```html
<html>
<head>
<title>Passing Parameters to Java Applets</title>
</head>
<body>
This applet gets a message from the HTML page and displays it.
<p>
<applet
  code = "DisplayMessage.class"
  width = 200
  height = 50
  alt="You must have a JDK 1.2-enabled browser to view the applet"
>
<param name=MESSAGE value="Welcome to Java">
<param name=X value=20>
<param name=Y value=30>
</applet>
</body>
</html>
```

To read the parameter from the applet, use the following method defined in the `Applet` class:

```java
public String getParameter("parametername");
```

This returns the value of the specified parameter.

Example 10.2 Passing Parameters to Java Applets

This example shows an applet that displays a message at a specified location. The message and the location (x, y) are obtained from the HTML source. The program creates a Java source file named **DisplayMessage.java**, as shown below. The output of a sample run is shown in Figure 10.8.

```java
// DisplayMessage.java: Display a message on a panel in the applet
import javax.swing.*;

public class DisplayMessage extends JApplet
{
  private String message = "A default message"; // Message to display
  private int x = 20; // Default x coordinate
  private int y = 20; // Default y coordinate
```

continues

```java
    // Initialize the applet
    public void init()
    {
      // Get parameter values from the HTML file
      message = getParameter("MESSAGE");
      x = Integer.parseInt(getParameter("X"));
      y = Integer.parseInt(getParameter("Y"));

      // Create a message panel
      MessagePanel messagePanel = new MessagePanel(message);
      messagePanel.setXCoordinate(x);
      messagePanel.setYCoordinate(y);

      // Add the message panel to the applet
      getContentPane().add(messagePanel);
    }
}
```

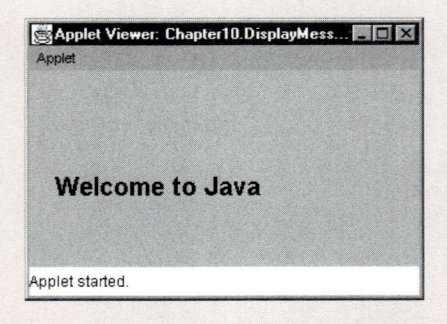

Figure 10.8 *The applet displays the message* Welcome to Java *passed from the HTML page.*

Example Review

The program gets the parameter values from the HTML in the `init()` method. The values are strings obtained using the `getParameter()` method. Because x and y are int, the program uses `Integer.parseInt(string)` to convert a digital string into an int value.

If you change Welcome to Java to Welcome to HTML in the HTML file and reload the HTML file in the Web browser, you should see Welcome to HTML displayed. Similarly, the x and y values can be changed to display the message in the desired location.

You can run this applet with Internet Explorer or view it in the Editor with Quick View, but you cannot run it with JVIEW because the HTML parameters cannot be passed to the applet in JVIEW.

Conversions between Applications and Applets

The JFrame class and the JApplet class have a lot in common despite some differences. Since they both are subclasses of the Container class, all the user interface components, layout managers, and event-handling features are the same for both classes. Applications, however, are invoked by the Java interpreter, and applets are invoked by the Web browser. In this section, you will learn how to convert between applets and applications.

In general, an applet can be converted to an application. The following are the steps in the conversion:

1. Eliminate the HTML page that invokes the applet. If the applet gets parameters from the HTML page, you can handle them from the command line.

2. Derive the main class named NewClass, for instance, from JFrame or MyFrame-WithExitHandling instead of from JApplet.

3. Write a constructor in the new class to contain the code in the init() and start() methods.

4. Place the codes from the stop() and destroy() methods in the windowClosing() method that handles the window-closing event.

5. Add a main method, as follows:

   ```
   public static void main()
   {
     NewClass frame = new NewClass();

     // width and height are from the <applet> tag
     frame.resize(width, height);
     frame.setVisible(true);
   }
   ```

6. Because applets do not have title bars, you can add a title for the window using the setTitle() method.

> **NOTE**
> When using frames in applications, specify an initial size in width and height using the setSize() method. After the frame is displayed, you can resize it. With applets, the viewing area is fixed on a Web page by the width and height values in the <applet> tag.

Example 10.3 Converting Applets to Applications

This example converts the Java applet MortgageApplet (from Example 10.1) to a Java application and displays the frame in the center of the screen. The program is given below, and its sample run is shown in Figure 10.9.

continues

```java
// MortgageApplication.java: Application for computing mortgage
   payments
import java.awt.*;
import java.awt.event.*;
import javax.swing.*;
import javax.swing.border.TitledBorder;

public class MortgageApplication extends MyFrameWithExitHandling
  implements ActionListener
{
  // Declare and create text fields for interest rate
  // year, loan amount, monthly payment, and total payment
  private JTextField jtfInterestRate = new JTextField(10);
  private JTextField jtfYear = new JTextField(10);
  private JTextField jtfLoan = new JTextField(10);
  private JTextField jtfMonthlyPay = new JTextField(10);
  private JTextField jtfTotalPay = new JTextField(10);

  // Add a main method
  public static void main(String[] args)
  {
    MortgageApplication frame =
      new MortgageApplication();
    frame.setSize(400, 200);
    frame.setTitle("Mortgage Application");
    frame.center();
    frame.setVisible(true);
  }

  // Declare and create a Compute Mortgage button
  private JButton jbtCompute = new JButton("Compute Mortgage");

  // Constructor (replacing the init() method in the applet
  public MortgageApplication()
  {
    // Set properties on the text fields
    jtfMonthlyPay.setEditable(false);
    jtfTotalPay.setEditable(false);

    // Panel p1 to hold labels and text fields
    JPanel p1 = new JPanel();
    p1.setLayout(new GridLayout(5,2));
    p1.add(new Label("Interest Rate"));
    p1.add(jtfInterestRate);
    p1.add(new Label("Years "));
    p1.add(jtfYear);
    p1.add(new Label("Loan Amount"));
    p1.add(jtfLoan);
    p1.add(new Label("Monthly Payment"));
    p1.add(jtfMonthlyPay);
    p1.add(new Label("Total Payment"));
    p1.add(jtfTotalPay);
    p1.setBorder(new
      TitledBorder("Enter interest rate, year and loan amount"));

    // Panel p2 to hold the button
    JPanel p2 = new JPanel();
    p2.setLayout(new FlowLayout(FlowLayout.RIGHT));
    p2.add(jbtCompute);
```

```java
      // Add the components to the applet
      getContentPane().add(p1, BorderLayout.CENTER);
      getContentPane().add(p2, BorderLayout.SOUTH);

      // Register listener
      jbtCompute.addActionListener(this);
    }

    // Handler for the "Compute" button
    public void actionPerformed(ActionEvent e)
    {
      if (e.getSource() == jbtCompute)
      {
        // Get values from text fields
        double interest =
          (Double.valueOf(jtfInterestRate.getText())).doubleValue();
        int year =
          (Integer.valueOf(jtfYear.getText())).intValue();
        double loan =
          (Double.valueOf(jtfLoan.getText())).doubleValue();

        // Create a mortgage object
        Mortgage m = new Mortgage(interest, year, loan);

        // Display monthly payment and total payment
        jtfMonthlyPay.setText(String.valueOf(m.monthlyPay()));
        jtfTotalPay.setText(String.valueOf(m.totalPay()));
      }
    }
  }
```

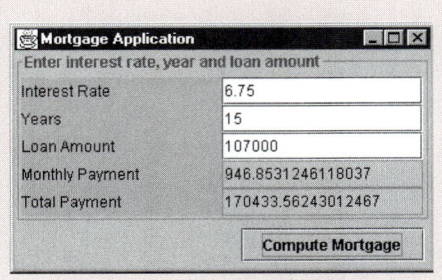

Figure 10.9 *The program is the same as Example 10.1 except that it is written as an application.*

Example Review

The program extends `MyFrameWithExitHandling`, a subclass of `JFrame` with exit handling, instead of extending `JApplet`.

The program uses a constructor to initialize the user interface instead of using the `init()` method. The `setTitle()` method is used to set a title for the frame in the constructor.

The program creates a main method to start the program by the Java interpreter.

Since `MyFrameWithExitHandling` was defined in c:\vjBook\Project8, you need to add c:\vjBook\Project8 in the Classpath in the Project10 Properties dialog box.

In Chapter 1, "Introduction to Java and Visual J++ 6," you learned that certain limitations are imposed on applets for security reasons. For example, applets are not allowed to access local files. If the conversion does not violate the security constraints imposed on applets, you can perform the following steps to convert an application to an applet:

1. Create an HTML page with the `<applet>` tag that invokes the applet. If command-line parameters are used in the application, add the parameters in the `<applet>` tag and get the parameters using `getParameter()` in the `init()` method.

2. Derive the main class from `JApplet` instead of from `JFrame` or from `MyFrameWithExitHandling`.

3. Replace the application's constructor by the `init()` method.

4. Eliminate the `main()` method, which usually contains the method to create and display the frame. The applet is automatically displayed in the size specified by the width and height in the `<applet>` tag. This step is optional. If you leave the `main()` method intact, it is simply ignored.

5. Because applets do not have title bars, eliminate the `setTitle()` method (if it is in the application).

Example 10.4 Converting Applications to Applets

This example converts the Java application `MenuDemo`, which performs arithmetic operations using buttons and menus (Example 9.10, "Using Menus," from Chapter 9, "Creating User Interfaces"), into a Java applet.

The following Java applet `AppletMenuDemo` is converted from the application `MenuDemo`. A sample run of the applet is shown in Figure 10.10.

```java
// AppletMenuDemo.java: Using menus in an applet
import java.awt.*;
import java.awt.event.*;
import javax.swing.*;

public class AppletMenuDemo extends JApplet
  implements ActionListener
{
  // Text fields for Number 1, Number 2, and Result
  private JTextField jtfNum1, jtfNum2, jtfResult;

  // Buttons "Add", "Subtract", "Multiply" and "Divide"
  private JButton jbtAdd, jbtSub, jbtMul, jbtDiv;

  // Menu items "Add", "Subtract", "Multiply","Divide" and "Close"
  private JMenuItem jmiAdd, jmiSub, jmiMul, jmiDiv, jmiClose;

  // Initialize the applet
  public void init()
  {
    // Create menu bar
    JMenuBar jmb = new JMenuBar();
```

```java
// Add menu "Operation" to menu bar
JMenu operationMenu = new JMenu("Operation");
operationMenu.setMnemonic('O');
jmb.add(operationMenu);

// Add menu "Exit" in menu bar
JMenu exitMenu = new JMenu("Exit");
exitMenu.setMnemonic('E');
jmb.add(exitMenu);

// Add menu items with mnemonics to menu "Operation"
operationMenu.add(jmiAdd= new JMenuItem("Add", 'A'));
operationMenu.add(jmiSub = new JMenuItem("Subtract", 'S'));
operationMenu.add(jmiMul = new JMenuItem("Multiply", 'M'));
operationMenu.add(jmiDiv = new JMenuItem("Divide", 'D'));
exitMenu.add(jmiClose = new JMenuItem("Close", 'C'));

// Set keyboard accelerators
jmiAdd.setAccelerator(
  KeyStroke.getKeyStroke(KeyEvent.VK_A, ActionEvent.CTRL_MASK));
jmiSub.setAccelerator(
  KeyStroke.getKeyStroke(KeyEvent.VK_S, ActionEvent.CTRL_MASK));
jmiMul.setAccelerator(
  KeyStroke.getKeyStroke(KeyEvent.VK_M, ActionEvent.CTRL_MASK));
jmiDiv.setAccelerator(
  KeyStroke.getKeyStroke(KeyEvent.VK_D, ActionEvent.CTRL_MASK));

// Panel p1 to hold text fields and labels
JPanel p1 = new JPanel();
p1.setLayout(new FlowLayout());
p1.add(new JLabel("Number 1"));
p1.add(jtfNum1 = new JTextField(3));
p1.add(new JLabel("Number 2"));
p1.add(jtfNum2 = new JTextField(3));
p1.add(new JLabel("Result"));
p1.add(jtfResult = new JTextField(4));
jtfResult.setEditable(false);

// Panel p2 to hold buttons
JPanel p2 = new JPanel();
p2.setLayout(new FlowLayout());
p2.add(jbtAdd = new JButton("Add"));
p2.add(jbtSub = new JButton("Subtract"));
p2.add(jbtMul = new JButton("Multiply"));
p2.add(jbtDiv = new JButton("Divide"));

// Add menu bar to the applet
setJMenuBar(jmb);

// Add panels to the applet
getContentPane().add(p1, BorderLayout.CENTER);
getContentPane().add(p2, BorderLayout.SOUTH);

// Register listeners
jbtAdd.addActionListener(this);
jbtSub.addActionListener(this);
jbtMul.addActionListener(this);
jbtDiv.addActionListener(this);
jmiAdd.addActionListener(this);
jmiSub.addActionListener(this);
```

continues

```java
      jmiMul.addActionListener(this);
      jmiDiv.addActionListener(this);
      jmiClose.addActionListener(this);
  }

  // Handling ActionEvent from buttons and menu items
  public void actionPerformed(ActionEvent e)
  {
    String actionCommand = e.getActionCommand();

    // Handling button events
    if (e.getSource() instanceof JButton)
    {
      if ("Add".equals(actionCommand))
        calculate('+');
      else if ("Subtract".equals(actionCommand))
        calculate('-');
      else if ("Multiply".equals(actionCommand))
        calculate('*');
      else if ("Divide".equals(actionCommand))
        calculate('/');
    }
    else if (e.getSource() instanceof JMenuItem)
    {
      // Handling menu item events
      if ("Add".equals(actionCommand))
        calculate('+');
      else if ("Subtract".equals(actionCommand))
        calculate('-');
      else if ("Multiply".equals(actionCommand))
        calculate('*');
      else if ("Divide".equals(actionCommand))
        calculate('/');
      else if ("Close".equals(actionCommand))
        System.exit(0);   //Ignored by the Web bro
    }
  }

  // Calculate and show the result in jtfResult
  private void calculate(char operator)
  {
    // Obtain Number 1 and Number 2
    int num1 = (Integer.parseInt(jtfNum1.getText().trim()));
    int num2 = (Integer.parseInt(jtfNum2.getText().trim()));
    int result = 0;

    // Perform selected operation
    switch (operator)
    {
      case '+': result = num1 + num2;
                break;
      case '-': result = num1 - num2;
                break;
      case '*': result = num1 * num2;
                break;
      case '/': result = num1 / num2;
    }

    // Set result in jtfResult
    jtfResult.setText(String.valueOf(result));
  }
}
```

Example Review

The following changes are made to convert the `MenuDemo` application to `AppletMenuDemo`:

1. Extend `JApplet` instead of `MyFrameWithExitHandling`.

2. Replace the constructor with the `init()` method and eliminate the `setTitle()` method.

3. Create an HTML file to run the applet.

Menus can only be used with applications in AWT programming. In Swing, menus can be used in both applications and applets.

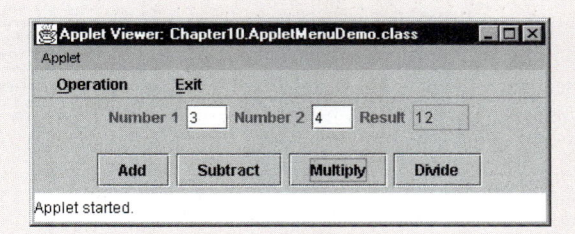

Figure 10.10 *The `AppletMenuDemo` class demonstrates using menus in an applet.*

Running a Program as an Applet and an Application

You can implement a main method in an applet that will run the applet as an application or as an applet using the same program. This feature has both theoretical and practical implications. Theoretically, it blurs the difference between applets and applications. You can write a class that is both an applet and an application. Practically, it is convenient to be able to run a program in two ways.

It is not difficult to write such types of programs on your own. Suppose you have an applet named `TestApplet`. To enable it to run as an application, all you need to do is add a main method in the applet with the implementation as follows:

```
public static void main(String[] args)
{
  // Create a frame
  MyFrameWithExitHandling frame = new MyFrameWithExitHandling(
    "Running a program as applet and frame");

  // Create an instance of TestApplet
  TestApplet applet = new TestApplet();

  // Add the applet instance to the frame
  frame.getContentPane().add(applet, BorderLayout.CENTER);
```

```java
      // Invoke init() and start()
      applet.init();
      applet.start();

      // Display the frame
      frame.setSize(300, 300);
      frame.setVisible(true);
   }
```

Since the `JApplet` class is a subclass of `Component`, it can be placed in a frame. You can invoke the `init()` and `start()` methods of the applet to run an `JApplet` object in an application.

Example 10.5 Running a Program as an Applet and as an Application

This example modifies the `DisplayMessage` applet in Example 10.2 to enable it to run both as an applet and as an application. The program is identical to `DisplayMessage` except for the addition of a new main method and of a variable named `isStandalone` to indicate whether it is running as an applet or as an application.

```java
// DisplayMessageApp.java:
// The program can run as an applet or application
import javax.swing.*;
import java.awt.BorderLayout;

public class DisplayMessageApp extends JApplet
{
   private String message = "A default message"; // Message to display
   private int x = 20; // Default x coordinate
   private int y = 20; // Default y coordinate

   // Determine if it is application
   private boolean isStandalone = false;

   // Initialize the applet
   public void init()
   {
      if (!isStandalone)
      {
         // Get parameter values from the HTML file
         message = getParameter("MESSAGE");
         x = Integer.parseInt(getParameter("X"));
         y = Integer.parseInt(getParameter("Y"));
      }

      // Create a message panel
      MessagePanel messagePanel = new MessagePanel(message);
      messagePanel.setXCoordinate(x);
      messagePanel.setYCoordinate(y);

      // Add the message panel to the applet
      getContentPane().add(messagePanel);
   }

   // Main method with three arguments:
   // args[0]: x coordinate
   // args[1]: y coordinate
```

```java
    // args[2]: message
    public static void main(String[] args)
    {
      // Create a frame
      MyFrameWithExitHandling frame = new MyFrameWithExitHandling(
        "DisplayMessageApp");

      // Create an instance of the applet
      DisplayMessageApp applet = new DisplayMessageApp();

      // It runs as an application
      applet.isStandalone = true;

      // Get parameters from the command line
      applet.getCommandLineParameters(args);

      // Add the applet instance to the frame
      frame.getContentPane().add(applet, BorderLayout.CENTER);

      // Invoke init() and start()
      applet.init();
      applet.start();

      // Display the frame
      frame.setSize(300, 300);
      frame.setVisible(true);
    }

    // Get command line parameters
    public void getCommandLineParameters(String[] args)
    {
      // Check usage and get x, y and message
      if (args.length != 3)
      {
        System.out.println(
          "Usage: java DisplayMessageApp x y message");
        System.exit(0);
      }
      else
      {
        x = Integer.parseInt(args[0]);
        y = Integer.parseInt(args[1]);
        message = args[2];
      }
    }
  }
```

Example Review

When you run the program as an applet, the `main()` method is ignored. When you run it as a frame, the `main()` method is invoked. A sample run of the program as an application and as an applet is shown in Figure 10.11.

The `main()` method creates a `JFrame` object `frame` and creates `applet`, an instance of the `JApplet`. The `main()` method then places the applet `applet` into the frame `frame` and invokes its `init()` method. The application runs just like an applet.

continues

The `main()` method sets `isStandalone` true so that it does not attempt to retrieve HTML parameters when the `init()` method is invoked.

The `setVisible(true)` method was invoked *after* the components had been added to the applet, and the applet has been added to the frame to ensure that the components will be visible. Otherwise, the components are not shown when the frame starts.

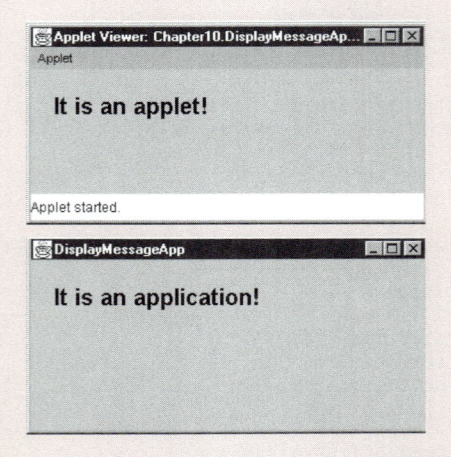

Figure 10.11 *The* `DisplayMessageApp` *class can run as an application or as an applet.*

> **NOTE**
> Since the applet has a main method, Visual J++ lets you choose to run it as applet or as application on the Launch page of the Project Properties dialog box, as shown in Figure 10.12.

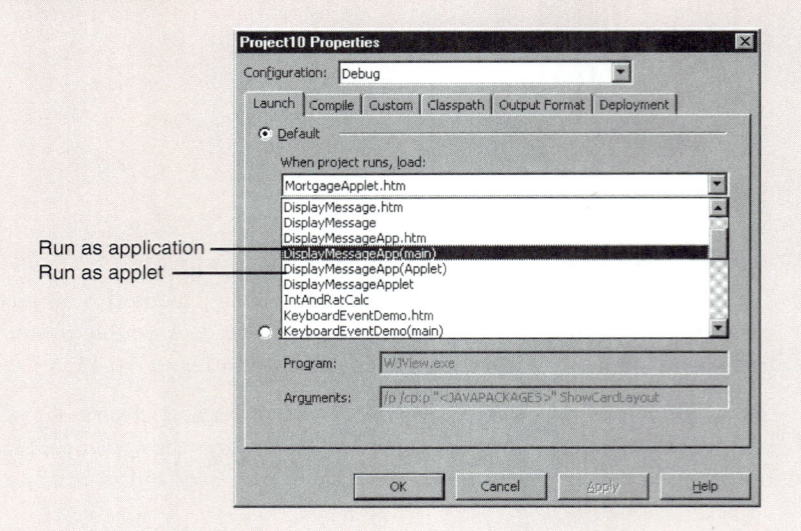

Figure 10.12 *Visual J++ lets you choose to run the program as an applet or as application in the Project Properties dialog box.*

Mouse Events

A mouse event is generated whenever a mouse is clicked, released, moved, or dragged on a component. The mouse event object captures the nature of the event, such as the number of clicks associated with it or the location (x and y coordinates) of the mouse. Java provides two listener interfaces, `MouseListener` and `MouseMotionListener`, to handle mouse events. Implement the `MouseListener` interface to listen for such actions as when the mouse is pressed, released, entered, exited, or clicked, and implement the `MouseMotionListener` interface to listen for such actions as dragging or moving the mouse.

The `MouseEvent` handlers are listed along with the handlers of other events in Table 8.2 in Chapter 8, "Getting Started with Graphics Programming." The following are the handlers:

- The `mouseEntered(MouseEvent e)` and `mouseExit(MouseEvent e)` handlers are invoked when a mouse enters a component or exits the component.

- The `mousePressed(MouseEvent e)` and `mouseReleased(MouseEvent e)` handlers are invoked when a mouse is pressed or released. The `mouseClicked(MouseEvent e)` handler is invoked when a mouse is pressed and then released.

- The `mouseMoved(MouseEvent e)` handler is invoked when the mouse is moved without a button being pressed. The `mouseDragged(MouseEvent e)` handler is invoked when the mouse is moved with a button pressed.

The `Point` class often is used for handling mouse events. The `Point` class encapsulates a point in a plane. The class contains two instance variables, x and y, for coordinates. To create a point object, use the following constructor:

```
Point(int x, int y)
```

This constructs a `Point` object with the specified x and y coordinates.

You can use the `move(int x, int y)` method to move the point to the specified x and y coordinates. You can use the following properties from a `MouseEvent` object when a mouse event occurs:

- `public int getClickCount()`

    This returns the number of mouse clicks associated with the event.

- `public Point getPoint()`

    This returns the x and y coordinates of the event relative to the source component.

- `public int getX()`

    This returns the x coordinate of the event relative to the source component.

- `public int getY()`

    This returns the y coordinate of the event relative to the source component.

Since the `MouseEvent` class inherits `InputEvent`, you can use the methods defined in the `InputEvent` class on a `MouseEvent` object. The following methods in `InputEvent` are often useful for handling mouse events:

- `public long getWhen()`

  This returns the time stamp of when the event occurred.

- `public boolean isAltDown()`

  This returns whether the Alt key is down on the event.

- `public boolean isControlDown()`

  This returns whether the Control key is down on the event.

- `public boolean isMetaDown()`

  This returns `true` if the right mouse button is pressed.

- `public boolean isShiftDown()`

  This returns whether the Shift key is down on the event.

Example 10.6 Handling Complex Mouse Events

This example shows a program that uses a mouse for drawing. It can be used to draw anything on a panel by dragging with the left mouse button pressed. The drawing can be erased by dragging with the right button pressed. A sample run of the program is shown in Figure 10.13.

```java
// MouseDrawingDemo.java: Drawing using mouse
import java.awt.*;
import javax.swing.*;
import java.awt.event.*;

public class MouseDrawingDemo extends JApplet
{
  // This main method enables the applet to run as an application
  public static void main(String[] args)
  {
    // Create a frame
    MyFrameWithExitHandling frame = new MyFrameWithExitHandling(
      "Mouse Drawing Demo");

    // Create an instance of the applet
    MouseDrawingDemo applet = new MouseDrawingDemo();

    // Add the applet instance to the frame
    frame.getContentPane().add(applet, BorderLayout.CENTER);

    // Invoke init() and start()
    applet.init();
    applet.start();

    // Display the frame
    frame.setSize(300, 300);
    frame.setVisible(true);
  }
```

```java
    // Initialize the applet
    public void init()
    {
      // Create a PaintPanel and add it to the applet
      getContentPane().add(new PaintPanel(), BorderLayout.CENTER);
    }
  }

  // PaintPanel for painting using the mouse
  class PaintPanel extends JPanel
    implements MouseListener, MouseMotionListener
  {
    final int CIRCLESIZE = 20; // Circle diameter used for erasing
    private Point lineStart = new Point(0, 0); // Line start point
    private Graphics g; // Create a Graphics object for drawing

    public PaintPanel()
    {
      // Register listener for the mouse event
      addMouseListener(this);
      addMouseMotionListener(this);
    }

    public void mouseClicked(MouseEvent e)
    {
    }

    public void mouseEntered(MouseEvent e)
    {
    }

    public void mouseExited(MouseEvent e)
    {
    }

    public void mouseReleased(MouseEvent e)
    {
    }

    public void mousePressed(MouseEvent e)
    {
      lineStart.move(e.getX(), e.getY());
    }

    public void mouseDragged(MouseEvent e)
    {
      g = getGraphics(); // Get graphics context

      if (e.isMetaDown()) // Detect right button pressed
      {
        // Erase the drawing using an oval
        g.setColor(getBackground());
        g.fillOval(e.getX() - (CIRCLESIZE/2),
          e.getY() - (CIRCLESIZE/2), CIRCLESIZE, CIRCLESIZE);
      }
      else
      {
        g.setColor(Color.black);
        g.drawLine(lineStart.x, lineStart.y,
          e.getX(), e.getY());
      }
```

continues

```
      lineStart.move(e.getX(), e.getY());

      // Dispose this graphics context
      g.dispose();
    }

    public void mouseMoved(MouseEvent e)
    {
    }
  }
```

Figure 10.13 *The program enables you to use the mouse to draw anything.*

Example Review

The program can run as an application and as an applet. The program creates a `PaintPanel` instance to capture mouse movements on the panel. Line are created or erased by dragging the mouse with the left or right button pressed.

When a button is pressed, the `mousePressed()` handler is invoked. This handler sets the `lineStart` to the current mouse point as the starting point. When the mouse is dragged with the left button pressed, drawing begins. In this case, the `mouseDragged()` handler sets the foreground color to black, and draws a line along the path of the mouse movement.

When the mouse is dragged with the right button pressed, erasing occurs. In this case, the `mouseDragged` handler sets the foreground color to the background color and draws an oval filled with the background color at the mouse pointer to erase the area covered by the oval.

The program does not use the `paintComponent(Graphics g)` method. Instead, it uses `getGraphics()` to obtain a `Graphics` instance and draws on this `Graphics` instance.

Because the `mousePressed()` handler is defined in the `MouseListener` interface, and the `mouseDragged()` handler is defined in the `MouseMotionListener` interface, the program implements both interfaces.

> The `dispose()` method disposes of this graphics context and releases any system resources it is using. Although the finalization process of the Java runtime system automatically disposes of the object after it is no longer used, I recommend that you manually free the associated resources by calling this method rather than rely on a finalization process that may not run to completion for a long time. In this program, a large number of `Graphics` objects can be created within a short time. The program would run fine if these objects were not disposed of manually, but it would consume a lot of memory.

Keyboard Events

Keyboard events are generated whenever a key is pressed. They enable the use of the keys to control and perform actions or get input from the keyboard.

The keyboard event object describes the nature of the event (namely, that a key is pressed, released, or typed) and the value of the key. The following handlers from the `KeyListener` interface are used to process keyboard events:

- `public void keyPressed(KeyEvent e)`

    This handler is called when a key is pressed.

- `public void keyReleased(KeyEvent e)`

    This handler is called when a key is released.

- `public void keyTyped(KeyEvent e)`

    This handler is called when a key is pressed and then released.

The keys captured in the event are integers representing Unicode character values, which include alphanumeric characters, function keys, the Tab key, the Enter key, and so on. Every keyboard event has an associated key character or key code, which is returned by the `getKeyChar()` or `getKeyCode()` method in `KeyEvent`, respectively.

Java defines many constants for normal keys and function keys in the `KeyEvent` class. Table 10.2 shows the most common ones.

TABLE 10.2 Key Constants

Constant	Description
VK_HOME	The Home key
VK_End	The End key
VK_PGUP	The Page Up key
VK_PGDN	The Page Down key
VK_UP	The up-arrow key
VK_DOWN	The down-arrow key

continues

Constant	Description
VK_LEFT	The left-arrow key
VK_RIGHT	The right-arrow key
VK_ESCAPE	The Esc key
VK_TAB	The Tab key
VK_BACK_SPACE	The Backspace key
VK_CAPS_LOCK	The Caps Lock key
VK_NUM_LOCK	The Num Lock key
VK_ENTER	The Enter key
VK_F1 to VK_F12	The function keys F1 to F12
VK_0 to VK_9	The number keys from 0 to 9
VK_A to VK_Z	The letter keys from A to Z

Example 10.7 Handling Keyboard Events

This example shows a program that displays a user-input character. The user can move the character up, down, left, and right, using arrow keys VK_UP, VK_DOWN, VK_LEFT, and VK_RIGHT. Figure 10.14 contains a sample run of the program.

```java
// KeyboardEventDemo.java: Receive key input
import java.awt.*;
import java.awt.event.*;
import javax.swing.*;

public class KeyboardEventDemo extends JApplet
{
  private KeyboardPanel keyboardPanel = new KeyboardPanel();

  // Main method used if run as an application
  public static void main(String[] args)
  {
    // Create a frame
    MyFrameWithExitHandling frame = new MyFrameWithExitHandling(
      "KeyboardEvent Demo");

    // Create an instance of the applet
    KeyboardEventDemo applet = new KeyboardEventDemo();

    // Add the applet instance to the frame
    frame.getContentPane().add(applet, BorderLayout.CENTER);

    // Invoke init() and start()
    applet.init();
    applet.start();

    // Display the frame
    frame.setSize(300, 300);
    frame.setVisible(true);
```

```java
      // Set focus on the keyboardPanel
      applet.focus();
    }

    // Initialize UI
    public void init()
    {
      // Add the keyboard panel to accept and display user input
      getContentPane().add(keyboardPanel);

      // Request focus
      focus();

    }

    // Set focus on the panel
    public void focus()
    {
      // It is required for receiving key input
      keyboardPanel.requestFocus();
    }
  }

  // KeyboardPanel for receiving key input
  class KeyboardPanel extends JPanel implements KeyListener
  {
    private int x = 100;
    private int y = 100;
    private char keyChar = 'A'; // Default key

    public KeyboardPanel()
    {
      addKeyListener(this); // Register listener
    }

    public void keyReleased(KeyEvent e)
    {
    }

    public void keyTyped(KeyEvent e)
    {
    }

    public void keyPressed(KeyEvent e)
    {
      switch (e.getKeyCode())
      {
        case KeyEvent.VK_DOWN: y += 10; break;
        case KeyEvent.VK_UP: y -= 10; break;
        case KeyEvent.VK_LEFT: x -= 10; break;
        case KeyEvent.VK_RIGHT: x += 10; break;
        default: keyChar = e.getKeyChar();
      }
      repaint();
    }

    // Draw the character
    public void paintComponent(Graphics g)
    {
      super.paintComponent(g);
```

continues

```
            g.setFont(new Font("TimesRoman", Font.PLAIN, 24));
            g.drawString(String.valueOf(keyChar), x, y);
    }
}
```

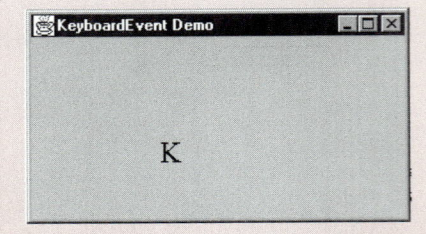

Figure 10.14 *The program responds to the keyboard events by displaying a character and moving it up, down, left, or right.*

Example Review

When a non-arrow key is pressed, the key is displayed. When an arrow key is pressed, the character moves in the direction indicated by the arrow key.

Because the program gets input from the keyboard, it listens for `KeyEvent` and implements `KeyListener` to handle key input.

When a key is pressed, the `keyPressed()` handler is invoked. The program uses `e.getKeyCode()` to obtain the `int` value for the key and `e.getKeyChar()` to get the character for the key. In fact, `(int)e.getKeyChar()` is the same as `e.getKeyCode()`.

Only the focused component can receive `KeyEvent`. When the program runs as an applet, the `keyboardPanel` component receives focus, because it is the last and only component added to the applet. When the program runs as an application, `keyboardPanel` is not focused, since `keyboardPanel` is added to the applet, and the applet is placed inside a frame. Thus you need to set focus to `keyboardPanel` using the `focus()` method defined in the `KeyboardEventDemo`. The `focus()` method sets the focus to `keyboardPanel` using the `requestFocus()` method defined in the `java.awt.Component` class.

Case Studies

You have learned objects, classes, arrays, class inheritance, graphics, event-driven programming, applets from the many examples in this chapter and the preceding chapters. Now it is time to put what you have learned to work in developing comprehensive projects. In this section, you will develop a Java applet to play the popular game of TicTacToe.

Example 10.8 The TicTacToe Game

This example creates a program for playing TicTacToe. In a game of TicTac-Toe, two players take turns marking an available cell in a 3×3 grid with their respective tokens (either X or O). When one player has placed three tokens in a horizontal, vertical, or diagonal row on the grid, the game is over and that player has won. A draw (no winner) occurs when all the spaces on the grid have been filled with tokens and neither player has achieved a win. Figures 10.15 and 10.16 are representative sample runs of the example.

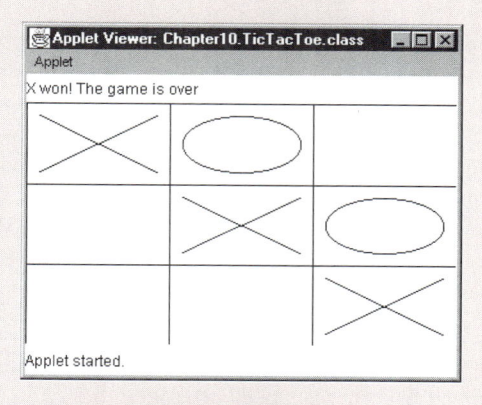

Figure 10.15 *This sample shows that the X player has won.*

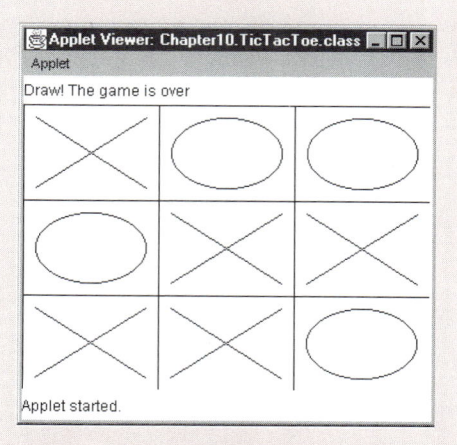

Figure 10.16 *This sample shows a draw with no winner.*

All the examples you have seen so far have simple behaviors that are easy to model with classes. The behavior of the TicTacToe game is somewhat more complex. To create the classes to model the behavior, you need to study and understand the game.

continues

Assume that all the cells are empty initially, and that the first player takes the X token, and the second player takes the O token. To mark a cell, the player points the mouse to the cell and clicks it. If the cell is empty, the token (X or O) is displayed. If the cell is already filled, the player's action is ignored.

From the preceding description, it is obvious that a cell is a GUI object that handles the mouse-click event and displays tokens. Such an object could be either a button or a panel. Drawing on panels is more flexible than on buttons. The token (X or O) can be drawn on a panel in any size, but it only can be displayed on a button as a label. Therefore, a panel should use to model a cell.

Let `Cell` be a subclass of `JPanel`. You can declare the 3×3 grid to be an array `Cell[][] = new Cell[3][3]` to model the game. How do you know the state of the cell (empty, X, or O)? You simply use a property named `token` of `char` type in the `Cell` class. The `Cell` class is responsible for drawing the token when an empty cell is clicked, so you need to write the code for listening to the `MouseEvent` and for painting the shape for token X and O. To determine which shape to draw, you can introduce a variable named `whoseTurn` of `char` type. `whoseTurn` is initially X, then changes to O, and subsequently changes between X and O whenever a new cell is occupied.

Finally, how do you know whether the game is over with or without a winner and who the winner, if any, is? You can create a method named `isWinning(char token)` to check whether a specified token has won and a method named `isFull()` to check whether all the cells are occupied.

Clearly, two classes emerge from the foregoing analysis. One is the `Cell` class, which handles operations for a single cell; and the other is the `TicTacToe` class, which plays the whole game and deals with all the cells. The `Cell` class has the following data fields and methods:

Data field:

   `char token`: Represent token used in the cell.

Methods:

   `public char getToken()`

   Return the token of the cell.

   `public void setToken(char token)`

   Set the token in the cell.

   `public char getToken()`

   Return the token of the cell.

   `public void paintComponent(Graphics g)`

   Override this method to display the token in the cell.

   `public void mouseClicked(MouseEvent e)`

Implement this method in the `MouseListener` to handle a mouse click on the cell.

The `TicTacToe` class has the following data fields and methods:

Data field:

```
char whoseTurn: Indicate which player has the turn.

Cell[][] cell: Represent the cells.

JLabel jlblStatus: A label for displaying game status.
```

Methods:

```
public void init()
```

Override this method to initialize variables and create UI.

```
public boolean isFilled()
```

Determine if the cells are all filled.

```
public boolean isWinning(char token)
```

Determine if the player with the specified token wins.

The program is given below:

```java
// TicTacToe.java: Play the TicTacToe game
import java.awt.*;
import java.awt.event.*;
import javax.swing.*;
import javax.swing.border.LineBorder;

public class TicTacToe extends JApplet
{
  // Indicate which player has a turn, initially it is the X player
  private char whoseTurn = 'X';

  // Create and initialize cells
  private Cell[][] cell =  new Cell[3][3];

  // Create and initialize a status label
  private JLabel jlblStatus = new JLabel("X's turn playing");

  // Initialize UI
  public void init()
  {
    // Panel p to hold cells
    JPanel p = new JPanel();
    p.setLayout(new GridLayout(3, 3, 0, 0));
    for (int i=0; i<3; i++)
      for (int j=0; j<3; j++)
        p.add(cell[i][j] = new Cell());

    // Set line borders on the cells panel and the status label
    p.setBorder(new LineBorder(Color.red, 1));
    jlblStatus.setBorder(new LineBorder(Color.yellow, 1));
```

continues

```java
    // Place the panel and the label to the applet
    this.getContentPane().add(p, BorderLayout.CENTER);
    this.getContentPane().add(jlblStatus, BorderLayout.NORTH);
  }

  // This main method enables the applet to run as an application
  public static void main(String[] args)
  {
    // Create a frame
    MyFrameWithExitHandling frame = new MyFrameWithExitHandling(
      "Tic Tac Toe");

    // Create an instance of the applet
    TicTacToe applet = new TicTacToe();

    // Add the applet instance to the frame
    frame.getContentPane().add(applet, BorderLayout.CENTER);

    // Invoke init() and start()
    applet.init();
    applet.start();

    // Display the frame
    frame.setSize(300, 300);
    frame.setVisible(true);
  }

  // Determine if the cells are all occupied
  public boolean isFull()
  {
    for (int i=0; i<3; i++)
      for (int j=0; j<3; j++)
        if (cell[i][j].getToken() == ' ')
          return false;

    return true;
  }

  // Determine if the player with the specified token wins
  public boolean isWinning(char token)
  {
    for (int i=0; i<3; i++)
      if ((cell[i][0].getToken()==token)
          && (cell[i][1].getToken()==token)
          && (cell[i][2].getToken()==token))
      {
        return true;
      }

    for (int j=0; j<3; j++)
      if ((cell[0][j].getToken()==token)
          && (cell[1][j].getToken()==token)
          && (cell[2][j].getToken()==token))
      {
        return true;
      }

    if ((cell[0][0].getToken()==token)
        && (cell[1][1].getToken()==token)
        && (cell[2][2].getToken()==token))
    {
      return true;
    }
```

```java
      if ((cell[0][2].getToken()==token)
          && (cell[1][1].getToken()==token)
          && (cell[2][0].getToken()==token))
      {
        return true;
      }

      return false;
    }

    // An inner class for a cell
    public class Cell extends JPanel implements MouseListener
    {
      // Token used for this cell
      private char token = ' ';

      public Cell()
      {
        setBorder(new LineBorder(Color.black, 1)); // Set cell's border
        addMouseListener(this);   // Register listener
      }

      // The getter method for token
      public char getToken()
      {
        return token;
      }

      // The setter method for token
      public void setToken(char c)
      {
        token = c;
        repaint();
      }

      // Paint the cell
      public void paintComponent(Graphics g)
      {
        super.paintComponent(g);

        if (token == 'X')
        {
          g.drawLine(10, 10, getSize().width-10, getSize().height-10);
          g.drawLine(getSize().width-10, 10, 10, getSize().height-10);
        }
        else if (token == 'O')
        {
          g.drawOval(10, 10, getSize().width-20, getSize().height-20);
        }
      }

      // Handle mouse click on a cell
      public void mouseClicked(MouseEvent e)
      {
        if (token == ' ') // If cell is not occupied
        {
          if (whoseTurn == 'X')  // If it is the X player's turn
          {
            setToken('X');  // Set token in the cell
            whoseTurn = 'O';  // Change the turn
```

continues

```java
          jlblStatus.setText("O's turn");  // Display status
          if (isWinning('X'))
            jlblStatus.setText("X won! The game is over");
          else if (isFull())
            jlblStatus.setText("Draw! The game is over");
        }
        else if (whoseTurn == 'O') // If it is the O player's turn
        {
          setToken('O'); // Set token in the cell
          whoseTurn = 'X';  // Change the turn
          jlblStatus.setText("X's turn"); // Display status
          if (isWinning('O'))
            jlblStatus.setText("O won! The game is over");
          else if (isFull())
            jlblStatus.setText("Draw! The game is over");
        }
      }
    }

    public void mousePressed(MouseEvent e)
    {
      // TODO: implement this java.awt.event.MouseListener method;
    }

    public void mouseReleased(MouseEvent e)
    {
      // TODO: implement this java.awt.event.MouseListener method;
    }

    public void mouseEntered(MouseEvent e)
    {
      // TODO: implement this java.awt.event.MouseListener method;
    }

    public void mouseExited(MouseEvent e)
    {
      // TODO: implement this java.awt.event.MouseListener method;
    }
  }
}
```

Example Review

The TicTacToe class initializes the user interface with nine cells placed in a panel of GridLayout. A label named jlblStatus is used to show the status of the game. The variable whoseTurn is used to track the type of next token to be placed on a cell. The methods isFull() and isWinning() are for checking the status of the game.

It is worth noting that the Cell class is declared as an inner class for TicTacToe. This is because the mouseClicked() method in Cell references variable whoseTurn and invokes isFull and isWinning in the TicTacToe class. Since Cell is an inner class in TicTacToe, the variable and methods defined in TicTacToe can be directly used in it. This approach makes programs simple and concise. If Cell were not declared as an inner class of TicTacToe, you would have to pass an object of TicTacToe to Cell for the variables and methods in TicTacToe to be used in Cell. You will rewrite the program without using inner class in Exercise 10.5.

> The `Cell` class implements `MouseListener` to listen for `MouseEvent`. When a cell is clicked, it draws a shape determined by variable `whoseTurn`, and then checks whether the game is won or all the cells are occupied.
>
> There is a problem in this program in that the user may continue to mark the cells even after the game is over. You will fix this problem in Exercise 10.5.

The *CardLayout* Manager (Optional)

Layout managers arrange components in a container. You have already used the `FlowLayout` manager, `GridLayout` manager, and `BorderLayout` manager. Java has two other layout managers like `CardLayout` and `GridBagLayout`. Java also enables you to directly place components in a specific position without using a layout manager. This section discusses the `CardLayout` manager; the following sections discuss the `GridBagLayout` manager and using no layout manager.

The `CardLayout` manager arranges components in a queue of cards. You can only see one card at a time. To construct a `CardLayout`, use the constructor `CardLayout()`.

Cards are usually placed in a container, such as a panel. Components are placed into the card queue in the order in which they are added. To add a component in the `CardLayout` container, use the following method:

```
public void add(Component component, String name)
```

This adds the specified component to the container. The `String` argument of the method, `name`, gives an explicit identity to the component in the queue.

To make a component visible in the container with `CardLayout`, use the following instance methods in the `CardLayout` object:

- `public void first(Container container)`

    This method views the first card in the container.

- `public void last(Container container)`

    This method views the last card in the container.

- `public void next(Container container)`

    This method views the next card in the container.

- `public void previous(Container container)`

    This method views the previous card in the container.

- `public void show(Container container, String name)`

    This method views the component with the specified name in the container. It can be used to directly display the component.

Example 10.9 Testing *CardLayout* Manager

This example shows a program that creates two panels in a frame. The first panel uses `CardLayout` to hold 15 labels for displaying images. The second panel uses `FlowLayout` to group four buttons named First, Next, Previous, and Last, and a combo box labeled `Image`.

These buttons control which image will be shown in the `CardLayout` panel. When the user clicks on the First button, for example, the first image in the `CardLayout` panel appears. The combo box enables the user to directly select an image.

The program follows, and the output of a sample run is shown in Figure 10.17.

```java
// ShowCardLayout.java: Using CardLayout to display images
import java.awt.*;
import java.awt.event.*;
import javax.swing.*;

public class ShowCardLayout extends JApplet
  implements ActionListener, ItemListener
{
  private CardLayout queue = new CardLayout();
  private JPanel cardPanel = new JPanel();
  private JButton jbtFirst, jbtNext, jbtPrevious, jbtLast;
  private JComboBox jcboImage;

  public void init()
  {
    // Use CardLayout for cardPanel
    cardPanel.setLayout(queue);

    // Add 15 labels for displaying images into cardPanel
    for (int i=1; i<=15; i++)
      cardPanel.add
        (new JLabel(new ImageIcon("images/L"+i+".gif")),
          String.valueOf(i));

    // Panel p to hold buttons and a combo box
    JPanel p = new JPanel();
    p.add(jbtFirst = new JButton("First"));
    p.add(jbtNext = new JButton("Next"));
    p.add(jbtPrevious= new JButton("Previous"));
    p.add(jbtLast = new JButton("Last"));
    p.add(new JLabel("Image"));
    p.add(jcboImage = new JComboBox());

    // Initialize combo box items
    for (int i=1; i<=15; i++)
      jcboImage.addItem(String.valueOf(i));

    // Place panels in the frame
    getContentPane().add(cardPanel, BorderLayout.CENTER);
    getContentPane().add(p, BorderLayout.NORTH);

    // Register listeners with the source objects
    jbtFirst.addActionListener(this);
    jbtNext.addActionListener(this);
```

```java
    jbtPrevious.addActionListener(this);
    jbtLast.addActionListener(this);
    jcboImage.addItemListener(this);
  }

  // This main method enables the applet to run as an application
  public static void main(String[] args)
  {
    // Create a frame
    MyFrameWithExitHandling frame = new MyFrameWithExitHandling(
      "CardLayout Demo");

    // Create an instance of the applet
    ShowCardLayout applet = new ShowCardLayout();

    // Add the applet instance to the frame
    frame.getContentPane().add(applet, BorderLayout.CENTER);

    // Invoke init() and start()
    applet.init();
    applet.start();

    // Display the frame
    frame.setSize(300, 300);
    frame.setVisible(true);
  }

  // Handle button actions
  public void actionPerformed(ActionEvent e)
  {
    String actionCommand = e.getActionCommand();
    if (e.getSource() instanceof JButton)
      if ("First".equals(actionCommand))
        // Show the first component in queue
        queue.first(cardPanel);
      else if ("Last".equals(actionCommand))
        // Show the last component in queue
        queue.last(cardPanel);
      else if ("Previous".equals(actionCommand))
        // Show the previous component in queue
        queue.previous(cardPanel);
      else if ("Next".equals(actionCommand))
        // Show the next component in queue
        queue.next(cardPanel);
  }

  // Handle selection of combo box item
  public void itemStateChanged(ItemEvent e)
  {
    if (e.getSource() == jcboImage)
      // Show the component at specified index
      queue.show(cardPanel, (String)e.getItem());
  }
}
```

continues

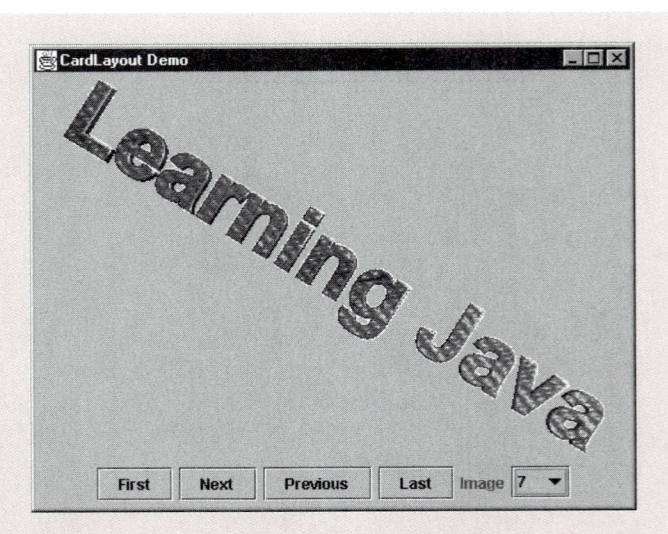

Figure 10.17 *The program shows images in a panel of* `CardLayout`.

Example Review

The program creates an instance of `CardLayout`, `queue = new CardLayout()`. The statement `cardPanel.setLayout(queue)` sets the `cardPanel` with the `CardLayout`; `cardPanel` is an instance of `JPanel`. You have already used such statements as `setLayout(new FlowLayout())` to create an anonymous layout object and set the layout for a container, instead of declaring and creating a separate instance of the layout manager, as in this program. The object `queue`, however, is useful later in the program to show components in `cardPanel`. You have to use `queue.first(cardPanel)`, for example, to view the first component in `cardPanel`.

The statement `cardPanel.add(new JLabel(new ImageIcon("images/L"+i+".gif")),String.valueOf(i))` adds the image label with identity `String.valueOf(i)`. Later, when the user selects an image with number `i`, the identity `String.valueOf(i)` is used in the `queue.show()` method to view the image with the specified identity.

The *GridBagLayout* Manager (Optional)

The `GridBagLayout` manager is the most flexible and the most complex. It is similar to the `GridLayout` manager in the sense that both layout managers arrange components in a grid. The components of `GridBagLayout` can vary in size, however, and can be added in any order. For example, with `GridBagLayout` you can create the layout shown in Figure 10.18.

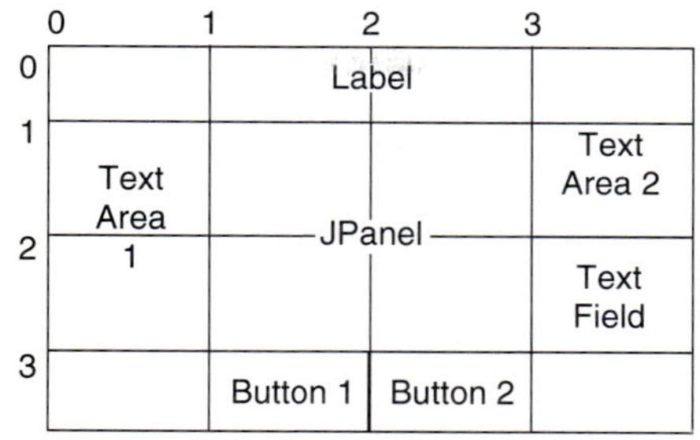

Figure 10.18 *A* `GridBagLayout` *manager divides the container into cells. A component can occupy several cells.*

The constructor `GridBagLayout()` is used to create a new `GridBagLayout`. In `GridLayout`, the grid size (the number of rows and columns) is specified in the constructor. It is not specified in `GridBagLayout`.

Each `GridBagLayout` uses a dynamic rectangular grid of cells, with each component occupying one or more cells called its *display area*. Each component managed by a `GridBagLayout` is associated with a `GridBagConstraints` instance that specifies how the component is laid out within its display area. How a `GridBagLayout` places a set of components depends on the `GridBagConstraints` and minimum size of each component, as well as the preferred size of the component's container.

To use `GridBagLayout` effectively, you must customize the `GridBagConstraints` of one or more of its components. You customize a `GridBagConstraints` object by setting one or more of its instance variables:

- **gridx** and **gridy**—Specifies the cell at the upper left of the component's display area, where the upper-leftmost cell has address `gridx=0`, `gridy=0`. Note that `gridx` specifies the column in which the component will be placed, and `gridy` specifies the row in which the component will be placed. In Figure 10.19, Button 1 has a `gridx` value of 1 and a `gridy` value of 3, and Label has `gridx` value of 0 and a `gridy` value of 0.

- **gridwidth** and **gridheight**—Specifies the number of cells in a row (for `gridwidth`) or column (for `gridheight`) in the component's display area. The default value is 1. In Figure 10.18, the JPanel in the center occupies two columns and two rows, and Text Area 2 occupies one row and one column.

- **weightx** and **weighty**—Specifies the extra space to allocate horizontally and vertically for the component when the window is resized. Unless you specify a weight for at least one component in a row (`weightx`) and a column (`weighty`), all the components clump together in the center of their container. This is because, when the weight is zero (the default), the `GridBagLayout` puts any extra space between its grid of cells and the edges of the container. You will see the effect of these parameters in Example 10.10.

- **fill**—Specifies how the component should be resized if its viewing area is larger than its current size. Valid values are `GridBagConstraints.NONE` (the default), `GridBagConstraints.HORIZONTAL` (makes the component wide enough to fill its display area horizontally, but doesn't change its height), `GridBagConstraints.VERTICAL` (makes the component tall enough to fill its display area vertically, but doesn't change its width), and `GridBagConstraints.BOTH` (makes the component totally fill its display area).

- **anchor**—Specifies where in the area the component is placed when it does not fill in the entire area. Valid values are as follows:

  `GridBagConstraints.CENTER` (the default)

  `GridBagConstraints.NORTH`

  `GridBagConstraints.NORTHEAST`

  `GridBagConstraints.EAST`

  `GridBagConstraints.SOUTHEAST`

  `GridBagConstraints.SOUTH`

  `GridBagConstraints.SOUTHWEST`

  `GridBagConstraints.WEST`

  `GridBagConstraints.NORTHWEST`

The `fill` and `anchor` parameters deal with how to fill and place the component when the viewing area is larger than the requested area. The `fill` and `anchor` parameters are class variables, whereas `gridx`, `gridy`, `width`, `height`, `weightx`, and `weighty` are instance variables.

Example 10.10 Testing the *GridBagLayout* Manager

This example shows a program that uses the `GridBagLayout` manager to create a layout for Figure 10.18. The output of the program is shown in Figure 10.19.

```java
// ShowGridBagLayout.java: Using GridBagLayout
import java.awt.*;
import java.awt.event.*;
import javax.swing.*;

public class ShowGridBagLayout extends MyFrameWithExitHandling
{
  private JLabel jlbl;
  private JTextArea jta1, jta2;
  private JTextField jtf;
  private JPanel jp;
  private JButton jbt1, jbt2;
  private GridBagLayout gbLayout;
  private GridBagConstraints gbConstraints;

  // Main method
  public static void main(String[] args)
  {
    ShowGridBagLayout frame = new ShowGridBagLayout();
    frame.setSize(350,200);
    frame.setVisible(true);
  }
```

```java
// Add a component to the conjtainer
private void addComp(Component c, GridBagLayout gbLayout,
                     GridBagConstraints gbConstraints,
                     int row, int column, int numRows,
                     int numColumns, int weightx, int weighty)
{
  // Set parameters
  gbConstraints.gridx = column;
  gbConstraints.gridy = row;
  gbConstraints.gridwidth = numColumns;
  gbConstraints.gridheight = numRows;
  gbConstraints.weightx = weightx;
  gbConstraints.weighty = weighty;

  // Set constraints in the GridBagLayout
  gbLayout.setConstraints(c, gbConstraints);

  // Add component to the container
  getContentPane().add(c);
}

// Constructor
public ShowGridBagLayout()
{
  setTitle("Show GridBagLayout");

  // Initialize UI components
  jlbl = new JLabel("Resize the Window and Study GridBagLayout",
              JLabel.CENTER);
  jp = new JPanel();
  jta1 = new JTextArea("Text Area", 5, 15 );
  jta2 = new JTextArea("Text Area", 5, 15 );
  jtf = new JTextField("JTextField");
  jbt1 = new JButton("Cancel" );
  jbt2 = new JButton("Ok" );

  // Create GridBagLayout and GridBagConstraints object
  gbLayout = new GridBagLayout();
  gbConstraints = new GridBagConstraints();
  getContentPane().setLayout(gbLayout);

  // Place JLabel to occupy row 0 (the first row)
  gbConstraints.fill = GridBagConstraints.BOTH;
  gbConstraints.anchor = GridBagConstraints.CENTER;
  addComp(jlbl, gbLayout, gbConstraints, 0, 0, 1, 4, 0, 0);

  // Place text area 1 in row 1 and 2, and column 0
  addComp(jta1, gbLayout, gbConstraints, 1, 0, 2, 1, 0, 0);

  // Place Panel in row 1 and 2, and column 1 and 2
  addComp(jp, gbLayout, gbConstraints, 1, 1, 2, 2, 100, 100);
  jp.setBackground(Color.red);

  // Place text area 2 in row 1 and column 3
  addComp(jta2, gbLayout, gbConstraints, 1, 3, 1, 1, 0, 100);

  // Place text field in row 2 and column 3
  addComp(jtf, gbLayout, gbConstraints, 2, 3, 1, 1, 0, 0);

  // Place JButton 1 in row 3 and column 1
  addComp(jbt1, gbLayout, gbConstraints, 3, 1, 1, 1, 0, 0);
```

continues

```
        // Place JButton 2 in row 3 and column 2
        addComp(jbt2, gbLayout, gbConstraints, 3, 2, 1, 1, 0, 0);
    }
}
```

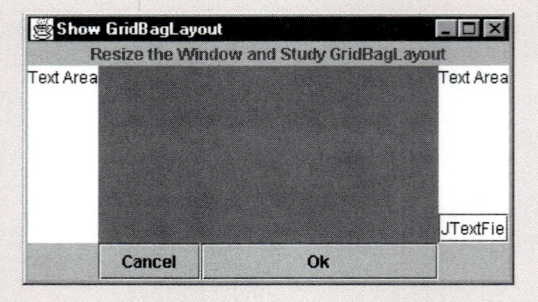

Figure 10.19 *The components are placed in the frame of* `GridBagLayout`.

Example Review

The program defines the `addComp()` method to add a component to the `GridBagLayout` with the specified constraints parameters.

Since the program creates a panel with a `weightx` of 100 and a `weighty` of 100, the component has extra space to grow horizontally and vertically up to 100 pixels. If you resize the window, the panel's viewing area will increase or shrink as the window grows or shrinks.

Since the program creates the second text area `jta2` with `weightx` 0 and `weighty` 100, this text area can grow vertically but not horizontally when the window is resized.

The `weightx` and `weighty` for all the other components are 0. Whether the size of these components grows or shrinks depends on the `fill` and `anchor` parameters. The program defines `fill = BOTH` and `anchor = CENTER`.

Because the `fill` and `anchor` parameters are class variables, their values are for all components. Consider this scenario: Suppose you enlarge the window. The panel is expanded, which causes the display area for text area `jta1` to increase. Because `fill` is `BOTH` for `jta1`, `jta1` fills in its new display area.

Using No Layout Manager (Optional)

Java enables you to place components in a container without using a layout manager. In this case, the component must be placed using the component's instance method `setBounds()`, as follows:

```
public void setBounds(int x, int y, int width, int height);
```

This sets the location and size for the component, as in the following example:

```
JButton jbt = new JButton("Help");
jbt.setBounds(10, 10, 40, 20);
```

The upper-left corner of the Help button is placed at (10, 10); the button width is 40, and the height is 20.

You perform the following steps in order not to use a layout manager:

1. Use the following statement to specify no layout manager:

   ```
   setLayout(null);
   ```

2. Add the component to the container:

   ```
   add(component);
   ```

3. Specify the location where the component is to be placed, using the setBounds() method, as follows:

   ```
   JButton jbt = new JButton("Help");
   jbt.setBounds(10, 10, 40, 20);
   ```

Example 10.11 Using No Layout Manager

This example shows a program that places the same components in the same layout as in the preceding example, but without using a layout manager. Figure 10.20 contains the sample output.

```
// ShowNoLayout.java: Place components without using a layout manager
import java.awt.*;
import java.awt.event.*;
import javax.swing.*;

public class ShowNoLayout extends MyFrameWithExitHandling
{
  private JLabel jlbl =
    new JLabel("Resize the Window and Study No Layout",
      JLabel.CENTER);;
  private JTextArea jta1 = new JTextArea("Text Area", 5, 10 );
  private JTextArea jta2 = new JTextArea("Text Area", 5, 10 );
  private JTextField jtf = new JTextField("TextField");
  private JPanel jp = new JPanel();
  private JButton jbt1 = new JButton("Cancel" );
  private JButton jbt2 = new JButton("Ok" );
  private GridBagLayout gbLayout;
  private GridBagConstraints gbConstraints;

  public static void main(String[] args)
  {
    ShowNoLayout frame = new ShowNoLayout();
    frame.setSize(400,200);
    frame.setVisible(true);
  }
```

continues

```
public ShowNoLayout()
{
  setTitle("Show No Layout");

  // Set background color for the panel
  jp.setBackground(Color.red);

  // Specify no layout manager
  getContentPane().setLayout(null);

  // Add components to frame
  getContentPane().add(jlbl);
  getContentPane().add(jp);
  getContentPane().add(jta1);
  getContentPane().add(jta2);
  getContentPane().add(jtf);
  getContentPane().add(jbt1);
  getContentPane().add(jbt2);

  // Put components in the right place
  jlbl.setBounds(0, 10, 400, 40);
  jta1.setBounds(0, 50, 100, 100);
  jp.setBounds(100, 50, 200, 100);
  jta2.setBounds(300, 50, 100, 50);
  jtf.setBounds(300, 100, 100, 50);
  jbt1.setBounds(100, 150, 100, 50);
  jbt2.setBounds(200, 150, 100, 50);
  }
}
```

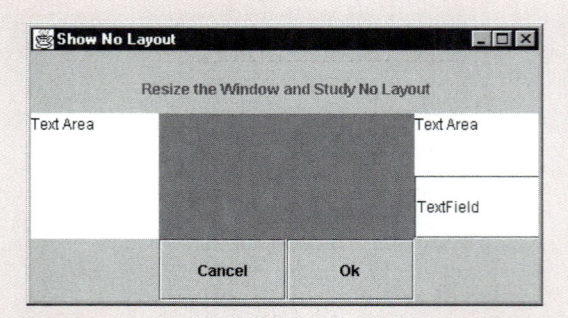

Figure 10.20 *The components are placed in the frame without using a layout manager.*

Example Review

If you run this program on Windows with 640×480 resolution, the layout size is desirable. If you run the program on Windows with a higher resolution, the components appear very small and clump together. If you run the program on Windows with a lower resolution, the components cannot be shown in their entirety.

If you resize the window, you will see that the components' location and size are not changed, as shown in Figure 10.21.

Figure 10.21 *With no layout, the components' size and positions are fixed, and can only be changed in the frame with a layout manager.*

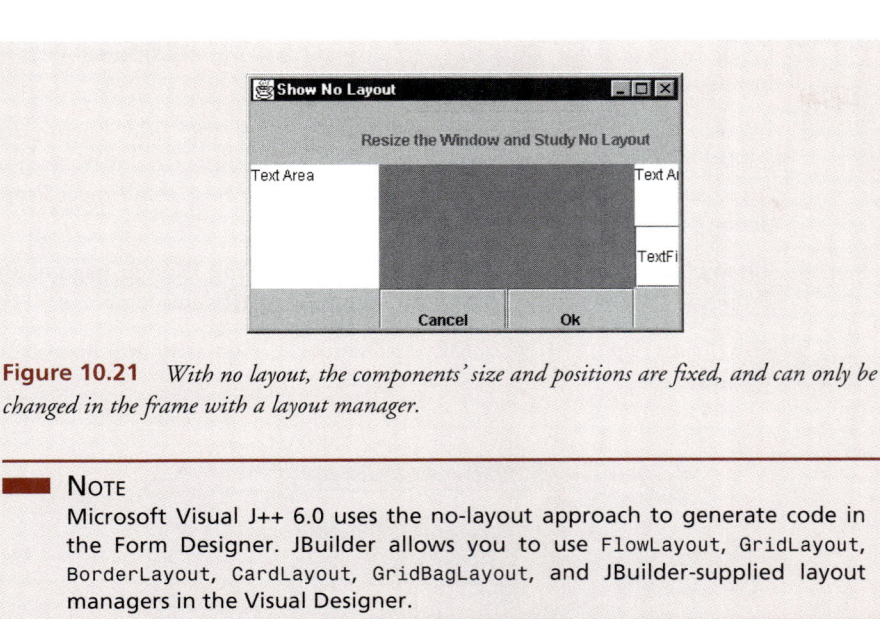

> ■ **NOTE**
> Microsoft Visual J++ 6.0 uses the no-layout approach to generate code in the Form Designer. JBuilder allows you to use `FlowLayout`, `GridLayout`, `BorderLayout`, `CardLayout`, `GridBagLayout`, and JBuilder-supplied layout managers in the Visual Designer.

> ■ **TIP**
> Do not use the no-layout-manager option to develop platform-independent applications.

Packaging and Deploying Visual J++ Projects (Optional)

Visual J++ projects with many files can be packaged into one file for convenient deployment. The output file can be a COM .dll file, a cabinet file, a setup file, a compressed .zip file, or a Windows .exe file. This section uses Example 10.7 to demonstrate how to package and deploy Visual J++ projects in .zip files and .exe files.

Packaging and Deploying as .exe files

Example 10.7 contains two classes, `KeyboardEventDemo` and `KeyboardPanel`. The `KeyboardEventDemo` can run either as a standalone application or as an applet.

Follow the steps below to package these two classes into a .exe file.

1. On the Output Format page of the Project Properties dialog box for Project10, choose Windows EXE in the packaging type field and type KeyboardEventDemo.exe in the File name field, as shown in Figure 10.22. Click the option "These outputs," and check the boxes for KeyboardPanel.class and KeyboardEventDemo.class.

2. Click Include Additional Files to display the Add Additional Files dialog box, as shown in Figure 10.23.

3. In the Add Additional Files dialog box, click the Add button to add c:\vjBook\Project8\MyFrameWithExitHandling.class. Click OK to close the Add Additional Files dialog box, and click OK to close the Project Properties dialog box.

4. Choose KeyboardEventDemo(main) to run on the Launch page of Project Properties. Build the project to generate KeyboardEventDemo.exe.

5. You can deploy KeyboardEventDemo.exe on any machine running Windows.

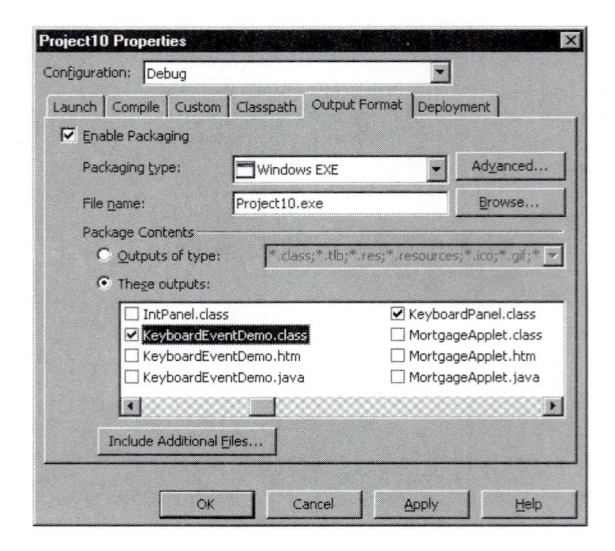

Figure 10.22   *You can specify the Output format in the Project Properties dialog box.*

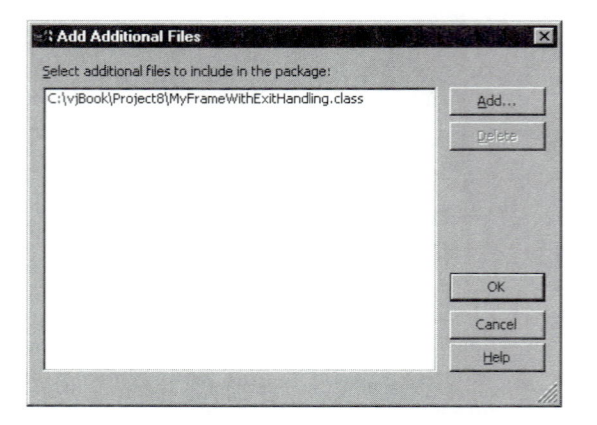

Figure 10.23   *The Add Additional Files dialog box lets you include additional files for packaging.*

> **NOTE**
> To be packaged into a Windows EXE file, a project consisting of several files must contain one and only one class with a main method.

Packaging and Deploying as .zip files

Windows EXE files can only run on Windows. To enable your Java programs to run on any Java VM, you need to package your projects into a .zip file that is equivalent to the Java archive file.

Follow the steps below to package KeyboardEventDemo and its associated files into a .zip file, and deploy it as a standalone application or as an applet.

1. On the Output Format page of the Project Properties dialog box for Project10, choose ZIP Archive (.zip) in the packaging type field, and type KeyboardEventDemo.zip in the File name field. Click the option "These outputs," and check the boxes for KeyboardPanel.class and KeyboardEventDemo.class.

2. Add c:\vjBook\Project8\MyFrameWithExitHandling.class in the Add Additional Files dialog box.

3. Choose KeyboardEventDemo(main) to run on the Launch page of Project Properties. Build the project to generate KeyboardEventDemo.zip.

4. You can deploy KeyboardEventDemo.zip on any machine with Java VM, and use the following command to run the program in JDK 1.1.x:

   ```
   jre -cp KeyboardEventDemo.zip KeyboardEventDemo
   ```

   In JDK 1.2, you have to use this command to run it:

   ```
   java -jar KeyboardEventDemo.zip KeyboardEventDemo
   ```

5. The program can also run as a Java applet. You can embed it in the <applet> tag as follows:

   ```
   <APPLET
   code=KeyboardEventDemo.class
   name=KeyboardEventDemo
   archive="KeyboardEventDemo.zip"
   width = 200
   height = 200
   >
   </applet>
   ```

Chapter Summary

In this chapter, you learned about applets and advanced graphics programming using mouse and keyboard events, `CardLayout` manager, `GridBagLayout` manager, and using no layout manager. You also learned how to package files to efficiently deploy Java projects.

The Web browser controls and executes applets through the `init()`, `start()`, `stop()`, and `destroy()` methods in the `Applet` class. Applets always extend the `Applet` class and implement these methods if applicable, so they can be run by the Web browser. The applet bytecode must be specified, using the `<applet>` tag in an HTML file to tell the Web browser where to find the applet. The applet can accept parameters from HTML using the `<param>` tag. `JApplet` is a subclass of `Applet`. It should be used for developing Java applets with Swing components.

The procedures for writing applications and writing applets are very similar. An applet can easily be converted into an application, and vice versa. Moreover, an applet can be written with the capability to run, additionally, as an application.

Two examples and a case study demonstrated how to handle mouse events and keyboard events. Mouse events and keyboard events have many uses in graphics programming. Clicking, pressing, or releasing a mouse button generates a `MouseEvent`; dragging or moving a mouse generates a `MouseMotionEvent`. Entering a key generates a `KeyEvent`. `MouseEvent`, `MouseMotionEvent`, and `KeyEvent` are subclasses of `InputEvent`, which contains several common methods useful in processing mouse and keyboard events.

The `CardLayout` manager arranges components in a queue of cards. You can see one component at a time. To add a component into the container, you need to use `add(component, string)`. You can see the components by using the methods `first(container)`, `last(container)`, `next(container)`, `previous(container)`, or `show(container, string)`. The `show(container, string)` method directly displays the component identified by the string.

The `GridBagLayout` manager provides the most flexible way to arrange components. It is similar to `GridLayout` in that the components are placed into cells, but it enables a component to occupy multiple cells. The components can vary in size and can be placed in any order.

Components can be placed without using a layout manager. In such cases, they are placed at a hard-coded location. If you use this approach, your program may look fine on one machine and be useless on others. For this reason it is advisable to use the layout managers to develop a platform-independent graphical user interface.

Finally, you also learned how to package and deploy Visual J++ projects.

Chapter Review

10.1. How do you run an applet?

10.2. Describe the `init()`, `start()`, `stop()`, and `destroy()` methods in the `Applet` class.

10.3. Is the `getParameter()` method defined in `Applet`? Is the `paintComponent()` method defined in `Applet`? Find where these methods are originally defined.

10.4. How do you add components to a `JApplet`?

10.5. Describe the `<applet>` HTML tag. How do you pass parameters to an applet?

10.5. Describe the procedure for converting an application to an applet, and vice versa.

10.6. How do you create a frame from an applet?

10.7. Can you place an applet in a frame?

10.8. Describe `CardLayout`. How do you create a `CardLayout`? How do you add a component to a `CardLayout`? How do you show a card in the `CardLayout` container?

10.9. Describe `GridBagLayout`. How do you create a `GridBagLayout`? How do you create a `GridBagConstraints` object? What are the constraints you learned in this chapter? Describe their functions. How do you add a component to a `GridBagLayout` container?

10.10. Is the order in which the components are added important for certain layout managers? Identify the layout managers.

10.11. Which layout manager allows the components in the container to be moved to other rows when the window is resized?

10.12. Can you place components without using a layout manager? What are the disadvantages of not using a layout manager?

Programming Exercises

10.1. Convert Example 9.7, "Using Radio Buttons," into an applet.

10.2. Rewrite Example 10.2, "Passing Parameters to Java Applets," to display a message with specified color, font, and size. The message, x, y, color, fontname, and fontsize are parameters in the `<applet>` tag, like this:

```
<applet
  code = "Exercise10_2.class"
  width = 200
  height = 50>
  <param name=MESSAGE value="Welcome to Java">
  <param name=X value=40>
  <param name=Y value=50>
  <param name=COLOR value="red">
  <param name=FONTNAME value="Monospaced">
  <param name=FONTSIZE value=20>
You must have a Java-enabled browser to view the applet
</applet>
```

10.3. Rewrite the `MortgageApplet` in Example 10.1, "Using Applets," to enable it to run as an application as well as an applet.

10.4. Write an applet to find a path in a maze, as shown in Figure 10.24. The applet can also run as an application. The maze is represented by an 8×8 board. The path must meet the following conditions:

- The path is between the upper-left corner cell and the lower-right corner cell in the maze.

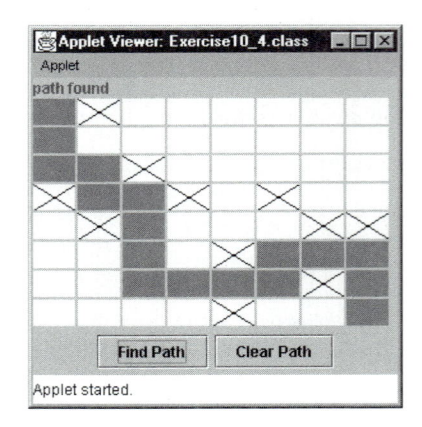

Figure 10.24 *The program finds a path from the upper-left corner to the bottom-right corner.*

- The applet enables the user to insert or remove a mark on a cell. A path consists of adjacent unmarked cells. Two cells are said to be adjacent if they are horizontal or vertical neighbors, but not diagonal neighbors.

- The path does not contain cells that form a square. The path in Figure 10.25, for example, does not meet this condition. (This condition makes a path easy to identify on the board.)

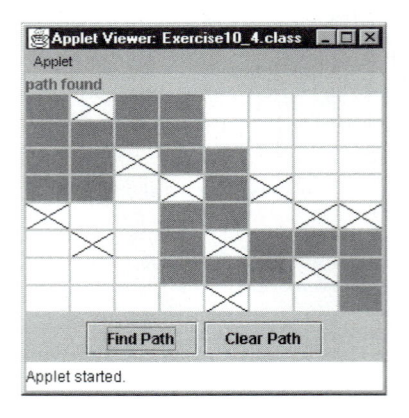

Figure 10.25 *The path does not meet the third condition for this exercise.*

10.5. Rewrite Example 10.8, "The TicTacToe Game," with the following modifications:

- Declare Cell as a standalone class rather than an inner class.
- When the game is over, the user cannot click to mark empty cells.

10.6. Write an applet that contains two buttons called Simple Calculator and Mortgage. When you click Simple Calculator, a frame for Example 9.9,

"Using Menus," appears in a new window so that you can perform arithmetic (see Chapter 9, "Creating User Interfaces"). When you click Mortgage, a frame for Example 10.4 appears in a separate new window so that you can calculate a mortgage (see Figure 10.26).

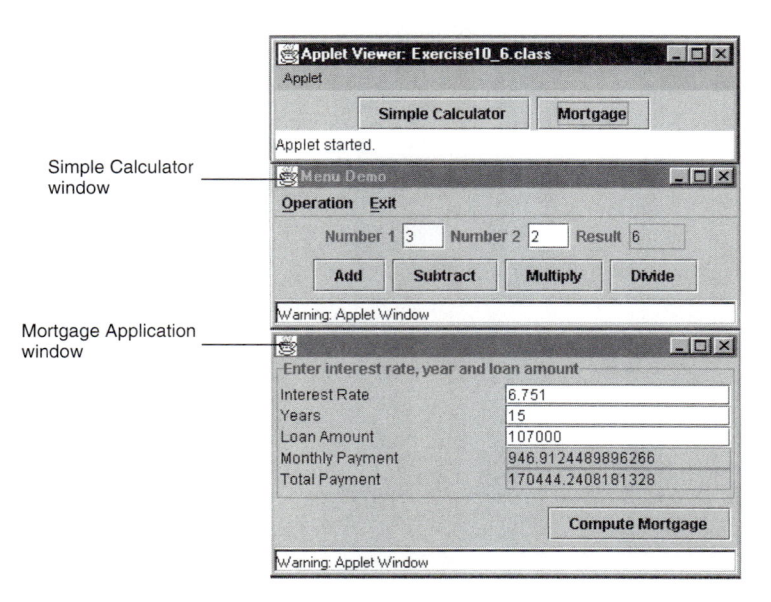

Figure 10.26 *You can show frames in the applets.*

10.7. Use various panels of `FlowLayout`, `GridLayout`, and `BorderLayout` to lay out the following calculator and to implement addition (+), subtraction (−), division (/), square root (sqrt), and modulus (%) functions (see Figure 10.27).

Figure 10.27 *This is a Java implementation of a popular calculator.*

10.8. Use `GridBagLayout` to lay out the preceding calculator.

10.9. Write a program to get character input from the keyboard and put the characters where the mouse points.

10.10. Write an applet to emulate a paint utility. Your program should enable the user to choose options, and to draw shapes or get characters from the keyboard based on the selected options (see Figure 10.28). Enable the applet to run as an application.

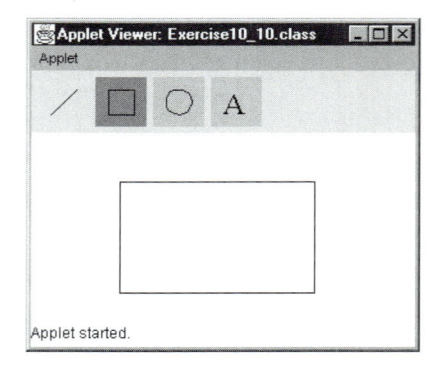

Figure 10.28 *This exercise produces a prototype drawing utility that enables you to draw lines, rectangles, ovals, and characters.*

10.11. Write an applet that does arithmetic on integers and rationals. The program uses two panels in a `CardLayout` manager, one for integer arithmetic and the other for rational arithmetic.

The program provides a menu labeled Operation that has two menu items, Integer and Rational, for selecting the two panels. When the user chooses the Integer menu item from the Operation menu, the integer panel is activated. When the user chooses the Rational menu item, the rational panel is activated. (See Figure 10.29)

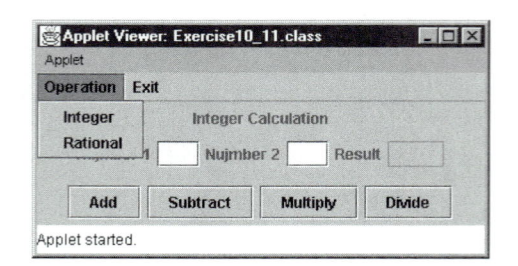

Figure 10.29 *This exercise uses `CardLayout` to select panels for performing integer operations or rational number operations.*

10.12. Rewrite the preceding example using tabbed panes instead of `CardLayout` (see Figure 10.30).

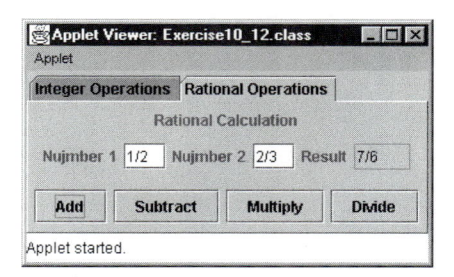

Figure 10.30 *This exercise uses tabbed panes to select panels for performing integer operations or rational number operations.*

PART IV

DEVELOPING COMPREHENSIVE PROJECTS

This part of the book is devoted to several advanced features of Java programming. You will learn how to use these features to develop comprehensive programs; for example, the use of exception handling to make your program robust, the use of internationalization support to develop projects for international audiences, the use of multithreading to make your program more responsive and interactive, the incorporation of sound and images to make your program user-friendly, the use of input and output to manage and process large quantities of data, and the creation of client/server applications with Java networking support.

CHAPTER 11 EXCEPTION HANDLING

CHAPTER 12 INTERNATIONALIZATION

CHAPTER 13 MULTITHREADING

CHAPTER 14 MULTIMEDIA

CHAPTER 15 INPUT AND OUTPUT

CHAPTER 16 NETWORKING

CHAPTER 11

Exception Handling

Objectives

- Understand the concept of exception handling.
- Become familiar with exception types.
- Claim exceptions in a method.
- Throw exceptions in a method.
- Use the `try-catch` block to handle exceptions.
- Create your own exception classes.
- Rethrow exceptions in a `try-catch` block.
- Use the `finally` clause in a `try-catch` block.
- Know when to use exceptions.

Introduction

There were no runtime errors in the program examples you have seen so far. Nonetheless, runtime errors are unavoidable, even for experienced programmers, and in Java they cause *exceptions*: events that occur during the execution of a program and disrupt the normal flow of control.

A program that does not provide the code to handle exceptions may terminate abnormally, causing serious problems. For example, if your program attempts to transfer money from a savings account to a checking account but, because of a runtime error, is terminated *after* the money is drawn from the savings account and *before* the money is deposited in the checking account, the customer will lose money.

Java provides programmers with the capability to handle runtime errors. With this capability, referred to as *exception handling*, you can develop robust programs for mission-critical computing.

This chapter introduces Java's exception-handling model. The chapter covers exception types, claiming exceptions, throwing exceptions, catching exceptions, creating exception classes, rethrowing exceptions, and the `finally` clause.

Exceptions and Exception Types

Runtime errors occur for various reasons. For example, the user may enter an invalid input, or the program may attempt to open a file that doesn't exist, or the network connection may hang up, or the program may attempt to access an out-of-bounds array element. When a runtime error occurs, Java raises an exception.

Exceptions are handled differently from the events of graphics programming. (In Chapter 8, "Getting Started with Graphics Programming," you learned the events used in graphics.) An *event* may be ignored in graphics programming, but an *exception* cannot be ignored. In graphics programming, a listener must register with the source object. External user action on the source object generates an event and the source object notifies the listener by invoking the handlers implemented by the listener. If no listener is registered with the source object, the event is ignored. However, when an exception occurs, the program may terminate if no handler can be used to deal with the exception.

A Java exception is an instance of a class derived from `Throwable`. The `Throwable` class is contained in the `java.lang` package, and subclasses of `Throwable` are contained in various packages. For example, errors related to graphics are included in the `java.awt` package; numeric exceptions are included in the `java.lang` package because they are related to the `java.lang.Number` class. You can create your own exception classes by extending `Throwable` or a subclass of `Throwable`. Figure 11.1 shows some of Java's predefined exception classes.

```
                          ┌── RuntimeException
              ┌─Exception─┼── IOException
              │           ├── AWTException
              │           └── ...
  Throwable ──┤
              │           ┌── LinkageError
              └── Error ──┼── Virtual MachineError
                          ├── AWTError
                          └── ...
```

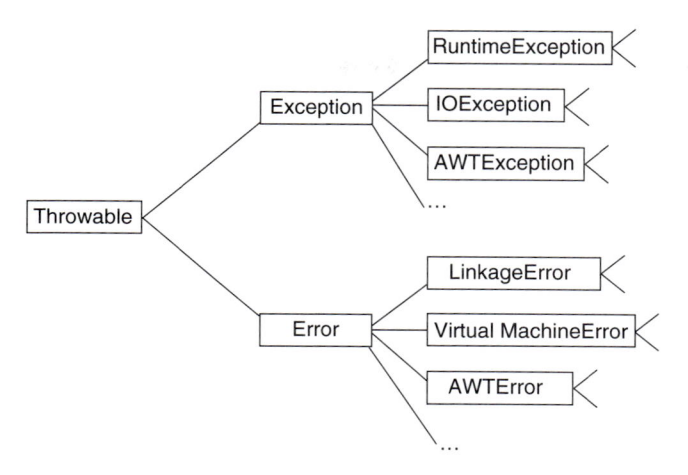

Figure 11.1 *The exceptions are instances of the classes shown in this diagram.*

> **NOTE**
> The class names `Error`, `Exception`, and `RuntimeException` are somewhat confusing. All the classes are exceptions. `Exception` is just one of these classes, and all errors discussed here occur at runtime.

The `Error` class describes internal system errors. Such errors rarely occur. If one does, there is little you can do beyond notifying the user and trying to terminate the program gracefully. Examples of subclasses of `Error` are `LinkageError`, `VirtualMachineError`, and `AWTError`. Subclasses of `LinkageError` indicate that a class has some dependency on another class, but that the latter class has changed incompatibly after the compilation of the former class. Subclasses of `VirtualMachineError` indicate that the Java Virtual Machine is broken or has run out of the resources necessary for it to continue operating. `AWTError` is caused by a fatal error in the graphics programs.

The `Exception` class describes the errors caused by your program and external circumstances. These errors can be caught and handled by your program. `Exception` has many subclasses. Examples are `RuntimeException`, `IOException`, and `AWTException`.

The `RuntimeException` class describes programming errors, such as bad casting, accessing an out-of-bound array, and numeric errors. Examples of subclasses of `RuntimeException` are `ArithmeticException`, `NullPointerException`, `IllegalArgumentException`, `ArrayStoreException`, and `IndexOutOfBoundsException`.

The `IOException` class describes errors related to input/output operations, such as invalid input, reading past the end of a file, and opening a nonexistent file. Examples of subclasses of `IOException` are `InterruptedIOException`, `EOFException`, and `FileNotFoundException`.

The `AWTException` class describes exceptions in graphics programs.

Understanding Exception Handling

Java's exception-handling model is based on three operations: *claiming an exception, throwing an exception,* and *catching an exception.*

In Java, the statement currently being executed belongs to a method—either to `main()` or to a method invoked by another method. The system invokes the `main()` method for a Java application and invokes the `init()` method for a Java applet. In general, every method must state the types of exceptions it can encounter. This process is called *claiming an exception,* which simply tells the compiler what can go wrong.

When a statement causes errors, the method containing the statement creates an exception object and passes it to the system. The exception object contains information about the exception, including its type and the state of the program when the error occurred. This process is called *throwing an exception.*

After a method throws an exception, the Java runtime system begins the process of finding the code to handle the error. The code that handles the error is called the *exception handler;* it is found by searching backward through a chain of method calls, starting from the current method. The handler must match the type of exception thrown. If no handler is found, the program terminates. The process of finding a handler is called *catching an exception.*

Claiming Exceptions

To claim an exception is to tell the compiler what might go wrong during the execution of a method. Because system errors and runtime errors can happen to any code, Java does not require you to claim `Error` and `RuntimeException` in the method. However, all the other exceptions must be explicitly claimed in the method declaration if they are thrown by the method.

To claim an exception in a method, you use the `throws` keyword in the method declaration, as in this example:

```
public void myMethod() throws IOException
```

The `throws` keyword indicates that `myMethod` might throw an `IOException`. If the method might throw multiple exceptions, you can add a list of the exceptions, separated by commas, after `throws`:

```
MethodDeclaration throws Exception1, Exception2,...,ExceptionN
```

Throwing Exceptions

In the method that has claimed the exception, you can throw an object of the exception if the exception arises. The following is the syntax to throw an exception:

```
throw new TheException();
```

Or if you prefer, you can use the following:

```
TheException ex = new TheException();
throw ex;
```

> **NOTE**
>
> The keyword to claim an exception is `throws`, and the keyword to throw an exception is `throw`.
>
> A method can only throw the exceptions claimed in the method declaration or throw `Error`, `RuntimeException`, or subclasses of `Error` and `RuntimeException`. For example, the method cannot throw `IOException` if it is not claimed in the method declaration, but a method can always throw `RuntimeException` or a subclass of it even if it is not claimed by the method.

Example 11.1 Throwing Exceptions

This example demonstrates the throwing of an exception by modifying the `Rational` class defined in Example 5.8, "Using the `Rational` Class" (see Chapter 5, "Programming with Objects and Classes") so that it can handle the zero-denominator exception.

You create a new `Rational` class in the package Chapter11. The new `Rational` class is the same except that the `divide()` method throws a zero-denominator exception if the client attempts to call the method with a zero denominator. The new `divide()` method is shown below:

```
// Divide a rational number from this rational
public Rational divide(Rational secondRational) throws Exception
{
  if (secondRational.getNumerator() == 0)
    throw new Exception("Denominator cannot be zero");

  long n = numerator*secondRational.getDenominator();
  long d = denominator*secondRational.getNumerator();
  return new Rational(n, d);
}
```

Example Review

The original class `Rational` remains intact except for the `divide()` method. The `divide()` method now claims an exception and throws it if the divisor is zero.

The `divide()` method claims the exception to be an instance of `Exception` by using `throws Exception` in the method signature. The method throws the exception by using the following statement:

```
throw new Exception("Denominator cannot be zero");
```

Catching Exceptions

You now know how to claim an exception and how to throw an exception. Next, you will learn how to handle exceptions.

When calling a method that explicitly claims an exception, you must use the try-catch block to wrap the statement, as shown in the next few lines:

```
try
{
  statements;   //statements that may throw exceptions
}
catch (Exception1 ex)
{
  handler for exception1;
}
catch (Exception2 ex)
{
  handler for exception2;
}
...
catch (ExceptionN ex)
{
  handler for exceptionN;
}
```

If no exceptions arise during the execution of the try clause, the catch clauses are skipped.

If one of the statements inside the try block throws an exception, Java skips the remaining statements and starts to search for a handler for the exception. If the exception type matches one listed in a catch clause, the code in the catch clause is executed. If the exception type does not match any exception in the catch clauses, Java exits this method, passes the exception to the method that invoked this method, and continues the same process to find a handler. If no handler is found in the chain of the calling method, the program terminates and prints an error message on the console.

Consider the scenario in Figure 11.2. Suppose that an exception occurs in the try-catch block that contains a call to method3. If the exception type is Exception3, it is caught by the catch clause for handling exception ex3. If the exception type is Exception2, it is caught by the catch clause for handling exception ex2. If the exception type is Exception1, it is caught by the catch clause for handling exception ex1 in the main() method. If the exception type is not Exception1, Exception2, or Exception3, the program terminates immediately.

If the exception type is Exception3, statement3 is skipped. If the exception type is Exception2, statement2 and statement3 are skipped. If the exception type is Exception1, statement1, statement2, and statement3 are skipped.

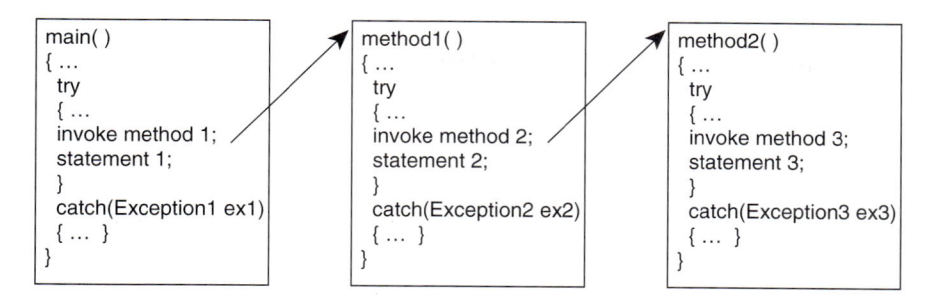

```
main( )                  method1( )              method2( )
{ ...                    { ...                   { ...
  try                      try                     try
  { ...                    { ...                   { ...
    invoke method 1;         invoke method 2;        invoke method 3;
    statement 1;             statement 2;            statement 3;
  }                        }                       }
  catch(Exception1 ex1)    catch(Exception2 ex2)   catch(Exception3 ex3)
  { ... }                  { ... }                 { ... }
}                        }                       }
```

Figure 11.2 *If an exception is not caught in the current method, it is passed to its caller. The process is repeated until the exception is caught or passed to the* `main()` *method.*

NOTE
If an exception of a subclass of `Exception` occurs in a graphics program, Java prints the error message on the console, but the program goes back to its user-interface-processing loop to run continuously. The exception is ignored.

The exception object contains valuable information about the exception. It may use the following instance methods in the `java.lang.Throwable` class to get information related to the exception.

- `public String getMessage()`

    This returns the detailed message of the `Throwable` object.

- `public String toString()`

    This returns a short description of the `Throwable` object, whereas `getMessage()` returns a detailed message.

- `public String getLocalizedMessage()`

    This returns a localized description of the `Throwable` object. Subclasses of `Throwable` can override this method in order to produce a locale-specific message. For subclasses that do not override this method, the default implementation returns the same result as `getMessage()`.

- `public void printStackTrace()`

    This prints the `Throwable` object and its trace information on the console.

NOTE
Various exception classes can be derived from a common superclass. If a `catch` clause catches exception objects of a superclass, it can catch all the exception objects of the subclasses of that superclass.

CAUTION
The order in which the exceptions are specified in a `catch` clause is important. You should specify an exception object of a class before the exception object of the superclass of that class; otherwise, a compilation error will result.

Example 11.2 Catching Exceptions

This program demonstrates catching exceptions, using the new `Rational` class given in Example 11.1. Figure 11.3 shows the output of a sample run of the program.

```java
// TestRationalException.java: Catch and handle exceptions
import Rational;

public class TestRationalException
{
  // Main method
  public static void main(String[] args)
  {
    // Create three rational numbers
    Rational r1 = new Rational(4,2);
    Rational r2 = new Rational(2,3);
    Rational r3 = new Rational(0,1);

    try
    {
      System.out.println(r1+" + "+ r2 +" = "+r1.add(r2));
      System.out.println(r1+" - "+ r2 +" = "+r1.subtract(r2));
      System.out.println(r1+" * "+ r2 +" = "+r1.multiply(r2));
      System.out.println(r1+" / "+ r2 +" = "+r1.divide(r2));
      System.out.println(r1+" / "+ r3 +" = "+r1.divide(r3));
      System.out.println(r1+" + "+ r2 +" = "+r1.add(r2));
    }
    catch(Exception ex)
    {
      System.out.println(ex);
    }

    // Display the result
    System.out.println(r1 + " - " + r2 + " = " + r1.subtract(r2));
  }
}
```

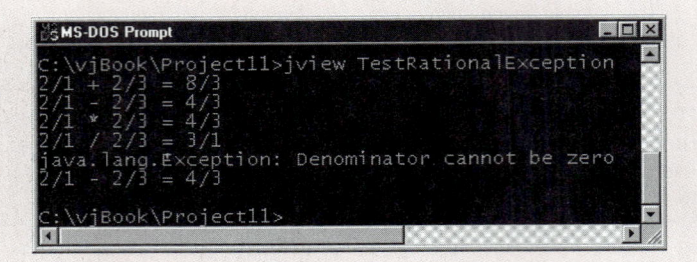

```
C:\vjBook\Project11>jview TestRationalException
2/1 + 2/3 = 8/3
2/1 - 2/3 = 4/3
2/1 * 2/3 = 4/3
2/1 / 2/3 = 3/1
java.lang.Exception: Denominator cannot be zero
2/1 - 2/3 = 4/3

C:\vjBook\Project11>
```

Figure 11.3 *The exception is raised when the divisor is zero.*

Example Review

The program creates two `Rational` numbers, r1 and r2, to test numeric methods (`add()`, `subtract()`, `multiply()`, and `divide()`) on rational numbers.

Invoking the `divide()` method with divisor 0 causes the method to throw an exception object. In the `catch` clause, the type of the object ex is `Exception`, which matches the object thrown by the `divide()` method. So this exception is caught by the `catch` clause.

The exception handler simply prints a short message, `ex.toString()`, about the exception, using `System.out.println(ex)`.

Note that the execution continues in the event of the zero denominator. If the handlers had not caught the exception, the program would have abruptly terminated.

Example 11.3 Exceptions in GUI Applications

Here Example 9.10, "Using Menus" (from Chapter 9, "Creating User Interfaces"), is used to demonstrate the effect of exceptions in GUI applications. Run the program and enter any number in the Number 1 field and 0 in the Number 2 field; then click the Divide button (see Figure 11.4). You will see nothing in the Result field, but an error message will appear on the console, as shown in Figure 11.5. The GUI application continues.

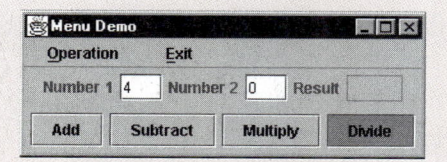

Figure 11.4 *In GUI programs, if an exception of the* `Exception` *class is not caught, it is ignored, and the program continues.*

continues

Figure 11.5 *In GUI programs, if an exception of the* `Exception` *class is not caught, an error message appears on the console.*

Example Review

If exceptions of the type `Exception` are not caught when Java graphics programs are running, the error messages are displayed on the console, but the program continues to run.

If you rewrite the `calculate()` method in the `MenuDemo` program of Example 9.9 with a `try-catch` block to catch `RuntimeException` as follows, the program will display Error in the Result text field in the case of a numerical error. No errors are shown on the console because they are handled in the program.

```java
// Calculate and show the result in jtfResult
private void calculate(char operator)
{
  // Obtain Number 1 and Number 2
  int num1 = (Integer.parseInt(jtfNum1.getText().trim()));
  int num2 = (Integer.parseInt(jtfNum2.getText().trim()));
  int result = 0;

  try
  {
    // Perform selected operation
    switch (operator)
    {
      case '+': result = num1 + num2;
              break;
      case '-': result = num1 - num2;
              break;
      case '*': result = num1 * num2;
              break;
      case '/': result = num1 / num2;
    }
```

```
      // Set result in jtfResult
      jtfResult.setText(String.valueOf(result));
    }
    catch (RuntimeException ex)
    {
      jtfResult.setText("Error ");
    }
  }
```

Creating Custom Exception Classes

Java provides quite a few exception classes. You should use them whenever possible instead of creating your own exception classes. However, if you run into a problem that cannot be adequately described by the predefined exception classes, you can create your own exception class, derived from `Exception` or from a subclass of `Exception`, such as `IOException`. This section shows how to create your own exception class.

Example 11.4 Creating Your Own Exception Classes

This program creates 10 accounts and transfers funds among them. If a transaction amount is negative, the program raises a negative-amount exception. If the account's balance is less than the requested transaction amount, an insufficient-funds exception is raised.

The example consists of four classes: `Account`, `NegativeAmountException`, `InsufficientAmountException`, and `TestMyException`. The `Account` class provides the information and operations pertaining to the account. `NegativeAmountException` and `InsufficientAmountException` are the exception classes dealing with transactions of negative or insufficient amounts. The `TestMyException` class utilizes all these classes to perform transactions, transferring funds among accounts.

The code for the `Account` class follows. This class contains two data fields: `id` (for account ID) and `balance` (for current balance). The methods for `Account` are `deposit` and `withdraw`. Both methods will throw `NegativeAmountException` if the transaction amount is negative. The `withdraw()` method will also throw `InsufficientFundException` if the current balance is less than the requested transaction amount.

```
// Account.java: The class for describing an account
public class Account
{
  // Two data fields in an account
  private int ID;
  private double balance;
```

continues

```java
  // Construct an account with specified ID and balance
  public Account(int ID, double balance)
  {
    this.ID = ID;
    this.balance = balance;
  }

  // Getter method for ID
  public int getID()
  {
    return ID;
  }

  // Setter method for balance
  public void setBalance(double balance)
  {
    this.balance = balance;
  }

  // Getter method for balance
  public double getBalance()
  {
    return balance;
  }

  // Deposit an amount to this account
  public void deposit(double amount)
    throws NegativeAmountException
  {
    if (amount < 0)
      throw new NegativeAmountException
        (this, amount, "deposit");
    balance = balance + amount;
  }

  // Withdraw an amount from this account
  public void withdraw(double amount)
    throws NegativeAmountException, InsufficientFundException
  {
    if (amount < 0)
      throw new NegativeAmountException
        (this, amount, "withdraw");
    if (balance < amount)
      throw new InsufficientFundException(this, amount);
    balance = balance - amount;
  }
}
```

The `NegativeAmountException` exception class follows. It contains information about the attempted transaction type (deposit or withdrawal), the account, and the negative amount passed from the method.

```java
// negative amount exception
public class NegativeAmountException extends Exception
{
  // Information to be passed to the handlers
  private Account account;
  private double amount;
  private String transactionType;
```

```java
    // Construct an negative amount exception
    public NegativeAmountException(Account account,
                                   double amount,
                                   String transactionType)
    {
      super("Negative amount");
      this.account = account;
      this.amount = amount;
      this.transactionType = transactionType;
    }
}
```

The `InsufficientFundException` exception class follows. It contains information about the account and the amount passed from the method.

```java
// InsufficientFundException.java: An exception class for describing
// insufficient fund exception
public class InsufficientFundException extends Exception
{
  // Information to be passed to the handlers
  private Account account;
  private double amount;

  // Construct an insufficient exception
  public InsufficientFundException(Account account, double amount)
  {
    super("Insufficient amount");
    this.account = account;
    this.amount = amount;
  }

  // Override the "toString" method
  public String toString()
  {
    return "Account balance is " + account.getBalance();
  }
}
```

The `TestMyException` class follows. It creates 10 accounts with account id 0, 1, and so on, to 9. Each account has an initial balance of $1,000. The program first attempts to deposit −$10 into account 0, raising the negative amount exception. The program then continuously withdraws $9 from account 0. When the balance of account 0 falls below $9, the program begins to withdraw from the next account, and finally the program terminates when the balances of all of the accounts are below $9. The output of the test program is shown in Figure 11.6.

```java
// TestMyException.java: Use custom exception classes
public class TestMyException
{
  // Main method
  public static void main(String[] args)
  {
    // Create 10 accounts with id 0 .. 9 and initial balance 1000
    Account[] account = new Account[10];
    for (int i=0; i<10; i++)
      account[i] = new Account(i, 1000);
```

continues

```java
      // Test negative deposit exception
      try
      {
        account[0].deposit(-10);
      }
      catch (NegativeAmountException ex)
      {
        System.out.println(ex);
      }

      // Test negative withdraw exception
      try
      {
        account[0].withdraw(-10);
      }
      catch (NegativeAmountException ex)
      {
        System.out.println(ex);
      }
      catch (InsufficientFundException ex)
      {
        System.out.println(ex);
      }

      // Keep withdrawing $9 dollars from the accounts
      for (int j=0; j<10; j++)
      {
        boolean enoughFund = true;
        while (enoughFund)
        {
          try
          {
            account[j].withdraw(9);
          }
          catch (InsufficientFundException ex)
          {
            enoughFund = false;
            System.out.println(ex);
          }
          catch (NegativeAmountException ex)
          {
            System.out.println(ex);
          }
        }
      }
    }
  }
```

Example Review

You need to create and save all the programs, either in one combined file or in separate files, and then compile the `TestMyException` class. The Java compiler will compile all the classes on which `TestMyException` depends. Therefore, the classes `Account`, `NegativeAmountException`, and `InsufficientFundException` will be compiled along with `TestMyException`.

```
MS-DOS Prompt
C:\jbBook>java Chapter11.TestMyException
Chapter11.NegativeAmountException: Negative amount
Chapter11.NegativeAmountException: Negative amount
Account balance is 1.0
Account balance is 1.0
Account balance is 1.0
Account balance is 1.0
Account balance is 1.0
Account balance is 1.0
Account balance is 1.0
Account balance is 1.0
Account balance is 1.0

C:\jbBook>
```

Figure 11.6 *The* TestMyException *program tests* NegativeAmountException *and* InsufficientFundException.

In the Account class, the deposit() method throws NegativeAmountException if the amount to be deposited is less than 0. The withdraw() method throws a NegativeAmountException if the amount to be withdrawn is less than 0, and throws an InsufficientFundException if the amount to be withdrawn is less than the current balance.

The user-defined exception class always extends Exception or a subclass of Exception. Therefore, both NegativeAmountException and InsufficientFund-Exception extend Exception.

Storing relevant information in the exception object is useful, enabling the handler to retrieve the information from the exception object. For example, NegativeAmountException contains the account, the amount, and the transaction type.

The NegativeAmountException occurs when the test program deposits −$10, using account[0].deposit(-10). The NegativeAmountException again occurs when the program withdraws −$10, using account[0].withdraw(-10). The exception handler in the test program displays the first two lines of the output to tell the user that these exceptions have occurred and were caught and properly handled.

The test program then repeatedly withdraws $9 from each account until the account balance is below $9. When the program attempts to withdraw from an account with a balance below $9, an exception is raised and caught by the handler, which displays the account balance.

Note that the test program continues its normal execution after an exception is handled. In the while loop, if the balance of one account is below $9, an exception is raised and handled in the try-catch block; then the program continues to stay in the for loop to withdraw from the next account until the balance of every account is below $9.

Example 11.5 Using Exceptions in Applets

This example demonstrates the use of exceptions in GUI applications. The applet presented here handles account transactions. It displays the account ID and balance, and lets the user deposit to or withdraw from the account. For each transaction, a message is displayed to indicate the status of the transaction: successful or failed. In case of failure, the failure reason is reported. A sample run of the program is shown in Figure 11.7.

```java
// AccountApplet.java: Use custom exception class
import java.awt.*;
import java.awt.event.*;
import javax.swing.*;
import javax.swing.border.*;

public class AccountApplet extends JApplet implements ActionListener
{
  // Declare text fields
  private TextField jtfID, jtfBalance, jtfDeposit, jtfWithdraw;

  // Declare Deposit and Withdraw buttons
  private JButton jbtDeposit, jbtWithdraw;

  // Create an account with initial balance $1000
  private Account account = new Account(1, 1000);

  // Create a label for showing status
  private JLabel jlblStatus = new JLabel();

  // Initialize the applet
  public void init()
  {
    // Panel p1 to group ID and Balance labels and text fields
    JPanel p1 = new JPanel();
    p1.setLayout(new GridLayout(2, 2));
    p1.add(new Label("Accout ID"));
    p1.add(jtfID = new TextField(4));
    p1.add(new Label("Account Balance"));
    p1.add(jtfBalance = new TextField(4));
    jtfID.setEditable(false);
    jtfBalance.setEditable(false);
    p1.setBorder(new TitledBorder("Display Account Information"));

    // Panel p2 to group deposit amount and Deposit button and
    // withdraw amount and Withdraw button
    JPanel p2 = new JPanel();
    p2.setLayout(new GridLayout(2, 3));
    p2.add(new Label("Deposit"));
    p2.add(jtfDeposit = new TextField(4));
    p2.add(jbtDeposit = new JButton("Deposit"));
    p2.add(new Label("Withdraw"));
    p2.add(jtfWithdraw = new TextField(4));
    p2.add(jbtWithdraw = new JButton("Withdraw"));
    p2.setBorder(new TitledBorder("Deposit or withdraw funds"));

    // Place panels p1, p2, and label in the applet
    this.getContentPane().add(p1, BorderLayout.WEST);
    this.getContentPane().add(p2, BorderLayout.CENTER);
    this.getContentPane().add(jlblStatus, BorderLayout.SOUTH);
```

```java
    // Refresh ID and Balance fields
    refreshFields();

    // Register listener
    jbtDeposit.addActionListener(this);
    jbtWithdraw.addActionListener(this);
  }

  // Handle ActionEvent
  public void actionPerformed(ActionEvent evt)
  {
    String actionCommand = evt.getActionCommand();
    if (evt.getSource() instanceof JButton)
      if ("Deposit".equals(actionCommand))
      {
        try
        {
          double depositValue = (Double.valueOf(
            jtfDeposit.getText().trim())).doubleValue();
          account.deposit(depositValue);
          refreshFields();
          jlblStatus.setText("Transaction Processed");
        }
        catch (NegativeAmountException ex)
        {
          jlblStatus.setText("Negative Amount");
        }
      }
      else if ("Withdraw".equals(actionCommand))
      {
        try
        {
          double withdrawValue = (Double.valueOf(
            jtfWithdraw.getText().trim())).doubleValue();
          account.withdraw(withdrawValue);
          refreshFields();
          jlblStatus.setText("Transaction Processed");
        }
        catch(NegativeAmountException ex)
        {
          jlblStatus.setText("Negative Amount");
        }
        catch (InsufficientFundException ex)
        {
          jlblStatus.setText("Insufficient Funds");
        }
      }
  }

  // Update the display for account balance
  public void refreshFields()
  {
    jtfID.setText(String.valueOf(account.getID()));
    jtfBalance.setText(String.valueOf(account.getBalance()));
  }
}
```

continues

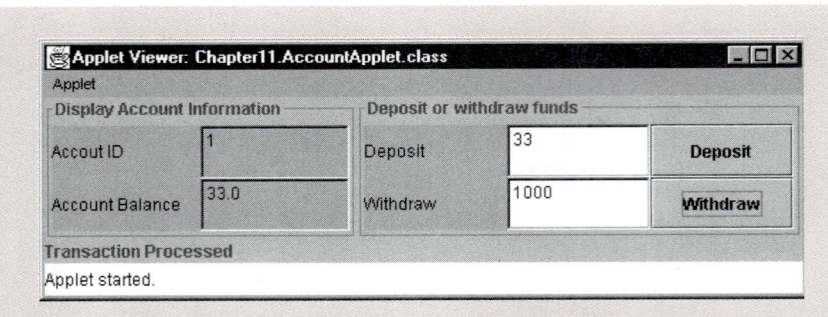

Figure 11.7 *The program lets you deposit and withdraw funds, and displays the transaction status on the label.*

Example Review

The program creates an applet with two panels (p1 and p2) and a label that displays messages. Panel p1 contains account ID and balance; panel p2 contains the action buttons for depositing and withdrawing funds.

With a click of the Deposit button, the amount in the Deposit text field is added to the balance. With a click of the Withdraw button, the amount in the Withdraw text field is subtracted from the balance.

For each successful transaction, the message Transaction Processed is displayed. For a negative amount, the message Negative Amount is displayed; for insufficient funds, the message Insufficient Funds is displayed.

Rethrowing Exceptions

When an exception occurs in a method, the method exits immediately if it does not catch the exception. If the method is required to perform any tasks before exiting, you can catch the exception in the method and then rethrow it to the real handler in a structure like this:

```
try
{
  statements;
}
catch(TheException ex)
{
  perform operations before exits;
  throw ex;
}
```

The statement throw ex rethrows the exception so that other handlers get a chance to process the exception ex.

The *finally* Clause

Occasionally, you may want some code to be executed regardless of whether the exception occurs and whether it is caught. Java has a `finally` clause that can be used to accomplish this objective. The syntax for the `finally` clause might look like this:

```
try
{
  statements;
}
catch(TheException ex)
{
  handling ex;
}
finally
{
  finalStatements;
}
```

The code in the `finally` block is executed under all circumstances, regardless of whether an exception occurs in the `try` block and whether it is caught. Consider three possible cases:

- If no exception arises in the `try` block, `finalStatements` is executed, and the next statement after the `try-catch` block is executed.

- If one of the statements causes an exception in the `try` block that is caught in a `catch` clause, the other statements in the `try` block are skipped, the `catch` clause is executed, and the `finally` clause is executed. If the `catch` clause does not rethrow an exception, the next statement after the `try-catch` block is executed. If it does, the exception is passed to the caller of this method.

- If one of the statements causes an exception that is not caught in any `catch` clause, the other statements in the `try` block are skipped, the `finally` clause is executed, and the exception is passed to the caller of this method.

> **NOTE**
> The `catch` clause may be omitted when the `finally` clause is used.

Cautions When Using Exceptions

Exception handling separates error-handling code from normal programming tasks, thus making programs easier to read and to modify. Be aware, however, that exception handling usually requires more time and resources because it requires instantiating a new exception object, rolling back the call stack, and propagating the errors to the calling methods.

Exception handling should not be used to replace simple tests. You should test simple exceptions whenever possible, and let exception handling deal with circumstances that cannot be handled with `if` statements.

Example 11.4 demonstrates the use of exception handling, but it is a bad example in the sense that its implementation is inefficient. Instead of letting the exceptions be caught by the other programs, you could simply check for a negative amount and insufficient balance before calling the `deposit()` and `withdraw()` methods in the test program. This would significantly improve the program's performance.

Example 11.6 Demonstrating Performance Differences with and without Exception Handling

This example compares the performance of the program in Example 11.4, which uses exception handling, with the performance of the same program without exception handling. Example 11.4 uses exception handlers to process negative amounts and insufficient funds. Here, the program is rewritten without the use of exceptions, and the execution time of the two programs is compared. The output of a sample run of the program is shown in Figure 11.8.

```java
import java.util.*;

public class UsingNoException
{
  //create 10 accounts with id 0 .. 9 and initial balance 1000
  public static void main(String[] args)
  {
    //create and initialize 10 accounts
    Account[] account = new Account[10];
    for (int i=0; i<10; i++)
      account[i] = new Account(i, 1000);

    //get start time
    long startTime = System.currentTimeMillis();

    //keep withdrawing $9 dollars from the accounts
    for (int j=0; j<10; j++)
    {
      boolean enoughFund = true;
      while (enoughFund)
        try
        {
          if (account[j].accountBalance() < 9)
          {
            System.out.println("Account balance is "+
              account[j].accountBalance());
            enoughFund = false;
          }
          else
            account[j].withdraw(9);
        }
        catch (InsufficientFundException ex)
        {
          enoughFund = false;
          System.out.println(ex);
        }
        catch (NegativeAmountException ex)
        {
          System.out.println(ex);
        }
    }
}
```

```
        //get end time
        long endTime = System.currentTimeMillis();

        //display elapsed time
        System.out.println("Elapsed time: "+ (endTime - startTime) +
          " Milliseconds");
    }
}
```

To compare the execution time with exception handling, replace the `if` statement (set in bold in the code) with the following code:

```
account[j].withdraw(9);
```

For convenience, rename the program `TestMyExceptionWithTiming`. A sample run of the output of the program is shown in Figure 11.9.

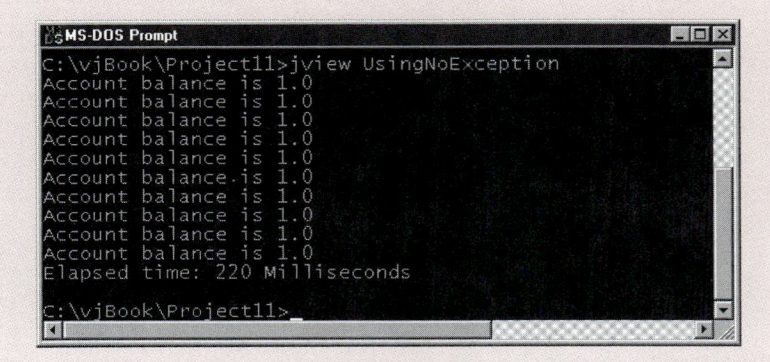

Figure 11.8 *The program uses `if` statements to test for negative amounts and insufficient funds.*

Figure 11.9 *The program takes a little more time because it uses exceptions to test for negative amounts and insufficient funds.*

continues

Example Review

The `UsingNoException` program uses the `if` statement to check whether the account has a sufficient balance before invoking the `withdraw()` method, whereas the `TestMyExceptionWithTiming` program lets the `catch` block handle the case. The `try-catch` block is required because the program invokes `withdraw()`, which claims two exceptions. Whenever you use a method that claims an exception, the `try-catch` block must be used. However, no exceptions are raised in the `UsingNoException` program because the program uses a simple `if` statement to check the account balance.

Since you want to see the time spent on the `for` loop, the program obtains the `startTime` before the `for` loop starts and the `endTime` after the `for` loop finishes.

The static `currentTimeMillis()` method in the `java.lang.System` class is used to obtain the current time in milliseconds. The `System` class provides access to the system's platform-independent resources, such as forcing garbage collection using the `gc()` method. All the variables and methods in `System` are static. You have already used `System.out` to print messages. The `out` variable represents the standard output stream, which will be further discussed in Chapter 15, "Input and Output."

The elapsed time is

```
endTime - startTime
```

Note that the elapsed time is not the exact CPU time spent on the loop. You may get a different elapsed time whenever you run the program, depending on the system load when the program is executed.

A comparison of the running times of these two programs clearly shows the performance benefits of not using exceptions. You should not use exception handling if a simple `if` statement will work instead.

TIP
Do not use exception handling to validate user input. The input can be validated with the use of simple `if` statements.

Chapter Summary

In this chapter, you learned how Java handles exceptions. When an exception occurs, Java creates an object that contains the information for the exception. You can use the information to handle the exception.

A Java exception is an instance of a class derived from `java.lang.Throwable`. You can create your own exception classes by extending `Throwable` or a subclass of `Throwable`. The Java system provides a number of predefined exception classes, such as `Error`, `Exception`, `RuntimeException`, and `IOException`. You can also define your own exception class.

Exceptions occur during the execution of a method. When defining the method, you have to claim an exception if the method might throw that exception, thus telling the compiler what can go wrong.

To use the method that claims exceptions, you need to enclose the method call in the `try` clause of a `try-catch` block. When the exception occurs during the execution of the method, the `catch` clause catches and handles the exception.

Exception handling takes time because it requires the instantiation of a new exception object. Exceptions are not meant to substitute for simple tests. Avoid using exception handling if an alternative solution can be found. Using an alternative would significantly improve the performance of the program.

Chapter Review

11.1. Describe the Java `Throwable` class, its subclasses, and the types of exceptions.

11.2. What is the purpose of claiming exceptions? How do you claim an exception, and where? Can you claim multiple exceptions in a method declaration?

11.3. How do you throw an exception? Can you throw multiple exceptions in one `throw` statement?

11.4. What is the keyword `throw` used for? What is the keyword `throws` used for?

11.5. What does the Java runtime system do when an exception occurs?

11.6. How do you catch an exception?

11.7. Does the presence of the `try-catch` block impose overhead when no exception occurs?

11.8. Suppose that `statement2` causes an exception in the following `try-catch` block:

```
try
{
  statement1;
  statement2;
  statement3;
}
catch (Exception1 ex1)
{
}
catch (Exception2 ex2)
{
}

statement4;
```

Answer the following questions:

- Will `statement3` be executed?

- If the exception is not caught, will `statement4` be executed?
- If the exception is caught in the catch clause, will `statement4` be executed?
- If the exception is passed to the caller, will `statement4` be executed?

11.9. Suppose that `statement2` causes an exception in the following `try-catch` block:

```
try
{
  statement1;
  statement2;
  statement3;
}
catch (Exception1 ex1)
{
}
catch (Exception2 ex2)
{
}
catch (Exception3 ex3)
{
  throw ex3;
}
finally
{
  statement5;
};
statement4;
```

Answer the following questions:

- Will `statement5` be executed?
- If the exception is of type `Exception3`, what will happen? Will `statement3` be executed? Will `statement4` be executed?

11.10. What is wrong in the following program?

```
class TestRationalWithException
{
  public static void main(String[] args)
  {
    Rational r1 = new Rational(4,2);
    Rational r2 = new Rational(2,3);
    Rational r3 = new Rational(0,1);

    try
    {
      System.out.println(
        r1 + " + " + r2 + " = " + r1.add(r2));
      System.out.println(
        r1 + " - " + r2 + " = " + r1.subtract(r2));
      System.out.println(
        r1 + " * " + r2 + " = " + r1.multiply(r2));
      System.out.println(
        r1 + " + " + r2 + " = " + r1.add(r2));
    }
  }
}
```

11.11. What is displayed on the console when the following program is run?

```
class Test
{
  public static void main(String[] args)
  {
    try
    {
      System.out.println("Welcome to Java");
    }
    finally
    {
      System.out.println("End of the block");
    }
  }
}
```

11.12. What is displayed on the console when the following program is run?

```
class Test
{
  public static void main(String[] args)
  {
    try
    {
      System.out.println("Welcome to Java");
      return;
    }
    finally
    {
      System.out.println("End of the block");
    }
  }
}
```

11.13. What is displayed on the console when the following program is run?

```
class Test
{
  public static void main(String[] args)
  {
    try
    {
      System.out.println("Welcome to Java");
      int i = 0;
      int y = 2/i;
      System.out.println("Welcome to HTML");
    }
    finally
    {
      System.out.println("End of the block");
    }
  }
}
```

11.14. What is displayed on the console when the following program is run?

```
class Test
{
  public static void main(String[] args)
  {
    try
    {
      System.out.println("Welcome to Java");
      int i = 0;
      double y = 2.0/i;
      System.out.println("Welcome to HTML");
    }
    finally
    {
      System.out.println("End of the block");
    }
  }
}
```

11.15. What is displayed on the console when the following program is run?

```
class Test
{
  public static void main(String[] args)
  {
    try
    {
      System.out.println("Welcome to Java");
      int i = 0;
      int y = 2/i;
      System.out.println("Welcome to Java");
    }
    catch (RuntimeException ex)
    {
      System.out.println("Welcome to Java");
    }
    finally
    {
      System.out.println("End of the block");
    }
  }
}
```

11.16. What is displayed on the console when the following program is run?

```
class Test
{
  public static void main(String[] args)
  {
    try
    {
      System.out.println("Welcome to Java");
      int i = 0;
      int y = 2/i;
      System.out.println("Welcome to Java");
    }
    catch (RuntimeException ex)
    {
      System.out.println("Welcome to Java");
    }
    finally
```

```
      {
        System.out.println("End of the block");
      }

      System.out.println("End of the block");
    }
  }
```

11.17. What is displayed on the console when the following program is run?

```
class Test
{
  public static void main(String[] args)
  {
    try
    {
      System.out.println("Welcome to Java");
      int i = 0;
      int y = 2/i;
      System.out.println("Welcome to Java");
    }
    finally
    {
      System.out.println("End of the block");
    }

    System.out.println("End of the block");
  }
}
```

In the following questions, assume that the modified `Rational` given in Example 11.1 is used.

11.18. What is wrong with the following code?

```
class Test
{
  public static void main(String[] args)
  {
    try
    {
      Rational r1 = new Rational(3, 4);
      Rational r2  = new Rational(0, 1);
      Rational x = r1.divide(r2);

      int i = 0;
      int y = 2/i;
    }
    catch (Exception ex)
    {
      System.out.println("Rational operation error ");
    }
    catch (RuntimeException ex)
    {
      System.out.println("Integer operation error");
    }
  }
}
```

11.19. What is displayed on the console when the following program is run?

```java
class Test
{
  public static void main(String[] args)
  {
    try
    {
      Rational r1 = new Rational(3, 4);
      Rational r2  = new Rational(0, 1);
      Rational x = r1.divide(r2);

      int i = 0;
      int y = 2/i;
      System.out.println("Welcome to Java");
    }
    catch (RuntimeException ex)
    {
      System.out.println("Integer operation error");
    }
    catch (Exception ex)
    {
      System.out.println("Rational operation error");
    }
  }
}
```

11.20. What is displayed on the console when the following program is run?

```java
class Test
{
  public static void main(String[] args)
  {
    try
    {
      method();
      System.out.println("After the method call");
    }
    catch (RuntimeException ex)
    {
      System.out.println("Integer operation error");
    }
    catch (Exception e)
    {
      System.out.println("Rational operation error");
    }
  }

  static void method() throws Exception
  {
    Rational r1 = new Rational(3, 4);
    Rational r2  = new Rational(0, 1);
    Rational x = r1.divide(r2);

    int i = 0;
    int y = 2/i;
    System.out.println("Welcome to Java");
  }
}
```

11.21. What is displayed on the console when the following program is run?

```
class Test
{
  public static void main(String[] args)
  {
    try
    {
      method();
      System.out.println("After the method call");
    }
    catch (RuntimeException ex)
    {
      System.out.println("Integer operation error");
    }
    catch (Exception ex)
    {
      System.out.println("Rational operation error");
    }
  }

  static void method() throws Exception
  {
    try
    {
      Rational r1 = new Rational(3, 4);
      Rational r2  = new Rational(0, 1);
      Rational x = r1.divide(r2);

      int i = 0;
      int y = 2/i;
      System.out.println("Welcome to Java");
    }
    catch (RuntimeException ex)
    {
      System.out.println("Integer operation error");
    }
    catch (Exception ex)
    {
      System.out.println("Rational operation error");
    }
  }
}
```

11.22. What is displayed on the console when the following program is run?

```
class Test
{
  public static void main(String[] args)
  {
    try
    {
      method();
      System.out.println("After the method call");
    }
    catch (RuntimeException ex)
    {
      System.out.println("Integer operation error");
    }
    catch (Exception ex)
    {
      System.out.println("Rational operation error");
    }
  }
```

```java
      static void method() throws Exception
      {
        try
        {
          Rational r1 = new Rational(3, 4);
          Rational r2   = new Rational(0, 1);
          Rational x = r1.divide(r2);

          int i = 0;
          int y = 2/i;
          System.out.println("Welcome to Java");
        }
        catch (RuntimeException ex)
        {
          System.out.println("Integer operation error");
        }
        catch (Exception ex)
        {
          System.out.println("Rational operation error");
          throw ex;
        }
      }
    }
```

11.23. If an exception was not caught in a non-GUI application, what would happen? If an exception was not caught in a GUI application, what would happen?

Programming Exercises

11.1. Example 6.10, "Using Command-Line Parameters," in Chapter 6, "Arrays and Strings," is a simple command-line calculator. Note that the program terminates if any operand is non-numeric. Write a program with an exception handler to deal with non-numeric operands; then write another program without using an exception handler to achieve the same objective. Your program should display a message to inform the user of the wrong operand type before exiting (see Figure 11.10).

Figure 11.10   *The program performs arithmetic operations and detects input errors.*

11.2. Example 9.10, "Using Menus," is a GUI calculator. Note that if Number 1 or Number 2 were a non-numeric string, the program would display errors on the console. Modify the program with an exception handler to catch ArithmeticException (i.e., divided by 0) and NumberFormatException (i.e., input is not an integer) and display the errors in a message dialog box.

11.3. Write a program that meets the following requirements:

- Create an array with 100 elements that are randomly chosen.
- Create a text field to enter an array index and another text field to display the array element at the specified index (see Figure 11.11).
- Create a Show button to cause the array element to be displayed. If the specified index is out of bounds, display the message Out of Bound.

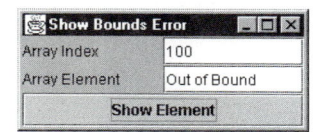

Figure 11.11 *The program displays the array element at the specified index or displays the message Out of Bound if the index is out of bounds.*

CHAPTER 12

INTERNATIONALIZATION

Objectives

- Understand the concept of Java's internationalization mechanism.
- Know how to construct a locale with language, country, and variant.
- Process date and time based on locales.
- Display numbers, currencies, and percentage based on locales.
- Use resource bundles.

Introduction

Java is an Internet programming language. Since the Internet has no boundaries, people who don't understand English may view your applet. What is useful for readers of English may be unusable for readers of French. Many Web sites maintain several versions of HTML pages so that readers can choose one written in a language they understand. Because there are so many languages in the world, it would be highly problematic to create and maintain enough different versions to meet the needs of all clients everywhere. Java comes to the rescue. Java is the first language designed from ground up to support internationalization. In consequence, it allows your programs to be customized for any number of countries or languages without requiring cumbersome changes in the code.

Here are the major Java features that support internationalization:

- Java characters use *Unicode,* a 16-bit encoding scheme established by the Unicode Consortium to support the interchange, processing, and display of written texts in the world's diverse languages. The use of Unicode encoding makes it easy to write Java programs that can manipulate strings in any international language.

- Java provides the `Locale` class to encapsulate information about a specific locale. A locale determines how locale-sensitive information, such as date, time, and number, is displayed, and how locale-sensitive operations, such as sorting strings, are performed. The classes for formatting date, time, and numbers, and for sorting strings are grouped in the `java.text` package.

- In this chapter, you will learn how to format date, numbers, currencies, and percentages for different regions, countries, and languages. You will also learn how to use resource bundles to define which images and strings are used by a component, depending on the user's locale and preferences.

Locale

A `Locale` object represents a geographical, political, or cultural region in which a specific language or custom is used. For example, Americans speak English, and the Chinese speak Chinese. The conventions for formatting dates, numbers, currencies, and percentages may differ from one country to another. The Chinese, for instance, use year/month/day to represent the date, while Americans use month/day/year. It is important to realize that a locale is not defined only by country. For example, Canadians speak Canadian English or Canadian French, depending on which region of Canada they reside in.

To create a `Locale` object, you can use the following constructors in the `java.util.Locale` class:

```
Locale(String language, String country)

Locale(String language, String country, String variant)
```

The `language` should be a valid language code, that is to say, one of the lowercase, two-letter codes defined by ISO-639. For example, zh stands for Chinese, da for

Danish, en for English, de for German, and ko for Korean. A complete list can be found at a number of sites, among them:

    http://www.indigo.ie/egt/standards/iso639/

    http://www.ics.uci.edu/pub/ietf/http/related/iso639.txt

The country should be a valid ISO country code, that is to say, one of the uppercase, two-letter codes defined by ISO-3166. For example, CA stands for Canada, CN for China, DK for Denmark, DE for Germany, and US for the United States. A complete list can be found at a number of sites, including:

    ftp://ftp.ripe.net/iso3166-countrycodes

    http://userpage.chemie.fu-berlin.de/diverse/doc/ISO_3166.html

The argument variant is rarely used and is needed only for exceptional or system-dependent situations to designate information specific to a browser or vendor. For example, the Norwegian language has two sets of spelling rules, a traditional one called *bokmål* and a new one called *nynorsk*. The locale for traditional spelling would be created as follows:

    Locale("no", "NO", "B");

For convenience, the Locale class contains many predefined locale constants. Locale.CANADA is for the country Canada and language English; Locale.CANADA_FRENCH is for the country Canada and language French.

At present Java supports the locales shown in Table 12.1.

TABLE 12.1 A list of supported locales

Locale	Language	Country
da_DK	Danish	Denmark
de_AT	German	Austria
de_CH	German	Switzerland
el_GR	Greek	Greece
en_CA	English	Canada
en_GB	English	United Kingdom
en_IE	English	Ireland
en_US	English	United States
es_ES	Spanish	Spain
fi_FI	Finnish	Finland
fr_BE	French	Belgium
fr_CA	French	Canada
fr_CH	French	Switzerland

continues

Locale	Language	Country
fr_FR	French	France
it_CH	Italian	Switzerland
it_IT	Italian	Italy
ja_JP	Japanese	Japan
ko_KR	Korean	Korea
nl_BE	Dutch	Belgium
nl_NL	Dutch	Netherlands
no_NO	Norwegian (*nynorsk*)	Norway
no_NO_B	Norwegian (*bokmål*)	Norway
pt_PT	Portuguese	Portugal
sv_SE	Swedish	Sweden
tr_TR	Turkish	Turkey
zh_CN	Chinese (Simplified)	China
zh_TW	Chinese (Traditional)	Taiwan

Several useful methods contained in the `Locale` class are listed below (note that the default locale is used if no locale is specified):

- `public static Locale getDefault()`

    This method returns the default locale as stored on the machine where the program is running.

- `public static void setDefault(Locale newLocale)`

    This method sets the default locale.

- `public String getLanguage()`

    This method returns a lowercase, two-letter language code.

- `public String getCountry()`

    This method returns an uppercase, two-letter country code.

- `public String getVariant()`

    This method returns the code for the variant.

- `public final String getDisplayLanguage()`

    This method returns the name of the language for the default locale.

- `public String getDisplayLanguage(Locale inLocale)`

    This method returns the name of the language for the specified locale.

- `public final String getDisplayCountry()`

This method returns the name of the country as expressed in the current locale.

- `public String getDisplayCountry(Locale inLocale)`

  This method returns the name of the country as expressed in the specified locale.

- `public final String getDisplayVariant()`

  This method returns the variant code.

- `public String getDisplayVariant(Locale inLocale)`

  This method returns the variant code for the specified locale.

- `public String getDisplayName(Locale l)`

  This method returns the name for the locale. For example, the name is `Chinese (China)` for the locale `Locale.CHINA`.

- `public String getDisplayName()`

  This method returns the name for the default locale.

An operation that requires a `Locale` to perform its task is called *locale-sensitive*. To display a number as a date or time, for example, is a locale-sensitive operation; the number should be formatted according to the customs and conventions of the user's locale.

Several classes in the Java class libraries contain locale-sensitive methods. For example, `Date`, `Calendar`, `Collator`, `DateFormat`, and `NumberFormat` are locale-sensitive. All the locale-sensitive classes contain a static method, `getAvailableLocales()`, which returns an array of the locales they support. For example,

```
Locale[] availableLocales = Calendar.getAvailableLocales();
```

returns all locales for which Calendars are installed.

Processing Date and Time

Your applications often need to obtain date and time. Java provides a system-independent encapsulation of date and time in the `java.util.Date` class; it also provides `java.util.TimeZone` for dealing with time zones, and `java.util.Calendar` for extracting detailed information from `Date`. Different locales have different conventions for displaying date and time. Should the year, month, or day be displayed first? Should slashes, periods, or colons be used to separate fields of the date? What are the names of the months in the language? The `java.text.DateFormat` class can be used to format date and time in a locale-sensitive way for display to the user.

A `Date` object represents a specific instant in time. The `Calendar` class contains the `get()` method to extract year, month, day, hour, minute, and second, using the `get()` method. For example, you can use `cal.get(Calendar.YEAR)` to get the year, and `cal.get(Calendar.MINUTE)` to get the minute from the `Calendar` object `cal`. Subclasses of `Calendar` interpret a `Date` according to the rules of a specific calendar system. `java.util.GregorianCalendar` is currently supported in Java. Future subclasses could represent other types of calendars used in some parts of the world.

`TimeZone` represents a time zone offset, and also figures out daylight savings. To set a time zone in a `Calendar` object, use the `setTimeZone()` method with a time zone ID. For example, `cal.setTimeZone("CST")` sets the time zone to Central Standard Time. To find all the available time zones, use the static method `getAvailableIDs()` in the `TimeZone` class. In general, the international time zone ID is a string in the form of continent/city like Europe/Berlin, Asia/Taipei, and America/Washington.

The `DateFormat` class can be used to format date and time in a number of styles. The `DateFormat` class supports several standard formatting styles. To format date and time using the `DateFormat` class, simply create an instance of `DateFormat` using one of the following three types of static methods:

- `public static final DateFormat getDateInstance(int dateStyle, Locale aLocale)`

    This method returns the date formatter with the formatting style for the specified locale.

- `public static final DateFormat getTimeInstance(int timeStyle, Locale aLocale)`

    This method returns the time formatter with the formatting style for the given locale.

- `public static final DateFormat getDateTimeInstance(int dateStyle, int timeStyle, Locale aLocale)`

    This method returns the date/time formatter with the formatting style for the given locale.

If the arguments are not present, the default style or default locale is used. The `dateStyle` and `timeStyle` are one of the following constants: FULL, LONG, MEDIUM, and SHORT. The exact result depends on the locale, but generally,

- SHORT is completely numeric, such as 7/24/98 (for date) and 4:49 PM (for time);
- MEDIUM is longer, such as 24-Jul-98 (for date) and 4:52:09 PM (for time);
- LONG is even longer, such as July 24, 1998 (for date) and 4:53:16 PM EST (for time);
- FULL is completely specified, such as Friday, July 24, 1998 (for date) and 4:54:13 o'clock PM EST (for time).

You can use the `getDateTimeInstance()` method to obtain a `DateFormat` object.

```
public static final DateFormat getDateTimeInstance(int dateStyle, int timeStyle, Locale aLocale)
```

This gets the date and time formatter with the formatting styles for the given locale.

The statements given below, for example, display current time with a specified time zone (CST), formatting style (full date and full time), and locale (US).

```
GregorianCalendar myCal = new GregorianCalendar();
DateFormat myFormat = DateFormat.getDateTimeInstance(
  DateFormat.FULL, DateFormat.FULL, Locale.US);
tz = TimeZone.getTimeZone("CST");
myFormat.setTimeZone(tz);
System.out.println("The local time is "+
  myFormat.format(myCal.getTime()));
```

The date and time formatting subclass, such as `SimpleDateFormat`, enables you to choose any user-defined pattern for date and time formatting. The following constructor can be used to create a `SimpleDateFormat` object, and the object can be used to convert a `Date` object into a string with the desired format:

```
public SimpleDateFormat(String pattern)
```

The parameter `pattern` is a string consisting of characters with special meanings. For example, y means year, M means month, d means day of the month, G is for era designator, h means hours, m means minute of the hour, s means second of the minute, and z means time zone. Therefore, the following code will display a string like "Current time is 1997.11.12 AD at 04:10:18 PST" because the pattern is "yyyy.MM.dd G 'at' hh:mm:ss z".

```
SimpleDateFormat formatter
  = new SimpleDateFormat ("yyyy.MM.dd G 'at' hh:mm:ss z");
Date currentTime = new Date();
String dateString = formatter.format(currentTime);
System.out.println("Current time is " + dateString);
```

The following two examples demonstrate how to display date, time, and calendar based on locale. The first example creates a clock and displays date and time in locale-sensitive format. The second example displays several different calendars with the names of the days shown in the appropriate local language.

Example 12.1 Displaying a Clock

This example presents a program that displays the clock to show current time based on the specified locale and time zone. The language, country, and time zone are passed to the program as parameters. The program can run as an applet or an application. When it runs as an applet, the parameters are passed from HTML tags. When it runs as an application, the parameters are passed as command-line arguments like this:

```
java CurrentTimeApplet en US CST
```

The program is given next, and its output is shown in Figure 12.1.

```
// CurrentTimeApplet.java: Display a still clock on the applet
import java.awt.*;
import java.util.*;
import javax.swing.*;
import MyFrameWithExitHandling;
```

continues

```java
public class CurrentTimeApplet extends JApplet
{
  protected Locale locale;
  protected TimeZone tz;
  protected StillClock stillClock;
  private boolean isStandalone = false;

  // Construct the applet
  public CurrentTimeApplet()
  {
  }

  // Initialize the applet
  public void init()
  {
    // Load native fonts. Uncomment the following two statements,
    // if native fonts such as Chinese fonts are not used
    // GraphicsEnvironment ge =
    //   GraphicsEnvironment.getLocalGraphicsEnvironment();
    // ge.getAllFonts();

    if (!isStandalone)
    {
      // Get locale and timezone from HTML
      getHTMLParameters();
    }

    // Add the clock to the applet
    createClock();
  }

  // Create a clock and add it to the applet
  public void createClock()
  {
    getContentPane().add(stillClock = new StillClock(locale, tz));
  }

  public void getHTMLParameters()
  {
    // Get parameters from the HTML
    String language = getParameter("language");
    String country = getParameter("country");
    String timezone = getParameter("timezone");

    // Set default values if parameters are not given in the HTML
    // file
    if (language == null)
      language = "en";

    if (country == null)
      country = "US";

    if (timezone == null)
      timezone = "CST";

    // Set locale and timezone
    locale = new Locale(language, country);
    tz = TimeZone.getTimeZone(timezone);
  }

  // Main method with three arguments:
  // args[0]: language such as en
```

```java
    // args[1]: country such as US
    // args[2]: timezone such as CST
    public static void main(String[] args)
    {
      // Create a frame
      MyFrameWithExitHandling frame = new MyFrameWithExitHandling(
        "Display Current Time");

      // Create an instance of the applet
      CurrentTimeApplet applet = new CurrentTimeApplet();

      // It runs as an application
      applet.isStandalone = true;

      // Get parameters from the command line
      applet.getCommandLineParameters(args);

      // Add the applet instance to the frame
      frame.getContentPane().add(applet, BorderLayout.CENTER);

      // Invoke init() and start()
      applet.init();
      applet.start();

      // Display the frame
      frame.setSize(300, 300);
      frame.setVisible(true);
    }

    // Get command line parameters
    public void getCommandLineParameters(String[] args)
    {
      // Declare locale and timezone with default values
      locale = Locale.getDefault();
      tz = TimeZone.getDefault();

      // Check usage and get language, country and time zone
      if (args.length > 3)
      {
        System.out.println(
          "Usage: java CurrentTimeApplet language country timezone");
        System.exit(0);
      }
      else if (args.length == 3)
      {
        locale = new Locale(args[0], args[1]);
        tz = TimeZone.getTimeZone(args[2]);
      }
      else if (args.length == 2)
      {
        locale = new Locale(args[0], args[1]);
        tz = TimeZone.getDefault();
      }
      else if (args.length == 1)
      {
        System.out.println(
          "Usage: java DisplayTime language country timezone");
        System.exit(0);
      }
      else
```

continues

```java
      {
        locale = Locale.getDefault();
        tz = TimeZone.getDefault();
      }
    }
  }

  // StillClock.java: Display a clock in JPanel
  import java.awt.*;
  import java.util.*;
  import java.text.*;
  import javax.swing.*;

  public class StillClock extends JPanel
  {
    protected TimeZone tz = TimeZone.getDefault();
    protected int xCenter, yCenter;
    protected int clockRadius;
    protected DateFormat myFormat;

    public StillClock()
    {
    }

    public StillClock(Locale locale, TimeZone tz)
    {
      setLocale(locale);
      this.tz = tz;
    }

    // Set timezone using a time zone id such as "CST"
    public void setTimeZoneID(String newTimeZoneID)
    {
      tz = TimeZone.getTimeZone(newTimeZoneID);
    }

    public void paintComponent(Graphics g)
    {
      super.paintComponent(g);

      // Initialize clock parameters
      clockRadius =
        (int)(Math.min(getSize().width, getSize().height)*0.7*0.5);
      xCenter = (getSize().width)/2;
      yCenter = (getSize().height)/2;

      // Draw circle
      g.setColor(Color.black);
      g.drawOval(xCenter - clockRadius,yCenter - clockRadius,
        2*clockRadius, 2*clockRadius);
      g.drawString("12",xCenter-5, yCenter-clockRadius);
      g.drawString("9",xCenter-clockRadius-10,yCenter+3);
      g.drawString("3",xCenter+clockRadius,yCenter+3);
      g.drawString("6",xCenter-3,yCenter+clockRadius+10);

      // Get current time using GregorianCalendar
      GregorianCalendar cal = new GregorianCalendar(tz);

      // Draw second hand
      int second = (int)cal.get(GregorianCalendar.SECOND);
      int sLength = (int)(clockRadius*0.9);
```

```java
      int xSecond =
        (int)(xCenter + sLength*Math.sin(second*(2*Math.PI/60)));
      int ySecond =
        (int)(yCenter - sLength*Math.cos(second*(2*Math.PI/60)));
      g.setColor(Color.red);
      g.drawLine(xCenter, yCenter, xSecond, ySecond);

      // Draw minute hand
      int minute = (int)cal.get(GregorianCalendar.MINUTE);
      int mLength = (int)(clockRadius*0.75);
      int xMinute =
        (int)(xCenter + mLength*Math.sin(minute*(2*Math.PI/60)));
      int yMinute =
        (int)(yCenter - mLength*Math.cos(minute*(2*Math.PI/60)));
      g.setColor(Color.blue);
      g.drawLine(xCenter, yCenter, xMinute, yMinute);

      // Draw hour hand
      int hour = (int)cal.get(GregorianCalendar.HOUR_OF_DAY);
      int hLength = (int)(clockRadius*0.6);
      int xHour = (int)(xCenter +
        hLength*Math.sin((hour+minute/60.0)*(2*Math.PI/12)));
      int yHour = (int)(yCenter -
        hLength*Math.cos((hour+minute/60.0)*(2*Math.PI/12)));
      g.setColor(Color.green);
      g.drawLine(xCenter, yCenter, xHour, yHour);

      // Set display format in specified style, locale and timezone
      myFormat = DateFormat.getDateTimeInstance
        (DateFormat.MEDIUM, DateFormat.LONG, getLocale());
      myFormat.setTimeZone(tz);

      // Display current date
      g.setColor(Color.red);
      String today = myFormat.format(cal.getTime());
      FontMetrics fm = g.getFontMetrics();
      g.drawString(today, (getSize().width -
        fm.stringWidth(today))/2, yCenter+clockRadius+30);
    }
  }
```

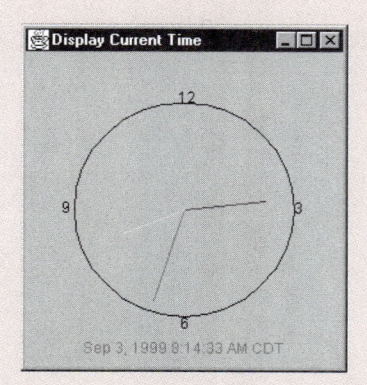

Figure 12.1 *The program displays a clock that shows the current time with specified locale and time zone.*

continues

Example Review

The program consists of two classes: `CurrentTimeApplet` and `StillClock`. The `CurrentTimeApplet` class can run as an applet or as an application. When it runs as an application, it sets `isStandalone true` so that it does not attempt to retrieve HTML parameters.

The program obtains language, country, and time zone as either an HTML parameter or a command-line parameter, and uses this information to create an instance of `StillClock`. `StillClock` is responsible for drawing the clock for the current time. `StillClock` is similar to the `DrawClock` class in Example 8.10, "Drawing a Clock," except that the time (hour, minute, and second) is passed as a parameter to `DrawClock`, but the time in `StillClock` is the current time for the specified locale and time zone.

This program uses the `GregorianCalendar` class to extract the hour, minute, and second from the current time, and the `DateFormat` class to format date and time in a string, with the locale and time zone specified by the user.

The date is displayed below the clock. The program uses font metrics to determine the size of the date/time string and center the display.

The `Component` class has a variable `locale`, which can be accessed through the `getLocale()` and `setLocale()` methods. Since `StillClock` is a `JPanel`, a subclass of `Component`, you can use these methods to work with the locale in `StillClock`.

The variables are purposely declared as protected so that they can be accessed by `StillClock`'s subclasses in later chapters. The `setTimeZoneID()` method defined in `StillClock` is not used here, but it will be used in Example 13.3, "Clock Groups," in Chapter 13, "Multithreading."

The clock is locale-sensitive. If you use the Chinese locale with language (zh) and country (CN), the date and time are displayed in Chinese, as shown in Figure 12.2.

The `CurrentTimeApplet` class is designed for reuse in future chapters. The `createClock()` method is purposely defined in such a way as to make it possible to create and add different types of clocks to the applet in Chapter 14, "Multimedia," by overriding this method.

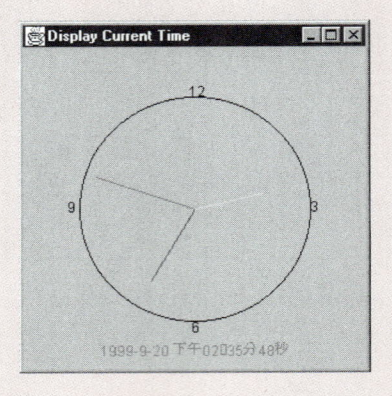

Figure 12.2 *The program displays a clock in the Chinese locale.*

Example 12.2 Displaying a Calendar

This example presents a program that displays a calendar based on the specified locale, as shown in Figures 12.3 and 12.4. The user can specify a locale from a combo box that consists of a list of all the available locales supported by the system.

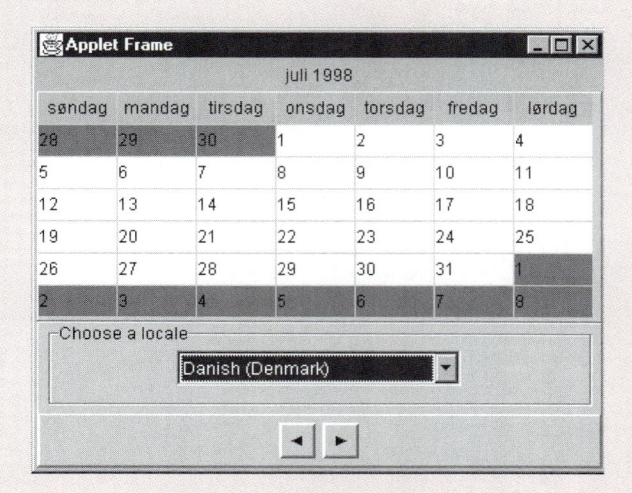

Figure 12.3 *The calendar applet displays a calendar with the Danish locale.*

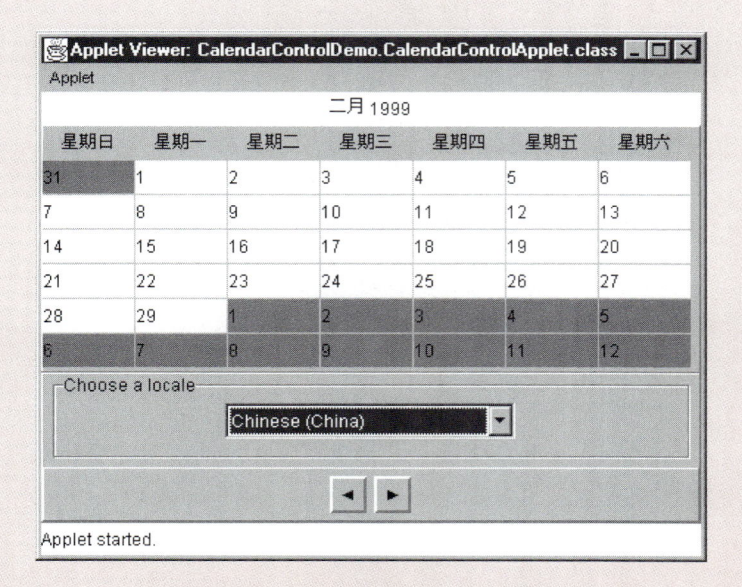

Figure 12.4 *The calendar applet displays a calendar with the Chinese locale.*

continues

```java
// CalendarApplet.java: Display a locale-sensitive calendar
import java.awt.*;
import java.awt.event.*;
import javax.swing.*;
import javax.swing.border.*;
import java.util.*;
import java.text.DateFormat;
import MyFrameWithExitHandling;

public class CalendarApplet extends JApplet
  implements ItemListener, ActionListener
{
  // Create a CalendarPanel for showing calendars
  private CalendarPanel calendarPanel = new CalendarPanel();

  // Combo box for selecting available locales
  private JComboBox jcboLocale = new JComboBox();

  // Declare locales to store available locales
  private Locale locales[] = Calendar.getAvailableLocales();

  // Buttons Prior and Next to displaying prior and next month
  private JButton jbtPrior = new JButton("Prior");
  private JButton jbtNext = new JButton("Next");

  // Initialize the applet
  public void init()
  {
    // Load native fonts. Uncomment the following two statements,
    // if native fonts such as Chinese fonts are not used
    // GraphicsEnvironment ge =
    //   GraphicsEnvironment.getLocalGraphicsEnvironment();
    // ge.getAllFonts();

    // Panel jpLocale to hold the combo box for selecting locales
    JPanel jpLocale = new JPanel();
    jpLocale.setBorder(new TitledBorder("Choose a locale"));
    jpLocale.setLayout(new FlowLayout());
    jpLocale.add(jcboLocale);

    // Initialize the combo box to add locale names
    for (int i=0; i<locales.length; i++)
      jcboLocale.addItem(locales[i].getDisplayName());

    // Panel jpButtons to hold buttons
    JPanel jpButtons = new JPanel();
    jpButtons.setLayout(new FlowLayout());
    jpButtons.add(jbtPrior);
    jpButtons.add(jbtNext);

    // Panel jpCalendar to hold calendarPanel and buttons
    JPanel jpCalendar = new JPanel();
    jpCalendar.setLayout(new BorderLayout());
    jpCalendar.add(calendarPanel, BorderLayout.CENTER);
    jpCalendar.add(jpButtons, BorderLayout.SOUTH);

    // Place jpCalendar and jpLocale to the applet
    this.getContentPane().add(jpCalendar, BorderLayout.CENTER);
    this.getContentPane().add(jpLocale, BorderLayout.SOUTH);
```

```java
      // Register listeners
      jcboLocale.addItemListener(this);
      jbtPrior.addActionListener(this);
      jbtNext.addActionListener(this);
    }

    // Main method
    public static void main(String[] args)
    {
      // Create a frame
      MyFrameWithExitHandling frame = new MyFrameWithExitHandling(
        "Calendar Demo");

      // Create an instance of the applet
      CalendarApplet applet = new CalendarApplet();

      // Add the applet instance to the frame
      frame.getContentPane().add(applet, BorderLayout.CENTER);

      // Invoke init() and start()
      applet.init();
      applet.start();

      // Display the frame
      frame.pack();
      frame.setVisible(true);
    }

    // Handle locale selection
    public void itemStateChanged(ItemEvent e)
    {
      // Set a new locale
      calendarPanel.setLocale(locales[jcboLocale.getSelectedIndex()]);
    }

    // Handle the Prior and Next buttons
    public void actionPerformed(ActionEvent e)
    {
      int currentMonth = calendarPanel.getMonth();

      if (e.getSource() == jbtPrior)
      {
        if (currentMonth==1)
        {
          calendarPanel.setMonth(12);
          calendarPanel.setYear(calendarPanel.getYear()-1);
        }
        else
          calendarPanel.setMonth(currentMonth-1);
      }
      else if (e.getSource() == jbtNext)
      {
        if (currentMonth==12)
        {
          calendarPanel.setMonth(1);
          calendarPanel.setYear(calendarPanel.getYear()+1);
        }
        else
          calendarPanel.setMonth(currentMonth+1);
      }
    }
}
```

continues

```java
// CalendarPanel.java: Display calendar for a month
import java.awt.*;
import javax.swing.*;
import javax.swing.border.LineBorder;
import java.util.*;
import java.text.*;

public class CalendarPanel extends JPanel
{
  private int month;
  private int year;
  private Locale locale = Locale.getDefault();   // Default locale

  // The header label
  private JLabel jlblHeader = new JLabel(" ", JLabel.CENTER);

  // Labels to display day names and days
  private JLabel[] jlblDay = new JLabel[49];

  // MyCalendar instance
  private MyCalendar calendar = new MyCalendar();

  // Constructor
  public CalendarPanel()
  {
    // Panel jpDays to hold day names and days
    JPanel jpDays = new JPanel();
    jpDays.setLayout(new GridLayout(7, 1));
    for (int i=0; i<49; i++)
    {
      jpDays.add(jlblDay[i] = new JLabel());
      jlblDay[i].setBorder(new LineBorder(Color.black, 1));
      jlblDay[i].setHorizontalAlignment(JLabel.RIGHT);
      jlblDay[i].setVerticalAlignment(JLabel.TOP);
    }

    // Place header and calendar body in the panel
    this.setLayout(new BorderLayout());
    this.add(jlblHeader, BorderLayout.NORTH);
    this.add(jpDays, BorderLayout.CENTER);

    // Set current month, and year
    calendar = new MyCalendar();
    month = calendar.get(Calendar.MONTH)+1;
    year = calendar.get(Calendar.YEAR);

    // Show calendar
    showHeader();
    showDayNames();
    showDays();
  }

  // Update the header based on locale
  private void showHeader()
  {
    SimpleDateFormat sdf = new SimpleDateFormat("MMMM yyyy", locale);
    String header = sdf.format(calendar.getTime());
    jlblHeader.setText(header);
  }
```

```java
// Update the day names based on locale
private void showDayNames()
{
  DateFormatSymbols dfs = new DateFormatSymbols(locale);
  String dayNames[] = dfs.getWeekdays();

  // Set calendar days
  for (int i=0; i<7; i++)
  {
    jlblDay[i].setText(dayNames[i+1]);
    jlblDay[i].setHorizontalAlignment(JLabel.CENTER);
  }
}

// Display days
public void showDays()
{
  // Set the calendar to the first day of the
  // specified month and year
  calendar.set(Calendar.YEAR, year);
  calendar.set(Calendar.MONTH, month-1);
  calendar.set(Calendar.DATE, 1);

  // Get the day of the first day in a month
  int startingDayOfMonth = calendar.get(Calendar.DAY_OF_WEEK);

  // Fill the calendar with the days before this month
  MyCalendar cloneCalendar = (MyCalendar)calendar.clone();
  cloneCalendar.add(Calendar.DATE, -1);
  for (int i=0; i<startingDayOfMonth-1; i++)
  {
    jlblDay[i+7].setForeground(Color.yellow);
    jlblDay[i+7].setText(
      cloneCalendar.daysInMonth()-startingDayOfMonth+2+i+"");
  }

  // Display days of this month
  for (int i=1; i<=calendar.daysInMonth(); i++)
  {
    jlblDay[i-2+startingDayOfMonth+7].setForeground(Color.black);
    jlblDay[i-2+startingDayOfMonth+7].setText(i+"");
  }

  // Fill the calendar with the days after this month
  int j = 1;
  for (int i=calendar.daysInMonth()-1+startingDayOfMonth+7;
    i<49; i++)
  {
    jlblDay[i].setForeground(Color.yellow);
    jlblDay[i].setText(j++ + "");
  }

  showHeader();
}

// Getter method for month
public int getMonth()
{
  return month;
}
```

continues

```java
      // Setter method for month
      public void setMonth(int newMonth)
      {
        month = newMonth;
        showDays();
      }

      // Getter method for year
      public int getYear()
      {
        return year;
      }

      // Setter method for year
      public void setYear(int newYear)
      {
        year = newYear;
        showDays();
      }

      // Set a new locale
      public void setLocale(Locale newLocale)
      {
        locale = newLocale;
        showHeader();
        showDayNames();
      }
    }

    // MyCalendar.java: A subclass of GregorianCalendar
    import java.awt.*;
    import java.util.*;

    public class MyCalendar extends GregorianCalendar
    {
      // Find the number of days in a month
      public int daysInMonth()
      {
        switch (get(MONTH))
        {
          case 0: case 2: case 4: case 6: case 7: case 9: case 11:
            return 31;
          case 1: if (isLeapYear(get(YEAR))) return 28;
                  else return 29;
          case 3: case 5: case 8: case 10: return 30;
          default: return 0;
        }
      }
    }
```

Example Review

When the program starts, the calendar for the current month of the year is displayed. The user can use the Prior and Next buttons to browse the calendar.

The program consists of three classes: CalendarApplet, CalendarPanel, and MyCalendar. MyCalendar is a subclass of GregorianCalendar, which has a new method dayInMonth() that computes the number of days in a month. Future versions of JDK may include this method in GregorianCalendar.

CalendarApplet creates the user interface and handles the button actions and combo box item selections for locales. The Calendar.getAvailableLocales()

method is used to find all available locales that have calendars. Its `getDisplay-Name()` method returns the name of each locale, and the name is added to the combo box. When the user selects a locale name in the combo box, a new locale is passed to `calendarPanel`, and a new calendar is displayed based on the new locale.

`CalendarPanel` is created to control and display the calendar. It displays the month and year in the header, and day names and days in the calendar body. The header and day names are locale-sensitive.

The `showHeader()` method displays the calendar title in a form like "MMMM yyyy". The `SimpleDateFormat` class used in the `showHeader()` method is a subclass of `DateFormat`. `SimpleDateFormat` allows you to customize the date format to display the date in various nonstandard styles.

The `showDayNames()` method displays the day names in the calendar. The `DateFormatSymbols` class used in the `showDayNames()` method is a class for encapsulating localizable date-time formatting data, such as the names of the months, the names of the days of the week, and the time zone data. The `getWeekdays()` method is used to get an array of the day names.

The `showDays()` method displays the days for the specified month of the year. As you can see in Figure 12.3, the labels before the current month are filled with the last few days of the previous month, and the labels after the current month are filled with the first few days of the next month.

To fill the calendar with the days before the current month, a clone of `calendar`, named `cloneCalendar`, was created to obtain the days for the previous month. `cloneCalendar` is a copy of `calendar` with separate memory space. Thus you can change the properties of `cloneCalendar` without corrupting the `calendar` object. The `clone()` method is defined in the `Object` class, which was introduced in Chapter 7, "Class Inheritance." You can clone any object as long as its defining class implements the `Cloneable` interface.

Formatting Numbers

Formatting numbers as currency or percentages is highly locale-dependent. For example, the number 5000.50 is displayed as $5,000.50 in US currency, but as 5 000,50 F in French currency.

Numbers are formatted using the `java.text.NumberFormat` class, an abstract base class that provides the methods for formatting and parsing numbers. With `NumberFormat`, you can format and parse numbers for any locale. Your code can be completely independent of locale conventions for decimal points, thousands-separators, or the particular decimal digits used, and even for whether the number format is decimal.

To format a number for the current locale, use one of the factory class methods to get a formatter. Use `getInstance()` or `getNumberInstance()` to get the normal number format. Use `getCurrencyInstance()` to get the currency number format.

And use `getPercentInstance()` to get a format for displaying percentages. With this format, a fraction like 0.53 is displayed as 53%.

For example, to display a number in percentages, you can use the following code to create a formatter for the given locale:

```
NumberFormat percForm = NumberFormat.getPercentInstance(locale);
```

You can then use `percForm` to format a number into a string like this:

```
String s = percForm.format(0.075);
```

Conversely, if you want to read a number entered or stored with the conventions of a certain locale, use the `parse()` method of a formatter to convert the formatted number into an instance of `java.lang.Number`. The `parse()` method throws a `ParseException` if parsing fails.

You can also control the display of numbers with such methods as `setMinimumFractionDigits()`. If you want even more control over the format or parsing, or want to give your users more control, try casting the `NumberFormat` you get from the factory methods to a `DecimalFormat`, which is a subclass of `NumberFormat`. You can then use the `applyPattern()` method of the `DecimalFormat` class to specify the patterns for displaying the number.

Example 12.3 Formatting Numbers

This example creates a mortgage calculator similar to the one in Example 10.1, "Using Applets." This new mortgage calculator allows the user to choose locales, and displays numbers in locale-sensitive format. As shown in Figure 12.5, the user enters interest rate, years, and loan amount, then presses Compute to display the interest rate in percentage format, the years in normal number format, and the loan amount, total payment, and monthly payment in currency format.

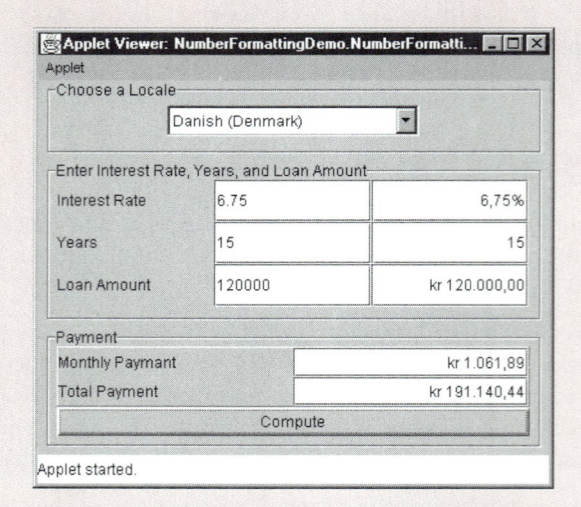

Figure 12.5 *The locale determines the format of the numbers displayed in the mortgage calculator.*

```java
// NumberFormattingDemo.java: Demonstrate formatting numbers
import java.awt.*;
import java.awt.event.*;
import javax.swing.*;
import javax.swing.border.*;
import java.util.*;
import java.text.*;
import MyFrameWithExitHandling;

public class NumberFormattingDemo extends JApplet
  implements ItemListener, ActionListener
{
  // Combo box for selecting available locales
  JComboBox jcboLocale = new JComboBox();

  // Text fields for interest rate, year, loan amount,
  JTextField jtfInterestRate = new JTextField(10);
  JTextField jtfYears = new JTextField(10);
  JTextField jtfLoanAmount = new JTextField(10);
  JTextField jtfFormattedInterestRate = new JTextField(10);
  JTextField jtfFormattedYears = new JTextField(10);
  JTextField jtfFormattedLoanAmount = new JTextField(10);

  // Text fields for monthly payment and total payment
  JTextField jtfTotalPay = new JTextField();
  JTextField jtfMonthlyPay = new JTextField();

  // Compute Mortgage button
  JButton jbtCompute = new JButton("Compute");

  // Current locale
  Locale locale = Locale.getDefault();

  // Declare locales to store available locales
  Locale locales[] = Calendar.getAvailableLocales();

  // Initialize the combo box
  public void initializeComboBox()
  {
    // Add locale names to the combo box
    for (int i=0; i<locales.length; i++)
      jcboLocale.addItem(locales[i].getDisplayName());
  }

  // Initialize the applet
  public void init()
  {
    // Load native fonts. Uncomment the following two statements,
    // if native fonts such as Chinese fonts are not used
    // GraphicsEnvironment ge =
    //   GraphicsEnvironment.getLocalGraphicsEnvironment();
    // ge.getAllFonts();

    // Panel p1 to hold the combo box for selecting locales
    JPanel p1 = new JPanel();
    p1.setLayout(new FlowLayout());
    p1.add(jcboLocale);
    initializeComboBox();
    p1.setBorder(new TitledBorder("Choose a Locale"));
```

continues

```java
    // Panel p2 to hold the input
    JPanel p2 = new JPanel();
    p2.setLayout(new GridLayout(3, 3));
    p2.add(new JLabel("Interest Rate"));
    p2.add(jtfInterestRate);
    p2.add(jtfFormattedInterestRate);
    p2.add(new JLabel("Years"));
    p2.add(jtfYears);
    p2.add(jtfFormattedYears);
    p2.add(new JLabel("Loan Amount"));
    p2.add(jtfLoanAmount);
    p2.add(jtfFormattedLoanAmount);
    p2.setBorder(new TitledBorder
      ("Enter Interest Rate, Years, and Loan Amount"));

    // Panel p3 to hold the result
    JPanel p3 = new JPanel();
    p3.setLayout(new GridLayout(2, 2));
    p3.setBorder(new TitledBorder("Payment"));
    p3.add(new JLabel("Monthly Payment"));
    p3.add(jtfMonthlyPay);
    p3.add(new JLabel("Total Payment"));
    p3.add(jtfTotalPay);

    // Set text field alignment
    jtfFormattedInterestRate.setHorizontalAlignment
      (JTextField.RIGHT);
    jtfFormattedYears.setHorizontalAlignment(JTextField.RIGHT);
    jtfFormattedLoanAmount.setHorizontalAlignment(JTextField.RIGHT);
    jtfTotalPay.setHorizontalAlignment(JTextField.RIGHT);
    jtfMonthlyPay.setHorizontalAlignment(JTextField.RIGHT);

    // Set editable false
    jtfFormattedInterestRate.setEditable(false);
    jtfFormattedYears.setEditable(false);
    jtfFormattedLoanAmount.setEditable(false);
    jtfTotalPay.setEditable(false);
    jtfMonthlyPay.setEditable(false);

    // Panel p4 to hold result payments and a button
    JPanel p4 = new JPanel();
    p4.setLayout(new BorderLayout());
    p4.add(p3, BorderLayout.CENTER);
    p4.add(jbtCompute, BorderLayout.SOUTH);

    // Place panels to the applet
    getContentPane().add(p1, BorderLayout.NORTH);
    getContentPane().add(p2, BorderLayout.CENTER);
    getContentPane().add(p4, BorderLayout.SOUTH);

    // Register listeners
    jcboLocale.addItemListener(this);
    jbtCompute.addActionListener(this);
  }

  // Main method
  public static void main(String[] args)
  {
    // Create a frame
    MyFrameWithExitHandling frame = new MyFrameWithExitHandling(
      "Number Formatting Demo");
```

```java
    // Create an instance of the applet
    NumberFormattingDemo applet = new NumberFormattingDemo();

    // Add the applet instance to the frame
    frame.getContentPane().add(applet, BorderLayout.CENTER);

    // Invoke init() and start()
    applet.init();
    applet.start();

    // Display the frame
    frame.setSize(300, 300);
    frame.setVisible(true);
  }

  // Handle locale selection
  public void itemStateChanged(ItemEvent e)
  {
    if (e.getSource() == jcboLocale)
    {
      locale = locales[jcboLocale.getSelectedIndex()];
      computeMortgage();
    }
  }

  // Handle button action
  public void actionPerformed(ActionEvent e)
  {
    if (e.getSource() == jbtCompute)
      computeMortgage();
  }

  // Compute payments and display results locale-sensitive format
  private void computeMortgage()
  {
    // Retrieve input from user
    double loan = new Double(jtfLoanAmount.getText()).doubleValue();
    double interestRate =
      new Double(jtfInterestRate.getText()).doubleValue()/1200;
    int years = new Integer(jtfYears.getText()).intValue();

    // Calculate payments
    double monthlyPay =
      loan*interestRate/(1-(Math.pow(1/(1+interestRate),years*12)));
    double totalPay = monthlyPay*years*12;

    // Get formatters
    NumberFormat percForm = NumberFormat.getPercentInstance(locale);
    NumberFormat currencyForm =
      NumberFormat.getCurrencyInstance(locale);
    NumberFormat numberForm = NumberFormat.getNumberInstance(locale);
    percForm.setMinimumFractionDigits(2);

    // Display formatted input
    jtfFormattedInterestRate.setText(
      percForm.format(interestRate*12));
    jtfFormattedYears.setText(numberForm.format(years));
    jtfFormattedLoanAmount.setText(currencyForm.format(loan));
```

continues

```java
      // Display results in currency format
      jtfMonthlyPay.setText(currencyForm.format(monthlyPay));
      jtfTotalPay.setText(currencyForm.format(totalPay));
    }
  }
```

Example Review

The `computeMortgage()` method gets the input on interest rate, years, and loan amount from the user, computes monthly payment and total payment, and displays interest in percentage format, years in normal number format, and loan amount, monthly payment, and total payment in locale-sensitive format.

The statement `percForm.setMinimumFractionDigits(2)` sets the minimum number of fractional parts to 2. Without this statement, 0.075 would be displayed as 7% rather than 7.5%.

Resource Bundles (Optional)

The `NumberFormattingDemo` in Example 12.3 displays the numbers, currencies, and percentages in local customs, but displays all the message strings, titles, and button labels in English. In this section, you will learn how to use resource bundles to localize message strings, titles, button labels, etc.

A *resource bundle* is a Java class file or a text file that provides locale-specific information. This information can be accessed by Java programs dynamically. When a locale-specific resource is needed—a message string, for example—your program can load it from the resource bundle appropriate for the desired locale. In this way, you can write program code that is largely independent of the user's locale, isolating most, if not all, of the locale-specific information in resource bundles.

With resource bundles, you can write programs that separate the locale-sensitive part of your code from the locale-independent part. The programs can easily handle multiple locales, and can be easily modified later to support even more locales.

The resources are placed inside the classes that extend the `ResourceBundle` class or a subclass of `ResourceBundle`. Resource bundles contain *key/value* pairs. Each key uniquely identifies a locale-specific object in the bundle. You can use the key to retrieve the object. `ListResourceBundle` is a convenient subclass of `ResourceBundle` that is often used to simplify the creation of resource bundles. Here is an example of a resource bundle that contains four keys using `ListResourceBundle`:

```java
// Resource.java: resource file
public class Resource extends java.util.ListResourceBundle
{
  static final Object[][] contents =
  {
    {"nationalFlag", "china.gif"},
    {"nationalAnthem", "china.au"},
    {"nationalColor", Color.red},
    {"annualGrowthRate", new Double(7.8)}
  };
```

```
      public Object[][] getContents()
      {
        return contents;
      }
    }
```

Keys are case-sensitive strings. In this example, the keys are `nationalFlag`, `nationalAnthem`, `nationalColor`, and `annualGrowthRate`. The values can be any type of `Object`.

If all the resources are strings, they can be placed in a convenient text file with extension.properties. A typical property file would look like this:

```
#Wed Jul 01 07:23:24 EST 1998
nationalFlag=us.gif
nationalAnthem=us.au
```

To retrieve values from a `ResourceBundle` in a program, you first need to create an instance of `ResourceBundle` using one of the following two static methods:

```
public static final ResourceBundle getBundle(String baseName)
   throws MissingResourceException

public static final ResourceBundle getBundle
   (String baseName, Locale locale) throws MissingResourceException
```

The first method returns a `ResourceBundle` for the default locale, and the second method returns a `ResourceBundle` for the specified locale. `baseName` is the base name for a set of classes, each of which describes the information for a given locale. These classes are named in Table 12.2.

TABLE 12.2 Resource Bundle Naming Conventions

1. BaseName_language_country_variant.class
2. BaseName_language_country.class
3. BaseName_language.class
4. BaseName.class
5. BaseName_language_country_variant.properties
6. BaseName_language_country.properties
7. BaseName_language.properties
8. BaseName.properties

For example, Resource_en_BR.class stores resources specific to the United Kingdom, Resource_en_US.class stores resources specific to the United States, and Resource_en.class stores resources specific to all the English-speaking countries.

The `getBundle()` method attempts to load the class that matches the specified locale by language, country, and variant by searching the file name in the order shown in Table 12.2. The files searched in this order form a *resource chain*. If no file is found in the resource chain, the `getBundel()` method raises a `MissingResourceException`.

Once a resource bundle object is created, you can use the `getObject()` method to retrieve the value according to the key. For example,

```java
String flagFile = (String)rb.getObject("nationalFlag");
String anthemFile = (String)rb.getObject("nationalAnthem");
Color color = (Color)rb.getObject("nationalColor");
double growthRate = (Double)rb.getObject("annualGrowthRate").
  toDouble();
```

> **TIP**
> If the resource value is a string, a convenient `getString()` method can be used to replace the `getObject()` method. The `getString()` method simply casts the value returned by `getObject` to a string.

What happens if a resource object you are looking for is not defined in the resource bundle? Java employs an intelligent look-up scheme that searches the object in the parent file along the resource chain. This search is repeated until the object is found or all the parent files in the resource chain have been searched. A `MissingResourceException` is raised if the search is unsuccessful.

Example 12.4 Using Resource Bundles

This example modifies the `NumberFormattingDemo` program in Example 12.3 so that it displays messages, title, and button labels in English, Chinese, and French, as shown in Figure 12.6.

The source code for ResourceBundleDemo.java is shown below:

```java
// ResourceBundleDemo.java: Demonstrate resource bundle
import java.awt.*;
import java.awt.event.*;
import javax.swing.*;
import javax.swing.border.*;
import java.util.*;
import java.text.*;

public class ResourceBundleDemo extends JApplet
  implements ItemListener, ActionListener
{
  // Combo box for selecting available locales
  JComboBox jcboLocale = new JComboBox();
  ResourceBundle res = ResourceBundle.getBundle("Res");

  // Create labels
  JLabel jlblInterestRate = new
    JLabel(res.getString("Interest_Rate"));
  JLabel jlblYears = new JLabel(res.getString("Years"));
  JLabel jlblLoanAmount = new JLabel(res.getString("Loan_Amount"));
  JLabel jlblMonthlyPay = new
    JLabel(res.getString("Monthly_Payment"));
  JLabel jlblTotalPay = new JLabel(res.getString("Total_Payment"));
```

```
// Create titled borders
TitledBorder comboBoxTitle = new
  TitledBorder(res.getString("Choose_a_Locale"));
TitledBorder inputTitle = new TitledBorder
  (res.getString("Enter_Interest_Rate"));
TitledBorder paymentTitle = new TitledBorder(res.getString
  ("Payment"));

// Text fields for interest rate, year, loan amount,
JTextField jtfInterestRate = new JTextField(10);
JTextField jtfYears = new JTextField(10);
JTextField jtfLoanAmount = new JTextField(10);
JTextField jtfFormattedInterestRate = new JTextField(10);
JTextField jtfFormattedYears = new JTextField(10);
JTextField jtfFormattedLoanAmount = new JTextField(10);

// Text fields for monthly payment and total payment
JTextField jtfTotalPay = new JTextField();
JTextField jtfMonthlyPay = new JTextField();

// Compute Mortgage button
JButton jbtCompute = new JButton(res.getString(
  "Compute_Mortgage"));

// Current locale
Locale locale = Locale.getDefault();

// Declare locales to store available locales
Locale locales[] = Calendar.getAvailableLocales();

// Initialize the combo box
public void initializeComboBox()
{
  // Add locale names to the combo box
  for (int i=0; i<locales.length; i++)
    jcboLocale.addItem(locales[i].getDisplayName());
}

// Initialize the applet
public void init()
{
  // Load native fonts. Uncomment the following two statements,
  // if native fonts such as Chinese fonts are not used
  // GraphicsEnvironment ge =
  //   GraphicsEnvironment.getLocalGraphicsEnvironment();
  // ge.getAllFonts();

  // Panel p1 to hold the combo box for selecting locales
  JPanel p1 = new JPanel();
  p1.setLayout(new FlowLayout());
  p1.add(jcboLocale);
  initializeComboBox();
  p1.setBorder(comboBoxTitle);

  // Panel p2 to hold the input for interest rate, years and
  // loan amount
  JPanel p2 = new JPanel();
  p2.setLayout(new GridLayout(3, 3));
  p2.add(jlblInterestRate);
  p2.add(jtfInterestRate);
```

continues

```java
    p2.add(jtfFormattedInterestRate);
    p2.add(jlblYears);
    p2.add(jtfYears);
    p2.add(jtfFormattedYears);
    p2.add(jlblLoanAmount);
    p2.add(jtfLoanAmount);
    p2.add(jtfFormattedLoanAmount);
    p2.setBorder(inputTitle);

    // Panel p3 to hold the payment
    JPanel p3 = new JPanel();
    p3.setLayout(new GridLayout(2, 2));
    p3.setBorder(paymentTitle);
    p3.add(jlblMonthlyPay);
    p3.add(jtfMonthlyPay);
    p3.add(jlblTotalPay);
    p3.add(jtfTotalPay);

    // Set text field alignment
    jtfFormattedInterestRate.setHorizontalAlignment
      (JTextField.RIGHT);
    jtfFormattedYears.setHorizontalAlignment(JTextField.RIGHT);
    jtfFormattedLoanAmount.setHorizontalAlignment(JTextField.RIGHT);
    jtfTotalPay.setHorizontalAlignment(JTextField.RIGHT);
    jtfMonthlyPay.setHorizontalAlignment(JTextField.RIGHT);

    // Set editable false
    jtfFormattedInterestRate.setEditable(false);
    jtfFormattedYears.setEditable(false);
    jtfFormattedLoanAmount.setEditable(false);
    jtfTotalPay.setEditable(false);
    jtfMonthlyPay.setEditable(false);

    // Panel p4 to hold result payments and a button
    JPanel p4 = new JPanel();
    p4.setLayout(new BorderLayout());
    p4.add(p3, BorderLayout.CENTER);
    p4.add(jbtCompute, BorderLayout.SOUTH);

    // Place panels to the applet
    getContentPane().add(p1, BorderLayout.NORTH);
    getContentPane().add(p2, BorderLayout.CENTER);
    getContentPane().add(p4, BorderLayout.SOUTH);

    // Register listeners
    jcboLocale.addItemListener(this);
    jbtCompute.addActionListener(this);
  }

  // Main method
  public static void main(String[] args)
  {
    // Create an instance of the applet
    ResourceBundleDemo applet = new ResourceBundleDemo();

    // Create a frame with a resource string
    MyFrameWithExitHandling frame = new MyFrameWithExitHandling(
      applet.res.getString("Number_Formatting"));

    // Add the applet instance to the frame
    frame.getContentPane().add(applet, BorderLayout.CENTER);
```

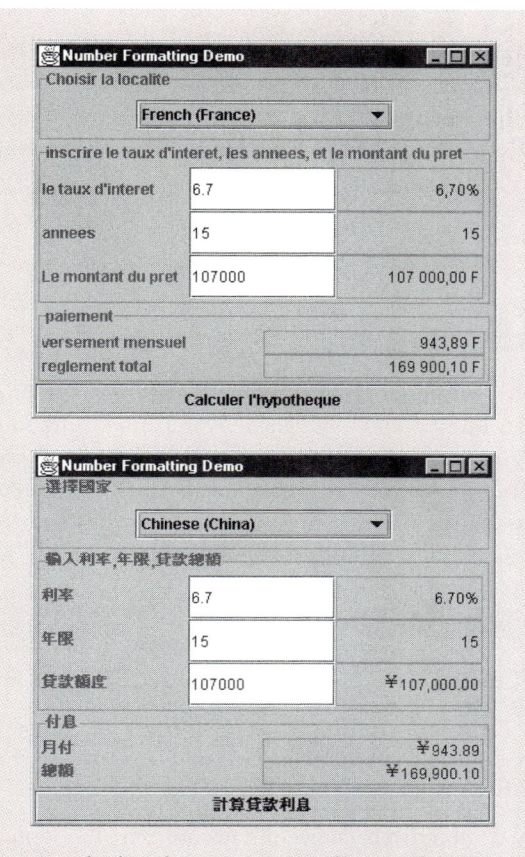

Figure 12.6 *The program displays the strings in French or in Chinese.*

Example Review

Property resource bundles are implemented as text files with a .properties extension, and are placed in the same location as the class files for the application or applet. `ListResourceBundles` are provided as Java source files. Because they are implemented as Java source code, new and modified `ListResourceBundles` need to be recompiled for deployment. With `PropertyResourceBundles`, there is no need for recompilation when translations are modified or added to the application. `ListResourceBundles` provide considerably better performance than `PropertyResourceBundles`.

If the resource bundle is not found or a resource object is not found in the resource bundle, a `MissingResourceException` is raised. Since `MissingResourceException` is a subclass of `RuntimeException`, you do not need to catch the exception explicitly in the code.

This example is the same as Example 12.3 except that the program contains the code for handling resource strings. The `updateString()` method is responsible for displaying the locale-sensitive strings. This method is invoked when a new

continues

locale is selected in the combo box. Since the variable res of the ResourceBundle class is an instance of ResourceBundleDemo, it cannot be directly used in the main() method, because the main() method is static. To fix the problem, create an applet (as an instance of ResourceBundleDemo) and you will then be able to reference res using applet.res.

Chapter Summary

This chapter introduced the subject of building Java programs that operate correctly for an international audience. You learned how to use the Locale object to represent a particular locale, how to localize date and time, and how to display numbers in normal format, currency format, and percentage format. You also learned how to use the Resource Wizard to create resource bundles and move the locale-specific strings, titles, and labels to them.

Chapter Review

12.1. How does Java support international characters in languages like Chinese and Arabic?

12.2. How do you construct a Locale object? How do you get all the available locales from a Calendar object?

12.3. How do you display current date and time in German?

12.4. How do you format and display numbers and percentages in Chinese?

12.5. How does the getBundle() method locate a resource bundle?

12.6. How does the getObject() method locate a resource?

Programming Exercises

12.1. Develop an applet that displays Unicode characters, as shown in Figure 12.7. The user specifies a Unicode in the text field and presses the Enter key to display a sequence of Unicode characters starting with the specified Unicode. The Unicode characters are displayed in a scrollable text area of 20 lines. Each line contains 16 characters preceded by a Unicode, which is the code for the first character on the line.

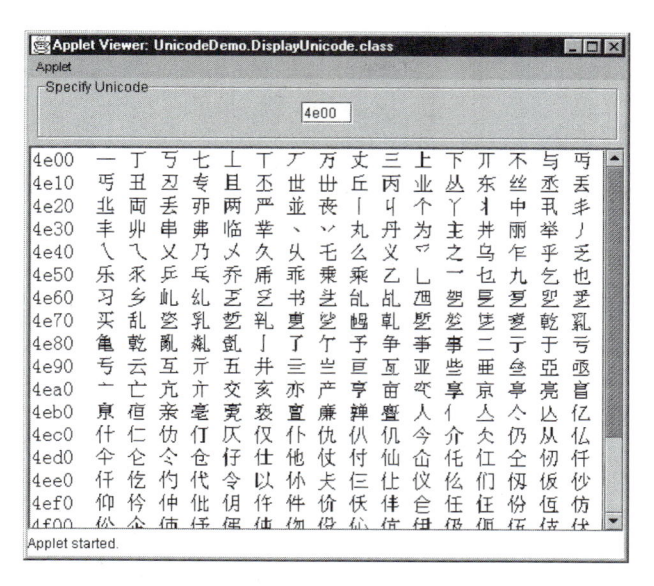

Figure 12.7 *The applet displays the Unicode characters.*

12.2. Modify Example 12.2, "Displaying a Calendar," to localize the labels "Choose a locale" and "Calendar Demo" in French, German, and Chinese, or a language of your choice.

12.3. Write a program that displays a calendar for a specified month using the `Date`, `Calendar`, and `GregorianCalendar` classes. Your program receives the month and year from the command line. For example:

```
java DisplayCalendar 5 1999
```

This displays the calendar shown in Figure 12.8.

You also can run the program without the year. In this case, the year is the current year. If you run the program without specifying a month and a year, the month is the current month.

Figure 12.8 *The program displays a calendar for May 1999.*

12.4. Write a program that converts US dollars to Canadian dollars, German marks, and British pounds, as shown in Figure 12.9. The user enters the US dollar amount and the conversion rates, and clicks the Convert button to display the converted amount.

Figure 12.9 *The program converts US dollars to Canadian dollars, German marks, and British pounds.*

12.5. Use a tabbed pane to write a program with two tabs. One, labeled Calendar, displays the calendar, and the other, labeled Clock, displays the current time on a clock (see Figure 12.10).

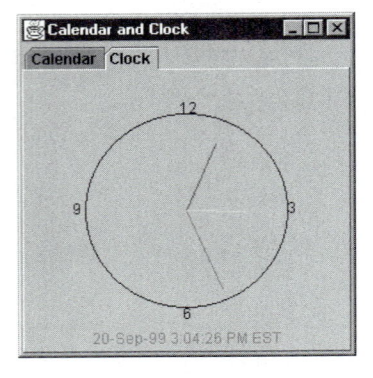

Figure 12.10 *The Calendar tab displays a calendar, and the Clock tab displays a clock.*

CHAPTER 13

MULTITHREADING

Objectives

- Understand the concept of multithreading and apply it to develop animation.
- Write threads by extending the `Thread` class.
- Debug Multithreaded Applications in Visual J++
- Write threads by implementing the `Runnable` interface in cases of multiple inheritance.
- Understand the life-cycle of thread states.
- Understand and set thread priorities.
- Use thread groups to manage a group of similar threads.
- Use thread synchronization to avoid resource conflicts.

Introduction

A *thread* is a flow of execution, with a beginning and an end, of a task in a program. The programs you have seen so far run in a single thread; that is, at any given time, a single statement is being executed. With Java, you can launch multiple threads from a program concurrently. These threads can be executed simultaneously in multiprocessor systems, as shown in Figure 13.1.

Figure 13.1   *Here, multiple threads are running on multiple CPUs.*

In single-processor systems, as shown in Figure 13.2, the multiple threads share CPU time, and the operating system is responsible for scheduling and allocating resources to them. This arrangement is practical because most of the time the CPU is idle. For example, it does nothing while waiting for the user to enter data.

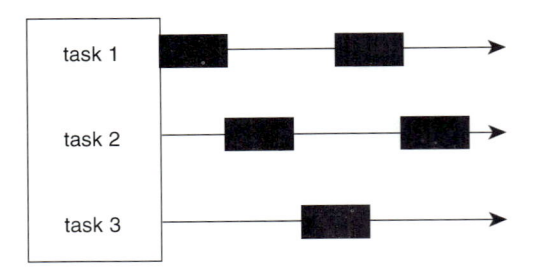

Figure 13.2   *Here, multiple threads share a single CPU.*

Multithreading can make your program more responsive and interactive, as well as enhance performance. For example, a good word processor lets you print or save the file while you are typing. In some cases, multithreaded programs run faster than single-threaded programs even on single-processor systems. Multithreading is particularly useful for animation in Java, which is designed to make computer animation easy. Java also provides exceptionally good support for programming with multiple threads of execution, including built-in support for creating threads and for locking resources to prevent conflicts.

You can create threads by extending the `Thread` class or implementing the `Runnable` interface. Both `Thread` and `Runnable` are defined in the `java.lang` package. `Thread` actually implements `Runnable`. In this chapter, you will learn how to use the `Thread` class and the `Runnable` interface to write multithreaded programs.

The *Thread* Class

The `Thread` class contains the constructor `Thread()`, as well as many useful methods that run, start, suspend, resume, interrupt, and stop threads. To create and run a thread, first define a class that extends the `Thread` class. Your thread class must override the `run()` method, which tells the system how the thread will be executed when it runs. You then need a client class that creates an object running on the thread. This object is referred to as a *runnable object*. Figure 13.3 illustrates the structure of a thread class and its client class.

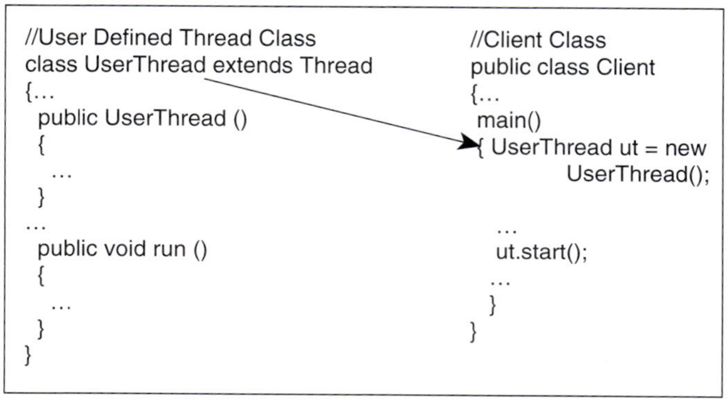

```
//User Defined Thread Class              //Client Class
class UserThread extends Thread          public class Client
{...                                     {...
  public UserThread ()                     main()
  {                                        { UserThread ut = new
    ...                                             UserThread();
  }                                          ...
  ...                                        ut.start();
  public void run ()                         ...
  {                                        }
    ...                                   }
  }
}
```

Figure 13.3 *A thread is defined as a subclass of the* `Thread` *class.*

You use the `Thread()` constructor to create a runnable object. The `start()` method tells the system that the thread is ready to run. The constructor and several methods in the `Thread` class are described in the next few paragraphs. The following constructs a new thread:

```
public Thread()
```

Usually, it is called from the client class to create a runnable object. If a user-defined thread class is used, the client program creates a thread by using the user-defined thread class constructor, as shown in Figure 13.3.

These methods in the `Thread` class are often useful:

- `public void run()`

  This method is invoked by the Java runtime system to execute the thread. You must override this method and provide the code you want your thread to execute in your thread class. This method is never directly invoked by the runnable object in the program, although it is an instance method of a runnable object.

- `public void start()`

  This method starts the thread, which causes the `run()` method to be invoked. This method is called by the runnable object in the client class.

- `public void stop()`

    This method stops the thread. As of Java 2, this method is deprecated, because it is known to be inherently unsafe. You should assign `null` to a `Thread` variable to indicate that it is stopped rather than using the `stop()` method.

- `public void suspend()`

    This method suspends the thread. As of Java 2, this method is deprecated, because it is known to be deadlock-prone. You should use the `wait()` method along with a `boolean` variable to indicate whether a thread is suspended rather than using the `suspend()` method. An example of implementing the `suspend()` method is introduced in the next section, "The `Runnable` Interface."

- `public void resume()`

    This method resumes the thread. As of Java 2, this method, along with the `suspend()` method, is deprecated because it is deadlock-prone. You should use the `notify()` method along with a `boolean` variable to indicate whether a thread is resumed rather than using the `resume()` method. An example of implementing the `resume()` method will be introduced in the next section, "The `Runnable` Interface."

- `public static void sleep(long millis) throws InterruptedException`

    This method puts the runnable object to sleep for a specified time in milliseconds. Note that `sleep()` is a class method.

- `public void interrupt()`

    This method interrupts the running thread.

- `public static boolean isInterrupted()`

    This method tests to see whether the current thread has been interrupted.

- `public boolean isAlive()`

    This method tests to see whether the thread is currently running.

- `public void setPriority(int p)`

    This method sets priority `p` (ranging from `1` to `10`) for this thread.

The `wait()` and `notify()` methods in the `Object` class are often used with threads.

- `public final void wait() throws InterruptedException`

    This method puts the thread to wait for notification by another thread of a change in the object.

- `public final void notify()`

    This method awakens a single thread that is waiting on this object.

Chapter 13 Multithreading

Example 13.1 Using the *Thread* Class to Create and Launch Threads

This program creates and runs the following three threads:

- The first thread prints the letter *a* 100 times.
- The second thread prints the letter *b* 100 times.
- The third thread prints the integers 1 through 100.

The program has three independent tasks. To run them concurrently, it needs to create a runnable object for each task. Because the first two threads have similar functionality, they can be defined in one thread class.

The program is given here, and its output is shown in Figure 13.4.

```java
// TestThreads.java: Define threads using the Thread class
public class TestThreads
{
  // Main method
  public static void main(String[] args)
  {
    // Create threads
    PrintChar printA = new PrintChar('a',100);
    PrintChar printB = new PrintChar('b',100);
    PrintNum  print100 = new PrintNum(100);

    // Start threads
    print100.start();
    printA.start();
    printB.start();
  }
}

// The thread class for printing a specified character
// in specified times
class PrintChar extends Thread
{
  private char charToPrint;  // The character to print
  private int times;  // The times to repeat

  // Construct a thread with specified character and number of
  // times to print the character
  public PrintChar(char c, int t)
  {
    charToPrint = c;
    times = t;
  }

  // Override the run() method to tell the system
  // what the thread will do
  public void run()
  {
    for (int i=1; i < times; i++)
      System.out.print(charToPrint);
  }
}

// The thread class for printing number from 1 to n for a given n
class PrintNum extends Thread
```

continues

```java
{
  private int lastNum;

  // Construct a thread for print 1, 2, ... i
  public PrintNum(int n)
  {
    lastNum = n;
  }

  public void run()
  {
    for (int i=1; i <= lastNum; i++)
      System.out.print(" " + i);
  }
}

// The thread class for printing number from 1 to n for a given n
class PrintNum extends Thread
{
  private int lastNum;

  public PrintNum(int i)
  {
    lastNum = i;
  }

  public void run()
  {
    for (int i=1; i <= lastNum; i++)
      System.out.print(" "+i);
  }
}
```

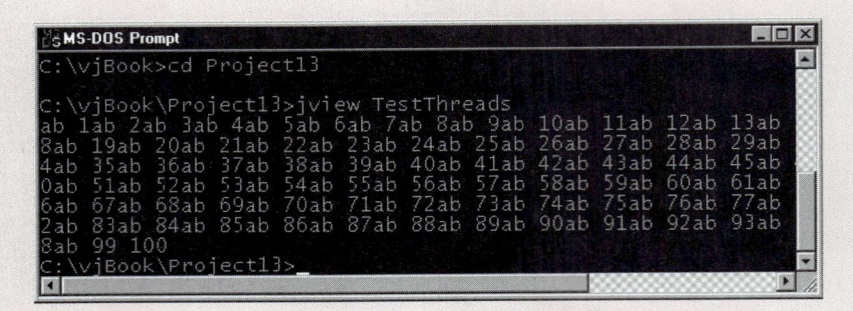

Figure 13.4 *The threads* printA, printB, *and* print100 *are executed simultaneously to display the letter* a *100 times, the letter* b *100 times, and the numbers from 1 to 100.*

Example Review

If you run this program on a multiple-CPU system, all three threads will execute simultaneously. If you run the program on a single CPU system, the three threads will share the CPU and take turns printing letters and numbers on the console.

The program creates thread classes by extending the `Thread` class. The `PrintChar` class, derived from the `Thread` class, overrides the `run()` method with the print-character action. This class provides a framework for printing any single character a given number of times. The runnable objects `printA` and `printB` are instances of the user-defined thread class `PrintChar`.

The `PrintNum` class overrides the `run()` method with the print-number action. This class provides a framework for printing numbers from *1* to *n*, for any integer *n*. The runnable object `print100` is an instance of `PrintNum`.

In the client program, the program creates a thread, `printA`, for printing the letter *a*; and a thread, `printB`, for printing the letter *b*. Both are objects of the `PrintChar` class. The `print100` thread object is created from the `PrintNum` class.

The `start()` method is invoked to start a thread, which causes the `run()` method to execute. When the `run()` method completes, the threads terminate.

> **NOTE**
> On some systems, the program may not terminate or print out all the characters and numbers. The problem has nothing to do with your program. It may be an OS problem or a Java Virtual Machine implementation problem. If the program does not seem to terminate, press Ctrl+C to stop it.

Debugging Multithreaded Applications in Visual J++

Visual J++ enables you to debug multithreaded applications. You can view and control the execution of the threads during debugging in the Thread window. This section uses Example 13.1 to demonstrate how to debug multithreaded applications.

Here are the steps in the demonstration:

1. Set breakpoints at the `print` statements in the `run` method of the `PrintChar` class and the run method of the `PrintNum` class.

2. On the Launch page of the Project13 Properties dialog box, choose Test-Threads to run and uncheck the option "Launch as a console application."

3. Click the Start button to start debugging. The program pauses at one of the two preset breakpoints, as shown in the Threads window in Figure 13.5. (You need to click the Start button several times to give all three threads a chance to run so you will see the three threads in the Threads window.)

4. To inspect a thread, double-click the thread in the Threads window. You will see a yellow arrow pointing to the thread in the Threads window. You can examine the variables associated with the thread in the Autos, Locals, and

Watch windows, and modify them in the Immediate window. For instance, double-click Thread-2 with location `PrintNum.run` in the Threads, and then choose the Locals tab to display the local variables in the thread, as shown in Figure 13.6.

5. You can suspend or resume the threads during debugging. For instance, to suspend Thread-2, right-click the mouse button to reveal a context menu, as shown in Figure 13.7. Choose Suspend in the menu to suspend Thread-2. Click the Continue button to execute the program.

6. The output of the program can be shown in the Output window during debugging, since you unchecked the option "Run as a console application" in the Project Properties box. To show the Output window, click the toolbar button ▤ in the Debug toolbar window. The output is shown in Figure 13.5.

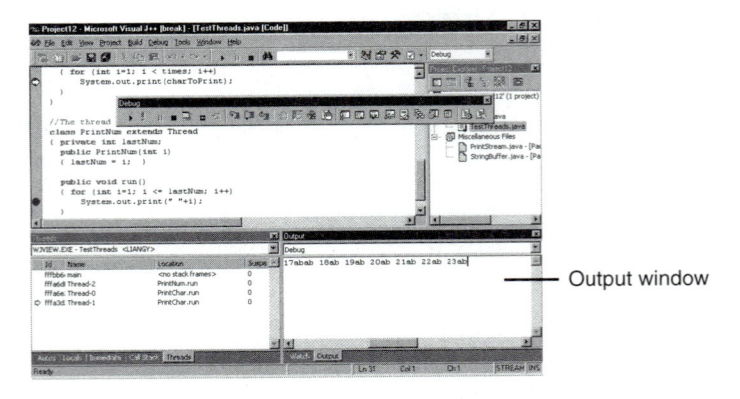

Figure 13.5 *The Threads window displays the threads in the application.*

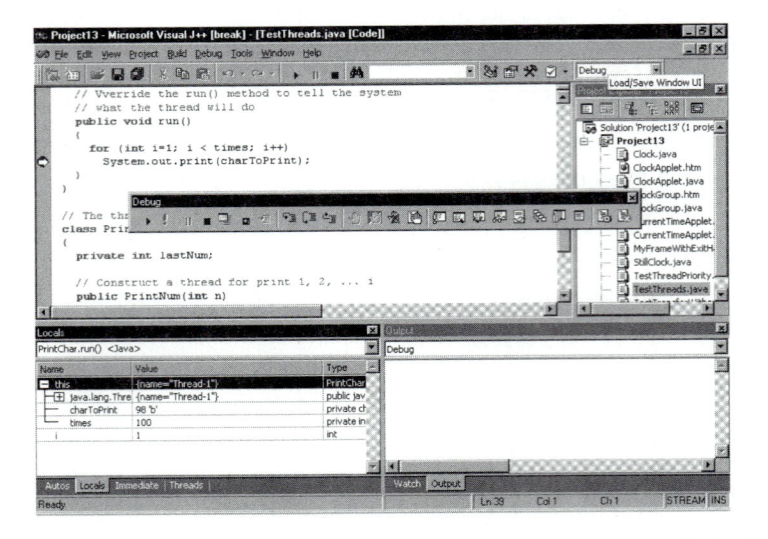

Figure 13.6 *With the thread activated in the Threads window, you can inspect the local variables in the thread in the Locals window.*

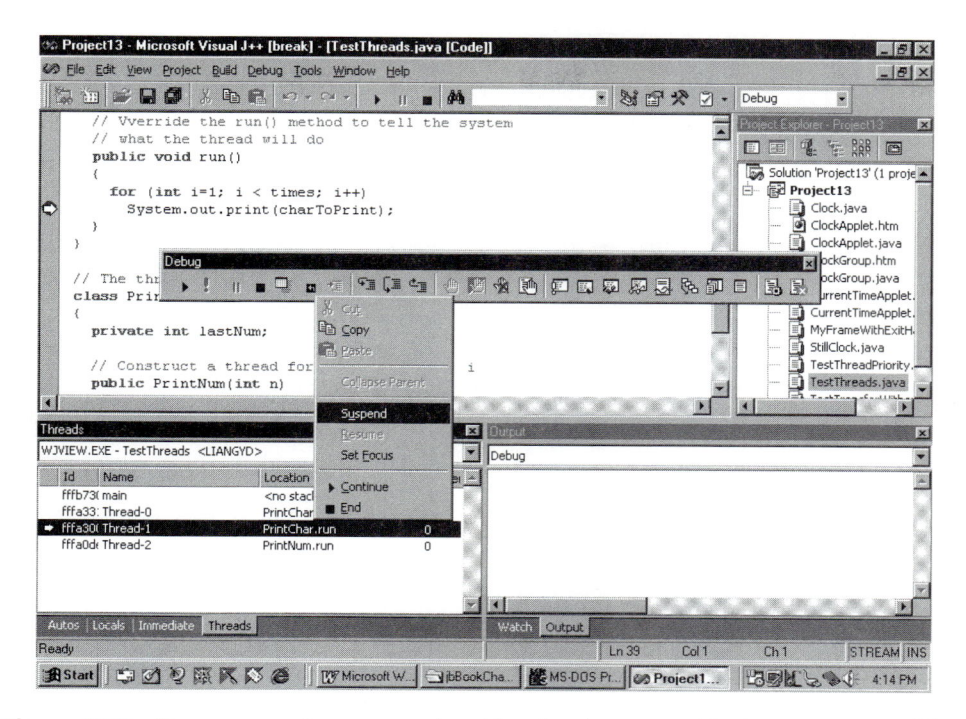

Figure 13.7 *You can suspend or resume a thread by using the command in the context menu of the thread in the Threads window.*

The *Runnable* Interface

In the preceding section, you created and ran a thread by declaring a user thread class that extends the `Thread` class. This approach works well if the user thread class inherits only from the `Thread` class, but not if the user thread class inherits multiple classes, as in the case of an applet. To inherit multiple classes, you have to implement interfaces. Java provides the `Runnable` interface as an alternative to the `Thread` class.

In Example 12.1, "Displaying a Clock," you drew a clock to show the current time in an applet. The clock does not tick after it is displayed. What can you do to let the clock display a new current time every second? The key to making the clock tick is to repaint it every second with a new current time. You can use the code given below to override the `start()` method in `CurrentTimeApplet`:

```
public void start()
{
  while (true)
  {
    stillClock.repaint();
    try
    {
      Thread.sleep(1000);
    }
```

```
        catch(InterruptedException ex)
        {
        }
      }
    }
  }
```

The `start()` method is called when the applet begins. The infinite loop repaints the clock every 1,000 milliseconds (in other words, at 1-second intervals). This appears to refresh the clock every second, but if you run the program, the browser hangs up. The problem is that as long as the `while` loop is running, the browser cannot serve any other event that might be occurring. Therefore, the `paintComponent()` method is not called. The solution is to move the `while` loop to another thread that can be executed in parallel with the `paintComponent()` method.

To create a new thread for the applet, you need to implement the `Runnable` interface in the applet. Here are the implementation guidelines for the `Runnable` interface:

1. Add `implements Runnable` in the applet class declaration:

    ```
    public class MyApplet extends JApplet implements Runnable
    ```

2. Declare a thread in `MyApplet`. For example, the following statement declares a thread instance, `thread`, with the initial value `null`:

    ```
    private Thread thread = null;
    ```

    By default, the initial value is `null`, so assigning `null` in this statement is not necessary.

3. Create a new thread in the applet's `init()` method and start it right away in `MyApplet`:

    ```
    public void init()
    {
      thread = new Thread(this);  // Create a thread
      thread.start();   // Start the thread
    }
    ```

    The `this` argument in the `Thread` constructor is required; it specifies that the run function of `MyApplet` should be called when the thread executes an instance of `MyApplet`.

4. Resume the thread in the applet's `start()` method by invoking `resume()` like this in `MyApplet`:

    ```
    public void start()
    {
      resume();
    }
    ```

    The `resume()` method resumes this thread if it was suspended. This method is ignored if the thread was not suspended. Since the `resume()` method in the `Thread` class has been deprecated, you have to create a new one in the program.

5. Create `resume()` and `suspend()` methods as follows:

   ```
   public synchronized void resume()
   {
     if (suspended)
     {
       suspended = false;
       notify();
     }
   }

   public synchronized void suspend()
   {
     suspended = true;
   }
   ```

   The variable `suspended` should be declared as a data member of the class, which indicates the state of the thread. The `synchronized` keyword ensures that the `resume()` and `suspend()` methods are serialized to avoid race conditions that could result in an inconsistent value for the variable `suspended`. The `synchronized` keyword is further discussed in the section titled "Synchronization," later in this chapter.

6. Write the code you want the thread to execute in the `run()` method:

   ```
   public void run()
   {
     while (true)
     {
       stillClock.repaint();

       try
       {
         thread.sleep(1000);
         synchronized (this)
         {
           while (suspended)
             wait();
         }
       }
       catch (InterruptedException ex)
       {
       }
     }
   }
   ```

   The `run()` method is invoked by the Java runtime system when the applet starts. The `while` loop repeatedly invokes the `stillClock.repaint()` method every second if the thread is not suspended. If `suspended` is true, the `wait()` method causes the thread to suspend and wait for notification by the `notify()` method invoked from the `resume()` method. The `repaint()` method runs on the system default thread, which is separate from the thread on which the `while` loop is running. The `synchronized` keyword eliminates potential conflicts that could cause the suspended thread to miss a notification and remain suspended.

7. Override the `stop()` method to suspend the running thread:

```
public void stop()
{
  suspend();
}
```

This code suspends the thread so that it does not consume CPU time when the Web page containing this applet becomes inactive.

8. Override the `destroy()` method to kill the thread:

```
public void destroy()
{
  thread = null;
}
```

This code releases all the resources associated with the thread when the Web browser exits.

Example 13.2 Implementing the *Runnable* Interface in an Applet

The applet presented here displays a clock. To simulate the clock running, a separate thread is used to repaint the clock. The output of the program is shown in Figure 13.8.

```
// ClockApplet.java: Display a running clock on the applet
import java.applet.*;
import java.awt.*;
import java.util.*;

public class ClockApplet extends CurrentTimeApplet
  implements Runnable
{
  // Declare a thread for running the clock
  private Thread thread = null;

  // Determine if the thread is suspended
  private boolean suspended = false;

  // Initialize applet
  public void init()
  {
    super.init();

    // Create the thread
    thread = new Thread(this);

    // Start the thread
    thread.start();
  }

  // Implement the start() method to resume the thread
  public void start()
  {
    resume();
  }

  // Implement the run() method to dictate what the thread will do
  public void run()
```

```java
  {
    while (true)
    {
      // Repaint the clock to display current time
      stillClock.repaint();

      try
      {
        thread.sleep(1000);
        synchronized (this)
        {
          while (suspended)
            wait();
        }
      }
      catch (InterruptedException ex)
      {
      }
    }
  }

  // Implement the stop method to suspend the thread
  public void stop()
  {
    suspend();
  }

  // Destroy the thread
  public void destroy()
  {
    thread = null;
  }

  // Resume the suspended thread
  public synchronized void resume()
  {
    if (suspended)
    {
      suspended = false;
      notify();
    }
  }

  // Suspend the thread
  public synchronized void suspend()
  {
    suspended = true;
  }
}
```

continues

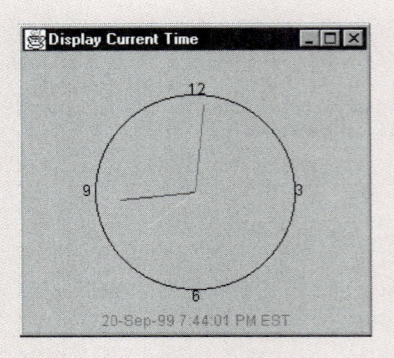

Figure 13.8 *The control of the clock drawing runs a thread separately from the* paintComponent() *method that draws the clock.*

Example Review

The CurrentTimeApplet class is presented in Example 12.1, "Displaying a Clock," to display the current time. The ClockApplet class extends CurrentTimeApplet with a control loop running on a separate thread to make the clock tick.

The run() method comes from the Runnable interface and is modified to specify what the separate thread will do. The paintComponent() method is called every second by the repaint() method to display the current time.

The init(), start(), stop(), and destroy() methods in the Applet class are modified for this program to work with the Web browser. The init() method is invoked to start the thread when the Web page is loaded. The stop() method is invoked to suspend the thread when the Web page containing the applet becomes inactive. The start() method is invoked to resume the thread when the Web page containing the applet becomes active. The destroy() method is invoked to terminate the thread when the Web browser exits.

The separate thread named thread is created and started in the applet's init() method:

```
thread = new Thread(this);
thread.start();
```

The ClockApplet's init() method calls super.init() defined in the CurrentTimeApplet class, which gets parameters for country, language, and time zone from HTML. Therefore, the ClockApplet class can get these parameters from HTML.

The resume() method sets the variable suspended to false and awakens the thread that is waiting on the notification by invoking the notify() method. The suspend() method sets the variable suspended to true, which causes the thread to suspend and wait for notification to resume.

> **NOTE**
> The start() method in thread.start() is different from the start() method in the applet. The former starts the thread and causes the run() method to execute, whereas the latter is executed by the Web browser when the applet starts for the first time or is reactivated.

> **TIP**
> Because it is easier and simpler to use the Thread class, I recommend that you use it unless your class uses multiple inheritance.

> **CAUTION**
> I recommend that you suspend the threads in the Applet's stop() method so that the applet does not consume CPU time when the Web page is inactive.

Case Studies

The preceding example shows how to implement the Runnable interface in an applet. You can implement the Runnable interface in any class. The next example shows you how to use the Runnable interface in a class other than applets. You will create a new class named Clock that extends StillClock and implements Runnable to make the clock self-running.

Example 13.3 Controlling a Group of Clocks

This program displays three clocks in a group. Each clock has individual Resume and Suspend control buttons. You can also resume or suspend all the clocks by using group-control Resume All and Suspend All buttons. Figure 13.9 contains the output of a sample run of the program.

```java
// ClockGroup.java: Display a group of international clocks
import java.awt.*;
import java.awt.event.*;
import java.util.*;
import javax.swing.*;

public class ClockGroup extends JApplet implements ActionListener
{
  // Declare three clock panels
  private ClockPanel clockPanel1, clockPanel2, clockPanel3;

  // Declare group control buttons
  private JButton jbtResumeAll, jbtSuspendAll;
```

continues

```java
// This main method enables the applet to run as an application
public static void main(String[] args)
{
  // Create a frame
  MyFrameWithExitHandling frame = new MyFrameWithExitHandling(
    "Clock Group Demo");

  // Create an instance of the applet
  ClockGroup applet = new ClockGroup();

  // Add the applet instance to the frame
  frame.getContentPane().add(applet, BorderLayout.CENTER);

  // Invoke init() and start()
  applet.init();
  applet.start();

  // Display the frame
  frame.setSize(600, 300);
  frame.setVisible(true);
}

// Initialize the applet
public void init()
{
  // Panel p1 for holding three clocks
  JPanel p1 = new JPanel();
  p1.setLayout(new GridLayout(1, 3));

  // Create a clock for Berlin
  p1.add(clockPanel1 = new ClockPanel());
  clockPanel1.setTitle("Berlin");
  clockPanel1.clock.setTimeZoneID("ECT");
  clockPanel1.clock.setLocale(Locale.GERMAN);

  // Create a clock for San Francisco
  p1.add(clockPanel2 = new ClockPanel());
  clockPanel2.clock.setLocale(Locale.US);
  clockPanel2.clock.setTimeZoneID("PST");
  clockPanel2.setTitle("San Francisco");

  // Create a clock for Taipei
  p1.add(clockPanel3 = new ClockPanel());
  clockPanel3.setTitle("\u6077\u6079");
  clockPanel3.clock.setLocale(Locale.CHINESE);
  clockPanel3.clock.setTimeZoneID("CTT");

  // Panel p2 for holding two group control buttons
  JPanel p2 = new JPanel();
  p2.setLayout(new FlowLayout());
  p2.add(jbtResumeAll = new JButton("Resume All"));
  p2.add(jbtSuspendAll = new JButton("Suspend All"));

  // Add panel p1 and p2 into the applet
  getContentPane().setLayout(new BorderLayout());
  getContentPane().add(p1, BorderLayout.CENTER);
  getContentPane().add(p2, BorderLayout.SOUTH);

  // Register listeners
  jbtResumeAll.addActionListener(this);
  jbtSuspendAll.addActionListener(this);
}
```

```java
    // Handlers for group control buttons
    public void actionPerformed(ActionEvent e)
    {
      if (e.getSource() == jbtResumeAll)
      {
        // Start all clocks
        clockPanel1.resume();
        clockPanel2.resume();
        clockPanel3.resume();
      }
      else if (e.getSource() == jbtSuspendAll)
      {
        // Stop all clocks
        clockPanel1.suspend();
        clockPanel2.suspend();
        clockPanel3.suspend();
      }
    }
  }

  // ClockPanel for holding a header, a clock, and control buttons
  class ClockPanel extends JPanel implements ActionListener
  {
    // Header title of the clock panel
    private JLabel jlblTitle;

    protected Clock clock  = null;

    // Individual clock Resume and Suspend control buttons
    private JButton jbtResume, jbtSuspend;

    // Constructor
    public ClockPanel()
    {
      // Panel jpButtons for grouping buttons
      JPanel jpButtons = new JPanel();
      jpButtons.add(jbtResume = new JButton("Resume"));
      jpButtons.add(jbtSuspend = new JButton("Suspend"));

      // Set BorderLayout for the ClockPanel
      setLayout(new BorderLayout());

      // Add title label to the north of the panel
      add(jlblTitle = new JLabel(), BorderLayout.NORTH);
      jlblTitle.setHorizontalAlignment(JLabel.CENTER);

      // Add the clock to the center of the panel
      add(clock = new Clock(), BorderLayout.CENTER);

      // Add jpButtons to the south of the panel
      add(jpButtons, BorderLayout.SOUTH);

      // Register ClockPanel as a listener to the buttons
      jbtResume.addActionListener(this);
      jbtSuspend.addActionListener(this);
    }

    // Set label on the title
    public void setTitle(String title)
```

continues

```java
      {
        jlblTitle.setText(title);
      }

      // Handlers for buttons "Resume" and "Suspend"
      public void actionPerformed(ActionEvent e)
      {
        if (e.getSource() == jbtResume)
        {
          clock.resume();
        }
        else if (e.getSource() == jbtSuspend)
        {
          clock.suspend();
        }
      }

      // Resume the clock
      public void resume()
      {
        if (clock != null) clock.resume();
      }

      // Resume the clock
      public void suspend()
      {
        if (clock != null) clock.suspend();
      }
    }

    // Clock.java: Show a running clock on the panel
    import java.util.*;

    public class Clock extends StillClock implements Runnable
    {
      // Declare a thread for running the clock
      private Thread timer = null;

      // Determine if the thread is suspended
      private boolean suspended = false;

      // Default constructor
      public Clock()
      {
        super();

        // Create the thread
        timer = new Thread(this);

        // Start the thread
        timer.start();
      }

      // Construct a clock with specified locale and time zone
      public Clock(Locale locale, TimeZone tz)
      {
        super(locale, tz);

        // Create the thread
        timer = new Thread(this);

        // Start the thread
        timer.start();
      }
```

```
// Implement the run() method to dictate what the thread will do
public void run()
{
  while (true)
  {
    repaint();
    try
    {
      timer.sleep(1000);
      synchronized (this)
      {
        while (suspended)
          wait();
      }
    }
    catch (InterruptedException ex)
    {
    }
  }
}

// Resume the clock
public synchronized void resume()
{
  if (suspended)
  {
    suspended = false;
    notify();
  }
}

// Suspend the clock
public synchronized void suspend()
{
  suspended = true;
}
}
```

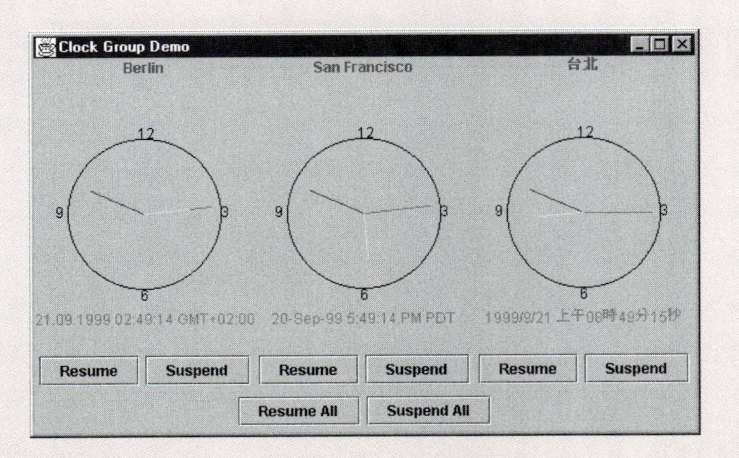

Figure 13.9 *Three clocks run independently with individual control and group control.*

continues

Example Review

The example consists of three classes: `ClockGroup`, `ClockPanel`, and `Clock`. The `Clock` class extends `StillClock` and implements `Runnable`. The `repaint()` method is invoked every second to call the `paintComponent()` method defined in `StillClock`. The `paintComponent()` method runs on a separate thread to draw a clock on a panel with the new current time.

The `ClockPanel` contains a title, a clock, and its control buttons, Resume and Suspend. You can use these two buttons to resume or suspend an individual clock.

The `ClockGroup` class creates and places three clock panels above two group-control buttons, Resume All and Suspend All, in the applet. You can use these two buttons to resume or suspend all the clocks. The three clocks are for Berlin, San Francisco, and Taipei. The titles and times displayed in the panel are locale-sensitive. The Unicode `"\u6077\u6079"` represents the Chinese characters for Taipei, and time is automatically displayed in Chinese because you have set the locale for the clock to `Locale.CHINESE`. If your machine does not support Chinese fonts, you cannot see the Chinese characters.

Thread States

Threads can be in one of five states: new, ready, running, inactive, or finished (see Figure 13.10).

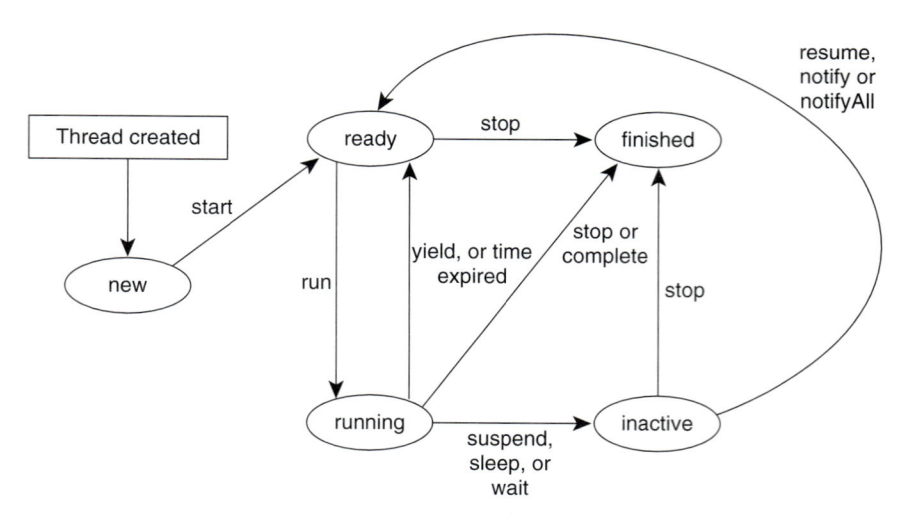

Figure 13.10 *A thread can be in one of five states: new, ready, running, inactive, or finished.*

When a thread is newly created, it enters the *new state*. After a thread is started by calling its `start()` method, it enters the *ready state*. A ready thread is runnable but may not be running yet. The operating system has to allocate CPU time to it.

When a ready thread begins executing, it enters the *running state*. A running thread may enter the ready state if its given CPU time expires or its `yield()` method is called.

A thread may enter the *inactive state* for several reasons. It may have invoked the `sleep()`, `wait()`, or `suspend()` method, or some other thread may have invoked its `sleep()` or `suspend()` method. It may be waiting for an I/O operation to finish. An inactive thread may be reactivated when the action inactivating it is reversed. For example, if a thread has been put to sleep and the sleep time has expired, the thread is reactivated and enters the ready state.

Finally, a thread is *finished* if it completes the execution of its `run()` method or if its `stop()` method is invoked.

The `isAlive()` method is used to find out the state of a thread. It returns `true` if the thread is in the ready, inactive, or running state; it returns `false` if the thread is new and has not started or if it is finished.

Thread Priority

Java assigns every thread a priority. By default, a thread inherits the priority of the thread that spawned it. You can increase or decrease the priority of any thread by using the `setPriority()` method, and you can get the thread's priority by using the `getPriority()` method. Priorities are numbers ranging from 1 to 10. The `Thread` class has `int` constants `MIN_PRIORITY`, `NORM_PRIORITY`, and `MAX_PRIORITY`, representing 1, 5, and 10, respectively. The priority of the main thread is `Thread.NORM_PRIORITY`.

> **TIP**
> The priority numbers may be changed in a future version of Java. To minimize the impact of any changes, use the constants in the `Thread` class to specify the thread priorities.

The Java runtime system always picks whatever currently runnable thread with the highest priority. If several runnable threads have equally high priorities, the CPU is allocated to all of them in round-robin fashion. A lower-priority thread can run only when no higher-priority threads are running.

Example 13.4 Testing Thread Priorities

This program creates three threads named `printA`, `printB`, and `printC` that print the letters *a*, *b*, and *c*, respectively. The program sets priority `NORM_PRIORITY` for `printA`, `NORM_PRIORITY + 1` for `printB`, and `NORM_PRIORITY + 2` for `printC`. Figure 13.11 contains the output of a sample run of the program.

continues

```java
// TestThreadPriority.java: Test thread priorities
public class TestThreadPriority
{
  // Main method
  public static void main(String[] args)
  {
    // Create three threads
    PrintChar printA = new PrintChar('a',200);
    PrintChar printB = new PrintChar('b',200);
    PrintChar printC = new PrintChar('c',200);

    // Set thread priorities
    printA.setPriority(Thread.NORM_PRIORITY);
    printB.setPriority(Thread.NORM_PRIORITY+1);
    printC.setPriority(Thread.NORM_PRIORITY+2);

    // Start threads
    printA.start();
    printB.start();
    printC.start();
  }
}
```

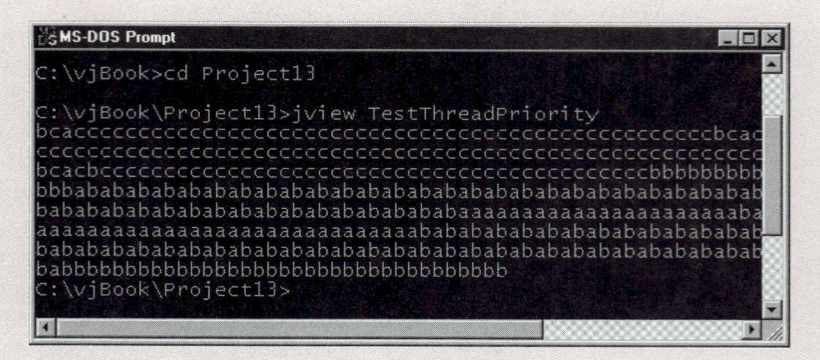

Figure 13.11 *The threads* `printA`, `printB`, *and* `printC` *are assigned different priorities.*

Example Review

The `PrintChar` class for repeatedly printing a character in a separate thread was given in Example 13.1.

The three threads are started in this order: `printA`, `printB`, and `printC`. The priority of these threads is `printC`, `printB`, and `printA`, so `printC` will be the first to get CPU time after it is ready to run.

In theory, `printC` should finish first, but the actual execution depends on the system load. The outputs may differ on different systems.

Thread Groups

A *thread group* is a set of threads. Some programs contain quite a few threads with similar functionality. For convenience, you can group them together and perform operations on the entire group. For example, you can suspend or resume all of the threads in a group at the same time.

Listed below are the guidelines for using thread groups:

1. Use the `ThreadGroup` constructor to construct a thread group:

    ```
    ThreadGroup g = new ThreadGroup("thread group");
    ```

    This creates a thread group g named `"thread group"`. The name is a string and must be unique.

2. Using the `Thread` constructor, place a thread in a thread group:

    ```
    Thread t = new Thread(g, new ThreadClass(), "This thread");
    ```

    The statement `new ThreadClass()` creates a runnable instance for the `ThreadClass`. You can add a thread group under another thread group to form a tree in which every thread group except the initial one has a parent.

3. To find out how many threads in a group are currently running, use the `activeCount()` method. The following statement displays the active number of threads in group g.

    ```
    System.out.println("The number of runnable threads in the group "
      + g.activeCount());
    ```

4. Each thread belongs to a thread group. By default, a newly created thread becomes a member of the current thread group that spawned it. To find which group a thread belongs to, use the `getThreadGroup()` method.

> **NOTE**
> You have to start each thread individually. There is no `start()` method in `ThreadGroup`. As of Java 2, the `stop()`, `suspend()`, and `resume()` methods are deprecated. You implemented the `stop()`, `suspend()`, and `resume()` methods in the `Thread` class. You can similarly implement these methods in the `ThreadGroup` class.

In the next section, you will see an example that uses the `ThreadGroup` class.

Synchronization

A shared resource may be corrupted if it is accessed simultaneously by multiple threads. The following example demonstrates the problem.

Example 13.5 Showing Resource Conflict

This program demonstrates the problem of resource conflict. Suppose that you launch 100 threads to transfer money from a savings account to a checking account, and 100 threads to transfer money from the checking account to the savings account, with each thread transferring $1. Assume that the savings account has an initial balance of $10,000 and the checking account has $0. The output of the program is shown in Figure 13.12.

```java
// TestTransferWithoutSync.java: Demonstrate resource conflict
import Account;
import NegativeAmountException;
import InsufficientFundException;

public class TestTransferWithoutSync
{
  // Main method
  public static void main(String[] args)
  {
    // Determine if all threads are finished
    boolean done = false;

    // Create a savings account with ID 1 and balance 10000
    Account saving = new Account(1, 10000);

    // Create a checking account with ID 2 and balance 0
    Account checking = new Account(2, 0);

    // Create 100 threads in t1 to transfer money from
    // savings to checking
    Thread t1[] = new Thread[100];

    // Create a thread group g1 for grouping t1's
    ThreadGroup g1 = new ThreadGroup("from savings to checking");

    // Create 100 threads in t2 to transfer money from
    // checking to savings
    Thread t2[] = new Thread[100];

    // Create a thread group g2 for grouping t2's
    ThreadGroup g2 = new ThreadGroup("from checking to savings");

    // Add t1[i] to g1, and start t1[i]
    for (int i=0; i<100; i++)
    {
      t1[i] = new Thread(g1,
        new TransferThread(saving, checking, 1), "t1");
      t1[i].start();
    }

    // Add t2[i] to g2, and start t2[i]
    for (int i=0; i<100; i++)
    {
      t2[i] = new Thread(g2,
        new TransferThread(checking, saving, 1),"t2");
      t2[i].start();
    }
```

```java
      // Exit the loop when all threads finished
      while (!done)
        if ((g1.activeCount() == 0) && (g2.activeCount() == 0))
          done = true;

      // Show the balance in the savings and checking accounts
      System.out.println("Savings account balance "+
        saving.getBalance());
      System.out.println("Checking account balance "+
        checking.getBalance());
   }
}

// Define the thread to transfer money between accounts
class TransferThread extends Thread
{
  private Account fromAccount, toAccount;
  private double amount;

  // Construct a thread transferring amount
  // from account s to account c
  public TransferThread(Account s, Account c, double amount)
  {
    fromAccount = s;
    toAccount = c;
    this.amount = amount;
  }

  // Override the run method
  public void run()
  {
    transfer(fromAccount, toAccount, amount);
  }

  // Transfer amount from fromAccount to toAccount
  public void transfer(Account fromAccount,
                       Account toAccount,
                       double amount)
  {
    // Record the balance before transaction for use in recovery
    double fromAccountPriorBalance = fromAccount.getBalance();
    double toAccountPriorBalance = toAccount.getBalance();

    try
    {
      toAccount.deposit(amount);
      sleep(10);
      fromAccount.withdraw(amount);
    }
    catch (NegativeAmountException ex)
    {
      // Reset the balance to the value prior to the exception
      fromAccount.setBalance(fromAccountPriorBalance);
      toAccount.setBalance(toAccountPriorBalance);
    }
    catch (InsufficientFundException ex)
    {
      // Reset the balance to the value prior to the exception
      fromAccount.setBalance(fromAccountPriorBalance);
```

continues

```
            toAccount.setBalance(toAccountPriorBalance);
        }
        catch (InterruptedException ex)
        {
        }
      }
    }
```

```
C:\vjBook\Project13>jview TestTransferWithoutSync
Savings account balance 10020.0
Checking account balance 0.0

C:\vjBook\Project13>
```

Figure 13.12 *The* `TestTransferWithoutSync` *program causes data inconsistency.*

Example Review

The program creates one `Account` object for a savings account with an initial balance of $10,000, and another `Account` object for a checking account with an initial balance of $0.00. The `Account` class was given in Example 11.4, "Creating Your Own Exception Classes" (see Chapter 11, "Exception Handling").

The program creates 100 identical threads in array `t1` to transfer $1 from the savings account to the checking account, and then creates 100 identical threads to transfer $1 from the checking account to the savings account. The program groups all the threads in `t1` in thread group `g1`, and then groups all the threads in `t2` in thread group `g2` (see Figure 13.13).

All the threads use the `transfer()` method to transfer money from one account to the other.

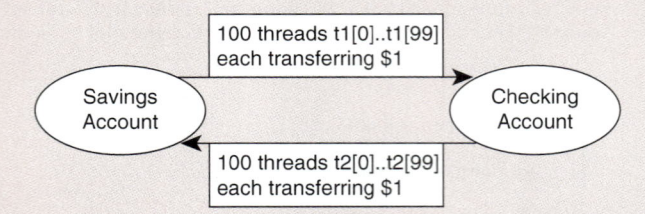

Figure 13.13 *The threads transfer funds between the savings account and the checking account.*

When all the threads finish, the sum of the balances of the two accounts should be $10,000, but the output is unpredictable. As can be seen in Figure 13.12, the answers are wrong in the sample run. This demonstrates the data-corruption problem that occurs when unsynchronized threads have access to the same data source.

> Interestingly, it is not easy to replicate the problem. The `sleep()` method in the `transfer()` method causes the transfer operation to pause for 10 milliseconds. The `sleep()` method is deliberately added to magnify the data-corruption problem and make it easy to see. If you run the program several times but still do not see the problem, put the `transfer()` method in a `for` loop to run 100 times in the `run()` method. This will dramatically increase the chances for resource contention.

So what caused the error in Example 13.5? Here is a possible scenario:

1. Thread `t1[i]` reads the savings account balances and checking account balances and loses CPU time to thread `t1[j]`.

2. Thread `t1[j]` reads the savings account balances and checking account balances and completes a transfer.

3. Thread `t1[i]` regains the CPU time and completes a transfer.

The effect of this scenario is that thread `t1[j]` did nothing, because in Step 3 thread `t1[i]` overrides `t1[j]`'s result. Obviously, the problem is that `t1[i]` and `t1[j]` are accessing a common resource, causing conflict.

To avoid resource conflicts, Java uses the keyword `synchronized` to synchronize method invocation so that only one thread can be in a method at a time. To correct the data-corruption problem in the example, put the keyword `synchronized` on the `transfer()` method and make `transfer` static, as follows:

```
public static synchronized void transfer(Account saving,
                                        Account checking,
                                        double amount)
```

With the keywords `static synchronized` in the method, the preceding scenario cannot happen. If thread `t1[j]` starts to enter the method, and thread `t1[i]` is already in the method, thread `t1[j]` is blocked until thread `t1[i]` finishes the method.

A synchronized method acquires a lock before it executes. In the case of an instance method, the lock is on the object for which the method was invoked. In the case of a class (static) method, the lock is on all the objects of the same class. The synchronized keyword in the `suspend()` and `resume()` methods in Example 13.2 ensures that the variable `suspended` is updated serially without corruption within the object. Adding the keywords `static synchronized` in the `transfer()` method in Example 13.5 ensures that only one object can transfer funds among all the objects in arrays `t1` and `t2`, which avoids the concurrent access of the checking and saving accounts that could corrupt these accounts.

> **NOTE**
> In the `run()` method of Example 13.2, a synchronized block was used. A synchronized block obtains the lock in the same way as a synchronized method. If a synchronized block is inside a static method, the lock is associated with the class; if it is inside an instance method, the lock is associated with the object.
> In operating systems and database systems, locks are often used to protect resources exclusively for write or shared-read operations. Java does not have a mechanism that lets you lock data.

Chapter Summary

In this chapter, you learned multithreading programming, using the `Thread` class and the `Runnable` interface. You can derive your thread class from the `Thread` class and create a thread instance to run a task on a separate thread. If your class needs to inherit multiple classes, you can implement the `Runnable` interface to run multiple tasks in the program simultaneously.

After a thread object is created, you can use `start()` to start a thread; use `sleep()` to put a thread to sleep so that other threads can get a chance to run. Since the `stop()`, `suspend()`, and `resume()` methods are deprecated in Java 2, you need to implement these methods to stop, suspend, and resume a thread.

Your thread object never directly invokes the `run()` method. The Java runtime system invokes the `run()` method when it is time to execute the thread. Your class must override the `run()` method to tell the system what the thread will do when it runs.

Threads can be assigned priorities. The Java runtime system always executes the ready thread with the highest priority. You can use a thread group to put relevant threads together for group control. To prevent threads from corrupting a shared resource, put the `synchronized` keyword into the method that may cause corruption.

Chapter Review

13.1. Why do you need multithreading capability in applications? In a single-processor system, how can multiple threads run simultaneously?

13.2. What are two ways to create threads? When do you use the `Thread` class, and when do you use the `Runnable` interface? What are the differences between the `Thread` class and the `Runnable` interface?

13.3. How do you create a thread and launch a thread object? Which of the following methods are instance methods? Which of them are deprecated in Java 2?

```
run(), start(), stop(), suspend(), resume(), sleep(),
  isInterrupted()
```

13.4. Will the program behave differently if `thread.sleep()` is replaced by `Thread.sleep()` in Example 13.2?

13.5. Describe the life-cycle of a thread object.

13.6. How do you set a priority for a thread? What is the default priority?

13.7. Describe a thread group. How do you create a thread group? Can you control an individual thread in a thread group (suspend, resume, stop, and so on)?

13.8. Give some examples of possible resource corruption when running multiple threads. How do you synchronize conflict threads?

13.9. Why does the following class have a syntax error?

```
class Test extends Thread
{
  public static void main(String[] args)
  {
    Test t = new Test();
    t.start();
    t.start();
  }

  public void run()
  {
    System.out.println("test");
  }
}
```

13.10. Why does the following class have a syntax error?

```
import javax.swing.*;

class Test extends JApplet implements Runnable
{
  public void init() throws InterruptedException
  {
    Thread thread = new Thread(this);
    thread.sleep(1000);
  }

  public synchronized void run()
  {
  }
}
```

Programming Exercises

13.1. Write an applet that displays a flashing label. Enable it to run as an application.

Hints: To make the label flash, you need to repaint the window alternately with the label and without the label (blank screen). You can use a `boolean` variable to control the alternation.

13.2. Write an applet to display a moving label. The label continuously moves from right to left in the applet's viewing area. Whenever the label disappears from the viewing area, it starts moving again on the right-hand side. The label freezes when the mouse is clicked on it, and moves again when the button is released. Enable it to run as an application.

Hints: Repaint the window with a new x coordinate.

13.3. Rewrite Example 13.1, "Using the `Thread` Class to Create and Launch Threads," to display the output on a text area, as shown in Figure 13.14.

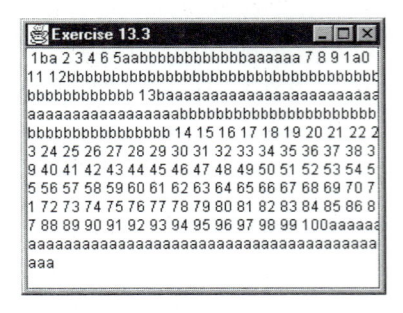

Figure 13.14 *The output from three threads is displayed on a text area.*

13.4. Write a program that launches 100 threads. Each thread adds 1 to a variable `sum` that initially is zero. You need to pass `sum` by reference to each thread. In order to pass it by reference, you need to define an `Integer` wrapper object to hold `sum`. Run the program with and without synchronization to see its effect.

13.5. Write an applet that simulates an elevator going up and down (see Figure 13.15). The buttons on the left indicate the floor where the rider is now located. The rider must click a button on the left to request that the elevator move to his or her floor. On entering the elevator, the rider clicks a button on the right to request that it go to the specified floor. Enable the applet to run standalone.

Figure 13.15 *The program simulates elevator operations.*

13.6. Write a Java applet that displays a stock index ticker (see Figure 13.16). The stock index information is passed from the `<param>` tag in the HTML file. Each index has four parameters: *Index Name* (for example, S&P 500), *Current Time* (for example, 15:54), the index from the previous day (for example, 919.01), and *Change* (for example, 4.54). Enable the applet to run standalone.

Use at least five indexes, such as Dow Jones, S&P 500, NASDAQ, NIKKEI, and Gold & Silver Index. Display positive change in green, and negative change in red. The indexes move from right to left in the applet's viewing area. Clicking anywhere on the applet freezes the ticker; it moves again when the mouse button is released.

Figure 13.16   *The program displays a stock index ticker.*

13.7. Write a Java applet that simulates a running fan, as shown in Figure 13.17. The buttons Start, Stop, and Reverse control the fan. The scrollbar controls the fan speed. Create a subclass of `JPanel` to display the fan. This subclass also contains the methods to suspend and resume the fan, set its speed, and reverse its direction. Enable the applet to run standalone.

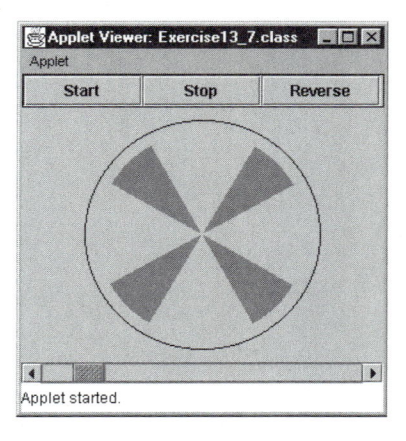

Figure 13.17   *The program simulates a running fan.*

CHAPTER 14

MULTIMEDIA

Objectives

- Develop multimedia applications with audio and images.
- Get audio files and play sound in Java applets.
- Get image files and display graphics in Java applets.
- Display images and play audio in Java applications.
- Use `MediaTracker` to ensure that images are completely loaded before they are displayed.

Introduction

Welcome to the fascinating world of *multimedia*. You have seen computer animation used every day in TV and movies. When surfing the Web, you have seen sites with texts, images, sounds, animation, and movie clips. These are examples of multimedia at work.

Multimedia is a broad term that describes making, storing, retrieving, transferring, and presenting various types of information—such as text, graphics, pictures, videos, and sound. Multimedia involves a complex weave of communications, electronics, and computer technologies. It is beyond the scope of this book to cover multimedia in great detail. This chapter concentrates on the presentation of multimedia in Java.

Whereas most programming languages have no built-in multimedia capabilities, Java was designed with multimedia in mind. It provides extensive built-in support that makes it easy to develop powerful multimedia applications. Java's multimedia capabilities include animation that uses drawings, audio, and images.

You have already used animation with drawings, in the examples that simulated a clock, and you used the image icons in the Swing components. In this chapter, you will learn how to develop Java programs with audio and images.

Playing Audio

Audio is stored in files. There are several formats of audio files. Prior to Java 2, sound files in the AU format used on UNIX machines were the only ones Java was able to play. With Java 2, you can also play sound files in WAV, AIFF, MIDI, AU, and RMF format with better sound quality.

To play an audio clip in an applet, you use the following `play()` method:

```
play(URL url, String filename);
```

This method downloads the audio file from the `url` and plays the audio clip. Nothing happens if the audio file cannot be found.

The URL (Universal Resource Locator) describes the location of a resource on the Internet. Java provides a class that is used to manipulate URLs: `java.net.URL`. Java's security mechanism restricts all files read via a browser to the directory where the HTML file is stored or to the subdirectory of that location. You can use `getCodeBase()` to get the URL of the applet, or `getDocumentBase()` to get the HTML file that contains the applet. These two methods are defined in the `Applet` class:

```
play(getCodeBase(), "soundfile.au");

play(getDocumentBase(), "soundfile.au");
```

The former method plays the sound file soundfile.au, which is located in the applet's directory. The latter method plays the sound file soundfile.au, which is located in the HTML file's directory.

The `play(url, filename)` statement downloads the audio file every time you play the audio. If you want to play the audio many times, you can create an *audio clip object* for the file. The audio clip is created once and can be played repeatedly without reloading the file. To create an audio clip, you can use either of the following methods:

```
public AudioClip getAudioClip(URL url);

public AudioClip getAudioClip(URL url, String name);
```

The former requires an absolute URL address for it to specify a sound file; the latter lets you use a relative URL with the filename. The relative URL is obtained by using `getCodeBase()` or `getDocumentBase()`. For example, the following statement creates an audio clip for the file soundfile.au that is stored in the same directory as the applet that contains the statement.

```
AudioClip ac = getAudioClip(getCodeBase(), "soundfile.au");
```

To manipulate a sound for an audio clip, you can use the following instance methods of `java.applet.AudioClip`.

- `public void play()`

    Play the clip once. Each time this method is called, the clip is restarted from the beginning.

- `public void loop()`

    Play the clip repeatedly.

- `public void stop()`

    Stop playing the clip.

Example 14.1 Incorporating Sound in Applets

This program displays a running clock, as shown in Example 12.1. In addition, the program plays sound files that announce the time at one-minute intervals.

```java
// ClockAppletWithAudio.java: Display a running clock on the applet
// with audio
import java.applet.*;
import java.awt.*;
import java.util.*;

public class ClockAppletWithAudio extends CurrentTimeApplet
{
  // Declare audio files
  protected AudioClip[] hourAudio = new AudioClip[12];
  protected AudioClip minuteAudio;
  protected AudioClip amAudio;
  protected AudioClip pmAudio;

  // Declare a clock
  ClockWithAudio clock;
```

continues

```java
// Initialize the applet
public void init()
{
  super.init();

  // Create audio clips for pronouncing hours
  for (int i=0; i<12; i++)
    hourAudio[i] = getAudioClip(getCodeBase(),
      "timeaudio/hour"+i+".au");

  // Create audio clips for pronouncing am and pm
  amAudio = getAudioClip(getCodeBase(), "timeaudio/am.au");
  pmAudio = getAudioClip(getCodeBase(), "timeaudio/pm.au");
}

// Override the createClock method defined in CurrentTimeApplet
public void createClock()
{
  getContentPane().add(clock =
    new ClockWithAudio(locale, tz, this));
}

// Announce the current time at every minute
public void announceTime(int s, int m, int h)
{
  if (s == 0)
  {
    // Announce hour
    hourAudio[h%12].play();

    // Load the minute file
    minuteAudio = getAudioClip(getCodeBase(),
      "timeaudio/minute"+m+".au");

    // Time delay to allow hourAudio play to finish
    try
    {
      Thread.sleep(1500);
    }
    catch(InterruptedException ex)
    {
    }

    // Announce minute
    minuteAudio.play();

    // Time delay to allow minuteAudio play to finish
    try
    {
      Thread.sleep(1500);
    }
    catch(InterruptedException ex)
    {
    }

    // Announce am or pm
    if (h < 12)
      amAudio.play();
    else
      pmAudio.play();
  }
}
```

```java
    // Implement Applet's start method to resume the thread
    public void start()
    {
      clock.resume();
    }

    // Implement Applet's stop method to suspend the thread
    public void stop()
    {
      clock.suspend();
    }
}

// ClockWithAudio.java: Display a clock and announce time
import java.awt.*;
import java.util.*;
import java.text.*;

public class ClockWithAudio extends Clock
{
  protected ClockAppletWithAudio applet;

  // Construct a clock with specified locale, timezone, and applet
  public ClockWithAudio(Locale locale, TimeZone tz,
    ClockAppletWithAudio applet)
  {
    // Invoke the Clock class's constructor
    super(locale, tz);

    this.applet = applet;
  }

  // Modify the paintComponent() method to play sound
  public void paintComponent(Graphics g)
  {
    // Invoke the paintComponent method in the Clock class
    super.paintComponent(g);

    // Get current time using GregorianCalendar
    GregorianCalendar cal = new GregorianCalendar(tz);

    // Get second, minute and hour
    int s = (int)cal.get(GregorianCalendar.SECOND);
    int m = (int)cal.get(GregorianCalendar.MINUTE);
    int h = (int)cal.get(GregorianCalendar.HOUR_OF_DAY);

    // Announce current time
    applet.announceTime(s, m, h);
  }
}
```

Example Review

This example contains two classes named ClockAppletWithAudio and ClockWithAudio. The ClockAppletWithAudio class extends the CurrentTimeApplet class with the capability to announce time. CurrentTimeApplet was given in Example 12.1, "Displaying a Clock." The ClockWithAudio class extends the Clock class and invokes the announceTime() method whenever it repaints the clock. The Clock class was given in Example 13.3, "Controlling a Group of Clocks."

continues

The `hourAudio` is an array of 12 audio clips that are used to announce the 12 hours of the day; the `minuteAudio` is an audio clip that is used to announce the minute in an hour. The `amAudio` announces A.M.; the `pmAudio` announces P.M.

For example, if the current time is 6:30:00, the applet announces, "The time is six-thirty A.M." If the current time is 20:20:00, the applet announces, "The time is eight-twenty P.M." The three audio clips are played in sequence in order to announce a time.

The `init()` method invokes `super.init()` defined in the `CurrentTimeApplet` class, and creates audio clips for announcing time. `super.init()` gets country, language, and time zone parameters from HTML, and creates and places a clock into the applet.

All of the audio files are stored in the directory `timeaudio`, a subdirectory of the applet's directory. The 12 audio clips that are used to announce the hours are stored in the files **hour0.au, hour1.au,** and so on, to **hour11.au.** They are loaded using the following loop:

```
for (int i=0; i<12; i++)
   hourAudio[i] = getAudioClip(getCodeBase(),
     "timeaudio/hour" + i + ".au");
```

Similarly, the `amAudio` clip is stored in the file **am.au,** and the `pmAudio` clip is stored in the file **pm.au;** they are loaded along with the hour clips in the `init()` method.

The program created an array of 12 audio clips to announce each of the 12 hours, but did not create 60 audio clips to announce each of the minutes. Instead, the program created and loaded the minute audio clip when needed in the `announceTime()` method. The audio files are very large. Loading all 60 audio clips at once may cause `OutOfMemoryError` exception.

In the `announceTime()` method, the `sleep()` method is purposely invoked to ensure that one clip finishes before the next clip starts so that the clips do not interfere with each other.

The constructor of `ClockWithAudio` contains an argument that points to `ClockAppletWithAudio`, which enables the `paintComponent()` method in `ClockWithAudio` to invoke `announceTime()` defined in `ClockAppletWithAudio`. This is a common programming technique for an object to reference methods and data from another class. You might declare `ClockWithAudio` as an inner class inside `ClockAppletWithAudio` to avoid passing `ClockAppletWithAudio` as a parameter. This is fine if `ClockWithAudio` is not reused elsewhere.

The `paintComponent()` method invokes `super.paintComponent()` and `announceTime()`. `super.paintComponent()` defined in `Clock` draws a clock for the current time. `announceTime(h, m, s)` announces the current hour, minute, and A.M. or P.M. if the second s is 0.

Running Audio on a Separate Thread

If you ran the preceding program, you noticed that the second hand did not display at the first, second, and third seconds of the minute. This is because `sleep(1500)` was invoked twice in the `announceTime()` method, which takes three seconds to announce the time at the beginning of each minute.

As a result of this delay, the `paintComponent()` method does not have time to draw the clock during the first three seconds of each minute. Clearly, the `announceTime()` method for playing audio interferes with repainting the clock. To avoid the conflict, you should announce the time on a separate thread. This problem is fixed in the following program.

Example 14.2 Announcing the Time on a Separate Thread

To avoid the conflict between painting the clock and announcing the time, the program in this example runs these tasks on separate threads.

```java
// ClockAppletWithAudioOnSeparateThread.java: Display a
//   running clock on the applet with audio on a separate thread
import java.applet.*;

public class ClockAppletWithAudioOnSeparateThread
  extends ClockAppletWithAudio
{
  // Declare a thread for announcing time
  AnnounceTime announceTime;

  // Initialize the applet
  public void init()
  {
    super.init();
  }

  // Override this method defined in ClockAppletWithAudio
  // to announce the current time at every minute
  public void announceTime(int s, int m, int h)
  {
    // Load the minute file
    minuteAudio = getAudioClip(getCodeBase(),
      "timeaudio/minute" + m + ".au");

    // Announce current time
    if (s == 0)
    {
      if (h < 12)
        announceTime = new AnnounceTime(hourAudio[h%12],
          minuteAudio, amAudio);
      else
        announceTime = new AnnounceTime(hourAudio[h%12],
          minuteAudio, pmAudio);
      announceTime.start();
    }
  }
}
```

continues

```java
// Define a thread class for announcing time
class AnnounceTime extends Thread
{
  private AudioClip hourAudio, minuteAudio, amPM;

  // Get Audio clips
  public AnnounceTime(AudioClip hourAudio,
                     AudioClip minuteAudio,
                     AudioClip amPM)
  {
    this.hourAudio = hourAudio;
    this.minuteAudio = minuteAudio;
    this.amPM = amPM;
  }

  public void run()
  {
    // Announce hour
    hourAudio.play();

    // Time delay to allow hourAudio play to finish
    // before playing the clip
    try
    {
      Thread.sleep(1500);
    }
    catch(InterruptedException ex)
    {
    }

    // Announce minute
    minuteAudio.play();

    // Time delay to allow minuteAudio play to finish
    try
    {
      Thread.sleep(1500);
    }
    catch(InterruptedException ex)
    {
    }

    // Announce am or pm
    amPM.play();
  }
}
```

Example Review

The program extends `ClockAppletWithAudio` with the capability to announce time without interfering with the `paintComponent()` method. The program defines a new thread class, `AnnounceTime`, which is derived from the `Thread` class. This new class plays audio.

To create an instance of the `AnnounceTime` class, you need to pass three audio clips. These are used to announce the hour, the minute, and A.M. or P.M. This instance is created only when s equals 0 at the beginning of each minute.

> When running this program, you discover that the audio does not interfere with the clock animation because an instance of `AnnounceTime` starts on a separate thread to announce the current time. This thread is independent of the thread on which the `paintComponent()` method runs.

Displaying Images

In Example 9.2, "Using Labels," and Example 9.13, "Using Scroll Pane," you used the `ImageIcon` class to create an icon from an image file and the `setIcon()` method to place the image in a UI component, such as a label. These examples are only applicable to Java applications and are not suitable for Java applets, because the image files are directly accessed from the local file system.

To display an image in Java applets, you need to load an image from an Internet source, using the `getImage()` method in the `Applet` class. This method returns a `java.awt.Image` object. Two versions of the `getImage()` method are shown below:

- `public Image getImage(URL url)`

    Load the image from the specified URL.

- `public Image getImage(URL url, String filename)`

    Load the image file from the specified file at the given URL.

> **NOTE**
> When the `getImage()` method is invoked, it launches a separate thread to load the image, which enables the program to continue while the image is being retrieved.

Once you have an `Image` instance for the image file, you can create an `ImageIcon` using the following method:

```
ImageIcon imageIcon = new ImageIcon(image);
```

You can now convert Examples 9.2 and 9.13 to Java applets and use the `getImage()` method to load the image files.

Using a label as an area for displaying images is simple and convenient, but you don't have much control over how the image is displayed. A more flexible way to display images is to use the `drawImage()` method of the `Graphics` class on a panel.

Here are four versions of the `drawImage()` method:

- `drawImage(Image img, int x, int y, Color bgcolor, ImageObserver observer)`

    Draw the image in the specified location. The image's top-left corner is at (x, y) in the graphics context's coordinate space. Transparent pixels in the image are drawn in the specified color `bgcolor`. The `observer` is the object on which the image is displayed. The image is cut-off if it is larger than the area it is being drawn on.

- `drawImage(Image img, int x, int y, ImageObserver observer)`

  Same as the preceding method except that it does not specify a background color.

- `drawImage(Image img, int x, int y, int width, int height, ImageObserver observer)`

  Draw a scaled version of the image that can fill all of the available space in the specified rectangle.

- `drawImage(Image img, int x, int y, int width, int height, Color bgcolor, ImageObserver observer)`

  Same as the previous method except that it provides a solid background color behind the image being drawn.

Example 14.3 Displaying Images in an Applet

The program in this example will display an image in an applet. The image is stored in a file located in the same directory as the applet. The user enters the filename in a text field and displays the image on a panel. Figure 14.1 contains a sample run of the program.

```
// DisplayImageApplet.java: Display an image on a panel in the applet
import java.awt.*;
import java.awt.event.*;
import javax.swing.*;
import javax.swing.border.LineBorder;

public class DisplayImageApplet extends JApplet
  implements ActionListener
{
  // The panel for displaying the image  private
  private ImagePanel imagePanel = new ImagePanel();

  // The text field for entering the name of the image file
  private JTextField jtfFilename = new JTextField(20);

  // The button for displaying the image
  private JButton jbtShow = new JButton("Show Image");

  // Initialize the applet
  public void init()
  {
    // Panel p1 to hold a text field and a button
    JPanel p1 = new JPanel();
    p1.setLayout(new FlowLayout());
    p1.add(new Label("Image Filename"));
    p1.add(jtfFilename);
    p1.add(jbtShow);

    // Place an ImagePanel object and p1 in the applet
    getContentPane().add(imagePanel, BorderLayout.CENTER);
    getContentPane().add(p1, BorderLayout.SOUTH);
```

```java
      // Set line border on the image panel
      imagePanel.setBorder(new LineBorder(Color.black, 1));

      // Register listener
      jbtShow.addActionListener(this);
      jtfFilename.addActionListener(this);
    }

    // Handle the ActionEvent
    public void actionPerformed(ActionEvent e)
    {
      if ((e.getSource() instanceof JButton) ||
        (e.getSource() instanceof JTextField))
        displayImage();
    }

    // Display image on the panel
    private void displayImage()
    {
      // Retrieve image
      Image image = getImage(getCodeBase(),
        jtfFilename.getText().trim());

      // Show image in the panel
      imagePanel.showImage(image);
    }
  }

  // Define the panel for showing an image
  class ImagePanel extends JPanel
  {
    // Image filename
    private String filename;

    // Image instance
    private Image image = null;

    // Default constructor
    public ImagePanel()
    {
    }

    // Set image and show it
    public void showImage(Image image)
    {
      this.image = image;
      repaint();
    }

    // Draw image on the panel
    public void paintComponent(Graphics g)
    {
      super.paintComponent(g);

      if (image != null)
        g.drawImage(image, 0, 0,
          getSize().width, getSize().height, this);
    }
  }
```

continues

Example Review

The image is loaded by using the `getImage()` method from the file in the same directory as the applet. The `showImage()` method defined in `ImagePanel` sets the image so that it can be drawn in the `paintComponent()` method.

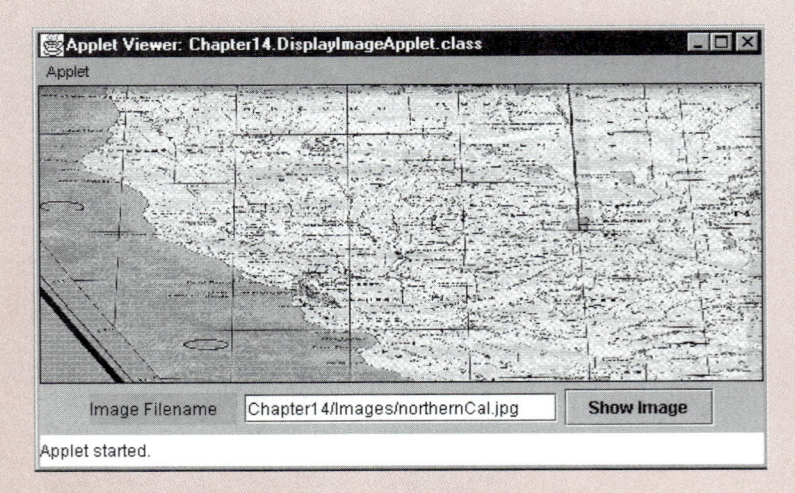

Figure 14.1 *Given the image filename, the applet displays an image.*

The statement `g.drawImage(image, 0, 0, getSize().width, getSize().height, this)` displays the image in the `Graphics` context g on the `ImagePanel` object. To display the image, you enter the filename in the text field, then press the Enter key or click the Show Image button. The filename you enter must be located in the same directory as the applet.

`ImageObserver` is an asynchronous update interface that receives notifications of image information as the image is constructed. The `Component` class implements `ImageObserver`. Therefore, `ImagePanel` (this) is an instance of `ImageObserver`.

Loading Image and Audio Files in Java Applications

The `getImage()` method used in Example 14.3 is defined in the `Applet` class, and thus is only available with the applet. The audio files in Example 14.1 "Incorporating Sound in Applets," are loaded through the URL specified by the `getCodeBase()` method, and thus this method of retrieving audio files cannot be used with Java applications.

When writing a Java application, you can use the `java.lang.Class` class to load an image or audio file. Whenever Java VM loads a class or an interface, it creates an instance of a special class named `Class`. The `Class` class provides access to useful information about the class, such as the data fields and method. It also contains the `getResource(filename)` method, which can be used to obtain the URL of a file name in the same directory with the class or in its subdirectory. Thus, you use this code to get the URL of an image or audio file:

```
URL url = this.getClass().getResource(filename);
```

To get an audio clip, use the static method `newAudioClip()` in the `java.applet.Applet` class:

```
AudioClip audioClip = Applet.newAudioClip(url);
```

> **NOTE**
> The `newAudioClip()` method is new in Java 2, which is not currently supported in Visual J++. You have to use Java 2 VM to compile and run any programs that use this new method.

You might attempt to use the `getImage()` method to obtain an `Image` object like this:

```
Image image = getImage(url);
```

This method would work fine for Java applets, but not for Java applications. To get an `Image` object from the URL in a Java application, you need to use `getImage()` method in the `Toolkit` class to create an `Image` object, as follows:

```
// Obtain a Toolkit instance
Toolkit toolkit = Toolkit.getDefaultToolkit();

// Get the image from the URL
Image image = toolkit.getImage(url);
```

You used the `java.util.Toolkit` to get the screen size in Example 8.1, "Creating a Centered Frame with Exit Handling," so as to display the frame in the center of the screen. Another good use of the `Toolkit` class is to get the image from a URL.

Example 14.4 Using Image and Audio in Applications and in Applets

This program uses the `Class` class to obtain the URL of the image and audio resource, which are located in the program's class directory. The program enables you to select a country from a combo box, and then displays the country's flag image. You can play the selected country's national anthem by clicking the Play Anthem button, as shown in Figure 14.2.

```
// ResourceLocatorDemo.java: Demonstrate using resource locator to
// load image files and audio files to applets and applications
import java.awt.*;
import java.awt.image.*;
import java.awt.event.*;
```

continues

```java
import javax.swing.*;
import javax.swing.border.*;
import java.net.URL;
import java.applet.*;

public class ResourceLocatorDemo extends JApplet
  implements ActionListener, ItemListener
{
  // Image panel for displaying an image
  private ImagePanel imagePanel = new ImagePanel();

  // Combo box for selecting a country
  private JComboBox jcboCountry = new JComboBox();

  // Button to play an audio
  private JButton jbtPlayAnthem = new JButton("Play Anthem");

  // Selected country
  private String country = "United States of America";

  // Initialize the applet
  public void init()
  {
    // Panel p to hold a label combo box and a button for play audio
    JPanel p = new JPanel();
    p.add(new JLabel("Select a country"));
    p.add(jcboCountry);
    p.add(jbtPlayAnthem);

    // Initialize the combo box
    jcboCountry.addItem("United States of America");
    jcboCountry.addItem("United Kingdom");
    jcboCountry.addItem("Denmark");
    jcboCountry.addItem("Norway");
    jcboCountry.addItem("China");
    jcboCountry.addItem("India");
    jcboCountry.addItem("Germany");

    // By default, a US flag is displayed
    imagePanel.showImage(createImage("us.gif"));
    imagePanel.setPreferredSize(new Dimension(300, 300));

    // Place p and an image panel in the applet
    getContentPane().add(p, BorderLayout.NORTH);
    getContentPane().add(imagePanel, BorderLayout.CENTER);
    imagePanel.setBorder(new LineBorder(Color.black, 1));

    // Register listener
    jbtPlayAnthem.addActionListener(this);
    jcboCountry.addItemListener(this);
  }

  // Handle ActionEvent
  public void actionPerformed(ActionEvent e)
  {
    // Get the file name
    String filename = null;

    if (country.equals("United States of America"))
      filename = "us.mid";
```

```java
    else if (country.equals("United Kingdom"))
      filename = "uk.mid";
    else if (country.equals("Denmark"))
      filename = "denmark.mid";
    else if (country.equals("Norway"))
      filename = "norway.mid";
    else if (country.equals("China"))
      filename = "china.mid";
    else if (country.equals("India"))
      filename = "india.mid";
    else if (country.equals("Germany"))
      filename = "germany.mid";

    // Create an audio clip and play it
    createAudioClip(filename).play();
  }

  // Handle ItemEvent
  public void itemStateChanged(ItemEvent e)
  {
    // Get selected country
    country = (String)jcboCountry.getSelectedItem();

    // Get the file name
    String filename = null;

    if (country.equals("United States of America"))
      filename = "us.gif";
    else if (country.equals("United Kingdom"))
      filename = "uk.gif";
    else if (country.equals("Denmark"))
      filename = "denmark.gif";
    else if (country.equals("Norway"))
      filename = "norway.gif";
    else if (country.equals("China"))
      filename = "china.gif";
    else if (country.equals("India"))
      filename = "india.gif";
    else if (country.equals("Germany"))
      filename = "germany.gif";

    // Load image from the file and show it on the panel
    imagePanel.showImage(createImage(filename));
  }

  // Create an audio from the specified file
  public AudioClip createAudioClip(String filename)
  {
    // Get the URL for the file name
    URL url = this.getClass().getResource("anthems/" + filename);

    // Return the audio clip
    return Applet.newAudioClip(url);
  }

  // Create an image from the specified file
  public Image createImage(String filename)
  {
    // Get the URL for the file name
    URL url = this.getClass().getResource("images/" + filename);
```

continues

```java
      // Obtain a Toolkit instance
      Toolkit toolkit = Toolkit.getDefaultToolkit();

      // Return the image
      return toolkit.getImage(url);
    }

    // Main method
    public static void main(String[] args)
    {
      // Create a frame
      MyFrameWithExitHandling frame = new MyFrameWithExitHandling(
        "Flags and Play Anthem");

      // Create an instance of the applet
      ResourceLocatorDemo applet = new ResourceLocatorDemo();

      // Add the applet instance to the frame
      frame.getContentPane().add(applet, BorderLayout.CENTER);

      // Invoke init() and start()
      applet.init();
      applet.start();

      // Display the frame
      frame.pack();
      frame.setVisible(true);
    }
  }
```

Figure 14.2 *The program displays the flag of the selected country and plays its national anthem.*

Example Review

The program can run as an applet or an application. Obtaining the URL using the `Class` class works not only for standalone applications, but also for Java applets.

The `createAudioClip(filename)` method obtains the URL instance for the filename and creates an `AudioClip` for the URL using the `newAudioClip` static method, which is a new method introduced in Java 2 to support playing audio in applications.

The `createImage(filename)` method obtains the URL instance for the filename and creates an `Image` object, using the `getImage()` method in the `Toolkit` class.

The program is not efficient if the user repeatedly chooses the same country and plays the same anthem, because a new `Image` instance is created for every newly selected country, and a new `AudioClip` instance is created every time an audio is played. To improve efficiency, load the image and audio files once and store them in the memory.

> **NOTE**
> Two features of this program are new in Java 2, which is not currently supported in Visual J++.
> - The newAudioClip() method.
> - The MIDI sound files.
>
> To compile and run the program, you have to use Java SDK v 1.2.x, which can be downloaded from **www.javasoft.com**.

Displaying a Sequence of Images

In the preceding section, you learned how to display a single image. Now you will learn how to display a sequence of images that will simulate a movie. You will use a control loop to continuously paint the viewing area with different images. As in the clock example, the loop and the `paintComponent()` method should run on separate threads so that the `paintComponent()` method can execute while the loop controls how the images are drawn. The two images should not be drawn at the same time. The first image should be seen before the next image is drawn.

Example 14.5 Using Image Animation

This example presents a program that will display a sequence of images in order to create a movie. The images are files stored in the `Images` directory that are named **L1.gif, L2.gif,** and so on, to **L52.gif.** When you run the program, you will see a phrase entitled "Learning Java" rotate. Figure 14.3 contains the output of a sample run of the program.

```java
// ImageAnimation.java: Display a sequence of images
import java.awt.*;
import java.awt.event.*;
import javax.swing.*;
import javax.swing.border.*;

public class ImageAnimation extends JApplet implements ActionListener
{
  private Image imageToDisplay;
  protected Image imageArray[]; // Hold images
```

continues

```java
    protected int numOfImages = 52, // Total number of images
                  currentImageIndex = 0, // Current image subscript
                  sleepTime = 100; // Milliseconds to sleep
    protected int direction = 1; // Image rotating direction

    // Text field for receiving speed
    protected JTextField jtfSpeed = new JTextField(5);

    // Button for reversing direction
    JButton jbtReverse = new JButton("Reverse");

    // Initialize the applet
    public void init()
    {
      // Load the image, the image files are named
      // L1 - L52 in Images directory
      imageArray = new Image[numOfImages];
      for (int i=0; i<imageArray.length; i++ )
      {
        imageArray[i] = getImage(getDocumentBase(),
          "Images/L" + (i+1) + ".gif" );
      }

      // Panel p to hold animation control
      JPanel p = new JPanel();
      p.setLayout(new BorderLayout());
      p.add(new JLabel("Animation speed in millisecond"),
        BorderLayout.WEST);
      p.add(jtfSpeed, BorderLayout.CENTER);
      p.add(jbtReverse, BorderLayout.EAST);

      // Add the image panel and p to the applet
      getContentPane().add(new PlayImage(), BorderLayout.CENTER);
      getContentPane().add(p, BorderLayout.SOUTH);

      // Register listener
      jtfSpeed.addActionListener(this);
      jbtReverse.addActionListener(this);
    }

    // Handle ActionEvent
    public void actionPerformed(ActionEvent e)
    {
      if (e.getSource() == jtfSpeed)
      {
        sleepTime = Integer.parseInt(jtfSpeed.getText());
      }
      else if (e.getSource() == jbtReverse)
      {
        direction = -direction;
      }
    }

    class PlayImage extends JPanel implements Runnable
    {
      private Thread thread = null;

      // Determine the thread status
      protected boolean suspended = false;
```

```java
// Constructor
public PlayImage()
{
  // Start with the first image
  currentImageIndex = 0;

  // Start the thread
  thread = new Thread(this);
  thread.start();

  // Set line border on the panel
  setBorder(new LineBorder(Color.red, 1));
}

public void start()
{
  resume();
}

public void stop()
{
  suspend();
}

public synchronized void resume()
{
  if (suspended)
  {
    suspended = false;
    notify();
  }
}

public synchronized void suspend()
{
  suspended = true;
}

public void destroy()
{
  thread = null;
}

public void run()
{
  while (true)
  {
    imageToDisplay =
      imageArray[currentImageIndex%numOfImages];

    // Make sure currentImageIndex is nonnegative
    if (currentImageIndex == 0) currentImageIndex = numOfImages;
    currentImageIndex = currentImageIndex + direction;
    repaint();

    try
    {
      thread.sleep(sleepTime);
      synchronized (this)
```

continues

```java
            {
              while (suspended)
                wait();
            }
          }
          catch (InterruptedException ex)
          {
          }
        }
      }

      // Display an image
      public void paintComponent(Graphics g)
      {
        super.paintComponent(g);

        if (imageToDisplay != null)
        {
          g.drawImage(imageToDisplay, 0, 0, getSize().width,
            getSize().height, this);
        }
      }
    }
  }
```

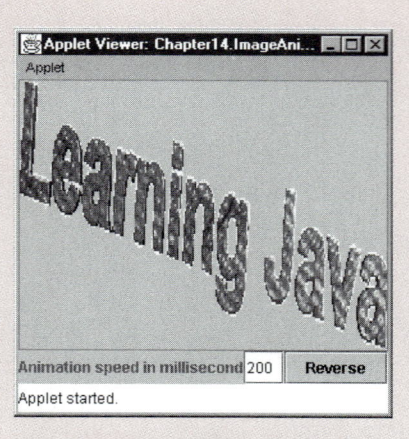

Figure 14.3 *The applet displays a sequence of images.*

Example Review

Fifty-two image files are located in the `Images` directory, which is a subdirectory of the `getDocumentBase()` directory. The images in these files are loaded to `imageArray` and then painted continuously on the applet on a separate thread.

The image is drawn to occupy the entire applet viewing area in a rectangle. It is scaled to fill in the area.

Since the `thread` for drawing images is created and started in the applet's `init()` method, and is suspended in the applet's `stop()` method, the images are not displayed when the browser leaves the applet's page. From then on, the thread releases CPU time when it is not active. When the applet becomes active again, the `thread` is resumed in the applet's `start()` method to display images.

You can adjust the `sleepTime` to control animation speed by entering a value in milliseconds and presssing the Enter key for the change to take place.

The display sequence can be reversed by clicking the Reverse button.

You can add a simple function to suspend a running `imageThread` with a mouse click. You can resume a suspended `imageThread` with another click. (See Exercise 14.4.)

> **NOTE**
>
> The `JComponent` class has a property named `doubleBuffered`. By default, this property is set to `true`. Double buffering is a technique for reducing animation flickering. It creates a graphics context off-screen and does all the drawings on the off-screen context. When the drawing is complete, it displays the whole context on the real screen. Thus, there is no flickering within an image because all the drawings are displayed at the same time. To see the effect of double buffering, set the `doubleBuffered` property to false. You will see a stunning difference.

Using MediaTracker

One problem you may face if you run the preceding example is that images are only partially displayed while being loaded. This occurs because the image has not yet been loaded completely. The problem is particularly annoying when you are downloading an image over a slow modem.

To resolve the problem, Java provides the `MediaTracker` class to track the status of a number of media objects. Media objects include audio clips as well as images, though currently only images are supported.

You can use `MediaTracker` to determine whether an image has been completely loaded. To use it, you must first create an instance of `MediaTracker` for a specific graphics component. The following is an example of creating a `MediaTracker`:

```
MediaTracker imageTracker = new MediaTracker(this);
```

To enable `imageTracker` (in order to determine whether the image has been loaded), you need to use the `addImage()` method to register the image with `imageTracker`. For example, the following statement registers `anImage` with `imageTracker`:

```
imageTracker.addImage(Image anImage, int id);
```

The second argument, `id`, is an integer ID that controls the priority order in which the images are fetched. Images with a lower ID number are loaded in preference to those with a higher ID number. The ID can be used to query `imageTracker` about the status of the registered image. To query, use the `checkID()` method. For example, the following method returns `true` if the image with the `id` is completely loaded:

```
checkID(id)
```

Otherwise, it returns `false`.

You can use the `waitForID(id)` method to force the program to wait until the image registered with the `id` is completely loaded, or you can use the `waitForAll()` method to wait for all of the registered images to be loaded completely. The methods shown below block the program until the image is completely loaded:

```
waitForID(int id) throws InterruptedException

waitForAll() throws InterruptedException
```

> **TIP**
> To track multiple images as a group, you can register them with a media tracker using the same ID.

Example 14.6 Using *MediaTracker*

This example uses `MediaTracker` to improve upon the preceding example. With `MediaTracker`, the user of this program can ensure that all of the images are fully loaded before they are displayed.

```java
// ImageAnimationUsingMediaTracker.java: Monitor loading images
// using MediaTracker
import java.awt.*;
import javax.swing.*;

public class ImageAnimationUsingMediaTracker extends ImageAnimation
{
  private MediaTracker imageTracker = new MediaTracker(this);

  // Initialize the applet
  public void init()
  {
    // Load the image, the image files are named
    // L1 - L52 in Images directory
    imageArray = new Image[numOfImages];
    for (int i=0; i<imageArray.length; i++ )
```

```
      {
        imageArray[i] = getImage(getDocumentBase(),
          "Images/L" + (i+1) + ".gif" );

        // Register images with the imageTracker
        imageTracker.addImage(imageArray[i], i);
      }

      // Wait for all the images to be completely loaded
      try
      {
        imageTracker.waitForAll();
      }
      catch (InterruptedException ex)
      {
        System.out.println(ex);
      }

      // Dispose of imageTracker since it is no longer needed
      imageTracker = null;

      // Panel p to hold animation control
      JPanel p = new JPanel();
      p.setLayout(new BorderLayout());
      p.add(new JLabel("Animation speed in millisecond"),
        BorderLayout.WEST);
      p.add(jtfSpeed, BorderLayout.CENTER);
      p.add(jbtReverse, BorderLayout.EAST);

      // Add the image panel and p to the applet
      getContentPane().add(new PlayImage(), BorderLayout.CENTER);
      getContentPane().add(p, BorderLayout.SOUTH);

      // Register listener
      jtfSpeed.addActionListener(this);
      jbtReverse.addActionListener(this);
    }
  }
```

Example Review

The `ImageAnimationUsingMediaTracker` class extends `ImageAnimation`, which was created in Example 14.5. The `ImageAnimationUsingMediaTracker` uses `MediaTracker` to monitor loading images.

The program creates an instance of `MediaTracker`, `imageTracker`, and registers images with `imageTracker` in order to track image loading. The program uses `imageTracker` to ensure that all of the images are completely loaded before they are displayed.

The `waitForAll()` method forces the program to wait for all of the images to be loaded before displaying any of them. Because the program needs to load 52 images, using `waitForAll()` results in a long delay before images are displayed. You should display something while the image is being loaded in order to keep the user attentive and/or informed. A simple approach is to use the `showStatus()`

continues

method in the `Applet` class to display some information on the Web browser's status bar. Here is a possibility:

```
showStatus("Please wait while loading images");
```

Put this statement before the `try/catch` block for `waitForAll()` in the program.

The `imageTracker` object is no longer needed after the images are loaded. The statement `imageTracker = null` notifies the garbage collector of the Java runtime system to reclaim the memory space previously occupied by the `imageTracker` object.

You can rewrite this example to enable it to run as an application. See Exercise 14.4.

Chapter Summary

In this chapter, you learned how to play audio and display images in Java multimedia programming. You also learned how to use the `Class` class to load image and audio files, and the media tracking mechanism to track loading images.

Audio and images files are accessible through an URL. The `getDocumentBase()` method returns the URL of the HTML file that invokes the applet. The `getCodeBase()` method returns the URL of the applet. The `Class` class can be used to obtain the URL of an image or audio file for Java applications. This approach also works for Java applets. Thus it is a good idea to develop programs that can run both as applications and as applets.

The `MediaTracker` class is used to determine whether one image or all of the images are completely loaded. The `MediaTracker` obtains this information in order to ensure that the images will be displayed fully.

Chapter Review

14.1. What types of audio files are used in Java?

14.2. How do you get an audio file? How do you play, repeatedly play, and stop an audio clip?

14.3. The `getAudioClip()` method is defined in the `Applet` class. If you want to use audio in Java applications, what options do you have?

14.4. What is the difference between `getDocumentBase()` and `getCodeBase()`?

14.5. What is the difference between the `getImage()` method in the `Applet` class and the `getImage()` method in the `Toolkit` class?

14.6. How do you get the URL of an image or audio file in Java applications?

14.7. Describe the `drawImage()` method in the `Graphics` class.

14.8. Can you create image icons and use the `setIcon()` method to set an icon in a `JLabel` instance in Java applets?

14.9. Describe the differences between displaying images in a `JLabel` instance and in a `JPanel` instance.

14.10. How do you get an audio clip in Java applications?

14.11. Why do you use `MediaTracker`? How do you add images to a media tracker? How do you know that an image or all of the images are completely loaded? Can you assign images the same ID in order to register them with a media tracker?

Programming Exercises

14.1. Write an applet that meets the following requirements:

- Get an audio file from the URL of the HTML base code.
- Place three buttons labeled Play, Loop, and Stop, as shown in Figure 14.4.
- If you click the Play button, the audio file is played once. If you click the Loop button, the audio file keeps playing repeatedly. If you click the Stop button, the playing stops.
- The applet can run as an application.

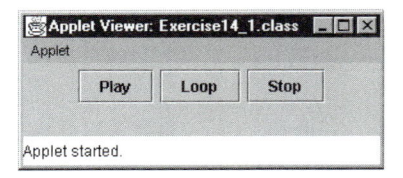

Figure 14.4 *Click Play to play an audio clip once, click Loop to play an audio repeatedly, and click Stop to terminate playing.*

14.2. Modify the elevator program in the fifth exercise in the "Programming Exercises" section of Chapter 13, "Multithreading," to add sound to the program. When the elevator stops on a floor, announce which floor the elevator is on.

14.3. Sometimes, when you repaint the entire viewing area of a panel, only a tiny portion of the viewing area is changed. You can improve the performance by only repainting the affected area. To do so, you should not invoke `super.paintComponent(g)` when repainting the panel. Invoking `super.paintComponent(g)` causes the entire viewing area to be cleared. Use this approach to write an applet to display the temperatures of each hour during the last 24 hours in a histogram. Suppose that the temperatures between 50 and 90 degrees Fahrenheit are obtained randomly and are updated every hour. The temperature of the current hour needs to be redisplayed, while others remain unchanged. Use a unique color to highlight the temperature for the current hour (see Figure 14.5).

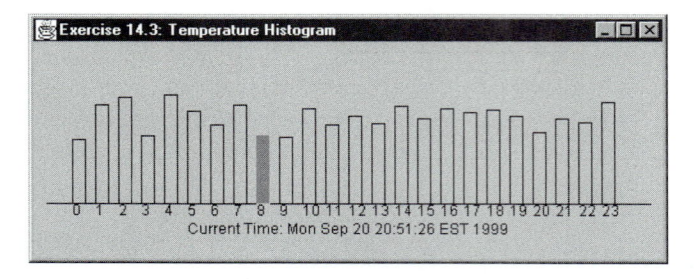

Figure 14.5 *The histogram displays the average temperature of every hour in the last 24 hours.*

14.4. Rewrite Example 14.6, "Using MediaTracker," to add the following new functions:

- The animation is suspended when the mouse is pressed and resumed when the mouse is released. To implement this feature, add the code in the `PlayImage` inner class of the `ImageAnimation` class to handle the mouse event for `mousePressed` and `mouseReleased` actions.

- Sound is incorporated into the applet so that it is played while images are displayed.

- Enable the applet to run standalone.

14.5. Write an applet that will display a digital clock with a large display panel that shows hour, minute, and second. This clock should allow the user to set an alarm. Figure 14.6 shows an example of such a clock. To turn on the alarm, check the Alarm check box. To specify the alarm time, click the "Set alarm" button to display a new frame, as shown in Figure 14.7. You can set the alarm time in the frame. Enable the applet to run standalone.

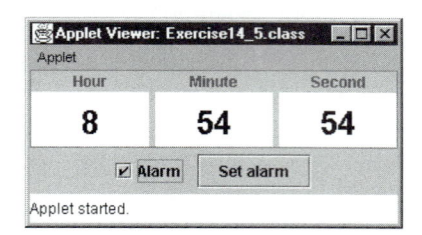

Figure 14.6 *The program displays current hour, minute, and second, and enables you to set an alarm.*

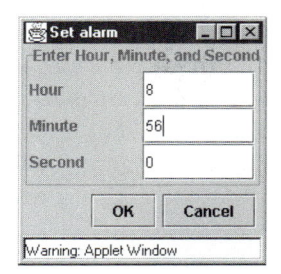

Figure 14.7 *You can set the alarm time by specifying hour, minute, and second.*

14.6. Create animation using the applet (see Figure 14.8) to meet the following requirements:

- Allow the user to specify the animation speed. The user can enter the speed in a text field.

- Get the number of frames and the image filename prefix from the user. For example, if the user enters **n** for the number of frames and **L** for the image prefix, then the files are **L1, L2,** and so on, to **Ln.** Assume that the images are stored in the Images directory, a subdirectory of the applet's directory.

- Allow the user to specify an audio filename. The audio file is stored in the same directory as the applet. The sound is played while the animation runs.

- Enable the applet to run standalone.

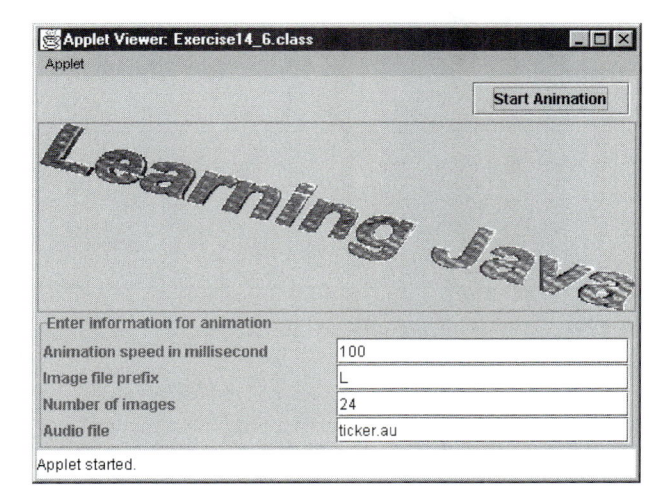

Figure 14.8 *This applet lets the user select image files, audio file, and animation speed.*

14.7. Write an applet that will display a sequence of images for a single image in different sizes. Initially, the viewing area for this image is of 300 width and 300 height. Your program should continuously shrink the viewing area by 10 in width and 10 in height until it reaches a width of 50 and a height of 50. At that point, the viewing area should continuously enlarge by 1 in width and 1 in height until it reaches a width of 300 and a height of 300. The viewing area should shrink and enlarge (alternately) to create animation for the single image. Enable the applet to run standalone.

14.8. Suppose that the instructor asks the students in a Java class to write short paragraphs stating their personal objectives for taking the course. Write an applet that introduces the students, one after the other, by presenting each one's photo, name, and paragraph (see Figure 14.9) along with audio that reads the paragraph.

Suppose there are 10 students in the class. Assume that the audio files, named **a1.au, a2.au,** and so on, up to **a10.au,** are stored in a subdirectory named audio in the applet's directory, and the photo image files, named **photo1.gif, photo2.gif,** and so on, up to **photo10.gif,** are stored in a subdirectory named photo in the applet's directory. Assume that the name and paragraph of each student is passed from the HTML. Here is an example for student **a1.**

```
<param name= "paragraph1"
   value="I am taking the class because I want to
     learn to write cool programs like this!">
<param name= "name1"  value = "Michael Liang">
```

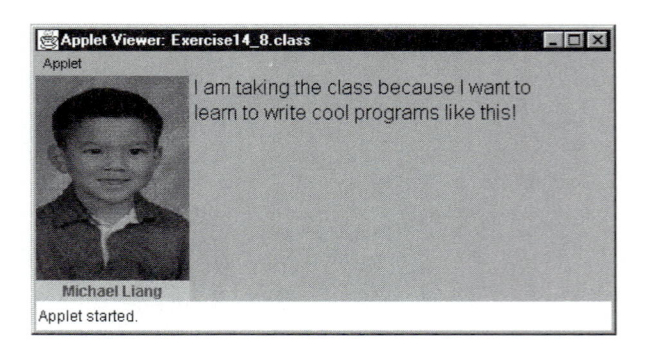

Figure 14.9 *This applet shows each student's photo, name, and paragraph, one after another, and reads the paragraph that is currently shown.*

14.9. Rewrite Example 14.4, "Using Image and Audio in Applications and in Applets." Use the resource bundle to retrieve image and audio files. (Hints: When a new country is selected, set an appropriate locale for the country. Have your program look for the flag and audio file from the resource file for the locale.)

CHAPTER 15

INPUT AND OUTPUT

Objectives

- Understand input and output streams and learn how to create them.
- Discover the uses of byte and character streams.
- Know how to read from or write to external files using file streams.
- Employ data streams for cross-platform data format compatibility.
- Identify print streams and use them to output data of primitive types in text format.
- Know how to parse text files using `StreamTokenizer`.
- Understand how to use `RandomAccessFile` for both read and write.
- Use `JFileChooser` to display open and save file dialog boxes.
- Become familiar with interactive I/O for input and output on the console.

PART IV   DEVELOPING COMPREHENSIVE PROJECTS

Introduction

In previous chapters, you used input and output only on the console. In Chapter 2, "Java Building Elements," you created the `MyInput` class and used `MyInput.readInt()` and `MyInput.readDouble()` to receive data from the console. You used `System.out.print()` to display output on the console. In this chapter, you will learn about many other forms of input and output as well as how these methods work.

In Java, all I/Os are handled in streams. A *stream* is an abstraction of the continuous one-way flow of data. Imagine a swimming pool with pipes that connect it to another pool. Let's consider the water in the first pool as the data, and the water in the second pool as your program. The flow of water through the pipes is called a *stream*. If you want input, just open the valve to let water out of the data pool and into the program pool. If you want output, just open the valve to let water out of the program pool and into the data pool.

It's a very simple concept, and a very efficient one. Since Java streams can be applied to any source of data, it is as easy for a programmer to input from a keyboard or output to a console as it is to input from a file or output to a file. Figure 15.1 shows the input and output streams between a program and an external file. Java streams are used liberally. There can even be input and output streams between two programs.

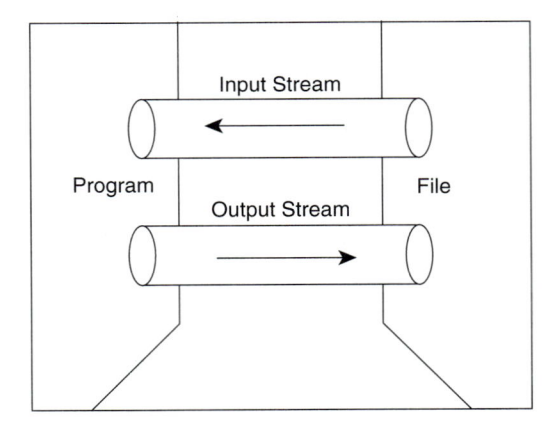

Figure 15.1 *The program receives data through the input stream and sends data through the output stream.*

In general, all streams except random-access file streams flow only in one direction; therefore, if you want to input and output, you need two separate stream objects. In Java, streams can be *layered*—that is, connected to one another in pipeline fashion. The output of one stream becomes the input of another stream.

This layering capability makes it possible to filter data along the pipeline of streams so that you can get data in the desired format. For instance, suppose you want to get integers from an external file. You can use a file input stream to get raw data in binary format, then use a data input stream to extract integers from the output of the input stream.

Streams are objects. Stream objects have methods that read and write data or do other useful things, such as flushing the stream, closing the stream, and counting the number of bytes in the stream.

Stream Classes

Java offers stream classes for processing all kinds of data. Figures 15.2 and 15.3 show the hierarchical relationship of these classes.

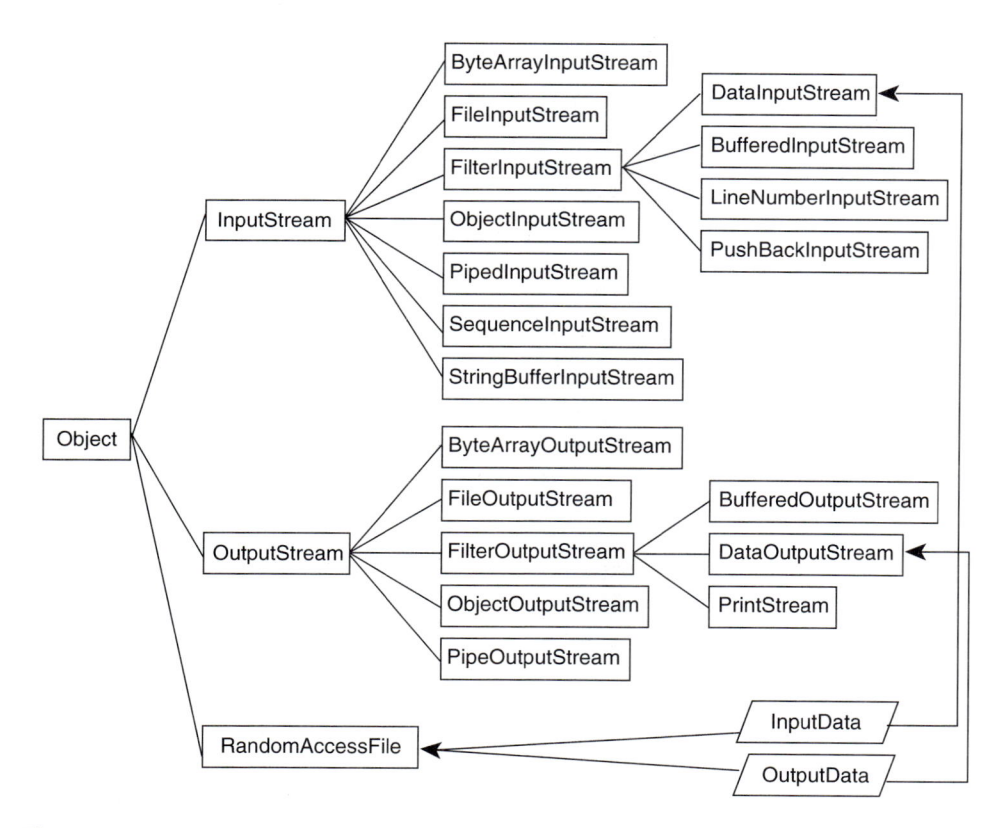

Figure 15.2 `InputStream`, `OutputStream`, `RandomAccessFile`, *and their subclasses deal with streams of bytes.*

Stream classes can be categorized either as *byte streams* or as *character streams*. The `InputStream/OutputStream` class is the root of all byte stream classes, and the `Reader/Writer` class is the root of all character stream classes. The subclasses of `InputStream/OutputStream` are analogous to the subclasses of `Reader/Writer`.

Many of these subclasses have similar method signatures and often can be used in the same way. The `RandomAccessFile` class extends `Object` and implements the

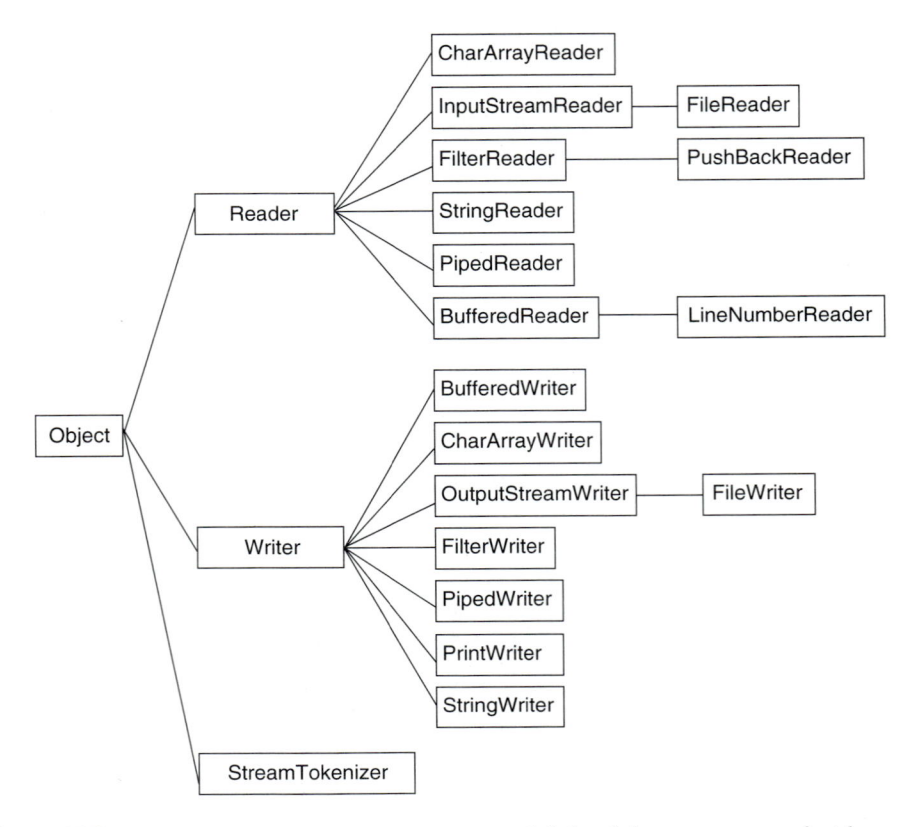

Figure 15.3 `Reader`, `Writer`, `StreamTokenizer`, *and their subclasses are concerned with streams of characters.*

`InputData` and `OutputData` interfaces. It can be used to open a file that allows both reading and writing. The `StreamTokenizer` class that extends `Object` can be used for parsing text files.

InputStream and Reader

The abstract `InputStream` and `Reader` classes, extending `Object`, are the base classes for all of the input streams of bytes and characters, respectively. These classes and their subclasses are very similar, except that `InputStream` uses bytes for its fundamental unit of information, and `Reader` uses characters. `InputStream` and `Reader` have many common methods with identical signatures. These methods have similar functionality, but `InputStream` is designed to read bytes, and `Reader` is designed to read characters.

The following methods, defined in `InputStream`, are often useful:

- `public abstract int read() throws IOException`

    This method reads the next byte and returns its value. The value of the byte is returned as an `int` in the range from 0 to 255. At the end of the stream, it returns -1. This method blocks the program from executing until input data is available, the end of the stream is detected, or an exception is thrown. A subclass of `InputStream` must provide an implementation of the method.

- `public int read(byte[] b) throws IOException`

  This method reads `b.length` bytes into array `b`, returns `b.length` if the number of available bytes is more than `b.length`, returns the number of bytes read if the number of available bytes is less than `b.length`, and returns -1 at the end of the stream.

- `public void close() throws IOException`

  This method closes the input stream.

- `public void int available() throws IOException`

  This method returns the number of bytes that can be read from the input stream without blocking.

- `public long skip(long n) throws IOException`

  This method skips over and discards `n` bytes of data from the input stream. The actual number of bytes skipped is returned.

> **NOTE**
> The `read()` method reads a byte from the stream. If no data are available, it blocks the thread from executing the next statement. The thread that invokes the `read()` method is suspended until the data become available.

The `Reader` class contains all of the methods listed previously except `available()`. These methods have the same functionality in `Reader` as in `InputStream`, but they are subject to character stream interpretation. For example, `read()` returns an integer in the range from 0 to 16,383, which represents a Unicode character.

OutputStream and *Writer*

Like `InputStream` and `Reader`, `OutputStream` and `Writer` are counterparts. They are the base classes for all output streams of bytes and characters, respectively. The following instance methods are in both `OutputStream` and `Writer`:

- `public abstract void write(int b) throws IOException`

  This method writes a byte (for `OutputStream`) or a character (for `Writer`).

- `public void write(byte[] b) throws IOException`

  This method writes all bytes in the array `b` to the output stream (for `OutputStream`) or characters in the array of characters (for `Writer`).

- `public void close() throws IOException`

  This method closes the output stream.

- `public void flush() throws IOException`

    This method flushes the output stream (that is, it sends any buffered data in the stream to its destination).

> **NOTE**
> In JDK 1.02, the methods in `OutputStream` do not throw exceptions. But all of the methods in the `OutputStream` class throw `IOException` in JDK 1.1 and JDK 1.2.

Processing External Files

You must use file streams to read from or write to a disk file. `FileInputStream` or `FileOutputStream` is used for byte streams, and `FileReader` or `FileWriter` for character streams. To create a file stream, you can use the following constructors:

```
public FileInputStream(String fileNameString)

public FileOutputStream(String fileNameString)

public FileReader(String fileNameString)

public FileWriter(String fileNameString)
```

For example, the following statements create `infile` and `outfile` streams for the input file **in.dat** and the output file **out.dat**, respectively:

```
FileInputStream infile = new FileInputStream("in.dat");

FileOutputStream outfile = new FileOutputStream("out.dat");
```

When a filename or a path is used, it is always assumed that the host's file-naming conventions are used. For example, a filename with a path on Windows could be **c:\data\in.dat.** If it had a path on UNIX, the same file might be **/username/data/in.dat.**

You can also use a file object to construct a file stream. For example, see the following statement:

```
FileInputStream infile = new FileInputStream(new File("in.dat"));
```

The `File` class is intended to provide an abstraction that deals with most of the machine-dependent complexities of files and path names in a machine-independent fashion.

An abstract method, such as `read(byte b)` in `InputStream`, is implemented in `FileInputStream`, and the abstract `write(int b)` method in the `OutputStream` class is implemented in `FileOutputStream`.

Example 15.1 Processing External Files

This example gives a program that uses `FileInputStream` and `FileOutputStream` to copy files. The user needs to provide a source file and a target file as command-line arguments. The program copies the source file to the target file and displays the number of bytes in the file. The output of sample runs, of the program is shown in Figure 15.4.

```java
// CopyFileUsingByteStream.java: Copy files
import java.io.*;

public class CopyFileUsingByteStream
{
  // Main method: args[0] for sourcefile and args[1] for target file
  public static void main(String[] args)
  {
    // Declare input and output file streams
    FileInputStream fis = null;
    FileOutputStream fos = null;

    // Check usage
    if (args.length !=2)
    {
      System.out.println(
        "Usage: java CopyFileUsingByteStream fromfile tofile");
      System.exit(0);
    }

    try
    {
      // Create file input stream
      fis = new FileInputStream(new File(args[0]));

      // Create file output stream if the file does not exist
      File outFile = new File(args[1]);
      if (outFile.exists())
      {
        System.out.println("file " + args[1] + " already exists");
        return;
      }
      else
        fos = new FileOutputStream(args[1]);

      // Display the file size
      System.out.println("The file " + args[0] + " has "+
        fis.available() + " bytes");

      // Continuously read a byte from fis and write it to fos
      int r;
      while ((r = fis.read()) != -1)
        fos.write((byte)r);
    }
    catch (FileNotFoundException ex)
    {
      System.out.println("File not found: " + args[0]);
    }
    catch (IOException ex)
```

continues

```
    {
      System.out.println(ex.getMessage());
    }
    finally
    {
      try
      {
        // Close files
        if (fis != null) fis.close();
        if (fos != null) fos.close();
      }
      catch (IOException ex)
      {
        System.out.println(ex);
      }
    }
  }
}
```

Figure 15.4 *The program copies a file using byte streams.*

Example Review

The program creates the `fis` and `fos` streams for the input file `args[0]` and the output file `args[1]` (see Figure 15.5).

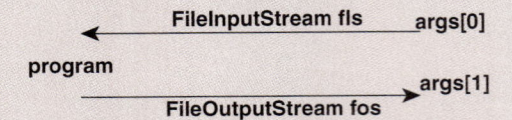

Figure 15.5 *The program uses* `FileInputStream` *to read data from the file and* `FileOutputStream` *to write data to the file.*

If the input file `args[0]` does not exist, `new FileInputStream(new File(args[0]))` will raise the exception `FileNotFoundException`. By contrast, `new FileOutputStream(new File(args[1]))` will always create a file output stream, whether or not the file `args[1]` exists.

To avoid writing into an existing file, the program uses the `exists()` method in the `File` class to determine whether `args[1]` exists. If the file already exists, the user would be notified; otherwise, the file should be created.

The program continuously reads a byte from the `fis` stream and sends it to the `fos` stream until all of the bytes have been read. (The condition (`fis.read() == -1`) signifies the end of a file.)

The program closes any open file streams in the `finally` clause. The statements in the `finally` clause are always executed, whether or not exceptions occur.

The program could be rewritten using `FileReader` and `FileWriter`. The new program would be almost exactly the same. (See Exercise 15.1.)

> **TIP**
> Always close files when they are not needed. In some cases, not closing them will cause programming errors. Files are usually closed in the `finally` clause.

Array Streams

Streams were first used for file input/output in the C language, but Java streams are not limited to this function. Array streams like `ByteArrayInputStream`, `CharArrayReader`, `ByteArrayOutputStream`, and `CharArrayWriter` are used to read and write bytes or characters from arrays. The following constructors can be used to create array streams:

```
public ByteArrayInputStream(byte[] byteArray)

public ByteArrayOutputStream(byte[] byteArray)

public ByteArrayReader(char[] byteArray)

public ByteArrayWriter(char[] byteArray)
```

For example, the following statements create the byte array input stream `bai` and the character array read stream `car`.

```
byte[] bArray = new byte[2048];
char[] cArray =  new char[2048];
ByteArrayInputStream bai = new ByteArrayInputStream(bArray);
ByteArrayReader car = new ByteArrayReader(cArray);
```

The streams can now be processed just as file streams would be processed. For example, `bai.read()` reads a byte, and `car.read()` reads a character from the array streams.

Filter Streams

Filter streams are streams that filter bytes or characters for some purpose. The basic input stream provides a read method that can only be used for reading bytes or characters. If you want to read integers, doubles, or strings, you need a filter class to wrap the input stream. Using a filter class enables you to read integers, doubles, and strings instead of bytes and characters.

When you need to process primitive numeric types, you should use `FilterInputStream` and `FilterOutputStream` to filter bytes. When you need to process strings, you should use `BufferedReader` and `PushbackReader` to filter characters. `FilterInputStream` and `FilterOutputStream` are abstract classes; their subclasses (listed below in Tables 15.1 and 15.2) are often used.

TABLE 15.1 `FilterInputStream` Subclasses

Subclass	Class Usage
`DataInputStream`	Handles binary formats of all the primitive data types.
`BufferedInputStream`	Gets data from the buffer and then reads it from the stream if necessary.
`LineNumberInputStream`	Keeps track of how many lines are read.
`PushbackInputStream`	Allows single-byte look-ahead. After the byte is looked at, this stream pushes the byte back to the stream so that the next read can read it.

TABLE 15.2 `FilterOutputStream` Subclasses

Subclass	Class Usage
`DataOutputStream`	Outputs the binary format of all of the primitive types, which is useful if another program uses the output.
`BufferedOutputStream`	Outputs to the buffer first and then to the stream if necessary. Programmers can also call the `flush()` method to write the buffer to the stream.
`PrintStream`	Outputs the Unicode format of all of the primitive types, which is useful if the format is output to the console.

Data Streams

The data streams (`DataInputStream` and `DataOutputStream`) read and write Java primitive types in a machine-independent fashion, thereby enabling you to write a data file on one machine and read it on another machine that has a different operating system or file structure.

`DataInputStream` extends `FilterInputStream` and implements the `DataInput` interface. `DataOutputStream` extends `FilterOutputStream` and implements the `DataOutput` interface. The `DataInput` and `DataOutput` interfaces are also implemented by the `RandomAccessFile` class, which is discussed in the section "Random Access Files," later in this chapter.

The following methods are defined in the `DataInput` interface:

```
public int readByte() throws IOException
public int readShort() throws IOException
```

```
public int readInt() throws IOException

public int readLong() throws IOException

public float readFloat() throws IOException

public double readDouble() throws IOException

public char readChar() throws IOException

public boolean readBoolean() throws IOException

public String readUTF() throws IOException
```

The following methods are defined in the `DataOutput` interface:

```
public void writeByte(byte b) throws IOException

public void writeShort(short s) throws IOException

public void writeInt(int i) throws IOException

public void writeLong(long l) throws IOException

public void writeFloat(float f) throws IOException

public void writeDouble(double d) throws IOException

public void writeChar(char c) throws IOException

public void writeBoolean(boolean b) throws IOException

public void writeBytes(String l) throws IOException

public void writeChars(String l) throws IOException

public void writeUTF(String l) throws IOException
```

Data streams are often used as wrappers on existing input and output streams to filter data in the original stream.

These are the data Input and Output stream constructors:

```
public DataInputStream(InputStream instream)

public DataOutputStream(OutputStream outstream)
```

The statements given below create data streams. The first statement creates an input stream for file **in.dat;** the second statement creates an output stream for file **out.dat.**

```
DataInputStream infile =
  new DataInputStream(new FileInputStream("in.dat"));
DataOutputStream outfile =
  new DataOutputStream(new FileOutputStream("out.dat"));
```

Example 15.2 Using Data Streams

This example presents a program that creates 10 random integers, stores them in a data file, retrieves data from the file, and then displays the integers on the console. Figure 15.6 contains the output of a sample run of the program.

The program uses a temporary file to store data. The temporary file is named **mytemp.dat**.

```java
// TestDataStreams.java: Create a file, store it in binary form, and
// display it on the console
import java.io.*;

public class TestDataStreams
{
  // Main method
  public static void main(String[] args)
  {
    // Declare data input and output streams
    DataInputStream dis = null;
    DataOutputStream dos = null;

    // Construct a temp file
    File tempFile = new File("mytemp.dat");

    // Check if the temp file exists
    if (tempFile.exists())
    {
      System.out.println("The file mytemp.dat already exists,"
        +" delete it, rerun the program");
      System.exit(0);
    }

    // Write data
    try
    {
      // Create data output stream for tempFile
      dos = new DataOutputStream(new
        FileOutputStream(tempFile));
      for (int i=0; i<10; i++)
        dos.writeInt((int)(Math.random()*1000));
    }
    catch (IOException ex)
    {
      System.out.println(ex.getMessage());
    }
    finally
    {
      try
      {
        // Close files
        if (dos != null) dos.close();
      }
      catch (IOException ex)
      {
      }
    }

    // Read data
    try
```

```
      {
        // Create data input stream
        dis = new DataInputStream(new FileInputStream(tempFile));
        for (int i=0; i<10; i++)
          System.out.print("  "+dis.readInt());
      }
      catch (FileNotFoundException ex)
      {
        System.out.println("File not found");
      }
      catch (IOException ex)
      {
        System.out.println(ex.getMessage());
      }
      finally
      {
        try
        {
          // Close files
          if (dis != null) dis.close();
        }
        catch (IOException ex)
        {
          System.out.println(ex);
        }
      }
    }
  }
```

```
C:\vjBook\Project15>jview TestDataStreams
   436   31  324  365  402  207  777  790  734  735
C:\vjBook\Project15>type mytemp.dat
...
C:\vjBook\Project15>
```

Figure 15.6 *The program creates 10 random numbers and stores them in a file named* ***mytemp.dat.*** *It then reads the data from the file and displays them on the console.*

Example Review

The program creates a `DataInputStream` object dis wrapped on `FileInputStream` and creates a `DataOutputStream` object dos wrapped on `FileOutputStream` (see Figure 15.7).

```
                    DataInputStream dis
program  <──────────────────────────────────────  mytemp.dat

         ──────────────────────────────────────>  mytemp.dat
                    DataOuputStream dos
```

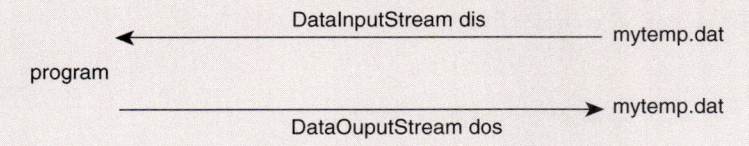

Figure 15.7 *The program uses* `DataOutputStream` *to write data to a file and* `DataInput-Stream` *to read the data from the file.*

continues

> The program first creates **mytemp.dat** if it does not exist. It writes 10 random integers into **mytemp.dat,** using the data output stream, and then closes the stream.
>
> The program creates a data input stream for **mytemp.dat,** reads integers from it, and displays it.
>
> **NOTE**
> The data stored in **mytemp.dat** are in binary format, which is machine-independent and portable. If you need to transport data between different systems, you should use data input and data output streams.

Print Streams

A data output stream outputs a binary representation of data, so you cannot view its contents as text. As shown in Figure 15.6, when you attempt to view the **mytemp.dat** file on the console, strange symbols are displayed. In Java, you can use print streams to output data into files. These files can be viewed as text.

The `PrintStream` and `PrintWriter` classes provide this functionality. You have already used `System.out.println()` to display data on the console. An instance of `PrintStream`, `out`, is defined in the `java.lang.System` class. `PrintStream` and `PrintWriter` have similar method interfaces. `PrintStream` is deprecated in JDK 1.1, but the `System.out` standard output stream is not, so you can continue to use it for output to the console.

Here are the constructors for `PrintWriter`:

```
public PrintWriter(Writer out)

public PrintWriter(Writer out, boolean autoFlush)

public PrintWriter(OutputStream out)

public PrintWriter(OutputStream out, boolean autoFlush)
```

The methods in `PrintWriter` are as follows:

```
public void print(Object o)

public void print(String s)

public void print(char c)

public void print(char[] cArray)

public void print(int i)

public void print(long l)

public void print(float f)
```

```
public void print(double d)

public void print(boolean b)
```

You can replace print with println. The println() method, which prints the object, is followed by a new line. When an object is passed to print or println, the object's toString() method converts it to a String object.

Example 15.3 Using Print Streams

The program in this example creates 10 random integers and stores them in a text data file. The file can be viewed on the console by using an OS command, such as type on Windows or cat on UNIX. Figure 15.8 contains the output of a sample run of the program.

```java
// TestPrintWriters.java: Create a text file using PrintWriter
import java.io.*;

public class TestPrintWriters
{
  // Main method: args[0] is the output file
  public static void main(String[] args)
  {
    // Declare print stream
    PrintWriter pw = null;

    // Check usage
    if (args.length != 1)
    {
      System.out.println("Usage: java TestPrintWriters file");
      System.exit(0);
    }

    File tempFile = new File(args[0]);

    if (tempFile.exists())
    {
      System.out.println("The file " + args[0] +
        " already exists, delete it, rerun the program");
      System.exit(0);
    }

    // Write data
    try
    {
      // Create data output stream for tempFile
      pw = new PrintWriter(new FileOutputStream(tempFile), true);
      for (int i=0; i<10; i++)
        pw.print(" "+(int)(Math.random()*1000));
    }
    catch (IOException ex)
    {
      System.out.println(ex.getMessage());
    }
    finally
```

continues

```
      {
        // Close files
        if (pw != null) pw.close();
      }
    }
  }
```

```
MS-DOS Prompt
C:\vjBook\Project15>jview TestPrintWriters t.dat
C:\vjBook\Project15>type t.dat
 946 952 451 406 520 136 914 965 758 213
C:\vjBook\Project15>
```

Figure 15.8 *The program creates 10 random numbers and stores them in a text file.*

Example Review

The program creates a print stream `pw` of `PrintWriter`—wrapped in `FileOutputStream`—for output data written in text format (see Figure 15.9).

```
                      PrintWriter    FileOutputStream
         program  ─────────────────▶─────────────────▶ args[0]
```

Figure 15.9 *The program uses the `PrintWriter` stream, which is wrapped in `FileOutputStream`, to write data in text format.*

The program creates the file **args[0]** if that file does not already exist. It writes 10 random integers into **args[0]** by using the data output stream, then closes the stream.

The output in **args[0]** is in text format. The data can be seen using the `type` command in DOS.

Buffered Streams

Java introduces buffered streams that speed input and output by reducing the number of reads and writes. Buffered streams employ a buffered array of bytes or characters that acts as a cache. In the case of input, the array reads a chunk of bytes or characters into the buffer before the individual bytes or characters are read. In the case of output, the array accumulates a block of bytes or characters before writing the entire block to the output stream.

The use of buffered streams enables you to read and write a chunk of bytes or characters at once instead of reading or writing the bytes or characters one at a time. The `BufferedInputStream`, `BufferedOutputStream`, `BufferedReader`, and `BufferedWriter` classes provide this functionality.

Chapter 15 Input and Output

The following constructors are used to create a buffered stream:

```
public BufferedInputStream(InputStream in)

public BufferedInputStream(InputStream in, int bufferSize)

public BufferedOutputStream(OutputStream in)

public BufferedOutputStream(OutputStream in, int bufferSize)

public BufferedReader(Reader in)

public BufferedReader(Reader in, int bufferSize)

public BufferedWriter(Writer out)

public BufferedWriter(Writer out, int bufferSize)
```

If no buffer size is specified, the default size is 512 bytes or characters. A buffered input stream reads as much data into its buffer as possible in a single read call. By contrast, a buffered output stream calls the write method only when its buffer fills up or when the `flush()` method is called.

The buffered stream classes inherit methods from their superclasses. In addition to using the methods from their superclasses, `BufferedReader` has a `readLine()` method to read a line.

Example 15.4 Displaying a File in a Text Area

This example presents a program that views a file in a text area. The user enters a filename in a text field and clicks the View button; the file is then displayed in a text area. Figure 15.10 contains the output of a sample run of the program.

```java
// ViewFile.java: Read a text file and store it in a text area
import java.awt.*;
import java.awt.event.*;
import java.io.*;
import javax.swing.*;

public class ViewFile extends MyFrameWithExitHandling
  implements ActionListener
{
  // Button to view view
  private JButton jbtView = new JButton("View");

  // Text field to receive file name
  private JTextField jtf = new JTextField(12);

  // Text area to display file
  private JTextArea jta = new JTextArea();

  // Main method
  public static void main(String[] args)
  {
    ViewFile frame = new ViewFile();
    frame.setTitle("View File");
```

continues

```java
      frame.setSize(400, 300);
      frame.setVisible(true);
    }

    // Constructor
    public ViewFile()
    {
      // Panel p to hold a label, a text field, and a button
      Panel p = new Panel();
      p.setLayout(new BorderLayout());
      p.add(new Label("Filename"), BorderLayout.WEST);
      p.add(jtf, BorderLayout.CENTER);
      jtf.setBackground(Color.yellow);
      jtf.setForeground(Color.red);
      p.add(jbtView, BorderLayout.EAST);

      // Add jta to a scroll pane
      JScrollPane jsp = new JScrollPane(jta);

      // Add jsp and p to the frame
      getContentPane().add(jsp, BorderLayout.CENTER);
      getContentPane().add(p, BorderLayout.SOUTH);

      // Register listener
      jbtView.addActionListener(this);
    }

    // Handle the "View" button
    public void actionPerformed(ActionEvent e)
    {
      if (e.getSource() == jbtView)
        showFile();
    }

    // Display the file in the text area
    private void showFile()
    {
      // Use a BufferedStream to read text from the file
      BufferedReader infile = null;

      // Get file name from the text field
      String filename = jtf.getText().trim();

      String inLine;

      try
      {
        // Create a buffered stream
        infile = new BufferedReader(new FileReader(filename));

        // Read a line
        inLine = infile.readLine();

        boolean firstLine = true;

        // Append the line to the text area
        while (inLine != null)
        {
          if (firstLine)
          {
            firstLine = false;
```

```
            jta.append(inLine);
        }
        else
        {
            jta.append("\n" + inLine);
        }

        inLine = infile.readLine();
      }
    }
    catch (FileNotFoundException ex)
    {
      System.out.println("File not found: " + filename);
    }
    catch (IOException ex)
    {
      System.out.println(ex.getMessage());
    }
    finally
    {
      try
      {
        if (infile != null) infile.close();
      }
      catch (IOException ex)
      {
        System.out.println(ex.getMessage());
      }
    }
  }
}
```

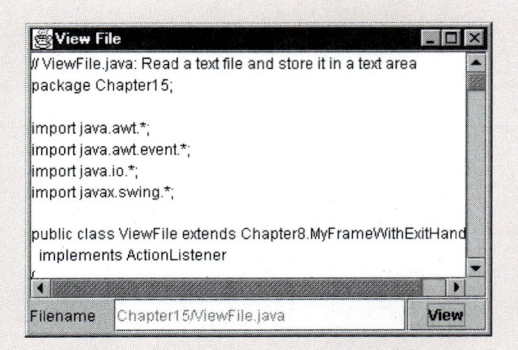

![View File window showing ViewFile.java source code with Filename field containing "Chapter15/ViewFile.java" and a View button]

Figure 15.10 *The program displays the specified file in the text area.*

Example Review

The user enters a filename into the Filename text field. When the View button is pressed, the program gets the input filename from the text field; it then creates a data input stream. The data are read one line at a time and appended to the text area for display.

The program uses a BufferedReader stream to read lines from a buffer. Instead of using BufferedReader and Reader classes, the BufferedInputStream and FileInputStream can also be used in this example.

continues

You are encouraged to rewrite the program without using buffers and then compare the performance of the two programs. This will show you the improvement in performance obtained by using buffers when reading from a large file.

> **TIP**
> Since physical input and output involving I/O devices are typically very slow compared with CPU processing speeds, you should use buffered input/output streams to improve performance.

Parsing Text Files

Occasionally you need to process a text file. For example, the Java source file is a text file. The compiler reads the source file and translates it into bytecode, which is a binary file. Java provides the `StreamTokenizer` class so that you can take an input stream and parse it into words, which are known as *tokens*. The tokens are read one at a time.

To construct an instance of `StreamTokenizer`, you can use `StreamTokenizer(Reader is)` on a given character input stream. The `StreamTokenizer` class contains the useful constants listed in Table 15.3.

TABLE 15.3 `StreamTokenizer` **Constants**

Constant	Description
TT_WORD	The token is a word.
TT_NUMBER	The token is a number.
TT_EOL	The end of the line has been read.
TT_EOF	The end of the file has been read.

The `StreamTokenizer` class also contains the useful variables listed in Table 15.4.

TABLE 15.4 `StreamTokenizer` **Variables**

Variable	Description
int ttype	Contains the current token type, which matches one of the constants listed previously.
double nval	Contains the value of the current token if the token is a number.
String sval	Contains a string that gives the characters of the current token if the token is a word.

Typically, the nextToken() method is used to retrieve tokens one by one in a loop until TT_EOF is returned. The following method parses the next token from the input stream of a StreamTokenizer:

```
public int nextToken() throws IOException
```

The type of the next token is returned in the ttype field. If ttype == TT_WORD, the token is stored in sval; if ttype == TT_NUMBER, the token is stored in nval.

Example 15.5 Using *StreamTokenizer*

The program in this example demonstrates parsing text files. The program reads a text file containing students' exam scores. Each record in the input file consists of a student's name, two midterm exam scores, and a final exam score. The program reads the fields for each record and computes the total score. It then stores the result in a new file. The formula for computing the total score is:

```
total score = midterm1*30% + midterm2*30% + final*40%;
```

Each record in the output file consists of a student's name and his or her total score. Figure 15.11 contains the output of a sample run of the program.

```java
// ParsingTextFile.java: Process text file using StreamTokenizer
import java.io.*;

public class ParsingTextFile
{
  // Main method
  public static void main(String[] args)
  {
    // Declare file reader and writer streams
    FileReader frs = null;
    FileWriter fws = null;

    // Declare streamTokenizer
    StreamTokenizer in = null;

    // Declare a print stream
    PrintWriter out = null;

    // For input file fields: student name, midterm1,
    // midterm2, and final exam score
    String sname = null;
    double midterm1 = 0;
    double midterm2 = 0;
    double finalScore = 0;

    // Computed total score
    double total = 0;

    try
    {
      // Create file input and output streams
      frs = new FileReader("in.dat");
      fws = new FileWriter("out.dat");
```

continues

```java
          // Create a stream tokenizer wrapping file input stream
          in = new StreamTokenizer(frs);
          out = new PrintWriter(fws);

          // Read first token
          in.nextToken();

          // Process a record
          while (in.ttype != in.TT_EOF)
          {
            // Get student name
            if (in.ttype == in.TT_WORD)
              sname = in.sval;
            else
              System.out.println("Bad file format");

            // Get midterm1
            if (in.nextToken() == in.TT_NUMBER)
              midterm1 = in.nval;
            else
              System.out.println("Bad file format");

            // Get midterm2
            if (in.nextToken() == in.TT_NUMBER)
              midterm2 = in.nval;
            else
              System.out.println("Bad file format");

            // Get final score
            if (in.nextToken() == in.TT_NUMBER)
              finalScore = in.nval;

            total = midterm1*0.3 + midterm2*0.3 + finalScore*0.4;
            out.println(sname + " " +total);

            in.nextToken();
          }
        }
        catch (FileNotFoundException ex)
        {
          System.out.println("File not found: in.dat");
        }
        catch (IOException ex)
        {
          System.out.println(ex.getMessage());
        }
        finally
        {
          try
          {
            if (frs != null) frs.close();
            if (fws != null) fws.close();
          }
          catch (IOException ex)
          {
            System.out.println(ex);
          }
        }
      }
    }
```

CHAPTER 15   INPUT AND OUTPUT

```
MS-DOS Prompt
C:\vjBook\Project15>jview ParsingTextFile

C:\vjBook\Project15>type in.dat
James 32 60 30
George 100 100 100
John 90 94 100

C:\vjBook\Project15>type out.dat
James 39.6
George 100.0
John 95.2

C:\vjBook\Project15>
```

Figure 15.11   *The program uses* `StreamTokenizer` *to parse the text file into strings and numbers.*

Example Review

Before running this program, make sure you have created the text file **in.dat.** To parse the text file **in.dat,** the program uses `StreamTokenizer` to wrap a `FileReader` stream. The `nextToken()` method is used on a `StreamTokenizer` object to get one token at a time. The token value is stored in the `nval` field if the token is numeric, and in the `sval` field if the token is a string. The token type is stored in the `ttype` field.

For each record, the program reads the name and the three exam scores and then computes the total score. A `FileWriter` stream is used to store the name and the total score in the text file **out.dat** (see Figure 15.12).

```
        in.dat                                    out.dat
┌──────────────────────┐              ┌──────────────────────┐
│ James 32 60 30       │              │ James 39.6           │
│ George 100 100 100   │ ───────────► │ George 100.0         │
│ John 90 94 100       │              │ John 95.2            │
└──────────────────────┘              └──────────────────────┘
                          30%                       ▲
                 30%                              +
            40%
```

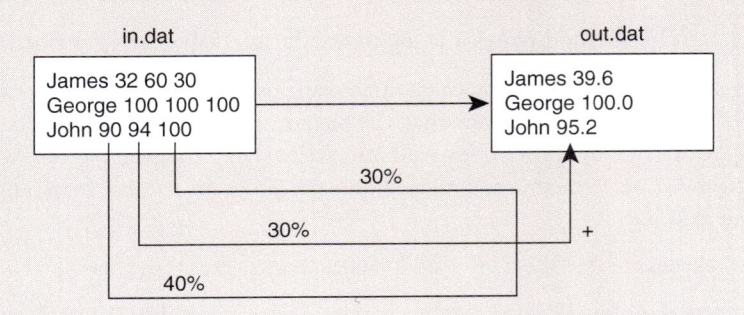

Figure 15.12   *The program reads two midterm scores and a final exam score, and then computes a total score.*

Random Access Files

All of the streams you have used so far are known as *read-only* or *write-only* streams. The external files of these streams are sequential files that cannot be updated without creating a new file. It is often necessary to modify files or to insert new records into the files. Java provides the `RandomAccessFile` class to allow a file to be read and updated at the same time.

The `RandomAccessFile` class extends `Object` and implements `DataInput` and `DataOutput` interfaces. Because `DataInputStream` implements the `DataInput` interface and `DataOutputStream` implements the `DataOutput` interface, many methods in `RandomAccessFile` are the same as those in `DataInputStream` and `DataOutputStream`. For example, `readInt()`, `readLong()`, `readDouble()`, `readUTF()`, `writeInt()`, `writeLong()`, `writeDouble()`, and `writeUTF()` can be used in data input streams or data output streams as well as in `RandomAccessFile` streams.

Additionally, `RandomAccessFile` provides the following methods to deal with random access:

- `public void seek(long pos) throws IOException`

  This method sets the offset from the beginning of the `RandomAccessFile` stream to where the next read or write occurs.

- `public long getFilePointer() throws IOException`

  This method returns the offset, in bytes, from the beginning of the file to where the next read or write occurs.

- `public long length() throws IOException`

  This method returns the length of the file.

- `public final void writeChar(int v) throws IOException`

  This method writes a character to the file as a two-byte Unicode, with the high byte written first.

- `public final void writeChars(String s) throws IOException`

  This method writes a string to the file as a sequence of characters.

When creating a `RandomAccessFile` stream, you can specify one of two modes (`"r"` or `"rw"`). Mode `"r"` means that the stream is read-only, and mode `"rw"` indicates that the stream allows both read and write. For example, the following statement creates a new stream, `raf`, that allows the program to read from and write to the file **test.dat**:

```
RandomAccessFile raf = new RandomAccessFile("test.dat", "rw");
```

If **test.dat** already exists, `raf` is created to access **test.dat**; if **test.dat** does not exist, a new file named **test.dat** is created, and `raf` is created to access the new file. The method `raf.length()` indicates the number of bytes in **test.dat** at any given time. If you append new data into the file, `raf.length()` increases.

> **NOTE**
> When you use `writeChar()` to write a character or `writeChars()` to write characters, a character occupies two bytes.

> **TIP**
> You should open the file with the `"r"` mode if the file is not intended to be modified. This prevents unintentional modification of the file.

Random access files are often used to process files of records. For convenience, fixed-length records are used in random access files so that a record can be located easily. A record consists of a fixed number of fields. A field can be a string or a primitive data type. A string in a fixed-length record has a maximum size. If a string is smaller than the maximum size, the rest of the string is padded with blanks.

Example 15.6 Using Random Access Files

This example presents a program that registers students and displays student information. The user interface consists of a tabbed pane with two tabs: Register Student and View Student. The Register Student tab enables you to store a student in the file, as shown in Figure 15.13. The View Student tab enables you to browse through student information, as shown in Figure 15.14.

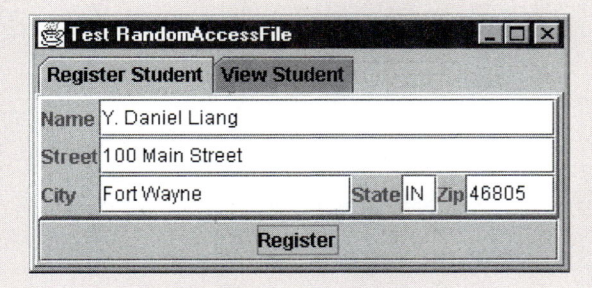

Figure 15.13 *The Register Student tab registers a student.*

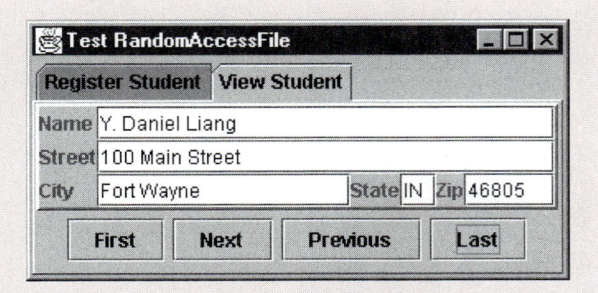

Figure 15.14 *The View Student tab displays student information.*

continues

The program is given as follows.

```java
// TestRandomAccessFile.java: Store and read data
// using RandomAccessFile
import java.io.*;
import java.awt.*;
import java.awt.event.*;
import javax.swing.*;
import MyFrameWithExitHandling;
import javax.swing.border.*;

public class TestRandomAccessFile extends MyFrameWithExitHandling
{
  // Create a tabbed pane to hold two panels
  private JTabbedPane jtpStudent = new JTabbedPane();

  // Random access file for access the student.dat file
  private RandomAccessFile raf;

  // Main method
  public static void main(String[] args)
  {
    TestRandomAccessFile frame = new TestRandomAccessFile();
    frame.pack();
    frame.setTitle("Test RandomAccessFile");
    frame.setVisible(true);
  }

  // Default constructor
  public TestRandomAccessFile()
  {
    // Open or create a random access file
    try
    {
      raf = new RandomAccessFile("student.dat", "rw");
    }
    catch(IOException ex)
    {
      System.out.print("Error: " + ex);
      System.exit(0);
    }

    // Place buttons in the tabbed pane
    jtpStudent.add(new RegisterStudent(raf), "Register Student");
    jtpStudent.add(new ViewStudent(raf), "View Student");

    // Add the tabbed pane to the frame
    getContentPane().add(jtpStudent);
  }
}

// Register student panel
class RegisterStudent extends JPanel implements ActionListener
{
  // Button for registering a student
  private JButton jbtRegister;

  // Student information panel
  private StudentPanel studentPanel;

  // Random access file
  private RandomAccessFile raf;
```

```java
    // Constructor
    public RegisterStudent(RandomAccessFile raf)
    {
      // Pass raf to RegisterStudent Panel
      this.raf = raf;

      // Add studentPanel and jbtRegister in the panel
      setLayout(new BorderLayout());
      add(studentPanel = new StudentPanel(),
        BorderLayout.CENTER);
      add(jbtRegister = new JButton("Register"),
        BorderLayout.SOUTH);

      // Register listener
      jbtRegister.addActionListener(this);
    }

    // Handle button actions
    public void actionPerformed(ActionEvent e)
    {
      if (e.getSource() == jbtRegister)
      {
        Student student = studentPanel.getStudent();

        try
        {
          raf.seek(raf.length());
          student.writeStudent(raf);
        }
        catch(IOException ex)
        {
          System.out.print("Error: " + ex);
        }
      }
    }
  }

  // View student panel
  class ViewStudent extends JPanel implements ActionListener
  {
    // Buttons for viewing student information
    private JButton jbtFirst, jbtNext, jbtPrevious, jbtLast;

    // Random access file
    private RandomAccessFile raf = null;

    // Current student record
    private Student student = new Student();

    // Create a student panel
    private StudentPanel studentPanel = new StudentPanel();

    // File pointer in the random access file
    private long lastPos;
    private long currentPos;

    // Constructor
    public ViewStudent(RandomAccessFile raf)
    {
      // Pass raf to ViewStudent
      this.raf = raf;
```

continues

```java
    // Panel p to hold four navigator buttons
    JPanel p = new JPanel();
    p.setLayout(new FlowLayout(FlowLayout.LEFT));
    p.add(jbtFirst = new JButton("First"));
    p.add(jbtNext = new JButton("Next"));
    p.add(jbtPrevious = new JButton("Previous"));
    p.add(jbtLast = new JButton("Last"));

    // Add panel p and studentPanel to ViewPanel
    setLayout(new BorderLayout());
    add(studentPanel, BorderLayout.CENTER);
    add(p, BorderLayout.SOUTH);

    // Register listeners
    jbtFirst.addActionListener(this);
    jbtNext.addActionListener(this);
    jbtPrevious.addActionListener(this);
    jbtLast.addActionListener(this);
  }

  // Handle navigation button actions
  public void actionPerformed(ActionEvent e)
  {
    String actionCommand = e.getActionCommand();
    if (e.getSource() instanceof JButton)
    {
      try
      {
        if ("First".equals(actionCommand))
        {
          if (raf.length() > 0)
            retrieve(0);
        }
        else if ("Next".equals(actionCommand))
        {
          currentPos = raf.getFilePointer();
          if (currentPos < raf.length())
            retrieve(currentPos);
        }
        else if ("Previous".equals(actionCommand))
        {
          currentPos = raf.getFilePointer();
          if (currentPos > 0)
            retrieve(currentPos - 2*2*Student.RECORD_SIZE);
        }
        else if ("Last".equals(actionCommand))
        {
          lastPos = raf.length();
          if (lastPos > 0)
            retrieve(lastPos - 2*Student.RECORD_SIZE);
        }
      }
      catch(IOException ex)
      {
        System.out.print("Error: " + ex);
      }
    }
  }

  // Retrieve a record at specified position
  public void retrieve(long pos)
```

```java
    {
      try
      {
        raf.seek(pos);
        student.readStudent(raf);
        studentPanel.setStudent(student);
      }
      catch(IOException ex)
      {
        System.out.print("Error: " + ex);
      }
    }
  }
}

// This class contains static methods for reading and writing
// fixed length records
class FixedLengthStringIO
{
  // Read fixed number of characters from a DataInput stream
  public static String readFixedLengthString(int size,
                                             DataInput in)
  throws IOException
  {
    char c[] = new char[size];

    for (int i=0; i<size; i++)
      c[i] = in.readChar();

    return new String(c);
  }

  // Write fixed number of characters (string s with padded spaces)
  // to a DataOutput stream
  public static void writeFixedLengthString(String s, int size,
    DataOutput out) throws IOException
  {
    char cBuffer[] = new char[size];
    s.getChars(0, s.length(), cBuffer, 0);
    for (int i=s.length(); i<cBuffer.length; i++)
      cBuffer[i] = ' ';
    String newS = new String(cBuffer);
    out.writeChars(newS);
  }
}

// StudentPanel.java: Panel for displaying student information
import javax.swing.*;
import javax.swing.border.*;
import java.awt.*;

public class StudentPanel extends JPanel
{
  JTextField jtfName = new JTextField(32);
  JTextField jtfStreet = new JTextField(32);
  JTextField jtfCity = new JTextField(20);
  JTextField jtfState = new JTextField(2);
  JTextField jtfZip = new JTextField(5);

  // Constuct a student panel
  public StudentPanel()
```

continues

```java
{
  // Set the panel with line border
  setBorder(new BevelBorder(BevelBorder.RAISED));

  // Panel p1 for holding labels Name, Street, and City
  JPanel p1 = new JPanel();
  p1.setLayout(new GridLayout(3, 1));
  p1.add(new JLabel("Name"));
  p1.add(new JLabel("Street"));
  p1.add(new JLabel("City"));

  // Panel jpState for holding state
  JPanel jpState = new JPanel();
  jpState.setLayout(new BorderLayout());
  jpState.add(new JLabel("State"), BorderLayout.WEST);
  jpState.add(jtfState, BorderLayout.CENTER);

  // Panel jpZip for holding zip
  JPanel jpZip = new JPanel();
  jpZip.setLayout(new BorderLayout());
  jpZip.add(new JLabel("Zip"), BorderLayout.WEST);
  jpZip.add(jtfZip, BorderLayout.CENTER);

  // Panel p2 for holding jpState and jpZip
  JPanel p2 = new JPanel();
  p2.setLayout(new BorderLayout());
  p2.add(jpState, BorderLayout.WEST);
  p2.add(jpZip, BorderLayout.CENTER);

  // Panel p3 for holding jtfCity and p2
  JPanel p3 = new JPanel();
  p3.setLayout(new BorderLayout());
  p3.add(jtfCity, BorderLayout.CENTER);
  p3.add(p2, BorderLayout.EAST);

  // Panel p4 for holding jtfName, jtfStreet, and p3
  JPanel p4 = new JPanel();
  p4.setLayout(new GridLayout(3, 1));
  p4.add(jtfName);
  p4.add(jtfStreet);
  p4.add(p3);

  // Place p1 and p4 into StudentPanel
  setLayout(new BorderLayout());
  add(p1, BorderLayout.WEST);
  add(p4, BorderLayout.CENTER);
}

// Get student information from the text fields
public Student getStudent()
{
  return new Student(jtfName.getText().trim(),
                     jtfStreet.getText().trim(),
                     jtfCity.getText().trim(),
                     jtfState.getText().trim(),
                     jtfZip.getText().trim());
}

// Set student information on the text fields
public void setStudent(Student s)
```

```java
      {
        jtfName.setText(s.getName());
        jtfStreet.setText(s.getStreet());
        jtfCity.setText(s.getCity());
        jtfState.setText(s.getState());
        jtfZip.setText(s.getZip());
      }
  }

  // Student.java: Student class encapsulates student information
  import java.io.*;

  public class Student
  {
    private String name;
    private String street;
    private String city;
    private String state;
    private String zip;

    // Specify the size of five string fields in the record
    final static int NAME_SIZE = 32;
    final static int STREET_SIZE = 32;
    final static int CITY_SIZE = 20;
    final static int STATE_SIZE = 2;
    final static int ZIP_SIZE = 5;

    // the total size of the record in bytes, a Unicode
    // character is 2 bytes size
    final static int RECORD_SIZE =
      (NAME_SIZE + STREET_SIZE + CITY_SIZE + STATE_SIZE + ZIP_SIZE);

    // Default constructor
    public Student()
    {
    }

    // Construct a Student with specified name, street, city, state,
    // and zip
    public Student(String name, String street, String city,
      String state, String zip)
    {
      this.name = name;
      this.street = street;
      this.city = city;
      this.state = state;
      this.zip = zip;
    }

    public String getName()
    {
      return name;
    }

    public String getStreet()
    {
      return street;
    }
```

continues

```java
    public String getCity()
    {
      return city;
    }

    public String getState()
    {
      return state;
    }

    public String getZip()
    {
      return zip;
    }

    // Write a student to a data output stream
    public void writeStudent(DataOutput out) throws IOException
    {
      FixedLengthStringIO.writeFixedLengthString(
        name, NAME_SIZE, out);
      FixedLengthStringIO.writeFixedLengthString(
        street, STREET_SIZE, out);
      FixedLengthStringIO.writeFixedLengthString(
        city, CITY_SIZE, out);
      FixedLengthStringIO.writeFixedLengthString(
        state, STATE_SIZE, out);
      FixedLengthStringIO.writeFixedLengthString(
        zip, ZIP_SIZE, out);
    }

    // Read a student from data input stream
    public void readStudent(DataInput in) throws IOException
    {
      name = FixedLengthStringIO.readFixedLengthString(
        NAME_SIZE, in);
      street = FixedLengthStringIO.readFixedLengthString(
        STREET_SIZE, in);
      city = FixedLengthStringIO.readFixedLengthString(
        CITY_SIZE, in);
      state = FixedLengthStringIO.readFixedLengthString(
        STATE_SIZE, in);
      zip = FixedLengthStringIO.readFixedLengthString(
        ZIP_SIZE, in);
    }
  }
```

Example Review

A random file, **student.dat,** is created to store student information if the file does not yet exist. If it does exist, the file is opened. The random file object, raf, is used in both registration and the viewing part of the program. The user can add a new student record to the file in the Register Student panel and view it immediately in the View Student panel.

Several classes are used in this example. The main class, TestRandomAccessFile, is a subclass of MyFrameWithExitHandling, and creates an instance of the RegisterStudent class and an instance of the ViewStudent class. These two instances are added to a tabbed pane with two tabs: Register Student and View Student. When the Register Student tab is clicked, the registration panel is shown. When the View Student tab is clicked, the viewing panel is shown.

The `RegisterStudent` class and the `ViewStudent` class have many things in common. They both extend the `JPanel` class, and they both use the `StudentPanel` class and the `Student` class.

The student information panels for registering and viewing student information are identical. Therefore, the program creates one class, `StudentPanel`, to lay out the labels and text fields, as shown in Figure 15.15. The `StudentPanel` class also provides the method `getStudent()` for getting student information from the text fields and the method `setStudent()` for setting student information text fields.

The `Student` class defines the student record structure and provides methods for reading and writing a record into the file. Each field in a student record has a fixed length. The `FixedLengthStringIO` class defines the methods for reading and writing fixed-length strings.

The size of each field in the student record is fixed. For example, zip code is set to a maximum of five characters. If you entered a zip code of more than five characters by mistake, the `ArrayIndexOutOfBounds` runtime error would occur when the program attempted to write the zip code into the file using the `writeFixedLengthString()` method defined in the `FixedLengthStringIO` class.

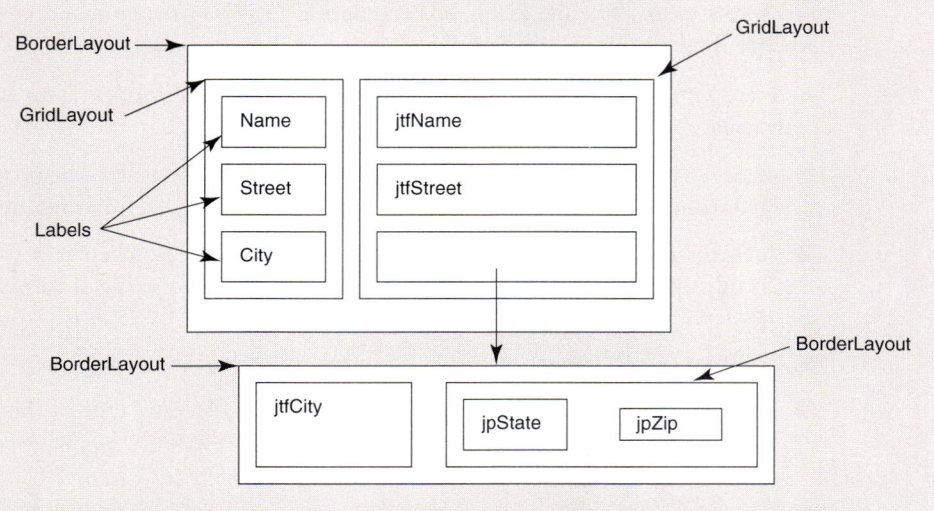

Figure 15.15 *The* `StudentPanel` *class uses several panels to group components to achieve desired layout.*

File Dialogs

Swing provides `javax.swing.JFileChooser`, which displays a dialog box from which the user can navigate through the file system and select files to load or save, as shown in Figure 15.16.

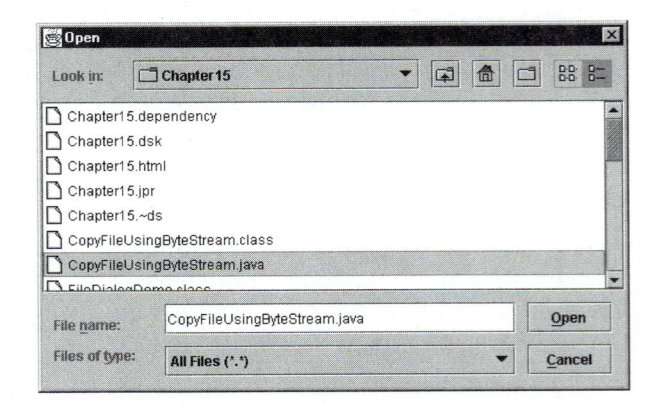

Figure 15.16 *The Swing* `JFileChooser` *shows files and directories, and enables the user to navigate through the file system visually.*

The file dialog box is modal; when displayed, it blocks the rest of the application until it disappears. The file dialog box can appear in two types: *open* and *save*. The *open type* is for opening a file, and the *save type* is for storing a file.

There are several ways to construct a file dialog box. The simplest is to use the `JFileChooser`'s default constructor.

`JFileChooser` is a subclass of `JComponent`. The `JFileChooser` class has the properties inherited from `JComponent`. Additionally, it has the following useful properties:

- `dialogType`—The type of this dialog. Use `OPEN_DIALOG` when you want to bring up a filechooser that the user can use to open a file. Likewise, use `SAVE_DIALOG` to let the user choose a file to save.

- `dialogTitle`—The string displayed in the title bar of the dialog box.

- `currentDirectory`—The current directory of the file. The type of this property is `java.io.File`. If you want the current directory to be used, use `setCurrentDirectory(new File("."))`.

- `selectedFile`—The selected file. You can use `getSelectedFile()` to return the selected file from the dialog box. The type of this property is `java.io.File`. If you have a default file name that you expect to use, use `setSelectedFile(new File(filename))`.

- `selectedFiles`—A list of selected files if the filechooser is set to allow multi-selection. The type of this property is `File[]`.

- `multiSelectionEnabled`—A `boolean` value indicating whether multiple files can be selected. By default, it is `false`.

To display the dialog box, use the following two methods.

```
public int showOpenDialog(Component parent)

public int showSaveDialog(Component parent)
```

The first method displays an "Open" dialog, and the second displays a "Save" dialog. Both methods return an `int` value `APPROVE_OPTION` or `CANCEL_OPTION`, which indicates whether the OK button or the Cancel button was clicked.

Example 15.7 Using File Dialogs

This example gives a program that creates a simple notepad using `JFileChooser` to open and save files. The notepad enables the user to open an existing file, edit the file, and save the note into the current file or to a specified file. You can display and edit the file in a text area.

A sample run of the program is shown in Figure 15.17. When you open a file, a file dialog box with the default title "Open" appears on-screen to let you select a file for loading, as shown in Figure 15.16. When you save a file, a file dialog box with the default title "Save" appears to let you select a file for saving, as shown in Figure 15.18. The status label below the text area displays the status of the file operations.

```java
// FileDialogDemo.java: Demonstrate using JFileDialog to display
// file dialog boxes for opening and saving files
import java.awt.*;
import java.awt.event.*;
import java.io.*;
import javax.swing.*;

public class FileDialogDemo extends MyFrameWithExitHandling
  implements ActionListener
{
  // Menu items Open, Save, exit, and About
  private JMenuItem jmiOpen, jmiSave,jmiExit, jmiAbout;

  // Text area for displaying and editing text files
  private JTextArea jta = new JTextArea();

  // Status label for displaying operation status
  private JLabel jblStatus = new JLabel();

  // File dialog box
  private JFileChooser jFileChooser = new JFileChooser();

  // Main method
  public static void main(String[] args)
  {
    FileDialogDemo frame = new FileDialogDemo();
    frame.setSize(300, 150);
    frame.setVisible(true);
  }
```

continues

```java
  public FileDialogDemo()
  {
    setTitle("Test JFileChooser");

    // Create a menu bar mb and attach to the frame
    JMenuBar mb = new JMenuBar();
    setJMenuBar(mb);

    // Add a "File" menu in mb
    JMenu fileMenu = new JMenu("File");
    mb.add(fileMenu);

    //add a "Help" menu in mb
    JMenu helpMenu = new JMenu("Help");
    mb.add(helpMenu);

    // Create and add menu items to the menu
    fileMenu.add(jmiOpen = new JMenuItem("Open"));
    fileMenu.add(jmiSave = new JMenuItem("Save"));
    fileMenu.addSeparator();
    fileMenu.add(jmiExit = new JMenuItem("Exit"));
    helpMenu.add(jmiAbout = new JMenuItem("About"));

    // Set default directory to the current directory
    jFileChooser.setCurrentDirectory(new File("."));

    // Set BorderLayout for the frame
    getContentPane().add(new JScrollPane(jta),
      BorderLayout.CENTER);
    getContentPane().add(jlblStatus, BorderLayout.SOUTH);

    // Register listeners
    jmiOpen.addActionListener(this);
    jmiSave.addActionListener(this);
    jmiAbout.addActionListener(this);
    jmiExit.addActionListener(this);
  }

  // Handle ActionEvent for menu items
  public void actionPerformed(ActionEvent e)
  {
    String actionCommand = e.getActionCommand();

    if (e.getSource() instanceof JMenuItem)
    {
      if ("Open".equals(actionCommand))
        open();
      else if ("Save".equals(actionCommand))
        save();
      else if ("About".equals(actionCommand))
        JOptionPane.showMessageDialog(this,
          "Demonstrate Using File Dialogs",
          "About This Demo",
          JOptionPane.INFORMATION_MESSAGE);
      else if ("Exit".equals(actionCommand))
        System.exit(0);
    }
  }

  // Open file
  private void open()
```

```java
    {
      if (jFileChooser.showOpenDialog(this) ==
        JFileChooser.APPROVE_OPTION)
      {
        open(jFileChooser.getSelectedFile());
      }
    }

    // Open file with the specified File instance
    private void open(File file)
    {
      try
      {
        // Read from the specified file and store it in jta
        BufferedInputStream in = new BufferedInputStream(
          new FileInputStream(file));
        byte[] b = new byte[in.available()];
        in.read(b, 0, b.length);
        jta.append(new String(b, 0, b.length));
        in.close();

        // Display the status of the Open file operation in jlblStatus
        jlblStatus.setText(file.getName() + " Opened");
      }
      catch (IOException ex)
      {
        jlblStatus.setText("Error opening " + file.getName());
      }
    }

    // Save file
    private void save()
    {
      if (jFileChooser.showSaveDialog(this) ==
        JFileChooser.APPROVE_OPTION)
      {
        save(jFileChooser.getSelectedFile());
      }
    }

    // Save file with specified File instance
    private void save(File file)
    {
      try
      {
        // Write the text in jta to the specified file
        BufferedOutputStream out = new BufferedOutputStream(
          new FileOutputStream(file));
        byte[] b = (jta.getText()).getBytes();
        out.write(b, 0, b.length);
        out.close();

        // Display the status of the save file operation in jlblStatus
        jlblStatus.setText(file.getName()  + " Saved ");
      }
      catch (IOException ex)
      {
        jlblStatus.setText("Error saving " + file.getName());
      }
    }
}
```

continues

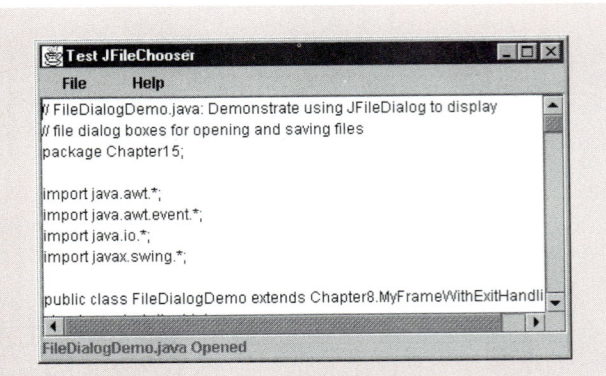

Figure 15.17 *The program enables you to open, save, and edit files.*

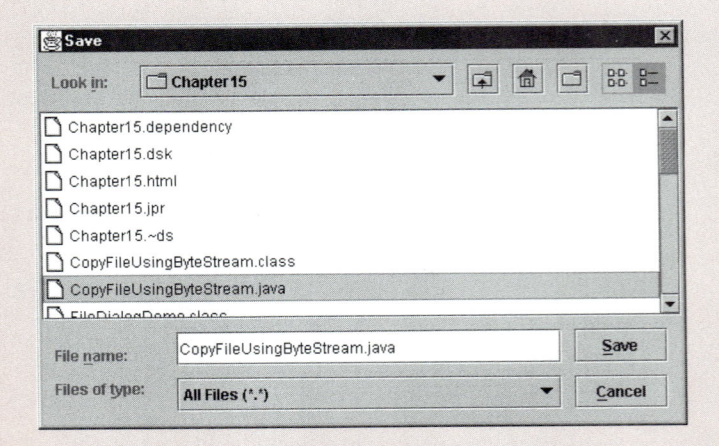

Figure 15.18 *The Save dialog box enables you to save to a new file or an existing file.*

Example Review

The program creates the File and Help menus. The File menu contains the menu commands Open for loading a file, Save for saving a file, and Exit for terminating the program. The Help menu contains the menu command About to display a message about the program, as shown in Figure 15.19.

An instance jFileChooser of JFileChooser is created for displaying the file dialog box to open and save files. The setCurrentDirectory(new File(".")) method is used to set the current directory to the directory where the class is stored.

The open() method is invoked when the user clicks the Open menu command. The showOpenDialog() method displays an Open dialog box, as shown in Figure 15.17. Upon receiving the selected file, the method open(file) is invoked to load the file to the text area, using a BufferedInputStream wrapped on a FileInputStream.

CHAPTER 15   INPUT AND OUTPUT

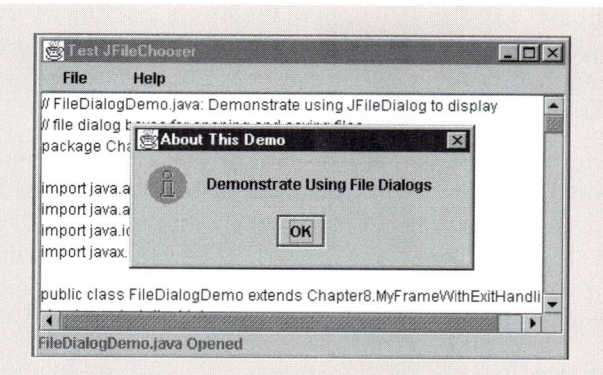

Figure 15.19   *Clicking the About menu item displays a message dialog box.*

The `save()` method is invoked when the user clicks the Save menu command. The `showSaveDialog()` method displays a Save dialog box, as shown in Figure 15.18. Upon receiving the selected file, the method `save(file)` is invoked to save the contents from the text area to the file, using a `BufferedOutputStream` wrapped on a `FileOutputStream`.

> **NOTE**
> The `JFileChooser` component does not work well in Visual J++. You will see an error message on the console when opening a file in the Open dialog box or saving a file in the Save dialog box. Ignore the message. The program runs fine on a Java 2 VM.

Interactive Input and Output

There are two types of *interactive I/O*. One involves simple input from the keyboard and simple output in a pure text form. The other involves input from various input devices and output to a graphical environment on frames and applets. The former is referred to as *text interactive I/O*, and the latter as *graphical interactive I/O*.

Graphical interactive I/O takes an entirely different approach from text interactive I/O. In the graphical environment, input can be received from an UI component, such as a text field, text area, list, combo box, check box, or radio button. It can also be received from a keystroke or a mouse movement. Output is usually displayed in the panel, in text fields, or in text areas.

Now turn your attention to text I/O. In all of the previous chapters, you used text input and output with the `System` class. The `System` class contains three I/O objects: `System.in`, `System.out`, and `System.err`. The objects `in`, `out`, and `err` are static variables. The variable `in` is of `InputStream` type, and `out` and `err` are of `PrintStream` type. These are the basic objects that all Java programmers use to input from the keyboard, output to the screen, and display error messages. Because the objects in this class are used in virtually all programs for simple console input and output, they are stored in the `java.lang` package, which is imported into a class automatically.

To perform console output, you can use any of the methods for `PrintStream` in `System.out`. However, keyboard input is more complicated. The `MyInput` class, which is used for getting `int` and `double` from the keyboard, was introduced in the section "Separate Classes" in Chapter 2, "Java Building Elements." In this section, `MyInput` class, as well as input for other primitive types and strings, will be described in more detail.

`BufferedReader` and `StringTokenizer` are used to input from the keyboard. `BufferedReader` takes the input of the character format of all of the primitive types, such as `integer`, `double`, `string`, and so on. The `StringTokenizer` class, introduced in Chapter 6, "Arrays and Strings," takes in a string, such as `"Welcome to Java"`, and breaks it into little pieces, which are known as *tokens*.

The tokens are usually separated by spaces (but the programmer can dictate what delimiter should be used). `StringTokenizer` objects are instantiated with the string, and each subsequent call to `nextToken()` of a `StringTokenizer` object returns a new token. In order to make input possible, you need to declare these two objects, as follows:

```
static private BufferedReader br =
    new BufferedReader(new InputStreamReader(System.in), 1);
static StringTokenizer stok;
```

> **NOTE**
> JavaSoft knows that some brands of PCs running Windows 95 are prone to cause input problems if the buffer size for the `BufferedReader` stream `br` is not set to 1. Therefore, the buffer size of 1 is purposely chosen to help eliminate input problems.

Table 15.5 shows the code for reading different primitive data types from the keyboard.

With the foregoing code, the programmer needs to add an exception handler in the `try/catch` wraparound because these I/O statements throw `IOException`.

TABLE 15.5 Input and Output of Primitive Types on the Console

Data Type	How to Read It
int	`String str = br.readLine();`
	`stok = new StringTokenizer(str);`
	`int i = Integer.parseInt(stok.nextToken());`

Data Type	How to Read It

byte	`String str = br.readLine();`
	`stok = new StringTokenizer(str);`
	`int i = Integer.parseInt(stok.nextToken());`
	`byte b = (byte)i;`

short	Same as the preceding entry, except that `byte b = (byte)i;` needs to be replaced with `short b = (short)i;`

boolean	`String str = br.readLine();`
	`stok = new StringTokenizer(str);`
	`boolean bo = new Boolean(stok.nextToken()).booleanValue();`

char	`char ch = br.readLine().charAt(0);`
long	`String str = br.readLine(); stok=new StringTokenizer(str)` `long lg = Long.parseLong(stok.nextToken());`

float	`String str = br.readLine();`
	`stok = new StringTokenizer(str);`
	`float fl = new Float(stok.nextToken()).floatValue();`

double	`String str = br.readLine();`
	`stok = new StringTokenizer(str);`
	`double db = new Double(stok.nextToken()).doubleValue();`

String	`String str = br.readLine();`

Piped Streams, String Streams, Pushback Streams, Line Number Streams, and Object Streams

You have learned many I/O streams in this chapter. Each stream has its intended application. There are several other stream classes that you might find useful. For example, you can use object streams to read or write whole objects from or to files. A brief discussion of these streams follows:

- **Piped streams**—A piped stream can be thought of as the two ends of a pipe that connects two processes. One process sends data out through the pipe, and the other receives data from the pipe. Piped streams are used in interprocess communication (IPC). Two processes running on separate threads can exchange data. Java provides `PipedInputStream`, `PipedOutputStream`, `PipedReader`, and `PipedWriter` to support piped streams.

- **String streams**—String streams (`StringReader` and `StringWriter`) are exactly like character array streams, except that the source of a string stream is a string, and the destination of a string stream is a string buffer.

- **Pushback streams**—These are commonly used in parsers to "push back" a single byte or character in the input stream after reading from the input stream. A pushback stream previews the input to determine what to do next. The number of bytes or characters pushed can be specified when the stream is constructed. By default, a single byte or a single character is pushed back. Java provides the classes `PushbackInputStream` and `PushbackReader` to support pushback streams.

- **Line number streams**—These allow you to track the current line number of an input stream. Java provides the `LineNumberReader` class for this purpose. This class is useful for such applications as editing and debugging. You can use the `getLineNumber()` method to get the current line number of the input, and the `getLine()` method to retrieve a line into a string.

- **Object streams**—Thus far, this chapter has covered input and output of bytes, characters, and primitive data types. Object streams enable you to perform input and output at the object level. The `ObjectInputStream` and `ObjectOutputStream` classes provide functionality to support object streams.

Chapter Summary

In this chapter, you learned about Java input and output. In Java, all I/O is handled in streams. Java offers many stream classes for processing all kinds of data.

Streams can be categorized as byte streams and character streams. The `InputStream` and `OutputStream` classes are the root of all byte stream classes, and the `Reader` and `Writer` classes are the root of all character stream classes. The subclasses of `InputStream` and `OutputStream` are analogous to the subclasses of `Reader` and `Writer`. Many of them have similar method signatures, and you can use them in the same way.

File streams—`FileInputStream` and `FileOutputStream` for byte streams, `FileReader` and `FileWriter` for character streams—are used to read from or write data to external files. Data streams—`DataInputStream` and `DataOutputStream`—read or write Java primitive types in machine-independent fashion, which enables you to write a data file on one machine and read it on a machine that has a different OS or file structure.

Since the data output stream outputs a binary representation of data, you cannot view its content as text. The `PrintStream` and `PrintWriter` classes allow you to print streams in text format. `System.out`, `System.in`, and `System.err` are examples of `PrintStream` objects.

The `BufferedInputStream`, `BufferedOutputStream`, `BufferedReader`, and `BufferedWriter` classes can be used to speed input and output by reducing the number of reads and writes. Typical physical input/output involving I/O devices is very slow compared with CPU processing, so using buffered I/O can greatly improve performance.

The `StreamTokenizer` class is useful in processing text files. This class enables you to parse an input stream into tokens and read them one at a time.

The `RandomAccessFile` class enables you to read and write data to a file at the same time. You can open a file with the `"r"` mode to indicate that the file is read-only, or you can open a file with the `"rw"` mode to indicate that the file is updateable. Since the `RandomAccessFile` class implements `DataInput` and `DataOutput` interfaces, many methods in `RandomAccessFile` are the same as those in `DataInputStream` and `DataOutputStream`.

You can use the `JFileChooser` class to display standard file dialog boxes from which the user can navigate through the file systems and select files to load or save.

Chapter Review

15.1. Which streams must always be used to process external files?

15.2. What type of data is read or written by `InputStream` and `OutputStream`? Can you use `read()` or `write(byte b)` in those streams?

15.3. `InputStream` reads bytes. Why does the `read()` method return an `int` instead of a byte?

15.4. What type of data is read or written by `Reader` and `Writer`? Can you use `read()` or `write(char c)` in those streams?

15.5. What are the differences between byte streams and character streams?

15.6. What type of data are read or written by file streams? Can you use `read()` or `write(byte b)` in file streams?

15.7. How are the data input and output streams used to read and write data?

15.8. What are the differences between `DataOutputStream` and `PrintStream`?

15.9. Answer the following questions regarding `StreamTokenizer`:

- When do you use `StreamTokenizer`?
- How do you read data using `StreamTokenizer`?
- Where is the token stored when you are using the `nextToken()` method?
- How do you find the data type of the token?

15.10. Can you close a `StreamTokenizer`?

15.11. Can `RandomAccessFile` streams read a data file that is created by `DataOutputStream`?

15.12. Create a `RandomAccessFile` stream for the file **student.dat** to allow the updating of student information in the file. Create a `DataOutputStream` for the file **student.dat**. Describe the differences between these two statements.

15.13. What are the data types for `System.in`, `System.out`, and `System.err`?

15.14. Is `JFileChooser` modal? What is the return type for `getSelectedFile()` and `getSelectedDirectory()`? How do you set the current directory as the default directory for a `JFileChooser` dialog?

15.15. What happens if the file test.dat does not exist when you attempt to compile and run the following code?

```java
import java.io.*;

class Test
{
  public static void main(String[] args)
  {
    try
    {
      RandomAccessFile raf =
        new RandomAccessFile("test.dat", "r");
      int i = raf.readInt();
    }
    catch(IOException ex)
    {
      System.out.println("IO exception");
    }
  }
}
```

Programming Exercises

15.1. Rewrite Example 15.1, "Processing External Files," using `FileReader` and `FileWriter` streams. Write another program with buffered streams to boost performance. Test the performance of these two programs (one with buffered streams and the other without buffered streams), as shown in Figure 15.20.

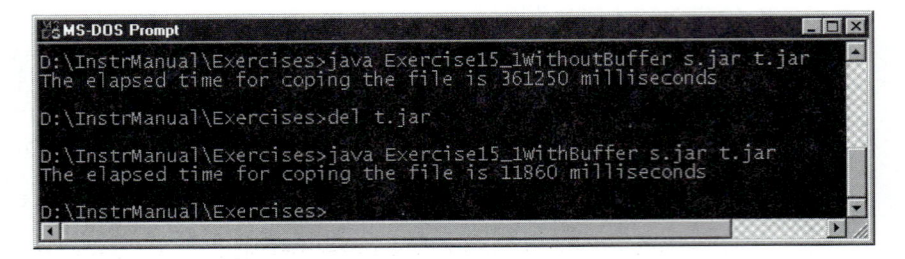

Figure 15.20 *Buffered streams can significantly boost performance.*

15.2. Write a program that will count the number of characters, including blanks, words, and lines, in a file. The filename should be passed as a command-line argument, as shown in Figure 15.21.

Figure 15.21 *The program displays number of characters, words, and lines in the given file.*

15.3. Use `StreamTokenizer` to write a program that will add all of the integers in a data file. Suppose that the integers are delimited by spaces. Display the result on the console. Rewrite the program, assuming this time that the numbers are `double`.

15.4. Rewrite Example 15.5, "Using `StreamTokenizer`," so that it reads a line as a string in a `BufferedReader` stream, and then use `StringTokenizer` to extract the fields.

15.5. Rewrite Example 15.4, "Displaying a File in a Text Area," to enable the user to view the file by opening it from a file open dialog box, as shown in Figure 15.22. A file open dialog box is displayed when the Browse button is clicked. The file is displayed in the text area, and the filename is displayed in the text field when the OK button is clicked in the file open dialog box. You can also enter the filename in the text field and press the Enter key to display the file in the text area.

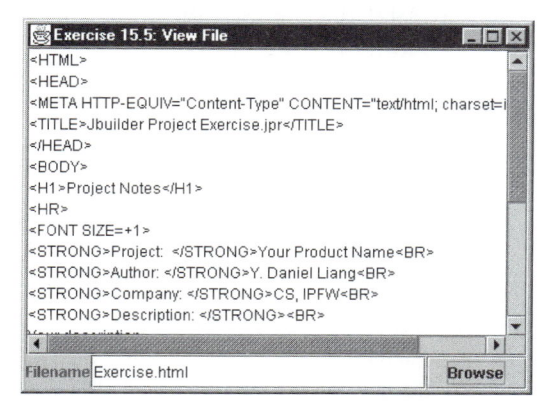

Figure 15.22 *The program enables the user to view a file by selecting it from a file open dialog box.*

15.6. Write a Java application that will display a stock index ticker, as shown in Figure 13.13 for Exercise 13.6. In that exercise, the stock index information is passed from the `<param>` tag in the HTML file.

Your program will get index information from an external text file. The first line in the file contains an integer, which indicates the number of stock indices given in the file. Each subsequent line should consist of four fields:

Index Name, Current Time, Previous Day Index, and Index Change. The fields are separated by the pound sign (#). The file could contain two lines, such as the following:

```
2
"S&P 500"#15:54#919.01#4.54
"NIKKEI"#04:03#1865.17#-7.00
```

15.7. Write a program that will display a histogram on a panel. The histogram should show the occurrence of each letter in a text file, as shown in Figure 15.23. Assume that the letters are not case-sensitive.

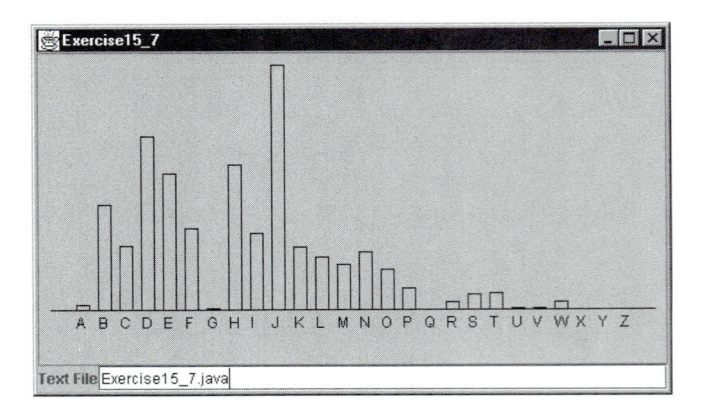

Figure 15.23 *The program displays a histogram that shows the occurrence of each letter in the file.*

- Place a panel that will display the histogram in the center of the frame.
- Place a label and a text field in a panel, and put the panel in the south side of the frame. The text file will be entered from this text field.
- Pressing the Enter key on the text field causes the program to count the occurrences of each letter and display the count in a histogram.

15.8. Modify the View Student panel in Example 15.6, "Using Random Access Files," to add an Update button for updating the student record that is being displayed, as shown in Figure 15.24. The Tab "View Student" is now changed to "View and Update Student."

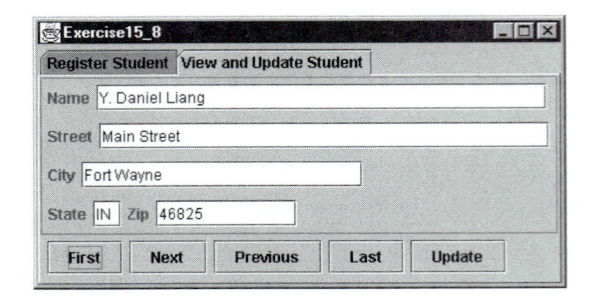

Figure 15.24 *You can browse student records and update the student record that is currently displayed.*

CHAPTER **16**

NETWORKING

Objectives

- Comprehend socket-based communication in Java.
- Understand client/server computing.
- Implement Java networking programs.
- Produce servers for multiple clients.
- Create applets that connect to servers.
- Write programs that will work with Web servers.

Introduction

Network programming in Java is tightly integrated. *Socket-based communication* is provided that enables programs to communicate through designated sockets. A *socket* is an abstraction that facilitates communication between a server and a client. Java treats socket communications much as it treats I/O operations; thus programs can read from or write to sockets as easily as they can read from or write to files.

Java supports *stream socket* and *datagram socket.* Stream sockets use TCP (Transmission Control Protocol) for data transmission, whereas datagram sockets use UDP (User Datagram Protocol). Since TCP can detect lost transmissions and resubmit them, transmissions are lossless and reliable. UDP, in contrast, cannot guarantee lossless transmission. Because of this, stream sockets are used in most areas of Java programming, and that is why the discussion in this chapter is based on stream sockets.

Client/Server Computing

Network programming usually involves a server and one or more clients. The client sends requests to the server, and the server responds to the requests. The client begins by attempting to establish a connection to the server. The server can accept or deny the connection. Once a connection is established, the client and server communicate through sockets.

The server must be running when a client starts. The server waits for a connection request from a client. The statements needed to create a server and a client and to exchange data between them are shown in Figure 16.1.

Server

```
int port = 8000;
BufferedReader in;
PrintWriter out;
ServerSocket serv;
Socket socket;

serv=new ServerSocket(port);
socket=serv.accept();
in=new new BufferedReader(
      new InputStreamReader(
         (socket.getInputStream())));
out=new PrintWriter
      (socket.getOutputStream());
System.out.println(in.readLine());
out.println("…");
```

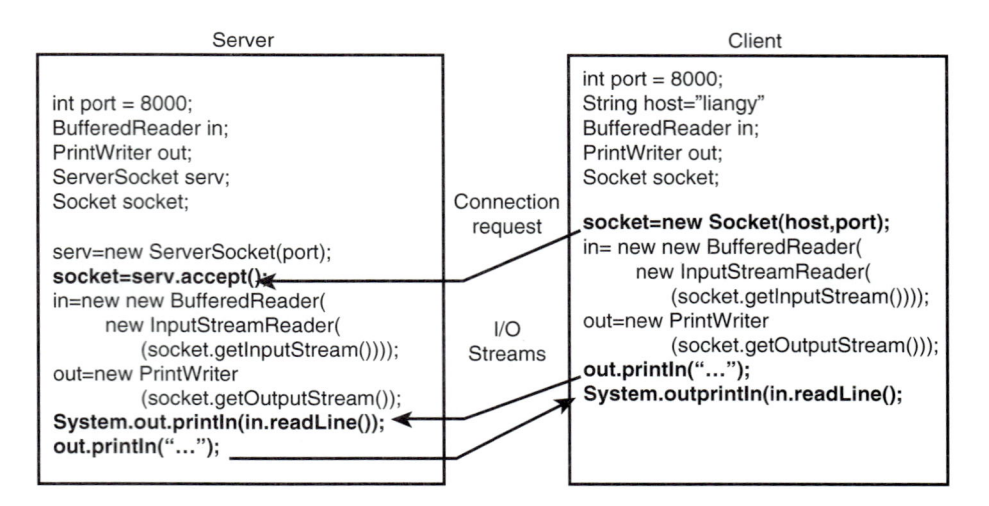

Client

```
int port = 8000;
String host="liangy"
BufferedReader in;
PrintWriter out;
Socket socket;

socket=new Socket(host,port);
in= new new BufferedReader(
       new InputStreamReader(
          (socket.getInputStream())));
out=new PrintWriter
       (socket.getOutputStream());
out.println("…");
System.outprintln(in.readLine());
```

Figure 16.1 *The server uses I/O streams to establish a server socket that facilitates communication between the server and the client.*

To establish a server, you need to create a server socket and attach it to a port, which is where the server listens for connections. The port identifies the TCP service on the socket. Port numbers between 0 and 1023 are reserved for privileged processes. For instance, the e-mail server runs on port 25, and the Web server usually runs on port 80. You can choose any port number that is not currently used by any other process. The following statement creates a server socket s:

```
ServerSocket s = new ServerSocket(port);
```

> **NOTE**
> Attempting to create a server socket on a port already in use would cause the `java.net.BindException` runtime exception.

After a server socket is created, the server can use the following statement to listen for connections:

```
Socket connectToClient = s.accept();
```

This statement waits until a client connects to the server socket. The client issues the following statement to request a connection to a server:

```
Socket connectToServer = new Socket(ServerName, port);
```

This statement opens a socket so that the client program can communicate with the server. *ServerName* is the server's Internet hostname or IP address. The following statement creates a socket at port 8000 on the client machine to connect to the host liangy.ipfw.edu:

```
Socket connectToServer = new Socket("liangy.ipfw.edu", 8000);
```

Alternatively, you can use the IP address to create a socket, as follows:

```
Socket connectToServer = new Socket("149.164.29.27", 8000)
```

An IP address, consisting of four dotted decimal numbers between 0 and 255, such as 149.164.29.27, is a computer's unique identity on the Internet. Since it is not easy to remember so many numbers, they are often mapped to meaningful names called *hostnames,* such as liangy.ipfw.edu.

> **NOTE**
> There are special servers on the Internet that translate hostnames into IP addresses. These servers are called Domain Name Servers (or DNS). The translation is done behind the scenes. When you create a socket with the hostname, the Java Runtime System asks the DNS to translate the hostname into the IP address.

After the server accepts the connection, communication between the server and the client is conducted the same as for I/O streams. To get an input stream and an output stream, use the `getInputStream()` and `getOutputStream()` methods on a socket object. For example, the following statements create an `InputStream` stream, isFromServer, and an OutputStream stream, osToServer, from the socket connect-ToServer:

```
InputStream isFromServer = connectToServer.getInputStream();

OutputStream osToServer = connectToServer.getOutputStream();
```

The InputStream and OutputStream streams are used to read or write bytes. You can use DataInputStream, DataOutputStream, BufferedReader, and PrintWriter to wrap on the InputStream, and OutputStream to read or write values of data, such as int, double, or String. The following statements, for instance, create a BufferedReader stream, isFromClient, and a PrintWriter stream, osToClient, to read and write primitive data values:

```
BufferedReader isFromClient = new BufferedReader(
  new InputStreamReader(connectToClient.getInputStream()));
PrintWriter osToClient = new PrintWriter(
  connectToClient.getOutputStream(), true);
```

The Boolean true is for auto flush, and the print() method flushes the output buffer. The server can use isFromClient.read() to receive data from the client, and osToClient.write() to send data to the client.

Example 16.1 A Client/Server Example

This example presents a client program and a server program. The client sends data to a server. The server receives the data, uses them to produce a result, and then sends the result back to the client. The client displays the result on the console. In this example, the datum sent from the client is the radius of a circle, and the result produced by the server is the area of the circle (see Figure 16.2).

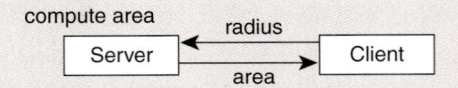

Figure 16.2 *The client sends the radius to the server; the server computes the area and sends it to the client.*

The server program follows. A sample run of the program is shown in Figure 16.3.

```
// Server.java: The server accepts data from the client, processes it
// and returns the result back to the client

import java.io.*;
import java.net.*;
import java.util.*;

public class Server
{
  // Main method
  public static void main(String[] args)
```

```java
{
  try
  {
    // Create a server socket
    ServerSocket serverSocket = new ServerSocket(8000);

    // Start listening for connections on the server socket
    Socket connectToClient = serverSocket.accept();

    // Create a buffered reader stream to get data from the client
    BufferedReader isFromClient = new BufferedReader(new
      InputStreamReader(connectToClient.getInputStream()));

    // Create a buffered writer stream to send data to the client
    PrintWriter osToClient = new PrintWriter(
      connectToClient.getOutputStream(), true);

    // Continuously read from the client and process it,
    // and send result back to the client
    while (true)
    {
      // Read a line and create a string tokenizer
      StringTokenizer st = new StringTokenizer
        (isFromClient.readLine());

      // Convert string to double
      double radius = new Double(st.nextToken()).doubleValue();

      // Display radius on console
      System.out.println("radius received from client: "
        +radius);

      // Compute area
      double area = radius*radius*Math.PI;

      // Send the result to the client
      osToClient.println(area);

      // Print the result to the console
      System.out.println("Area found: "+area);
    }
  }
  catch(IOException ex)
  {
    System.err.println(ex);
  }
 }
}
```

The client program follows. A sample run of the program is shown in Figure 16.4.

```java
// Client.java: The client sends the input to the server and receives
// result back from the server

import java.io.*;
import java.net.*;
import java.util.*;
import MyInput;
```

continues

```java
public class Client
{
  // Main method
  public static void main(String[] args)
  {
    try
    {
      // Create a socket to connect to the server
      Socket connectToServer = new Socket("localhost",8000);

      // Create a buffered input stream to receive data
      // from the server
      BufferedReader isFromServer = new BufferedReader(
        new InputStreamReader(connectToServer.getInputStream()));

      // Create a buffered output stream to send data to the server
      PrintWriter osToServer =
        new PrintWriter(connectToServer.getOutputStream(), true);

      // Continuously send radius and receive area
      // from the server
      while (true)
      {
        // Read the radius from the keyboard
        System.out.print("Please enter a radius: ");
        double radius = MyInput.readDouble();

        // Send the radius to the server
        osToServer.println(radius);

        // Get area from the server
        StringTokenizer st = new StringTokenizer(
          isFromServer.readLine());

        // Convert string to double
        double area = new Double(
          st.nextToken ()).doubleValue();

        // Print area on the console
        System.out.println("Area received from the server is "
          +area);
      }
    }
    catch (IOException ex)
    {
      System.err.println(ex);
    }
  }
}
```

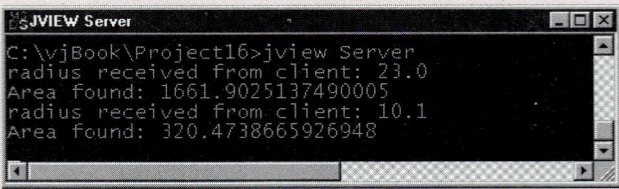

```
C:\vjBook\Project16>jview Server
radius received from client: 23.0
Area found: 1661.9025137490005
radius received from client: 10.1
Area found: 320.4738665926948
```

Figure 16.3 *The server receives a radius from the client, computes the area, and sends the area to the client.*

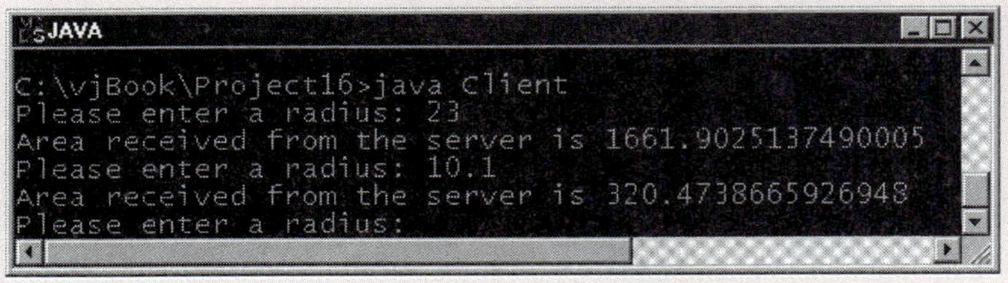

```
C:\vjBook\Project16>java Client
Please enter a radius: 23
Area received from the server is 1661.9025137490005
Please enter a radius: 10.1
Area received from the server is 320.4738665926943
Please enter a radius:
```

Figure 16.4 *The client sends the radius to the server and receives the area from the server.*

Example Review

You should start the server program first, then start the client program. The client program prompts the user to enter a radius, which is sent to the server. The server computes the area and sends it back to the client. This process is repeated until one of the two programs terminates. To terminate a program, press Ctrl+C on the console.

The networking classes are in the package `java.net`. This should be imported when writing Java network programs.

The `Server` class creates a `ServerSocket` `serverSocket` and attaches it to port 8000, using the following statement:

```
ServerSocket serverSocket = new ServerSocket(8000);
```

The server then starts to listen for connection requests, using the following statement:

```
Socket connectToClient = serverSocket.accept();
```

The server waits until a client requests a connection. After it is connected, the server reads radius from the client through an input stream, computes area, and sends the result to the client through an output stream.

The `Client` class uses the following statement to create a socket that will request a connection to the server at port 8000.

```
Socket connectToServer = new Socket("localhost", 8000);
```

The hostname `localhost` refers to the machine on which the client is running. If you run the server and the client on different machines, replace `localhost` with the server machine's hostname or IP address. In this example, the server and the client are running on the same machine.

If the server is not running, the client program terminates with an `IOException`. After it is connected, the client gets input and output streams—wrapped by buffered reader and writer streams—in order to receive and send data to the server.

Serving Multiple Clients

Multiple clients are quite often connected to a single server at the same time. Typically, a server runs constantly on a server computer, and clients from all over the Internet may want to connect to it. You can use threads to handle the server's multiple clients simultaneously. Simply create a thread for each connection. Here is how the server should handle the establishment of a connection:

```
while (true)
{
  Socket connectToClient = serverSocket.accept();
  Thread t = new ThreadClass(connectToClient);
  t.start();
}
```

The server socket can have many connections. Each iteration of the `while` loop creates a new connection. Whenever a connection is established, a new thread is created to handle communication between the server and the new client; and this allows multiple connections to run at the same time.

Example 16.2 Serving Multiple Clients

This example shows how to serve multiple clients simultaneously. For each connection, the server starts a new thread. This thread continuously receives input (the radius of a circle) from a client and sends the result (the area of the circle) back to the client (see Figure 16.5).

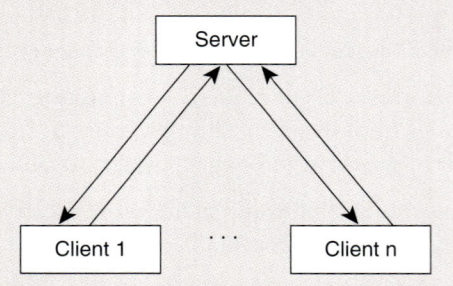

Figure 16.5 *Multithreading enables a server to handle multiple independent clients.*

The new server program follows. A sample run of the server is shown in Figure 16.6, and sample runs of two clients are shown in Figures 16.7 and 16.8.

```
// MultiThreadsServer.java: The server can communicate with
// multiple clients concurrently using the multiple threads
import java.io.*;
import java.net.*;
import java.util.*;

public class MultiThreadsServer
{
  // Main method
  public static void main(String[] args)
```

```java
    {
      try
      {
        // Create a server socket
        ServerSocket serverSocket = new ServerSocket(8000);

        // To number a thread
        int i = 0;

        while (true)
        {
          // Listen for a new connection request
          Socket connectToClient = serverSocket.accept();

          // Print the new connect number on the console
          System.out.println("Starting thread "+i);

          // Create a new thread for the connection
          ThreadHandler thread = new ThreadHandler(connectToClient, i);

          // Start the new thread
          thread.start();

          // Increment i to number the next connection
          i++;
        }
      }
      catch(IOException ex)
      {
        System.err.println(ex);
      }
    }
  }

  // Define the thread class for handling a new connection
  class ThreadHandler extends Thread
  {
    private Socket connectToClient; // A connected socket
    private int counter; // Number the thread

    // Construct a thread
    public ThreadHandler(Socket socket, int i)
    {
      connectToClient = socket;
      counter = i;
    }

    // Implement the run() method for the thread
    public void run()
    {
      try
      {
        // Create data input and print streams
        BufferedReader isFromClient = new BufferedReader(
          new InputStreamReader(connectToClient.getInputStream()));
        PrintWriter osToClient =
          new PrintWriter(connectToClient.getOutputStream(), true);

        // Continuously serve the client
        while (true)
```

continues

```java
        {
          // Receive data from the client in string
          StringTokenizer st = new StringTokenizer
            (isFromClient.readLine());

          // Get radius
          double radius = new Double(st.nextToken()).doubleValue();
          System.out.println("radius received from client: "+radius);

          // Compute area
          double area = radius*radius*Math.PI;

          // Send area back to the client
          osToClient.println(area);
          System.out.println("Area found: "+area);
        }
      }
      catch(IOException ex)
      {
        System.err.println(ex);
      }
    }
  }
}
```

Figure 16.6 *The server spawns a thread in order to serve a client.*

Figure 16.7 *The first client communicates to the server on thread 0.*

Figure 16.8 *The second client communicates to the server on thread 1.*

Example Review

The server creates a server socket at port 8000 and waits for a connection. When a connection with a client is established, the server creates a new thread to handle the communication. It then waits for another connection.

The threads, which run independently of one another, communicate with designated clients. Each thread creates buffered reader and writer streams that receive and send data to the client.

This server accepts an unlimited number of clients. To limit the number of concurrent connections, you can use a thread group to monitor the number of active threads and modify the `while` loop, as follows:

```
ThreadGroup g = new ThreadGroup("serving clients");

while (g.activeCount() < maxThreadLimit)
{
  // Listen for a new connection request
  Socket connectToClient = serverSocket.accept();

  // Print the new connect number on the console
  System.out.println("Starting thread " + i);

  // Create a new thread for the connection
  Thread t = new Thread(g, new ThreadHandler(connectToClient, i));

  // Start the new thread
  t.start();

  // Increment i to label the next connection
  i++;
}
```

Windows has a Telnet utility. Telnet can be used to log onto another host and to communicate with other services on the host. Telnet can be used as clients to test the server. This is convenient if you don't have the client program in place.

You can enter the `telnet` command from the DOS prompt to display a Telnet window, as shown in Figure 16.9. In the Telnet window, choose Connect, Remote System to display the Connect dialog box. Enter the server's hostname and port number, and press Connect. You must have the server already running. Here is a sample run with a server running, as shown in Figure 16.10, and with the Telnet session running, as shown in Figure 16.11.

continues

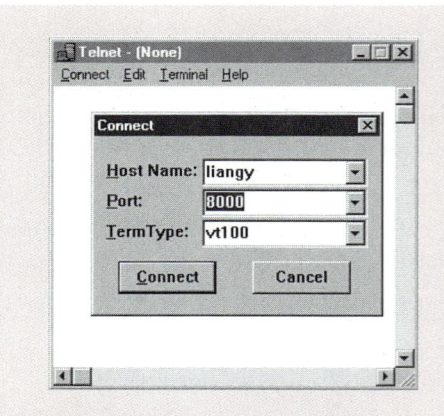

Figure 16.9 *A Telnet client connects to the server on port 8000.*

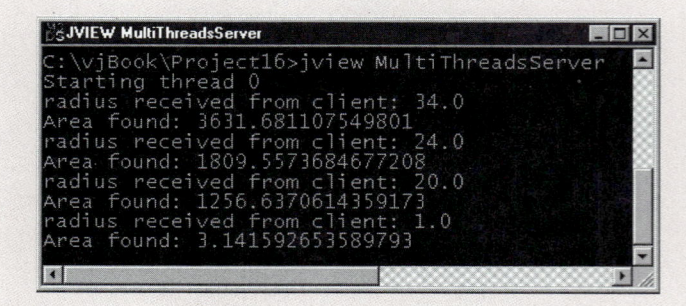

Figure 16.10 *The server receives the radii 34, 24, 20, and 1 from the Telnet client and sends the corresponding areas to the client.*

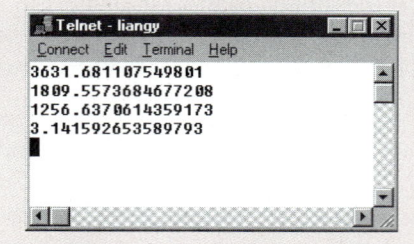

Figure 16.11 *The user enters the radius (not echo printed in the window). The Telnet client sends the radius to the server and receives the area that is displayed in the Telnet window.*

Applet Clients

Due to security constraints, applets can only connect to the host from which they were loaded. Therefore, the HTML file must be located on the machine on which the server is running. Directly below is an example of how to use an applet to connect to a server.

Example 16.3 Networking in Applets

This example, which is similar to Example 15.6, "Using Random Access Files," in Chapter 15, "Input and Output," shows how to use an applet to register students. The client collects and sends registration information to the server. The server appends the information to a data file using a random access file stream. The server program follows. A sample run of this program is shown in Figure 16.12.

```java
// RegServer.java: The server for the applet responsible for
// writing on the server side
import java.io.*;
import java.net.*;
import Student;

public class RegServer
{
  // Main method
  public static void main(String[] args)
  {
    // A random access file
    RandomAccessFile raf = null;

    // Open the local file on the server side
    try
    {
      // Open the file if the file exists, create a new file
      // if the file does not exist
      raf = new RandomAccessFile("student.dat", "rw");
    }
    catch(IOException ex)
    {
      System.out.println("Error: " + ex);
      System.exit(0);
    }

    // Establish server socket
    try
    {
      // Create a server socket
      ServerSocket serverSocket = new ServerSocket(8000);

      // Count the number of threads started
      int count = 1;

      while (true)
      {
        // Connect to a client
        Socket socket = serverSocket.accept();

        // Start a new thread to register a client
        new RegistrationThread(raf, socket, count++).start();
      }
    }
    catch (IOException ex)
    {
      System.err.println(ex);
    }
  }
}
```

continues

```java
// Define a thread to process the client registration
class RegistrationThread extends Thread
{
  // The socket to serve a client
  private Socket socket;

  // The file to store the records
  static RandomAccessFile raf = null;

  private int num; // The thread number

  // Buffered reader to get input from the client
  private BufferedReader in;

  // Create a registration thread
  public RegistrationThread(RandomAccessFile raf,
    Socket socket, int num)
  {
    this.raf = raf;
    this.socket = socket;
    this.num = num;

    System.out.println("Thread " + num + " running");

    // Create an input stream to receive data from a client
    try
    {
      in = new BufferedReader
        (new InputStreamReader(socket.getInputStream()));
    }
    catch(IOException ex)
    {
      System.out.println("Error: " + ex);
    }
  }

  public void run()
  {
    String name;
    String street;
    String city;
    String state;
    String zip;

    try
    {
      // Receive data from the client
      name = new String(in.readLine());
      street = new String(in.readLine());
      city = new String(in.readLine());
      state = new String(in.readLine());
      zip = new String(in.readLine());

      // Display data received
      System.out.println(
        "The following data received from the client");
      System.out.println("name: " + name);
      System.out.println("street: " + street);
      System.out.println("city: " + city);
      System.out.println("state: " + state);
      System.out.println("zip: " + zip);
```

```
      // Create a student instance
      Student student = new Student(name, street, city, state, zip);

      writeToFile(student);
    }
    catch (IOException ex)
    {
      System.out.println(ex);
    }
  }

  private synchronized static void writeToFile(Student student)
  {
    try
    {
    // Append it to "student.dat"
    raf.seek(raf.length());
    student.writeStudent(raf);
    }
    catch (IOException ex)
    {
      System.err.println(ex);
    }
  }
}
```

The applet client follows, and its sample run is shown in Figure 16.13.

```
// RegClient.java: The applet client for gathering student
// informationthe and passing it to the server
import java.io.*;
import java.net.*;
import java.awt.BorderLayout;
import java.awt.event.*;
import javax.swing.*;

public class RegClient extends JApplet implements ActionListener
{
  // Button for registering a student in the file
  private JButton jbtRegister = new JButton("Register");

  // Create student information panel
  private StudentPanel studentPanel = new StudentPanel();

  public void init()
  {
    // Add the student panel and button to the applet
    getContentPane().add(studentPanel, BorderLayout.CENTER);
    getContentPane().add(jbtRegister, BorderLayout.SOUTH);

    // Register listener
    jbtRegister.addActionListener(this);
  }

  // Handle button action
  public void actionPerformed(ActionEvent e)
  {
    if (e.getSource() == jbtRegister)
    {
      try
```

continues

```java
    {
      // Establish connection with the server
      Socket socket = new Socket("localhost", 8000);

      // Create an output stream to the server
      PrintWriter toServer =
        new PrintWriter(socket.getOutputStream(), true);

      // Get text field
      Student s = studentPanel.getStudent();

      // Get data from text fields and send it to the server
      toServer.println(s.getName());
      toServer.println(s.getStreet());
      toServer.println(s.getCity());
      toServer.println(s.getState());
      toServer.println(s.getZip());
    }
    catch (IOException ex)
    {
      System.err.println(ex);
    }
  }
}

// Run the applet as an application
public static void main(String[] args)
{
  // Create a frame
  MyFrameWithExitHandling frame = new MyFrameWithExitHandling(
    "Register Student Client");

  // Create an instance of the applet
  RegClient applet = new RegClient();

  // Add the applet instance to the frame
  frame.getContentPane().add(applet, BorderLayout.CENTER);

  // Invoke init() and start()
  applet.init();
  applet.start();

  // Display the frame
  frame.pack();
  frame.setVisible(true);
  }
}
```

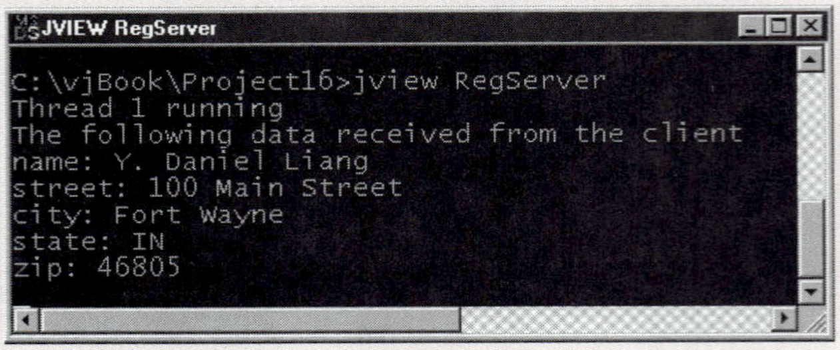

```
C:\vjBook\Project16>jview RegServer
Thread 1 running
The following data received from the client
name: Y. Daniel Liang
street: 100 Main Street
city: Fort Wayne
state: IN
zip: 46805
```

Figure 16.12 *The server receives information (name, street, city, state, and zip code) from the client, and stores it in a file.*

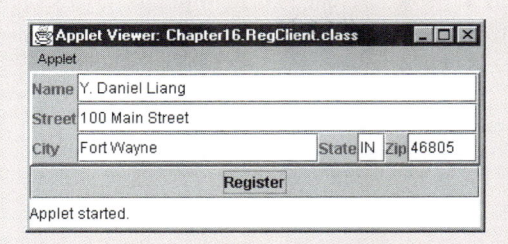

Figure 16.13 *The client gathers the name and address and sends them to the server.*

Example Review

The server handles multiple clients. It waits for a connection request from the client in the `while` loop. After the connection with a client is established, the server creates a thread to serve the client. The server then stays in the `while` loop to listen for the next connection request.

The server passes `raf` (random access file stream), `socket` (connection socket), and `num` (thread number) to the thread. The `num` argument is nonessential; its only use is to identify the thread. The thread receives student information from the client through the `BufferedReader` stream and appends a student record to **student.dat,** using the random access file stream `raf`.

The `StudentPanel` and `Student` classes are defined in Example 15.6. The statement given below creates an instance of `Student`:

```
Student s = new Student(name, street, city, state, zip);
```

The next code writes the student record into the file:

```
s.writeStudent(raf);
```

The client is an applet and can run standalone. The data are entered into text fields (name, street, city, state, and zip). When the Register button is clicked, the data from the text fields are collected and sent to the server.

When multiple clients register students simultaneously, data may be corrupted. To avoid this, the `writeToFile()` method is synchronized and defined as a static method. The synchronization is at the class level, meaning that only one object of the `RegistrationThread` at a time can execute the `writeToFile()` method to write a student to the file.

Viewing Web Pages

Given the URL, a Web browser can view an HTML page, for example, **http://www.sun.com.** HTTP is the common standard used for communication between Web servers and the Internet. You can open a URL and view a Web page in a Java applet. A URL is a description of a resource location on the Internet. Java provides a class, `java.net.URL`, to manipulate URLs. The following code can be written to create a URL:

```java
try
{
  URL location = new URL(URLString);
}
catch(MalformedURLException ex)
{
}
```

The following statement creates a Java URL object:

```java
try
{
  URL location = new URL("http://www.sun.com");
}
catch(MalformedURLException ex)
{
}
```

A `MalformedURLException` is thrown if the URL string has a syntax error. For example, the URL string `"http:/www.sun.com"` would cause the `MalformedURLException` runtime error because two slashes (//) are required.

To actually view the contents of an HTML page, you would need to write the following code:

```java
AppletContext context = getAppletContext();
context.showDocument(location);
```

The `java.applet.AppletContext` class provides the environment for displaying Web page contents. The `showDocument()` method displays the Web page in the environment.

Example 16.4 Viewing HTML Pages from Java

This example demonstrates an applet that views Web pages. The Web page's URL is entered, the Go button is clicked, and the Web page is displayed (see Figures 16.14 and 16.15).

```java
// ViewingWebPages.java: Access HTML pages through applets
import java.net.*;
import java.awt.*;
import java.awt.event.*;
import javax.swing.*;
import java.applet.*;

public class ViewingWebPages extends JApplet implements
  ActionListener
{
  // Button to display an HTML page on the applet
  private JButton jbtGo = new JButton("Go");

  // Text field for receiving the URL of the HTML page
  private JTextField jtfURL = new JTextField(20);
```

```
     // Initialize the applet
     public void init()
     {
       // Add URL text field and Go button
       getContentPane().setLayout(new FlowLayout());
       getContentPane().add(new JLabel("URL"));
       getContentPane().add(jtfURL);
       getContentPane().add(jbtGo);

       // Register listener
       jbtGo.addActionListener(this);
     }

     // Handle the ActionEvent
     public void actionPerformed(ActionEvent evt)
     {
       if (evt.getSource() == jbtGo)
         try
         {
           AppletContext context = getAppletContext();

           // Get the URL from text field
           URL url = new URL(jtfURL.getText());
           context.showDocument(url);
         }
         catch(Exception ex)
         {
           showStatus("Error " + ex);
         }
     }
   }
```

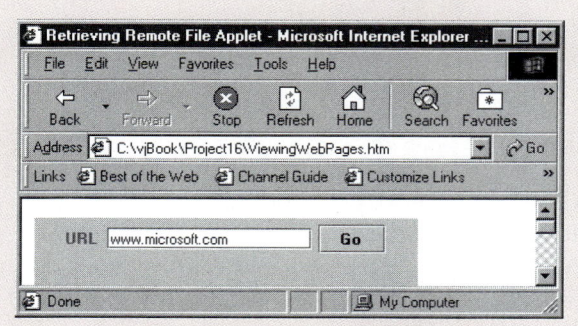

Figure 16.14 *Given the URL, the applet can display a Web page.*

continues

Figure 16.15 *The Web page specified in the applet is displayed in the browser.*

Example Review

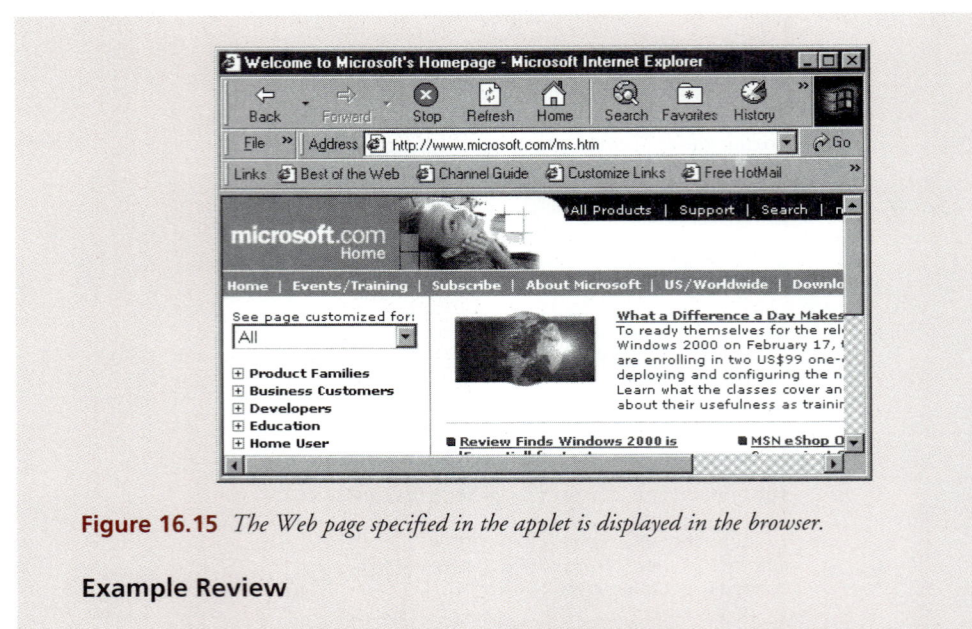

When the URL of a publicly available HTML file is entered and the Go button is clicked, a new HTML page is displayed. The page containing the applet becomes the previous page. A user could return to the previous page to enter a new URL and then view the new page.

Anyone using this program would have to run it from a Web browser, not from the Applet Viewer utility.

Retrieving Files from Web Servers

You can display an HTML page from an applet, as shown in the preceding section. But sometimes you need the Web server to give you access to the contents of a file. This access allows you to pass dynamic information from the server to the applet clients or the standalone application clients, as shown in Figure 16.16. The file stored on the server side can be a normal text file or a binary file that is created using `DataOutput` streams. To access the file, you would use the `openStream()` method defined in the URL class to open a stream to the file's URL.

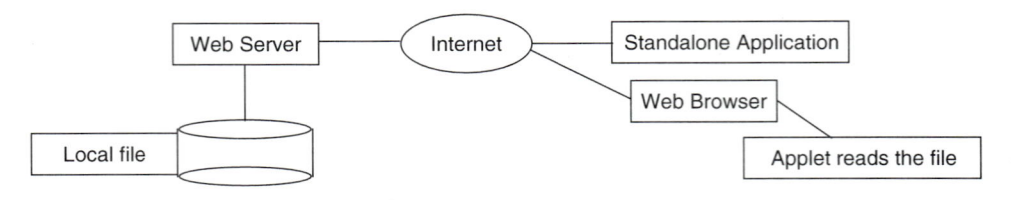

Figure 16.16 *The applet client or application client retrieves files from a Web server.*

The following method opens a connection to the file's URL and returns an `InputStream` so that you can read from the connection:

```
public final InputStream openStream() throws IOException
```

The following statements, for example, open an input stream for the URL **http://www.ipfw.edu/kt2/liangy/web/java/in.dat** for the file **in.dat,** which is stored on the author's Web server.

```
try
{
  String urlString = "http://www.ipfw.edu/kt2/liangy/web/java/in.dat";
  url = new URL(urlString);
  InputStream is = url.openStream();
}
catch (MalformedURLException ex)
{
  System.out.println("Bad URL : " + url);
}
catch (IOException ex)
{
  System.out.println("IO Error : " + ex.getMessage());
}
```

Example 16.5 Retrieving Remote Data Files

This example, which is similar to Example 15.5, "Using `StreamTokenizer`," in Chapter 15, "Input and Output," demonstrates an applet that computes and displays student exam scores.

The example reads the file from a Web server rather than from the local system. The file contains student exam scores. Each record in the input file consists of a student name, two midterm exam scores, and a final exam score. The program reads the fields for each record, computes the total score, and displays the result in a text area. Figure 16.17 contains the output of a sample run of the program.

```java
// RetrievingRemoteFile.java: Retrieve remote files in applets.
// This program can also run as an application.
import java.applet.Applet;
import java.awt.*;
import java.io.*;
import java.net.*;
import javax.swing.*;

public class RetrievingRemoteFile extends JApplet
{
  // The author's Web site URL string for the input file
  private String urlString =
    // Get in.dat from a remote host
    "http://www.ipfw.edu/kt2/liangy/web/java/in.dat";
    // Get in.dat from the local file system
    //"file:/C:\\vjBook\\Project16\\in.dat";

  // Declare a Java URL object
  private URL url;
```

continues

```java
// The StreamTokenizer for parsing input
private StreamTokenizer in;

// The fields in the file
private String sname = null;
private double midterm1 = 0;
private double midterm2 = 0;
private double finalScore = 0;

// Total score for a student
private double total = 0;

// Text area for displaying result
JTextArea jta = new JTextArea(5, 10);

// Initialize the applet
public void init()
{
  try
  {
    url = new URL(urlString);  // Create a URL
    InputStream is = url.openStream();  // Create a stream

    // Create streamtokenizer
    in = new StreamTokenizer(
      new BufferedReader(new InputStreamReader(is)));
  }
  catch (MalformedURLException ex)
  {
    System.out.println("Bad URL : " + url);
  }
  catch (IOException ex)
  {
    System.out.println("IO Error : " + ex.getMessage());
  }

  // Create a scroll pane and add text area to the scroll pane
  JScrollPane jsp = new JScrollPane(jta);

  // Add the scroll pane to the applet
  getContentPane().add(jsp);

  try
  {
    // Read first token
    in.nextToken();

    // Process a record
    while (in.ttype != in.TT_EOF)
    {
      // Get student name
      if (in.ttype == in.TT_WORD)
        sname = in.sval;
      else
        System.out.println("Bad file format");

      // Get midterm1
      if (in.nextToken() == in.TT_NUMBER)
        midterm1 = in.nval;
      else
        System.out.println("Bad file format");
```

```java
      // Get midterm2
      if (in.nextToken() == in.TT_NUMBER)
        midterm2 = in.nval;
      else
        System.out.println("Bad file format");

      // Get final score
      if (in.nextToken() == in.TT_NUMBER)
        finalScore = in.nval;

      // Compute total score
      total = midterm1*0.3 + midterm2*0.3 + finalScore*0.4;

      // Display result
      jta.append(sname + " " + total + '\n');

      // Get the next token
      in.nextToken();
    }
  }
  catch (IOException ex)
  {
    System.out.println("IO Errors " + ex.getMessage());
  }
}

// Run the applet as an application
public static void main(String[] args)
{
  // Create a frame
  MyFrameWithExitHandling frame = new MyFrameWithExitHandling(
    "Retrieve Remote File Demo");

  // Create an instance of the applet
  RetrievingRemoteFile applet = new RetrievingRemoteFile();

  // Add the applet instance to the frame
  frame.getContentPane().add(applet, BorderLayout.CENTER);

  // Invoke init() and start()
  applet.init();
  applet.start();

  // Display the frame
  frame.setSize(300, 300);
  frame.setVisible(true);
  }
}
```

continues

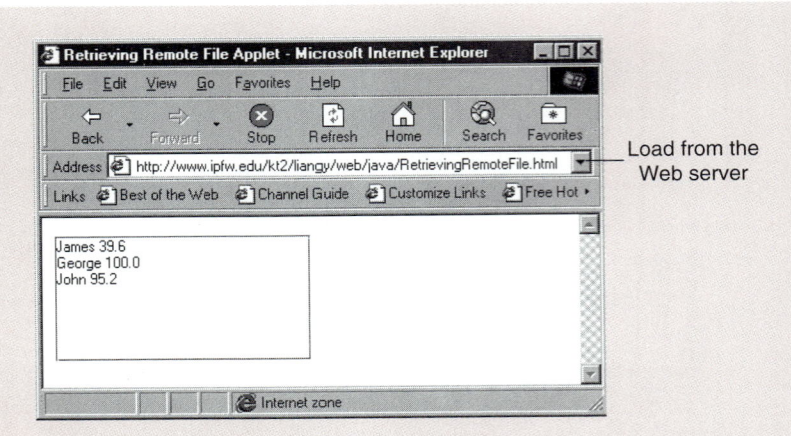

Figure 16.17 *The applet retrieves the file from the Web server and processes it.*

Example Review

This program can run as an applet or an application. In order for it to run as an applet, a user would need to place three files on the Web server:

RetrievingRemoteFile.class
RetrievingRemoteFile.html
in.dat

For convenience, the program assumes that these files are to be placed in one directory.

RetrievingRemoteFile.html can be browsed from any JDK 1.2-aware Web browser.

The `url = new URL(urlString)` statement creates a URL. The `InputStream is = url.openStream()` opens an input stream to read the remote file. After the input stream is established, reading data from the remote file is just like reading data locally.

The program uses `StreamTokenizer` to extract a student's name, two midterm exam scores, and the final exam score from the input stream; it computes the total score and displays it on the text area.

For this program to run as an application, you must place the following two files in the same directory:

RetrievingRemoteFile.class
in.dat

> **TIP**
> If you have no Internet access when testing this example, you can place all the files on your local disk and replace the urlString as follows:
>
> ```
> private String urlString = "file:/C:\\vjBook\\Project16\\in.dat";
> ```

Chapter Summary

In this chapter, you learned how to write client/server applications and programs that work with a Web server. In client/server computing, the server must be running when the client starts. The server waits for a connection request from a client.

To create a server, you must first obtain a server socket, using `new ServerSocket(port)`. After a server socket is created, the server can start to listen for connections, using the `accept()` method on the server socket. The client requests a connection to a server by using `new socket(ServerName, port)` to create a client socket.

Stream socket communication is very much like input/output stream communication after the connection between a server and a client is established. Server and client use `BufferedReader` and `PrintWriter` to communicate through input and output streams.

A server must often work with multiple clients at the same time. You can use threads to handle the server's multiple clients simultaneously by creating a thread for each connection.

Applets are recommended for deploying multiple clients. They can be run anywhere with a single copy of the program. However, an applet client can only connect to the server where the applet is loaded, due to security restrictions.

Java programs can get HTML pages through HTTP by directly connecting with a Web server. The URL can be used to view a Web page in a Java applet. To retrieve data files on the Web server from applets, you can open a stream on the file's URL on the Web server.

Chapter Review

16.1. How do you create a server socket? What port numbers can be used? What happens if a requested socket number is already in use? Can a port connect to multiple clients?

16.2. What are the differences between a server socket and a client socket?

16.3. How does a client program initiate a connection?

16.4. How does a server accept a connection?

16.5. How are data transferred between a client and a server?

16.6. How do you make a server serve multiple clients?

16.7. Can an application retrieve a file from a remote host? Can an application update a file on a remote host?

Programming Exercises

16.1. Rewrite Example 16.2 using GUI for the server and the client rather than console input and output. Display a message in the text area on the server side when the server receives a message from a client, as shown in Figure 16.18. On the client side, you can use a text field to enter the radius, as shown in Figure 16.19.

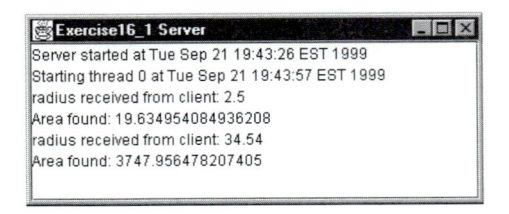

Figure 16.18 *The server receives a radius from a client, computes the area, and sends the area to the client.*

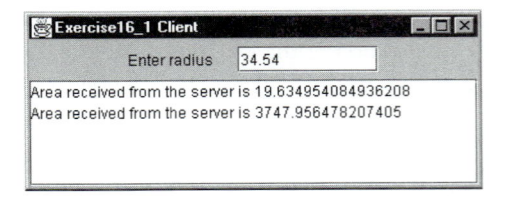

Figure 16.19 *The client sends the radius to the server and receives the area from the server.*

16.2. Write a client/server application. The client should retrieve a file from the Web server. The client can run as an application or as an applet—like the one in Example 15.4, "Displaying a File in a Text Area"—that includes a text field in which to enter the URL of the filename, a text area in which to show the file, and a button that can be used to submit an action. Also, add a label at the bottom of the frame to indicate the status, such as File loaded successfully or Network connection problem. Figure 16.20 is an example of how the file looks when viewed at **www.ipfw.edu/kt2/liangy/default.htm** located on the Web server. Swing provides a new component named `javax.swing.JEditorPane`, which can be used to render HTML files. For more information, see Chapter 5, "Swing Components," in my *Rapid Java Application Development Using JBuilder 3.*

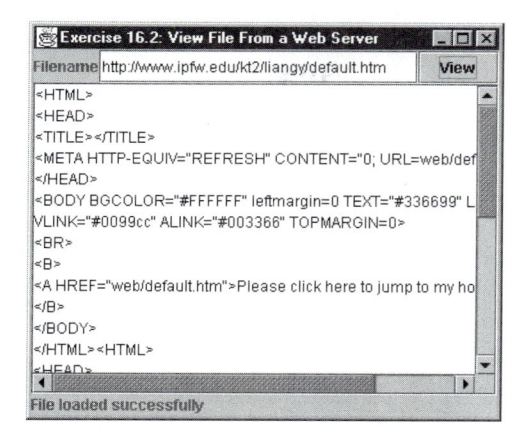

Figure 16.20 *The program displays the contents of a specified file on the Web server.*

16.3. Modify Example 16.3, "Networking in Applets," by adding the following features:

1. Add a View button to the user interface that allows the client to view a record for a specified name. The user will be able to enter a name in the Name field and click the View button to display the record for the student, as shown in Figure 16.21.

2. Limit the concurrent connections to two clients.

3. Display the status of the submission (Successful or Failed) on a label.

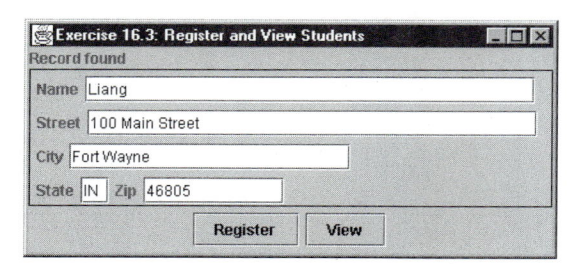

Figure 16.21 *You can view or register students in this applet.*

16.4. Write an applet—like the ones in Exercise 15.6. Ensure that the applet gets the stock index from a file stored on the Web server. Enable the applet to run standalone.

16.5. Write an applet that shows the number of visits made to a Web page. The count should be stored in a file on the server side. Every time the page is visited or reloaded, the applet should send a request to the server, and the server should increase the count and send it to the applet. The applet should then display the new count in a message, such as You are visitor number: 1000. The server can use a random file access stream to read or write to the file.

APPENDIXES

The appendixes cover a mixed bag of topics. Appendix A lists Java keywords. Appendix B gives tables of ASCII characters and their associated codes in decimal and in hex. Appendix C shows the operator precedence. Appendix D summarizes Java modifiers and their usage. Appendix E introduces HTML basics. Appendix F provides information on using the companion CD-ROM and installing the Swing library for graphics programming. Appendix G demonstrates rapid Java application development using Visual J++ 6.0. Finally, Appendix H provides a glossary of key terms and their definitions.

APPENDIX A   JAVA KEYWORDS

APPENDIX B   THE ASCII CHARACTER SET

APPENDIX C   OPERATOR PRECEDENCE CHART

APPENDIX D   JAVA MODIFIERS

APPENDIX E   AN HTML TUTORIAL

APPENDIX F   USING THE COMPANION CD-ROM AND INSTALLING THE SWING LIBRARY

APPENDIX G   RAPID JAVA APPLICATION DEVELOPMENT USING VISUAL J++ 6.0

APPENDIX H   GLOSSARY

APPENDIX A

JAVA KEYWORDS

The following 47 keywords are reserved for use by the Java language:

abstract	finally	public
boolean	float	return
break	for	short
byte	goto	static
case	if	super
catch	implements	switch
char	import	synchronized
class	instanceof	this
const	int	throw
continue	interface	throws
default	long	transient
do	native	try
double	new	void
else	package	volatile
extends	private	while
final	protected	

The keywords `goto` and `const` are C++ keywords reserved, but not currently used, in Java. This enables Java compilers to identify them and to produce better error messages if they appear in Java programs.

The Boolean literal values `true` and `false` are not keywords. Similarly, the `null` object value is not classified as a keyword. You cannot use them for other purposes, however.

APPENDIX B

THE ASCII CHARACTER SET

Tables B.1 and B.2 show ASCII characters and their respective decimal and hexadecimal codes. The decimal or hexadecimal code of a character is a combination of its row index and column index. For example, in Table B.1, the letter A is at row 6 and column 5, so its decimal equivalent is 65; in Table B.2, letter A is at row 4 and column 1, so its hexadecimal equivalent is 41.

TABLE B.1 ASCII Character Set in the Decimal Index

	0	1	2	3	4	5	6	7	8	9
0	nul	soh	stx	etx	eot	enq	ack	bel	bs	ht
1	nl	vt	ff	cr	so	si	dle	dcl	dc2	dc3
2	dc4	nak	syn	etb	can	em	sub	esc	fs	gs
3	rs	us	sp	!	"	#	$	%	&	'
4	(	)	*	+	,	-	.	/	0	1
5	2	3	4	5	6	7	8	9	:	;
6	<	=	>	?	@	A	B	C	D	E
7	F	G	H	I	J	K	L	M	N	O
8	P	Q	R	S	T	U	V	W	X	Y
9	Z	[	\	]	^	_	`	a	b	c
10	d	e	f	g	h	i	j	k	l	m
11	n	o	p	q	r	s	t	u	v	w
12	x	y	z	{	|	}	~	del		

APPENDIX B THE ASCII CHARACTER SET

TABLE B.2 ASCII Character Set in the Hexadecimal Index

	0	1	2	3	4	5	6	7	8	9	A	B	C	D	E	F
0	nul	soh	stx	etx	eot	enq	ack	bel	bs	ht	nl	vt	ff	cr	so	si
1	dle	dc1	dc2	dc3	dc4	nak	syn	etb	can	em	sub	esc	fs	gs	rs	us
2	sp	!	"	#	$	%	&	'	(	)	*	+	,	-	.	/
3	0	1	2	3	4	5	6	7	8	9	:	;	<	=	>	?
4	@	A	B	C	D	E	F	G	H	I	J	K	L	M	N	O
5	P	Q	R	S	T	U	V	W	X	Y	Z	[	\	]	^	_
6	`	a	b	c	d	e	f	g	h	i	j	k	l	m	n	o
7	p	q	r	s	t	u	v	w	x	y	z	{	|	}	~	del

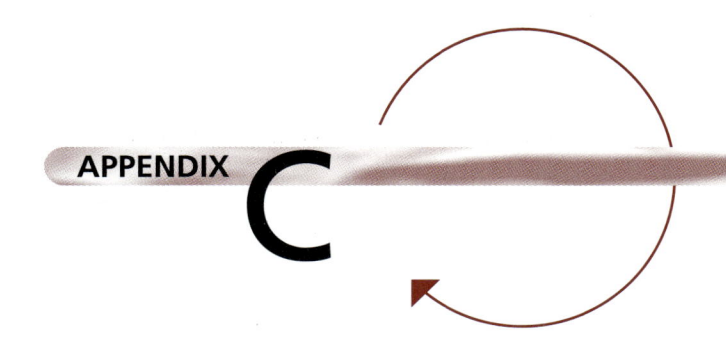

Operator Precedence Chart

The operators are shown in decreasing order of precedence from top to bottom. Operators in the same group have the same precedence and are executed from left to right.

Operator	Type
`()`	Parentheses
`()`	Function call
`[]`	Array subscript
`.`	Object member access
`++`	Prefix increment
`--`	Prefix decrement
`+`	Unary plus
`-`	Unary minus
`!`	Unary logical negation
`(type)`	Unary casting
`new`	Creating object
`*`	Multiplication
`/`	Division
`%`	Integer modulus
`+`	Addition
`-`	Subtraction
`<`	Less than
`<=`	Less than or equal to
`>`	Greater than
`>=`	Greater than or equal to
`instanceof`	Checking object type
`==`	Equal comparison
`!=`	Not equal
`&&`	Boolean AND
`||`	Boolean OR
`?:`	Ternary condition (Conditional expression)

Operator	Type
=	Assignment
+=	Addition assignment
-=	Subtraction assignment
*=	Multiplication assignment
/=	Division assignment
%=	Integer modulus assignment
++	Postfix increment
--	Postfix decrement

APPENDIX D

Java Modifiers

Modifiers are used on classes and class members (methods and data), but the `final` modifier can also be used on local variables in a method. A modifier that can be applied to a class is called a *class modifier*. A modifier that can be applied to a method is called a *method modifier*. A modifier that can be applied to a data field is called a *data modifier*. Some modifiers can be applied to all three entities. The following table gives a summary of the modifiers covered in this book.

Modifier	class	method	data	Explanation
`(default)`	✓	✓	✓	A class, method, or data field is visible in this package.
`public`	✓	✓	✓	A class, method, or data field is visible to all the programs in any package.
`private`		✓	✓	A method or data field is only visible in this class.
`protected`		✓	✓	A method or data field is visible in this package and in subclasses of this class in any package.
`static`		✓	✓	Define a class method or a class data field.
`final`	✓	✓	✓	A final class cannot be extended. A final method cannot be modified in a subclass. A final data field is a constant.
`abstract`	✓	✓		An abstract class must be extended. An abstract method must be overridden.
`synchronized`		✓		Only one thread can execute this method at a time.

APPENDIX E

AN HTML TUTORIAL

Java applets are embedded in HTML files. HTML (HyperText Markup Language) is a markup language used to design Web pages for creating and sharing multimedia-enabled, integrated electronic documents over the Internet. HTML allows documents on the Internet to be hyperlinked and presented using fonts and image and line justification appropriate for the systems on which they are displayed. The World Wide Web is a network of static and dynamic documents, including texts, sound, and images. The Internet has been around for more than thirty years, but has only recently become popular. The Web is the major reason for its popularity.

HTML documents are displayed by a program called a *Web browser*. When a document is coded in HTML, a Web browser interprets the HTML to identify the elements of the document and render it. The browser has control over the document's look and feel. At present there is no absolute unifying HTML standards. Different vendors have rushed to introduce their own features interpretable by their proprietary browsers. However, the differences aren't significant. This tutorial introduces some frequently used HTML features that have been adopted by most browsers.

There are many easy-to-use authoring tools for creating Web pages. For example, you may create HTML files using Microsoft Word. The Internet Explorer and Netscape Navigator have simple authoring tools to let you create and edit HTML files. Microsoft FrontPage is a comprehensive and fully loaded tool that enables you to design more sophisticated Web pages. Authoring tools can greatly simplify the task of creating Web pages, but do not support all features of HTML. Since you will probably end up editing the source text produced by the tools, it is imperative to know the basic concept of HTML. In this tutorial, you will learn how to use HTML to create your own Web pages.

Getting Started

Let us begin with an example that demonstrates the structure and syntax of an HTML document.

Example E.1 An HTML Example

The following HTML document displays a message and a list of Web browsers: Netscape, Internet Explorer, and Mosaic. You may use any text editor, such as Microsoft NotePad on Windows, to create HTML documents, as long as it can save the file in ACSII text format.

```
<html>
<head>
<title>My First Web Page</title>
</head>
<body>
<i>Welcome to</i> <b>HTML</b>. Here is a list of popular Web
browsers.
<ul>
  <li>Netscape
  <li>Internet Explorer
  <li>Mosaic
</ul>
<hr size=3>
Created by <A HREF=www.ipfw.edu/kt2/liangy>Y. Daniel Liang</A>.
</body>
</html>
```

Assume that you have created a file named **ExampleE1.html** for this HTML document. You may use any Web browser to view the document. To view it on Internet Explorer, start up your browser, choose Open from the File menu. A popup window opens to accept the filename. Type the full name of the file (including path), or click the Browser button to locate the file. Click OK to load and display the HTML file. Your document should be displayed as shown in Figure E.1.

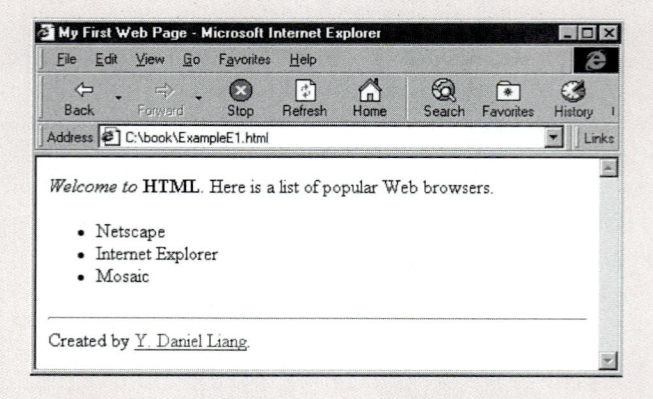

Figure E.1 *The HTML page is rendered by a Web browser.*

> **CAUTION**
> HTML filenames are case-sensitive on UNIX but not on other operating systems. HTML files end with .html or .htm.

> **NOTE**
> The same document may be rendered differently subject to the capabilities of the Web browser. Regardless of the difference, the power of HTML is that your document can be viewed on a variety of browsers and on most platforms, and can be formatted to suit any reader. This tutorial uses Internet Explorer 4.0 for illustrations.

What makes *Welcome to* appear in italic in Figure E.1? What makes the document appear in the desired style? HTML is a document-layout and hyperlink-specification language; that is, it tells the Web browser how to display the contents of the document, including text, images, and other media, using instructions called *tags*. The browser interprets the tags and decides how to display or otherwise treat the subsequent contents of the HTML document. Tags are enclosed in brackets; `<html>`, `<i>`, `<b>`, and `</html>` are tags that appear in the preceding HTML example. The first word in a tag, called the *tag name*, describes tag functions. Tags may have additional attributes, sometimes with values after an equals sign, which further define the tag's action. For example, in Example E.1, the attribute size in the tag `<hr>` defines the size of the bar as 3 inches.

Most tags have a *start tag* and a corresponding *end tag*. A tag has a specific effect on the region between the start tag and the end tag. For example, `<b>text</b>` advises the browser to display the word "text" in bold. `<b>` and `</b>` are the start and end tags for displaying boldface text. An end tag is always the start tag's name preceded by a forward slash (/). A few tags do not have end tags. For example, `<hr>`, a tag to draw a line, has no corresponding end tag.

A tag can be embedded inside another tag; for example, all tags are embedded within `<html>` and `</html>`. However, tags cannot overlap; it would be wrong, for instance, to use `<b>bold and <i>italic</b></i>`; the correct use should be `<b><i>bold and italic</i></b>`.

> **TIP**
> Tags are not case-sensitive. However, it is good practice to use case consistently for clarity and readability. This tutorial uses lowercase for tags.

The following types of tags are introduced in the upcoming sections:

- **Structure tags**—Define the structure of the documents.
- **Text appearance tags**—Define the appearance of text.

- **Paragraph tags**—Define headings, paragraphs, and line breaks.
- **Font tags**—Specify font sizes and colors.
- **List tags**—Define ordered or unordered lists and definition lists.
- **Table tags**—Define tables.
- **Link tags**—Specify navigation links to other documents.
- **Image tags**—Specify where to get images and how to display images.

Structure Tags

An HTML document begins with the `<html>` tag, which declares that the document is written with HTML. Each document has two parts—*head* and *body*—defined by `<head>` and `<body>` tags, respectively. The head part contains the document title (using the `<title>` tag) and other parameters the browser may use when rendering the document; the body part contains the actual contents of the document. An HTML document may have the following structure:

```
<html>
<head>
<title>My First Web Page</title>
</head>
<body>
<!-- document body -->
</body>
</html>
```

Here the special starting tag `<!--` and ending tag `-->` are used to enclose comments in the HTML documents. The comments are not displayed.

> **NOTE**
> Your documents may be displayed properly even if you don't use the `<html>`, `<head>`, `<title>`, and `<body>` tags. However, use of these tags is strongly recommended because they communicate certain information about the properties of a document to the browser; the information they provide is helpful for the effective use of the document.

Text Appearance Tags

HTML provides tags to advise the appearance of text. At present, some text tags have the same effect. For example, `<em>`, `<cite>`, and `<i>` will all display the text in italic. However, a future version of HTML may make these tags distinct. Text tag names are fairly descriptive. Text tags can be classified into two categories: *content-based tags* and *physical tags*.

Content-Based Tags

Content-based tags inform the browser to display the text based on semantic meaning, such as citation, program code, and emphasis. Here is a summary of content-based tags:

- `<cite>`—Indicates that the enclosed text is a bibliographic citation, displayed in italic.
- `<code>`—Indicates that the enclosed text is a programming code, displayed in monospace font.
- `<em>`—Indicates that the enclosed text should be displayed with emphasis, displayed in italic.
- `<strong>`—Indicates that the enclosed text should be strongly emphasized, displayed in bold.
- `<var>`—Indicates that the enclosed text is a computer variable, displayed in italic.
- `<address>`—Indicates that the enclosed text is an address, displayed in italic.

Table E.1 lists the content-based tags and provides examples of their use.

TABLE E.1 Using Content-Based Tags

Tag	Example	Display
`<cite>...</cite>`	`<cite>bibliographic</cite>`	*bibliographic*
`<code>...</code>`	`<code>source code</code>`	source code
`<em>...</em>`	`<em>emphasis</em>`	*emphasis*
`<strong>...</strong>`	`<strong>strongly emphasized</strong>`	**strongly emphasized**
`<var>...</var>`	`<var>programming variable</var>`	*programming variable*
`<address>...</address>`	`<address>Computer Dept</address>`	*Computer Dept*

Physical Tags

Physical tags explicitly ask the browser to display text in bold, italic, or other ways. Following are six commonly used physical tags:

- `<i>` (italic)
- `<b>` (bold)
- `<u>` (underline)
- `<tt>` (monospace)
- `<strike>` (strike-through text)
- `<blink>` (blink)

Table E.2 lists the physical tags and provides examples of their use.

TABLE E.2 Using Physical Tags

Tag	Example	Display
`<i>...</i>`	`<i>italic</i>`	*italic*
`<b>...</b>`	`<b>bold</b>`	**bold**
`<u>...</u>`	`<u>underline</u>`	underline
`<tt>...</tt>`	`<tt>monospace</tt>`	`monospace`
`<strike>...</strike>`	`<strike>strike</strike>`	~~strike~~
`<blink>...</blink>`	`<blink>blink</blink>`	blink (causes it to blink)

Paragraph Style Tags

There are many tags in HTML to deal with paragraph styles. There are six heading tags (`<h1>`, `<h2>`, `<h3>`, `<h4>`, `<h5>`, `<h6>`) for different sizes of headings, a line break tag *(`<br>`),* a paragraph start tag (`<p>`), a preformat tag (`<pre>`), and a block quote tag (`<blockquote>`).

The six heading tags indicate the highest (`<h1>`) and lowest (`<h6>`) precedence a heading may have in the document. Heading tags may be used with an align attribute to place the heading toward *left*, *center*, or *right*. The default alignment is left. For example, `<h3 align=right>Heading</h3>` tells the browser to right-align the heading.

The line break tag `<br>` tells the browser to start displaying from the next line. This tag has no end tag.

The paragraph start tag `<p>` signals the start of a paragraph. This tag has an optional end tag `</p>`.

The `<pre>` tag and its required end tag (`</pre>`) define the enclosed segment to be displayed in monospaced font by the browser.

The `<blockquote>` tag is used to contain text quoted from another source. The quote will be indented from both left and right.

Example E.2 HTML Source Code Using Structure Tags

The following HTML source code illustrates the use of paragraph tags. The text the code creates is displayed in Figure E.2.

```
<html>
<head>
<title>Demonstrating Paragraph Tags</title>
</head>
```

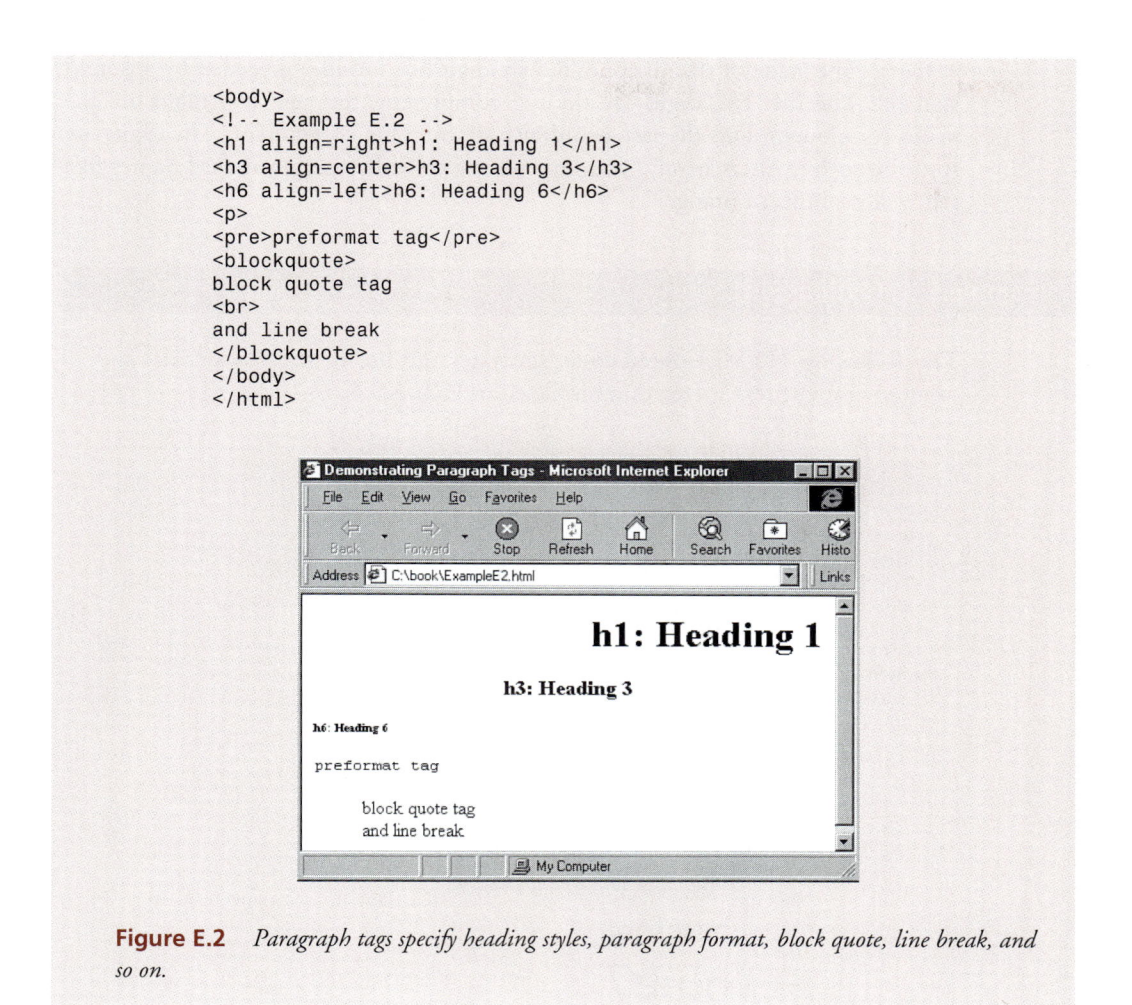

```
<body>
<!-- Example E.2 -->
<h1 align=right>h1: Heading 1</h1>
<h3 align=center>h3: Heading 3</h3>
<h6 align=left>h6: Heading 6</h6>
<p>
<pre>preformat tag</pre>
<blockquote>
block quote tag
<br>
and line break
</blockquote>
</body>
</html>
```

Figure E.2 *Paragraph tags specify heading styles, paragraph format, block quote, line break, and so on.*

Font, Size, and Color Tags

With HTML you can specify font size and colors using font tags. There are two font tags: `<basefont>` and `<font>`.

The `<basefont>` tag is typically placed in the head of an HTML document, where it sets the base font size for the entire document. However, it may appear anywhere in the document, and it may appear many times, each time with a new size attribute. Many browsers use a relative model for sizing fonts, ranging from 1 to 7; the default base font size is 3. Each successive size is 20 percent larger than its predecessor in the range.

The `<font>` tag allows you to specify the size and color of the enclosed text using size and color attributes. The size attribute is the same as the one for `<basefont>` tag. The color attribute sets the color for the enclosed text between `<font>` and

</font>. The value of the attribute is a six-digit hex number preceded by a pound sign (#). The first two digits are the red component, the next two digits are the green component, and the last two digits are the blue component. The digits are from 00 to FF. Alternatively, you may set the color by using standard names like red, yellow, blue, or orange.

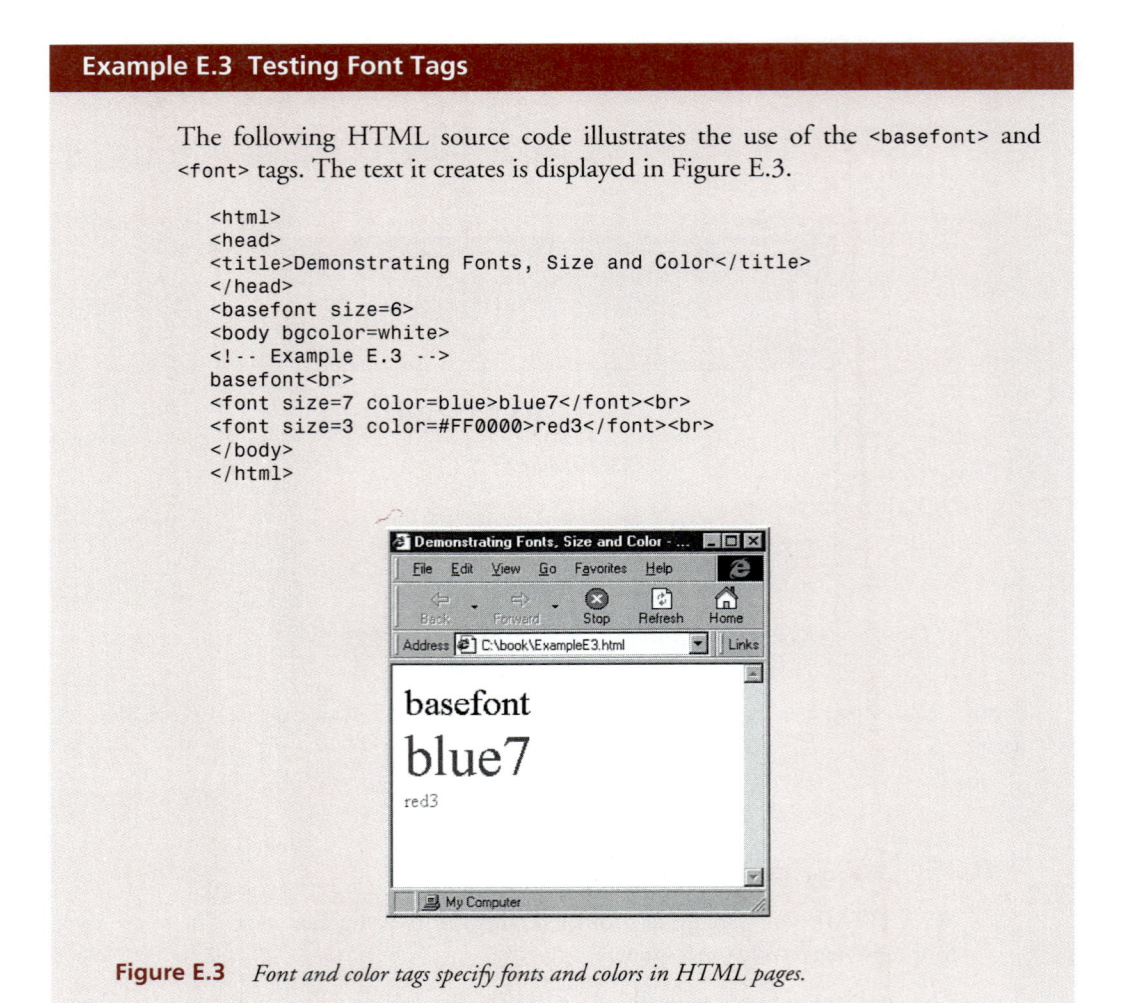

> **Example E.3 Testing Font Tags**
>
> The following HTML source code illustrates the use of the `<basefont>` and `<font>` tags. The text it creates is displayed in Figure E.3.
>
> ```
> <html>
> <head>
> <title>Demonstrating Fonts, Size and Color</title>
> </head>
> <basefont size=6>
> <body bgcolor=white>
> <!-- Example E.3 -->
> basefont<br>
> <font size=7 color=blue>blue7</font><br>
> <font size=3 color=#FF0000>red3</font><br>
> </body>
> </html>
> ```
>
> **Figure E.3** *Font and color tags specify fonts and colors in HTML pages.*

List Tags

HTML allows you to define three kinds of lists: *ordered lists, unordered lists,* and *definition lists.* You can also build nested lists. Example E.1 contains an unordered list of three Web browsers.

Ordered Lists

Ordered lists label the items they contain. An ordered list is used when the sequence of the listed items is important. For example, chapters are listed in order. An ordered list starts with the tag `<ol>` and ends with `</ol>`, and items are placed in between. Each item begins with an `<li>` tag. The browser automatically numbers list items starting from numeric 1. Instead of using the default numeric numbers for labeling, you may associate the tag `<ol>` with a type attribute. The value of the type determines the style of the label.

- Type value `A` for uppercase letter labels A, B, C, ...
- Type value `a` for lowercase letter labels a, b, c, ...
- Type value `I` for capital Roman numerals I, II, III, ...
- Type value `i` for lowercase Roman numerals i, ii, iii, ...
- Type value `1` for Arabic numerals 1, 2, 3, ...

Unordered Lists

When the sequence of the listed items is not important, you may use an unordered list. For example, a list of Web browsers may be given in any order. An unordered list starts with the tag `<ul>` and ends with `</ul>`. Inside, you use `<li>` tags for items. By default, the browser uses bullets to mark each item. You may use `disc`, `circle`, or `square` as type values to indicate the use of markers other than bullets.

Definition Lists

A definition list is used to define terms. The list is enclosed between `<dl>` and `</dl>` tags. Inside the tags are the terms and their definition. The term and definition have leading tags `<dt>` and `<dd>`, respectively. Browsers typically render the term name at the left margin and render the definition below it and indented.

Example E.4 Using Various List Tags

This example illustrates the use of tags for ordered lists, unordered lists, definition lists, and nested lists. The output of the following code is displayed in Figure E.4.

```
<html>
<head>
<title>Demonstrating List Tags</title>
</head>
<body bgcolor=white>
<!-- Example E.4 List Tags -->
<center><b>List Tags</b></center>
An ordered List
```

continues

```
<ol type=A>
  <li>Chapter 1: Introduction to Java
  <li>Chapter 2: Java Building Elements
  <li>Chapter 3: Control Structures
</ol>
An unordered List
<ul type=square>
  <li>Apples
  <li>Oranges
  <li>Peaches
</ul>
Definition List
<dl>
   <dt>What is Java?
   <dd>An Internet programming language.
</dl>
</body>
</html>
```

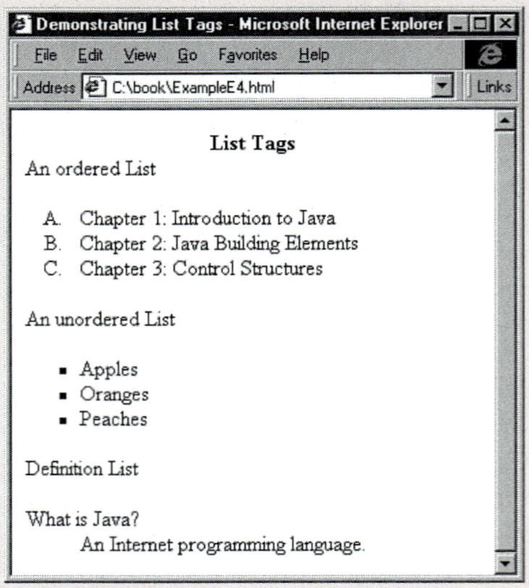

Figure E.4 *HTML list tags can display ordered lists, unordered lists, and definition lists.*

Table Tags

Tables are useful features supported by many browsers. Tables are collections of numbers and words arranged in rows and columns of cells. In HTML, table elements, including data items, row and column headers, and captions, are enclosed between `<table>` and `</table>` tags. Several table tags may be used to specify the layout of tables. Each row in the table is wrapped by `<tr>` and `</tr>`. Inside the row, data or words in a cell are enclosed by `<td>` and `</td>`. You may use `<caption>...</caption>` to display a caption for the table and `<th>...</th>` to display column headers.

Table tags may be used with attributes to obtain special effects. Here are some useful attributes:

- **border**—Can appear in the `<table>` tag to specify that all cells are surrounded with a border.

- **align**—Can appear in the `<caption>`, `<tr>`, `<th>`, or `<td>` tag. If it appears in `<caption>`, it specifies whether the caption appears above or below the table using values `top` or `bottom`. The default is `align=top`. If it appears in `<tr>`, `<th>`, or `<td>`, `align` specifies whether the text is aligned to the left, the right, or centered inside the table cell(s).

- **valign**—Can appear in `<tr>`, `<th>`, or `<td>`. The values of the attribute are `top`, `middle`, and `bottom` to specify whether text is aligned to the top, the bottom, or centered inside the table cell(s).

- **colspan**—Can appear in any table cell to specify how many columns of the table the cell should span. The default value is 1.

- **rowspan**—Can appear in any column to specify how many rows of the table the cell should span. The default value is 1.

Example E.5 Illustration of Table Tags

This example creates an HTML table. The output of the code is displayed in Figure E.5.

```
<html>
<head>
<title>Demonstraitng Table Tags</title>
</head>
<body bgcolor=white>
<!-- Example E.5 Table Tags -->
<center>Table Tags</center>
<br>
<table border=2>
<caption>This is a Table</caption>
<tr>
  <th>Table heading</th>
  <td>Table data</td>
</tr>
<tr>
  <th valign=bottom>Second row
  <td>Embedded Table
     <table border=3>
     <tr>
       <th>Table heading</th>
       <td align=right>Table data</td>
     </tr>
     </table>
  </td>
</tr>
</table>
</body>
</html>
```

continues

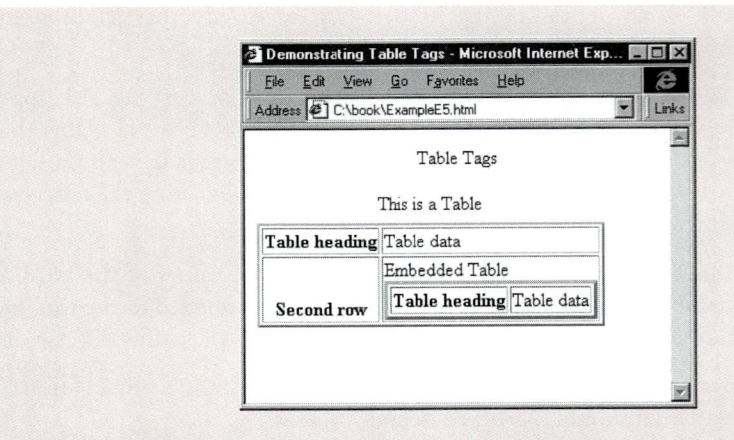

Figure E.5 *Table tags are useful for displaying tables in HTML pages.*

Hyperlink Tags

The true power of HTML lies in its capability to join collections of documents together into a full electronic library of information, and to link documents with other documents over the Internet. This is called *hypertext linking*, which is the key feature that makes the Web appealing and popular. By adding hypertext links, called *anchors*, to your HTML document, you can create a highly intuitive information flow and guide users directly to the information they want. You can link documents on different computers or on the same computer, and can jump within the same document using anchor tags.

Linking Documents on Different Computers

Every document on the Web has a unique address, known as its *Uniform Resource Locator* (URL). To navigate from a source document to a target document, you need to reference the target's URL inside the anchor tags `<a>` and `</a>` using attribute `href`. The following example displays a list of database vendors:

```
<ul>
 <li><a href="http://www.oracle.com">Oracle</a>
 <li><a href="http://www.sybase.com">Sybase</a>
 <li><a href="http://www.informix.com">Informix</a>
</ul>
```

In this example, clicking on Oracle will display the Oracle home page. The URL of Oracle's home page Internet address is **http://www.oracle.com**. The general format of a URL is:

method://*servername*:*port*/*pathname*/*fullfilename*

method is the name of the operation that is performed to interpret this URL. The most common methods are `http`, `ftp`, and `file`.

- **http**—Accesses a page over the network using the HTTP protocol. For example, **http://www.microsoft.com** links to Microsoft's homepage. **http://** can be omitted.
- **ftp**—Downloads a file using anonymous FTP service from a server, for example: **ftp://hostname/directory/fullfilename**.
- **file**—Reads a file from the local disk. For example, `file://home/liangy/liangy.html` displays the file **liangy.html** from the directory `/home/liangy` on the local machine.

servername is a computer's unique Internet name or Internet Protocol (IP) numerical address on the network. For example, **www.sun.com** is the hostname of Sun Microsystem's Web server. If a server name is not specified, it is assumed that the file is on the same server.

port is the TCP port number that the Web server is running on. Most Web servers use port number 80 by default.

pathname is optional and indicates the directory under which the file is located.

fullfilename is optional and indicates the target filename. Web servers usually use **index.html** on UNIX and **default.htm** on Windows for a default filename. For example, `<a href="http://www.oracle.com">Oracle</a>` is equivalent to `<a href="http://www.oracle.com/index.html">Oracle</a>`.

Linking Documents on the Same Computer

To link documents on the same computer, you should use the `file` method rather than the `http` method in the target URL. There are two types of links: *absolute link* and *relative link*.

When linking to a document on a different machine, you must use an absolute link to identify the target document. An absolute link uses a URL to indicate the complete path to the target file.

When you are linking to a document on the same computer, it is better to use a relative link. A relative URL omits method and server name and directories. For instance, assume that the source document is under directory `~liangy/teaching` on the server `sewrk01.ipfw.indiana.edu`. The URL

```
file://sewrk01.ipfw.indiana.edu/~liangy/teaching/teaching.html
```

is equivalent to

```
file://teaching.html
```

Here, `file://` can be omitted. An obvious advantage of using a relative URL is that you can move the entire set of documents to another directory or even another server and never have to change a single link.

Jumping Within the Same Document

HTML offers navigation within the same document. This is helpful for direct browsing of interesting segments of the document.

Example E.6 Navigation Within the Same Document

This example shows a document with three sections. The output of the following code is shown in Figure E.6. When the user clicks Section 1: Introduction on the list, the browser jumps to Section 1 of the document. The name attribute within the <a> tag labels the section. The label is used as a link to the section. This feature is also known as *using bookmarks.*

When you test this example, make the window small so that you can see the effects of jumping to each reference through the link tags.

```
<html>
<head>
<title>Deomonstrating Link Tags</title>
</head>
<body>
<ol>
  <li><a href="#introduction">Section 1: Introduction</a>
  <li><a href="#methodology">Section 2: Methodology</a>
  <li><a href="#summary">Section 3: Summary</a>
</ol>

<h3><a name="introduction"><b>Section 1</b>: Introduction</a></h3>
an introductory paragraph

<h3><a name="methodology"><b>Section 2</b>: Methodology</a></h3>
a paragraph on methodology

<h3><a name="summary"><b>Section 3</b>: Summary</a></h3>
a summary paragraph
</body>
</html>
```

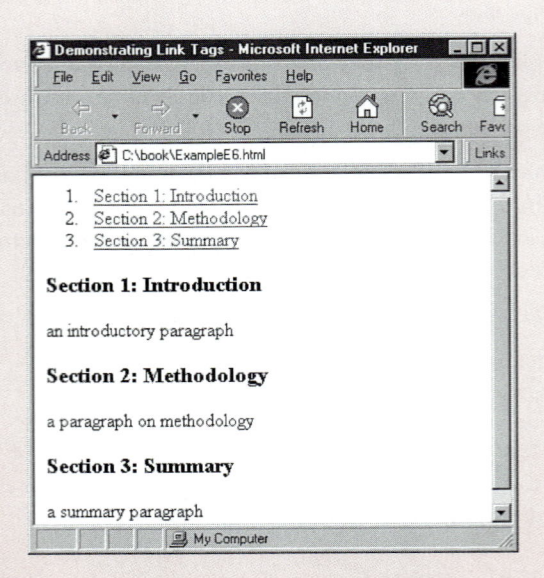

Figure E.6 *Hyperlink tags link documents.*

Embedding Graphics

One of most compelling features of the Web is its ability to embed graphics in a document. You may use graphics for icons, pictures, illustrations, drawings, and so on. Graphics bring a live dimension to your documents. You may use an image as a visual map of hyperlinks. This section introduces the use of *horizontal bar tags* and *image tags*.

Horizontal Bar Tags

The horizontal bar tag (`<hr>`) is used to display a rule. It is useful to separate sections of your document with horizontal rules. You may associate attributes `size`, `width`, and `align` to achieve the desired effect. You may thicken the rule using the `size` attribute with values in pixels. The `width` attribute specifies the length of the bar with values in either absolute number of pixels or extension across a certain percentage of the page. The `align` attribute specifies whether the bar is `left`, `centered`, or `right` aligned.

Example E.7 Illustration of Horizontal Bar Tags

This example illustrates the use of the `size`, `width`, and `align` attributes in horizontal bar tags. The output of the following code is shown in Figure E.7.

```
<html>
<head>
<title>Demonstrating Horizontal Rules</title>
</head>
<body bgcolor=white>
<! -- Example E.7 Horizontal Rule -- >
<center>Horizontal Rules</center>
<hr size=3 width=80% align=left>
<hr size=2 width=20% align=right noshade>
<hr>
</body>
</html>
```

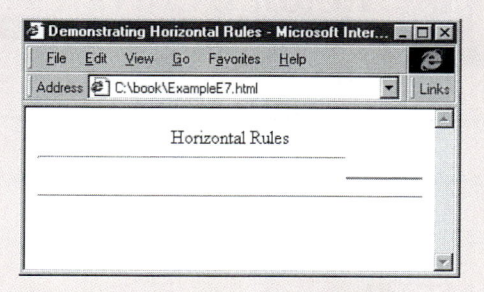

Figure E.7 *Horizontal bar tags are often used to separate contents in documents.*

continues

Image Tags

The image tag, `<img>`, lets you reference and insert images into the current text. The syntax for the tag is:

```
<img src=URL alt=text align = [top ¦ middle ¦ bottom ¦ texttop ]>
```

Most browsers support GIF and JPEG image format. Format is an encoding scheme to store images. The attribute `src` specifies the source of the image. The attribute `alt` specifies an alternative text message to be displayed in case the client's browser cannot display the image. The attribute `alt` is optional; if omitted, no message is displayed. The attribute `align` tells the browser where to place the image.

Example E.8 Illustration of Image Tags

This example creates a document with image tags. The output of the code is shown in Figure E.8.

```
<html>
<head>
<title>Demonstrating Image Tags</title>
</head>
<body bgcolor=white>
<!-- Example E.8 Image Tags -->
<center>Image Tags</center>
<img src="ipfwlogo.gif" align=middle>
</body>
</html>
```

Figure E.8 *Image tags display images in HTML pages.*

More on HTML

This tutorial is not intended to be a complete reference manual on HTML. It does not mention many interesting features, such as *forms* and *frames*. You will find dozens of books on HTML in your local bookstore. *Special Edition Using HTML* by Mark Brown and John Jung, published by QUE, is a comprehensive reference; it covers all the new HTML features supported by Netscape Navigator and Microsoft Internet Explorer. *HTML Quick Reference* by Robert Mullen, also published by QUE, contains all the essential information you need to build Web pages with HTML in 100 pages. Please refer to these and other books for more information. You can also get information on-line at the following Web sites:

- www.ncsa.uiuc.edu/General/Internet/WWW/HTMLPrimer.html
- www.w3.org/pub/WWW/MarkUp/
- www.mcli.dist.maricopa.edu/tut/lessons.html
- www.netscape.com/assist/net_sites/frames.html

APPENDIX F

USING THE COMPANION CD-ROM AND INSTALLING THE SWING LIBRARY

The companion CD-ROM contains Visual J++ 6 Student Edition, and the entire source code in the text. To use Swing components in Visual J++, you need to install the Swing standalone library in J++. This appendix covers installing Visual J++ 6 and the Swing standalone library, and using source code.

Installing Visual J++ 6

To install Visual J++ 6 on Windows 95, Windows 98, or Windows NT 4.0, you need a Pentium 90 MHz or faster processor, a minimum of 24 megabytes of RAM, and at least 82 MB megabytes of free disk space.

To start the installation, insert the companion CD into your CD-ROM drive. The Visual J++ 6 Installation Wizard automatically starts. Should it not automatically start, click the CD-ROM drive from the My Computer Folder. Follow the straightforward instructions and choose the default settings to install Visual J++ 6.

Installing Swing Library in Visual J++ 6

Visual J++ does not support Java 2, but you can use Swing components by adding the JAR file for the Swing components in the classpath, as follows:

```
set classpath=.;c:\swingall.jar;%classpath%
```

swingall.jar is a Java archive file, which contains all the classes for Swing components. Java archive files are introduced in Chapter 10, "Applets and Advanced Graphics." Swing components are built into Java VM in Java 2, but they can also be used in JDK 1.1.7 or JDK 1.1.8 as separate add-ons. JavaSoft provides swingall.jar for the use of Swing as add-ons in JDK 1.1.7 or JDK 1.1.8, which can be downloaded from

www.javasoft.com/products/jfc/download.html

Using the Examples in the Book

The source code for the examples in the text can be found in one compressed filename vjBook.zip. You can unpack the files by using an appropriate compressing/decompressing utility, such as unzip, gunzip, pkunzip, or WinZip. Your utility must support long filenames. WinZip can be downloaded from **www.winzip.com**.

You should extract the files into the C:\vjBook directory so that you can run the programs without modifications. For instance, if installing the documents using WinZip, enter C:\ in the Extract to field of the Extract dialog box, as shown in Figure F.1.

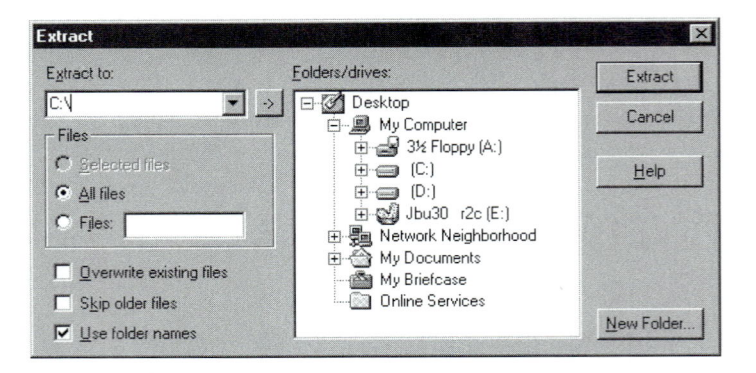

Figure F.1 *The WinZip utility unpacks the text examples in the C:\vjBook directory.*

The files are located and named as follows:

1. The Java source code in Chapter *X* is located in directory vjBook\Project*X*.

2. If the example contains a single class, the class name is the filename. For instance, the class name in Example 1.1 is Welcome, thus the filename for this example is Welcome.java.

2. If the example is a Java application with multiple classes, the class that contains the main method determines the filename on the CD-ROM. For instance, the filename for Example 9.1 is ButtonDemo.java because the main class is ButtonDemo.

3. If the example is a Java applet, the filename is the applet class name. For instance, the filename for Example 10.1 is MortgageApplet.java because the applet class is `MortgageApplet`.

4. For each applet, the associated HTML file is also provided on the CD-ROM. The HTML file is named according to the applet name. For instance, the HTML filename for Example 10.1 is MortgageApplet.htm because the applet class is `MortgageApplet`.

Appendix F Using the Companion CD-ROM and Installing the Swing Library

> **Note**
> To run the code from the book, add the following in a single line in the autoexec.bat file on Windows 95 or Windows 98:
>
> ```
> SET ClassPath=.;c:\swingall.jar;c:\vjBook\Project2;c:\vjBook\
>     Project5; c:\vjBook\Project8;c:\vjBook\Project11;c:\vjBook\
>     Project12;c:\vjBook\Project13; c:\vjBook\Project15;%classpath%
> ```

APPENDIX G

RAPID JAVA APPLICATION DEVELOPMENT USING VISUAL J++ 6.0

The *Form Designer* is Microsoft's answer to rapid Java application development. Rapid Application Development, or RAD, is a software technology for developing programs efficiently and effectively that has been successfully implemented in Visual Basic, Delphi, Power Builder, Oracle Developer 2000, and many other program development tools. Using a RAD tool, projects can be developed quickly and efficiently with minimum coding. Projects developed with RAD are easy to modify and easy to maintain. The key elements in a RAD tool are the software components, such as buttons, labels, combo boxes, lists, check boxes, and menus. These components can be visually manipulated and tailored during design time in order to develop customized programs.

The Form Designer provides you with a dynamic way to visually create graphic user interfaces for your applications with minimum coding for maximum productivity. Instead of writing code to create a button or some other user interface component, you simply drag the button icon in the Toolbox window and place it on the form. The Form Designer automatically generates the associated Java source code for creating the button and placing it on the form.

The code generated by the Form Designer is based on Microsoft *Windows Foundation Classes* for Java or WFC. Windows Foundation Classes is a set of class libraries that access the Microsoft Windows API. WFC works efficiently and seamlessly on Windows NT and Windows 95, but does not work on other platforms. Thus you should not use WFC and the Form Designer if you want to deploy your Java applications on platforms other than Windows.

Form Designer makes programming in Java easier and more productive. Since no tool can do everything, however, you will have to modify the programs your tools produce. Therefore, it is imperative to know the basic concepts of Java graphics programming before starting to use the visual tools.

This appendix introduces you to rapid Java application development using the Form Designer.

Form Designer Basics

The Form Designer is very similar to designing forms and writing code in Microsoft Visual Basic. Instead of using the Visual Basic Language, you use the Java language to implement code in Visual J++.

To use the Form Designer, you need to create a form. The form can be created when the project is created or can be added to a project by choosing Add, Add Form from the project's context menu. Suppose you create a new project using the New Project dialog box, as shown in Figure G.1. Type AppendixG in the Name field and choose the Windows Application icon to create a project AppendixG with a new startup form named Form1.java. Double-click Form1.java in the Project Explorer window to display the Form Designer, as shown in Figure G.2.

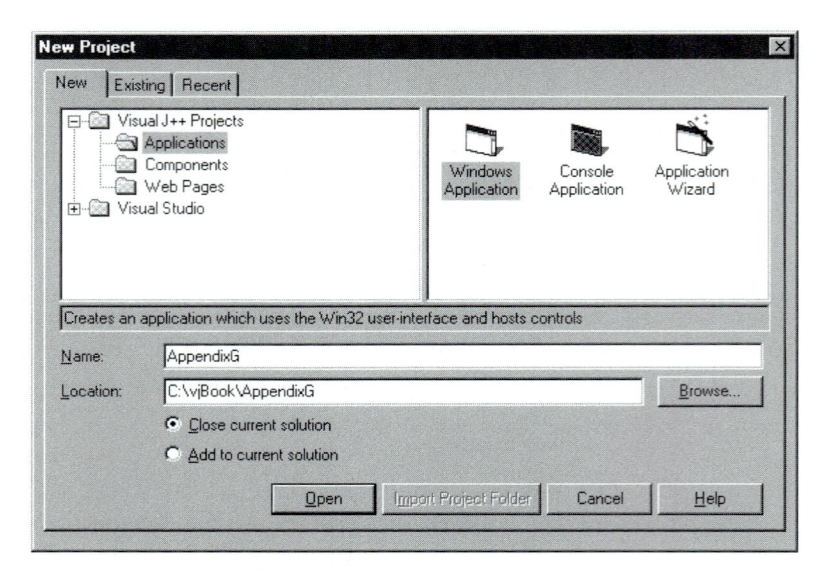

Figure G.1 *You can create a new form using the New Project dialog box.*

Form1.java is a special type of Java program that extends the WFC `Form` class, which contains:

- A main method that runs the form.
- A constructor that invokes the `initForm()` method.
- The `initForm()` method that specifies the properties for the items in the form.

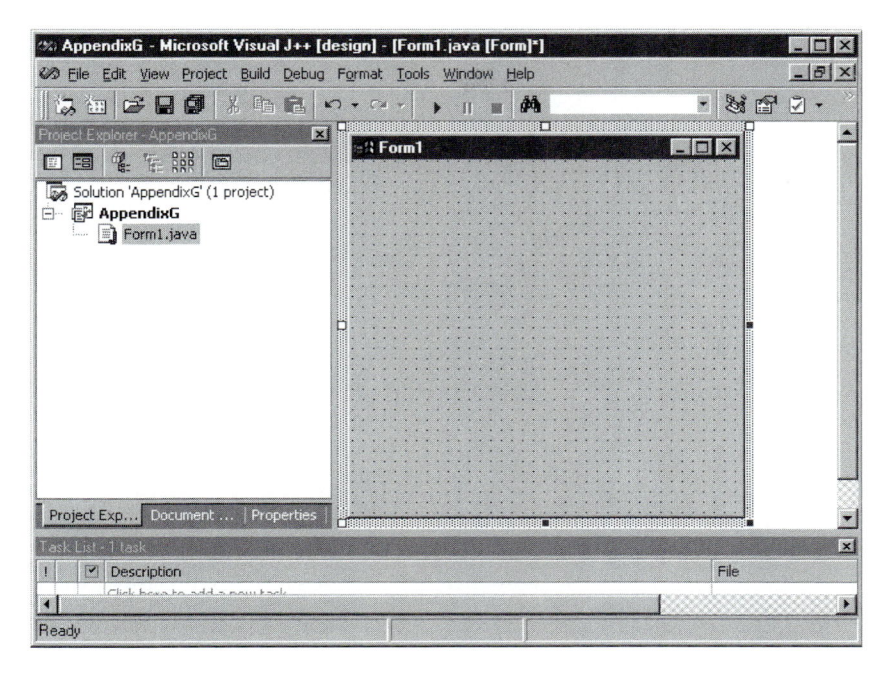

Figure G.2 *Double-clicking Form1.java in the Project Explorer displays Form Designer for Form1.java.*

Switching between Form Designer and Code Editor

You can view and modify the code in the Code editor. There are three ways to switch from the Form Designer to the Code editor:

- With Form1.java selected in the Project explorer, choose View, Code from the main menu bar.

- Right-click in the Form Designer to display a context menu, and choose View Code from the menu.

- Right-click Form1.java in the Project explorer window to display a context menu, and choose View Code from the menu.

Similarly, you can switch back to the Form Designer by choosing View, Designer from the main menu or from the context menu.

The Toolbox Window

The Toolbox window contains the components that you can drag-and-drop to the form. By default, the Toolbox window is displayed when the Form Designer is displayed. If the Toolbox window is closed, choose View, Toolbox from the main menu bar to open it, as shown in Figure G.3.

To add a component to a form, click the component in the Toolbox that you want to add and drag it onto the form. The component will appear on the form in its default size. You can resize it and place it in the desired location on the form. Figure G.4 shows that a button was added to the form.

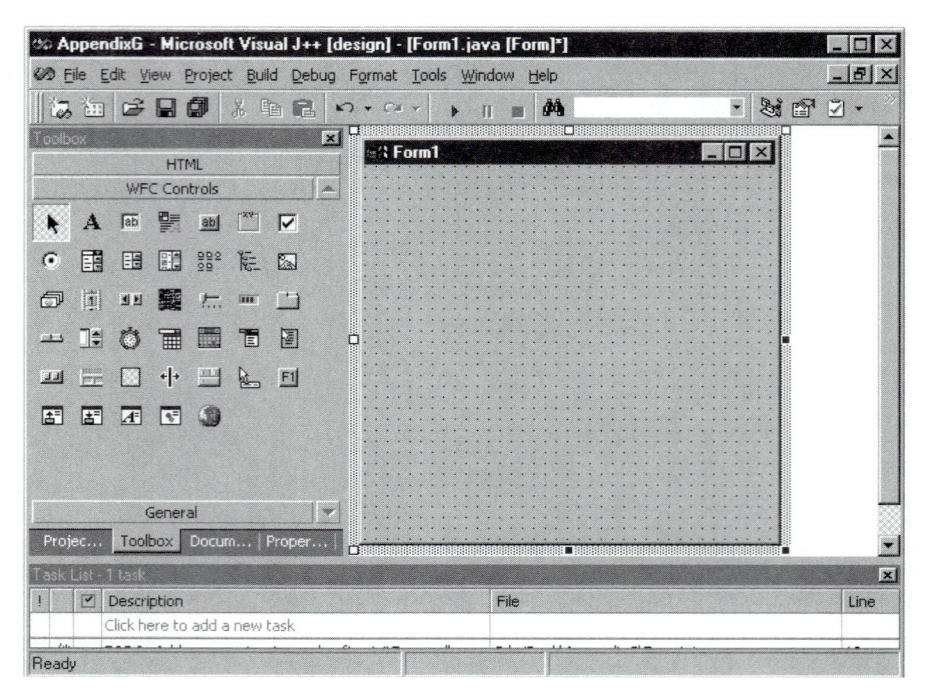

Figure G.3 *The Toolbox window contains a set of WFC components that you can use in the Form Designer.*

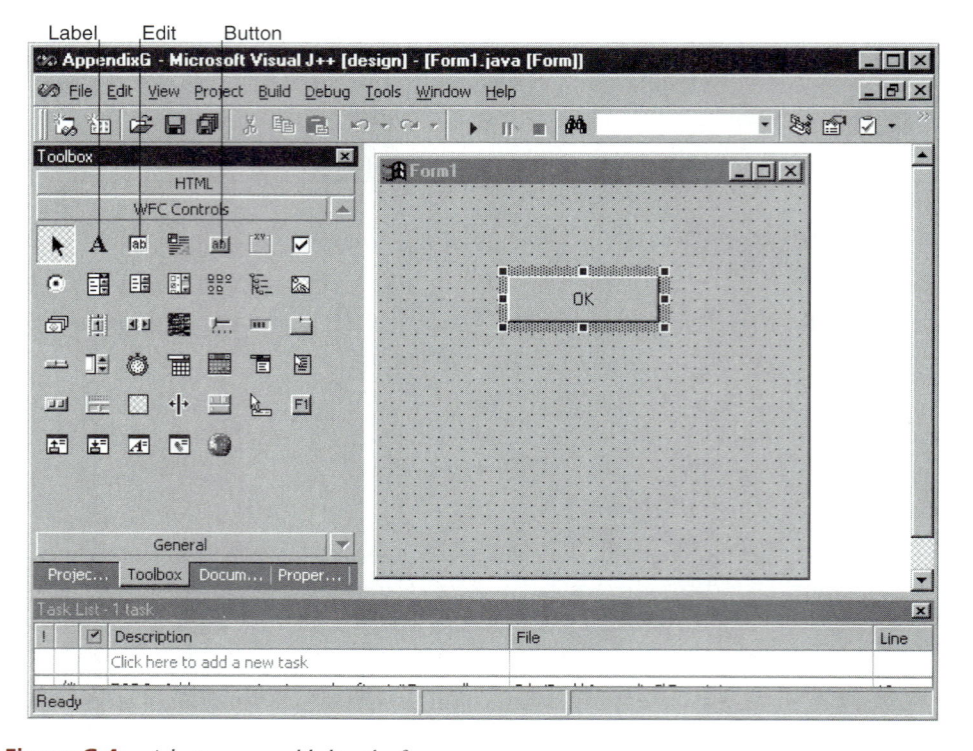

Figure G.4 *A button was added to the form.*

The source code was updated in response to the changes in the form. If you switch to the Code editor, you will see that the statement `Button button1 = new Button()` was created as a result of a button being dropped to the form.

The Toolbox window contains many WFC components. The WFC classes were developed by Microsoft at the same time that the Java Swing components were developed by Sun. Swing sets are pure Java, but the WFC classes are Windows-specific. The WFC classes run much faster than the Swing components on Windows. If your projects are run only on Windows, the WFC classes are good candidates for implementing high-performance Java applications.

The Properties Window

The Properties window enables you to view properties for selected objects and modify their current settings at design time. To display the Properties window for an object, right-click the object on the form to reveal a context menu and choose Properties to display the object's Properties window. Figure G.5 shows the Properties window for `button1`.

The Choice menu at the top of the Properties window lists the currently selected object. You can select other visible objects from the form. The properties can be listed in alphabetical order or by category. To list properties in alphabetical order,

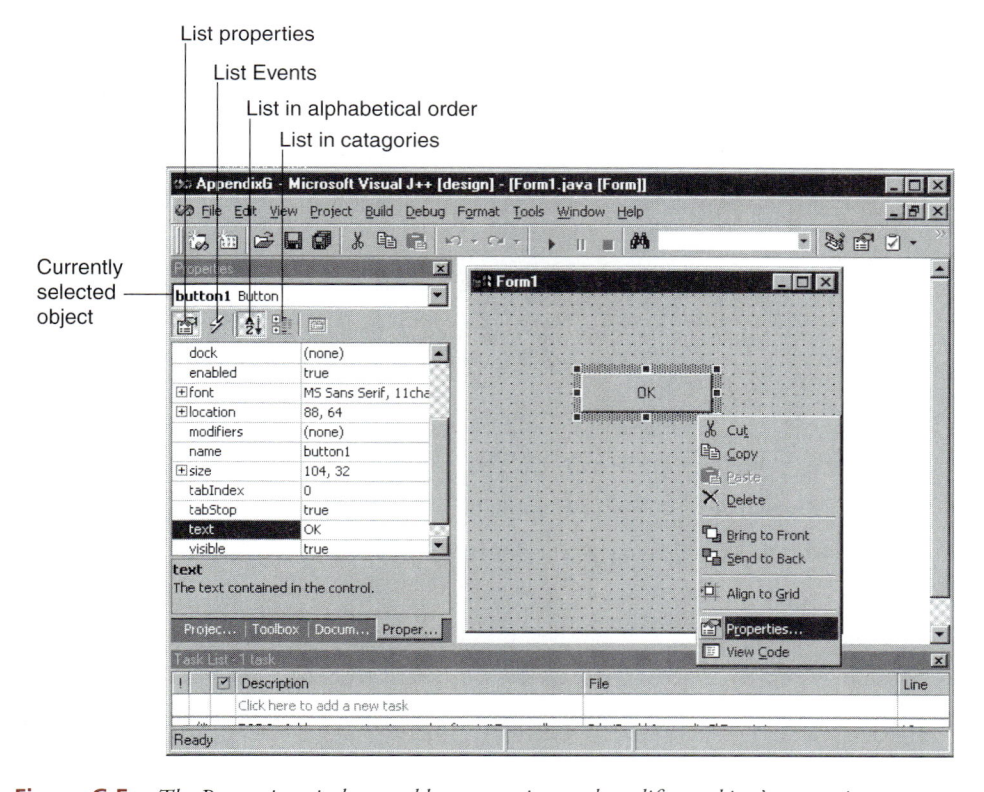

Figure G.5 *The Properties window enables you to view and modify an object's properties.*

click the Alphabetical icon. To list properties by category, click the Categorized icon. You can list the events associated with the object by clicking the Event icon on the Property window.

Changes in a property's value are automatically updated in the source code. For example, if you change the `text` property of `button1` to OK, the statement in the `initForm()` method

```
button1.setText("button1");
```

is changed to

```
button1.setText("OK");
```

> **NOTE**
> All the properties listed in the Properties window can be accessed programmatically using the getter and setter methods. For example, the text property is accessed using `getText()` and `setText()` methods.

Implementing Handlers

Every user interface component is associated with various types of events. The events are handled by event handlers.

You can click the Event icon in the Properties window to view the handlers associated with the object. The Properties window in Figure G.6 displays the handlers for `button1`. To generate the code for implementing the handler, double-click the handler in the Properties window. For example, the handler `button1_click()` for the button-click action on `button1` was generated, as shown in Figure G.6.

Type

```
System.out.println("Mouse clicked");
```

in `button1_click()` to implement the method.

Double-click the mouseEnter handler in the Properties window to generate `button1_mouseEnter()` method for handling the mouse-enter event on `button1`.

Type

```
System.out.println("Mouse entered");
```

in `button1_mouseEnter()` to implement the method.

A sample run of Form1.java is shown in Figure G.7.

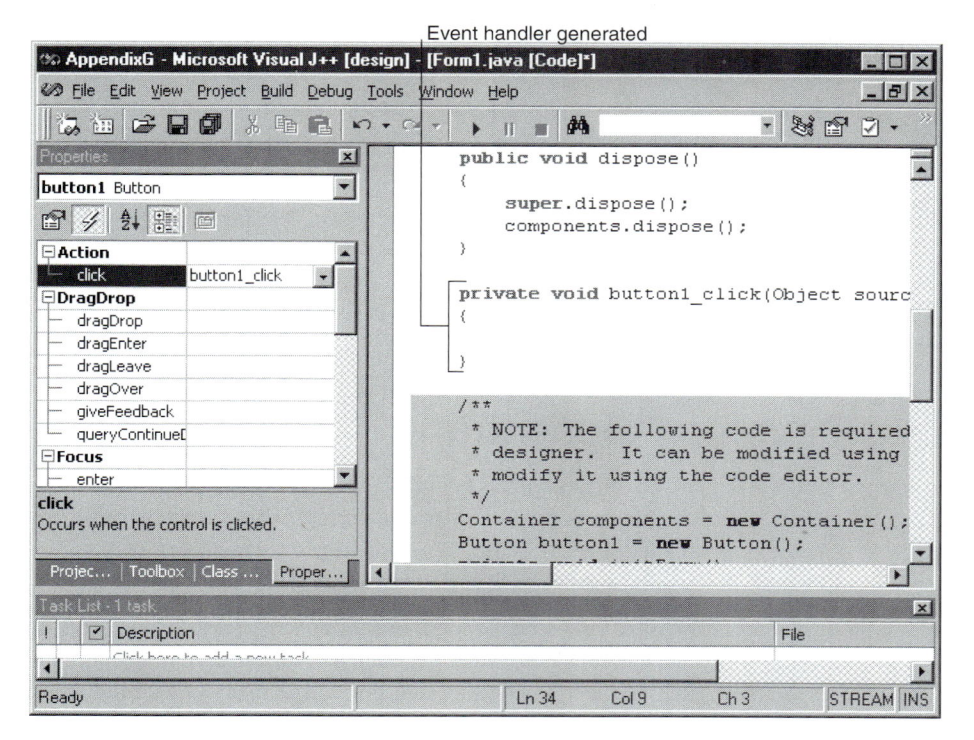

APPENDIX G RAPID JAVA DEVELOPMENT USING VISUAL J++ 6.0

Figure G.6 *Clicking the Event icon in the Properties window displays the handlers associated with the object. Double-clicking the handler generates the code template for the handler.*

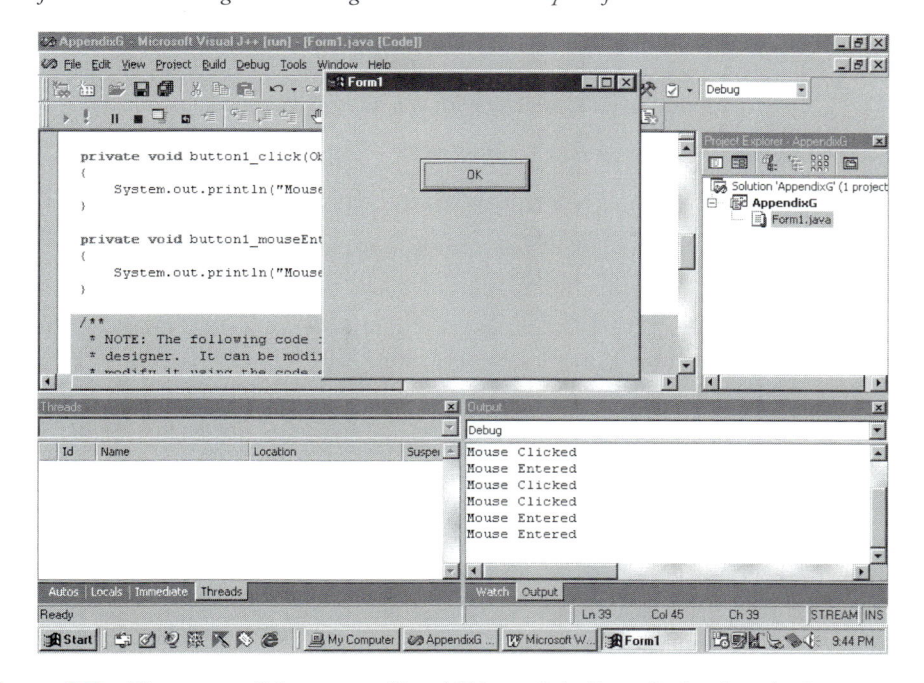

Figure G.7 *The messages "Mouse entered" and "Mouse clicked" are displayed on the Output window when the mouse enters the button or the button is clicked.*

> **NOTE**
> In the Visual J++ Form Designer, the components are placed using absolute positions and sizes, whereas in Java they are placed using the layout managers, such as `FlowLayout`, `GridLayout`, `BorderLayout`, `CardLayout`, and `GridBagLayout`. The use of absolute positions and sizes is fine if the application is developed and deployed on the same platform, but what looks fine on the development system may not look right on a different platform. The layout manager places the components in a way that is independent of fonts, screen resolutions, and platform differences.

Using the Form Designer to Develop Applications

When using the Form Designer to develop a project, you should carefully plan the project before implementing it. Designing the user interface constitutes the major part of the planning process. One approach is to draw a sketch of the screens that shows all the visible components you plan to use.

Implementation is a two-step process that involves creating user interfaces and writing code. To create a user interface, drag-and-drop the components, such as a button and a label, from the Toolbox window to the form and set the component's properties through the Properties window. Write code to implement event handlers to carry out the actions required by your applications.

This section provides an example that will demonstrate how to develop applications. The example is identical to Example 9.11, "Using Menus," in Chapter 9, "Creating User Interfaces." Instead of coding that uses the Swing classes, the example will use the Form Designer with the WFC classes.

The task for completing this application is divided into three phases:

1. Create user interface, as shown in Figure G.8.
2. Implement handlers for carrying out the actions of the Add, Subtract, Multiply, and Divide buttons.
3. Create and implement menu commands for Add, Subtract, Multiply, and Divide under the Operation menu.

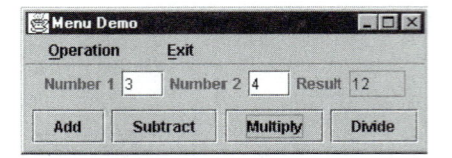

Figure G.8 *A numeric operation can be performed either by clicking a button or by choosing a menu command in the Operation menu.*

Phase 1: Creating User Interface

Follow the steps below to create a new form and design user interface on it:

1. Reopen project AppendixG if necessary. Right-click at project AppendixG in the Project Explorer window to display its context menu. Choose Add Class, Add Form to display the Add Item dialog box, as shown in Figure G.9. Type MenuDemo.java in the Name filed. Click Open to create a form named MenuDemo.java, as shown in Figure G.10.

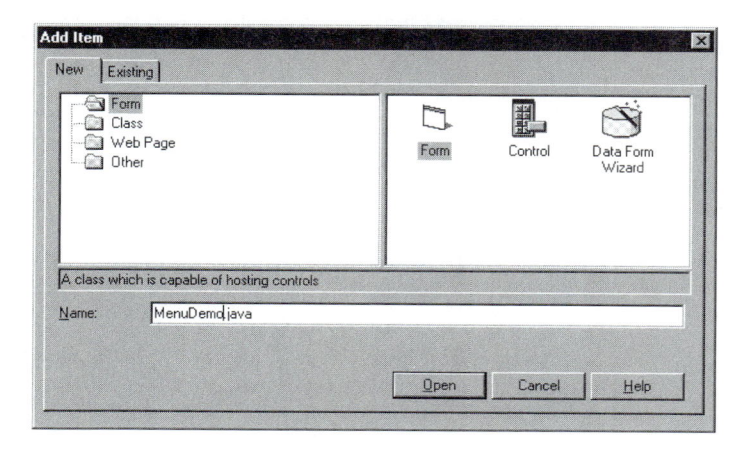

Figure G.9 *You can use the Add Item dialog box to create a new form.*

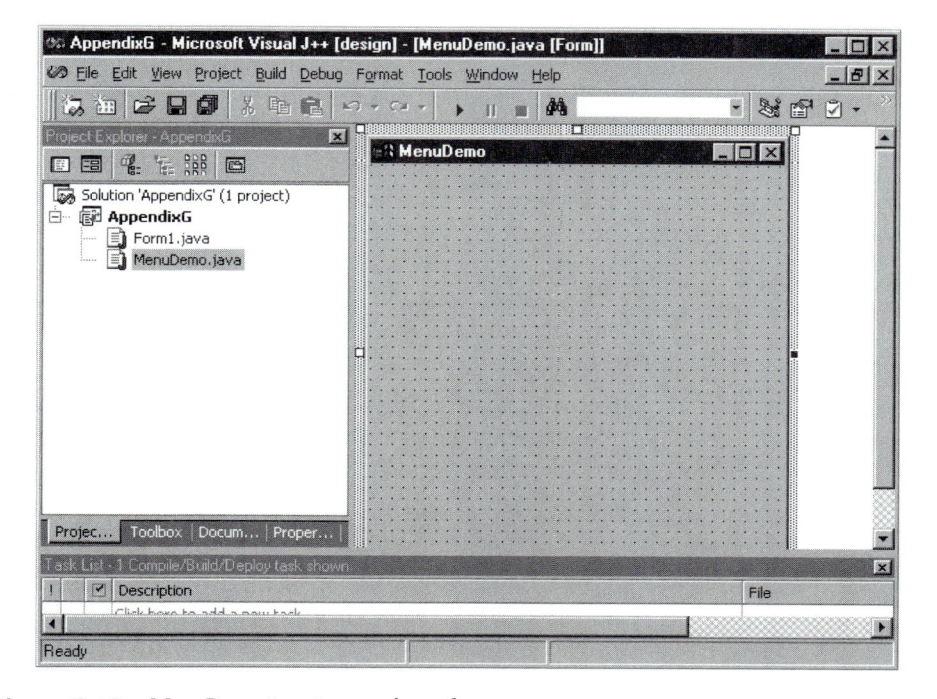

Figure G.10 *MenuDemo.java is created as a form.*

2. Create the user interface, as shown in Figure G.11. Add three Labels and change their text properties to Number 1, Number 2, and Result, respectively. Add three Edits, set their text properties to empty, and change their name properties to edtNum1, edtNum2, and edtResult. Add four Buttons, change their text properties to Add, Subtract, Multiply, and Divide, and change their name properties to btAdd, btSub, btMul, and btDiv.

3. Save the project by choosing File, Save All.

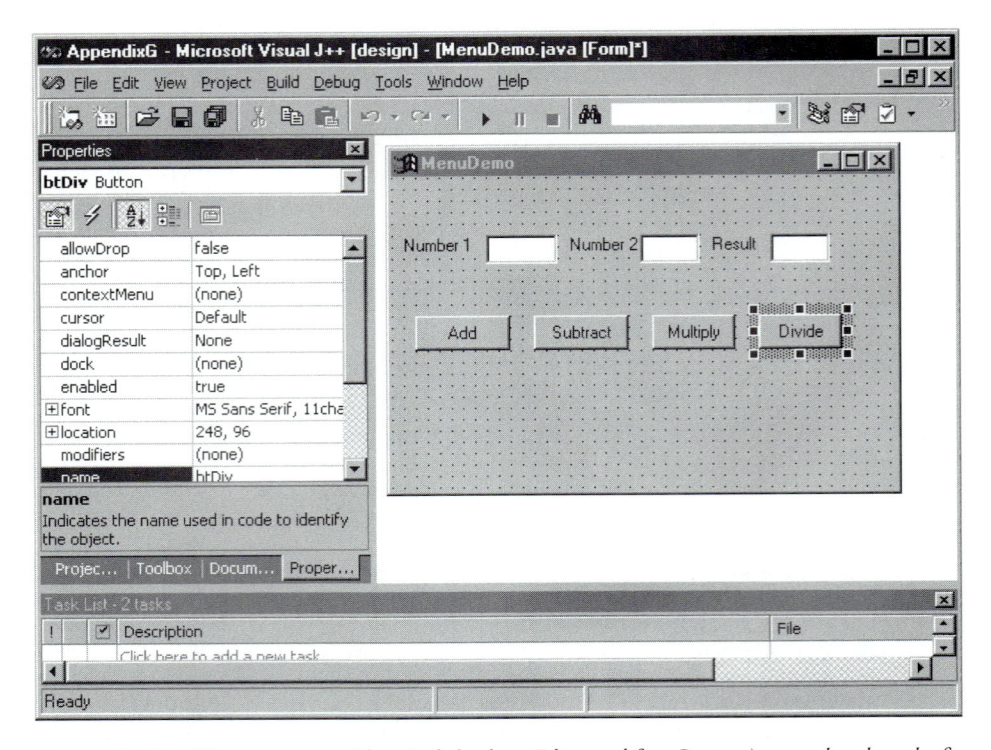

Figure G.11 *The components (three Labels, three Edits, and four Buttons) were placed on the form.*

Phase 2: Implementing Handlers

Follow the steps below to write the code for implementing the handlers for the four buttons:

1. Double-click the Add button to let Visual J++ generate the btAdd_Click() handler. Implement the btAdd_Click handler, as follows.

```
private void btAdd_click(Object source, Event e)
{
  add();
}

private void add()
{
  int num1 = new Integer(edtNum1.getText()).intValue();
  int num2 = new Integer(edtNum2.getText()).intValue();
  edtResult.setText(new Integer(num1+num2).toString());
}
```

2. The handlers for the Subtract, Multiply, and Divide buttons can be coded similarly.

3. Save the project by choosing File, Save All.

> **TIP**
> Once the handler is created, its signature cannot be updated automatically in Visual J++. For example, if the name of the `btAdd` button is changed to *newAdd*, the handler btAdd_click cannot be changed. This certainly would cause a problem, because the button-click action should be handled by a method named `newAdd_Click`. Therefore, avoid changing an object's name after the handler is implemented. If you must change the name, you should also manually change the handler's name. In other tools such as JBuilder, the object's name and its handler signatures are synchronized.

Phase 3: Creating Menus

Follow the steps below to create menus:

1. Click the MainMenu component in the Toolbox window and drop it on the Form Designer, as shown in Figure G.12.

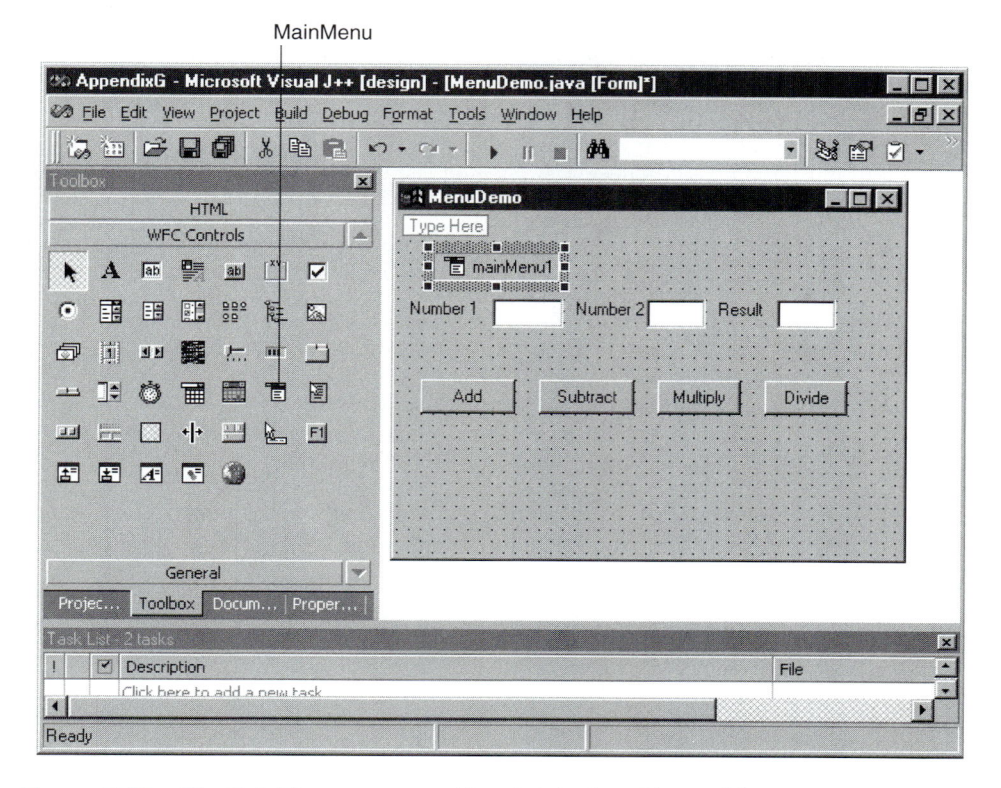

Figure G.12 *The MainMenu components (three Labels, three Edits, and four Buttons) were placed on the form.*

2. Create the menus Operation and Exit. Add menu items Add, Subtract, Multiply, and Divide in the Operation menu, and add menu item Close in the Exit menu.

3. Select Add, as shown in Figure G.13. In the Property window, change the name property to `miAdd`. Similarly, change the name properties for Subtract, Multiply, Divide, and Close to `miSub`, `miMul`, `miDiv`, and `miClose`.

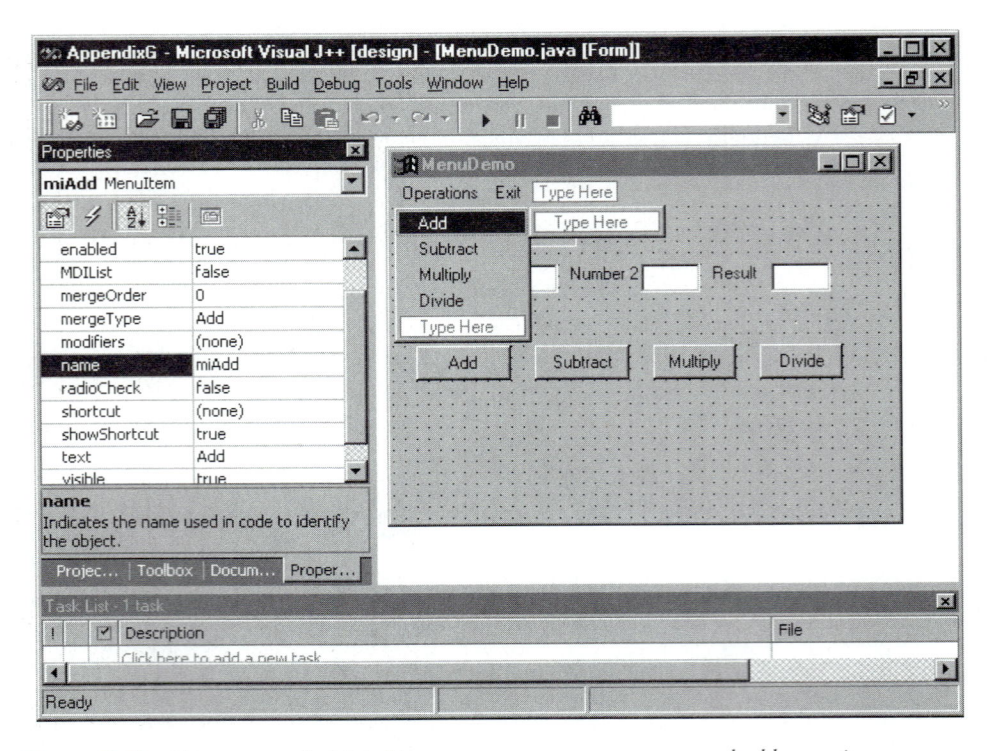

Figure G.13 *You can use the MainMenu component to create menus and add menu items.*

4. In the Properties window for `miAdd`, click the Event button to list the handlers for `miAdd`. Choose btAdd_click in the drop-down menu of the click handler, as shown in Figure G.14.

5. The handlers for the menu commands Subtract, Multiply, Divide, and Close can be similarly created and implemented.

6. In the Properties window for `miClose`, click the Event button to list the handlers for `miClose`. Double-click the value field of the click handler to generate handler miClose_Click, as shown in Figure G.14.

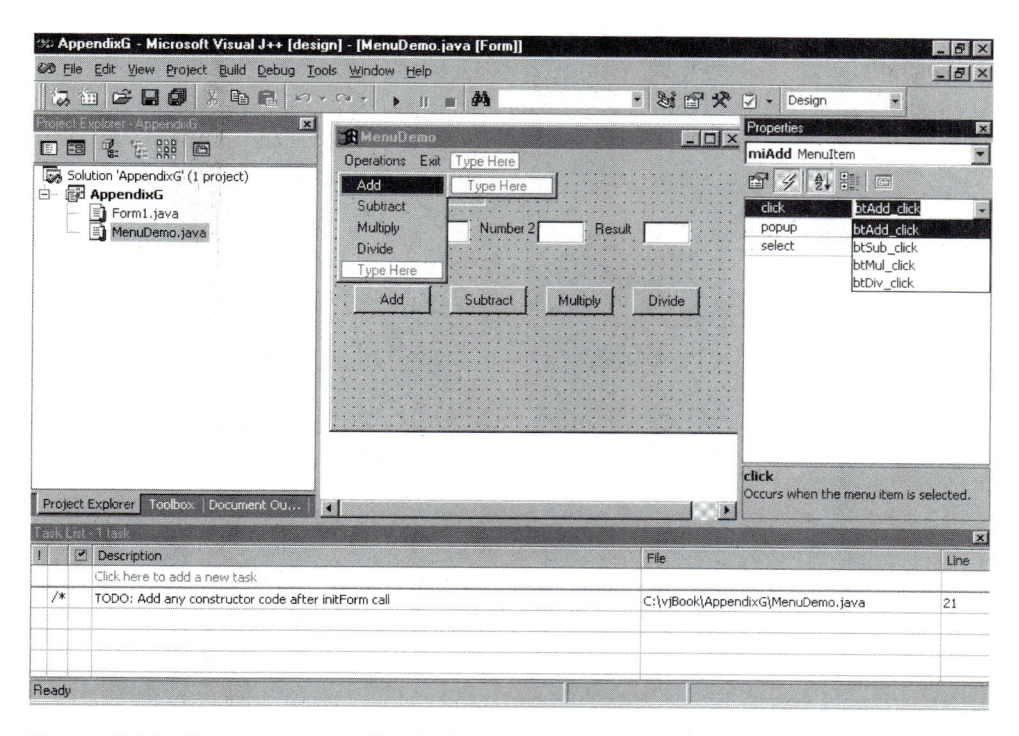

Figure G.14 *You can create handlers for the menu items in the Event page of the Properties window.*

7. The complete code is shown as follows:

```java
import com.ms.wfc.app.*;
import com.ms.wfc.core.*;
import com.ms.wfc.ui.*;
import com.ms.wfc.html.*;

/**
 * This class can take a variable number of parameters on the
     command
 * line. Program execution begins with the main() method.
    The class
 * constructor is not invoked unless an object of type
     'MenuDemo'
 * created in the main() method.
 */
public class MenuDemo extends Form
{
    public MenuDemo()
    {
        super();

        // Required for Visual J++ Form Designer support
        initForm();

        // TODO: Add any constructor code after initForm call
    }
```

```java
/**
 * MenuDemo overrides dispose so it can clean up the
 * component list.
 */
public void dispose()
{
        super.dispose();
        components.dispose();
}

// Handler for the Add button
private void btAdd_click(Object source, Event e)
{
        add();
}

//  Add Number 1 and Number 2 and show the result
private void add()
{
        int num1 = new Integer(edtNum1.getText()).intValue();
        int num2 = new Integer(edtNum2.getText()).intValue();
        edtResult.setText(new Integer(num1+num2).toString());
}

// Handler for the Subtract button
private void btSub_click(Object source, Event e)
{
  subtract();
}

  // Subtract Number 2 from Number 2 and show the result
  private void subtract()
  {
        int num1 = new Integer(edtNum1.getText()).intValue();
        int num2 = new Integer(edtNum2.getText()).intValue();
        edtResult.setText(new Integer(num1-num2).toString());
 }

// Handler for the Multiply button
private void btMul_click(Object source, Event e)
{
  multiply();
}

  // Multiply Number 1 and Number 2 and show the result
  private void multiply()
  {
        int num1 = new Integer(edtNum1.getText()).intValue();
        int num2 = new Integer(edtNum2.getText()).intValue();
        edtResult.setText(new Integer(num1*num2).toString());
  }

  // Handler for the Divide button
private void btDiv_click(Object source, Event e)
{
  divide();
}

  // Divide Number 2 from Number 1 and show the result
  private void divide()
  {
        int num1 = new Integer(edtNum1.getText()).intValue();
        int num2 = new Integer(edtNum2.getText()).intValue();
        edtResult.setText(new Integer(num1/num2).toString());
  }
```

```java
      private void miClose_click(Object source, Event e)
      {
        System.exit(0);
      }

      /**
       * NOTE: The following code is required by the Visual J++ form
       * designer.  It can be modified using the form editor.  Do not
       * modify it using the code editor.
       */
      Container components = new Container();
      Label label1 = new Label();
      Edit edtNum1 = new Edit();
      Label label2 = new Label();
      Edit edtNum2 = new Edit();
      Label label3 = new Label();
      Edit edtResult = new Edit();
      Button btAdd = new Button();
      Button btSub = new Button();
      Button btMul = new Button();
      Button btDiv = new Button();
      MainMenu mainMenu1 = new MainMenu();
      MenuItem menuItem1 = new MenuItem();
      MenuItem miAdd = new MenuItem();
      MenuItem miSub = new MenuItem();
      MenuItem miMul = new MenuItem();
      MenuItem miDiv = new MenuItem();
      MenuItem menuItem6 = new MenuItem();
      MenuItem miClose = new MenuItem();

      private void initForm()
      {
        label1.setLocation(new Point(8, 40));
        label1.setSize(new Point(56, 16));
        label1.setTabIndex(0);
        label1.setTabStop(false);
        label1.setText("Number 1");

        edtNum1.setLocation(new Point(64, 40));
        edtNum1.setSize(new Point(48, 20));
        edtNum1.setTabIndex(1);
        edtNum1.setText("");

        label2.setLocation(new Point(120, 40));
        label2.setSize(new Point(56, 16));
        label2.setTabIndex(2);
        label2.setTabStop(false);
        label2.setText("Number 2");

        edtNum2.setLocation(new Point(168, 40));
        edtNum2.setSize(new Point(40, 20));
        edtNum2.setTabIndex(3);
        edtNum2.setText("");

        label3.setLocation(new Point(216, 40));
        label3.setSize(new Point(40, 16));
        label3.setTabIndex(4);
        label3.setTabStop(false);
        label3.setText("Result");

        edtResult.setLocation(new Point(256, 40));
        edtResult.setSize(new Point(40, 20));
        edtResult.setTabIndex(5);
        edtResult.setText("");
```

```java
btAdd.setLocation(new Point(16, 96));
btAdd.setSize(new Point(64, 24));
btAdd.setTabIndex(6);
btAdd.setText("Add");
btAdd.addOnClick(new EventHandler(this.btAdd_click));

btSub.setLocation(new Point(96, 96));
btSub.setSize(new Point(64, 24));
btSub.setTabIndex(7);
btSub.setText("Subtract");
btSub.addOnClick(new EventHandler(this.btSub_click));

btMul.setLocation(new Point(176, 96));
btMul.setSize(new Point(56, 24));
btMul.setTabIndex(8);
btMul.setText("Multiply");
btMul.addOnClick(new EventHandler(this.btMul_click));

btDiv.setLocation(new Point(248, 96));
btDiv.setSize(new Point(56, 24));
btDiv.setTabIndex(9);
btDiv.setText("Divide");
btDiv.addOnClick(new EventHandler(this.btDiv_click));

miAdd.setText("Add");
miAdd.addOnClick(new EventHandler(this.btAdd_click));

miSub.setText("Subtract");
miSub.addOnClick(new EventHandler(this.btSub_click));

miMul.setText("Multiply");
miMul.addOnClick(new EventHandler(this.btMul_click));

miDiv.setText("Divide");
miDiv.addOnClick(new EventHandler(this.btDiv_click));

menuItem1.setMenuItems(new MenuItem[] {
                        miAdd,
                        miSub,
                        miMul,
                        miDiv});
menuItem1.setText("Operations");

miClose.setText("Close");
miClose.addOnClick(new EventHandler(this.miClose_click));

menuItem6.setMenuItems(new MenuItem[] {
                        miClose});
menuItem6.setText("Exit");

mainMenu1.setMenuItems(new MenuItem[] {
                        menuItem1,
                        menuItem6});
/* @designTimeOnly mainMenu1.setLocation(new Point(40, 8));
*/

this.setText("MenuDemo");
this.setAutoScaleBaseSize(new Point(5, 13));
this.setClientSize(new Point(340, 218));
this.setMenu(mainMenu1);
```

```
            this.setNewControls(new Control[] {
                            btDiv,
                            btMul,
                            btSub,
                            btAdd,
                            edtResult,
                            label3,
                            edtNum2,
                            label2,
                            edtNum1,
                            label1});
    }

    /**
     * The main entry point for the application.
     *
     * @param args Array of parameters passed to the application
     * via the command line.
     */
    public static void main(String args[])
    {
            Application.run(new MenuDemo());
    }
}
```

# APPENDIX H

GLOSSARY

This glossary lists and defines the key terms used in *Introduction to Java Programming with Microsoft Visual J++6*.

abstract class   When you are designing classes, a superclass should contain common features that are shared by subclasses. Sometimes the superclass is so abstract that it cannot have any specific instances. These classes are called *abstract classes* and are declared using the `abstract` modifier. Abstract classes are like regular classes with data and methods, but you cannot create instances of abstract classes using the `new` operator.

abstraction   A technique in software development that hides detailed implementation. Java supports method abstraction and class abstraction. *Method abstraction* is defined as separating the use of a method from its implementation. The client can use a method without knowing how the method is implemented. If you decide to change the implementation, the client program will not be affected. Similarly, class abstraction hides the implementation of the class from the client.

abstract method   A method signature without implementation. Its implementation is provided by its subclasses. An abstract method is denoted with an `abstract` modifier and must be contained in an abstract class. In a nonabstract subclass extended from an abstract class, all abstract methods must be implemented, even if they are not used in the subclass.

Abstract Window Toolkit (AWT)   The set of components for developing simple graphics applications that were in use before the introduction of Swing components. These components have now been replaced by the Swing components.

accessor method   The getter and setter methods for retrieving and setting private fields in an object.

actual parameter   The value passed to a method when it is invoked. Actual parameters should match formal parameters in type, order, and number.

algorithm   Pseudocode that describes how a problem is solved in terms of the actions to be executed, and specifies the order in which these actions should be executed. Algorithms can help the programmer plan a program before writing it in a programming language.

applet   A special kind of Java program that can run directly from a Web browser or an applet viewer. Various security restrictions are imposed on applets. For example, applets cannot perform input/output operations on a user's system and therefore cannot read or write files or transmit computer viruses.

application   Standalone programs, such as any program written using a high-level language. Applications can be executed from any computer with a Java interpreter. Applications are not subject to the security restrictions imposed on Java applets. An application class must contain a main method.

argument   Same as actual parameter.

array   A container object that stores an indexed sequence of the same types of data. Typically, the individual elements are referenced by an index value. The index is an int value starting with 0 for the first element, 1 for the second, and so on.

assignment statement   A simple statement that assigns a value to a variable.

block   A sequence of statements enclosed in braces ({}).

bytecode   The result of compiling Java source code. The bytecode is machine-independent and can run on any machine that has a Java running environment.

casting   The process of converting a primitive data type value into another primitive type or converting an object of one data type into another object type. For example, (int)3.5 converts 3.5 into an int value and (Cylinder)c converts an object c into the Cylinder type. In Java, an object of a class can be cast to an instance of another class as long as the latter is a subclass of the first class or, if an interface, implements it.

child class   Same as subclass.

class   An encapsulated collection of data and methods that operate on data. A class may be instantiated to create an object that is an instance of the class.

class hierarchy   A collection of classes organized in terms of superclasses and subclass relationships.

class method   A method that can be invoked without creating an instance of the class. To define class methods, put the modifier static in the method declaration.

class variable   A data member declared using the static modifier. A class variable is global to a class and to all instances of that class. Class variables are used to communicate between different objects with the same class and to handle global states among these objects.

comment Comments document what a program is and how it is constructed. They are not programming statements and are ignored by the compiler. In Java, comments are preceded by two slashes (//) in a line or enclosed between /* and */ in multiple lines.

compiler A software program that translates Java source code into bytecode.

constant A variable declared `final` in Java. Since a class constant is usually shared by all objects of the same class, a class constant is often declared `static`. A local constant is a constant declared inside a method.

constructor A special method for initializing objects when creating objects using the `new` operator. The constructor has exactly the same name as its defining class. Constructors can be overloaded, making it easier to construct objects with different kinds of initial data values.

data type Data type is used to define variables. Java supports primitive data types and object data types.

debugging The process of finding and fixing errors in a program.

declaration Defines variables, methods, and classes in a program.

default constructor A constructor that has no parameters. A default constructor is required for a JavaBeans component.

definition Alternative term for a declaration.

design To plan how a program can be structured and implemented by coding.

double buffering A technique to reduce flickering in image animation in Java.

encapsulation Combining of methods and data into a single data structure. In Java, this is known as a *class*.

event A signal to the program that something has happened. Events are generated by external user actions, such as mouse movements, mouse button clicks, and keystrokes, or by the operating system, such as a timer. The program can choose to respond to an event or ignore it.

event adapter A class used to filter event methods and handle only specified ones.

event delegation In Java event-driven programming, events are assigned to the listener object for processing. This is referred to as event delegation.

event-driven programming Java graphics programming is event-driven. In event-driven programming, codes are executed upon the activation of events, such as clicking a button or moving the mouse.

event handler A method in the listener's object that is designed to do some specified processing when a particular event occurs.

event listener The object that receives and handles the event.

event listener interface An interface implemented by the listener class to handle the specified events.

event registration To become a listener, an object must be registered as a listener by the source object. The source object maintains a list of listeners and notifies all the registered listeners when an event occurs.

event source The object that generates the event.

exception An unexpected event indicating that a program has failed in some way. Exceptions are represented by exception objects in Java. Exceptions can be handled in a `try/catch` block.

handler *See* event handler.

`final` A modifier for classes, data, methods, and local variables. A final class cannot be extended, a final data or local variable is a constant, and a final method cannot be overridden in a subclass.

formal parameter The parameters defined in the method signature.

getter method For retrieving private data in a class.

graphical user interface (GUI) An interface to a program that is implemented using AWT or Swing components, such as frames, buttons, labels, text fields, and so on.

HTML (Hypertext Markup Language) A script language to design Web pages for creating and sharing multimedia-enabled, integrated electronic documents over the Internet.

identifier A name of a variable, method, class, interface, or package.

information hiding A software engineering concept for hiding and protecting an object's internal features and structure.

inheritance In object-oriented programming, the use of the `extends` keyword to derive new classes from existing classes.

inner class A class embedded in another class. Inner classes enable you to define small auxiliary objects and pass units of behavior, thus making programs simple and concise.

instance An object of a class.

instance method A nonstatic method in a class. Instance methods belong to instances and can only be invoked by them.

instance variable A nonstatic data member of a class. A copy of an instance method exists in every instance of the class that is created.

instantiation The process of creating an object of a class.

Integrated Development Environment (IDE) Software that helps programmers write code efficiently. IDE tools integrate editing, compiling, building, debugging, and online help in one graphical user interface.

interface An interface is treated like a special class in Java. Each interface is compiled into a separate bytecode file, just like a regular class. You cannot create an instance for an interface. The structure of a Java interface is similar to that of an abstract class in that you can have data and methods. The data, however, must be constants, and the methods can have only declarations without implementation. Single inheritance is the Java restriction wherein a class can inherit from a single superclass. This restriction is eased by use of interface.

interpreter Software for interpreting and running Java bytecode.

JavaBean A public class that has a default constructor and is serializable.

Java Development Toolkit (JDK) Defines the Java API and contains a set of command-line utilities, such as javac (compiler) and java (interpreter). With Java 2, Sun renamed JDK 1.2 to Java 2 SDK v 1.2. SDK stands for Software Development Toolkit.

Just-in-Time compiler Capable of compiling each bytecode once, and then reinvoking the compiled code repeatedly when the bytecode is executed.

keyword A reserved word defined as part of Java language. (See Appendix A, "Java Keywords," for a full list of keywords.)

local variable A variable defined inside a method definition.

main class A class that contains a main method.

method A collection of statements grouped together to perform an operation. *See* class method; instance method.

method overloading Method overloading means that you can define methods with the same name in a class as long as there is enough difference in their parameter profiles.

method overriding Method overriding means that you can modify a method in a subclass that was originally defined in a superclass.

modal dialog box A dialog box that prevents the user from using other windows before it is dismissed.

modifier A Java keyword that specifies the properties of data, methods, and classes and how they can be used. Examples of modifiers are public, private, and static.

multithreading The capability of a program to perform several tasks simultaneously within a program.

object Same as instance.

object-oriented programming (OOP) An approach to programming that involves organizing objects and their behavior into classes of reusable components.

operator Operations for primitive data type values. Examples of operators are +, -, *, /, and %.

operator precedence Defines the order in which operators will be evaluated in an expression.

package A collection of classes.

parent class Same as superclass.

pass-by-reference A term used when an object reference is passed as a method parameter. Any changes to the local object that occur inside the method body will affect the original object that was passed as the argument.

pass-by-value A term used when a copy of a primitive data type variable is passed as a method parameter. The actual variable outside the method is not affected, regardless of the changes made to the formal parameter inside the method.

primitive data type The primitive data types are `byte`, `short`, `int`, `long`, `float`, `double`, `boolean`, and `char`.

`private` A modifier for members of a class. A private member can only be referenced inside the class.

`protected` A modifier for members of a class. A protected member of a class can be used in the class in which it is declared or any subclass derived from that class.

`public` A modifier for classes, data, and methods that can be accessed by all programs.

recursive method A method that invokes itself, directly or indirectly.

reserved word Same as keyword.

setter method For updating private data in a class.

signature The combination of the name of a method and the list of its parameters.

socket The facilitation of communication between a server and a client.

statement A unit of code that represents an action or a sequence of actions.

static method Same as class method.

static variable Same as class variable.

stream The continuous one-way flow of data between a sender and receiver.

subclass A class that inherits from or extends a superclass.

superclass A class inherited from a subclass.

Swing component The Swing GUI components are painted directly on canvases using Java code except for components that are subclasses of `java.awt.Window` or `java.awt.Panel`, which must be drawn using native GUI on a specific platform. Swing components are less dependent on the target platform and use less resource of the native GUI. Swing components are more flexible and versatile than their AWT counterparts.

tag An HTML instruction that tells a Web browser how to display a document. Tags are enclosed in brackets such as <html>, <i>, <b>, and </html>.

thread A flow of execution of a task, with a beginning and an end, in a program.

Unicode A code system for international characters managed by the Unicode Consortium. Java supports Unicode.

INDEX

SYMBOLS

\+ (addition operator), 46
[] (array subscript), 192
= (assignment statement), 45, 51
\b (backspace operator), 50
{ (beginning of blocks), 27
/* (block comment beginning indicator), 26
*/ (block comment ending indicator), 26, 56
\r (carriage return), 50
// (comments), 26
/ (division operator), 46
} (ends of blocks), 27
; (ends of statements), 27
== (equal operator), 51, 210
^ (exclusive OR operator), 52
\> (greater than operator), 51
\>= (greater than or equal to operator), 51
/** (javadoc comments), 56
< (less than), 51
<= (less than or equal to), 51
\n (linefeed character), 50
&& (logical AND), 51
& (logical AND operator), 52–53
% (modulus operator), 46
* (multiplication operator), 46
!= (not equal to operator), 51
! (not operator), 51
|| (OR operator), 51
| (OR operator), 51–52
++ (preincrement/postincrement), 48
-- (predecrement/postdecrement), 48
\- (subtraction operator), 46
\t (tab character), 50

abs () method, 178
Abstract classes, 239, 240
    Example 7.5 (Designing Abstract Classes), 254–256
    Example 7.6 (Extending Abstract Classes), 256–261
Abstract method, 240, 241
Abstract modifier, 238, 239, 690
Actual parameters, 113
Adapter class, 302–304, 303, 304
Adding
    data member, 267, 271
    methods, 267
    new classes, 267, 268, 269
Adjustment statement, 90
Algorithms, writing programs using, 46
Anchors, 702
Anonymous inner class, 304, 305

Applets, 41, 418
    clients, 660
        Example 16.3 (Networking in Applets), 661–665
    components, program, 39–41
    conversions
        Example 10.3 (Converting Applets to Applications), 431–433
        Example 10.4 (Converting Applications to Applets), 434–437
    conversions between applets and applications, 431
    creating and compiling, 33, 34
    definition, 9
    Example 10.1 (Using Applets), 420–424
    Example 13.2 (Implementing the Runnable Interface in Applet), 554–556
    Example 14.1 (Incorporating Sound in Applets), 577–580
    Example 14.4 (Using Image and Audio in Applications and Applets), 587–591
    Example 1.2 (A Simple Applet), 32–33
    exception handling
        Example 11.5 (Using Exceptions in Applets), 492–494
    HTML page, 10
    JApplet Class, 420
    Javasoft web site, 9
    limitations, 42
    methods
        destroy () method, 420
        init () method, 419
        start () method, 419
        stop () method, 420
    parameters, passing, 428, 429
        Example 10.2 (Passing Parameters to Java Applets), 429–430
    running in Java Plug-In, 425–428
    running programs
        Example 10.5 (Running Program as Applet and Application), 438–440
    running programs as applet and application, 437, 438
    structure, 418
    TicTacToe game, developing, 448
        Example 10.8 (The TicTacToe Game), 449–455
    versus applications, 42
    viewing, 37, 38, 39
    applet HTML tag, 34, 424, 425
Application programmer interface, 10
Applications
    components, 30
    conversions
        Example 10.3 (Converting Applets to Applications), 431–433
        Example 10.4 (Converting Applications to Applets), 434–437
    conversions between applets and applications, 431
    Example 14.4 (Using Image and Audio in Applications and Applets), 587–591
    Example 1.1 (A Simple Application), 23
    loading image and audio files, 586, 587
    running programs
        Example 10.5 (Running Program as Applet and Application), 438–440

Index

Applications (*cont.*)
   running programs as applet and application, 437, 438
   versus applets, 42

Arcs, drawing, 329, 330

Arguments, passing, 212, 213
   Example 5.4 (Passing Objects as Arguments), 153–155
   Example 6.10 (Using Command-Line Parameters), 213–215

Array streams, 611

Arrays
   copying, 199, 202
      Example 6.6 (Copying Arrays), 200–201
   creating arrays of objects, 198
   declaring and creating, 186
   definition, 186
   Example 6.1 (Assigning Grades), 189–190
   Example 6.5 (Adding an Array of Rationals), 198–199
   for loop, using, 188
   initializing and processing, 187
   multidimensional arrays, 202, 203
      Example 6.7 (Adding Two Matrices), 203–204
      main subscript, 203
      secondary subscript, 203
   searching, 193
      binary search approach, 195
      Example 6.3 (Testing Linear Search), 194–195
      Example 6.4 (Testing Binary Search), 196–197
      linear search, 193
   selection sort, 190, 191
   size, 188
   sorting, 190
      Example 6.2 (Using Arrays in Sorting), 191–193

ASCII character set, 681
   decimal index, 682
   hexadecimal index, 683

Assignment statement, 50, 51

Audio
   Example 14.1 (Incorporating Sound in Applets), 577–580
   Example 14.2 (Announcing the Time on a Separate Thread), 581–583
   Example 14.4 (Using Image and Audio in Applications and Applets), 587–591
   loading image and audio files in applications, 586, 587
   playing, 576, 577
   separate thread, running on, 581

AWT (Abstract Window Toolkit), 284
   JApplet Class, 420
   replacement by swing components, 284

AWTException class, 480

Base case, 127

Base class, 232

Behaviors, 5

Binary search approach, 195
   Example 6.4 (Testing Binary Search), 196–197

Block styles, 66

Blocks, 31

body tags, 694

Boolean data type, 57

Boolean expressions, if statement application, 8

BorderLayout, 310
   Example 8.6 (Testing the BorderLayout Manager), 311–312

Borders, 375, 376
   Example 9.9 (Using Borders), 377–381

Break
   Example 3.5 (Testing a break statement), 99

Break mode, 63

Break statement, 97, 98

Breakpoints, 219, 220

Buffered streams, 618, 619

Buttons, 347
   Example 9.1 (Using Buttons), 348–351
   properties, 348

Byte streams, 605

Bytecodes, 6

Bytecodes, extensions, file, 32

Calendar
   Example 12.2 (Displaying a Calendar), 521–527

CardLayout Manager, 455
   Example 10.9 (Testing CardLayout Manager), 456–458

Case-sensitivity, 31, 65

Casting objects, 243, 244
   Example 7.4 (Casting Objects), 244–247
   explicit casting, 243
   implicit casting, 243

Character data type, 55, 56

Character set, ASCII, 681
   decimal Index, 682
   hexadecimal Index, 683

Character streams, 605

Characteristics, 4
   architecture-neutral, 8
   distributed, 6
   dynamic, 9
   interpreted, 6
   multithreaded, 8
   object oriented programming, 6
   object-oriented, 5
   performance, 8
   portable, 8
   robustness, 7
   secure, 7
   simplicity, 5

Characters, special, 56

Check boxes, 367
   Example 9.7 (Using Check Boxes), 368–370

Child class, 232

Choice, 360, 361

Circle, 143
   class, 143
      class variables, 157
      instance variables, 157
   Example 5.2 (Using Constructors), 148, 149
   Example 5.6 (Testing Instance and Class Variables), 158–161
   object
      Example 5.1 (Using Objects), 145–17

Class abstraction, 163

Class inheritance, 41

Class instance, 40

Class methods, 161

Class modifier, 689

Class variables, 157, 158
   Example 5.6 (Testing Instance and Class Variables), 158–161

Classes
   abstract class, 239, 240
   color class, 318
   Java class, 345
   JComponent, 346
   JDialog, 286
   JFileChooser, 636

JFrame, 286
JPanel, 286
KeyEvent Class, 445, 446
main class, 143
Math class, 177
    abs () method, 178
    exponent methods, 177
    max () method, 178
    min () method, 178
    random () method, 178
    trigonometric methods, 177
modifiers, 150
    Example 5.3 (Using the Private Modifier), 151, 152
    private, 151
    public, 151
    static, 150
mortgage
    Example 5.7 (Using the Mortgage Class), 164–166
nested classes, 266
number class, 250
object class, 247, 248
OutputStream class, 607
packages, 170
    classes into packages, putting, 172
    Example 5.10 (Using your own packages), 174–175
    Example 5.9 (Putting Classes into Packages), 172–173
    Java Application Programmer Interface, 175, 176
    package naming conventions, 171
    using packages, 174
parent class, 232
rational
    Example 5.8 (Using the Rational Class), 166–170
Reader class, 606, 607
RuntimeException class, 479
stream classes, 605
    byte streams, 605
    character streams, 605
String class, 205
    string comparisons, 206
    string concatenation, 206
    string length and retrieving individual characters, 207
    string object, 205
    StringBuffer class, 207
    substrings, 206
StringBuffer class
    appending and inserting new contents, 208
    capacity() method, 208
    charAt() method, 208
    Example 6.8 (Testing StringBuffer), 209–210
    length() method, 208
    reverse() method, 208
    setCharAt() method, 208
    setLength() method, 208
StringTokenizer class, 210
    Example 6.9 (Testing StringTokenizer), 211–212
subclass, 232
superclass, 232
Thread class, 544
    Example 13.1 (Using Thread class to create and launch threads), 547–549
Window, 285
    JDialog, 285
    JFrame, 285

wrapper class, 250
Writer class, 607
Classes, separate, 66, 67
CLASSPATH environment variable, 171, 172
Clocks
    drawing demonstration, 333–334
        Example 8.10 (Drawing a clock), 334–337
    Example 12.1 (Displaying a Clock), 515–520
    Example 13.3 (Controlling a Group of Clocks), 557–562
    Example 14.1 (Incorporating Sound in Applets), 577–580
clone() method, 249
Coding, 46
Color, 286
Color class, 285, 318
Combo boxes, 360, 361
    Example 9.5 (Using Combo boxes), 361–363
Commands, debugging, 218, 219
Command-line arguments
    Example 8.10 (Drawing a clock), 334–337
Comments, 30, 64
Comments, javadoc, 267
Compilation errors, 60
Component, 285
Component class, 285
Concatenation, string, 206
Conditional expression, 87
Constants
    numeric wrapper class, 251
    StreamTokenizer Constants, 622
    syntax, 52
Constructors, 147
    Example 5.2 (Using Constructors), 148, 149
    numeric wrapper class, 251
    StringBuffer, 207
    superclass constructors, 234
Container class, 285
Containers, 285
    panels as containers, using, 312
        Example 8.7 (Testing Panels), 313–314
Content-based tags, 694, 695
Continue statement, 97, 98
    Example 3.6 (Using a Continue Statement), 100, 101
Control structures
    conditional expression, 87
    if statements, 80
        Example 3.1 (Using Nested if Statements), 83, 84
        if . . . statements, 81, 82
        nested if statements, 82, 83
        shortcut if statements, 87
        simple if statements, 80, 81
    introduction, 80
    keywords
        break, 97, 98
        continue, 97, 98
        Example 3.5 (Testing a Break Statement), 99
        Example 3.6 (Using a Continue Statement), 100, 101
    loop constructs, 80
    loop structures, 89
        do loop, 96, 97
        elements, required, 91
        Example 3.2 (Using for loops), 91, 92
        Example 3.3 (Using nested for loops), 92, 93, 94

Control structures (*cont.*)
  loop structures (*cont.*)
    Example 3.4 (Using a while loop), 95, 96
    Example 3.7 (Finding the Sales Amount), 101, 102, 103
    Example 3.8 (Displaying a triangle), 103, 104
    for loop, 89, 90, 91
    while loop, 94, 95
  switch statements, using, 87, 88, 89
Conversions
  applets and applications, between, 431
  Example 10.3 (Converting Applets to Applications), 431–433
  Example 10.4 (Converting Applications to Applets), 434–437
Conversion, numeric type, 54, 55
Creating
  instance of the class, 144
  methods in separate classes, 119
  object of the class, 144
  projects, 13
C++ language, *versus* **Java, 5**

Data, 5
Data fields, 142
Data files
  Example 16.5 (Retrieving Remote Data Files), 669–672
Data modifier, 689
Datagram socket, 650
Datastreams, 612, 613
  Example 15.2 (Using Data Streams), 614–616
Date and time, processing, 513–515
Debugging
  break mode, 63
  breakpoints, 219, 220
  commands, debugging, 218, 219
  demonstration, 223, 224
  inspecting and modifying data values, 220
    autos window, 221
    immediate window, 222
    locals window, 221
    threads window, 222
    watch window, 221
  logic errors, 64
  logical errors, 215
  multithreaded applications, 549, 550
  starting the debugger, 216, 217, 218
  utilities, debugging, 215, 216
Decimal index, 682
Declaring and creating objects, 143
Declaring object syntax, 143
Default modifier, 690
Definition, 143
Definition lists, 698, 699
Derived class, 232
Design guidelines, 252, 253
Design mode, 63
Developmental tools, 11
  JBuilder by Borland, 11
  JFactory by Rouge Wave, 11
  Sun Java Workshop, 11
  Visual Age for Java by IBM, 11
  Visual Cafe' by Symantec, 11
  Visual J++ by Microsoft, 11
Dialog boxes
  add class dialog box, 268, 269
  add member variable dialog box, 271, 272
  add method dialog box, 270, 271
  edit parameter list dialog box, 270
  error message, 63
  file dialogs, 636, 637
    Example 15.7 (Using File Dialogs), 637–641
  help button, 74
  message dialog boxes, 382
    Example 9.10 (Using Message Dialogs), 383–386
  options, integrated development environment, 74
Do loop, 96, 97
Document windows, 17, 21
Drawing
  lines, 324
  ovals, 327, 328
  rectangles, 324, 325, 326
Dynamic syntax checking, 61

Embedding graphics, 705
  Example E.7 (Illustration of Horizontal Bar Tags), 705
  horizontal bar tags, 705
  image tags, 706
End tag, 35, 693
equals() method, 248
Error class, 479
Errors, programming, 60
  compilation errors, 60
  error help, 62
  error tips, receiving, 62
  input error, 63
  logic errors, 64
  logical errors, 215
  runtime errors, 63
  syntax errors, 60
Events
  keyboard events, 445
    Example 10.7 (Handling Keyboard Events), 446–448
  mouse events, 441, 442
    Example 10.6 (Handling Complex Mouse Events), 442–445
Event-driven programming, 289
  adapter class, 302, 303, 304
  anonymous inner class, 304, 305
  event and event source, 290
  event registration, 291
  event types, listeners, and listener methods table, 292, 293
  Example 8.1 (Creating a Centered Frame with Exit Handling), 294–297
  Example 8.2 (Handling Simple Mouse Events), 297–300
  Example 8.3 (Handling Simple Action Events), 300–301
  handler, 291
  handling events, 293
  listener, 291
  listener object, 292
  source object, 292
  target object, 302
  user action, source object, and event type table, 291
Example programs
  1.1 (A Simple Application), 23
  1.2 (A Simple Applet), 32–33
  2.1 (Computing the Area of a Circle), 47–49
  2.2 (Computing a mortgage), 67–69
  2.3 (Breaking down a sum of money), 69, 70
  3.1 (Using Nested if Statements), 83, 84
  3.2 (Using for Loops), 91
  3.3 (Using Nested for Loops), 92
  3.4 (Using a while Loop), 95, 96
  3.5 (Testing a break Statement), 99
  3.6 (Using a continue Statement), 100, 101

3.7 (Finding the Sales Amount), 101, 102, 103
3.8 (Displaying a Triangle), 103, 104
4.1 (Testing the max() Method), 114, 115
4.2 (Testing Pass by Value), 117
4.3 (Overloading the max() Method), 118, 119
4.4 (Computing Square Roots), 119, 120
4.5 (Illustrating Method Abstraction in Large Projects), 121–126
4.6 (Computing Fibonacci Numbers), 128–130
4.7 (Solving the Towers of Hanoi problem), 130–133
5.1 (Using Objects), 145–147
5.2 (Using Constructors), 148, 149
5.3 (Using the private Modifier), 151, 152
5.4 (Passing Objects as Arguments), 153–155
5.5 (Using a Setter Method to Change Data in a Private Field), 156–157
5.6 (Testing Instance and Class Variables), 158–161
5.7 (Using the Mortgage Class), 164–166
5.8 (Using the Rational Class), 166–170
5.9 (Putting Classes into Packages), 172–173
5.10 (Using Your Own Packages), 174–175
6.1 (Assigning Grades), 189–190
6.2 (Using Arrays in Sorting), 191–193
6.3 (Testing Linear Search), 194–195
6.4 (Testing Binary Search), 196–197
6.5 (Adding an Array of Rationals), 198–199
6.6 (Copying Arrays), 200–201
6.7 (Adding Two Matrices), 203–204
6.8 (Testing StringBuffer), 209–210
6.9 (Testing StringTokenizer), 211–212
6.10 (Using Command-Line Parameters), 213–215
7.1 (Demonstrating Inheritance), 232–233
7.2 (Testing Inheritance), 234–235
7.3 (Overriding the Methods in the Superclass), 236–237
7.4 (Casting Objects), 244–247
7.5 (Designing Abstract Classes), 254–256
7.6 (Extending Abstract Classes), 256–261
7.7 (Using Interfaces), 262–265
8.1 (Creating a Centered Frame with Exit Handling), 294–297
8.2 (Handling Simple Mouse Events), 297–300
8.3 (Handling Simple Action Events), 300–301
8.4 (Testing the FlowLayout Manager), 307–308
8.5 (Testing the GridLayout Manager), 309–310
8.6 (Testing the BorderLayout Manager), 311–312
8.7 (Testing Panels), 313–314
8.8 (Drawing on Panels), 315–316
8.9 (Using FontMetrics), 320–323
8.10 (Drawing a clock), 334–337
9.1 (Using Buttons), 348–351
9.2 (Using Labels), 352–354
9.3 (Using Text Fields), 355–357
9.4 (Using Text Areas), 358–359
9.5 (Using Combo Boxes), 361–363
9.6 (Using Lists), 364–366
9.7 (Using Check Boxes), 368–370
9.8 (Using Radio Buttons), 371–375
9.9 (Using Borders), 377–381
9.10 (Using Message Dialogs), 383–386
9.11 (Using Menus), 390–394
9.12 (Creating Multiple Windows), 394–396
9.13 (Using Scrollbars), 398–400
9.14 (Using Scroll Panes), 402–405
9.15 (Using Tabbed Panes), 406–409
10.1 (Using Applets), 420–424
10.2 (Passing Parameters to Java Applets), 429–430
10.3 (Converting Applets to Applications), 431–433
10.4 (Converting Applications to Applets), 434–437
10.5 (Running Program as Applet and Application), 438–440
10.6 (Handling Complex Mouse Events), 442–445
10.7 (Handling Keyboard Events), 446–448
10.8 (The TicTacToe Game), 449–455

10.9 (Testing CardLayout Manager), 456–458
10.10 (Testing the GridBagLayout Manager), 460–462
10.11 (Using No Layout Manager), 463–465
11.1 (Throwing Exceptions), 481
11.2 (Catching Exceptions), 484–487
11.3 (Exceptions in GUI Applications), 485–487
11.4 (Creating your Own Exception Classes), 487–492
11.5 (Using Exceptions in Applets), 492–494
11.6 (Performance Differences with and without Exception Handling), 496–498
12.1 (Displaying a Clock), 515–520
12.2 (Displaying a Calendar), 521–527
12.3 (Formatting Numbers), 528–532
12.4 (Using Resource Bundles), 534–540
13.1 (Using Thread Class to Create and Launch Threads), 547–549
13.2 (Implementing the Runnable Interface in an Applet), 554–556
13.3 (Controlling a Group of Clocks), 557–562
13.4 (Testing Thread Priorities), 563–564
13.5 (Showing Resource Conflict), 566–569
14.1 (Incorporating Sound in Applets), 577–580
14.2 (Announcing the Time on a Separate Thread), 581–583
14.3 (Displaying Images in an Applet), 584–586
14.4 (Using Image and Audio in Applications and Applets), 587–591
14.5 (Using Image Animation), 591–595
14.6 (Using MediaTracker), 596–598
15.1 (Processing External Files), 609–611
15.2 (Using Data Streams), 614–616
15.3 (Using Print Streams), 617–618
15.4 (Displaying a File in a Text Area), 619–622
15.5 (Using StreamTokenizer), 623–625
15.6 (Using Random Access Files), 627–635
16.1 (A Client/Server Example), 652–655
16.2 (Serving Multiple Clients), 656–660
16.3 (Networking in Applets), 661–665
16.4 (Viewing HTML Pages from Java), 666–668
16.5 (Retrieving Remote Data Files), 669–672
E.1 (An HTML Example), 692
E.2 (HTML Source Code Using Structure Tags), 696–697
E.3 (Testing Font Tags), 698
E.4 (Using Various List Tags), 699–700
E.5 (Illustration of Table Tags), 701–702
E.6 (Navigation Within Same Document), 704
E.7 (Illustration of Horizontal Bar Tags), 705
E.8 (Illustration of Image Tags), 706
Examples, using in book, 710–711

Exception classes, 479
    creating your own, 487
        Example 11.4 (Creating your Own Exception Classes), 487–492
        Example 11.5 (Using Exceptions in Applets), 492–494

Exception handling, 478
    AWTException class, 480
    catching an exception, 480
    catching exceptions, 482, 483
    claiming an exception, 480
    Error class, 479
    Example 11.1 (Throwing Exceptions), 481
    Example 11.2 (Catching Exceptions), 484–487
    Example 11.5 (Using Exceptions in Applets), 492–494
    Example 11.6 (Differences with and without Exception Handling), 496–498
    exception classes, 479
        creating your own, 487
        Example 11.4 (Creating your Own Exception Classes), 487–492
    exception types, 478
    finally clause, 495

Index

Exception handling (*cont.*)
    InstantiationException class, 480
    IOException class, 479
    models, operational, 480
    precautions, 495, 496
    rethrowing exceptions, 494
    RuntimeException class, 479
    throwing an exception, 480, 481
Exceptions
    Example 11.3 (Exceptions in GUI Applications), 485–487
.exe files, packaging and deploying, 465–466
Exponent methods, 177
Extended class, 232
extends keyword, 41
External files, processing, 608
    Example 15.1 (Processing External Files), 609–611

Fibonacci series, 127
    Example 4.6 (Computing Fibonacci Numbers), 128–130
Fibonacci, Leonardo, 127
File dialogs, 636, 637
    Example 15.7 (Using File Dialogs), 637–641
Files, saving, 15
Filter streams, 611
FilterInputStream subclasses, 612
FilterOutputStream subclasses, 612
Final modifier, 238, 239, 690
Finished, 563
FlowLayout manager
    Example 8.4 (Testing the FlowLayout Manager), 307–308
Font, 286
Font class, 285, 319
Font tags, 694
    Example E.3 (Testing Font Tags), 698
    basefont tags, 697
    font tags, 697
FontMetrics, 286
FontMetrics class, 285, 319, 320
    Example 8.9 (Using fontMetrics), 320–323
for loop, 90
    Example 3.2 (Using for loops), 92
Formal parameters, 113
Formatting numbers based on locales, 527
    Example 12.3 (Formatting Numbers), 528–532
Frame creation, 288, 289
Ftp, 703
Fullfilename, 703

Geometric figures, drawing, 318, 319
Getter method, 345
Gosling, James, 4
Graphical interactive input and output, 641
Graphics, 40, 286
Graphics class, 40, 285
GridBagLayout manager, 458–460
    Example 10.10 (Testing the GridBagLayout Manager), 460–462
GridLayout manager, 308, 309
    Example 8.5 (Testing the GridLayout Manager), 309–310
GUI (graphical user interface), 261, 262
    arcs, drawing, 329, 330
    borders, 375, 376

    Example 9.9 (Using Borders), 377–381
buttons, 347
    Example 9.1 (Using Buttons), 348–351
check boxes, 367
    Example 9.7 (Using Check Boxes), 368–370
clocks
    Example 8.10 (Drawing a clock), 334–337
Color class, 318
combo boxes, 360, 361
    Example 9.5 (Using Combo Boxes), 361–363
Component class, 285
container, 305
Container class, 285
creating, 288
declaring, 261
defining, 266
drawing lines, 324
drawing ovals, 327, 328
drawing rectangles, 324, 325, 326
Example 11.3 (Exceptions in GUI Applications), 485–487
Example 7.7 (Using Interfaces), 262–265
Font class, 319
FontMetrics class, 319, 320
    Example 8.9 (Using FontMetrics), 320–323
frame creation, 288, 289
geometric figures, drawing, 318, 319
Graphics class, 285
    Color class, 285
    Font class, 285
    FontMetrics class, 285
image icons, 389, 390
JApplet class, 285
JComponent, 346
JComponent and subclasses, 287
JComponent class, 285
    JButton, 285
    JCheckBox, 285
    JLabel, 285
    JList, 285
    JMenu, 285
    JRadioButton, 285
    JScrollPane, 285
    JTextArea, 285
    JTextField, 285
JDialog class, 285
JFrame class, 285
JPanel class, 285
keyboard accelerators, 389, 390
keyboard mnemonics, 389, 390
labels, 352
    Example 9.2 (Using Labels), 352–354
layout managers, 305
    BorderLayout manager, 310
    CardLayout manager, 455
    Example 10.10 (Testing GridBagLayout*)*, 460–462
    Example 10.11 (Using No Layout Manager), 463–465
    Example 10.9 (Testing CardLayout Manager), 456–458
    Example 8.4 (Testing FlowLayout Manager), 307–308
    Example 8.5 (Testing GridLayout Manager), 309–310
    Example 8.6 (Testing BorderLayout Manager), 311–312
    FlowLayout manager, 306
    GridBagLayout manager, 458, 459, 460
    GridLayout manager, 308, 309
    no layout manager, using, 462

lists, 364
    Example 9.6 (Using Lists), 364–366
menus, 386–389
    Example 9.11 (Using Menus), 390–394
message dialog boxes, 382
    Example 9.10 (Using Message Dialogs), 383–386
methods
    paint() method, 317
    paintComponent() method, 317
    repaint() method, 317
    update() method, 317
multiple windows, 394
    Example 9.12 (Creating multiple windows), 394–396
no layout manager, using, 462
panels
    containers, using, 312
    draw graphics, using, 314
    Example 8.7 (Testing Panels), 313–314
    Example 8.8 (Drawing on Panels), 315–316
polygons, drawing, 330, 331, 332
radio buttons, 370, 371
    Example 9.8 (Using Radio Buttons), 371–375
scroll panes, 400, 401, 402
    Example 9.14 (Using Scroll Panes), 402–405
scrollbars, 396, 397, 398
    Example 9.13 (Using Scrollbars), 398–400
    horizontal, 396
    vertical, 396
tabbed panes, 405, 406
    Example 9.14 (Using Tabbed Panes), 406–409
text areas, 357, 358
    Example 9.4 (Using Text Areas), 358–359
text fields, 354, 355
    Example 9.3 (Using Text Fields), 355–357
Window class, 285

Handlers, 291
    keyboard events, 445
        Example 10.7 (Handling Keyboard Events), 446–448
    mouse events, 441, 442
        Example 10.6 (Handling Complex Mouse Events), 442–445
Handling events, 293
    Example 8.1 (Creating a Centered Frame with Exit Handling), 294–297
    Example 8.2 (Handling Simple Mouse Events), 297–300
    Example 8.3 (Handling Simple Action Events), 300–301
head tags, 694
Help
    error help, receiving, 62
    favorites list, 73
    menu, 74
    online help, 71, 72, 73
    viewer, help, 71, 72
Hexadecimal Index, 683
Hierarchical relationship, 285
History, java, 4
HTML tag, applet, 424, 425
HTML (Hypertext Markup Language), 9
    creating files, 34, 35, 36, 37
    embedding graphics, 705
        Example E.7 (Illustration of Horizontal Bar Tags), 705

Example 16.4 (Viewing HTML Pages from Java), 666–668
Example E.1 (An HTML Example), 692
Example E.2 (HTML Source Code Using Structure Tags), 696–697
Example E.5 (Illustration of Table Tags), 701–702
Example E.6 (Navigation Within Same Document), 704
image tags
    Example E.8 (Illustration of Image Tags), 706
retrieving files from web servers, 668, 669
source containing applet, 10
tutorial, creating web page, 691–707
applet tag, 34
html tag, 35
Http, 703
Hyperlink tags, 702
Hypertext linking, 702
    absolute link, 703
    anchors, 702
    jumping within the same document, 703
    linking documents on same computer, 703
    relative link, 703
    same document, within
        Example E.6 (Navigation Within Same Document), 704

Identifiers, naming rules, 49
if statements, 80
    Boolean expressions, 80
    if ... else statements, 81, 82
    nested if statements, 82, 83
        Example 3.1 (Using Nested if Statements), 83, 84
    shortcut if statements, 87
    simple if statements, 80
Image icons, 389, 390
Image tags, 694
    Example E.8 (Illustration of Image Tags), 706
Images
    displaying, 583, 584
        Example 14.3 (Displaying Images in an Applet), 584–586
        Example 14.4 (Using Image and Audio in Applications and Applets), 587–591
    displaying a sequence of, 591
        Example 14.5 (Using Image Animation), 591–595
    loading image and audio files in applications, 586, 587
import statement, 39, 40
Inactive state, 563
Indentation, proper, 65
Information hiding, 120
Inheritance, 232
    Example 7.1 (Demonstrating Inheritance), 232–233
    Example 7.2 (Testing Inheritance), 234–235
Inheritance, class, 41
Inner class, 266, 267
Input and output, 604
    array streams, 611
    buffered streams, 618, 619
    datastreams, 612, 613
        Example 15.2 (Using Data Streams), 614–616
    Example 15.4 (Displaying a File in a Text Area), 619–622
    Example 16.5 (Retrieving Remote Data Files), 669–672
    external files, processing, 608
        Example 15.1 (Processing External Files), 609–611
    file dialogs, 636, 637
        Example 15.7 (Using File Dialogs), 637–641

Input and output (*cont.*)
    filter streams, 611
    FilterInputStream subclasses, 612
    FilterOutputStream subclasses, 612
    InputStream class, 606, 607
    interactive input and output, 641, 642
        graphical interactive input and output, 641
        text interactive input and output, 641
    layering, 604
    OutputStream class, 607
    parsing text files, 622
    primitive types on the console, 642, 643
    print streams, 616, 617
        Example 15.3 (Using Print Streams), 617–618
    random access files, 625, 626, 627
        Example 15.6 (Using Random Access Files), 627–635
    Reader class, 606, 607
    stream classes, 605
        byte streams, 605
        character streams, 605
    streams, 604
        line number streams, 644
        object streams, 644
        piped streams, 643
        pushback streams, 644
        string streams, 643
    StreamTokenizer
        Constants, 622
        Example 15.5 (Using StreamTokenizer), 623–625
        Variables, 622, 623
    Writer class, 607
Input errors, 63
InputStream class, 606, 607
Inspecting and modifying data values
    autos window, 221
    immediate window, 222
    locals window, 221
    threads window, 222
    Watch window, 221
Installing Swing Library in Visual J++6, 709
Installing Visual J++6, 709
Instance methods, 161
Instance variables, 157
    Example 5.6 (Testing Instance and Class Variables), 158–161
Instantiation, 5, 143
InstantiationException class, 480
Integrated development environment, 11, 12
    options, customizing, 74
    windows, 17
Interactive input and output, 641, 642
    graphical interactive input and output, 641
    text interactive input and output, 641
Internationalization
    calendar
        Example 12.2 (Displaying a Calendar), 521–527
    clock
        Example 12.1 (Displaying a Clock), 515–520
    date and time, processing, 513–515
    formatting numbers based on locales, 527
        Example 12.3 (Formatting Numbers), 528–532
    locales, 510, 511
        methods, 512
        object constructors, 510
        supported locales, 511, 512
    resource bundles, 532
        Example 12.4 (Using Resource Bundles), 534–540
        naming conventions, 533
    resource chain, 533
    support features, 510
IOException class, 479

JApplet class, 420
JApplet subclass, 285, 286
Java 2 API, 175, 176
Java Application Programmer Interface, 175, 176
Java Development Toolkit, 11
Java Plug-In
    running applets, 425–428
JavaBeans
    getter method, 345
    JComponent
        properties, 346
    minimum JavaBeans component requirements, 345
    requirements, 344, 345
    setter method, 345
Javadoc comments, 64, 267
Javasoft web site, 9, 10
JBuilder by Borland, 11
JComponent, 285
    JButton, 285
    JCheckBox, 285
    JLabel, 285
    JList, 285
    JMenu, 285
    JRadioButton, 285
    JScrollPane, 285
    JTextArea, 285
    JTextField, 285
    properties, 346
    subclasses, 287
JDialog class, 285
JFactory by Rouge Wave, 11
JFileChooser, 636
JFrame class, 285
JPanel class, 285

Keyboard accelerators, 390
Keyboard events, 445
    Example 10.7 (Handlig Keyboard Events), 446–448
Keyboard mnemonics, 389, 390
Keywords, 30
    break, 97, 98
        Example 3.5 (Testing a break Statement), 99
    continue, 97, 98
    continue statement
        Example 3.6 (Using a continue Statement), 100, 101
    extends, 41
    listing, 679
    return, 113
    super, 234
    this, 237
    void, 113

Labels, 352
    Example 9.2 (Using Labels), 352–354
Language specification, 10

Language, Hypertext Markup Language, 9
Layout manager
    BorderLayout, 310
        Example 8.6 (Testing the BorderLayout Manager), 311–312
    CardLayout manager, 455
        Example 10.9 (Testing the CardLayout Manager), 456–458
    FlowLayout manager, 306
        Example 8.4 (Testing the FlowLayout Manager), 307–308
    GridBagLayout Manager, 458–460
    GridBagLayout manager
        Example 10.10 (Testing the GridBagLayout Manager), 460–462
    GridLayout manager, 308, 309
        Example 8.5 (Testing the GridLayout Manager), 309–310
    No Layout manager
        Example 10.11 (Using No Layout Manager), 463–465
    no layout manager, using, 462
Layout, defining window, 22, 23
Line number streams, 644
Linear search, 193
    Example 6.3 (Testing Linear Search), 194–195
Link tags, 694
Linking, hypertext, 702
    absolute link, 703
    anchors, 702
    jumping within the same document, 703
    linking documents on same computer, 703
    relative link, 703
    same document, within
        Example E.6 (Navigation Within Same Document), 704
List tags, 694, 698
    definition lists, 698, 699
    Example E.4 (Using Various List Tags), 699–700
    ordered lists, 698, 699
    unordered lists, 698, 699
Listener, 291
Lists, 364
    Example 9.6 (Using Lists), 364–366
Literals, numeric, 53
Loading image and audio files in applications, 586, 587
Locale, 510, 511
    Example 12.1 (Displaying a Clock), 515–520
    Example 12.2 (Displaying a Calendar), 521–527
    methods, 512, 513
    object constructors, 510
    supported locales, 511, 512
Logic errors, 64
Loop constructs, 80
Loop structures, 89
    do loop, 96, 97
    elements, required, 91
    for loop, 89, 90, 91
        Example 3.2 (Using for Loops), 91, 92
    nested for loops
        Example 3.3 (Using Nested for Loops), 92, 93, 94
    nested loops
        Example 3.8 (Displaying a Triangle), 103, 104
    while loop, 94, 95
        Example 3.4 (Using a While Loop), 95, 96

Main class, 143
Main() method, 32, 47
Math class, 177
    abs() method, 178
    max() method, 178
    min() method, 178
    random() method, 178
    trigonometric methods, 177
max() method, 114, 115
max() methods, 178
MediaTracker, using, 595, 596
    Example 14.6 (Using MediaTracker), 596–598
Menu bar, 15
Menus, 386, 387, 388, 389
    Example 9.11 (Using Menus), 390–394
Message dialog boxes, 382
    Example 9.10 (Using Message Dialogs), 383–386
Method abstraction, 120
    Example 4.5 (Illustrating Method Abstraction in Large Projects), 123
Method heading, 112
Method modifier, 689
Methods, 32, 142
    abstract, 240, 241
    adding new methods, 270, 271
    calling, 113, 114
    capacity() method, 208
    charAt() method, 208
    clone() method, 249
    constructors, 147
    creating, 112
    creating methods in separate classes, 119
    destroy() method, 420
    equals() method, 248
    Example 4.1 (Testing the max() Method), 114, 115
    Example 4.3 (Overloading the max() Method, 118, 119
    Example 4.6 (Computing Fibonacci Numbers), 128–130
    Example 4.7 (Solving the Towers of Hanoi problem), 130–133
    Example 5.2 (Using Constructors), 148, 149
    Example 5.4 (Passing Objects as Arguments), 153–155
    Example 5.5 (Using a Setter Method to Change Data in a Private Field), 156–157
    Example 5.7 (Using the Mortgage Class), 164–166
    Example 5.8 (Using the Rational Class), 166–170
    Example 7.3 (Overriding the Methods in the Superclass), 236–237
    information hiding, 120
    init() method, 419
    instance methods, 161
    length() method, 208
    locale, 512, 513
    Math class, 177
        abs() method, 178
        exponent method, 177
        max() method, 178
        min() method, 178
        random() method, 178
        trigonometric method, 177
    max() method, 114
    method abstraction, 120
        Example 4.5 (Illustrating Method Abstraction in large projects), 121–126
    method heading, 112
    method overloading, 117

Methods (*cont.*)
    modifiers, 112, 150
        Example 5.3 (Using the Private Modifier), 151, 152
        private, 151
        public, 151
        static, 150
    mouse events, 442
    overloading methods, 117, 118, 119
    overriding methods, 235
    overriding, within superclass, 272, 273
    paint() method, 317
    paintComponent() method, 317
    parameter order association, 115
    parameters
        actual parameters, 113
        formal parameters, 113
        passing, 115, 116
    parseDouble() methods, 252
    parseInt() methods, 252
    pass by value, 116
        Example 4.2 (Testing Pass by Value), 116, 117
    passing objects to methods, 152, 153
    readDouble, 112
    readDouble(), 47
    recursion, 126, 127
        base case, 127
        characteristics, 129
        Example 4.6 (Computing Fibonacci Numbers), 128–130
        recursive call, 127
        stopping condition, 127
    recursion *versus* iteration, 133, 134
    repaint() method, 317
    return a value, 114
    return a void, 114
    reverse() method, 208
    setCharAt() method, 208
    setLength() method, 208
    start() method, 419
    static methods for creating borders, 376
    stop() method, 420
    superclass methods, 234
    terminating, 113
    thread class, 545, 546
    toString() method, 248, 249
    update() method, 317
    valueOf() methods, 252

Method, local variable, 163
min() method, 178
Modes
    break mode, 63
    design mode, 63
    run mode, 63
Modifiers, 31, 112, 150, 689, 690
    abstract modifier, 238, 239, 690
    class modifier, 689
    data modifier, 689
    Example 5.3 (Using the private Modifier), 151, 152
    final modifier, 238, 239, 690
    method modifier, 689
    private, 151
    private modifier, 690
    protected modifier, 238, 690
    public, 151
    public modifier, 690
    static, 150
    static modifier, 690
    synchronized modifier, 690

    visibility modifier, 238
    (default) modifier, 690
Money, breaking down sum
    Example 2.3 (Breaking down a sum of money), 69, 70
Mortgage class
    Example 5.7 (Using the Mortgage Class), 164–166
Mortgages, computing
    Example 10.1 (Using Applets), 420–424
Mortgage, computing
    Example 2.2 (Computing a mortgage), 67–69
Mouse events, 441, 442
    Example 10.6 (Handling Complex Mouse Events), 442–445
Multidimensional arrays, 202, 203
    Example 6.7 (Adding Two Matrices), 203–204
Multimedia
    audio
        Example 14.1 (Incorporating Sound in Applets), 577–580
        Example 14.2 (Announcing the Time on a Separate Thread), 581–583
        playing, 576, 577
        separate thread, running, 581
    Example 14.4 (Using Image and Audio in Applications and Applets), 587–591
    images, displaying, 583, 584
        Example 14.3 (Displaying Images in an Applet), 584–586
    images, displaying a sequence of, 591
        Example 14.5 (Using Image Animation), 591–595
    introduction, 576
    loading image and audio files in applications, 586, 587
    MediaTracker, using, 595, 596
        Example 14.6 (Using MediaTracker), 596–598
Multiple clients, serving, 656
    Example 16.2 (Serving Multiple Clients), 656–660
Multiple windows, creating, 394
    Example 9.12 (Creating multiple windows), 394–396
Multithreading
    debugging multithreaded applications, 549, 550
    definition, 8
    Example 13.1 (Using Thread Class to Create and Launch Threads), 547–549
    Example 13.2 (Implementing the Runnable Interface in Applet), 554–556
    methods, 545, 546
    program benefits, 544
    runnable interface, 551–554
        Example 13.3 (Controlling a Group of Clocks), 557–562
    synchronization, 565, 569
        Example 13.5 (Showing Resource Conflict), 566–569
    Thread class, 545
    thread groups, 565
    thread priority, 563
        Example 13.4 (Testing Thread Priorities), 563–564
    thread states, 562
        finished, 563
        inactive state, 563
        new state, 562
        ready state, 562
        running state, 563

Naming conventions, 65
Nested, 31
Nested class, 266

Nested for loops
Example 3.3 (Using nested for loops), 92, 94
Nested if statements, 82, 83
Example 3.1 (Using Nested if Statements), 83, 84
Nested loops
Example 3.8 (Displaying a Triangle), 103, 104
Networking, 652
applet clients, 660
Example 16.3 (Networking in Applets), 661–665
client/server computing, 650
Example 16.1 (A Client/Server Example), 652–655
connection to a server, 651
datagram socket, 650
integration, 650
multiple clients, serving, 656
Example 16.2 (Serving Multiple Clients), 656–660
server establishment, 651
socket-based communications, 650
stream socket, 650
New project dialog box, 13
New state, 562
No Layout manager
Example 10.11 (Using No Layout Manager), 463–465
Number class, 250
Numeric wrapper class
constants, 251
constructors, 251
conversion methods, 251
parseDouble() methods, 252
parseInt() methods, 252
valueOf() methods, 252
Numerical data types, 52

Object class, 247
instance methods, 248
Object-oriented programming
characteristics, 142
class abstraction, 163
flexibility, 4
Object streams, 644
Objects, 142
anonymous objects, creating, 144
arrays, 186
casting objects, 243, 244
Example 7.4 (Casting Objects), 244–247
explicit casting, 243
implicit casting, 243
constructors, 147
creating an instance of the class, 144
creating an object of the class, 144
creating arrays of objects, 198
data fields, 142
declaring and creating objects, 143
Example 5.1 (Using Objects), 145–147
Example 5.2 (Using Constructors), 148, 149
Example 5.4 (Passing Objects as Arguments), 153–155
Example 5.5 (Using a Setter Method to Change Data in a Private Field), 156–157
listener object, 292
methods, 142
passing objects to methods, 152, 153
source object, 292
target object, 302
Online help, 71, 72, 73
Operator precedence, 59
Operator precedence chart, 59, 685, 686, 687

Operators
Boolean, 57
comparison, 57
shortcut, 53
! truth, 58
&& truth, 58
^ truth, 58
¦¦ truth, 58
Option buttons, 370, 371
Options, integrated development environment, 74
Ordered lists, 698, 699
OutputStream class, 607
Overloading methods, 118, 119
Overriding inherited methods, 273
Overriding methods, 235
Example 7.3 (Overriding the Methods in the Superclass), 236–237
superclass, within, 272

Packages, 170
classes into packages, putting, 172
Example 5.10 (Using Your Own Packages), 174–175
Example 5.9 (Putting Classes into Packages), 172–173
Java Application Programmer Interface, 175
naming conventions, 171
using packages, 174
Packaging and deploying Visual J++ projects, 465
as .exe files, 465–466
as .zip files, 467
paint() method, 40, 317
paintComponent() method, 317
Panels
containers, using, 312
Example 8.7 (Testing Panels), 313–314
draw graphics, using, 314
Example 8.8 (Drawing on Panels), 315–316
Paragraph style tags, 696
Example E.2 (HTML Source Code Using Structure Tags), 696–697
Paragraph tags, 694
Parameter order association
Parameters
actual parameters, 113
formal parameters, 113
passing, 115, 116
Example 10.2 (Passing Parameters to Java Applets), 429–430
to applets, 428, 429
Parent class, 232
parseDouble() methods, 252
parseInt() methods, 252
Parsing text files, 622
Pass by value, 116
Example 4.2 (Testing Pass by Value), 116
Pathname, 703
Performance, Java, 8
Physical tags, 694, 695, 696
Piped streams, 643
Polygons, drawing, 330, 331, 332
Polymorphism, 242, 243
Port, 703
Portability, 8
Precedence chart, operator, 685, 686, 687

Primitive data type values, processing, 249, 250
Primitive data types
    creating variables, 144
Primitive types on the console, 642, 643
Print streams, 616, 617
    Example 15.3 (Using Print Streams), 617–618
private modifier, 690
Programs
    compiling and executing a Java, 28–30
    creating a Java, 24–28
    Example 2.1 (Computing the Area of a Circle), 47–49
    writing simple, 46, 47
Project explorer window, 17
Project files, displaying, 14
Project, creating, 13
Properties, 5
Property window, 17
protected modifier, 238, 690
public modifier, 690
Pushback streams, 644

RAD (Rapid Application Development), 713
    applications, developing, 720, 722
        handlers, implementing, 722, 723
        interfaces, creating user, 721
        menus, creating, 723–729
    form designer, 713
        basics, 714
    handlers, implementing, 718, 719
    properties window, 717, 718
    switching between form designer and code editor, 715
    toolbox window, 715, 716, 717
Radio buttons, 370, 371
    Example 9.8 (Using Radio Buttons), 371–375
Random access files, 625, 626, 627
    Example 15.6 (Using Random Access Files), 627–635
random() method, 178
Rational class
    Example 5.8 (Using the Rational Class), 166–170
Rationals
    Example 6.5 (Adding an Array of Rationals), 198–199
readDouble() method, 47
Reader class, 606, 607
Ready state, 562
Recursion, 126, 127
    characteristics, 129
    recursion *versus* iteration, 133, 134
Recursive call, 127
repaint() method, 317
Reserved words, 30
Resource bundles, 532, 533
    Example 12.4 (Using Resource Bundles), 534–540
    naming conventions, 533
Resource chain, 533
Resource conflict, 569
    Example 13.5 (Showing Resource Conflict), 566–569
Rethrowing exceptions, 494
Run mode, 63
Runnable interface, 551, 552, 553, 554
    Example 13.2 (Implementing the Runnable Interface in an Applet), 554–556
    Example 13.3 (Controlling a Group of Clocks), 557–562

Running state, 563
Runtime errors, 63
RuntimeException class, 479

Sales amount, finding
    Example 3.7 (Finding the Sales Amount), 101, 102, 103
Saving files, 15
Scope of a variable, 162
Scroll panes, 400, 401, 402
    Example 9.14 (Using Scroll Panes), 402–405
Scroll Bars, 396, 397, 398
    Example 9.13 (Using Scroll Bars), 398–400
    horizontal, 396
    vertical, 396
Searching
    binary search approach, 195
        Example 6.4 (Testing Binary Search), 196–197
    linear search, 193
        Example 6.3 (Testing Linear Search), 194–195
Security team, Java, 7
Selection sort, 190, 191
    Example 6.2 (Using Arrays in Sorting), 191–193
Servername, 703
Setter method, 156–157
    Example 5.5 (Using a Setter Method to Change Data in a Private Field), 156-1
    JavaBeans, 345
Shortcut operators, 53, 54
Simplicity, 5
Socket-based communications, 650
Sorting, 190
    Example 6.2 (Using Arrays in Sorting), 191–193
Square roots
    Example 4.4 (Computing Square Roots), 119, 120
Start tag, 35, 693
Statement completion assistant, 61
Statements, 31
Static methods for creating borders, 376
Static modifier, 690
Stopping condition, 127
Stream classes, 605
    byte streams, 605
    character streams, 605
    InputStream class, 606, 607
    OutputStream class, 607
    Reader class, 606, 607
    Writer class, 607
Stream socket, 650
Streams, 604
    array streams, 611
    Buffered streams, 618, 619
    datastreams, 612, 613
        Example 15.2 (Using Data Streams), 614–616
    filter streams, 611
    FilterInputStream subclasses, 612
    FilterOutputStream subclasses, 612
    layering, 604
    line number streams, 644
    object streams, 644
    piped streams, 643
    print streams, 616, 617
        Example 15.3 (Using Print Streams), 617–618
    pushback streams, 644
    string streams, 643

StreamTokenizer
    Constants, 622
    Example 15.5 (Using StreamTokenizer), 623–625
    Variables, 622, 623

String, 55, 56
    StringBuffer class
        capacity() method, 208
        charAt()method, 208
        Example 6.8 (Testing StringBuffer), 209–210
        length() method, 208
        reverse()method, 208
        setCharAt() method, 208
        setLength() method, 208

String class, 205
    string length and retrieving individual characters, 207
    stringbuffer class, 207
    stringBuffer class
        appending and inserting new contents, 208
    substrings, 206

String comparisons, 205, 206
String concatenation, 206
String object, 205
String streams, 643
StringBuffer class, 207
StringTokenizer
    constructors, 211
    Example 6.9 (Testing StringTokenizer), 211–212

StringTokenizer Class, 210
Structure tags, 693, 694
    body tags, 694
    head tags, 694

Style, programming
    block styles, 66
    comment style, 64
    comments, 64
    indentation, proper, 65
    introduction to, 64
    naming conventions, 65

Subclass, 232
Sun Java Workshop, 11
Sun Microsystems, 4
super keyword, 234
Superclass, 232
    constructors, 234
    Example 7.3 (Overriding the Methods in the Superclass), 236–237
    methods, 234

Swing components, 284
    JComponent class
        properties, 346

Swing Library, installing in Visual J++ 6, 709
Switch statements, using, 87, 88, 89
Symbols
    i++ (adjustment statement), 90
    ! operators, 58
    ! truth, 58
    && truth, 58
    (x++) postincrement operator, 54
    (x–) postdecrement operator, 54
    (%) modulus, 52
    (*) multiplication, 52
    (+) addition, 52
    (++x) preincrement operator, 54
    (+-) shortcut operators, 53
    (-) subtraction, 52
    (–x) predecrement operator, 54
    (/) division, 52
    ^ truth, 58
    || truth, 58

Synchronization, 565, 569
    Example 13.5 (Showing Resource Conflict), 566–569

synchronized modifier, 690
Syntax checking, dynamic, 61
Syntax errors, 60

Tabbed panes, 405, 406
    Example 9.14 (Using Tabbed Panes), 406–409

Table tags, 694, 700, 701
    Example E.5 (Illustration of Table Tags), 701–702

Tag name, 693
Tags
    end tag, 35, 693
    Example E.7 (Illustration of Horizontal Bar Tags), 705
    Example E.8 (Illustration of Image Tags), 706
    font tags, 694, 697
        Example E.3 (Testing Font Tags), 698
        basefont tags, 697
        font tags, 697
    hyperlink tags, 702
    image tags, 694
    link tags, 694
    list tags, 694, 698
        definition lists, 698
        Example E.4 (Using Various List Tags), 699–700
        ordered lists, 698, 699
        unordered lists, 698, 699
    names, 693
    paragraph style tags, 696
        Example E.2 (HTML Source Code Using Structure Tags), 696–697
    paragraph tags, 694
    start tag, 35, 693
    structure tags, 693, 694
        body tags, 694
        head tags, 694
    table tags, 694, 700, 701
        Example E.5 (Illustration of Table Tags), 701–702
    text appearance tags, 693, 694
        content-based tags, 694, 695
        physical tags, 694, 695, 696
    applet tag, 34
    html tag, 35

Tasklist window, 17
Text appearance tags, 693, 694
    content-based tags, 694
    physical tags, 694

Text areas, 357, 358
    Example 9.4 (Using Text Areas), 358–359

Text fields, 354, 355
    Example 9.3 (Using Text Fields), 355–357

Text interactive input and output, 641
this keyword, 237
Thread, 544, 581
    Example 14.2 (Announcing the Time on a Separate Thread), 581–583

Thread class, 544
    Example 13.1 (Using Thread Class to Create and Launch Threads), 547–549
    methods, 545, 546

Index

Thread groups, 565
Thread priority, 563
   Example 13.4 (Testing Thread Priorities), 563–564
Thread states, 562
   finished, 563
   inactive state, 563
   new state, 562
   ready state, 562
   running state, 562
TicTacToe game, developing
   Example 10.8 (The TicTacToe Game), 449–455
Tokens, 210
Tool bar, 15
Tool windows, 17, 18, 19, 20
   project explorer window, 17
   property window, 17
   tasklist window, 17
   toolbox window, 17
Toolbar, 16
Toolbox window, 17
Tooltips, displaying, 15
toString() method, 248, 249
Towers of Hanoi
   Example 4.7 (Solving the Towers of Hanoi problem), 130–133
Trigonometric methods, 177
Truths
   operator !, 58
   operator &&, 58
   operator ^, 58
   operator ¦¦, 58
Type casting, 55

Unicode, 56
Unicode web site, 56
Unordered lists, 698, 699
update() method, 317
URL (Uniform Resource Locator), 702
   fullfilename, 703
   methods, 702, 703
      file, 703
      ftp, 703
      http, 703
   pathname, 703
   port, 703
   servername, 703

Utilities, debugging, 215, 216

valueOf() methods, 252
Variables, 47, 50, 163
   declaring, 50
   declaring and initializing, one step, 51
   local variables, 163
   scope, 162
   StreamTokenizer Variables, 622, 623
Visibility modifier, 238
Visual Age for Java, 11
Visual Cafe,' 11
Visual J ++, 11
Visual J++
   starting, 12

Web
   URL (Uniform Resource Locator), 702
Web browser
   running Java, 9
Web page
   creating web page tutorial, 691–707
   viewing, 665, 666
      Example 16.4 (Viewing HTML Pages from Java), 666–668
Web servers
   retrieving files from web servers, 668, 669
while loop, 94, 95
   Example 3.4 (Using a while loop), 95, 96
Window class, 285
Window layout, defining, 22, 23
Windows Start button, 12
World Wide Web
   Java and, 9
Wrapper class, 250
Writer class, 607
Writing programs
   Example 2.2 (Computing a Mortgage), 67–69
   Example 2.3 (Breaking Down a Sum of Money), 69, 70

.zip files, packaging and deploying, 467

END USER LICENSE AGREEMENT

You should carefully read the following terms and conditions before breaking the seal on the CD-ROM envelope. Among other things, this Agreement licenses the enclosed software to you and contains warranty and liability disclaimers. By breaking the seal on the CD-ROM envelope, you are accepting and agreeing to the terms and conditions of this Agreement. If you do not agree to the terms of this Agreement, do not break the seal. You should promptly return the package unopened.

LICENSE

Prentice-Hall, Inc. (the "Company") provides this Software to you and licenses its use as follows:

a. use the Software on a single computer of the type identified on the package;

b. make one copy of the Software in machine-readable form solely for back-up purposes.

LIMITED WARRANTY

The Company warrants the physical CD-ROM(s) on which the Software is furnished to be free from defects in materials and workmanship under normal use for a period of sixty (60) days from the date of purchase as evidenced by a copy of your receipt.

DISCLAIMER

THE SOFTWARE IS PROVIDED "AS IS" AND COMPANY SPECIFICALLY DISCLAIMS ALL WARRANTIES OF ANY KIND, EITHER EXPRESS OR IMPLIED, INCLUDING, BUT NOT LIMITED TO, THE IMPLIED WARRANTIES OF MERCHANTABILITY AND FITNESS FOR A PARTICULAR PURPOSE. IN NO EVENT WILL COMPANY BE LIABLE TO YOU FOR ANY DAMAGES, INCLUDING ANY LOSS OF PROFIT OR OTHER INCIDENTAL, SPECIAL OR CONSEQUENTIAL DAMAGES EVEN IF COMPANY HAS BEEN ADVISED OF THE POSSIBILITY OF SUCH DAMAGES.

SOME STATES DO NOT ALLOW THE EXCLUSION OF IMPLIED WARRANTIES OR LIMITATION OR EXCLUSION OF LIABILITY FOR INCIDENTAL OR CONSEQUENTIAL DAMAGES, SO THE ABOVE EXCLUSIONS AND/OR LIMITATIONS MAY NOT APPLY TO YOU.

LIMITATIONS OF REMEDIES

The Company's entire liability and your exclusive remedy shall be:

1. the replacement of such CD-ROM if you return a defective CD-ROM during the limited warranty period, or

2. if the Company is unable to deliver a replacement CD-ROM that is free of defects in materials or workmanship, you may terminate this Agreement by returning the Software.

GENERAL

You may not sublicense, assign, or transfer the license of the Software or make or distribute copies of the Software. Any attempt otherwise to sublicense, assign, or transfer any of the rights, duties, or obligations hereunder is void.

Should you have any questions concerning this Agreement, you may contact Prentice-Hall, Inc. by writing to:

Prentice Hall
Computer Science/ Engineering
One Lake Street
Upper Saddle River, NJ 07458
Attention: Mechanical Engineering Editor

YOU ACKNOWLEDGE THAT YOU HAVE READ THIS AGREEMENT, UNDERSTAND IT, AND AGREE TO BE BOUND BY ITS TERMS AND CONDITIONS. YOU FURTHER AGREE THAT IT IS THE COMPLETE AND EXCLUSIVE STATEMENT OF THE AGREEMENT BETWEEN US THAT SUPERSEDES ANY PROPOSAL OR PRIOR AGREEMENT, ORAL OR WRITTEN, AND ANY OTHER COMMUNICATIONS BETWEEN US RELATING TO THE SUBJECT MATTER OF THIS AGREEMENT.

Borland® JBuilder™3 University Edition

Authorized Book Publisher License Statement and
Limited Warranty for Inprise Products

IMPORTANT—READ CAREFULLY

This license statement and limited warranty constitutes a legal agreement ("License Agreement") for the software product ("Software") identified above (including any software, media, and accompanying on-line or printed documentation supplied by Inprise) between you (either as an individual or a single entity), the Book Publisher from whom you received the Software ("Publisher"), and Inprise International, Inc. ("Inprise").

BY INSTALLING, COPYING, OR OTHERWISE USING THE SOFTWARE, YOU AGREE TO BE BOUND BY ALL OF THE TERMS AND CONDITIONS OF THE LICENSE AGREEMENT. If you are the original purchaser of the Software and you do not agree with the terms and conditions of the License Agreement, promptly return the unused Software to the place from which you obtained it for a full refund.

Upon your acceptance of the terms and conditions of the License Agreement, Inprise grants you the right to use the Software solely for educational purposes, in the manner provided below. No rights are granted for deploying or distributing applications created with the Software.

This Software is owned by Inprise or its suppliers and is protected by copyright law and international copyright treaty. Therefore, you must treat this Software like any other copyrighted material (e.g., a book), except that you may either make one copy of the Software solely for backup or archival purposes or transfer the Software to a single hard disk provided you keep the original solely for backup or archival purposes.

You may transfer the Software and documentation on a permanent basis provided you retain no copies and the recipient agrees to the terms of the License Agreement. Except as provided in the License Agreement, you may not transfer, rent, lease, lend, copy, modify, translate, sublicense, time-share or electronically transmit or receive the Software, media or documentation. You acknowledge that the Software in source code form remains a confidential trade secret of Inprise and/or its suppliers and therefore you agree not to modify the Software or attempt to reverse engineer, decompile, or disassemble the Software, except and only to the extent that such activity is expressly permitted by applicable law notwithstanding this limitation.

Though Inprise does not offer technical support for the Software, we welcome your feedback.

This Software is subject to U.S. Commerce Department export restrictions, and is intended for use in the country into which Inprise sold it (or in the EEC, if sold into the EEC).

LIMITED WARRANTY

The Publisher warrants that the Software media will be free from defects in materials and workmanship for a period of ninety (90) days from the date of receipt. Any implied warranties on the Software are limited to ninety (90) days. Some states/jurisdictions do not allow limitations on duration of an implied warranty, so the above limitation may not apply to you.

The Publisher's, Inprise's, and the Publisher's or Inprise's suppliers' entire liability and your exclusive remedy shall be, at the Publisher's or Inprise's option, either (a) return of the price paid, or (b) repair or replacement of the Software that does not meet the Limited Warranty and which is returned to the Publisher with a copy of your receipt. This Limited Warranty is void if failure of the Software has resulted from accident, abuse, or misapplication. Any replacement Software will be warranted for the remainder of the original warranty period or thirty (30) days, whichever is longer. Outside the United States, neither these remedies nor any product support services offered are available without proof of purchase from an authorized non-U.S. source.

TO THE MAXIMUM EXTENT PERMITTED BY APPLICABLE LAW, THE PUBLISHER, INPRISE, AND THE PUBLISHER'S OR INPRISE'S SUPPLIERS DISCLAIM ALL OTHER WARRANTIES AND CONDITIONS, EITHER EXPRESS OR IMPLIED, INCLUDING, BUT NOT LIMITED TO, IMPLIED WARRANTIES OF MERCHANTABILITY, FITNESS FOR A PARTICULAR PURPOSE, TITLE, AND NON-INFRINGEMENT, WITH REGARD TO THE SOFTWARE, AND THE PROVISION OF OR FAILURE TO PROVIDE SUPPORT SERVICES. THIS LIMITED WARRANTY GIVES YOU SPECIFIC LEGAL RIGHTS. YOU MAY HAVE OTHERS, WHICH VARY FROM STATE/JURISDICTION TO STATE/JURISDICTION.
LIMITATION OF LIABILITY

TO THE MAXIMUM EXTENT PERMITTED BY APPLICABLE LAW, IN NO EVENT SHALL THE PUBLISHER, INPRISE, OR THE PUBLISHER'S OR INPRISE'S SUPPLIERS BE LIABLE FOR ANY SPECIAL, INCIDENTAL, INDIRECT, OR CONSEQUENTIAL DAMAGES WHATSOEVER (INCLUDING, WITHOUT LIMITATION, DAMAGES FOR LOSS OF BUSINESS PROFITS, BUSINESS INTERRUPTION, LOSS OF BUSINESS INFORMATION, OR ANY OTHER PECUNIARY LOSS) ARISING OUT OF THE USE OF OR INABILITY TO USE THE SOFTWARE PRODUCT OR THE PROVISION OF OR FAILURE TO PROVIDE SUPPORT SERVICES, EVEN IF INPRISE HAS BEEN ADVISED OF THE POSSIBILITY OF SUCH DAMAGES. IN ANY CASE, INPRISE'S ENTIRE LIABILITY UNDER ANY PROVISION OF THIS LICENSE AGREEMENT SHALL BE LIMITED TO THE GREATER OF THE AMOUNT ACTUALLY PAID BY YOU FOR THE SOFTWARE PRODUCT OR U.S. $25; PROVIDED, HOWEVER, IF YOU HAVE ENTERED INTO A INPRISE SUPPORT SERVICES AGREEMENT, INPRISE'S ENTIRE LIABILITY REGARDING SUPPORT SERVICES SHALL BE GOVERNED BY THE TERMS OF THAT AGREEMENT. BECAUSE SOME STATES AND JURISDICTIONS DO NOT ALLOW THE EXCLUSION OR LIMITATION OF LIABILITY, THE ABOVE LIMITATION MAY NOT APPLY TO YOU.

HIGH RISK ACTIVITIES

The Software is not fault-tolerant and is not designed, manufactured or intended for use or resale as on-line control equipment in hazardous environments requiring fail-safe performance, such as in the operation of nuclear facilities, aircraft navigation or communication systems, air traffic control, direct life support machines, or weapons systems, in which the failure of the Software could lead directly to death, personal injury, or severe physical or environmental damage ("High Risk Activities"). The Publisher, Inprise, and their suppliers specifically disclaim any express or implied warranty of fitness for High Risk Activities.

U.S. GOVERNMENT RESTRICTED RIGHTS

The Software and documentation are provided with RESTRICTED RIGHTS. Use, duplication, or disclosure by the Government is subject to restrictions as set forth in subparagraphs (c)(1)(ii) of the Rights in Technical Data and Computer Software clause at DFARS 252.227-7013 or subparagraphs (c)(1) and (2) of the Commercial Computer Software-Restricted Rights at 48 CFR 52.227-19, as applicable.

GENERAL PROVISIONS

This License Agreement may only be modified in writing signed by you and an authorized officer of Inprise. If any provision of this License Agreement is found void or unenforceable, the remainder will remain valid and enforceable according to its terms. If any remedy provided is determined to have failed for its essential purpose, all limitations of liability and exclusions of damages set forth in the Limited Warranty shall remain in effect.

This License Agreement shall be construed, interpreted and governed by the laws of the State of California, U.S.A. This License Agreement gives you specific legal rights; you may have others which vary from state to state and from country to country. Inprise reserves all rights not specifically granted in this License Agreement.